STUDIES ON ETHNIC GROUPS IN CHINA

Stevan Harrell, Editor

STUDIES ON ETHNIC GROUPS IN CHINA

Cultural Encounters on China's Ethnic Frontiers
Edited by Stevan Harrell

Guest People: Hakka Identity in China and Abroad
Edited by Nicole Constable

Familiar Strangers:
A History of Muslims in Northwest China
Jonathan N. Lipman

Lessons in Being Chinese: Minority Education
and Ethnic Identity in Southwest China
Mette Halskov Hansen

Manchus and Han: Ethnic Relations and Political Power
in Late Qing and Early Republican China, 1861–1928
Edward J. M. Rhoads

Manchus & Han

Ethnic Relations and Political Power in Late Qing
and Early Republican China, 1861–1928

EDWARD J. M. RHOADS

UNIVERSITY OF WASHINGTON PRESS

Seattle and London

This publication was supported in part by the

Donald R. Ellegood International Publication Endowment.

Library of Congress Cataloging-in-Publication Data
Manchus and Han : ethnic relations and political power in late Qing
and early republican China, 1861–1928 / Edward J. M. Rhoads.
p.   cm. — (Studies on ethnic groups in China)
Includes bibliographical references (p.) and index.
ISBN 0-295-97938-0
1. Manchus.   2. China—Ethnic relations.
3. China—History—1861–1912.   4. China—History—1912–1928.
I. Rhoads, Edward J. M.   II. Title.   III. Series.
DS761.2.M36   2000
951'.035—DC21   00-008470

For my wife, Patty,

and my daughter, Jennifer,

with love

Contents

Acknowledgments

In the course of doing this research I have incurred a large number of debts, which I am delighted to be able at this time to acknowledge. The most obvious debts are to the archives and libraries housing and caring for the documents and books on which this study is based. These include China's No. 1 Historical Archives in Beijing and the U.S. National Archives in Washington, D.C., as well as the following libraries: the Harvard-Yenching Library at Harvard University, the Butler and East Asian Libraries at Columbia University, the Hillman Library at the University of Pittsburgh, the Beijing Library, the library of People's University and that of its Institute for Qing History, the Beijing University Library, the library of the Institute of Modern History, Academia Sinica (Taipei), and, above all, the Perry-Castañeda Library of the University of Texas at Austin and its Asian Studies librarians, Kevin Lin and Merry Burlingham. I am particularly grateful to the Institute for Qing History, People's University, and to its director, Dai Yi, for inviting me to spend the academic year 1982–83 with them.

I also acknowledge with gratitude the financial support of the American Council of Learned Societies, the Committee for Scholarly Communication with China, the University Research Institute of the University of Texas at Austin, and the University Center for International Studies at the University of Pittsburgh.

Several people kindly read and commented on all or parts of this book prior to its publication: Steve MacKinnon, Lynn Struve, Steve Harrell, Betsy Bartlett, and Patty Stranahan, as well as an anonymous reviewer for the University of Washington Press. Their criticisms, coupled with those of my editor at the Press, Lorri Hagman, have resulted in a shorter, tighter, and more accurate study, for which all its readers should rejoice. Any remaining imperfections are, of course, my responsibility.

Yet other people have helped and sustained me in less direct ways. Among them are Bill Braisted, Li Wenhai, Jennifer Rhoads, Suzanne Kain Rhoads, Art Rosenbaum, David Strand, the late Sun Yutang, Phil Woodruff, and, not least, the members of the Southwestern and Western conferences of the Association for Asian Studies, who year after year heard me grapple with my elusive topic with forbearance and good humor. But my chief helpmate and sustainer has been my wife, Patty Stranahan, who offered not only constructive criticisms but also constant encouragement. Without her support and enthusiasm, completion of this project would have taken even longer than it has.

Manchus & Han

Introduction

In late December 1898, soon after the bitter disappointment of the Hundred Days, when the Guangxu emperor had tried and failed to introduce institutional changes from above, Liang Qichao founded *The China Discussion* (Qingyibao) in Japan as a forum for the exploration of new ideas for political reform in Qing China. Liang's own recommendation, announced in the lead commentary of the inaugural issue, was not, as one might have expected, to elevate the level of social consciousness among the Chinese citizenry or to transform the autocratic structure of the Qing state. It was, rather, to "tear down the boundaries between Manchus and Han" (*ping Man-Han zhi jie*).[1]

Liang's surprising prescription was based upon a social Darwinist reading of history. "Racial competition," in which races necessarily struggled with one another for existence, was considered the driving force of history. In this competition, which occurs not only on a worldwide basis but also within individual countries, only "superior races" will survive, while "inferior" ones will inevitably perish. When life began, all races were equal. Why, then, did some "improve" to become superior, differentiated from and triumphant over the inferior ones? The key was race mixing. "Racial improvement arises from the amalgamation of many different races." The more extensive the mixing, the more successful the improvement. Races that do not mix face extinction.

Liang Qichao drew a historical parallel between contemporary China and China during the ancient Spring and Autumn era. Then, the inhabitants of the peripheral states and the people of the Central Plain looked upon each other as racially different. "They [the various races] were mutually suspicious and had nothing to do with each another. They were no different from today's Manchus and Han." Since then the people of China (Zhina) "have gradually advanced to civilization and become a superior race." The reason was that "all these races had mixed together; only because they had mixed together were they able to survive." Meanwhile, numerous other groups had perished because they had not intermixed. Liang pointed out that there still are some races—such as the Miao, Tong, and Yao—who live inter-spersed among people of a superior race and do not mix. Their extinction, however, cannot be long delayed. Why? Because if they do not amalgamate, they must struggle; and when they struggle, one side must lose. Victory or defeat depends entirely upon who is superior or inferior. Today, as between the Manchus [Manren] and the Han [Hanren], it takes no expert to establish which is the superior race and which the inferior.

Admittedly, at the time of Liang's writing, the Manchus ruled over the Han, but this was a temporary aberration. Racial conflicts were not resolved in a single moment; resolution might take as long as several centuries. In the end, brain would inevitably triumph over brawn. By extension, so would the supe-rior Han eventually prevail over the inferior Manchus.

Liang suggested that it was not too late for the Manchu rulers of China to take remedial action, which, in view of the imperialist threat, would affect not only the Manchus but all of Asia. The worldwide struggle for survival had come down to that between the white race and the yellow race, with the outcome yet to be decided. The fate of the entire yellow race depended on the survival of China, whose population makes up 70 to 80 percent of the race. However, as the Manchus were in control of China, the prospects were grim. With brain being superior to brawn, "were those valiant Manchus [Manzhou] of a cou-ple hundred years ago alive today, they still could not stand up intellectually to the foreign powers. As for today's Manchus [Manren], they have lost their fierceness but have not changed their dull nature. Even if they wished to avoid the disaster of extinction, how could they do so?" Although the key to success in the racial struggle was racial improvement through mixing, China's rulers would rather that the entire yellow race suffer eternal destruction than change one day of their life of pleasure and luxury.

Liang lamented the shortsightedness of the Manchu rulers. "They look upon the Han, without reason, as an alien race who mean them ill; all the while they are oblivious that the harm that the truly alien race [i.e., the whites] will inflict will be a hundred million times greater." Liang concluded by speculating on the catastrophic consequences that awaited the Manchus from both the Han and the white race if they did not begin to reform by eliminating Manchu-Han differences:

If their oppressive policies continue much longer, they will engender a great upheaval, in which resolute scholars all over the country will either declare independence, as in America, or start a revolution, as in France and Spain. By then, of course, it will be too late for the Manchus to regret. Or if it does not happen like this, then after a few more years of today's reactionary government, there will be partition. As partition takes place, the secret societies will rise and run amok. Since the government's authority cannot penetrate to the local level, the people will have free rein to take their revenge. Whatever else might happen, the Manchus in the provincial garrisons will surely be annihilated.

After partition both Han and Manchus will be enslaved. But the Han, because they have a large population and are not lacking in intelligence, will still be able to conspire to join together to regain their independence. The Manchus, on the other hand, are not only few in number but also stupid and weak. Although they will have escaped the vengeance of the Han, they will forever serve as beasts of burden for the white people.

Moreover, Han farmers and artisans are industrious and frugal. In the past the Han have been critical to the success of labor-intensive enterprises the world over; it was they who developed the wasteland in South America, Africa, and around the Pacific Ocean. Consequently, even if the Han territory is partitioned, the Han people will still have some influence in the world; though subjugated, they will survive in the end. The Manchus [on the other hand] have for the past two centuries eaten without farming and been clothed without weaving. Not one among their five million people is capable of being a scholar, farmer, artisan, or merchant. When partition occurs and their political, financial, and military powers have all fallen into the hands of the white race, if they want some food or lodging then, will they still get it? Therefore, what the Manchus themselves have decided to do is precisely a self-chosen road to destruction. This truly is an example of "quenching one's thirst by drinking poisoned wine."

Liang Qichao's short article is noteworthy because it not only helped introduce the concepts and terminology of social Darwinism to the Chinese reading public but also was the first reasoned critique since the Taiping Rebellion of the Manchu court and the Manchu people and, more generally, of Manchu-Han relations. Moreover, his condemnation of the five million Manchus for their parasitic lifestyle (they "eat without farming and are clothed without weaving") foreshadowed the anti-Manchu propaganda that the republican revolutionaries unleashed soon afterward. And his prophecy that a "great upheaval" awaited the Manchus if the court refused, as a start toward other reforms, to remove the barriers between Manchus and Han came true a decade later in the Revolution of 1911.

This book addresses many of the issues that Liang Qichao raised or touched upon. Who were the Manchus, and who, correspondingly, were the Han? What did opponents of the Qing, notably the republican revolutionaries in the post-Boxer era, criticize the Manchus *qua* Manchus for? How valid were those criticisms; that is, to what extent and in what ways were Manchus and Han, after more than two hundred years of Manchu rule over China, still significantly different from each other? How effectively did the Qing court deal with those criticisms? Did it, as Liang urged, tear down the boundaries between Manchus and Han? With regard to Manchu-Han relations, what did the court do, or fail to do, that estranged it from China's elite and thus brought on the revolution in 1911? What happened to the Manchu rulers and to the broad masses of the Manchu people during the revolution as well as afterward? In sum, what can be learned about the late Qing court from the way it handled, or rather mishandled, this thorny and controversial issue of Manchu-Han relations? Thus, the book is concerned equally with ethnic relations and political power as they pertain to Manchus and Han, especially in the ten or so years before the Republican revolution.

Studies of the 1911 Revolution have evolved greatly over the last several decades. Early works, particularly those by Chinese historians (such as Xiao Yishan's comprehensive history of the Qing dynasty), focused almost exclusively upon the role of the revolutionaries, particularly Sun Yat-sen.[2] Then, in the late 1960s, scholarly attention began to shift away from the revolutionaries, who necessarily had conducted most of their conspiratorial activities from abroad, and toward the nonrevolutionary reformers who operated within China. They were what Joseph Esherick, in his study of Hubei and Hunan, calls the "urban reformist elite" and what Marxist historians in the post-Mao era (such as Hou Yijie, in his history of the constitutionalist movement in the late Qing) see as an emergent "national bourgeoisie" at war with feudal conditions.[3] The 1911 Revolution thus came to be seen no longer as the last in the series of military insurrections and popular uprisings that the revolutionaries had organized but rather as the consequence of the reformist elite's growing dissatisfaction with and alienation from the Qing court. Such revisionist studies, however, generally paid no more attention to the court than had those by the earlier generation of orthodox historians. As a result, it was never quite clear what the court did, and why, that so alienated the reformist elite and caused them to withdraw their critical support, without which the dynasty was doomed.

In contrast to the relative abundance of studies on the early Qing rulers, there are only a couple of monographs in English on the late Qing court: Mary Wright's on the Tongzhi Restoration and Luke Kwong's on the palace intrigues surrounding the Hundred Days of 1898.[4] Despite the longevity and the political importance of her rule, there is, as yet, no book-length published study of the empress dowager Cixi, though popular biographies of dubious veracity (often traceable back to the 1910 account by Bland and Backhouse) abound.[5] Such neglect, particularly for the last decade of the dynasty, prevails among Chinese scholars as well.

The principal reason is, of course, the progressive weakening of the central authority during the nineteenth century and the accompanying (it is widely assumed) growing impotence of the Qing court. Hence, research on the post-Boxer decade generally focuses not on Cixi or other equally unstudied court figures, such as Yikuang (Prince Qing), but rather on such ostensibly powerful provincial officials as Zhang Zhidong and Yuan Shikai, about whom Daniel Bays, Ralph Powell, Jerome Ch'en, and Stephen MacKinnon have written.[6] When historians have considered the late Qing court at all, it has usually been to emphasize one or both of two themes: the attempt begun by Cixi, dating from the suppression of the Taiping Rebellion, to reverse the long-term trend toward political decentralization; and the incompetence of Cixi's young and inexperienced successor, Zaifeng, whose brief regency ended in revolution. These two themes can be seen as converging in January 1909, when Zaifeng abruptly, perhaps foolishly, stripped Yuan Shikai of all of his political and military posts. Yet Yuan's dismissal, which he neither contested nor resisted, also shows beyond a doubt that as late as three years before its demise, the Qing court was hardly so impotent as it is usually portrayed.

This book casts new light on the late Qing court by examining how Cixi and Zaifeng dealt with the issue of Manchu-Han relations that Liang Qichao raised in late 1898 and on which the revolutionaries subsequently focused much of their propaganda. In particular, the assassination in the summer of 1907 of the Manchu governor, Enming, prompted Cixi to conduct a full-scale review of the issue. She (and later, Zaifeng) tried to undercut the revolutionaries' appeal by reducing various differences between the Manchu minority and the Han majority. At the same time, however, they undermined their own efforts by not only recentralizing authority but also "reimperializing" it. Begun in 1861, when Yixin (Prince Gong) was appointed to the Grand Council, the court's long-term attempt at reimperialization—which historians heretofore have overlooked as they focused on the parallel trend of recentralization—culminated in the naming of the immensely unpopular "imperial kinsmen's cabinet" in May 1911. This was one of the court's key decisions that greatly disappointed the reformist elite and led to their withdrawal of support when the revolution broke out five months later. This book considers how the court responded, both militarily and politically, to the Wuchang Revolt in October and what role it played in hammering out the agreement that paved the way to the Qing abdication the following February. Finally, it discusses the fate of the court after the revolution, down to the expulsion of the "last emperor" from the

Forbidden City in 1924 and the unpunished desecration of the Qing imperial tombs in 1928.

As for the broad masses of the Manchu people, whose relations with the Han is the other main subject of this book, their history and identity are inextricably intertwined with the Eight Banner system. Started by Nurhaci, from whom all Qing emperors were descended, the banners were the armed force that in 1644 conquered China proper for the Qing and that subsequently, when garrisoned throughout the empire, served as an army of occupation. The founding members of the banner system were the Jurchen of eastern and northern Manchuria, whom Nurhaci's son and successor Hong Taiji renamed "Manchus" (Manzhou). They were soon joined by members of other ethnic groups in the region, principally Mongols and Han Chinese. The banners, however, were composed of not only banner soldiers but also all of their dependents, male and female, old and young, who were collectively known as the "banner people" (*qiren*). Membership in the system was hereditary, and the banner people as a group were classified differently from most of the rest of the population, the "civilians" (*min*). The question of the relationship between the banner people and the Manchus is a vexing one. It is complicated by the inability of the English language to distinguish among several different Chinese terms—notably Manzhou, Manren, and Manzu—all of which can justifiably be rendered into English as "Manchu." This book contends that the banner people (of whom Hong Taiji's Manzhou were one component) were synonymous with the Manchus of the post-Boxer decade (whom Liang Qichao in 1898 generally labeled as "Manren") and also that they constitute the defining basis for the Manchu "nationality" or ethnic group (Manzu), who in the 1980s became the second largest minority ethnic group (after the Zhuang) in the People's Republic of China. It shows how the Manchus were transformed from a hereditary military caste—which they were for most of the Qing period, as members of the banner system—into the ethnic group that they are today. Correspondingly, if the Manchus are thus defined as equivalent to the banner people, then the Han may be equated, by and large, with the nonbanner "civilians."

Although the Manchus *qua* banner people loom large in the writings about the early Qing, they practically disappear from history by the early nineteenth century.[7] Until now, for example, only three books in English have focused to any significant extent on the Manchus in the late Qing. One is Robert Lee's examination of the effect of Han migration to the Manchus' homeland, Manchuria; another is Roger Des Forges's political biography of the Mongol bannerman Xiliang; the third is Pamela Crossley's history of one Manchu banner family from the Hangzhou garrison from the 1790s to the end of the Qing and beyond.[8] While there are a greater number of Chinese-language studies of the banner system in the late Qing, as might be expected, they are only a fraction as numerous as those on the early Qing. The leading researchers are Chen Yishi, Jin Qicong, Ma Xiedi, Wang Zongyou, and Zheng Chuanshui, whose writings are cited throughout this study.

The Manchus became an all-but-forgotten people by the beginning of the nineteenth century. It is widely believed that they had become so assimilated into the culture of the majority Han population that they were no longer identifiable as a separate and distinct group. This belief rests, in part, upon the undeniable degeneration of the Eight Banners as an effective fighting force in the course of the eighteenth century (if not earlier) and their displacement by various other, predominantly Han, armies that emerged in the nineteenth century. Since the issue of Manchu identity was tightly bound up with the Eight Banners, the collapse of that system leads easily to the conclusion that the Manchu people who comprised the system had lost their raison d'être and, along with it, their distinctive identity. In particular, Chinese historians, motivated perhaps by cultural defensiveness, have long emphasized both the rapidity and the degree of the Manchus' decline. Zheng Tianting, for example, dates the military disintegration of the Manchus as early as one generation after their conquest of China proper: "By 1673, when the Rebellion of the Three Feudatories began, the Eight Banner troops (including the Hanjun) were nearly incapable of waging war, and the Manchu Qing rulers could only make use of the Han people's Army of the Green Standard." Similarly, Ch'en Chieh-hsien points to the extent of the Manchus' acculturation in the core area of language. Noting that "modern linguists have estimated that fully one-third of Manchu vocabulary is derived from Chinese," he concludes that "the mother language of the Manchus, like some other aspects of their primitive culture, proved unable to resist assimilation after contact with the [Han] Chinese." Chinese historians are not alone in proclaiming the Manchus' absorption into Han culture. Mary Wright, in her influential study of the Tongzhi Restoration, categorically states that by 1865, when an edict was issued that seemingly liberated the banner people from the constraints of the banner system, "most of the last restrictions separating the Manchus from the [Han] Chinese" had been eased.[9]

If this were so, why then would Liang Qichao at the end of 1898 still be calling for the erasure of Manchu-Han differences? And how could the anti-Manchu propaganda of the post-Boxer decade be justified? The revolutionaries claimed that the Manchus were an alien ruling minority who enjoyed a privileged existence separate from the subject Han majority. The republicans were opposed not only to the Qing court but also to the Manchu people as a whole. Zou Rong's widely circulated pamphlet of 1903, *The Revolutionary Army* (Gemingjun), expressed this broad anti-Manchu sentiment most vividly, as he called for the "annihilation of the five million and more of the furry and horned Manchu race [*Manzhou zhong*]."[10] Similarly, the leading revolutionary organization, the Alliance (Tongmenghui), in 1905 demanded, along with the overthrow of the dynasty and the establishment of a republic, the "expulsion of the Tartars," by whom it meant, of course, the Manchus. Scholars who minimize the continuing differences between Manchus and Han generally dismiss the revolutionaries' anti-Manchu rhetoric as sheer propaganda, devoid of content and lacking in substance. In her thoughtful introduction to a collection of essays on the revolution, Mary Wright characterizes such anti-Manchu expressions as unimportant and groundless. Reiterating her earlier view that a "Sino-Manchu amalgam" had achieved "full maturity in the mid-nineteenth century," Wright concludes that "the ethnic issue was irrelevant."[11]

This book refutes Mary Wright on both of these points: that is, the extent of the Manchus' acculturation after the mid-nineteenth century and the relative importance of the "ethnic issue" in the 1911 Revolution. The process of cultural assimilation was not all one way. Just as the Manchus were unquestionably "Sinicized" (or, more precisely, "Hanified"), so also were the Han to some (though admittedly far less) extent "Manchufied." Nevertheless, despite the cumulative effect of mutual acculturation, down through the nineteenth and into the early twentieth century Manchus and Han were still sufficiently different from each other as to justify many of the revolutionaries' criticisms of the Manchus as Manchus. Consequently, if the alleged amalgamation of Manchus and Han was by no means complete at the turn of the century, or even at the time of the revolution, then the ethnic issue was hardly irrelevant. It most assuredly was relevant to the vast numbers of Manchus who, as Zou Rong had demanded, were hunted down and slaughtered during the revolution. The establishment of the Republic was not nearly so bloodless as it is usually described.

In sum, the continuing inability of the Qing court—beginning with Yixin's appointment to the Grand Council in 1861 and the edict of 1865 on the Eight Banners cited by Mary Wright and coming down through the New Policies of the post-Boxer decade—to solve the problem of Manchu-Han differences helped to undermine elite confidence in the regime and thus to create the conditions that enabled the revolution to succeed. Even so, the problem was not entirely resolved until more than a decade after the revolution, as it was only in the mid- and late 1920s, concurrent with the expulsion of the emperor from the Forbidden City in 1924 and the desecration of the Qing tombs in 1928, that the Eight Banner system was completely disbanded. Only then, thirty years after Liang Qichao's commentary in *The China Discussion*, were the boundaries between Manchus and Han fully torn down.

1 / Separate and Unequal

Anti-Manchuism, narrowly defined as ethnic opposition among China's Han majority toward the "alien" Manchus, figured prominently in the critique of the Manchus' Qing regime in the years immediately following the antiforeign Boxer uprising of 1899–1900.[1] As Zou Rong (1885–1905), for example, complained in his pamphlet *The Revolutionary Army* (Gemingjun) of 1903, "Unjust! Unjust! What is most unjust and bitter in China today is to have to put up with this inferior race of nomads with wolfish ambitions, these thievish Manchus [Manzhouren], as our rulers."[2] The revolutionaries, to be sure, were never narrowly or exclusively anti-Manchu. While "expulsion of the Tartar caitiffs" (*quzhu Dalu*) was the first of its stated goals, the revolutionary Alliance (Tongmenghui) in 1905 had three other, no-less-important objectives: revival of China, establishment of a republic, and equalization of land rights. Furthermore, the revolutionaries advanced numerous reasons other than ethnic opposition to justify ousting the ruling Manchus: they were incompetent; corrupt; oppressive and arbitrary; and, above all, incapable of defending China's national interests against the rapacious foreign powers. Nevertheless, apart from and in addition to such criticisms, the revolutionaries time and time again asserted simply that the Manchus had to go because they were not "Chinese."

But who, exactly, were the Manchus? They are often described as the descendants of the scattered Jurchen tribes in the northeastern frontier of China, bordering Korea, whom Nurhaci (1559–1626) began in the 1590s to unify and whom his son and successor Hong Taiji (1592–1643) renamed in 1635 "Manju" ("Manzhou" in Chinese). They were, in fact, a much broader, more heterogeneous group; they encompassed the total membership of the Eight Banners (Baqi), of whom the Manzhou were only one (though, admittedly, the core) group. Members of the system were known, collectively as well as individually, as "banner people" (*qiren*). Thus, the issue of Manchu identity is inextricably bound up with the Eight Banner system.

How valid were the revolutionaries' criticisms of the Manchus as an alien people? To what extent and in what ways were the Manchus in the late Qing dynasty (1644–1912) separate and distinct from the Han, particularly in view of the 1865 edict cited by Mary Wright in *The Last Stand of Chinese Conservatism* that purportedly had abolished most remaining differences between the two groups?

THE CASE AGAINST THE MANCHUS

Anti-Manchuism was a loud chorus among the young, revolutionary-minded intellectuals who gathered to study in Japan in the early post-Boxer years. Their immediate concern was the menace of imperialism. Following the multinational invasion of north China to suppress the Boxers and the Russian occupation of Manchuria in 1900, China seemed to be on the verge of being partitioned among the foreign powers. The perilous condition of their homeland could easily be blamed upon the Qing government, the Manchu court, and the Manchu people as a whole. An article in *Enlightenment Journal* (Kaizhilu) in 1900–1901 spelled out the link between anti-imperialism and anti-Manchuism: "People of our country speak daily of the shame of becoming the slaves of the foreigners, but they overlook the shame of being the slaves of the Manchus. They speak daily of expelling the foreign race but ignore the expelling of the foreign Manchu race [*Manzhou zhi waizhong*]."[3]

The most outspoken of the anti-Manchu critics in the early post-Boxer years were Zhang Binglin (1868–1936), Zou Rong, and Chen Tianhua (1875–1905). Zhang Binglin, the oldest and most persistent of the three, had been loosely associated with the radical reformers of 1898 and, like them, had had to flee China after the Hundred Days of Reform. He did not become a revolutionary until the summer of 1900, when, distressed by the empress dowager's mishandling of the Boxer crisis, he published his first attack on the Manchus. In one of two statements written for *China Daily* (Zhongguo ribao), the newly founded organ of the Revive China Society (Xing-Zhong Hui) in Hong Kong, he announced that he had cut off his queue—thus severing his ties to the Qing dynasty—and explained why he had done so. Later on, as part of his assault on the monarchical reformers, he published other criticisms of the Manchus, such as a 1901 article on Liang Qichao (1873–1929) in the Tokyo *Citizens' News* (Guominbao) and a 1903 Shanghai pamphlet on Kang Youwei (1858–1927). For his anti-Manchu writings, Zhang was arrested in 1903 in Shanghai as part of the *Jiangsu News* (Subao) censorship case. Following his release from prison in 1906, he joined forces with Sun Yat-sen (1866–1925) in Tokyo and became editor of *The People's Journal* (Minbao), the organ of Sun's year-old revolutionary Alliance.[4] Zou Rong, the second of the three chief anti-Manchu critics, was the author of *The Revolutionary Army*, which was published in 1903 in

Shanghai as a pamphlet, with a laudatory preface by Zhang Binglin. Zou had written the tirade a year or two earlier while a student in Japan. Because of his unrestrained criticism of the Manchus, he too was arrested as part of the *Jiangsu News* case. He died in 1905, at twenty years of age, in prison. In part because of his youthful martyrdom, in the post-Boxer decade Zou's *The Revolutionary Army* became the most widely circulated of the anti-Manchu writings.[5] Finally, Chen Tianhua, who was Zou's elder by ten years, was the author of two pamphlets, *A Sudden Look Back* (Meng huitou) and *An Alarm to Awaken the Age* (Jingshi zhong), both published in 1903 in Tokyo, where Chen had been studying for about a year. He subsequently, in 1905, joined Sun Yat-sen's Alliance in Tokyo and wrote extensively for the first issue of *The People's Journal*. Shortly afterward Chen committed suicide in protest against Japanese press reports that denigrated the patriotism of the Chinese students in Japan. His unfinished novel *Lion's Roar* (Shizi hou) was published posthumously.[6]

The revolutionaries complained a great deal about the Manchus *qua* Manchus but seldom in a systematic fashion. Their condemnation of the Manchus, even in a tract so unremittingly hostile as *The Revolutionary Army*, was usually scattered throughout a broader condemnation of the Qing regime, one that criticized the Qing, for example, for being corrupt, oppressive, or incapable of standing up to the imperialists. However, a sampling of the revolutionary literature of the early post-Boxer years shows that their critique of the Manchus may be summarized in a seven-point indictment. The specifics come largely from the writings of Zou Rong, Chen Tianhua, and Zhang Binglin, supplemented by other publications of the period. Except for Chen's novel *Lion's Roar*, all of these sources appeared prior to the formation of the Alliance in mid-1905.[7]

The Seven-Point Indictment against the Manchus

First, the Manchus were an alien, barbarian group who were different from the Chinese and did not belong in China. "Why do I find fault with the Manchu people [Manzhouren]?" Zhang Ji asked bluntly in the *Jiangsu News* in 1903. "Because China belongs to the Chinese people [Zhongguoren]."[8] This stance was what distinguished the anti-Manchu revolutionaries from the anti-imperialist reformers, whose foremost concern was to exclude the imperialist powers (and not necessarily the Manchus) from China; so far as the reformers were concerned, the Manchu rulers were no less "Chinese" than their subjects. For revolutionaries such as Zhang Ji, the Manchus most definitely were not "Chinese" and they had no more right to be in China than the imperialists had.

The revolutionaries differentiated the Manchus from themselves terminologically in two ways. One was to refer to them by epithets traditionally applied to the various "barbarians" on the periphery surrounding China's civilized core. Thus, Zou Rong asserted,

> What our compatriots today call court, government, and emperor, we used to call Yi, Man, Rong, and Di [barbarians of the east, south, west, and north] as well as Xiongnu and Dada. Their tribes lived beyond Shanhaiguan and fundamentally are of a different race from our illustrious descendants of the Yellow Emperor. Their land is barren; their people, furry; their minds, bestial; their customs, savage.[9]

Other labels of a similar sort that were commonly used to designate and denigrate the Manchus were "Donghu" (Eastern Barbarians), which Zhang Binglin often used, and "Dalu," as in the Alliance membership oath, which combined "Dada" (Tartar) with *lu* (caitiffs), an archaic term used in the Northern Song period to refer to the Khitan.[10] As for the corresponding terms of self-reference, those revolutionaries who equated the Manchu "other" with barbarians generally identified themselves as "Chinese," which they usually rendered, as Zhang Ji did, as "Zhongguoren" or, as Liang Qichao had done in his 1898 *China Discussion* commentary, as "Zhina" or "Zhinaren," from the Chinese reading of "Shina," the prevalent Japanese term in the Meiji era for China.[11] Interestingly, they hardly ever referred to themselves as "Hua" and/or "Xia," the traditional terms for the people of the civilized central core when they were being contrasted with the barbarians of the periphery.

The other way the revolutionaries differentiated the Manchus from themselves was by drawing upon the imported doctrine of social Darwinism, which Liang Qichao had helped to introduce. According to their understanding of those teachings, as exemplified in Chen Tianhua's *Lion's Roar*, the world's population was divided, on the basis of location and skin color, among five large racial groups (*zhongzu*), or peoples: yellow, white, black, brown, and red; and each of these five peoples was in turn divided into a number of races (*zu*) and further subdivided into yet smaller groupings such as ethnic groups (*minzu*) and tribes. Thus, for example, the white people, living in Europe and North America, were made up of three races: Aryans, Teutons, and Slavs. Similarly, according to Zou Rong, the yellow people, in East and Southeast Asia, were composed of two races (*renzhong*): those of China (Zhongguo) and those of Siberia. The Chinese race included the Han (Hanzu)—with Koreans and Japanese as subgroups of the Han—as well as Tibetans and Vietnamese; the Siberian race included the Mongols, Turks, and Tungus, with the Manchus (Manzhouren) as a subgroup of the Tungus.[12] Chen Tianhua generally referred to the Manchus as "Manzhouren," but for Zou Rong and many others, the usual term was "Manren," which Liang Qichao had popularized. The most widely used corresponding term of self-reference in this instance was, again following Liang Qichao, "Hanren." Chen Tianhua, in *Lion's Roar*, thus rephrased Zhang Ji's slogan: "China belongs to the Han people [Hanren]."[13] The term "Hanzu," which is how the Han are classified today in the People's Republic, was seldom used; even more rare was the correlative term "Manzu" for the Manchus. The range of terms that were used to identify Manchus and Han and their relative frequency of use will become clear in the course of this study.

Second, the Manchus had committed a number of heinous crimes against the Chinese people, particularly in the course of their conquest in the mid-seventeenth century. Their barbarous actions marked the Manchus as the ancestral enemies of the Han, and though those deeds happened a long time ago, they demanded to be avenged. The worst of such crimes were the savage massacres of defenseless civilians at various cities in central and south China as the Manchus marched through in 1645. Citing the recently reprinted chronicles of the slaughter at Yangzhou and Jiading (both in Jiangsu), Zou Rong claimed that the Manchu troops had been "let loose, burning and plundering" and that "wherever the cavalry of the thievish Manchus [Manren] reached, there was murder and pillage." Nor, according to Zhang Binglin in 1903, were these atrocities attributable to only a few individual Manchu commanders; instead, every Manchu person had been responsible and thus culpable. Therefore, "when the Han race [Hanzu] wants revenge against the Manchus [Manzhou], they want revenge against their entire group."[14]

Third, the Manchus had barbarized China by imposing their savage customs upon their Han subjects. Unlike previous foreign conquerors of China who had assimilated the ways of the Chinese, the Qing had forced the Han to adopt their alien Manchu customs, notably their male hairstyle and their official dress. As Zou Rong noted indignantly,

> When a man with a braid and wearing barbarian clothes loiters about in London, why do all the passersby cry out [in English], "Pig-tail" or "Savage"? And if he loiters about in Tokyo, why do all the passersby say, "Chanchanbotsu" [lit., "a slave with a tail"]? Alas, the dignified appearance of the Han official has vanished utterly; the dress instituted by the Tang has gone without a trace! When I touch the clothes I wear, the hair on my head, my heart aches! . . . Ah, these queues, these barbarian clothes, these banner gowns [*qipao*], these peacock feathers, these red hat buttons, these necklaces. Are they the costume of China's cultural tradition, or are they the loathsome dress of the nomadic and thievish Manchus [Manren]?[15]

Fourth, the Manchus had set themselves up as a privileged minority separate from and superior to the Han. According to Zou Rong, "Although it has been over two hundred years, the Manchus stick with the Manchus and the Han stick with the Han; they have not mingled. Clearly there is a feeling that a lower race does not rank with a noble one." That is, the Manchus did not consider the Han their equal. As an example of the continuing failure of Manchus and Han to intermix, Zou referred to the provincial garrisons, where Manchus stationed in various major cities lived in their own quarters and were residentially segregated from the Han. Chen Tianhua, in *Lion's Roar*, cited a ban on intermarriage as another device by which Manchus kept apart from Han. The revolutionaries, furthermore, claimed that the Manchus, from their own separate world, lorded over and indeed lived off the Han. Echoing Liang Qichao's earlier criticism, Chen Tianhua, in *A Sudden Look Back*, charged, "They require that the inhabitants of the eighteen provinces collectively provide for their five million people. But up to now they themselves have not farmed or labored. All they do is sit and feed off the Han people [Hanren]. Is this not absolutely hateful?"[16]

Fifth, the Manchus subjugated the Han in the manner of a foreign military occupation. They maintained their domination over the Han by keeping their banner soldiers separate and concentrating them in a few strategic places around the country. Chen Tianhua, in *Lion's Roar*, commented on the careful thought the early Qing rulers had given to the placement of their troops:

> Aware that the Jurchen, by being dispersed, had opened themselves to be killed by the Han [Hanren], they took the several million Manchus [Manzhouren] that they had brought to China and stationed one-half of them in Beijing, where they are called the "palace guard" and the other half in the provinces, where they are called "provincial garrisons" [*zhufang*].

Zou Rong drew attention to the term used for these provincial encampments:

> Suppose we try to explain the meaning of the term *zhufang*. It is as if they are terrified and are constantly fearful lest the Han people [Hanren] rebel against them, and so they hold them in check like bandits. Otherwise, whom are they defending [*fang*] against? And why do they need to be stationed [*zhu*] somewhere?

The obvious intent of these provincial garrisons, as a *Jiangsu News* article in 1903 summed up, was "to suppress the slaves."[17]

Sixth, the Manchus practiced political discrimination against their Han subjects in at least three ways. They were a numerical minority ruling over the Han majority. According to Zou Rong, "The world recognizes only the principle that a minority submits to a majority. . . . If only the thievish Manchus [Manren] were a majority, but they number merely five million, scarcely the population of a single department or county." The Manchus discriminated against the Han also by their monopoly of the highest governmental posts, in contravention of the Qing court's own professed commitment to Manchu-Han equality. According to Chen Tianhua, in *Lion's Roar*, "Official posts are supposed to be evenly divided between Manchus and Han, but all the important responsibilities are held by Manchus [Manren]." Following a detailed analysis of the metropolitan administration, Zou Rong concluded, "Opportunities for an official career for a Manchu in comparison with those for a Han are hardly less far apart than the sky is from the ground or clouds are from mire." The Manchus discriminated against the Han in promotions as well. According to Zou again,

> One may often find Manchus and Han of similar grades, graduates of the same year and employed in the same office. The Han [Hanren], however, may be held back for decades, without being transferred to a higher post, whereas the Manchu [Manren] in a twinkling becomes first a board vice-president, and then a board president, and finally a grand secretary. . . . If, by good fortune and against all odds, some [Han] officials do finally rise to the position of grand secretary or board president or vice-president, they are all white-haired and toothless, old and weak, and they share whatever is left over from the hands of the Manchus.[18]

Seventh, and last, the Manchus, despite their pretense at accommodation, were fundamentally at odds with and hostile toward the Han people. As evidence, the revolutionaries repeatedly cited a remark that Liang Qichao, in an essay of 1900, attributed to Gangyi (1837–1900), the reactionary Manchu leader at Cixi's court after 1898: "If the Han get strong, the Manchus are doomed; if the Han grow weak, the Manchus get plump."[19] Zou Rong claimed that Gangyi's statement embodied the single underlying rationale behind the court's successive policies toward the Taiping Rebellion (1851–64), the Sino-Japanese War (1894–95), and the Boxer Rebellion, for in every instance the Manchus derived all the rewards while the Han made all the sacrifices. As for the court's recent efforts to achieve "wealth and power" (*fuqiang*): "Today's strengthening [*qiang*] is the strengthening of the Manchus [Manren]; it has nothing to do with us Han [Hanren]. Today's enrichment [*fu*] is the enrichment of the Manchus; it has nothing to do with us Han."[20] It was, according to the revolutionaries, the Manchus' anti-Han posture that explained the court's inability, indeed unwillingness, to defend China's national sovereignty and territory from the foreign powers. Their policy was epitomized by another of Gangyi's alleged sayings: "Rather than hand over our land to household slaves [i.e., the Han], let us present it to neighboring friends."[21] Having thus sold out to their foreign "friends," the Qing had become, in the words of Chen Tianhua, "the foreigners' court," and the Han had become, in Zou's words, "slaves of barbarous slaves."[22]

MANCHUS AND BANNER PEOPLE

Among the numerous terms that the revolutionaries of the early post-Boxer era applied to the Manchus, one—"banner people" (qiren)—was strikingly absent. This was odd because it is clear that four of the seven counts in their indictment of the Manchus clearly equated them with the membership of the Eight Banner system. It was soldiers of the banner army who committed the atrocities against the Han during the Qing conquest of China proper (no. 2) and who then kept the conquered Han under continuous subjugation from their various garrisons (no. 5), and it was the broad masses of the banner population who lived a privileged existence segregated from the Han (no. 4) and who benefited from the Qing dynasty's policy of political discrimination (no. 6). Thus, in the eyes of the revolutionaries, the Manchus were identical to the banner people, and so it was in the eyes of the Manchus, too. As a descendant of the Qing imperial clan recalls, "The Manchus [Manren] called themselves, and were called by others, 'banner people' [qiren]." Or, as stated by James Lee and Robert Eng, "The banner system was the principal institution which unified the Manchu people and defined Manchu identity."[23]

The Eight Banner system as it existed in the late nineteenth century was fundamentally little changed from when it was first set up by the founders of the dynasty, Nurhaci and Hong Taiji, prior to the invasion of Ming dynasty (1368–1644) China. Nurhaci created the system in 1615 when he divided all the scattered Jurchen tribes in the mountains of eastern and northern "Manchuria" that he had dominated into eight groups called "banners" (qi), each with a number of companies (zuoling). Twenty years later, when Hong Taiji bestowed the new name "Manzhou" (from the Manchu "Manju") upon his people, they became the "Eight Banner Manchus" (Baqi Manzhou). Meanwhile, as Nurhaci and Hong Taiji extended their authority into the plains of southern Manchuria and began overrunning Han settlements and enslaving their inhabitants, they apportioned these captives among the leaders of the original Manchu Eight Banners. Such household slaves of Han origin were known as "bondservants"

(*baoyi*, from the Manchu *booi*, "of the household"), some of whom were organized into separate banner companies of their own that became a part of their
master's Manchu banner. Still later, in 1642, as more and more Han in southern Manchuria either defected to or were defeated by him, Hong Taiji stopped
enslaving them and organized them instead into their own set of banners; these
Eight Banners composed of Han personnel were known as the Hanjun.
Meanwhile, in 1635, Hong Taiji similarly had established another separate Eight
Banner organization for those Mongols of western Manchuria and eastern
Mongolia who had submitted to his rule. Although other peoples were incor-
porated into the banner system later on, its basic framework was thus already
in place by the time Hong Taiji's successors "entered through the pass" into
China proper in 1644. It had three ethnic components—Manchu, Mongol, and
Hanjun—each with its own set of eight banners, for a total of twenty-four ban-
ners in the entire banner force.[24]

The Eight Banner system, though simple in structure, was extremely heterogeneous in composition. In addition to the tripartite division among the
Manchu banners, Mongol banners, and Hanjun, there were numerous other
significant internal differences: between the Upper Three and the Lower Five
Banners, between Old and New banner people, between the imperial lineage
and ordinary banner people, between the regular banner companies and the
bondservant companies, between the core banners and the affiliated banners,
between the Metropolitan Banners (Jingqi) and the provincial garrisons, and
between the banner soldiers and their dependents.

In all three ethnic components, each of the Eight Banners was identified
by the color (yellow, white, red, or blue) of its flag, which was either "plain"
(solid) or "bordered" with a red or white fringe. The Eight Banners were
ranked in descending order of social importance: Bordered Yellow, Plain Yellow,
Plain White, Plain Red, Bordered White, Bordered Red, Plain Blue, and Bordered Blue. The first three—Bordered Yellow, Plain Yellow, and Plain White—
constituted the Upper Three Banners, which from an early date had been under
the direct command of the emperor; the Lower Five Banners were originally
commanded by various imperial princes and did not come under direct imperial command until the Yongzheng reign (1722–35). The Upper Three Banners
were more prestigious than the Lower Five.[25]

Of the three ethnic components, the Manchu banners were in the late Qing
the largest by far. According to *The Draft History of the Qing* (Qingshigao),
compiled after the revolution, 53.5 percent of the officers and soldiers in the
Metropolitan Banners belonged to the Manchu banners, 31.8 percent to the
Hanjun, and 14.7 percent to the Mongol banners.[26] However, when the banner troops in the provinces are taken into account, the Hanjun's share was con-

siderably less, because the partial demobilization of the Hanjun that took place during the Qianlong reign (1735–96) had a significantly greater effect upon the provincial garrisons than among the Metropolitan Banners. Therefore, it may be roughly estimated that 60 percent of the entire banner force was made up of Manchu banners and the other 40 percent was divided roughly equally between the Mongol banners and the Hanjun.

The Manchu banners were not only the oldest and the most numerous but, not surprisingly, also the most prestigious. They outranked the Mongol banners, who in turn outranked the Hanjun.[27] However, just as the entire banner force was not a homogeneous body, neither were the Manchu banners. For example, apart from the Jurchen who formed the founding core, the Eight Banner Manchus also included thirty-seven companies of Mongols, six of Koreans (Chaoxian), one of Russians (Eluosi), and one of Tibetans (*fanzi*). These "foreign" units in the Manchu banners were in addition to the many individual Mongols and Han Chinese who were scattered among the Manchu banner companies.[28] The major difference within the Manchu banners was that between the Old and the New Manchus, depending on the date of their adherence to the Qing cause. The Old Manchus ("Fo Manzhou," from the Manchu *fe*, "old") were those whose ancestors had joined up and been organized into banners during the time of Nurhaci and Hong Taiji; they were principally descended from the Jianzhou and other Jurchen tribal groups. On the other hand, the New Manchus ("Yiche Manzhou," from the Manchu *ice*, "new") were principally the descendants of those northeastern tribes who submitted only after the Qing had invaded China proper; they were relocated southward into the Amur River basin and brought into the banner system during the Shunzhi (1644–61) and Kangxi (1661–1722) reigns to defend against Czarist Russia's expansionism in the region. These New Manchus included two non-Jurchen Tungusic groups—the Hezhe and Kiakar (Kuyala)—who lived by hunting and fishing amidst the mountains and streams of northeastern Manchuria and adjacent parts of Siberia; and four groups of intermixed Mongols and Tungus— the Daur (Dawoer), Solun (Suolun), Oroqen (Elunchun), and Xibe (Xibo)—who lived on either side of the Greater Xing'an Mountains separating the Mongolian steppe to the west and the Manchurian forests to the east. Because their association with the Qing rulers was more recent as well as more distant, the New Manchus were less prestigious than the Old, but they were allowed a degree of organizational autonomy denied the Old Manchus; even after they had been incorporated into the banner system, they remained under the leadership of their own tribal and clan chiefs.[29]

One notable subset of the Old Manchus was the imperial lineage (*huangzu*), which consisted of two large categories of relatives. One was the imperial clan (*zongshi*), the Aisin Gioro ("Aixin Jueluo" in Chinese), who traced their descent directly from Nurhaci's father, Taksi. The rest of the imperial lineage, consisting of the collateral lines descended from Nurhaci's uncles and brothers, were known as the *gioro* (Ch. *jueluo*). Members of these two groups multiplied rapidly. At the end of the dynasty, there were twenty-nine thousand members of the imperial lineage in the main line and another twenty thousand in the collateral lines. Although each of the two categories of the imperial lineage were assigned to their own separate banner companies, all members, whether main line or collateral, were subject to the jurisdiction of the Imperial Clan Court (Zongrenfu) rather than that of the regular banner authorities.[30] The most exalted of the imperial clan were the titled princes and nobles, who were divided into twelve ranks, the top four of which were *qinwang, junwang, beile* (a Manchu term), and *beizi* (from the Manchu *beise*) respectively. With some exceptions, notably the eight "iron-capped princes" (*tiemaozi wang*) who had the right of perpetual inheritance, these ranks were inheritable only on a descending scale. The eldest son of a third-rank *beile*, for example, became a fourth-rank *beizi*, while all of the younger sons dropped down to "nobles of the ninth rank" (*zhenguo jiangjun*).[31] Consequently, only a minuscule number of imperial clan members held a title.

In the post-Boxer era the most prominent member of the imperial clan, aside from the emperor and his immediate family, was unquestionably Yikuang (Prince Qing; see chart 1.1.). Born in 1836, Yikuang was a great-grandson of the Qianlong emperor and belonged to the Manchu Plain Blue Banner, one of the Five Lower Banners to which direct descendants of emperors were assigned. His grandfather, Yonglin, was the first Prince Qing, an honor conferred on him in 1799 after his brother had become the Jiaqing emperor. Yikuang inherited the family estate in 1850 when his uncle, Mianti, died without a male heir. By then, however, due to the impact of the Qing inheritance rules, Yikuang was a mere noble of the tenth rank (*fuguo jiangjun*). His subsequent rise to prominence came about as a result of his long association with Empress Dowager Cixi (1835–1908). When in 1884 he succeeded Yixin (1832–98), the first Prince Gong, as head of the Zongli Yamen (or proto–Foreign Office), he was made a prince of the second rank, thus reclaiming the family title of Prince Qing. Ten years later, on the occasion of Cixi's sixtieth birthday, his position was raised to that of prince of the first rank. Finally, in December 1908, at the beginning of the Xuantong reign, he reached the top of the princely ladder and was given the rare right of perpetual inheritance. When a cabinet was formed in early 1911, Yikuang became China's first prime minister.[32] Among the collateral lines of the imperial lineage, the most notable figure in the post-Boxer period was probably Liangbi (1877–1912), a member of the Bordered Yellow Banner,

CHART 1.1.   Prominent Members of the Imperial Clan in the Late Qing

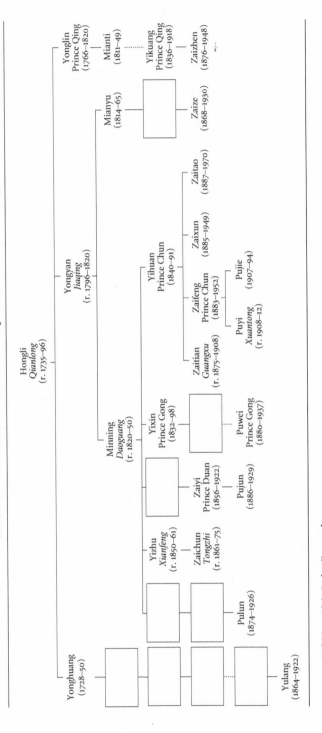

SOURCE: Li Zhiting, *Aixin Jueluo jiazu*, vols. 2–3.

NOTE: Dotted line = descent by adoption. Reign titles are set in italic type.

whose ancestor was a younger brother of Nurhaci and whose grandfather, Yilibu, negotiated and signed the Treaty of Nanjing, ending the First Opium War (1839–42). At the time of the 1911 Revolution, Liangbi was a leading proponent of resistance to the Republicans. It was his assassination in late January 1912 that, as much as anything, convinced the court to abdicate.[33]

The second ethnic component of the banner system was the Mongol Eight Banners. They were drawn mostly from the horse-riding, sheep-herding peoples of eastern Mongolia bordering on Manchuria. The Mongol banners were also divided between Old and New, depending on whether they had submitted to the Qing before or after the invasion of China proper. The Old Mongols included early adherents such as the Khorchin (Keerqin) and Chahar (Chahaer); the New Mongols were late joiners such as the Barga (Baerhu) and Olot (Elute). The most prominent Mongol bannerman in the post-Boxer era was Xiliang (1853–1917), of the Bordered Blue Banner, who in early 1911 was the governor-general of the three northeastern provinces.[34]

The third ethnic component of the Eight Banners was the Hanjun (often translated as "Chinese banners").[35] Depending again on when they were enrolled into the system, they too were differentiated between Old and New. The Old Hanjun were descended from the Han frontiersmen living in southern Manchuria who had been captured by Hong Taiji. The New Hanjun were descended from captives of later wars, principally the invasion of China proper in 1644 and the suppression of the Rebellion of the Three Feudatories (1673–81). (Other Han prisoners of war after 1644 were put into the non-banner Army of the Green Standard [Lüying].) The Hanjun were the least well regarded of the three ethnic components of the banner system. It was they, particularly the New Hanjun, who bore the brunt of the Qianlong emperor's reorganization of the banner system. Despite their relatively low status, the Hanjun were no less a part of the system than its other components.[36] The highest-ranking Hanjun among the officials of the post-Boxer era were the two Zhao brothers, Erxun and Erfeng, both members of the Plain Blue Banner. Zhao Erxun (1844–1927) became in 1911 the governor-general of the three northeastern provinces, succeeding the Mongol bannerman Xiliang; after the revolution, he supervised the compilation of *The Draft History of the Qing*. His younger brother, Erfeng (1846–1911), was the governor-general of Sichuan at the time of the revolution and was killed shortly afterward.[37]

The last element of the banner system, ranking lower than even the Hanjun, comprised the bondservants. Bondservants owned by the emperor belonged to the Upper Three Banners and were under the jurisdiction of the Imperial Household Department (Neiwufu); they generally served in the palace. Those owned by various imperial princes belonged to the Lower Five Banners.

Bondservants were not, strictly speaking, a separate part of the Eight Banner system, but were part of their master's banner. Because they were hereditarily servile, bondservants as a group, even those in the Upper Three Banners, did not rank with the regular banners. While bondservants had played a crucial role as intermediaries for the Qing rulers during the early part of the dynasty, they were politically insignificant in the late Qing.[38]

The Eight Banner organization provided the institutional framework within which its members, the banner people, lived out their lives. All banner people—men, women, and children alike—belonged to one of the twenty-four banners. Except for members of the imperial lineage and the bondservants of the Upper Three Banners, who were governed by the Imperial Clan Court and the Imperial Household Department respectively, all were subject to the jurisdiction of their banner. Membership in a particular banner was hereditary and, except when women changed banner affiliation on marriage, was largely immutable.[39] To the banner people, the banner and its subunits, particularly the company, were only slightly less important than the lineage and the family.

The Eight Banner system was organized along military lines. Each of the twenty-four banners was commanded by a lieutenant-general (*dutong*, rank 1B [within a nine-rank system]) and two deputy lieutenant-generals (*fudutong*, rank 2A), who were almost always themselves bannermen, often imperial princes and high officials, though not necessarily members of that particular banner or even that ethnic component within the banner system.[40] Each banner looked after its own affairs, while the Banner Duty Office (Zhinianqi), composed of representatives from the Eight Banners, provided overall coordination.[41] The banner commanders were located in Beijing.

For the banner people, the banner was one of two basic social units. It determined, in part, the social standing of individuals because the different banners varied in prestige depending on ethnicity and color. The color and ethnicity of a banner also determined where its members lived, as each banner was assigned a residential area according to the Manchu system of correlation between color and compass direction. Under this system, which differed from that of both the Chinese and the Mongols, yellow was associated with north, white with east, red with west, and blue with south. Thus, within Beijing's Inner City surrounding the Forbidden City (the emperor's Winter Palace), the two yellow banners (the most prestigious) were assigned land in the north, the white banners in the east, the red banners in the west, and the blue banners (the least prestigious) in the south.[42] This explains why, for example, the Manchu novelist Lao She (1899–1966), whose family belonged to the Plain Red Banner, was born and grew up in the west-northwest sector of Beijing.[43] The distribution of the banners by color provided the basis for the further division of the Eight Banners into two "wings" (*yi*), with the Bordered Yellow, the two Whites, and the Plain Blue forming the east (or, when facing south, left) wing, and the Plain Yellow, the two Reds, and the Bordered Blue forming the west (or right) wing.[44] A banner's ethnicity was another, though secondary, factor in determining its residential location. In Beijing, each of the eight sectors into which the Inner City was divided by the color of the banner was further divided into three districts, one for each of the ethnic components of that banner. The result was the creation in Beijing's Inner City of twenty-four residential zones, one for each of the banners, with the Manchu, Mongol, and Hanjun banners interspersed throughout the city but each living in their own separate quarters.[45] This spatial arrangement by the color and ethnicity of banners was replicated in most other places where banner soldiers were garrisoned.

Each banner was divided into battalions (*jiala*, from the Manchu *jalan*), then subdivided into companies (*zuoling*). In a Manchu or Hanjun banner, there were five battalions; in a Mongol banner, only two. Each battalion was headed by a colonel (*canling*, rank 3A), who was appointed from within the banner, as were all subordinate officials. The number of companies within a battalion varied from fourteen to nineteen in the Manchu banners, eleven to fifteen in the Mongol banners, and five to nine in the Hanjun.[46] Altogether, as we shall see, there were over two thousand banner companies.

More so than the banner, the company was the primary social organization for the banner people. Membership in a company, as in a banner, was hereditary, and members of a company "resided together within the area designated for their banner."[47] The company was the banner person's primary focus of identification, in the same way that the county was for most other Chinese. Whereas a Han would be identified as "So-and-so of X county in Y province," a banner person would be known by his or her company and its parent banner. Each company was headed by a captain (also known as *zuoling*, rank 4A), assisted by a lieutenant (*xiaoqixiao*, rank 6A). Just as the magistrate was the "father and mother official" to the inhabitants of his county, so the captain was to the members of his banner company. So closely was a banner company associated with its leader, who unlike the county magistrate was not subject to rotation, that it was more likely to be identified by the name of its captain than by its unit designation; for example, the Fifteenth Company in the Third Battalion of the Manchu Plain Red Banner was, in 1904, better known as "Yizhen's company."[48]

Finally, the basic unit of the banner organization was the banner soldier (*qibing*). Each company was assigned a quota of soldiers. In the late Qing, according to Zhang Deze, a company in a Manchu banner had about 260 soldiers; in a Mongol company, more than 100; and in a Hanjun company, about 140.[49] One of the main functions of a company captain was to maintain a register of all the members of his company, which he submitted to his banner headquarters and to the Board of Revenue every three years. The register recorded the name, age, occupational status, and family relationship of every member of the company. In particular, it classified the men according to their availability for military service: those who were not yet sixteen years (*sui*) in age were classified as "young males" (*youding*); those who were between sixteen and sixty as "able-bodied males" (*zhuangding*); those who were older than sixty as "retired" (*tuiding*); and those who were ill as "handicapped" (*feiding*). The purpose of the register was to keep track of those who were eligible for selection as new banner soldiers in the company when old ones retired or died.[50] Except in the Hanjun, another purpose of the register was to assist the captain in recommending young women from his company who might be eligible for service in the emperor's palace.[51]

All banner personnel, apart from their membership in one of the twenty-four banners, were assigned to a specific geographical location, usually a military garrison, depending on which type of banner company they belonged to. Also, all banner soldiers were enrolled in one of several service branches. These additional affiliations served to further differentiate the banner population. For example, Lao She's father was a member not only of the Manchu Plain Red Banner but also of the Metropolitan Banners in Beijing and the Guards Division (Hujunying). Just as the statutory strength of the banner system had long been fixed by the late Qing, so had the geographical distribution of the companies, the number and size of individual garrisons, and (except for a few creations of the Self-Strengthening Movement in the late nineteenth century) the size and duties of the service branches. Consequently, the descriptions of the banner system in the 1899 edition of *The Collected Statutes of the Great Qing* (Da-Qing huidian) and in *The Draft History of the Qing* differ hardly at all from Thomas Wade's detailed account in the 1851 volume of the English-language *Chinese Repository*, which was based on the 1812 edition of *The Collected Statutes*.

Banner companies were customarily divided among three types—outer, inner, and garrison—but there was a fourth type as well, which may be called "affiliated." Outer companies (*wai zuoling*) consisted of the regular banner units located in and around Beijing; they were commonly called the Metropolitan Banners. They were the most numerous of the four types, totaling 1,147 companies. Inner companies (*nei zuoling*) were composed of bondservants and hence were also known as bondservant companies. They, too, were located in Beijing as well as in Zhili and Fengtian. *The Draft History of the Qing* suggests that they numbered 115 companies.[52] Garrison companies (*zhufang zuoling*) were regular banner units stationed outside Beijing at various locations in the provinces; they added up to 817. These three types of banner companies, which altogether totaled 2,079, are usually thought of as constituting the totality of the banner force. However, as *The Collected Statutes* also indicates, there was a fourth type of banner company, which consisted of various frontier peoples who belonged to the banner system but were not formally counted among the provincial garrisons. There is no complete accounting of the strength of such affiliated banner companies.

Soldiers of the Metropolitan Banners were divided principally among five long-established service branches (listed in order of prestige): the Escorts (Qinjunying), Vanguard (Qianfengying), Guards (Hujunying), Light Cavalry (Xiaoqiying), and Infantry or Gendarmerie (Bujunying), all of which date from the days of Nurhaci and Hong Taiji. Subsequently, in the early Qing, several new units were created: the Firearms Division (Huoqiying), Yuanmingyuan Guards, and Scouts (Jianruiying). During the Self-Strengthening Movement in the late Qing, yet another new unit, which contemporary Westerners called the Peking Field Force (Shenjiying), was added to the Metropolitan Banners. All of these units, including the Peking Field Force, served principally in one capacity or another as palace guards for the emperor and his residences. Thus, nine-tenths of the Metropolitan Banners were stationed in Beijing's Inner City. The remainder were quartered near the emperor's Summer Palace in the northwestern suburb.

The total strength of the Metropolitan Banners, according to different estimates, ranged between 125,000 and 150,000 soldiers and officers (see table 1.1). T. F. Wade's statistics for the various divisions indicate that the Metropolitan Banners consisted of 7,305 officers, 90,333 regular soldiers, 31,064 reservists, and 2,497 artisans and others, for a total of 131,199. An 1849 source cited by Wang Zhonghan said that the total was 149,425. Yang Du, writing in 1907, quoted figures for the banner units in Beijing that add up to 139,430. *The Draft History of the Qing* asserts that the Metropolitan Banners numbered 126,989.[53] On the basis of these sources, it may be estimated that the total strength of the Metropolitan Banners in the late Qing was about 130,000 soldiers and officers. If the roughly 20,000 bondservants (derived from Wade and *The Draft History of the Qing*) are added to this figure, then altogether the banner personnel in and around Beijing totaled about 150,000.

Banner personnel who were not in the Metropolitan Banners or in bondservant companies belonged to either garrison companies or, in some instances, affiliated banner detachments. According to *The Collected Statutes*, the garrison companies numbered 817, divided among ninety-one garrisons, with each garrison assigned a certain number of companies and a quota of soldiers and

TABLE 1.1. Composition and Strength of the Banner Troops in Beijing

	Wade			The Draft History of the Qing				
	Officers	Soldiers	Total	Officers	Soldiers	Total	Yang	Liu
METROPOLITAN BANNERS								
Escorts (Qinjunying)	1,201	1,756	2,957	—	—	—	1,756	1,742
Vanguards (Qianfengying)	160	1,764	1,924	230	1,668	1,898	1,764	1,764
Guards (Hujunying)	1,199	14,075	15,274	1,502	14,081	15,583	15,975	15,975
Light Cavalry (Xiaoqiying)	3,340	65,437	68,777	—	—	—	80,538	75,427
Infantry (Bujunying)	575	23,012	23,587	—	—	—	21,238	23,122
Firearms (Huoqiying)	297	7,814	8,111	—	—	—	—	—
Inner Detachment	—	—	—	148	3,920	4,068	4,021	4,016
Outer Detachment	—	—	—	145	3,700	3,845	3,797	3,797
Yuanmingyuan Guards	350	6,108	6,458	336	6,408	6,744	6,508	4,108
Scouts (Jianruiying)	183	3,928	4,111	102	3,878	3,980	3,833	3,833
Guards at Prince Chun's tomb	—	—	—	3	48	51	—	—
Subtotal	7,305	123,894	131,199	6,680	120,309	126,989	139,430	133,784
BONDSERVANT COMPANIES								
Upper Three Banners	404	7,480	7,884	278	8,477	8,755	—	—
Lower Five Banners	212	9,705	9,917	918	10,740	11,658	—	—
Subtotal	616	17,185	17,801	1,196	19,217	20,413	—	—
Grand Total	7,921	141,079	149,000	7,876	139,526	147,402	—	—

SOURCES: Wade, "Army of the Chinese Empire," 254, 308; Qingshigao, 130: 3886–89; Yang Du, Yang Du ji, 425; Liu Fenghan, "Qingji ziqiang yundong," 346–47.

officers.[54] As was previously noted, there is no complete accounting of the affiliated companies. The ninety-one provincial garrisons varied greatly in size. The largest ones—namely, Shengjing (7,031), Xi'an (6,588), and Jingzhou (5,668)—had more than five thousand soldiers each; the smallest ones, such as Shunyi in Zhili, had only fifty soldiers. The larger or more important provincial garrisons typically were commanded by a general (*jiangjun*, often translated into English as "Tartar-general"; rank 1B) or a brigade-general (also *fudutong*; rank 2A); the smaller garrisons, by a military commandant (*chengshouwei*, rank 3A; or *fangshouwei*, rank 4A) or a platoon captain (*fangyu*, rank 5A).[55] The commander of a larger garrison often had one or more smaller nearby garrisons within his overall jurisdiction. In the most extreme case, the general at Shengjing was responsible for twenty-four other garrisons in Fengtian. The garrison commander was usually appointed from outside the garrison; his subordinates came from within the garrison.

As with the Metropolitan Banners, the banner soldiers in the provinces were divided among several service branches, principally the Light Cavalry, the Vanguard, and the Infantry, with the Light Cavalry as the principal unit. Unlike the Metropolitan Banners, the provincial garrisons did not include Escorts and Guards, and they also largely excluded the Hanjun. Following the large-scale demobilization of the Hanjun during the Qianlong era, almost all of the provincial garrisons were staffed solely by Manchu and Mongol banner soldiers. Only the garrisons in the three northeastern territories (particularly Fengtian) and in Guangzhou and Fuzhou had any Hanjun.[56]

The garrison at Jingzhou (present-day Jiangling), the historically strategic city in Hubei up the Yangzi River from Wuhan, was, except for its large size, a representative provincial garrison. Established by the Kangxi emperor in 1683 following the suppression of the Rebellion of the Three Feudatories, it was headed by a general and consisted of fifty-six companies: forty from the Manchu banners, sixteen from the Mongol banners, and none from the Hanjun. Assisting the general were two brigade-generals, each responsible for one of the two wings into which the companies were divided by banner color. Below the two brigade-generals were ten regimental colonels (*xieling*, rank 3B), one for each of the eight Manchu banners and one for each of the two wings of Mongol banners. Each of the fifty-six companies was headed by a captain, with ten of the captains serving concurrently as regimental colonels. Each company also had one platoon captain and one lieutenant. Aside from the officers, the garrison was made up of—according to *The Collected Statutes of the Great Qing*—5,668 soldiers, two-thirds of whom (3,800) were either privates (*majia*) or corporals (*lingcui*) in the Light Cavalry. The remaining soldiers consisted of 200 vanguards, 700 infantrymen, 80 artillerymen, 168 artisans, and 720 reservists (*yangyubing*).[57] Insofar as they were members of one of the Eight Banners, they were under the jurisdiction of the commander of their respective banner in Beijing. At the same time, because they were stationed in the provinces, they were also under the jurisdiction of the general of their garrison. Thus, no less than their peers in Beijing, the banner soldiers in the provinces possessed multiple identities, depending on their banner, geographical location, and service branch. During the post-Boxer era, probably the most prominent bannerman who came from the provinces was Tieliang (1863–1938), a member of the Manchu Bordered White Banner from the Jingzhou garrison. He rose to the position of grand councilor in 1905 and was both a bitter rival of Yuan Shikai (1859–1916) and a hated enemy of the republican revolutionaries.[58]

By the late Qing, the assignment of soldiers to a garrison was hereditary and permanent.[59] The last large-scale uprooting of banner soldiers was after the Taiping Rebellion, when the ranks of such decimated garrisons as Hangzhou and Nanjing were replenished by recruits from other garrisons. The Hangzhou garrison, whose statutory strength was 2,216 soldiers, was virtually reconstituted between 1865 and 1880 by 1,461 transfers from Zhapu, Fuzhou, Dezhou, Qingzhou, Jingzhou, and Chengdu. The destroyed garrisons, however, were not always restored to full strength. The Nanjing garrison originally had 4,666 soldiers in 40 companies, but when it was restocked by transfers from Jingzhou following the Taiping massacre, it had only 2,424 soldiers in 24 companies.[60]

The provincial garrisons were widely distributed among four geographical regions: the "capital region" (*jifu*), northeast China, northwest China, and the rest of China proper (see table 1.2).[61] According to *The Collected Statutes of the Great Qing*, the banner soldiers in the capital region, which encompassed most of Zhili Province outside Beijing, were divided among 25 garrisons, with a total of 14,238 soldiers organized into 54 banner companies. The largest of these garrisons, with 2,100 soldiers and headed by a brigade-general, was at Miyun, north of the capital. Also within the region were two large affiliated banner detachments, both stationed outside the Great Wall. One was a detachment of 1,000 soldiers at the Mulan imperial hunting grounds, north of Rehe, commanded by the Rehe lieutenant-general. (It is unclear from *The Collected Statutes* how many banner companies these 1,000 soldiers constituted.) The other, consisting of 10,800 Chahar, Olot, Barga, and other Mongols organized into 120 companies, was under the jurisdiction of the Chahar lieutenant-general at Zhangjiakou. Finally, although they were not formally counted among the capital region contingent of garrisons or among the affiliated detachments, a group of 1,460 banner soldiers guarded the two sets of Qing imperial tombs in Zhili: the Eastern Tombs near Zunhua (where the Shunzhi, Kangxi, Qianlong,

TABLE 1.2. Disposition and Strength of the Provincial Banners

	Garrisons	Companies	Officers	Soldiers	Total
Qing tombs	—	—	402	1,999	2,401
Capital region	25	54	293	14,238	14,531
Fengtian	25	125	426	18,340	18,766
Jilin	11	122	349	10,279	10,628
Heilongjiang	8	91	228	6,742	6,970
Willow Palisade	—	—	20	700	720
Northwest China	8	119	369	15,642	16,011
North China plain	3	26	93	3,323	3,416
Northwest highlands	3	60	214	10,652	10,866
Lower Yangzi	4	104	304	10,272	10,576
Middle Yangzi	1	56	180	5,668	5,848
Upper Yangzi	1	24	75	1,990	2,065
Southeast coast	1	18	61	2,720	2,781
South China	1	18	101	5,254	5,355
Total	91	817	3,115	107,819	110,934

SOURCES: *Da-Qing huidian*, 84: 4b-8a; 86: 4b-8a; Wade, "Army of the Chinese Empire," 315, 321, 324–25.

Xianfeng, and Tongzhi emperors are buried) and the Western Tombs near Yixian (where the Yongzheng, Jiaqing, and Daoguang emperors are buried).[62]

The banner contingent in the northeast (or Manchuria) consisted of 338 companies, totaling 35,361 soldiers in forty-four garrisons, six of which were attached "water forces" (*shuishiying*). They were divided among the three territories of Fengtian, Jilin, and Heilongjiang, each headed by a general. Slightly more than half of the banner troops in Manchuria were located in the southernmost territory, Fengtian, whose capital, Shengjing (also known as Mukden, now Shenyang), was the site of the largest provincial garrison in the country. Yet other banner soldiers not counted among the regular banner companies were located in the northeast. These included three large affiliated detachments. One was the Buteha [Hunting] Eight Banners, made up of Solun, Daur, and Oroqen; another was a "herding" detachment composed of Barga and Olot. Both were located in the Greater Xing'an Mountains in what is now Inner Mongolia, and both were under the jurisdiction of the Heilongjiang general at Qiqihar. The third affiliated detachment was made up of the Hezhe and Kiakar along the coast of the Japan Sea, who were under the authority of the brigade-general at Sanxing in Jilin (now Yilan in present-day Heilongjiang). Also counted as part of the banner force in the northeast were two other groups: the seven hundred soldiers stationed in detachments of twenty to fifty under platoon captains at nineteen gates (*bianmen*) along the length of the Willow Palisade (Liutiaobian), which enclosed southern Manchuria; and the 539 soldiers guarding the three early Qing imperial tombs in Fengtian (including those of Nurhaci and Hong Taiji).[63]

The banner contingent in the northwest consisted of eight garrisons, with 15,642 soldiers organized into 119 companies, stretched out along a vast arc from Ningxia in the east to the Yili River valley on the Xinjiang-Russian border in the west. These eight garrisons were distributed among three subregions: Ningxia and the Gansu corridor, eastern Xinjiang, and western Xinjiang. The largest of the northwestern garrisons was at Huiyuan (also Kuldja, now Yining), on the Yili River, with forty companies under the command of a general. Also under the authority of the general at Yili were two tribal detachments, one Solun and one Daur, relocated from northern Manchuria in the mid-eighteenth century; they were encamped along the south bank of the Yili River and were considered as part of the Yili garrison rather than as affiliated banner soldiers.[64]

Finally, the banner contingent in China proper (exclusive of Zhili) consisted of 39,879 soldiers, organized into 306 companies and divided among fourteen garrisons and two attached water forces. Except for Yunnan-Guizhou in the southwest, there was at least one banner garrison in each of G. William Skinner's "macro-regions," usually (but not always) in the core city of the region. Each of the three regions closest to the capital had more than one garrison. In the plains of north China, excluding the Metropolitan Banners in Beijing and the capital-region contingents in Zhili, the banner forces were stationed in three cities: Qingzhou (now Yidu), in east-central Shandong; Dezhou, on the Grand Canal in western Shandong; and Kaifeng. In the northwest highlands, the banner forces were stationed in three cities also: Xi'an, Suiyuan (now Hohhot), and Taiyuan. In the lower Yangzi region of east-central China, the banner troops were divided among four garrisons: Nanjing (or Jiangning), Zhenjiang (or Jingkou), Hangzhou, and Zhapu, on the Zhejiang coast halfway between Hangzhou and Shanghai. Each of the other four macro-regions had only one garrison. In the middle Yangzi region, the garrison was at Jingzhou; in the upper Yangzi region, at Chengdu; along the southeast coast, at Fuzhou; and in the West River region of south China, at Guangzhou. At both Fuzhou and Guangzhou the garrison included an attached water force.[65]

The total strength of the ninety-one provincial garrisons was about 110,000 (see table 1.2). Together with the 150,000 soldiers in the Metropolitan Banners and the bondservant companies, the total banner force (exclusive of the affiliated detachments) adds up to 260,000 soldiers. Of these, roughly 55 percent were concentrated in Beijing and 45 percent were scattered among the provinces, with 5 percent in the capital region, 19 percent in the northeast, 6 percent in the northwest, and 15 percent in the rest of China proper. This finding accords well with Wang Zhonghan's estimates for 1849: 149,425 (52 percent) in Beijing, 52,552 (18 percent) in the northeast, and 85,219 (30 percent) everywhere else in China. If an estimated forty thousand soldiers in the affiliated detachments are added to the others to produce a grand total of three hundred thousand banner soldiers, then the banner troops would have been evenly divided between the capital and the provinces, which is what Zheng Tianting and numerous other scholars have concluded.[66]

These three hundred thousand banner soldiers constituted the core personnel of the Eight Banner system, but they were by no means all of the banner people, for the Eight Banners were not only a military organization made up of banner soldiers but also an administrative system that incorporated the banner soldiers' numerous dependents. In addition to bannermen's wives and daughters, the system also included many men who were not soldiers. It is a common misconception that every able-bodied adult bannerman was a soldier. As the banner population proliferated over the course of the Qing period while the size of the banner army remained more or less fixed, it was not even the case (contrary to the recollection of Aixin Jueluo Zongkui) that every banner family produced a banner soldier. Those bannermen who failed to be selected as soldiers and who were not otherwise employed (e.g., as officials) were known as *xiansan* or (from the Manchu) *sula*, that is, unsalaried or "idle" bannermen.[67]

These idle bannermen loomed large among the banner soldiers' dependents, but how numerous were they in the late Qing? Different sets of information yield very different answers. At one extreme, several banner company records from the Beijing area in 1904 suggest that the unsalaried may have constituted no more than one-third or one-half of all adult bannermen. Thus, in one Manchu banner company (perhaps of the Plain White Banner) headed by the *gioro* Juntong, only 49 out of 128 adult men (38 percent) were *xiansan*; in another company of unspecified ethnicity commanded by Songhua, 100 out of 216 (46 percent) were *xiansan*. In a third company, Yizhen's in the Manchu Plain Red Banner, of 168 able-bodied adult men, 79 were soldiers; the other 89 (53 percent) were presumably *xiansan*. Viewed from a different angle, these company rosters suggest that the ratio of banner soldiers to adult bannermen

was roughly one to two or two to three.[68] At the other extreme, some authorities suggest, though without much supporting evidence, that this ratio of no
fewer than one banner soldier to two adult bannermen is much too narrow.
A Short History of the Manchus (Manzu jianshi), for example, asserts that already
in the days of Hong Taiji only one in three adult males was selected as a banner soldier and that by the Qianlong reign in the mid-eighteenth century, only
one in eight was so selected. Wang Zhonghan similarly estimates that by the
late 1840s the ratio of banner soldiers to adult bannermen had widened to one
to fifteen.[69]

Yet another type of source, family genealogies from the northeast, yields
statistics that fall between these two extremes. According to the records of three
banner families in eastern Fengtian—the Guan (Guaerjia, or Gūwalgiya) and
the Wu (Wushu) in Xinbin and the Wang (Wanyan, or Wanggiya) in Xiuyan—
only about 10 percent of the males in each of the three families ever qualified
as soldiers or officials. Among the Guan, for example, over the course of eight
generations stretching from before 1644 and to 1825, there were altogether 230
males in the family, of whom only 24 were soldiers and 7 were officials; the
other 199 (87 percent) were xiansan. In the eighth generation alone, living in
the early nineteenth century, there were 87 Guan males, of whom only 3 were
soldiers; 84 were xiansan. Among the Wu, of 226 males going back twelve generations, only 23 were soldiers or officials; among the Wang, of 123 males over
four generations, all but 12 were xiansan. Similarly, in Daoyi, a banner village
in Fengtian near Shengjing, according to a detailed analysis of its banner registers in the eighteenth century, only about 10 percent of the males were or
had been in military or administrative service. In short, the three northeastern family genealogies and the Daoyi registers agree that the ratio of banner
soldiers to bannermen was about one to ten.[70]

If one were to accept one to ten as the approximate ratio of banner soldiers
to bannermen and then factor in the female half of the system, the banner soldiers would have accounted for about one-twentieth (5 percent) of the entire
population of banner people. Indeed, records of the Banner Affairs Office
(Qiwuchu) in Fengtian in 1910 confirm that banner soldiers and officials made
up 4.9 percent of all the banner people of the province.[71] Consequently, if the
total number of banner soldiers was three hundred thousand and the ratio of
soldiers to banner people was one to twenty, then the total banner population
in the late Qing would have been six million. This is roughly comparable to
the figure of five million that Liang Qichao, Zou Rong, and other anti-Manchu
critics of the early post-Boxer era regularly gave as the number of Manchus.
If so, the banner people constituted slightly more than 1 percent of the total
population of China at the time.

SEPARATE . . .

On 23 July 1865 an edict issued in the name of the nine-year-old Tongzhi emperor (r. 1861–75) endorsed a memorial from Governor Shen Guifen (1817–81) of Shanxi urging a fundamental reform of the Eight Banner system. The governor had proposed that

> hereafter all banner people [*qiren*] who wish to go out and make their own living . . . be permitted by the lieutenant-general [of their banner] to venture forth. If they wish to settle down and work in the provinces, they should be permitted to notify the local county magistrate and be registered as banner people. . . . In all litigation, they should then come under the jurisdiction of the county magistrate. If some do not attend to their own affairs but stir up trouble, they should be punished by the local officials on the same basis as civilians [*minren*]. Those who wish to be reclassified as civilians should be entered in the local registers as civilians.

It is on the basis of this "important" edict that Mary Wright concludes, "Most of the last restrictions separating the Manchus from the [Han] Chinese were removed in 1865."[72] The Tongzhi emperor's decree did not, however, have the far-reaching impact that Wright ascribes to it, simply because it was never carried out. Consequently, even after 1865, the Manchus continued, as before, to live lives that were separate from and unequal to those of the Han.[73]

Manchus were segregated from Han in four important respects: administratively, occupationally, residentially, and socially. First, they were kept apart from Han administratively by a system known as "separate governance of banner people and civilians" (*qimin fenzhi*). As the 1865 edict indicates, Manchus were classified differently from Han. They were registered as "banner people," whereas the non-banner people, who were nearly all Han, were generally registered as "civilian." These classifications were hereditary and essentially permanent. Not since the seventeenth century had Han been enrolled into the banner system. As for the Manchus, they had rarely been permitted to leave the system, and this had occurred only on the explicit instruction of the ruler, such as when the Qianlong emperor ordered the demobilization of a large number of Hanjun and their reclassification as civilians. The 1865 edict cited by Wright admittedly made it easier than before for a banner person to resign from the system, because it gave blanket authorization to the commanders of the twenty-four banners to approve individual requests to get out. The decree, however, merely permitted— it did not order—the reclassification of the banner population. There is no evidence that many members asked or were allowed to resign from their banners.

Due to their different classifications, Manchus were governed separately from Han. As civilians, the Han were under the jurisdiction of the regular local administrative hierarchy, which ranged upward from the county magistrate to the provincial governor; as banner people, the Manchus were subject to their own set of officials, from the captain of their banner company to the lieutenant-general of their banner in Beijing. Generally speaking, civilian officials had no jurisdiction over banner people, nor did banner officials have authority over civilians. For example, at Xiuyan, a garrison town in eastern Fengtian with between five hundred and six hundred banner soldiers, the banner people were under the command of their garrison's senior military commandant and ultimately the general at Shengjing; the civilian population, on the other hand, was governed by a second-class subprefect (*tongpan*) locally and by the metropolitan prefect of Fengtian at Shengjing. Legal cases involving members of both populations in Xiuyan required joint adjudication by the garrison's commandant and the subprefect.[74] On the face of it, the 1865 edict did away with at least part of this administrative segregation when it extended the judicial authority of local civil officials to cover those banner people who had opted to settle in the provinces but had kept their banner classification. It appears, however, that few banner members exercised this option either. Consequently, both the separate classification and the separate governance of banner people and civilians continued in force down to the end of the century.

Second, Manchus were segregated from Han occupationally in that they, in essence, constituted a hereditary military caste from which non-banner civilians were excluded. As members of the Eight Banner system, their primary responsibility was to fight, when needed, as soldiers in the banner army, and when they were not soldiering, they were permitted only to serve as officials in the Qing government or to farm. They were specifically barred from engaging in trade or other occupations.[75] These prohibitions applied not only to the banner soldiers but to other members of the banner system as well. Although the 1865 edict explicitly allowed the banner people "to go out and make their own living," it does not appear to have had any practical consequences. Manchus in the late nineteenth century still labored under the old occupational restrictions, which by and large set them apart from Han.

Third, Manchus were segregated from Han residentially. Half of the banner population were hereditarily assigned to the Metropolitan Banners in Beijing, and most of the rest to one or another of the ninety-one provincial garrisons that were unevenly distributed throughout the Qing empire. Whether in Beijing or in the provinces, all banner people were tightly bound to their respective garrisons. In particular, they were not allowed to travel beyond a certain distance of their garrison headquarters without the explicit approval of their superiors. In Beijing they were restricted to within forty li (about thirteen miles) of the capital, and in the provinces to within twenty li of their garrison (although in the northeast it was one hundred li, or thirty-three miles). These limits applied as well to the location of banner settlements away from a garrison city. For example, Sanjiazitun (Three Family Village, in present-day Fuyu County), whose banner personnel were under the jurisdiction of the Heilongjiang general, was located ninety-five li north of Qiqihar, near the outer limit of the permissible range for Manchuria. Any banner person who ventured beyond these specified distances without permission was considered a deserter. Manchus thus lacked the Han's freedom of movement. When the expectant prefect Jitai, of the Hanjun Bordered Red Banner, died in Shandong in 1888, his son had to petition his banner commander for a travel permit to accompany the coffin back to the capital. As the Shandong governor observed in a covering letter forwarding the petition,

> If the family of the deceased had been classified as civilian, there would have been no need to request permission to begin their journey. This youth, however, belongs to a banner. Heretofore, each banner person, when leaving the capital on official business, has been required to report in writing to his lieutenant-general's headquarters before he can proceed.[76]

In the urban centers where they were garrisoned, except in Manchuria, the banner soldiers and their dependents lived in special quarters known as "Manchu cities" (Mancheng), which may be classified into four types depending on their spatial relationship to the indigenous population.[77] One type was the "attached twin city," where the Manchus lived in a walled enclosure that was external to but contiguous with another walled city that the non-banner people inhabited. Beijing's Inner (or "Tartar") City is the sole example of this type. When the Qing forces captured the Ming capital in the seventeenth century, they expelled all of the residents of the Inner City, which they took over entirely for their own people, and they relegated the Han and other non-banner people to the old walled addition to the south known as the Outer (or "Chinese") City.[78] A second, and related, type was the "detached twin city," where the banner people were quartered in a new, specially built walled city that was near to but separate from an existing walled city where the other people lived. In Shanxi, for example, the Manchus were garrisoned at Suiyuan, built in the 1730s, while Han, Mongols, and others lived about a mile and a half to the northeast in the Ming-era city of Guihua; known locally as the New and Old Cities respectively, these two settlements are now districts of the city of Hohhot in Inner Mongolia. Other Manchu cities of this second type were at Qingzhou (Shandong), Ningxia, and, until it was destroyed in the 1860s, Urumqi (Xinjiang).[79]

Two other types of Manchu cities, which Mark Elliott aptly calls "intramural," were located within an existing walled city. One type was a walled compound entirely enclosed within the larger Han city, such as in Kaifeng and Zhenjiang.[80] The other type, by far the most common, was not fully surrounded by its own set of walls but instead shared a part of the larger Han city's external walls. The amount of land occupied by the banner people in these intramural Manchu cities varied greatly. As depicted on maps, the Manchu city in Jingzhou took up the entire eastern half of the walled city; in Xi'an, the northeastern third; in Guangzhou, the western fourth; in Nanjing, a substantial portion of the southeastern sector within the old Ming imperial city; and in Taiyuan, merely the southwestern corner.[81] As in Beijing, wherever the banner people occupied portions of an existing city, they had first cleared the area of its former residents; they then built a set of internal walls, which were not so high nor so massive as the external ramparts but which nevertheless clearly demarcated one group of people from the other. Fuzhou and Guangzhou were exceptional in that their Manchu cities were not walled.[82]

In principle, Manchu cities were the exclusive residential quarters of the banner people. In Beijing, non-banner people originally could visit the Inner City during the day but not dwell there. At Hohhot, non-banner people, who lived at the Old City of Guihua, could not enter the new Manchu city of Suiyuan at will. Similarly, at Zhenjiang, the Manchu garrison "was off limits to Han."[83] In reality, with the passage of time, a growing number of non-banner civilians did live in the Manchu cities. In the capital, some high-ranking Han officials were, by imperial grace, allowed to reside within the Inner City. For example, Zhang Zhidong (1837–1909), who served on the Grand Council during 1907–9, lived on Baimixie Street just outside Di'anmen, the northern entrance into the Imperial City.[84] More commonly, shopkeepers managed in time to gain admission into the Manchu cities, especially since the banner people themselves were prohibited from engaging in commerce. In Beijing, by the mid-nineteenth century the population of the Inner City included some fifteen thousand non-Manchu shopkeeper households, in addition to the seventy-six thousand regular banner households.[85] Nevertheless, despite this Han influx, the Manchu cities remained down to the late Qing predominantly Manchu in population, even if they were no longer exclusively so, as the scattered census returns from 1908 and 1910 reveal. In Beijing, as late as 1908, the banner people still constituted 54 percent of the 414,528 individuals in the Inner City. In Chengdu, they were 53 percent of the households in the Manchu City; and in Xi'an, 64 percent.[86] Non-banner civilian immigration, therefore, had eroded but did not destroy the Manchu cities' fundamental characteristic as ethnic ghettoes.

Another characteristic of Manchu cities was that even with their Han inhabitants, they were sparsely populated, particularly when contrasted with the rest of their host city. (Beijing was an exception: the population of the Inner City slightly exceeded that of the Outer City.)[87] Intramural Manchu cities, as noted, sometimes took up as much as one-quarter or even one-half of an entire city, yet proportionately their resident population was considerably less. In Guangzhou, where they occupied about one-fourth of the city's area within the walls, the banner people probably numbered no more than one-tenth, or perhaps even one-twentieth, of the city's estimated total population of six hundred thousand. Foreign visitors in the late nineteenth century often commented on the parklike atmosphere of the spacious yet sparsely populated Manchu cities. One lauded the Manchu City in Xi'an for "its wide, healthy spaces, its lovely gardens, its grand old trees." Of Chengdu, where the banner people took up one-fifth of the city, another wrote, "The Manchu quarter is one of the most picturesque parts of the city, with the charm of a dilapidated village set in untidy gardens and groves of fine trees."[88] The sharp difference in population density and in the pace of life between the Manchu and Han quarters in Chengdu was captured well in a novel by Li Jieren (1891–1962), *Ripples across Stagnant Water* (Sishui weilan), written in 1935 but set at the end of the Qing. Separated by a low wall, the two areas were known locally as the Small City (Shaocheng) and the Big City (Dacheng):

> The low wall created two entirely different worlds. In the Big City, there were houses and shops everywhere and numerous pedestrians would be moving to and fro on the cobblestone streets. Not a drop of green could be seen in the whole district. By contrast, as soon as one entered the Manchu City, there were trees in abundance. . . . Everywhere was one vast expanse of green. A broad unpaved road [probably present-day Changshun Street] flanked by low yellow earthen walls extended itself among the shadows far into the distance. Inside the walls, flowers and trees complemented the low houses, interspersed with ponds covered with lotus blossoms. And human beings were rarely to be seen. Unlike, for example, the Big City where pedestrians would be everywhere and on some of the downtown streets you would have to squeeze through shoulder to shoulder. In the Manchu City, you could walk down whole streets without encountering other pedestrians. In any case, those whom you did meet were utterly different from people in the Big City where, except for some cultured older types, everyone was invariably in a hurry. Here [in the Small City] most of the male pedestrians would be strolling with a bird cage in their hands or

a fishing-rod on their shoulders. As for the females, dressed in long gowns, waists cinched and hair tied back, they would walk along slowly in their slippers smoking long bamboo pipes. The Manchu City was indeed a different world.[89]

In sum, in an urban environment such as Chengdu, Manchus and Han lived out their lives in separate worlds and generally had little to do with one another. Because the Manchu City had few stores and workshops, it was economically dependent on the rest of the host city. Aside from commerce, however, the two populations did not interact much. As one longtime resident of Chengdu recalls, "Before the Xuantong era [1908–12], the Han people very rarely entered the Small City for recreation; similarly, the banner people hardly ever went to the Big City for activity. The line between the two was very strict."[90]

As for the sizable minority of banner people who did not live in urban garrisons, they too were residentially segregated. Those in Zhili Province outside Beijing lived on land that long ago was cleared of its Han inhabitants, for in the mid-seventeenth century, the newly established Qing, in a move that paralleled the expulsion of previous residents from Beijing's Inner City, had "enclosed" (quanzhan) much of the land within a five-hundred-li (170–mile) radius of the capital, evicting the Han farmers and reallocating the land to its banner soldiers and bondservants to farm.[91] Although many Han farmers subsequently managed to filter back into the region and, despite a prohibition on the sale of banner land, even regain control of the land from their Manchu proprietors, Manchus and Han lived apart from each other in separate settlements. Thus, near the Summer Palace, soldiers of the Outer Detachment of the Firearms Division resided in walled villages whose inhabitants were entirely banner people. The bondservants working on imperial or princely estates in various parts of Zhili, such as Xiaoyingzi in Qinglong County and Zhoujiazhuang in present-day Yi County, likewise lived in separate communities composed of banner people. Such ethnic enclaves were also widespread in Fengtian. For example, the village of Daoyi, north of Shengjing, was composed predominantly, if not exclusively, of Hanjun.[92]

The most extensive example of the Manchus' residential segregation was central and northern Manchuria, which, even more so than the five-hundred-li zone around Beijing, was supposed to be an exclusively banner domain from which non-banner civilians were barred. This was the region north and east of the Willow Palisade. The palisade, an earthen levee about a yard high planted with a row of willow trees with a parallel trench about three yards deep, was composed of three sections radiating outward from the vicinity of Kaiyuan, north of Shengjing, dividing Manchuria into three distinct regions. To the south was the Liao River plain of Fengtian, which the Han had long cultivated. To the west was the arid steppe occupied by Mongols. Finally, to the east and north-east was the forested region of Jilin and Heilongjiang, from which the origi-nal (or Old) Manchus had come. The Qing rulers were determined to maintain this third region of Manchuria, in Robert Lee's words, as "a fountainhead of ancestral virtues and a reservoir of military power," by prohibiting Han immi-gration beyond the Willow Palisade.[93]

The Qing's efforts at keeping northern Manchuria a Manchu preserve free of the Han were a mixed success. On the one hand, the Willow Palisade was no Great Wall; it was lightly guarded, poorly maintained, and easily penetrated. There were along the entire length of the barrier only nineteen gates, through which all traffic into and out of the region was supposed to be funneled, and each was guarded by fifty or fewer banner soldiers. Furthermore, by the nine-teenth century, the palisade itself was run-down at so many points as to be all but useless. The British consular official Alexander Hosie (1853–1925) observed in 1896 that "little but the gates, each with its guard of a few soldiers, remains." Long before then, Robert Lee says, the palisade had been "breached at will," as Han from overcrowded north China ignored the ban in search of land to farm. On the other hand, notwithstanding its porosity and deterioration, the Willow Palisade could not be, and was not, ignored with impunity. Thus, even though the barrier had supposedly been breached at will for over a century, there were still very few Han immigrants living in Jilin and Heilongjiang in the 1860s.[94] Indeed, it was the very success of the Qing in keeping the Han out of the northernmost parts of Manchuria that allowed the Russians in 1860 to walk off with the extensive territory north of the Amur River and east of the Ussuri.[95] Even when afterward the Qing began to allow Han immigration into north-ern Manchuria to forestall the Russians from further encroachments, the effect was geographically limited. The opening-up started with the Lalin district along the middle reaches of the Songhua River (in Jilin) in 1860 and the Hulan basin (in Heilongjiang) in 1862; it was subsequently extended to the upper Mudan valley, the Tumen valley, and the upper Ussuri (all in Jilin) between 1878 and 1882 and the Tongken valley (in Heilongjiang) in 1896.[96] However, aside from these specific areas where Han immigration was now unrestricted, much of northern Manchuria beyond the Willow Palisade was still in the late nineteenth century populated largely, though no longer exclusively, by banner people.

Last, Manchus were segregated socially from Han. In particular, they were forbidden to marry Han. For example, the Manchus at Xiuyan, the garrison town in eastern Fengtian, observed four "big taboos" concerning marriage. Along with prohibitions against marrying someone with the same surname, someone from the same generation, or a minor was a prohibition against mar-rying a Han. According to local informants, the ban on Manchu-Han intermarriage was "a regulation of the dynasty and could never, ever, be contravened." The prohibition does not appear in the Qing code as such, but successive Qing rulers, including the Yongzheng emperor and Empress Dowager Cixi, declared it to be imperial policy. As Ding Yizhuang asserts, "The prohibition against marriage between banner people and civilians was indeed extraordinarily severe."[97]

As a cumulative consequence of the various aspects of segregation, Manchus and Han generally lived in separate communities and kept apart from each other. Indeed, the banner garrisons were so isolated from the local population that they often became "language islands," where, as in Jingzhou, the banner people, after two and a half centuries, still spoke the standard Chinese (Mandarin; Putonghua) dialect of north China, from which their ancestors had been dispatched, rather than the dialect of the people among whom they were living. In Guangzhou, according to a 1959 field survey, "prior to the 1911 Revolution the Manchus all spoke standard Chinese. Although they could understand and talk Cantonese, they normally did not speak it." Similarly, according to the journalist Harry A. Franck in the early 1920s, the Manchus at Xi'an were "recognizable to the others by their Peking dialect."[98] The persistence of such linguistic distinctions is additional evidence that the two groups had rarely interacted.

. . . AND UNEQUAL

In addition to keeping Manchus and Han separate, the Qing rulers dealt with the two populations unequally. Their policy was not so much anti-Han as pro-Manchu, but their favoritism toward the Manchus occurred unavoidably at the expense of the Han. Thus, down to the end of the nineteenth century, the banner people received preferential treatment over the non-banner civilians in three broad areas: legal, political, and economic.

Legally, Manchus (as banner people) were treated differently as well as better than Han (as civilians). If, for example, a Manchu and a Han were brought before a court on a legal matter, the Han was required to kneel before the magistrate, whereas the Manchu was permitted to stand.[99] More important, if found guilty of a crime, a Manchu was subject to a lesser punishment than a Han. According to the Qing code, banner people could opt for a beating with a whip instead of a bamboo rod, and they could substitute wearing the cangue in place of penal servitude or even military exile. In one early nineteenth-century case, a Manchu in Heilongjiang was found guilty in the accidental death of a boy. If the defendant had been a Han, he would have been beaten with one hundred blows of the heavy bamboo rod and exiled for life at a distance of three thousand li (one thousand miles), but because he was a bannerman, his sentence was reduced to an equal number of blows of the whip and the wearing of the cangue for sixty days.[100] The 1865 edict permitting banner members to leave the system would have greatly reduced such forms of discrimination between Manchus and Han, because it specified that those banner people who had asked to be reclassified as civilians, as well as those who had resettled in the provinces but had kept their banner status, would be subject to the same laws as the civilians. However, since the edict was not widely implemented, the special consideration that Manchus received in legal matters remained in force down to the end of the century.

Politically, Manchus benefited from preferential treatment in recruitment, appointment, and tenure. In recruitment, there were four methods by which Manchus could enter the civil bureaucracy much more easily than could Han. First, when bannermen participated in the regular (or "literary") examinations, they were assigned separate quotas that were more generous than those for the Han. Thus, among the 4,457 who passed the triennial metropolitan examinations and were awarded the *jinshi* degree between 1862 and 1894 were 242 bannermen, who constituted 5.4 percent of all successful candidates, which was several times greater than their share of China's total population. They included the previously noted Xiliang and Zhao Erxun, both of the class of 1874. Two other bannermen officials of the post-Boxer era who entered the civil service by way of the regular examinations were Duanfang (1861–1911), governor-general of Zhili in 1909, and Natong, a grand councilor during the Zaifeng regency (1908–11) at the end of the dynasty; they gained their provincial, or *juren*, degrees in 1882 and 1885 respectively.[101]

Second, Manchus were allowed to take a separate set of examinations that were less demanding than the literary ones and from which the Han were excluded. These "translation" (*fanyi*) examinations led to degrees that were identical to those awarded under the literary examinations except for the addition of the prefix *fanyi* (e.g., *fanyi jinshi*). As their name suggests, they were an exercise in translation: from Chinese to Manchu for Manchu bannermen and Hanjun, and from Manchu to Mongol for Mongol bannermen. They typically asked for a commentary on and a translation from the Four Books of the Confucian classics. Compared with their literary counterpart, the translation examinations were shorter, consisting of, for example, two rather than three sessions for the metropolitan examination; moreover, their success rate was several times higher. In the early nineteenth century, about one in fifteen bannermen passed the translation examination for the provincial degree, and about one in five or six passed the metropolitan examination. Because they were less difficult, the translation examinations lacked prestige and did not attract the most capable of bannermen candidates. Nevertheless, they were no less effective a way for bannermen to enter government service than were the literary examinations. For example, the Hanjun Fengshan (d. 1911), who in 1907 replaced Yuan Shikai as commander of four Beiyang New Army divisions, acquired his provincial degree via a translation examination.[102]

Third, Manchus were also allowed to enter the government by taking yet another translation test that qualified them for employment as low-ranking metropolitan officials known as Manchu-language scribes (*bitieshi*, from the Manchu *bithesi*). The test itself was quite easy, and while it was open to holders of the translation examination degree, it could be taken by other bannermen as well. It was, however, closed to Han. Among the officials in the post-Boxer era who obtained their first posts as Manchu-language scribes were Fuqi, the acting general of the Guangzhou garrison when he was assassinated in 1911, and Songshou, governor-general of Fujian-Zhejiang in 1911.[103]

Finally, yet other Manchus entered government service without having been certified by any sort of examination; they did so by taking advantage of their father's hereditary *yin* privilege (granted for meritorious service) or by purchasing a degree or position of their own. Thus, Empress Dowager Cixi's confidant Ronglu (1836–1903) started his career as an honorary licentiate (*yinsheng*), a degree bestowed upon him in 1852 in recognition of his father's death while resisting the Taiping rebels; this led to an initial appointment to the Board of Public Works as a second-class secretary and culminated in his appointment as a grand councilor in 1898. Similarly, Zhao Erfeng, younger brother of the metropolitan degree holder Zhao Erxun, began his career by purchasing a post in the salt administration in Guangdong.[104] The purchase of degrees and offices in order to enter the civil service was not, of course, a Manchu monopoly. Yuan Shikai, for example, started by buying the title of secretary of the Imperial Patent Office attached to the Grand Secretariat.[105] Yuan's "irregular" beginning, however, was an exception among high-ranking Han officials in the late Qing. Such was not the case among their Manchu peers, for whom an "irregular" beginning was more often the norm than the exception.

Because they had more numerous as well as less demanding ways of entering the government, Manchu officeholders were, not surprisingly, less academically qualified than Han. Over the course of the Qing period, 72.1 percent of Han governors-general held either the metropolitan or the provincial examination degree, whereas only 33.9 percent of Manchu bannermen and even fewer Mongol bannermen and Hanjun did. For the same reasons, Manchus also began their official careers four to six years sooner than did Han. Whereas the average age at first appointment of a Han as governor-general was just over fifty-six, that of a bannerman was between 49.5 and 52.1 years.[106]

In appointment, as in recruitment, Manchus had an advantage over Han because many posts in the government, particularly in the capital, were reserved for them. In the metropolitan administration, the Qing allocated most positions among members of six ethnic or status categories, namely, imperial clansmen, Manchu bannermen, Mongol bannermen, Hanjun, bondservants of the Upper Three Banners, and Han.[107] These might be called "ethnic slots." In most instances, half of all of the top posts in the metropolitan bureaucracy were reserved for members of the first five categories, and the other half were allocated to the Han. This was the well-known institution of Manchu-Han dyarchy, with the five various groups of bannermen collectively making up the Manchu half of the structure. On the basis of a detailed analysis of the top personnel of the Grand Council, the Grand Secretariat, and the Six Boards in the mid-nineteenth century, John Fairbank confirmed that "a roughly equal balance was in fact maintained between Manchus and [Han] Chinese in the official posts at the capital." The principle of dyarchy was observed among the top ranks of the Censorate as well.[108] Insofar as an equal number of Han were allowed to serve with Manchus, dyarchy can be considered nondiscriminatory. Indeed, with regard to official appointments, successive Qing emperors prided themselves on their alleged impartiality; their guiding thought, they claimed, was that "Manchus and Han were as one family" (*Man-Han yijia*).[109] But since the Manchus were only 1 percent of China's population, their half-share of the top metropolitan posts was obviously disproportionate to their numbers.

In any case, the principle of dyarchy applied only to a few posts at or near the top of the metropolitan administration. It did not, for example, extend to the shadowy post of board supervisor (*zongli*), who outranked a board's two presidents and oversaw the operations of their ministry; when the appointment (which was more common in the eighteenth than the nineteenth century) was made, the board supervisor was almost always a Manchu.[110] More commonly, dyarchy did not apply to the far more numerous positions at the middle and lower echelons of the Qing's nine-rank administrative system, where Manchus greatly outnumbered Han both absolutely and proportionately. At the Grand Secretariat, for example, twenty of the twenty-four mid-level positions (83 percent) were reserved for Manchus (fourteen Manchu bannermen, four Mongol bannermen, two Hanjun) and only four were for Han. The situation at the Six Boards was similar. At the Board of Revenue, of the 141 statutory positions in the three middle ranks, ninety-seven (69 percent) were reserved for Manchus (four imperial clansmen, ninety-one Manchu bannermen, two Mongol bannermen); the remaining forty-four slots (31 percent) were to be filled by Han. The Censorate and the Hanlin Academy were the only metropolitan agencies where at the middle ranks Manchus were not more numerous than Han.[111] The Manchus' preponderance was most egregious among the bottom three ranks, where in particular the post of Manchu-language scribe was set aside exclusively for bannermen. The scribe's primary duty was to translate documents, including memorials addressed to the throne, from Chinese into Manchu; he also served as copyist and archivist. Though lowly, the post existed in large numbers in every metropolitan agency. At the Board of Revenue, Manchu scribes numbered 141, almost half of the ministry's statutory officials; they comprised one imperial clansman, 120 Manchu bannermen, four Mongol bannermen, and sixteen Hanjun.[112] Manchus thus monopolized the bottom of the metropolitan bureaucracy to the almost total exclusion of Han.

Not only did the principle of dyarchy not extend below the top ranks of most organs of the metropolitan government, but it did not apply to certain agencies at all. Except for some clerical posts requiring a knowledge of Chinese that were held by Han, only imperial clansmen were appointed to the Imperial Clan Court, which had jurisdiction over members of the imperial lineage, and only bondservants of the Upper Three Banners were appointed to the Imperial Household Department, which served the needs of the court. The broader group of bannermen similarly filled all 161 posts at the Court of Colonial Affairs (Lifanyuan), which was responsible for dealing with the Mongols, Turks, and Tibetans living in the outlying realms of the Qing empire.[113] Of course, no Han was appointed to the Eight Banners either. Overall, according to Chen Wenshi's exhaustive analysis of 2,277 posts in the fourteen most important metropolitan agencies, 1,559 (68.4 percent) were earmarked for Manchus—1,255 imperial clansmen and Manchu bannermen, 196 Mongol bannermen, 108 Hanjun—and only 416 (18.3 percent) for Han, with the remaining 302 (13.3 percent) unspecified.[114]

Away from the capital, there were also some (though not nearly so many) posts that were set aside for Manchus and from which Han were excluded. These were typically located along the frontiers of the empire, especially the three regions of Manchuria—Fengtian, Jilin, and Heilongjiang—which were governed as territories, outside the regular provincial administration, down to the end of the nineteenth century. Each of the three territories was ruled by its respective banner general, each in command of a large banner force. With the Qing rulers determined to maintain Manchuria, especially its northern part, as a Manchu preserve, civil administration was largely dominated by bannermen as well. For example, the prefect of Fengtian, the chief civilian official in the entire northeast, was always a Manchu. At the garrison town of Xiuyan, in eastern Fengtian, of the forty-six second-class subprefects who had jurisdiction over the non-banner population from 1772 to 1856, thirty-six were

Manchus and only ten were Han. Even when the civilian administrative apparatus was extended into northern Manchuria in the late nineteenth century to keep pace with the influx of Han immigrants, most of the local officials continued to be Manchus. At Hulan, Heilongjiang, the subprefect—from the time the post was created in 1863 to oversee the affairs of the Han settlers, until its abolition in 1905–was never a Han.[115] Of course, the banner administration in the provinces, as in the capital, was another exclusive preserve of the Manchus.[116]

Because most provincial and local posts were not earmarked as "ethnic slots," Manchus were not nearly so dominant there as they were in the capital; still, their presence was disproportionately large. It was greatest among the top two ranks of the provincial administration, where dyarchy prevailed informally. Thus, over the course of the Qing dynasty, Manchus were 57 percent of all governors-general and 48.4 percent of all governors; in terms of length of tenure, they were in office 61.6 percent of the time as governors-general and 51 percent as governors. The Manchu presence diminished below the level of governor, particularly as the post declined in importance. Thus, among provincial financial commissioners and judges, 28 to 29 percent were bannermen; among prefects, 21 percent; and among county magistrates, only 6 percent. However, even at 6 percent, Manchus as local administrators exceeded their share of the population.[117]

Once they were appointed, Manchus also received preferential treatment politically, in that they were likely to have longer tenure than Han. Among governors-general, for example, the average length of service of a bannerman was five years five months, while that of a Han was eleven months shorter. Among county magistrates, 26.4 percent of Manchus (as against 20.9 percent of Han) served longer than three years.[118] Probably the main reason why Manchu officials had greater longevity than Han was the difference in their mourning requirement. Whereas Han officials had to give up their post and return home for twenty-seven months when a parent died, bannermen mourned for only one hundred days and could then resume their duties or receive immediate reassignment. Thus, out of 1,052 commanders of provincial banner garrisons (i.e., generals and brigade-generals) spanning 113 years from 1796 to 1908, only four left office because of mourning.[119]

It is widely, if mistakenly, assumed that the preferential treatment of Manchus at the expense of Han in the political realm greatly diminished during and after the Tongzhi Restoration, the period of dynastic recovery in the 1860s. The belief rests, in part, on the indisputable fact that far fewer bannermen were appointed as provincial rulers after 1851, as the Qing court began to recognize the power of the new Han "regional" armies and their commanders that arose during the suppression of the Taiping Rebellion. Thus, whereas Manchus constituted 57 percent of all governors-general over the entire Qing period, they were only 34.6 percent during 1851–1912; similarly, the percentage of Manchus as governors declined from 48.4 percent for all of the Qing to 22.2 percent for the last sixty years of the dynasty. There was, however, no parallel shift from Manchus to Han at the metropolitan level of government, where appointments were still made on the basis of dyarchy. When, for example, the Zongli Yamen was established in 1860 as a subcommittee of the Grand Council to handle China's burgeoning foreign relations, its staff of forty-two secretaries was evenly divided between Manchus and Han.[120]

Indeed, not only did the post-Taiping court continue to favor Manchus at the expense of Han by making metropolitan (if not provincial) appointments on the basis of ethnic slots, it exhibited even greater favoritism toward Manchus when it excluded practically all Han from several of its Self-Strengthening reforms. Thus, both the Peking Field Force (formed in 1862) and the Kunming Lake Naval School (Kunminghu Shuishi Xuetang, opened in 1888) drew their personnel entirely from the ranks of the Metropolitan Banners, while the Translators College (Tongwenguan, founded in Beijing in 1862 and in Guangzhou two years later) recruited most, though not all, of its students from the local banner population. The court's exclusion of Han from its efforts at modernization was also evident at the Navy Yamen, founded in 1885 after the naval debacle of the Sino-French War (1883–85). Unlike the Zongli Yamen, where the staff was evenly split, the Navy Yamen's administration was practically all Manchu. While the top five commissioners were divided roughly equally (in the spirit of dyarchy) between Manchus and Han, with the Manchus usually holding an edge of three to two, only one of the thirty-one secretaries who served during the yamen's ten-year history was a Han.[121]

Finally, economically, too, Manchus were treated preferentially over Han. The clearest example of economic favoritism was the subsidy paid to the banner soldiers, which went to support not only the soldiers but the rest of the banner population. The Manchus were thus hereditary stipendiaries of the state. Most banner soldiers, particularly those stationed in China proper, received two kinds of compensation: a monthly payment in silver and a semiannual distribution of grain. Compensation varied with service branch and rank. According to the published pay scale for a normal year (i.e., without an extra intercalary month), an Escort, the most prestigious among the Metropolitan Banner soldiers, received forty-eight taels of silver (at a rate of four taels a month) and 22.2 piculs of grain; a private in the Light Cavalry, the banners' common soldier, received thirty-six taels and also 22.2 piculs. The pay of an officer was, of course, higher. A lieutenant in the Metropolitan Banners, for example, received sixty taels of silver in regular salary (probably with an additional amount of "integrity nourishing" money) and seventy-two piculs of grain. Compared with the Army of the Green Standard, a Han unit, the pay scale of the banner force was at least twice as high.[122]

A minority of banner personnel, particularly those in less populated areas such as Manchuria, received a part of their pay in land, in lieu of the grain distribution. This was known as "emolument land" (*suiquedi*) and "soldiers land" (*wutiandi*), which they could farm themselves or, more likely, rent out to others. The land was theirs so long as they remained in active service, but when they retired or died, it reverted to their garrison for redistribution to others. Like the monetary payment, which they also received, the land allocation was graduated according to rank. At the Baishizui Gate along the Willow Palisade in the Liaoxi corridor, the garrison commander (a platoon captain) received eighty taels annually in silver and nineteen acres in emolument land; an ordinary banner soldier, twenty-four taels and thirteen acres.[123] As another example of economic favoritism, Manchu landholders were generally exempt from the land tax. All banner land in China proper as well as in central and northern Manchuria was entirely tax free, while banner land in southern Manchuria was taxed only nominally and at a lower rate than non-banner land.[124] In an attempt to ensure that Manchus remained economically independent, the Qing prohibited the transfer of property from banner people to civilians (*qimin bujiao chan*). Although widely ignored and even occasionally revoked within China proper, where banner land was relatively scarce, the prohibition was enforced in Manchuria, where banner land was much more plentiful. It seems to have kept much of the land in the hands of the Manchus; thus, in Shuangcheng (then in Jilin but now in Heilongjiang), 83 percent of the arable land was still owned by Manchus well past the 1911 Revolution.[125]

Apart from his stipend, whether paid in silver, grain, or land, the banner soldier enjoyed other economic benefits as well. He was given monetary grants to help defray the cost of weddings and funerals. If he had distinguished himself in battle and then retired because of illness, he was entitled to disability benefits of one tael a month for the rest of his life. When he died, his widow received half of his stipend. His orphans, too, received a small monthly stipend.[126]

In yet another expression of the regime's policy of economic favoritism, when the Manchus, despite their stipends, fell into economic difficulties, they could look to the Qing state to come to their rescue, or at least to try to help them out. The banner people, particularly the majority who were garrisoned in urban centers, became impoverished in different ways. They lived beyond their means, spending more than their stipends permitted and going into debt to grain merchants and other lenders. They could not keep up with inflation, as their stipends remained fixed while the cost of living increased. They, ignoring the ban on the transfer of property to civilians, sold off their allotted banner land to their Han tenants. And, perhaps most commonly, they proliferated in numbers far beyond the capacity of the banner system to accommodate. Because the banners did not expand in size to keep pace with the increased population, employment opportunities within the system became increasingly scarce. By the late Qing, as previously explained, perhaps only one in ten bannermen could become a banner soldier. Since only the banner soldier was compensated, and since others in the banner system were barred from any occupation other than soldiering, officeholding, and farming, the economic situation of the banner people became increasingly difficult over time.[127]

Successive Qing emperors, from the late seventeenth to the late nineteenth century, undertook a variety of measures to try to solve what came to be called the "problem of the Eight Banners' livelihood" (*Baqi shengji wenti*). Early Qing emperors canceled monetary debts to the central treasury that impoverished Manchus had incurred. They redeemed banner land that had been mortgaged to non-banner civilians. They demobilized a large part of the Hanjun in the provinces and replaced them with Manchu and Mongol bannermen from Beijing. They created new positions in the banner system, such as that of reservist, to provide additional employment and income opportunities. They relocated unsalaried bannermen and their families from Beijing to virgin lands in Manchuria.[128] At best, these early measures slowed down but did not reverse the Manchus' long-term trend toward impoverishment. The economic plight of the banner people worsened in the late nineteenth century. The post-Taiping court itself was in such financial straits that it was obliged to cut back on its payments to the banner soldiers. The outright grants of money for weddings and funerals were replaced by loans, which were deducted from the soldiers' subsequent pay. The stipends themselves were reduced by 30 to 40 percent.[129] The 1865 edict permitting the banner people to leave the system and find work on their own was one more attempt, ultimately ineffective, to solve the problem of the Eight Banners' livelihood.

In Beijing and other urban garrisons of China proper, where they had no other source of income than the banner soldiers' stipends, the Manchus sank deeper and deeper into the state of genteel poverty that Lao She, in *Beneath the Red Banner* (Zhenghongqi xia), recalls so graphically from his Beijing childhood. As a member of the Guards Division, Lao She's father received a stipend of three taels a month and two semiannual distributions of rice. The land the family had been given, amounting to twenty to thirty *mu* (three to five acres) north of the city, "had been sold generations ago, leaving only a little more

than one *mu* on which there now stood a few gravestones." Entirely dependent on his father's meager stipend, they lived continually on credit: "Buying
on credit and running up debts had become our way of life. . . . As soon as the
monthly allowances came in, we paid our debts, which left us so little cash that
we needed credit again."[130] The poor but proud bannerman became a stock
figure in late Qing fiction.[131]

Eyewitness accounts of China's Manchu cities in the late nineteenth century dwell not only on their spacious, parklike qualities but also on the poverty
and indolence of their inhabitants. The British consular official Alexander Hosie,
after a visit to the banner garrison in Chengdu in the early 1880s, observed that
its residents were "slip-shod, down-at-heel, lazy-looking" and that "the people,
especially the women, were badly, even slovenly, dressed; everything announced
the presence of parasites battening on Government pay, without affording any
adequate return." Seasoned traveler Elizabeth Kendall, speaking in 1911 of
Chengdu also, concurred with Hosie's observations: "Loafing in the streets and
doorways are tall, well-built men and women, but they had a rather down-at-
heel air, for their fortunes were at a low ebb when I was at Chengtu." Regarding
the Manchu quarters in Guangzhou, the American missionary B. C. Henry
wrote, "Their part of the city shows a marked contrast to the purely Chinese
portion. Their houses are smaller and poorer, and an air of neglect, thriftless-
ness, and decay spreads over all."[132]

Banner people living in rural areas were not so stricken as their urban peers.
On the one hand, they were spared the seductive extravagances of urban life.
On the other, they could fend for themselves; they were not absolutely dependent on the soldiers' stipend and the largess of the state. In Manchuria, where
the population was sparse and land was plentiful, many banner soldiers lived
not in the garrison town to which they were assigned but rather in outlying villages, which was permissible so long as they were within one hundred li of the
garrison. There, the soldiers and their families could farm or, as local circumstances allowed, make their living in yet other ways. For example, the Manchus
of Sanjiazitun, who belonged to the Qiqihar garrison of Heilongjiang, supplemented their soldiers' income of twenty-four taels a year by trapping fish in the
Nen River. Other Manchus farmed. In Daoyi, the Hanjun community north of
Shengjing, according to a reconstruction of its population in the late eighteenth
century, only 4 percent of all the men were soldiers, and 3 percent were hereditary craftsmen. "The vast majority of the men . . . were clearly farmers who tilled
plots of Banner land." Bondservants on imperial and princely estates, too, made
their living from farming; ironically, though their social status among Manchus
was low, they may have been better off economically than the more prestigious,
but sedentary, banner soldiers in the cities.[133]

TWO PEOPLES, TWO CULTURES

Manchus and Han were, at the beginning of the Qing period, two very different peoples with very different cultures. During the more than two hundred years that the Qing ruled over China, each group necessarily affected the other. It is well known that the Manchus over time underwent a process of "Sinicization" (or, more accurately, "Hanification"); it is less well known that the Han were subject to the reverse process of "Manchufication." Such mutual acculturation, however, was never complete. As a result, down to the end of the nineteenth century, Manchus and Han remained, to a greater extent than is generally realized, culturally different from each other.

The Qing rulers, from the beginning, were much worried about the possibility of becoming culturally absorbed by their far more numerous Han subjects. They were keenly aware of what had happened to previous conquest dynasties, including the Jurchen Jin (1127–1234), from whom they claimed descent. When Hong Taiji in 1636 lectured his officials on the perils of acculturation, he admonished them to heed the warnings of the fifth Jurchen emperor, Shizong (r. 1161–90) and to learn from the ultimate fate of the Jin:

> Fearing that his descendants would imitate the customs of the Han, he [Shizong] prohibited this, and many times urged his people not to forget Taizu and Taizong [the dynastic founders]. He ordered them to follow the old customs in clothing and language, to practice horsemanship and archery regularly so they would be ready for warfare. In spite of these imperial admonitions, later generations disregarded him and forgot their horsemanship and archery. Thus we come to Aizong, where the gods of grain were threatened, and subsequently the dynasty was wiped out.[134]

The Qing therefore attempted, on the one hand, to inculcate the ways of the original (or Old) Manchus among the rest of the banner population and, on the other, to preserve this distinctive culture of the banner people from being eroded by the Han.

The Manchu way of life was summed up in the Chinese phrase *guoyu qishe*, "national speech and mounted archery."[135] "National speech" during the Qing period was Manchu. It differed greatly from Chinese in grammar and orthography. Manchu, an Altaic language, is inflected, agglutinative, and atonal; Chinese, a Sino-Tibetan language, is none of these. Manchu is written with a modified form of the Mongolian alphabet; Chinese, with characters. The Qing rulers were concerned that every bannerman know Manchu—not just every Old Manchu whose ancestral speech it was, but all other banner people as well.

Thus, schools for banner youths were set up to teach the language. At the Jingzhou garrison in Hubei, it was required that "all bannermen, regardless of their personal background or status, study Manchu writing in order to look after the fundamentals."[136] Examinations in translation were instituted to screen bannermen who were prospective officials. Those who excelled at the language earned bonuses, rewards, advancement, and other material benefits. As the Yongzheng emperor once explained, "If some special encouragement as this is not offered, the ancestral language will not be passed on and learned." Conversely, those who performed poorly on such tests were penalized. Every five years, soldiers and officers in the banner force were supposed to take an oral examination in Manchu. Those who failed were given until the next review to achieve competence; if they failed again, they faced dismissal.[137] The Xibe, a New Manchu group of Mongol origin, were so adept at learning and absorbing Manchu that it eventually replaced Mongolian as their "native" language.[138]

The effort to inculcate and preserve the Manchu language among the banner population at large was generally not so successful as among the Xibe. The declining use of Manchu among the banner people was already marked in the early eighteenth century and only became worse thereafter, as successive emperors lamented. The Jiaqing emperor, for example, complained that "officials in the Imperial Household are simply not versed in the Manchu language, and when copying they must write stroke by stroke, and letter by letter; not only do they not comprehend the sense, but they do not even recognize the very graphs." The extant memorials in the Palace Archives (in Taiwan) confirm the steady decline of the Manchu language among bannermen officials, most of whom wrote only in Manchu in the early Qing, then in both Manchu and Chinese in the mid-Qing, and finally only in Chinese in the late Qing. The archives of the Hulan banner detachment in Heilongjiang, far from the center of Han cultural influence, exhibit a nearly identical pattern of change. By the end of the nineteenth century, only about 1 percent of the Manchus in Hulan could read Manchu, and no more than two-tenths of 1 percent could speak it. At around the same time, at the office of the Shengjing general in southern Manchuria, reportedly the sole occasion for using Manchu was to write the memorial wishing the reigning emperor a long life; all other public business at the yamen was conducted in Chinese. By then, too, banner-family genealogies in Fengtian were no longer written in Manchu but in Chinese. In Beijing, Lao She's cousin Fuhai "knew only a smattering of Manchu and always spoke Chinese, which he used for any occasional writing he did."[139]

However, the Manchus' linguistic acculturation, though far along, was never complete; Fuhai, after all, still knew "a smattering" of Manchu. The banner people, while taking up Chinese, did not stop using Manchu altogether, particularly those living in out-of-the-way places. Manchu was widely spoken in the Yili valley of western Xinjiang among the Xibe; it was also used, though less widely, in Manchuria. In Fengtian in 1870, the Scottish missionary Alexander Williamson observed that "some of the more aged still speak the Manchu language." He also noted that in "rare" instances some of the young people, if they already knew Chinese, were given additional instruction in the Manchu script. The British consular official Alexander Hosie, after a tour of the northeast in the 1890s, asserted that "the Manchu language . . . is to all intents and purposes a thing of the past" but admitted that it was still spoken in "remote corners" of Jilin and Heilongjiang "where Tartar tribes have kept themselves isolated and beyond the tide of Chinese immigration." Even within China proper, Manchu was not entirely a dead language in the late nineteenth century. In Beijing, some, though admittedly not many, official documents continued to be produced in Manchu. As Ch'en Chieh-hsien concedes, "The conservative instincts of the Manchus were very strong, and so the official archives and the Historiography Office contain numerous records written in Manchu, dating as late as the last years of the dynasty." Also, students in banner schools were still taught the Manchu language. Thus, prior study of Manchu writing was one of the principal prerequisites when the Beijing Translators College started recruiting banner students for European language study in 1862. The Guangzhou Translators College similarly stipulated that its banner students, in addition to learning English, should also study, as time allowed, written and spoken Manchu (Qingzi Qingyu). Because banner soldiers were routinely tested in spoken Manchu, minimum proficiency was sufficiently widespread in the Peking Field Force, the semimodern banner army organized in the 1860s, for its officers to be able to issue voice commands to their troops in Manchu. Indeed, the Peking Field Force's promoter, Yixin (Prince Gong), in 1878 commended this practice to other Qing military units of the time as a way of keeping secrets from inquisitive Westerners.[140]

Manchu name-giving practices reflected the process as well as the limits of their linguistic acculturation. Whereas Han typically had three-character names made up of a monosyllabic surname and a disyllabic personal name, Manchus originally had surnames and personal names that were generally both polysyllabic. Furthermore, their surnames were made up of two components: a lineage name preceded by a sublineage name. For example, the Aisin Gioro, the imperial clan, were a subset of the larger Gioro lineage. Finally, Manchus seldom used their surnames in public, such as when memorializing the throne; instead, they usually referred to themselves by their personal names, for example, Ronglu, a member of the Suwan Gūwalgiya.[141]

Other members of the banner population besides the Old Manchus adopted and went by Manchu-style names. The ancestors of the post-Boxer official Duanfang, for example, were Han Chinese from Zhejiang who, when they moved to southern Manchuria in the late Ming, became subjects of the Qing and were enrolled in the Manchu Plain White Banner; they then Manchufied their surname from Tao to Tohoro (Tuohuoluo in Chinese). Members of the Hanjun often altered an originally monosyllabic Han family name by adding to it the two-syllable suffix *giya* (*jia* in Chinese) to make it sound Manchu; thus, the monosyllabic surname Li would become (in Chinese) the disyllabic Lijia.[142] Despite such examples, the Qing rulers seemingly did not require all of their bannermen followers who were of Han origin to adopt Manchu-style names. Thus, the bondservant family of Cao Xueqin (1715–63), author of *Dream of the Red Chamber* (Hongloumeng), evidently never changed their surname. Neither did the Hanjun family of the late-Qing officials Zhao Erxun and Zhao Erfeng. Nevertheless, many members of the Hanjun did go by Manchu names. For example, six of the seven Hanjun who were sent to study police matters in Japan in 1901 had Manchu-style two-syllable names, and so did two of the six students who were identified as Hanjun in the school directory of the Metropolitan University (Jingshi Daxuetang) for 1906. And the Hanjun graduate of the Beijing Translators College who was China's minister to the United Kingdom in 1902–5 had both a Han-style name (Zhang Deyi) and a Manchu name (Deming [1847–1918]).[143]

Manchu men's names, like the Manchu language in general, underwent a process of acculturation that was substantial but by no means complete. In the beginning, among the first couple of generations, Manchu men had polysyllabic personal names (e.g., Nurhaci) that in their native language may have been meaningful but when transliterated by sound into Chinese characters were gibberish; furthermore, they did not arrange their personal names in generational order, as Han often did.[144] In time, however, Manchu names began to show Han traits. With the imperial clan itself taking the lead, Manchus started to shorten their personal names to disyllabic ones (e.g., Yinzhen, for the future Yongzheng emperor), to adopt names that were meaningful and felicitous in Chinese, and to assign names on a generational basis. By the time of the Guangxu emperor (r. 1875–1908), all the males of his generation in the imperial clan had the character *zai* in their personal names, such as Zaitian (the emperor), Zaifeng (1883–1952; his brother and future regent), and Zaizhen (1876–1948; his cousin). By contrast, the previous generation had used the character *yi* (e.g., Yikuang, Yixin, and Yihuan), while the following generation used the character *pu* (e.g., the future Xuantong emperor Puyi [1906–67] and his brother Pujie [1907–94]).

In a further refinement of the generational principle, the second character in the personal name of each person in the direct line of succession contained a radical that distinguished these names from all others of their generation in the imperial clan. Thus, the *tian* character in "Zaitian" and the *feng* character in "Zaifeng" shared the "water" radical; however, the *zhen* in "Zaizhen" (written with the "hand" radical) did not, because as the son of Yikuang (Prince Qing), Zaizhen was not in the direct line of succession.[145]

Among nonimperial Manchu families, a similar process was at work. At Xiuyan, in eastern Fengtian, the Manchus in the seventh or eighth generation continued as before to give their sons polysyllabic Manchu personal names that were meaningless when transliterated into Chinese, but at the same time they began to also give them Chinese names that were disyllabic and meaningful and that conformed to the generational principle. Thus, in the seventh generation of the Gūwalgiya lineage were sons with two names, one Manchu and one Chinese, such as Duolunbu/Shiman, Delinbu/Shizhu, and Tehengbu/Shizhen. Within the family and the banner, these boys used their Manchu name, but outside they used their Han-style name. Then, from the eighth or ninth generation on, at the beginning of the nineteenth century, the Gūwalgiya at Xiuyan stopped giving polysyllabic Manchu names to their sons, who thereafter used Chinese names exclusively.[146]

Some Manchus, though not the imperial clan, went further toward acculturation by replacing their polysyllabic surname with a Han-type monosyllabic surname to go along with their Chinese disyllabic personal name, as the Hanjun often did.[147] The Qing rulers, somewhat surprisingly, found serious fault with this practice; though they themselves had led in adopting Han-style personal names, they drew the line at family names. The Qianlong emperor repeatedly warned the Manchus "not to succumb to Han surnames, which will cause confusion," and when the ancient and politically prominent Manchu lineage of Niohuru adopted the Han-style surname Lang, he ridiculed them for having "forgotten their roots." (The Niohuru, whose name was derived from *niohe*, Manchu for "wolf," had chosen Lang as their surname because it was a homophone for the Chinese word for "wolf.")[148]

With regard to name-giving, therefore, Sinicization had proceeded apace for more than two hundred years. Manchu men had abandoned their original polysyllabic personal names in favor of Han-style disyllabic names; they had adopted the Han practice of choosing characters with auspicious meanings for the names; and they had assigned names on a generational basis. For all that, however, there remained down to the end of the nineteenth century one feature of Manchu name-giving that had not changed. Except among some Hanjun such as the two Zhao brothers, bannermen still did not, by and large, use their family name but called themselves only by their personal name—for example, Yikuang, Ronglu, Gangyi, Duanfang, Xiliang, and Tieliang. In this respect, most Manchus remained conspicuously different from Han.

Besides "national speech," the other core element of the Manchu way of life—one that differentiated them even more from the Han—was mounted archery. Mid-Qing emperors repeatedly insisted that horsemanship and archery constituted the "fundamental essence of us Manchus" (*wo Manzhou genben*), which had to be preserved. The Jiaqing emperor in 1820 even admonished the banner soldiers in Jilin not to use the musket in hunting but to use the ancestral bow and arrow instead. It was not only the Old Manchus but the rest of the banner system as well—not only banner soldiers but also ordinary bannermen—who were expected to maintain competency in riding a horse and shooting a bow and arrow. Among the Scouts Division of the Metropolitan Banners, young boys began such training at the age of seven. Students at banner schools, such as those in the Jingzhou garrison, practiced mounted archery as part of their regular curriculum. Candidates for the civil service examinations (literary and translation) were required to demonstrate minimum competence in archery, both mounted and on foot, before they were permitted to sit for the tests.[149]

For most banner soldiers, military training focused almost exclusively on horsemanship and archery. They practiced those skills on a regular (if rather relaxed) schedule and at different levels of organizational complexity. Among the Metropolitan Banners, for example, the Vanguards were supposed to practice archery on foot every fifth day (or six times a month) and archery from horseback twice a year, in the spring and fall. They also held joint maneuvers with other units once a year. Every third year there was a grand review at the imperial hunting park at Nanyuan, south of the capital, in which nearly twenty thousand banner soldiers participated. Similarly, in Manchuria, the troops of an entire garrison got together in the second and the eighth lunar month for month-long field exercises, and in the winter they went on collective hunting expeditions.[150]

However, the effort to preserve the Manchu martial tradition fell victim to the same forces that undermined the concurrent effort to maintain the Manchu language. In the late nineteenth century, the Qing rulers finally overcame their scruples about modern weaponry and allowed the newly organized Peking Field Force in Beijing and similar "foreign-rifle detachments" (*yangqiangdui*) in various provincial garrisons to substitute the rifle and the cannon for the bow and arrow. In the rest of the banner army, banner soldiers continued down to the end of the century to practice the traditional skills of horse riding and archery, but these exercises had become formalistic and meaningless. Moreover, the emperor himself had long ceased to take his equestrian heritage seriously. Jiaqing was the last ruler to go regularly on the traditional annual or biennial month-long expedition to the imperial hunting grounds at Mulan, one hundred miles north of the Great Wall. The expeditions were terminated altogether in 1821, and the Mulan hunting grounds were thrown open to cultivation in 1863. In Manchuria, the last annual hunts in Jilin and Heilongjiang were held in 1875.[151] Bannermen, living off the stipends paid to banner soldiers and barred from most other occupations, began instead to cultivate in their ample leisure time a variety of nonmilitaristic interests, such as raising birds, collecting cricket-feeding vessels and pigeon whistles, and singing Beijing opera. As Lao She observed sardonically of his Manchu elders, "The true meaning of life was to be found in the daily pursuit of their hobbies, in which they sought out what was exquisite, refined, and enchanting." It was these aesthetic activities, rather than horse riding and archery, with which the Manchus came to be associated in the late Qing.[152]

As the tradition of the Manchu mounted archer declined, so too, as is well known, did the efficacy of the banner army. The conquest of Xinjiang in the 1750s was the last military engagement in which banner soldiers constituted the main fighting force. They were, for example, ineffective in the 1790s against the White Lotus Rebellion (1796–1804). The Qing dynasty thereafter was forced to rely on a succession of non-banner forces: first the Army of the Green Standard, then locally raised militias, and finally regional armies. Neverthe-less, the banner soldiers were not so effete or so militarily inept in the mid-nineteenth century as they are usually portrayed. In the two Opium Wars and the Taiping Rebellion, the Manchus unavoidably did much of the fighting, and they often battled bravely against heavy odds. During the First Opium War, the banner garrisons at Guangzhou, Zhapu, and Zhenjiang carried the burden of the defense on the Chinese side. At Zhenjiang, where the garrison had been reinforced by banner soldiers from Qingzhou in Shandong, the banner troops, according to Peter Ward Fay, "fought bitterly and skillfully even after the walls had been scaled and one gate blown in, and would neither surrender nor run but died where they stood, or else managed to avoid the English long enough to regain their own quarter and there make an end to themselves and their fam-ilies." In the Second Opium War (1856–60), it was once again the banner troops who led the resistance against the British and French both at Guangzhou and at Beijing. Banner soldiers from Qiqihar, for example, were part of the army of Senggelinqin (d. 1865), which in 1858 repelled the invaders at Tianjin and Dagu.[153]

Meanwhile, other banner garrisons in central China were engaged in a long and even more desperate struggle against the Taiping rebels, whose heaven-sent mission was to slay the Manchu demons. In March 1853 the garrison at Nanjing fought off the Taipings for thirteen days; when it finally succumbed, the banner people paid dearly for their resistance. As described by Jen Yu-wen,

> The revolutionaries, in a fury of revenge for the bloody battle, carried out a brutal massacre of all but a few hundred people lucky enough to escape into the Outer City. At one point several thousand Manchu women were surrounded and driven through one of the gates, there to be burned, stabbed, or drowned. According to the later investigations of Tseng Kuo-fan [Zeng Guofan, 1811–72], more than thirty thousand lost their lives in this great massacre of Bannermen.

(The Taipings were to be treated no less terribly when Zeng Guofan recaptured the city for the Qing in 1864.) At Hangzhou, the banner garrison staved off a bitter two-month siege in 1860, only to capitulate a year later. A majority of the banner people in the city, numbering eight to ten thousand, committed suicide rather than fall into Taiping hands. The nearby garrison at Zhapu, already victimized in the First Opium War, was also decimated.[154]

Banner troops elsewhere participated in the struggle against the Taiping and other rebels as well, and suffered similarly. The small garrison at Cangzhou, in the capital region southeast of Beijing, lost over two hundred soldiers trying to halt the Taipings' northern expedition in 1853. Troops from the Manchurian garrisons that were sent south also absorbed tremendous (though improbably high) casualties. In Jilin, according to its general in 1865, "over 10,000 banner troops had died in the campaigns, and of those who returned, almost half were disabled." Likewise, in Heilongjiang, according to the gazetteer, "the number of troops sent to China proper totaled about 67,730 men; of those, only about 10 to 20 percent survived." The banner garrisons in the northwest similarly fought against the Chinese Muslim rebels and the invading force of Yacob Beg (1820–77) in the 1860s and early 1870s. Casualties at the Xinjiang garrisons rivaled those at Nanjing and Hangzhou.[155] In sum, the banner soldiers' role in both Opium Wars and the mid-century rebellions was by no means inconsequential.

Even as they tried to keep their Manchu followers from succumbing to Han ways, the rulers of the Qing dynasty were making several efforts in the opposite direction, that is, to Manchufy (or alternatively, as Mark Elliott puts it, "Manjurify") their Han subjects. The Manchus made three cultural impositions upon the Han: men's hairstyle, official dress, and Manchu language. The first was universally and stringently enforced; the other two were more limited in scope and effect.

The queue was the male hairstyle of the original Manchus, a variant of the way men of the northern tribes, including the Jurchen, had traditionally worn their hair; it involved shaving the front and sides of the head, letting the rest of the hair grow long, and braiding it into a plait. The Chinese style current in the Ming period was to let all the hair grow out, coil it up into a topknot on the crown of the head, and hold it in place with a cap made of horsehair. Within a year after they fought their way into China proper, the Qing demanded, on pain of death, that the men among their defeated subjects wear their hair the Manchu way. At first the queue requirement was tremendously unpopular among the Han, who protested that shaving the head was contrary to the "system of rites and music" of ancient China and that it violated the Confucian injunction against harming the body that had been bestowed by one's parents. The Qing rulers, however, viewed the queue as a visible emblem of submission and would neither withdraw nor modify the regulation. When a former Ming official, Chen Mingxia, in 1654 voiced his disapproval of the queue ordinance and urged a return to the Ming fashion, the Shunzhi emperor had him executed for treason. (Chen was also accused of corruption.) As the Qianlong emperor reaffirmed in 1768, when confronted by a baffling outbreak in Zhejiang and Jiangsu of queue-clipping (not queue-cutting), "Wearing the queue is a fundamental institution of this dynasty." The only ones exempt were men in mourning, young boys, Buddhist monks (who shaved off all their hair), and Taoist priests (who let their hair grow). All other Han males in Qing China were coerced into abiding by the requirement. (Among the non-Han peoples in the empire, such as the Turks in Xinjiang and the Miao in the southwest, only leaders were obliged to wear the queue, not commoners.)[156] As a result, notwithstanding their initial opposition, most Han came to accept the Manchu hairstyle. The "long-haired" Taiping rebels were an obvious exception; otherwise, by the end of the nineteenth century, as the anti-Manchu critics themselves admitted ruefully, the queue had become a part of the inherited tradition of China.[157]

Official dress was the second aspect of Han culture that was Manchufied. Like the hairstyle, the clothing style of the Manchus differed greatly from that of the Chinese during the Ming. In general, the Ming style of men's clothing, among both officials and scholars, was wide, bulky, and loose, as suited a sedentary population. The Ming official's formal dress consisted, in part, of a fulllength, loose-fitting, wide-sleeved robe, a stiff hooplike belt around the mid-section, a double-crowned hat with two "fins" protruding perpendicularly from the rear, and soft slippers with upturned toes. The scholar's casual wear lacked the hoop belt and substituted a square cap for the finned hat, but was similarly ample and flowing (see plates 1 and 2).[158] The Manchu style was narrow and tight and reflected its equestrian origins: it was close-fitting on top to conserve body heat; loose-fitting at the bottom and slit in front and back as well as along the sides to facilitate riding a horse; and had long, tapered sleeves flaring into "horse-hoof cuffs" that protected the back of the rider's hands from the cold. This full-length robe was worn over trousers that were all but concealed, and it was sometimes worn under a half- or three-quarter-length front-fastening surcoat called a "horse jacket" (*magua*). Qing officials dressed differently from Ming officials in yet other ways. They did not wear the hoop belt. They wore rigid-soled boots, not soft slippers. They wore hats of two seasonal types, neither with protruding fins: one was a cone-shaped, brimless summer hat made of bamboo, the other a round winter hat with an upturned brim made of animal fur. Both types of hat were topped with a glass or jewel ball, the color of which indicated the wearer's rank. Finally, officials of the fifth rank or higher also wore a long necklace of 108 beads. Both the hat knob and the necklace were Qing innovations. As for the Qing scholar, he wore a gown that was cut like the official robe—with tapered sleeves and slit below the waist— and a round cap rather than the square cap of the Ming (see plates 3 and 4).[159]

The Qing rulers demanded that their clothing style, like the queue, be adopted. As with Chen Mingxia a century earlier, Liu Zhenyu was executed during the Qianlong reign for urging that the costume be changed, presumably by returning to the Ming fashion.[160] However, the dress code was required only of the scholar-official elite and not of the entire male population. Therefore, the great majority of Han men were free to continue to dress as they had during the Ming. Nevertheless, in the course of the Qing period, they too, on their own, took to the Manchu style of dress, typified by the long gown with tapered sleeves worn under the three-quarter-length "horse jacket." As a result, by the late Qing, not only officials and scholars, but a great many commoners as well, had been Manchufied in their attire.[161]

The third instance of the Manchufication of Han culture was the elevation of Manchu to an equal status as Chinese as one of the two primary official languages of the Qing empire. Thus, the Qing rulers required that many official documents be rendered not only in Chinese but in Manchu as well. Consequently, throughout the Qing period, as summed up by Ch'en Chieh-hsien, "Imperial edicts, memorials to the throne, official documents, and even coins and stone inscriptions all bore Manchu writing." Furthermore, early Qing rulers had insisted that some of their Han subjects learn the Manchu language. The scope of the language requirement, however, was even more limited than that of the dress code. It applied to only a tiny elite among the officials. When on one occasion it was proposed that "all literati, whether Han Chinese or Manchu," be ordered to study the Manchu language, the Jiaqing emperor decided otherwise.[162] Only some members of the Hanlin Academy—the Han metropolitan degree holders most likely to reach the highest posts—were obliged to enroll in a three-year course on the Manchu language. This requirement was still in effect in the early nineteenth century, as one of the Hanlin academicians ordered to study Manchu was Lin Zexu (1785–1850), a metropolitan graduate of 1811.[163] By the late nineteenth century, however, Han officials seemingly were no longer required to study Manchu. Nevertheless, because of the state's extensive efforts to popularize its use throughout the Qing period, the Manchu language inevitably left its mark on the Chinese language. A number of Manchu words thus found their way into Chinese, particularly the specialized vocabulary of governmental administration, such as *zhangjing* (from *janggin*, "secretary"), *bitieshi* (from *bithesi*, "Manchu scribe"), *jiala* (from *jalan*, "banner battalion"), and *niulu* (from *niru*, "banner company"). The Manchu imprint was also evident in the speech of Han Chinese from Beijing and Shengjing, the two cities with the largest banner population, where the local dialects include many Manchu loan-words and their morphology and syntax exhibit some features that, according to Stephen Wadley, "suggest that they were influenced" by Manchu and other Altaic languages.[164]

Sinicization of the Manchus thus was not the only process of cultural change occurring during the Qing period; concurrent with it, on a much smaller though not insignificant scale, was the reverse process, the Manchufication of the Han. Furthermore, as of the late nineteenth century, neither culture had triumphed over the other. Each of the two peoples retained cultural elements that made them distinct despite more than two centuries of living together.

Manchus and Han differed particularly in women's clothing. Manchu women typically wore a one-piece gown. Also, as described by A. C. Scott, they "tended to build their hair up in elaborate shapes on top of their heads, using wire frames, false hair and ornate decorations." (The "bat-wing shapes" of this headdress, known colloquially as *liangbatou*, was, according to Valery Garrett, "characteristic of nomadic headwear from the Eurasian steppe.") Finally, Manchu women did not bind their feet, and they wore platform shoes that were two or three inches high. The attire of fashionable Han women differed in all three respects. Following Ming custom, they dressed in a two-piece outfit, with a loose three-quarter-length garment worn over a pair of trousers; they combed their hair back and coiled it into a bun at the rear or two buns on the sides; and they bound their feet and wore tiny cloth shoes (see plate 5).[165] Han women were not required to adopt Manchu dress, and, unlike the men, they never did. Nor, by and large, did Manchu women emulate Han fashion. Thus, down to the end of the nineteenth century, Manchu and Han women retained their distinctive costumes.

Yet other cultural differences divided Manchus and Han. For example, they differed in how they styled themselves when addressing the emperor in writing. When memorializing the throne, a bannerman referred to himself, in Chinese, as *nucai* (your slave), whereas a Han utilized the term *chen* (your minister). The Qianlong emperor once directed all his officials to call themselves *chen*, but for some reason the directive never took effect.[166] Manchus and Han also differed in where they placed the position of honor, with Manchus locating it on the right side and Han on the left.[167] And they greeted people differently. Manchus greeted a fellow Manchu (one who was socially superior) by dropping the right knee to the ground and letting the arms hang down; this was known in Chinese as *daqian*, which David Hawkes, in his translation of *Dream of the Red Chamber* (also known as *Story of the Stone* [Shitou ji]), calls the "Manchu salute." The Han greeting consisted of clasping both hands in front of the chest and bowing.[168]

POSTWAR ATTEMPTS AT REFORM

The clearest evidence that down to the end of the nineteenth century Manchus and Han were still separate peoples, who kept apart from each other and who retained some distinctive cultural traits, comes from some of the reforms that were proposed in the wake of China's loss in the Sino-Japanese War of 1894–95. The defeat, which led to the cession of Taiwan and then the Scramble for Concessions, had opened the floodgates of Japanese and Western imperialism. These alarming events alerted some members of the Chinese elite to the possibility, indeed likelihood, that their country would be partitioned among the imperialist powers. To prevent this from occurring, various scholars and officials began offering suggestions for reform, some of which went far beyond the limited aims of the Self-Strengthening Movement. The reformers soon found a receptive audience in the youthful Guangxu emperor, who had been freed from the constraints of his aunt Cixi's regency since 1889. On 18 December 1897, after the German seizure of Jiaozhou Bay in Shandong, the emperor issued a rambling edict that, inter alia, called on all officials who were knowledgeable in military affairs to suggest changes.[169] Six months later, on 11 June 1898, he greatly broadened his appeal for reform proposals, thus beginning the Hundred Days.

The postwar reformers, led by the new metropolitan degree holder Kang Youwei, organized political clubs in the guise of "study societies," such as the Society for the Study of Self-Strengthening (Qiangxuehui) in Beijing in late 1895, and they founded political journals, such as *Current Affairs News* (Shiwubao) in Shanghai in August 1896. One bannerman who was active in this unprecedented reform effort from below was the imperial clansman Shoufu (1865–1900), who was to pass the regular metropolitan examinations in 1898. In May 1897 Shoufu published an article in *Current Affairs News* titled "An Address to the Worthies of the Eight Banners Concerning Current Trends," in which he, like many others at the time, warned of the peril of partition. He focused generally on the threat that partition posed for all Chinese, but at one point he spoke to the self-interest of the banner people. He prophesied, "If the present dynasty is invigorated, then the Eight Banners will continue as the aristocracy." The unstated alternative, of course, was that if China were partitioned and the Qing dynasty extinguished, then the banner people would lose their privileged status.[170] In Beijing in the same year, Shoufu, together with Kang Youwei, founded the Study Society to Know Shame (Zhichi Xuehui); its purpose was to heighten popular consciousness about the "shame" of China's defeat by Japan.[171]

Some of the changes these popular agitators called for verged on what in the past would have been regarded as treasonous. One proposed reform involved the Qing's sumptuary laws. Previous scholars and officials who had recommended a change in the dynastic dress code had run the risk of severe punishment, including, in the case of Liu Zhenyu in the Qianlong era, even execution. Nevertheless, in the summer of 1896 a certain Jiang Shuzi published a short article in Young J. Allen's Shanghai reformist monthly *A Review of the Times* (Wanguo gongbao) that dared to suggest abandoning the Manchu-style official dress. Jiang asserted that it was only after Peter the Great had altered his country's clothing style to accord with the rest of Europe that Russia became strong, and that the Meiji emperor by following Peter's lead had achieved similar results in Japan. Such changes, including a change in the calendar (presumably from lunar to solar), would symbolize both an imperial determination to make drastic changes and a willingness to involve the entire population in that reform effort. They would help bring about a "new citizenry." Jiang then asked rhetorically, "If China wishes to reform, should it not begin with the calendar and the costume?" He admitted, in conclusion, that a commoner such as himself ought not intrude in "matters of institutions and rituals," which were the sole prerogative of the court; nevertheless, he proceeded to recommend that the Qing learn from the experiences of Petrine Russia and Meiji Japan. While Jiang did not specify how the clothing style should be changed, undoubtedly it would have meant abandoning the Manchu gown and, as Japan had done, adopting European garb.[172]

Kang Youwei went even further and suggested abolishing the dynasty's queue requirement. In a lengthy account of the Meiji reforms titled *A Study of the Governmental Reforms in Japan* (Riben bianzheng kao), which he offered to the court in 1898, Kang too alluded to the desirability of the Qing emperor's emulating the Japanese ruler, but unlike Jiang Shuzi, he referred not only to court dress but also to hairstyle. He wrote that in Japan "the official dress had all been changed to the Western style and the Japanese emperor had personally cut short his hair." He implied that the Guangxu emperor should follow suit.[173] (Kang Youwei supposedly submitted three other, much more detailed memorials on Manchu-Han relations in 1898, but they, unlike *A Study of the Governmental Reforms in Japan*, are thought to be later fabrications.)[174]

The most comprehensive reform proposal concerning Manchu-Han relations came in a memorial to the throne presented by Zhang Yuanji (1867–1959) on 5 September 1898. A metropolitan degree holder (class of 1892) from Zhejiang and founder of a foreign-language school (the Tongyi Xuetang) in Beijing in 1897, Zhang Yuanji had only recently been appointed to the Zongli Yamen. He proposed five sets of reforms, the second of which was "to dissolve Manchu-Han differences" (*rong Man-Han zhi jian*) so that China could unite in common opposition to the aggression of the foreign powers. Zhang, in this section of his memorial, recommended six reforms.[175] First, he urged an end to the administrative separation of Manchus and Han by reclassifying the "various Manchu and Mongol banner people in China proper" as civilians and transferring them to the jurisdiction of local officials. Only the imperial clan were to be exempt because they were too exalted to be treated as ordinary civilians; they would continue to be under the Imperial Clan Court. Second, he called for an end to the social and occupational segregation of Manchus and Han. There was no better way to integrate the two populations than for the emperor to issue a command that "banner people and Han [*qi-Han*] intermarry." He also urged the emperor to "lift the prohibition on venturing forth to trade so that the banner people may make their own living, and to permit those who wish to live elsewhere [than the garrison cities] to petition the local authorities to be reclassified as civilians."

Third, Zhang proposed an end to dyarchy. He conceded that it might have been sensible at the beginning of the dynasty to maintain separate slots for Manchu and Han officials. But the practice had become a source of "mutual discord between banner people and Han." Furthermore, the system no longer benefited the Manchus (Manren) themselves. Because they generally began their careers earlier, they were not as well educated as the Han (Hanren), and they were often assigned to posts in desolate places beyond the Great Wall. He recommended that henceforth only one qualified person, without regard to whether he was Manchu or Han, be appointed to each position. Fourth, Zhang seemed to call for a phasing out of the banner soldiers' stipends. Current soldiers would continue to be paid in full, but when vacancies in the banner units occurred, they should be allowed to lapse. Fifth, he urged that industrial schools be set up in Beijing and in the provincial garrisons to give vocational training to unemployed banner people. Last, he recommended that, pending the outcome of the reforms within China proper, the current institutions be left intact in Inner and Outer Mongolia, Xinjiang, and Qinghai (and presumably Manchuria as well).

Zhang Yuanji's was one of only two known memorials submitted during the Hundred Days that focused on Manchu-Han relations. The other came from Yuan Chang (1846–1900), the Jiangsu provincial treasurer at Nanjing. The text of Yuan's memorial has not been published, but its existence is known because it elicited an important edict from the emperor on 14 September 1898. Yuan apparently had brought up the vexing problem of the Eight Banners' livelihood. The emperor, in response, took note of the increase in the banner population and attributed their plight to their being "prohibited from engaging in trade in the provinces." Officials in previous reigns—notably Songyun (1752–1835) and Fujun (1749–1834) in the Jiaqing and Daoguang (1820–50) periods, and Shen Guifen in the Tongzhi period—had addressed the problem. Now that China was inaugurating a comprehensive renovation, it was time to relax the prohibition in order that the banner people might learn the vocational skills of the four classes (scholars, farmers, artisans, and merchants) so that they could provide for themselves. The emperor, furthermore, called on the Board of Revenue to develop specific programs to resettle the banner population based on the experiences from the Jiaqing and Daoguang eras.[176]

The emperor's edict responding to Yuan Chang's memorial greatly alarmed the banner people, especially those in Beijing. It seemed to augur an end to the banner stipends and perhaps even—if Zhang Yuanji's more radical ideas were enacted—an end to the banner system, to dyarchy and ethnic slots, and to the separation of Manchus and Han. According to Lao She, in *Beneath the Red Banner*,

> Several months before I was born [in 1899], my maternal uncle, [my elder sister's husband] Duofu, and his father were all in a state of great agitation. They fervently opposed the Reforms of 1898. . . . They had heard that when the changes came, bannermen were going to have to go out and earn their own keep. No longer would the Imperial government provide them with allowances.

Similarly, in Lao She's historical pageant *Teahouse* (Chaguan), the first act of which is set in Beijing in 1898 right after the Hundred Days, one bannerman observes to another that the reforms would have meant "cutting off our stipends and making us work for a living."[177]

Lao She's relatives and friends need not have fretted. One week after this edict was issued, the emperor's reform effort came to an abrupt end. On 21 September, Empress Dowager Cixi, fearful of where all the proposed changes might lead, came out of retirement, put the emperor under house arrest, and resumed her regency. The emperor never acted on Zhang Yuanji's memorial to reduce Manchu-Han differences. Nor had he, as Jiang Shuzi and Kang Youwei had recommended, shed his queue and abandoned the Manchu-style court dress.

CONCLUSION

The Eight Banner system was, originally, a heterogeneous, multiethnic organization. The founding members were the Jurchen whom Nurhaci united and organized into banners and whom Hong Taiji later renamed Manzhou. Also known as Old Manchus, they were the largest and most prestigious group within the system, but they were not the only group. The Eight Banner Manchus themselves included the New Manchus as well; these were generally either "Mongolized" Tungusic peoples (such as the Xibe) or "Tungusized" Mongols (such as the Daur), but some were Korean, Tibetan, and even Russian. Furthermore, in addition to the Manchu banners, the overall system had two other ethnic components—the Mongol banners and the Hanjun.

Despite these as well as other internal divisions, the Eight Banners by and large presented a united front to the outside world. With some exceptions, such as the addition of the Tibetan company to the Manchu banners in the 1770s, membership in the system was based on birth and was closed to new recruits. Thus, regardless of their ethnic origins, all members of the Eight Banner system shared a common status and a common identity that set them hereditarily apart from the rest of China's population. Thus, both individually and collectively, they called themselves and were called by others "banner people." Since their primary function was to hold themselves in readiness to protect and defend the Qing emperor and his court, the banner people, in this regard, constituted a hereditary military caste. They were differentiated from the non-banner people, who were generally known as "civilians."

Finally, by the end of the nineteenth century, the banner people also came to be called Manchus. These Manchus were not the Manzhou of Hong Taiji or even the Eight Banner Manchus, who were only part of the banner personnel. Rather, they were thought of as constituting the total membership of the banner system and were most often referred to in Chinese as Manren. In short, what was originally a multiethnic military organization (the Eight Banners) was also a hereditary caste (the banner people) that was increasingly being viewed (at least in the eyes of non-banner people) as an ethnic group (the

Manchus).[178] By a similar process, the non-banner "civilians" came to be equated with the correlative of the Manchus, the Han. In Zhang Yuanji's memorial of 1898, for example, the terms "Manchu" and "banner people" were used interchangeably, both in common opposition to "Han."

The Guangxu emperor's decree of 14 September 1898 proves conclusively that Mary Wright was very wrong when she asserted that "most of the last restrictions separating the Manchus from the [Han] Chinese were removed in 1865." If the Tongzhi emperor's edict permitting banner people to leave the Eight Banner system, be reclassified as civilians, and make their own living had indeed been implemented, it would have been unnecessary for his successor to issue a nearly identical decree thirty years later. Also, if most "restrictions" separating Manchus and Han had been removed in 1865, there would have been no need for Zhang Yuanji's six proposals to "dissolve Manchu-Han differences." The Tongzhi edict, however, had never been carried out. As a result, down to the end of the nineteenth century, Manchus and Han remained in many ways separate populations.

The continuing differences between Manchus and Han serve to confirm the essential validity of much of the revolutionaries' seven-point indictment against the Manchus in the early post-Boxer era. Although they had absorbed much of Han culture, the Manchus were, as charged, an alien people who in some respects were still manifestly different from the Han; their men, for example, did not use Han-style surnames, and their women dressed differently from Han and did not bind their feet. The Manchus had, as charged, barbarized (i.e., Manchufied) the Han when they successfully imposed their hairstyle upon Han men and their costume upon Han officials. The Manchus were, as charged, a privileged minority separate from and superior to the Han; they were administratively and residentially segregated, they were barred from marrying Han, and they were stipendiaries of the Qing state who were prohibited from any employment other than soldiering, serving as officials, and, in some regions, farming. The Manchus did, as charged, constitute a foreign occupying force; they were a hereditary military caste and were garrisoned within their own walled citadels that were strategically distributed throughout the empire. The Manchus did, as charged, receive preferential treatment that was denied to the Han; they were dealt with more leniently under the law, and they had more opportunities to enter and advance in government service. In short, the revolutionaries' indictment against the Manchus *qua* Manchus was not a mere propaganda ploy devoid of substance; rather, it did have a basis in contemporary social reality.

It was, however, not the revolutionaries but the postwar reformers such as Jiang Shuzi, Kang Youwei, and Zhang Yuanji who first raised what can be called the "Manchu issue" and brought it out into the open for public discussion. Previously, Manchu-Han relations had been a taboo subject. Chen Mingxia, for example, had been executed in 1654 for criticizing the queue; so had Liu Zhenyu in the Qianlong reign for proposing a change in the Manchu-style official costume. But in the late 1890s, not only did Jiang Shuzi and Kang Youwei suggest abolishing the queue and adopting Western dress, but Zhang Yuanji urged ending dyarchy and encouraging intermarriage between Manchus and Han. In making such proposals, they knew that they were treading on thin ice, as Jiang Shuzi acknowledged. They spoke up cautiously. Thus, Jiang's and Kang's separate recommendations to get rid of the queue, though unambiguous, were indirect: the Guangxu emperor should do as the Meiji emperor had done. Furthermore, the postwar reformers held back from the obvious. Thus, no one dared call for the outright disbandment of the banner army, even though it had become patently useless as a military force.[79] The closest that anyone came to suggesting an end to the banner system was when Zhang Yuanji proposed that as vacancies in the banner units occurred they be left unfilled. Nevertheless, despite the cautiousness of their approach and the moderation of their proposals, the postwar reformers presented the most serious challenge to Manchu-Han relations since the anti-Manchu Taiping Rebellion.

2 / Cixi and the "Peculiar Institution"

In the aftermath of the September palace coup, the erstwhile reformers of 1898 placed most of the blame for their failure upon the Manchus. Liang Qichao directed his ire at Associate Grand Secretary Gangyi, whose alleged declaration—that he would rather hand the empire over to "neighboring friends" than let it be seized by "household slaves"—epitomized what seemed to be the Manchus' narrow-minded ethnic bias. It was then that Liang wrote his commentary calling for tearing down the boundaries between Manchus and Han. Empress Dowager Cixi ignored all such criticisms as she repudiated or shelved many of the Guangxu emperor's attempted reforms. Her reactionary course soon led her to support the Boxer Rebellion in common opposition to Westerners and to Westernizing reforms. Her refusal to follow up on the emperor's reforms, of course, simply reinforced the notion among the growing number of critics that the ruling Manchus were the principal, perhaps the only, obstacle to China's regeneration through reform. The anti-Manchu movement intensified after the Boxer fiasco and reached an initial crescendo around the time of the anti-Russian agitation in the spring of 1903, when the revolutionaries' indictment against the Manchus was developed. As opposition to the Qing increased, Cixi was forced not only to initiate the comprehensive program of reforms known as the New Policies (Xinzheng) but also to face up to the "Manchu issue" that both reformers and revolutionaries had raised. In the early years of the post-Boxer decade, she began to make some changes in the framework of Manchu-Han relations, but these were rather modest. However, by late 1907, following the assassination of the Manchu governor of Anhui, she was driven to issue two edicts reforming the banner system that went considerably beyond that promulgated by the emperor nine years earlier. Meanwhile, others of Cixi's New Policies were affecting the banner people no less than they were the civilian population at large.

IN THE WAKE OF THE COUP

The Guangxu emperor's tentative effort at reforming the banner system was a casualty of Cixi's coup d'état. The empress dowager, who retrieved the reins of power on 22 September 1898, purged many of the leaders of the reform effort, including those who had spoken up about Manchu-Han relations. Zhang Yuanji was "dismissed permanently" from office and sent home to Shanghai in disgrace; Kang Youwei, of course, fled the country. However, Yuan Chang, the official whose memorial elicited the edict on the banner people's livelihood, was not punished; to the contrary, he was summoned to Beijing, commended, and assigned to the Zongli Yamen. Yuan was to fall victim to reactionary officials two years later; he was beheaded in July 1900 for criticizing the court's support of the Boxers. Except for the emperor himself, nearly all of the victims of Cixi's purge in 1898 were Han. This gave rise to rumors that her court was "treating Manchus as insiders and Han as outsiders" (*nei-Man wai-Han*), a charge she categorically denied on 8 October.[1]

With respect to the banner people, on the one hand Cixi shelved the emperor's plan for solving their economic problems. The decree had lifted the prohibition on their seeking outside employment and appointed Yikuang and others to explore resettlement as a long-term solution. In November 1898, when Yikuang's committee submitted a proposal for relocating the Metropolitan Banners, Cixi praised their memorial for its thoroughness but asked for additional information.[2] Thereafter, nothing more was said or done. The edict of 1898 met the same fate as that of 1865: though never revoked, it was never implemented either. On the other hand, Cixi encouraged the further military modernization of the Metropolitan Banners. In December 1898 she endorsed a proposal by Grand Councilor Ronglu to recruit a new ten-thousand-person army, known as the Center Division of the Guards Army (Wuwei Zhongjun), that was to be made up mostly of banner soldiers. In June 1899 she commended Zaiyi (Prince Duan, 1856–1922) for organizing the Tiger Spirit Division (Hushenying), also ten thousand strong, which was composed entirely of soldiers from the Metropolitan Banners.[3]

Soon afterward, Cixi embraced the Boxers and their attempt to expel the foreigners from China by force. A disproportionately large number of her supporters in this xenophobic endeavor were Manchus. One was the Tiger Spirit Division commander, Zaiyi, whose wife was Cixi's niece; in January 1900, their eldest son, Pujun (1886–1929), was designated as heir to the Tongzhi emperor (who had died without issue in 1875) and thus was also the presumptive heir apparent to the ailing Guangxu emperor.[4] Another supporter was Grand Secretary Gangyi, who, as the Boxers converged on the capital in June, mediated between them and the court. Not all leading Manchus, however, favored the Boxers. Shanqi (Prince Su, 1866–1922), one of the iron-capped princes, was outspokenly opposed, while Yikuang, head of the Zongli Yamen, was characteristically noncommittal.[5] On 20 June 1900, following a series of court conferences, Cixi declared war on the foreign powers.

Many Manchus, particularly in Beijing and Manchuria, took part in the conflict. In the capital, members of the Metropolitan Banners joined forces with the Boxers to attack the Catholic cathedral and besiege the Legation Quarters, both located within the Inner City; it was a soldier in Zaiyi's Tiger Spirit Division who shot and killed the German minister, Baron von Ketteler.[6] Metropolitan Banner soldiers, including those in the Peking Field Force (organized in the 1860s), the Tiger Spirit Division, and the Center Division of the Guards Army later defended the capital from the foreign troops sent to lift the siege. In the process, all three semimodern banner armies were decimated.[7] Among the Manchus killed in the valiant but futile defense of Beijing was Lao She's father. Another casualty was Shoufu, the reform-minded imperial clansman who in 1897 had written of the perils of partition; he committed suicide as the invaders fought their way into the capital.[8] Meanwhile, in Manchuria, where the Russians took advantage of the rebellion to overrun the region, it was the banner soldiers who similarly bore the brunt of the attack. As the Russians advanced southward along five routes, one banner garrison after another was destroyed. In Aihun (now Heihe), the garrison on the Amur River in Heilongjiang, which the anthropologist S. M. Shirokogoroff visited fifteen years later,

> the Manchu population ... sustained great losses,—thousands of refugees, in fact all the present population, left their homes and started to the south. Months later they came back only to find their houses in ashes. The Cossacks had come in, burnt the villages and stolen the cattle and horses. On account of this exodus they lost most of their personal property.[9]

As Cixi and the Guangxu emperor, escorted by a thousand banner soldiers, fled westward toward Xi'an, the victorious allied troops on 14 August 1900 entered Beijing, where they were to remain for thirteen months. The difficult task of negotiating with the foreigners, who were led by the German commander-in-chief, Count von Waldersee, was left to Yikuang and the former governor of Zhili, Li Hongzhang (1823–1901). When they finally met in mid-November, interpreting for the Chinese was the Manchu bannerman Yinchang (1859–1928), an early graduate of the German-language training program at the Beijing Translators College and head of the Tianjin Military Preparatory School.[10] In the ensuing negotiations, the foreigners, in addition to demanding heavy reparations, insisted that the Qing punish the principal instigators of the war. Among the pro-Boxer leaders at court, Zaiyi was exiled to Xinjiang, and Gangyi, who had recently died, was dishonored posthumously. Also, Zaiyi's son, Pujun, was stripped of his designation as Tongzhi's heir and expelled from the palace.[11] Local supporters of the Boxers were punished as well. At Suiyuan, where two hundred banner soldiers had joined an attack on a Catholic church, the garrison's general and brigade-general were cashiered, while the circuit intendant, a Han, was executed.[12] At the same time, former opponents of the Boxers and of the court's war policy were exonerated; Yuan Chang, for example, was posthumously rehabilitated.[13] Cixi herself, however, was not punished. Nor did the Guangxu emperor regain his power, though he was no longer threatened with involuntary abdication.

The victorious powers also demanded that a diplomatic mission be sent to Germany to apologize for the death of Baron von Ketteler and that the envoy be a prince of the first rank. Selected for the task was the emperor's younger brother, the eighteen-year-old Zaifeng, who had succeeded their father, Yihuan, as the second Prince Chun in 1891; he was accompanied to Berlin by Yinchang. On 4 September 1901, Zaifeng presented China's formal regrets to Kaiser Wilhelm II. He afterwards toured Germany and attended several military reviews, including one at Danzig in which both Wilhelm and his brother, Prince Heinrich, took a personal part. This three-week visit to Europe was to loom large in Zaifeng's thinking when he became regent in 1908.[14] Yinchang stayed on in Germany, where he served two tours (1901–6 and 1908–10) as China's minister; he later headed the Ministry of the Army.

Three days after Zaifeng's audience with the kaiser, the Boxer Protocol was signed. Thirteen days later, on 17 September 1901, the foreign powers withdrew most of their troops from Beijing, leaving only a small detachment to guard the Legation Quarters. Russia, however, remained in occupation of Manchuria. Separate negotiations between China and Russia were not concluded until the following April, when the Russians agreed to pull out in three phases over an eighteen-month period.[15] It was the Russian refusal to honor this promise in the spring of 1903 that sparked the first mass nationalist demonstrations within China and among the Chinese students in Japan. Only after the Russians were defeated in the Russo-Japanese War in 1905 did they withdraw from Manchuria. Meanwhile, Cixi and the Guangxu emperor had returned to Beijing on 7 January 1902.

CHANGES IN MANCHU-HAN RELATIONS

Before her arrival in the capital, Cixi had already begun to change her stance with regard to reform. A year earlier, on 29 January 1901, she issued in the name of the emperor a watershed edict in which she acknowledged the inevitability of change. Now that peace negotiations had commenced, the edict said, the whole system of government must be radically transformed so that wealth and power might eventually be attained. To this end, the strong points of foreign nations should be absorbed in order to make up for China's shortcomings. Heretofore those who studied Western ways had focused only on language and technology; these, however, were only the superficial elements of Western technique, not the essence of Western statecraft. By adopting only Western superficialities, how could China achieve wealth and power? Cixi now ordered all high-ranking officials to scrutinize the core institutions of China and the West and to suggest changes in any and all aspects of Qing administration.[16] Shortly afterward a new agency, the Office of Governmental Affairs (Zhengwuchu), was created to screen reform proposals and make recommendations to the court. Named to the office were six metropolitan officials, three Manchus (Yikuang, Ronglu, and Kungang [d. 1907]) and three Han (Li Hongzhang, Wang Wenshao [1830–1908], and Lu Chuanlin [1836–1910]). Except for Yikuang, all were concurrently members of the Grand Council and/or the Grand Secretariat. Also appointed, as consultants to the office, were Liu Kunyi (1830–1902) and Zhang Zhidong, governors-general at Nanjing and Wuchang respectively.[17]

Officials soon flooded the court with suggestions for reform. Over the course of the next six years, in response to such proposals, Cixi initiated a vast number of changes in a wide range of fields. In part because some of these New Policies harked back to the abortive reform movement of 1898, Cixi was obliged, though with obvious reluctance, to reconsider her harsh treatment of the Hundred Days. In her edict of 29 January 1901, she had insisted that "the new laws [xinfa] propounded by the rebel Kang [Youwei] were mutinous laws [luanfa], not true reforms [bianfa]." By June 1904, on the occasion of her seventieth birthday, she had been persuaded to issue a blanket pardon for everyone guilty of involvement in what she vaguely called the "1898 affair." The only exceptions were Kang Youwei, Liang Qichao, and Sun Yat-sen, whose crimes were said to be too odious to be forgiven. Otherwise, those who had been dismissed from office (such as Zhang Yuanji) were to be restored to their original rank, and those who had been detained were to be freed.[18] This, however, was not to be the last word on the political rehabilitation of the 1898 reformers, which remained a source of controversy down to the end of the dynasty.

Although many officials proposed reforms on a wide variety of subjects during the first half of the post-Boxer decade, only two broached the sensitive issue of Manchu-Han relations: Governor-General Zhang Zhidong of Hubei and Hunan and Governor Zhou Fu (1837–1921) of Shandong. Zhang Zhidong had been greatly disturbed by the conduct of the court and its Manchu supporters during the Boxer Rebellion, and, in an effort to prevent the foreign powers from extending their military operations into his jurisdiction, he had so informed the British consul-general at Hankou, Everard Fraser (1859–1922). In mid-December 1900 Fraser summarized Zhang's sentiments:

> He hates the Manchus as do all the Chinese officials I have met because of their hanging on to and eating up China and the absurd way in which they are promoted irrespective of their ability or fitness. There is only one way to reform China—abolish all Manchu privileges—whether of Banner pay or easy entrance to office.

According to Fraser, Zhang would then use the money thus saved from the banner soldiers' stipends to finance other reforms.[19] Seven months later, Zhang Zhidong incorporated these ideas into the second of three wide-ranging and influential memorials that he submitted with Liu Kunyi, his fellow consultant to the Office of Governmental Affairs. Though a joint memorial, it was authored principally by Zhang.[20]

In their memorial, Zhang and Liu recommended twelve reforms that were "absolutely vital for China," of which the ninth was "to deal with the Eight Banners' livelihood." They noted that the banner people were in dire economic straits and had suffered particular hardships in recent times because of the Taiping and Boxer rebellions. Since the Qianlong era there had been various proposals to improve their livelihood, but all of them had been impractical because they required resettlement beyond the Great Wall. Like Shen Guifen in 1865 and Zhang Yuanji in 1898, Zhang and Liu proposed that the banner people be permitted, if they so wished, to leave Beijing or their provincial garrisons and be reclassified as civilians. As banner soldiers opted out of the system, their places would not be filled. The savings thus realized would then be invested in schools to teach the remaining banner personnel vocational or military skills. Banner soldiers enrolled in such schools would continue to receive their pay, but as they acquired the ability to make their own living, their stipends would cease. In five or ten years, Zhang and Liu concluded, the banner people should be able to overcome most of their economic problems.

Two years later, on 14 December 1903, as he neared the end of a lengthy stay in Beijing, where he had gone to lobby the court on educational matters, Zhang Zhidong reportedly took advantage of a personal audience with Cixi to urge her again to "eradicate the boundaries between Manchus and Han" (*huaqu Man-Han zhenyu*). This time he proposed that administrative positions in the Eight Banner system not be restricted to Manchus but be opened to Han as well; he also suggested that the banner people be subject to the same criminal law as Han.[21] A few months later, in August 1904, Governor Zhou Fu, the only other official to comment on Manchu-Han relations at this time, memorialized that "banner people without a fixed domicile" should be permitted to study or farm as they wished and even to engage in trade. He, too, urged that the banner people come under the legal jurisdiction of the local civil authorities, though they would still be subject to banner regulations.[22]

Cixi's response to these proposals from Zhang Zhidong and Zhou Fu was mixed. On the one hand, she blithely insisted, after her 1903 audience with Zhang, that only the ignorant could believe that the Qing court discriminated in favor of Manchus and against Han.[23] On the other, she did initiate a few changes that helped to narrow differences between Manchus and Han. These reforms included the granting of permission for Manchus and Han to marry, the appointment of several Han to posts in the banner system, and a departure from the institution of dyarchy.

On 1 February 1902 Cixi issued an edict on Manchu-Han intermarriage. Though claiming that "the court has never distinguished between Manchu and Han," she nevertheless acknowledged that "ancient precedents [rather than the Qing code] have not permitted intermarriage." The original reason for the ban, according to the edict, was unfamiliarity with one another's customs and language, but such was no longer the case. The court therefore ought to heed popular sentiment and "eliminate this prohibition." She accordingly decreed that henceforth "all Manchus and Han, both officials and commoners, are permitted to marry each other."[24] Cixi's edict, however, had little immediate effect. When Grand Secretary Natong in early 1907 married his daughter to Li Hongzhang's grandson, the recently widowed Li Guojie (1881–1939), it was acclaimed in *Beijing Women's News* (Beijing nübao), a Manchu reformist daily, as the first Manchu-Han marriage among the top officials. Contemporary newspapers cited only two other marital alliances between prominent Manchu and Han families in this period: that between Duanfang's younger brother and a great-granddaughter of a Daoguang-era governor-general, and that between the children of Tieliang and Yuan Shikai. Such occasions were newsworthy precisely because they were so rare. As *Eastern Miscellany* (Dongfang zazhi), the Shanghai reformist monthly, commented in February 1905, Manchu-Han intermarriage had not occurred at the various banner garrisons despite the edict: "The racial boundaries are clearly demarcated and constitute a stout barrier; they can withstand any force."[25]

On 29 December 1903, two weeks after her audience with Zhang Zhidong, the empress dowager eliminated another instance of Manchu-Han difference when, perhaps on his recommendation, she abolished the Manchus' monopoly on posts in the Eight Banner system. She appointed Cheng Dequan (1860–1930), a veteran Han military officer in the northeast, as the brigade-general in the Qiqihar garrison in Heilongjiang. (When the Qiqihar post was abolished in 1905, Cheng was promoted to the position of general of Heilong-jiang.) Another Han who was named to a position in the provincial garrisons was Li Guojie, who at the time of his marriage to Natong's daughter in 1907 was brigade-general of the Hanjun contingent at Guangzhou.[26] Han officials were appointed for the first time to metropolitan banner posts as well. In January 1906, when Feng Guozhang (1859–1919) became superintendent of the Nobles Military School, he was named concurrently the acting deputy lieutenant-general of the Mongol Plain Yellow Banner. Ten months later, after the metro-politan administration was restructured, several leading Han whose offices had been abolished were assigned to posts of equivalent rank in the Mongol banners and the Hanjun.[27]

Cixi similarly ended the northeast's status as a Manchu preserve. By the early post-Boxer era, particularly in view of the Russian invasion, the ban on Han entering Manchuria, which had already been partially relaxed in the late nine-teenth century, was no longer in effect. Furthermore, as Han immigrants from over-populated north China flooded into the relatively open spaces of the region, the prohibition on the transfer of property from banner people to civil-ians, which had been in force in Manchuria even as it was widely ignored within China proper, was lifted in 1905.[28] Indeed, the Qing court itself, in an effort to raise money for its depleted treasury, began to sell off some of its extensive land holdings in the northeast. In 1906 it set up a bureau in Jinzhou, in the Liaoxi corridor in Fengtian, to survey the numerous imperial estates nearby preparatory to their sale; by 1909, it had disposed of over two hundred thou-sand acres.[29] Finally, the government of the region was completely restructured. Previously, Manchuria had been divided into three territories, each governed by a banner garrison general who had always been a Manchu. In April 1907 the court reorganized the three territories into provinces, eliminated the three gar-rison generals, and created a new civilian administration composed of a sin-gle governor-general for the entire region and three provincial governors. Named as the first governor-general was Xu Shichang (1855–1939), a Han; the three new provincial governors were also all Han. *Beijing Women's News*, speak-ing for the Manchus, commented that these appointments to a regional administration heretofore monopolized by bannermen demonstrated that the court "harbored not one iota of partiality with regard to Manchus and Han."[30]

Last, Cixi departed from, but did not abolish, the ancestral institution of dyarchy when she sanctioned the creation of four new ministries as additions to the existing Six Boards. The first was the Ministry of Foreign Affairs, estab-lished in July 1901 at the insistence of the foreign powers. The foreigners had long been dissatisfied with the irregular nature of the Zongli Yamen, which was only a nonstatutory committee of the Grand Council; they demanded that the yamen be upgraded into an independent ministry. The new body differed organizationally from the Six Boards in two ways. It revived and formalized the post of supervisor (*zongli dachen*), the shadowy, ad hoc post that had been widely used in the eighteenth century to oversee the work of a board; both he and his assistant supervisor outranked the ministry's president. More to the point, the new ministry had only one president, one senior vice-president, and one junior vice-president. This, of course, was contrary to the principle of dyarchy, whereby each board or ministry was headed by two presidents and two sets of vice-presidents, all evenly divided between Manchus and Han. Three other ministries—Commerce, Police, and Education—were created in the early post-Boxer era, and, except that none had a supervisor, they were organized the same way as the Ministry of Foreign Affairs.[31]

Cixi's departure from dyarchy, however, was quite limited. The structural change was confined to the four new ministries. In the fall of 1905 Zaizhen, the founding minister of commerce, proposed that in the interest of administrative efficiency, dyarchy be eliminated from the rest of the metropolitan administration so that all slots would "not distinguish between Manchus and Han" (*bufen Man-Han*).[32] Zaizhen's proposal, which harked back to an idea of Zhang Yuanji's in 1898, was not acted upon at this time. Furthermore, though ethnic slots no longer existed at these new agencies, no radical alteration in the numerical distribution of Manchu and Han ministers resulted. The initial appointees to the two supervisory and three ministerial posts in the Ministry of Foreign Affairs, for example, were two Manchus (Yikuang and Lianfang) and three Han (Wang Wenshao, Qu Hongji [1850–1918], and Xu Shoupeng [d. 1901]). At the other three new ministries, too, the founding presidents and vice-presidents were almost equally divided between Manchus (four) and Han (five).[33] Thus, the spirit of dyarchy lived on, even as its formal structure was dismantled.

If the initial appointments to the four new ministries resulted in only a slight shift toward Han preponderance over Manchus, they nevertheless represented a sharp increase in princely involvement in government, because two of the six Manchu appointees, Yikuang and Zaizhen, were imperial princes. In the early Qing, it had been common for imperial princes to participate directly in state affairs. But after the creation of the Grand Council in the 1720s and 1730s, they all but ceased to do so. In 1799, after naming his brother Yongxing (Prince Cheng, 1752–1823) to the Grand Council, the Jiaqing emperor abruptly rescinded his action, and as he did so he announced that the appointment of an imperial prince to the council contradicted the "established institutions of our state."[34] Thus, from the 1730s to 1861, aside from Yongxing, only one other prince, Yixin, in 1853, was named to the Grand Council, and his tenure on the council (1853–55), like Yongxing's, was relatively brief. Princes were excluded not only from the Grand Council but also from the Six Boards; thus, according to Qian Shifu's data for 1830–60, not a single prince was a board president or vice-president during those three decades.[35] It should, however, be noted that the prohibition did not bar imperial princes from participating in court politics from behind the scenes. Nor did it apply to those imperial clansmen who were not princes; indeed, as previously explained, they were assigned their own set of "slots" in the metropolitan bureaucracy.

The century-old dynastic tradition articulated by the Jiaqing emperor was first contravened in a significant way at the beginning of the Tongzhi Restoration, when in 1861 Yixin, the boy emperor's uncle, was reappointed to the Grand Council. In retrospect, we can see that this was the beginning of a long-term trend that culminated, during the regency of Zaifeng, in the "reimperialization" of political authority. Except for brief interruptions, Yixin remained on the Grand Council until ousted by Cixi in 1884, and he was succeeded by another prince, Shiduo (Prince Li, 1843–1914), one of the iron-capped princes, who served until 1901. Also, on two occasions Shiduo was joined on the council by a second prince: first Yixin, for three years during and after the Sino-Japanese War, and later Zaiyi, for one month at the height of the Boxer Rebellion in the summer of 1900. By then, the prohibition against princely participation in the Grand Council had clearly been breached.[36] However, imperial princes were still barred from the Six Boards. To be sure, they had been put in charge of the Zongli Yamen (Yixin, followed by Yikuang) and the Navy Yamen (Yihuan), but these two organizations were irregular, nonstatutory bodies, unlike the Six Boards.[37]

In the early post-Boxer years, the breach with the mid-Qing tradition of princely nonparticipation in state affairs grew considerably wider. At the Grand Council, when Shiduo was dismissed in August 1901, it first appeared as if the tradition had reasserted itself, for the one remaining Manchu on the council was Ronglu, who, though he was soon to marry his daughter to Zaifeng, was himself only an ordinary Manchu bannerman and not a prince.[38] However, such was not to be. When Ronglu died in April 1903, he was immediately succeeded by Yikuang, who was to remain on the council for the rest of the decade. More important, the breach with tradition had spread from the Grand Council to the ministries. The catalyst for this came from the foreign powers, who during the Boxer Protocol negotiations insisted not only that the Zongli Yamen be regularized and upgraded into a ministry but also that the new body be headed by an imperial prince. They may have reasoned that the Zongli Yamen had always been presided over by a prince and so therefore should its successor. Whatever the explanation, the appointment in July 1901 of Yikuang as supervisor of the Ministry of Foreign Affairs broke new ground, for it marked the first time that an imperial prince headed a statutory administrative office. When his son Zaizhen, a fourth-rank prince, became minister of commerce two years later, the prohibition was violated once more.[39]

Apart from several other minor changes that called for equality of treatment between Manchus and Han as provincial censors, as honorary licentiates, and regarding home leave for metropolitan officials, these were the only steps that Cixi took during the first half of the post-Boxer era to ameliorate Manchu-Han differences.[40] Considering the virulent anti-Manchu propaganda that the revolutionaries were then putting out, it is remarkable how few in number, how narrow in scope, and how limited in effect they were. It is especially noteworthy that Cixi failed to act on the main recommendations of Zhang Zhidong and Zhou Fu to erase the administrative and judicial barriers between banner people and civilians, lift the prohibition on outside employment for banner personnel, phase out the banner stipends, and perhaps even do away with the banner system itself.

With Cixi paying no heed to the problem, the economic plight of the Manchus worsened significantly. On the one hand, the banner people in Beijing and the northeast—who together accounted for the vast majority of the total banner population—had suffered enormous casualties, and their homes and communities had been uprooted and destroyed during the wars with Japan, Russia, and the allied powers. On the other hand, the Qing treasury, burdened by the costs of the wars as well as the postwar indemnities, was not only incapable of helping them with their economic recovery but was forced to cut yet again its payment to the banner soldiers. As well summarized by Pamela Crossley, "Living conditions for the Manchu populations in general [went] from desperate poverty to true misery." Consequently, more and more Manchus were driven to ignore the ban on outside employment. In Beijing, many poor bannermen, including soldiers whose reduced stipends had been further devalued by inflation, took up rickshaw pulling in order to make ends meet. Yet others became peddlers, petty artisans, day laborers, and trash collectors.[41]

In the absence of guidance from the central authorities, local banner officials developed various ad hoc solutions to the economic difficulties of the Manchus. One was to resettle banner personnel on wasteland. In Hubei, the Jingzhou garrison decided to send unsalaried banner people to cultivate its pasture lands in Jianli and Gongan Counties, south of the garrison. In Shandong, Governor Zhou Fu planned to allocate wasteland at nearby Guanshan to banner personnel from Qingzhou and Dezhou for them to develop and cultivate. These resettlement plans, however, seem not to have worked. According to Zhou Fu's successor, the idea of transferring banner personnel to the wasteland near Guanshan was never carried out.[42] Another solution was to rent out banner land to civilians to farm, with the rental income going to fund a variety of banner expenses. In Jiangsu, the Nanjing general turned the pasture land at Wanqinghu, near Wuhu, into an "agricultural colony" for tenant farmers whose rental payment would be earmarked for the care of widows and orphans in the Nanjing and Zhenjiang garrisons. In Shandong, as a substitute for relocating banner personnel to Guanshan, Governor Yang Shixiang (1860–1909) proposed to rent out six hundred *qing* (ten thousand acres) of banner land in Lijin and Lean (now Guangyao) Counties, north of Qingzhou, to tenant farmers. It is unclear if these plans were any more successful than the resettlement schemes. At Wanqinghu, for various reasons including flooding in early 1907 and rioting against onerous rents later the same year, tenants still had not begun providing a rental income to the banner authorities as of 1908.[43] Yet another solution was to promote vocational training. In Sichuan, the Chengdu general started a sericulture bureau and encouraged the banner people to plant mulberry trees on the plentiful vacant land inside the Manchu City and raise silkworms. At Zhenjiang, the brigade-general established a vocational training office to teach local bannermen how to dye and weave cloth and draw silk from cocoons; his superior, the Nanjing general, founded a similar agency to instruct banner women in weaving.[44]

In sum, down to early 1907 Cixi's New Policies had done relatively little to reduce, let alone eliminate, the various differences between Manchus and Han, or to alleviate the worsening economic distress of the banner population. However, other aspects of the New Policies, notably the military and education reforms, did have a substantial impact upon the banner people.

MILITARY AND POLICE REFORMS

The Boxer Rebellion and the consequent foreign invasion completed the long-term decline of the Metropolitan Banners, whose basic mission was to protect the emperor and his capital. The old elite units—the Escorts, Vanguards, and Guards—had failed miserably in their duties as a palace guard within the Forbidden City, as had the Infantry Division as a police force for the Inner City. Furthermore, all three of the semimodernized armies that had been carved out of the Metropolitan Banners—the Peking Field Force, Tiger Spirit Division, and Center Division of the Guards Army—had been destroyed, as they bore the brunt of the foreigners' assault. In the wake of this overwhelming military disaster, the court attempted the near herculean task of revitalizing the Metropolitan Banners. It set about finding a new palace guard, developing a new modern-trained, modern-equipped banner army, and establishing a new police force. Local banner garrisons were encouraged to make similar reforms.

These changes unavoidably affected the "mounted archery" component of the old Manchu way.

The court's immediate problem was what to do about a palace guard. When it returned to Beijing in early 1902, it had no option but to rely initially upon Han soldiers, since the banner forces had been shattered. It looked to Jiang Guiti (1843–1922), commander of the Left Division of the Guards Army, who provided a detachment of one thousand soldiers to serve as a palace guard. Known as the Suweiying, this unit later became a part of the Sixth Division, when the new national army was decreed in 1905, and its duties at the palace were assumed by the entire division on a rotating basis.[45] The reliance on the Sixth Division, however, was intended as no more than a stopgap measure. Meanwhile, the court was hard at work developing a new, modern banner army that in time could take over its guard duty. On 6 December 1902 it issued an edict assigning up to three thousand soldiers from the Metropolitan Banners to Yuan Shikai for training. Since becoming Zhili governor-general the year before, Yuan had embarked on a program to establish in his province two divisions of "standing army" (changbeijun). By October 1902 he had recruited the first of the two divisions, the Left Division of the Beiyang Standing Army. It was soon after this that the court asked him to take on the additional task of training the Metropolitan Banner soldiers. The edict directed six high-ranking Manchus to confer with Jiang Guiti in selecting the banner personnel to send to Yuan.[46]

To assist him with the training program, Yuan Shikai requested and obtained the services of Tieliang, the most junior of these six Manchus.[47] Tieliang, then about thirty-nine years old, was a Manchu bannerman from the Jingzhou (Hubei) garrison with a licentiate degree that he had acquired by purchase. By the late 1880s he had gravitated to the capital, where he served as a secretary at the Navy Yamen; later, he was on the staff of Zhili governor-general Ronglu. In 1901, along with about forty other Chinese, he was sent to Japan by the Hubei government to attend the Army Officers School (Shikan Gakkō), where he studied infantry for a year or so. He had just returned to China in 1902 when Yuan asked for his help.[48] Thus began a long, and eventually stormy, relationship between the two men. On 4 June 1903, Cixi's court formalized their joint effort by creating the Office for the Training of the Metropolitan Banners (Jingqi Lianbingchu), with Yuan Shikai as head and Tieliang as his assistant. This office, in turn, seems to have been the model for the powerful Office of Military Training (Lianbingchu), which was founded six months later to coordinate and standardize all military reforms throughout the country and which superseded the Board of War as the policy-making body for the military. The Office of Military Training was led jointly by Yuan and Tieliang as well, but with Yikuang as their supervisor.[49] In the meantime, Tieliang had returned to Japan to observe the 1903 autumn military maneuvers. He was accompanied by Fengshan and Feng Guozhang, both of whom were to play important roles in banner military affairs.[50]

The prototype for the new banner force was Yuan Shikai's Beiyang Standing Army; he and Tieliang accordingly asked that it be designated the Metropolitan Banners Standing Army (Jingqi Changbeijun). The ultimate objective was the formation of a Japanese-style division, with 11,184 soldiers and officers divided among two infantry brigades, one regiment each of artillery and cavalry, one engineer battalion, and one transport battalion. Yuan and Tieliang began at once by organizing one infantry regiment (or half of a brigade). On 21 February 1903, soon after the court's initial decision, Edmund Backhouse (1872–1944), an informant for G. E. Morrison (1862–1920) of the London *Times*, wrote that Tieliang had taken "about 1400 young men of good physique and morals" to Baoding, the Zhili provincial capital, for two years of drilling. "In all, I believe about 10,000 Manchus [equivalent to a division] are to be trained, and by the time the training is complete the Throne will have a powerful contingent for the defence of the capital."[51]

The training of the new banner force progressed smoothly and was mostly completed in three years. In July 1904 Yuan and Tieliang reported that they had organized one infantry brigade. The following November, half of the brigade took part in China's first modern war game, the Beiyang Army's division-strength maneuvers at Hejian, southeast of Baoding. In July 1905, when the various provincial "new armies" (*xinjun*) were incorporated into the framework of a new thirty-six-division national army, the Metropolitan Banners Standing Army was, in recognition of its ties to the court, redesignated the First Division. Yuan's Beiyang Army, which in the meantime had increased to five divisions, became the Second through the Sixth Divisions. However, despite its new name, the First Division was then only a "mixed brigade," since it was still missing a second infantry brigade. In October 1905 it participated as a mixed brigade in the fall maneuvers of the Beiyang Army, which were again held at Hejian.[52]

A year later, when a second infantry brigade had been trained, the First Division was close to statutory strength. According to the British military attaché, George Pereira (1865–1923), it lacked only an engineer and a transport battalion. Western opinion about the quality of the force was divided. To Pereira, as summarized by Edmund Fung, the infantry battalions were "smart on parade and well drilled." The American attaché, Henry Leonard, was not so impressed: "Officers and men are physically less fine than the Chinese troops. Years of rice pension, which the Manchus have enjoyed under this Dynasty, have left their mark." Leonard, however, conceded that the division was well supplied with up-to-date weapons. The infantry was armed with 1903–model Japanese rifles; other units were equipped with Japanese arms also. At the 1906 war games in Zhangde Prefecture, northern Henan, which pitted China's two best forces—Yuan Shikai's and Zhang Zhidong's—against each other, the First Division supplied more personnel to Yuan's contingent than any other.[53]

Except for the top command, the First Division was an all-banner army. Ninety percent of the rank-and-file soldiers, according to Pereira, came from the Metropolitan Banners, and the rest from various small banner garrisons in Zhili—such as Shanhaiguan, Baoding, and Miyun—which had arranged to send some of their soldiers to train with Yuan Shikai.[54] The overall commander of the division was also a bannerman, Fengshan, the Hanjun who had accompanied Tieliang on his inspection tour of Japan in 1903, whose only prior experience in military affairs was a minor post in the Beijing police department. Perhaps compensating for Fengshan's relative inexperience, all of the other top officers were Han military professionals. The commanders of the First and Second Brigades were Cao Kun (1862–1938) and He Zonglian (1861–1931) respectively; the chief of staff was Wang Tingzhen (1876–1940). All three were products of the old Tianjin Military Preparatory School; Wang, in addition, had attended the Japanese Army Officers School. All three were also close associates of Yuan Shikai.[55]

As the First Division reached full strength in 1907, the Qing court was at last able to cut its dependence on the Sixth Division and return the duty of protecting the palace to a banner force. As the Board of War had noted earlier, although the First Division was not intended as a formal palace guard, it could nevertheless function as such until a new separate guard unit was organized. Accordingly, in October 1907, the division was transferred from Baoding, its training site, to Beijing, where it assumed most of the responsibility for guarding the emperor.[56]

Parallel with and contributing to this successful effort to revitalize the Metropolitan Banners by organizing the First Division were four programs to improve their military education. The first, begun in early 1903 at the urging of Yuan Shikai, was to send a number of "intelligent and literate" soldiers to attend Yuan's new Military Preparatory School at Baoding.[57] Another was to set up a military primary school for the Beijing metropolitan region that would cater to its large banner population. This school was part of the new nationwide hierarchy of military schools decreed in 1904, but unlike the other primary schools (one in each province, to be operated by their respective provincial authorities), the metropolitan school was under the direct control of the Office of Military Training. It offered a three-year course to graduates of a civilian primary school. Though Han natives of Shuntian, the metropolitan prefecture, were also eligible to enroll in the school, its students were predominantly banner people. In 1908, when it had 404 students, three-quarters of them were Manchus. Upon graduation, they were assigned to the first six divisions of the national New Army.[58]

Yet another program was to establish the Nobles Military School (Lujun Guizhou Xuetang) for the "sons and brothers of nobles and high officials."[59] Like the Metropolitan Military Primary School, the Nobles School was administered directly by the Office of Military Training. Since Yikuang was supervisor of the office, he was nominally the overseer of the school as well, but the actual direction of the school lay with its superintendent, Feng Guozhang. Another graduate of the Tianjin Military Preparatory School and a prefectural degree-holder, Feng was most recently a high-ranking subordinate of Yuan Shikai, with special responsibility for military training and education; he was, however, also on good terms with Tieliang, whom he had accompanied to Japan in 1903. The school began operations on 15 June 1906.[60] Roughly equivalent to a military middle school, it offered a five-year course to 120 students between eighteen and twenty-five years of age. The students were an elite group drawn from hereditary princes, imperial clansmen of the fourth rank and above, and civil and military officials of the second rank and above. Though open to both Manchus and Han, the Nobles School was, like the Metropolitan Military Primary School, overwhelmingly Manchu in composition. Edmund Fung, based apparently on a British Foreign Office document, says that of its 120 students in 1908, seventy belonged to the imperial family, twenty-three were sons of Manchu officials, and only twenty-seven were sons of Han officials. When the first class graduated in mid-1909, after its five-year course had been shortened to three, the *Political Gazette* (Zhengzhi guanbao) listed ninety-six students as having achieved superior or middling grades; the vast majority had Manchu-style names.[61]

The fourth program to improve the Metropolitan Banners' military education was study abroad. In early 1904 the Office of Military Training developed an ambitious plan for sending one hundred military students to Japan annually for four years. The plan included members of the Metropolitan Banners, who were assigned an annual quota of six students, the same as a populous province such as Zhili or Jiangsu. The students were supposed to attend the Shinbu School, a preparatory school set up by the Japanese, before transferring to the Army Officers School.[62] The first group of students went in the fall of 1904, followed by other groups in later years. As a result, the number of Chinese who graduated each year from the Shinbu School increased steadily from forty-nine in 1904 to 330 in 1907, most of whom then went on to the Army

Officers School. At least some of these students were Metropolitan Bannermen. Thus, among the 108 candidates certified by the Office of Military Training in 1905 for military study in Japan were sixteen (not six, as under the original plan) nominees of the Metropolitan Banners' Training Office.[63]

Concurrent with the establishment of the First Division as a new (if perhaps only temporary) palace guard were similar efforts to create a new police force for the capital. Previously, law and order in the Inner (or Manchu) City of Beijing had been the responsibility of the Infantry Division, which, like other units of the Metropolitan Banners, had disintegrated amidst the disorder of the Boxer Rebellion and the subsequent foreign invasion. On 29 June 1901, with Beijing still occupied by the foreign powers, the refugee court at Xi'an appointed Hu Yufen (d. 1906), a former prefect of Shuntian and military advisor to Yuan Shikai, to "take charge of troop affairs in the metropolitan region." In early 1902, after the foreign troops had withdrawn, Hu proposed, and the court agreed, that a Public Works and Patrolling Bureau (Gongxunju) be set up in the capital. Hu's bureau amalgamated and reorganized the various ad hoc police forces that the foreign powers had installed in the city during the occupation. As its name indicates, the bureau was responsible not only for patrolling the streets but also for building and repairing them. Its jurisdiction was the Inner City. Later, in August 1905, a second bureau was set up for the Outer (or Chinese) City as well. Shortly afterward, both bureaus were merged into the new Ministry of Police. The police reforms were a resounding success. According to G. E. Morrison in 1911, "The police force cannot be too highly praised—a well-paid, well equipped, well disciplined body of men."[64]

Beijing's new Inner City police force was a Manchu organization. It numbered over three thousand, all or nearly all of whom were drawn from soldiers of the Metropolitan Banners who were older than twenty-five. (Those who were younger were reserved for the army recruiters.)[65] Not only were the rank and file all Manchus, but so was the top command, even though the original proponent of the police (Hu Yufen) was a Han. The first head of the Public Works and Patrolling Bureau was Shanqi, the iron-capped prince who in 1900 had opposed Cixi's decision to support the Boxers.[66] When Shanqi resigned in January 1904, he was replaced by Natong, a Manchu bannerman and provincial degree holder. However, with Natong preoccupied with his other duties as assistant supervisor at the Ministry of Foreign Affairs, the de facto chief of the bureau was the imperial clansman Yulang (1864–1922), who was appointed its director in April 1903, after a three-month tour of Japan to learn about police matters and road building.[67] When the bureau was incorporated into the Ministry of Police in 1905, Yulang became the senior vice-minister.

Officers for the Beijing police came from the Police Academy (Jingwu

Xuetang), which, like the police force itself, had its origins during the foreign occupation following the Boxer Rebellion. The Japanese, controlling the northern sector of the Inner City, had formed an especially effective police force under the direction of Kawashima Naniwa (1865–1949), an ex-samurai who had gone to China in 1886. To train the financially desperate bannermen who had flocked to join his force, Kawashima early in 1901 had founded a police academy. Yikuang, who (along with Li Hongzhang) had been deputized to deal with the foreigners, was greatly impressed. On 14 August 1901, as the foreign troops were preparing to withdraw, he signed Kawashima to a three-year contract, subsequently extended to five years, to continue to operate the school. The Japanese-staffed academy offered two police courses as well as a class for firefighters, all of which drew most of their students from the Metropolitan Banners.[68] As director of the Police Academy, Kawashima worked closely with the Beijing police bureau and its successor, the Ministry of Police. He developed a life-long relationship with the bureau's first head, Shanqi. And he accompanied Yulang, the bureau's prospective director, on his study tour of Japan. When the Ministry of Police was founded in 1905, he was named its chief advisor.[69]

As a part of his contract with the Qing government, Kawashima Naniwa also arranged for the Kōbun Institute in Tokyo to provide police training to a large group of bannermen, whom he escorted to Japan at the end of 1901. The group consisted of twenty-six Manchus and one Han and was headed by a thirty-three-year-old imperial clansman, Changfu. They were one of the largest contingents of Chinese sent to study in Japan in the early post-Boxer years.[70] They were still there in May 1903 when the anti-Russian agitation flared up among the Chinese students in Tokyo; indeed, three of these Manchus, among them Changfu, joined the Society for the Education of a Militant Citizenry (Junguomin Jiaoyuhui), an anti-imperialist organization whose members included the anti-Manchu propagandist Chen Tianhua. Changfu also published an open letter to the "young men of the Eight Banners in Zhili and Fengtian" encouraging them to come to Japan to "study for the sake of the nation." He and his fellow imperial clansman Liangbi (at the Army Officers School) were the two most politically active banner students then in Tokyo. They appear as characters, thinly disguised, in Chen Tianhua's novel *Lion's Roar*.[71] Shortly after the anti-Russian protests, Changfu returned to China and to his former employer, the Ministry of Foreign Affairs; later on, he was one of the imperially appointed members of the National Assembly. Though he himself did not go into police work, at least one of his fellow Manchu students at the Kōbun Institute, Yanhong, eventually served in the Ministry of Police.[72]

Kawashima Naniwa's tight personal control of the Beijing Police Academy ended in 1906, when his contract expired and the Ministry of Police reorganized and renamed the school the Metropolitan Higher Police Academy (Jingshi Gaodeng Xunjing Xuetang). He was given a new three-year contract whereby he retained his title as director, but his responsibilities were restricted to matters of curriculum, including that of liaison with the school's remaining Japanese instructors. Overall control of the school passed into the hands of a Chinese superintendent.[73]

Altogether, in the early post-Boxer years, well over fourteen thousand Metropolitan Bannermen were retrained for the First Division of the New Army and Beijing's Inner City police; educated in the Metropolitan Primary Military School, the Nobles Military School, or the Police Academy in Beijing; or sent to Japan to study military and police matters. The New Army and police did not, however, replace the traditional units into which the Metropolitan Banners were divided. The Infantry Division, for example, continued to exist, even though its primary duty had been assumed by the police.[74] Meanwhile, similar types of military and police reforms were taking place at various provincial banner garrisons.

Many garrisons reorganized some of their banner troops into the new military formations, modeled on Yuan Shikai's Beiyang Standing Army in Zhili, that the Qing court had decreed in 1901. The Jingzhou garrison in Hubei, for example, formed the Awe-Inspiring New Army (Zhenwei Xinjun), which, according to the British military attaché George Pereira in 1907 was "more or less equal to the New Army in training and drill."[75] Furthermore, in accord with a plan devised by Hubei governor Duanfang in early 1904, the Jingzhou garrison sent a thousand soldiers to be trained with the new provincial army in Wuchang. Duanfang's idea was for the banner soldiers to serve with the army at Wuchang for three years, after which they would return to Jingzhou and be replaced by a fresh batch of bannermen trainees. When Tieliang, the associate head of the Office of Military Training, toured central China in late 1904 and early 1905, he noted with satisfaction that almost 10 percent (more than eight hundred soldiers and twenty officers) of the Hubei Standing Army were from his native garrison. In 1910–11, banner troops from Jingzhou still constituted about 10 percent of the Hubei New Army.[76]

Some garrisons promoted military education. According to the detailed regulations for military education issued by the Office of Military Training in 1905, three widely separated garrisons—Chahar, Jingzhou, and Fuzhou—were authorized to set up their own military primary schools. The school in Chahar was reorganized from an existing "military preparatory school" and opened in 1905. The Jingzhou school, reconstituted from a training course attached to the garrison's Awe-Inspiring New Army, began operation in May 1906. Its three-year course was supposed to have ninety students, who on graduation were to go on to the regional military middle school in Wuchang. After the middle school opened in 1909, more than forty of its seven hundred students were indeed from the Jingzhou garrison. The Fuzhou garrison, though permitted to establish a military primary school, failed to do so for lack of funds. Instead, it annually sent ten students to the school operated by Fujian Province. Those garrisons without their own military primary school were entitled, according to the 1905 regulations, to enroll a number of their banner soldiers in the appropriate provincial military schools, much as the Fuzhou garrison did.[77]

Some garrisons sent their banner personnel to study in Japan. In this, as in most other reform efforts, the Jingzhou garrison was the most active, perhaps because of the dynamic leadership of Zhang Zhidong, who was governor-general of Hubei-Hunan until mid-1907, and Duanfang, the fast-rising Manchu bannerman who was Hubei governor during 1901–4. As of mid-1904, the garrison had sent more than fifty bannermen abroad. Among them were at least five of the first Chinese students (including Tieliang and Liangbi) to attend the Japanese Army Officers School.[78] Under the plan drawn up by the Office of Military Training in May 1904, whereby a hundred students were to be selected annually to go to Japan for military training, thirteen garrisons were authorized to nominate one student each. When at the end of 1905 the office had certified 108 candidates as qualified for the program, eleven were nominees of provincial garrisons: three from Shengjing, two from Jingzhou, and one each from Rehe, Suiyuan, Nanjing, Hangzhou, Fuzhou, and Chengdu. They were nominated in addition to the sixteen candidates from the Metropolitan Banners.[79]

Finally, provincial garrisons also carried out police reforms. On 17 October 1904, at the behest of the Beijing police director, Yulang, the court reportedly ordered each banner garrison to set up its own new police force. In response, the Xi'an garrison in 1905 transformed its traditional infantry unit into a "police division." A year later, the Nanjing garrison announced plans to form a police force to patrol the Manchu City. Personnel from the provincial garrisons were also dispatched to Japan to study police matters, but they seemed to have been relatively few. One was Tingqi, sent to the Kōbun Institute by the Hubei government, though he himself was from the Zhenjiang garrison in Jiangsu.[80]

One major consequence of the various military and police reforms among the banner population in both Beijing and the provinces was the further erosion of their ancestral tradition of mounted archery. Perhaps mindful of Hong Taiji's warning against cultural contamination by the Han, the Qing court in 1901 had clung to the traditional military examinations—with their emphasis upon physical strength and archery skills—for the Eight Banners, even as it did away with them for the Army of the Green Standard. On 21 July 1905, however, it finally issued an edict abolishing the mounted archery requirement for the banners as well. The court noted that formerly military officials had been trained in horse riding and archery, but that in recent years the art of war had changed steadily and so had military technology. It ordered the Board of War to devise new methods for selecting banner soldiers. In a wide-ranging memorial dated 16 December 1905, the board recommended—and the court agreed— that banner soldiers be chosen henceforth on the basis of their ability not to shoot a bow and arrow but to fire a "rapid rifle" (*kuaiqiang*). Because the new skill could not be attained at once and also because live ammunition was expensive, the board proposed that as a transitional measure banner soldiers be tested first with a Chinese-made, foreign-style "air rifle" (*qiqiang*), which it said was similar to the "rapid rifle" in accuracy and technique. It allowed the banner soldiers three months to familiarize themselves with the new weapon before they would be tested on its use.[81]

The board's expectation of a rapid transition to the new technology was, predictably, far too optimistic. The timetable for the implementation of the new requirement was extended several times. Every five years, all banner personnel were subject to a military review. In February 1907, as the Ministry of the Army, successor to the Board of War, prepared for the next review scheduled for later in the year, it found that at the capital although some units, such as the Outer Detachment of the Firearms Division, claimed to be ready to be examined using at least the ersatz "air rifle," others, such as the Infantry Division, admitted that they were not prepared to be tested even with the "air rifle" and asked for an extension to the next review five years hence. The ministry advised that, in the provinces as well as at the capital, those who were ready should be examined and those who were not should be given an extension. This concession did not satisfy many banner soldiers. Various metropolitan units, claiming that they lacked both weaponry and training, asked for a postponement of the military review itself. The ministry in May 1907 promised to remedy the shortcomings in arms and training, and although it opposed a delay of the review, it agreed to allow an extra year of training before subjecting the soldiers to a "supplemental" review. However, it appears that as of March 1908 the promised retraining program had not yet begun.[82]

Nevertheless, despite the difficulty in disseminating the new skills, what was significant was that the traditional skills were no longer prized, that the "mounted archery" portion of the old Manchu way of life had, at long last, been jettisoned. Among the Manchus of Beijing, according to Edmund Backhouse, the decree of July 1905 abolishing the archery competition was not well received: "No reform has excited more indignation than this," not even the ending of the civil service examinations two months later.[83]

EDUCATIONAL REFORMS

The post-Boxer New Policies also included extensive educational reforms, in which both Metropolitan Banners and provincial banner garrisons participated. The reforms consisted of, on the one hand, abolishing the traditional examination system (including both the literary as well as the translation examinations) and, on the other, establishing in its place a hierarchy of Japanese-style schools teaching modern subjects. In Beijing as well as in the garrisons, old schools were reorganized to conform to the new system, and new ones, among them schools for banner women, were founded. As with the military and police academies, graduates of these schools were encouraged to go abroad for additional study. Despite such reforms, the court tried to cling to the "national speech" component of the ancestral ways.

Banner schools in Beijing were reorganized and new ones established. In response to an imperial decree on 19 February 1902, existing government schools were amalgamated and converted into new schools, with one primary school for each of the Eight Banners. When the entire educational system was reconfigured in 1904, these eight schools were apparently redesignated as senior primary schools, and fifteen additional junior primary schools were founded. Also, bondservants belonging to the Upper Three Banners, the Light Cavalry Division, and the Firearms Division each established their own primary school. Above these various primary schools were an Eight Banner Middle School and an Eight Banner Higher School.[84] Apart from the government, private individuals also founded a number of schools that recruited from among the banner people in Beijing's Inner City. These included the Chongshi School (Chongshi Xuetang), established in 1905 by the imperial clansman Hengchang, and the Jiaxian School (Jiaxian Xuetang), founded by Shanqi in 1906. The latter school admitted Han students as well as Manchus.[85]

In the same edict of February 1902 ordering that the banner schools in Beijing be restructured, the Qing court called for similar educational reforms in the provincial banner garrisons.[86] Here too, as in military reforms, the Jingzhou garrison was a pacesetter. Spurred by Hubei governor Duanfang, it extensively reorganized its schools in 1903 to conform with the current system. Previously, each of the garrison's fifty-six banner companies had its own government school; these were amalgamated into eight four-year "elementary" schools, presumably one for each of the Eight Banners, each with 135 pupils ranging in age between seven and eleven years. The garrison's ten charitable schools were similarly consolidated and converted into four four-year "primary" schools for those between eleven and fourteen. When the national school system was restructured in 1904, the eight elementary schools became junior primary schools, and the four primary schools probably became senior primary schools. Meanwhile, the Fuwen Academy (Fuwen Shuyuan) had been transformed into a four-year middle school for those between fourteen and twenty-four. Later, again at Governor Duanfang's urging, the garrison established two additional schools—an industrial arts school and a language school—both of which were equivalent to a middle school and which offered a five-year course intended to broaden the vocational opportunities for the garrison's inhabitants. The Jingzhou garrison, however, did not have its own "higher" school; its middle-school graduates were sent instead to the provincial Higher School at Wuchang.[87] Other garrisons carried out similar reforms, but not on the same scale as at Jingzhou. In the Hangzhou garrison, for example, four junior primary schools were established, each with seventy to eighty pupils, and the Meiqing Academy (Meiqing Shuyuan) was converted into a senior primary school to accommodate graduates of the junior schools.[88]

The pinnacle of the new school system, for both banner and non-banner people in the capital and the provinces, was the Metropolitan University. Founded during the Hundred Days in 1898 but destroyed amidst the Boxer troubles in 1900, it was revived and reorganized in 1902, when it absorbed the old Translators College, which became the university's translation department. Located within the Inner City of Beijing, the university had a special relationship with the surrounding banner population. For example, to give the graduates of its teachers training class an opportunity for practice teaching, it set up an attached senior primary school that drew its pupils from graduates of the junior primary school operated by the bondservants of the Upper Three Banners. Despite such ties to the banner people, the Metropolitan University, like the Beijing Translators College in its later history, was not itself a banner school. Probably no more than 10 percent of its students were Manchus; among the 105 students of the class that graduated in 1907, for example, only nine were bannermen, of whom three or four were from the Metropolitan Banners and the rest from the provincial garrisons.[89]

Students at the civilian banner schools in Beijing and elsewhere, like those at the military and police academies, also went abroad for additional study. According to the 1906 alumni directory of the Metropolitan University, four of its graduates who were Beijing bannermen were then in Japan for teachers training. Earlier, in 1902, two Manchus from the Jingzhou garrison had attended the teachers training course at the Kōbun Institute. While most students went to Japan, twelve Manchus and Mongols from the Yangzheng School (Yangzheng Xuetang) in the Yili garrison were sent in 1903 to nearby Alma Ata to study Russian.[90]

In a radical departure from tradition, a few of the newly founded schools catered to the female half of the banner population. Two of these in Beijing were the Zhenyi Girls School (Zhenyi Nü Xuetang) and the Shushen Girls School (Shushen Nü Xuetang). According to a list of attendees at a memorial service for Empress Dowager Cixi at the end of 1908, all of the students at the Zhenyi School and half of those at the Shushen School were Manchus.[91] Two of the new schools in the Zhenjiang garrison in Jiangsu were also for women.[92] Unquestionably the most well-known school for banner women was the Zhenwen Girls School (Zhenwen Nüxue) in Hangzhou, founded in 1904 by Huixing, a widow influenced by Zhang Zhidong's ideas on the importance of education to China's future. Financed by private contributions from the local banner population, the Zhenwen Girls School taught basic literacy to the women of the garrison. A year later, however, the school was forced to close when it ran out of funds and garrison officials refused to come to its rescue. In despair but also to protest the indifference of her Manchu compatriots, Huixing committed suicide. Her ultimate sacrifice on behalf of women's education both shamed and stirred the Hangzhou garrison. At a local memorial service, she was lauded as a hero who had given her life for progress and acclaimed as a shining exemplar of "our great Qing dynasty," "our Tungusic race [Tonggusizu]," and "our East Asian womankind."[93]

Huixing's suicide caught the attention of banner people far and wide. *Beijing Women's News* published several reports about her. The young reform-minded Manchu bannerman Jinliang (1878–1962), a fellow native of the Hangzhou garrison and a member of the same Gūwalgiya lineage as Huixing, coauthored a play about her life and, together with another Manchu bannerman, Guilin, had it staged in Beijing in May 1907 at a fund-raising event. By then, Guilin and other supporters of Huixing's cause had come up with enough money and had also succeeded in securing the support of contrite garrison officials to reopen the school in April 1906 as a government institution. It was renamed in her memory as the Huixing Girls School. At the May 1907 benefit in Beijing, Guilin, the school's new superintendent, announced that it had six teachers and sixty students. Guilin ran the school until 1911, when he was killed while resisting the revolution. His daughter, for several years at least, continued his work. The Huixing Girls School survived as a middle school down to the mid-1950s.[94]

As shown by its interest in Huixing, an especially enthusiastic supporter of education for women was *Beijing Women's News*, a Manchu feminist daily founded in August 1905 and still publishing at the end of 1908. It is unclear if the newspaper's publisher and editor, Zhang Zhanyun, was herself a Manchu, but many of its contributors, some of them men, were Manchus, and its coverage was very definitely slanted toward the banner population, particularly women.[95] In November 1905, for example, it carried an article titled "On the

Degeneracy of Manchu Women" by someone who called herself a "daughter of Changbai," referring to the mountains along the Korean border from which the Old Manchus had originated. Her article criticized her sister Manchus for thinking that they were better than Han women. She wrote that although Manchu women (*Manzhou nüzi*) prided themselves on not binding their feet, the "willow-branch feet" they aspired to were not very different from bound feet. Furthermore, their use of rouge on the face would embarrass a stage actor: "I urge our Manchu sisters [*Manzhou jiemei*] henceforth to stop distinguishing between Manchus and Han [*bufen Man-Han*] and instead to work together to enliven our spirit and awaken our two hundred million fellow women." The newspaper did not entirely concur with the "daughter of Changbai," for it added a brief comment at the end of her piece that took issue with her plea to not make ethnic distinctions: "In our view, there are areas where Han women [*Hanren nüzi*] really do not measure up to Manchu women." Yet, it agreed with her on the importance of education as the means by which both Manchu and Han women could attain "civilization."[96]

Though *Beijing Women's News* presented a Manchu point of view, it was primarily a feminist journal. It was less concerned with Manchu-Han issues than with women's issues, notably education for women, equality of the sexes, and women's independence. In 1908 it printed the speech of a second-year student at the Huixing Girls School, a banner woman named Foying, discussing why Chinese parents, regardless of ethnicity, preferred sons over daughters. One reason, according to Foying, was women's inability to own property, which made them economically dependent on men; the other reason was social customs, whether they be the three-inch bound feet of Han women (Hannü) or the piled-up hairdo and high platform shoes of banner women (*qixia de nüzi*), both of which constricted and "harmed us women." She lauded her own school for prohibiting students from wearing makeup and flowery clothing and binding their feet, because only in this way could "women become human." If, in addition, they could learn to make their own living, she concluded, then they would truly be free.[97] *Beijing Women's News* was outspoken in its admiration for Empress Dowager Cixi, who reportedly helped finance the paper. It praised her as the foremost woman of China; when she died in 1908, it hailed her, referring to China's legendary cultural heroes, as "a Yao or Shun among women."[98]

In its support for the empress dowager, *Beijing Women's News* differed greatly from another Manchu-founded reformist daily newspaper of the time, *L'Impartial* (Dagongbao) of Tianjin. Begun in June 1902 by Ying Lianzhi (Vincent Ying, 1866–1926), a Manchu bannerman married into the Qing imperial clan and a convert to Roman Catholicism, *L'Impartial* supported many of the same reform causes, including women's education, as did *Beijing Women's News*, but, from the relative safety of Tianjin's foreign concessions, it bitterly criticized Cixi for having curtailed the 1898 reforms and it repeatedly called on her to return the reins of power to the Guangxu emperor. Thus, though founded by a bannerman, *L'Impartial*, unlike *Beijing Women's News*, did not focus on banner issues. It was to become one of China's leading newspapers in the Republican era.[99]

The Qing court was clearly committed to the new learning, but at the same time it was unwilling to allow the educational reforms to vitiate the "national speech" aspect of the dynasty's ancestral tradition in the way that the military reforms were undermining the "mounted archery" component. Thus, on the one hand, the Ministry of Education in the spring of 1907 issued a directive that graduates of the new primary schools should henceforth be given first priority when positions in the banner system were being filled. On the other hand, the ministry, headed by the conservative Mongol bannerman Rongqing (1859–1916), urged in 1906 that Manchu-language training, instead of being phased out as new schools were established, should be intensified, particularly since the translation examinations had been abolished. The aim was to make "every son and brother of the Eight Banners aware of the importance of the national speech and the Manchu script [*guoyu Manwen*]." The ministry stated that all government-operated banner schools in the capital ought to offer a course to teach Manchu to their pupils, and it recommended that schools in the provincial garrisons do likewise.[100] Indeed, at the Jingzhou garrison, spoken Manchu (Qingyu) was one of the required subjects taught at all three levels of the new school system, as was written Manchu (Qingwen) at the Language School.[101] Other garrisons had similar, if less intensive, programs. The Ministry of Education also founded in Beijing in 1907 the Higher School for Manchu and Mongol Literature (Man-Mengwen Gaodeng Xuetang) so that middle-school graduates could gain advanced training in the subject.[102] At the same time, the Ministry of the Army announced that all banner soldiers, even as they were trying to master the new skill of shooting a rifle, were still expected to be competent in the Manchu language. It specified that officials testing the soldiers for marksmanship should also, as before, conduct an oral examination in Manchu. Those soldiers who could not reply appropriately in Manchu would be told to learn the language or face dismissal.[103]

ADMINISTRATIVE REFORMS
AND THE POLITICAL STORM OF 1907

Cixi's New Policies, which in the beginning were hardly more than an extension of the kinds of military and educational reforms associated with Self-

Strengthening, eventually led to a far-reaching transformation of the Chinese polity, as the empress dowager was driven to declare in September 1906 her adherence to the cause of constitutionalism. As the Qing prepared to remake itself into a constitutional monarchy, it carried out an extensive reorganization of the metropolitan administration, in the course of which one of the pillars of Manchu-Han relations, dyarchy, was greatly modified. These political reforms also brought into the open a simmering dispute between Tieliang and Yuan Shikai that had overtones of a Manchu-Han dispute.

The empress dowager took the tentative first steps toward adopting a constitutional system in mid-1905, when, following Meiji Japan's startling victory over Czarist Russia, she came under mounting pressure from both Han and Manchu officials to take Japan as a model. On 2 July the country's three most powerful governors-general—Yuan Shikai, Zhang Zhidong, and Zhou Fu— submitted a joint memorial recommending that a constitutional regime be established within twelve years.[104] While Yuan, Zhang, and Zhou were all Han, Manchus played no less important a role in convincing Cixi of the desirability of constitutionalism. Indeed, according to the Shanghai reformer Zhang Jian (1853–1926), three of the four individuals who had the most influence over Cixi on this matter were Manchus. They were Tieliang (the Manchu senior vice-president of the Board of War and concurrently associate head of the Office of Military Training), Duanfang (governor-general of Fujian and Zhejiang), and Zaizhen (minister of commerce); the non-Manchu among the four was Xu Shichang, Tieliang's Han counterpart at the Board of War. When, for example, the empress dowager asserted at an audience, "We have inaugurated our New Policies, and we have not overlooked anything," Duanfang pointed out, "You have not instituted constitutionalism." She then asked, "What is constitutionalism about?" He answered reassuringly, "If constitutionalism is implemented, then the imperial institution may last forever."[105]

As a result of such lobbying, the Qing court, on 16 July 1905, issued an edict complaining that its previous reform decrees had thus far produced few solid results and appointing four leading officials to go abroad "to investigate all aspects of governmental administration with the intention of selecting the best for adoption." The appointees consisted of two Manchus (the imperial prince Zaize [1868–1930] and Governor-General Duanfang) and two Han (Dai Hongci [1853–1910], a junior vice-president of the Board of Revenue; and Xu Shichang, the Board of War vice-president, newly elevated to the Grand Council as a probationary member). Eleven days later, this ethnic balance was disturbed when a third Manchu, Shaoying, an obscure junior councilor at the Board of Commerce, was, without explanation, added to the group. Zaize, who was married to Cixi's niece, represented the interests of the imperial clan on the commission. He was a great-grandson of the Jiaqing emperor and a fifth-rank prince (*zhenguo gong*). (Because of the element *gong* in his title, he was often mistakenly referred to in the Western-language press as "Duke" Zaize.)[106]

As the five constitutional study commissioners were about to depart Beijing on 24 September, they were assaulted by the assassin Wu Yue (1878–1905). A member of the revolutionary Restoration Society (Guangfuhui), Wu Yue was incensed at the anti-Han policies of the Qing government. Wu's original target, according to his valedictory essay entitled "The Age of Assassination," had been Tieliang, whose sole purpose in life was "to control and annihilate us Han people [Hanren]" and whose distrust of the Han was reminiscent of Gangyi's. His recent inspection tour of central China, like Gangyi's a few years earlier, extorted the wealth of the region so that it might be squandered by "their race [*zu*]." Wu alleged that Tieliang's aim in organizing the Metropolitan Banners Standing Army was to defend against "household bandits," not China's foreign aggressors, and he claimed that Tieliang was trying to monopolize police positions all over the country for Manchus and to deny Han the opportunity to study police matters in Japan. Abetting Tieliang in these anti-Han measures was his young Manchu associate, Liangbi. A collateral member of the imperial lineage, Liangbi was, like Tieliang, a native of the Jingzhou garrison and a graduate of the Japanese Army Officers School. After his graduation in 1903, a year behind Tieliang, he had returned to China to work for the Office of Military Training and had become quite close to its associate head; he accompanied Tieliang on his tour of central China. Liangbi was, according to Wu Yue, behind "all matters relating to the strength and weakness, safety and danger of the Han race [Hanzu]" as well as the policy at the Office of Military Training of "strengthening the Manchus and excluding the Han" (*qiang-Man pai-Han*). However, by the time Wu Yue was ready to take action, he had turned his attention from Tieliang to the constitutional study commissioners. He wanted to deflate the widespread optimism that their impending trip was generating. As the commissioners prepared to leave for Tianjin, Wu Yue managed to penetrate their security and make his way onto their railroad car. Just then, the train lurched forward, causing the device hidden on Wu's body to detonate prematurely. He was killed instantly, along with several bystanders. Two commissioners, Zaize and Shaoying, were slightly injured.[107]

One immediate consequence of the assassination attempt was a tightening of security in Beijing. The wall around the Yiheyuan Summer Palace was heightened.[108] And it was then that the court created the Ministry of Police, which, in addition to its national responsibilities, took charge of police matters in the capital as well. The new ministry was headed by Grand Councilor Xu Shichang, with Yulang and Zhao Bingjun (1865–1914) as vice-ministers. Yulang had been police director for the Inner City of Beijing, while Zhao had organized a modern police force in Tianjin for Yuan Shikai. The two existing Public Works and Patrolling Bureaus in Beijing were reorganized as Central Police Bureaus, one for the Inner City and one for the Outer.[109]

Dramatic as it was, Wu Yue's assassination attempt had hardly any immediate effect on Manchu-Han relations. The Qing court did call on local officials to curb all talk of "revolution and anti-Manchuism" (geming pai-Man), but this edict was not issued until two months later and may not have been linked to the attack.[110] The reason for the court's surprising nonchalance was that the anti-Manchu motives of the assassin were not then known. Wu Yue had died in the explosion, and his testamentary account, "The Age of Assassination," and his farewell letter were not published until 1907 in the special Heaven's Punishment (Tiantao) supplement to The People's Journal, organ of the revolutionary Alliance.

Wu Yue's assault delayed the departure of the constitutional investigative tour by only a couple of months. Xu Shichang and Shaoying, who was still recovering from his wounds, were dropped from the commission and replaced by the Shuntian prefect (and former minister to Japan) Li Shengduo (1860–1937) and the Shandong treasurer Shang Qiheng, a Hanjun whose sister was married to Cixi's brother. Joined with the other original appointees (Zaize, Duanfang, and Dai Hongci), they still constituted three Manchus and two Han. The commissioners, accompanied by a staff of thirty-eight, left Beijing in early December 1905. Dividing into two groups, one led by Zaize and the other by Dai Hongci, they visited Japan, the United States, Britain, and other European countries.[111]

When the commissioners returned to China eight months later, they predictably recommended to the court that it emulate the constitutional system of Japan. In particular, they urged the creation of a "responsible cabinet" (zeren neige), which they claimed, based on the experience of Meiji Japan, would strengthen, rather than weaken, the authority of the emperor, because it would deflect political criticisms to the cabinet and its prime minister that otherwise would be directed at the emperor himself. This was probably what Duanfang had meant earlier when he reassured the empress dowager that with constitutionalism the imperial institution might last forever.[112]

In addition, Zaize and Duanfang separately urged Cixi to reform Manchu-Han relations. In a memorial of 23 August 1906, which dwelled on the benefits to the sovereign of a representative system, Zaize addressed the anxious concern of the general banner population that "if a constitutional government were implemented, it would harm the interests of the Manchus [Manren]." Zaize pointed out that, first of all, Manchu-Han differences were now minimal. It had been mostly Han officers and soldiers who suppressed the Taiping, Nian, and Muslim rebellions in the mid-nineteenth century. More recently, the court had lifted the ban on Manchu-Han intermarriage and had opened up posts in the Eight Banners to Han appointees. Furthermore, in the face of imperialist pressure, China needed to be united, not divided. How then, Zaize asked rhetorically, could one consider the narrow interests of the Manchus at the expense of the future of the nation? Zaize finished with a muted call for an end to dyarchy and ethnic slots. As his kinsman Zaizhen had previously advised the court, it was only proper to appoint officials on the basis of ability, not ethnicity.[113]

Duanfang, in a secret memorial dated 1 September, was far more blunt and detailed in his recommendations than was Zaize. He had come back from his travels in Europe keenly aware of the consequences of ethnic discord upon a country's political stability. Manchus and Han were comparable to the Austrians and Hungarians, whose strife was tearing the Hapsburg empire apart. Because Manchus and Han had lived in close proximity for more than two hundred years, their language, religion, and customs were largely identical; yet, due to the previous prohibition on intermarriage they remained ethnically distinct. As a result, a few unscrupulous people had falsely charged that the power and privileges of Manchus and Han were unequal. The speeches of the rebel Sun Yat-sen and the publications of the revolutionary party reached and deceived a wide audience. Repression, however, was not the solution. In all countries where the aristocracy and the common people were in conflict, the aristocracy might win the first battles, but the common people inevitably would win the war, as was the case in France. The Qing court had always treated Manchus and Han impartially, but there were "one or two small instances" where the two groups were not equal. The rebel party had seized on these instances as proof of their contention. There were, Duanfang concluded, two remedies for China's current problems. One was to restore hope to alienated youth by implementing constitutionalism; the other, to undercut the revolutionaries' charges of ethnic favoritism. With regard to the latter, Duanfang proposed two reforms. Like Zaize, he called for the abolition of dyarchy; ethnic slots had already been eliminated from the four new ministries and so should they be from the rest of the metropolitan administration. In addition, perhaps harking back to the 1901 proposal of Zhang Zhidong, he recommended that the provincial garrisons (though apparently not the Metropolitan Banners) be disbanded. He cited as a recent precedent the disbandment and pensioning off of the Japanese samurai following the Meiji Restoration.[114]

By the time Duanfang submitted his memorial, Cixi's court had already, on 25 August 1906, appointed Zaifeng to chair a large ad hoc committee composed of all the leading officials—the grand councilors, the members of the newly created Office of Governmental Affairs, the grand secretaries, and Zhili governor-general Yuan Shikai—to review the findings of the constitutional study commissioners and to make recommendations. This was Zaifeng's first significant political responsibility since his mission of apology to Germany in 1901. It followed by only a few months the birth on 7 February of his son Puyi, the future Xuantong emperor. After only two meetings, Zaifeng's committee made its report on the 29th. Three days later, on 1 September, Empress Dowager Cixi issued her historic edict promising, though without as yet specifying a date, to set up a constitutional system. Thus began the age of constitutional preparation in China.[115]

As a first step toward constitutionalism, Cixi called for a reorganization of the administrative system. On 2 September the court appointed fourteen officials (all of them metropolitan officials except for Zaize and Yuan Shikai) to draw up the plans for the reorganization and another three officials to review those plans. The larger group of fourteen included eight Manchus and six Han. (Zaifeng was not among them.) Six other governors-general were asked to send representatives to Beijing to participate in the deliberations. The smaller group of three charged to review the recommendations was composed of one Manchu and two Han: Grand Councilors Yikuang and Qu Hongji and Grand Secretary Sun Jia'nai (1827–1909).[116]

The two groups deliberated for two months. One controversial issue that they had to resolve was whether to do away with the Grand Secretariat and the Grand Council and replace them both, as the constitutional study commissioners had recommended, with a "responsible cabinet" headed by a strong, executive prime minister. Another contentious issue was whether to roll back the independent authority of the provincial officials in an attempt to recentralize authority in Beijing. In the thick of both debates was Yuan Shikai, who clashed with Qu Hongji over the former issue and with Tieliang over the latter. While Yuan favored adopting the new cabinet, Qu preferred retaining the existing system; and while Yuan supported the current division of authority between the center and the provinces, Tieliang urged that the independent authority of the provincial officials be curbed. Neither of these was a Manchu-Han issue, as Manchus and Han were ranged on both sides of both questions. Thus, Yikuang, the most likely candidate as prime minister, supported Yuan against Qu in favoring the cabinet proposal, and Duanfang, himself a provincial official, evidently sided with Yuan against Tieliang in opposing the recentralization of authority.[117]

These bitter deliberations culminated in a report from Yikuang's three-man committee on 6 November. Their report was notable for what it did not say. It said nothing about reorganizing the provincial administration or about doing away with the provincial banner garrisons, as Duanfang had proposed, and it shied away from replacing the Grand Secretariat and the Grand Council with a cabinet. Its one major reform proposal was to abolish dyarchy and ethnic slots in the core agencies of the metropolitan government. As Duanfang (and, before him, Zhang Yuanji and Zaizhen) had urged, it called for each ministry to be headed by one president and two vice-presidents (as was already the case with the four new ministries), rather than the traditional system of two presidents and four vice-presidents, evenly divided between Manchus and Han. It also recommended that all heads of ministries be barred from holding other important concurrent positions, so that they might concentrate on the affairs of their respective agencies. The only exception would be the Ministry of Foreign Affairs, whose president was, by the terms of the Boxer settlement, required to sit on the Grand Council.[118]

Cixi largely went along with the recommendations of Yikuang's committee. She ordered that the metropolitan agencies be reorganized as his committee had proposed, but she made explicit what had only been implicit in their report, that ministry heads should be appointed "without distinction between Manchus and Han" (*bufen Man-Han*). Otherwise, she saw no need to create a cabinet. She left unchanged the Eight Banners and several other Manchu-dominated agencies, such as the Imperial Clan Court and the Imperial Household Department. And she postponed restructuring the provincial administration, except that she did reorganize the government of Manchuria the following April.[119]

Cixi's court promptly reshuffled the membership of the Grand Council. In line with the proposal from Yikuang's committee that all heads of ministries be barred from holding other important positions, it dismissed from the council four members who were concurrently board presidents, including Tieliang at the Board of Revenue. It retained on the council only Yikuang and Qu Hongji, both of whom held top posts at the Ministry of Foreign Affairs, the one ministry that was exempt from the prohibition. To replace the others, the court named Grand Secretary Shixu (1853–1921), a Manchu bannerman, as a full member and, in a surprise move, the relatively low-ranking governor of Guangxi, Lin Shaonian (1849–1916), as a probationary member. This new four-member Grand Council was evenly divided between Manchus and Han.[120]

The court also reorganized the metropolitan administration by expanding the traditional Six Boards to eleven ministries.[121] Except again for the Ministry of Foreign Affairs with its two additional supervisors, each of these ministries was headed by a single president and two vice-presidents, who were to be appointed without regard to whether they were Manchus or Han. However, as earlier in the post-Boxer era, the ending of dyarchy and the elimination of ethnic slots at these core agencies of the metropolitan administration did not result in any dramatic reduction in the Manchu presence among the top officials. On the contrary, in an extraordinary display of political insensitivity, Cixi's court proceeded to appoint more Manchus than would have been possible under the old system of dyarchy. Of the thirteen ministry heads (including the two supervisors at the Ministry of Foreign Affairs), eight were Manchus and only five were Han. The eight Manchus were Yikuang and Natong (at Foreign Affairs), Puting (Finance), Puliang (b. 1854; Rites), Rongqing (Education), Tieliang (Army), Zaizhen (Agriculture, Industry, and Commerce), and Shouqi (Colonial Affairs). The retention of Yikuang and his son Zaizhen as ministry heads also continued to contravene the mid-Qing dynastic tradition of princely nonparticipation in state affairs.[122] The revolutionaries greeted these appointments gleefully as confirming their contention that the Qing court was inherently untrustworthy. Writing in *The People's Journal*, Wang Jingwei (1883–1944) offered ironic "congratulations" to those reformers who had placed their hopes in "Manchu constitutionalism."[123] There is no evidence that the court had any second thoughts about the appointments.

Meanwhile, the controversy over reorganizing the government had brought the simmering rivalry between Tieliang and Yuan Shikai to the surface. Tieliang had started out as a protégé and ally of Yuan. He was Yuan's assistant at the Office of Military Training, and their children had married. However, by the time of his highly publicized tour of central China in 1904–5, Tieliang, as senior vice-president of the Board of War, had risen in the central government to where he was beginning to equal his former patron in power. Then, while continuing to oversee the training of the Metropolitan Banners Standing Army (soon to be the First Division), he was promoted to the position of president of the Board of Revenue and appointed to the Grand Council. In mid-1906 both he and Yuan served on the committee that sifted through the findings of the constitutional study commission and made recommendations for the restructuring of the government. It was then that Tieliang openly clashed with Yuan Shikai. He not only favored curbing the independent authority of provincial officials such as Yuan but also opposed the creation of a strong cabinet lest Yuan, who would likely be the deputy prime minister behind Yikuang, accumulate too much power. Tieliang emerged from this initial confrontation victorious by a narrow margin. Although Yuan managed to sidetrack the proposal to reorganize the provincial administration and to get Tieliang removed from the Grand Council, he nevertheless failed to push through the creation of a cabinet. Tieliang, though no longer a grand councilor, became minister of the army.[124]

Soon afterward, following the October 1906 war games at Zhangde with

Zhang Zhidong's army, Yuan Shikai acknowledged his political defeat. He relinquished control over four of the six Beiyang divisions, including the predominantly Manchu First Division, and turned them over to Tieliang's Ministry of the Army. He retained only his two oldest units, the Second and Fourth Divisions.[125] Tieliang strove quickly to consolidate his control over the army. He created the Metropolitan Training Office (Jinji Dulian Gongsuo) under the jurisdiction of his Ministry of the Army in order to provide a unified command over these four divisions, and he put Fengshan, the Hanjun who had been commander of the First Division, in charge of the office.[126] Fengshan was replaced at the First Division by He Zonglian, who, in turn, was replaced as commander of the Second Brigade by Zhu Panzao. Cao Kun remained head of the First Brigade.[127]

Tieliang's victory did not go unchallenged. The following summer, in what is known as the "political storm of 1907," Yuan Shikai, supported by Yikuang, managed to bring about the downfall of many of their political opponents, including Grand Councilor Qu Hongji and his protégé Lin Shaonian, by alleging or fabricating a link between them and the still-blacklisted 1898 reformers.[128] Yuan also went after Tieliang, both directly and indirectly. In May 1907 Yuan's ally, Yikuang, was appointed to the Ministry of the Army as supervisor, thus outranking Tieliang. Then, at the end of July, in a memorial on the appropriate use of human talent, Yuan cited Fengshan, Tieliang's appointee to the Metropolitan Training Office, as a glaring negative example. He criticized Fengshan, whose provincial examination degree was of the translation variety, for his poor education and for his lack of field experience as a military commander. In a perhaps related move, Yuan Shikai's associate, Duan Qirui (1865–1936), resigned as commander of the Third Division rather than serve under Fengshan. Finally, in early November, Yuan, perhaps by way of the Ministry of the Army's supervisor, Yikuang, secured an imperial decree removing Fengshan and transferring him to the Xi'an garrison.[129]

Unlike Qu Hongji, whose political career ended in 1907, Tieliang managed to beat back these attacks on himself. He reportedly warned the empress dowager that if Yuan were not held in check, the authority of the Manchus would be jeopardized. Also, he seems not to have been unduly constrained by his princely supervisor, Yikuang, who was concurrently supervisor at the Ministry of Foreign Affairs and who may have been stretched too thin. Defending Fengshan's qualifications, Tieliang persuaded the court to rescind its decision to ship him off to Xi'an, allowing him to remain "temporarily" in Beijing. And he replaced Duan Qirui at the Third Division with Cao Kun, whose former position as commander of the First Brigade of the First Division was filled by Li Kuiyuan (d. 1925). Meanwhile, on 1 August 1907, Tieliang memorialized that the predominantly Manchu First Division had reached full statutory strength. In late October, a mixed brigade from the division, along with mixed brigades from the other three divisions directly controlled by the Ministry of the Army, participated in the 1907 maneuvers, the first not to be conducted by Yuan Shikai. It was also around this time that the First Division relocated to Beijing and took over as palace guard. Thus, contrary to Stephen MacKinnon's conclusion, Tieliang's attempt to wrest control of Yuan Shikai's Beiyang Army had by no means been "thwarted."[30]

ENMING'S ASSASSINATION AND ITS REPERCUSSIONS

On 6 July, in the midst of the "political storm of 1907," the Manchu governor of Anhui, Enming (1846–1907), was assassinated at his provincial capital, Anqing. His assassin Xu Xilin (1873–1907) was no more (or less) anti-Manchu than Wu Yue had been two years earlier, but whereas Wu Yue's attempt, though occurring at the heart of the capital, had had remarkably few repercussions, Xu Xilin's brought Manchu-Han relations to center stage. Until then, the Qing court had done relatively little to address the Manchu issue as raised by its critics. Specifically, it had only lifted the ban on intermarriage, opened up the Eight Banners to a few Han appointees, and eliminated ethnic slots from the core agencies of the metropolitan government. The assassination of Enming let loose a flood of proposals for the removal of many other Manchu-Han differences, which in turn led to the issuance of two important edicts in September and October that called for radical changes in the banner system and in Manchu-Han relations.

Xu Xilin's assassination of Enming was an inside job. The governor was killed as he presided over the graduation ceremony of the provincial police academy; his murderer was the academy's superintendent. Xu, who was from a wealthy merchant family in Zhejiang, had visited Japan during the Osaka Exhibition in the spring of 1903, when the anti-Russian agitation among the Chinese students was at its height. He became politically radicalized as a result and, like Wu Yue, subsequently joined the Restoration Society. It was through family connections—Xu's older cousin, Yu Liansan, had once been Enming's superior—that he obtained his position as superintendent of the Anhui police academy at the end of 1906. Once installed in Anqing, Xu Xilin connived with another cousin, the radical feminist Qiu Jin (1875–1907) in Shaoxing, Zhejiang, to launch a coordinated revolt against the Qing. Their plot, however, was poorly planned and executed. The uprising at Anqing, of which the killing of Enming was to be only the prelude, was easily suppressed, while that at Shaoxing never materialized. Xu was captured almost immediately and, after a brief interrogation, was beheaded later the same day; his heart was cut out and offered as a sacrifice to the dead governor. Qiu Jin, at Shaoxing, was beheaded six days later.[131] The severity and barbarity of their punishment horrified many. The Manchu-founded *L'Impartial* of Tianjin exclaimed, "Such savage ferocity is inconceivable in twentieth-century China!"[132]

Xu Xilin, during his interrogation, readily confessed that he had killed Enming simply because he was a Manchu. Enming was a Manchu bannerman from the Jinzhou garrison in the Liaoxi corridor outside Shanhaiguan. He had obtained a regular provincial degree in 1873, after which he had risen steadily through the ranks of the provincial bureaucracy. In 1903 he was transferred to Jiangsu, where he was successively provincial judge and treasurer; he was promoted to the position of Anhui governor in early 1906.[133] Xu Xilin professed no grudge against Enming personally, nor did he claim that the governor had been particularly hostile toward Han. Rather, Xu's enmity was directed toward the Manchus in general:

> The Manchus [Manren] have enslaved us Han [Hanzu] for nearly three hundred years. On the surface they seem to be implementing constitutionalism, but that's only to ensnare people's minds. In reality they are upholding the centralization of authority so as to enhance their own power. The Manchus' presumption is that once there is constitutionalism, then revolution will be impossible. . . . If constitutionalism means centralization, then the more constitutionalism there is, the faster we Han people [Hanren] will die. . . . I have harbored anti-Manchu feelings for more than ten years. Only today have I achieved my goal. My intention was to murder Enming, then to kill Duanfang, Tieliang, and Liangbi, so as to avenge the Han people. . . . You say that the governor was a good official, that he treated me very well. Granted. But since my aim is to oppose the Manchus, I cannot be concerned with whether a particular Manchu was a good or bad official. As for his treating me well, that was the private kindness of an individual person. My killing of the governor, on the other hand, expresses the universal principle of anti-Manchuism [*pai-Man*].[134]

The murder of Enming caused tremendous unease among Manchu officials. Unlike Wu Yue, whose anti-Manchu intentions were not disclosed until much later and indeed whose identity was unknown at the time, Xu Xilin freely acknowledged his thirst for racial vengeance. His confession, with its explicit threats against the Manchus, received wide publicity; it was published, for example, in the 22 July issue of *Beijing Women's News*, except that the names of his other intended victims—Duanfang, Tieliang, and Liangbi—had been deleted.[135]

Because it coincided with a series of revolutionary uprisings in Guangdong that Sun Yat-sen had launched in early May, the assassination was especially upsetting. According to British diplomats, "Everywhere throughout the country the Manchu officials are living closely guarded in their Yamens." Perhaps none was more worried than Duanfang, who had been promoted to the position of governor-general of Liang-Jiang (hence Enming's superior) and who was next on Xu Xilin's hit list. Already unnerved by Wu Yue's assault two years earlier, he reportedly sent his family back to Beijing, and though he remained at his post in Nanjing, he was accompanied by a special bodyguard everywhere he went.[136]

Cixi was particularly anxious about Xu Xilin's anti-Manchuism. At an audience a month later with her foreign minister, Lü Haihuan (1840–1927), the empress dowager was reportedly still wrestling with Xu's ghost. She insisted to Lü, "The bandit Xu Xilin claimed that there is prejudice between Manchus and Han, but really when we select provincial officials there is no prejudice whatsoever."[137] More to the point, she issued within five weeks of each other two edicts that were clearly prompted by Enming's murder. The first, promulgated on 8 July, two days after the assassination, called once more upon her subjects to present proposals for reform, but this time her appeal went beyond the elite of top officials who were authorized to memorialize the throne to the much broader group of junior officials and scholar commoners, who were now permitted to have their ideas forwarded to her by either the Censorate or the provincial officials. As evidence of her sincerity with regard to constitutional reform, she noted that she had just the day before ordered the restructuring of the government in Manchuria.[138]

The initial response to Cixi's change of direction was tepid, as only a few people responded with suggestions. However, those few who did respond included the three most influential governors-general in the realm: Yuan Shikai of Zhili, Duanfang of Liang-Jiang, and Zhang Zhidong of Hu-Guang. To help achieve constitutionalism, they separately urged the court to take immediate steps to improve Manchu-Han relations. Yuan Shikai's memorial, dated 28 July, proposed ten sets of reforms, of which one was that "Manchu-Han differences must be dissolved" (Man-Han bixu ronghua ye). He observed that the rebel Sun Yat-sen was stirring up anti-Manchu sentiments among the overseas Chinese by spreading allegations of Manchu plots to exterminate the Han and that Sun was also prodding the Manchus to retaliate against the Han. He suggested that in this situation the empress dowager revert to the policies she had used successfully half a century earlier against the Taiping and Nian rebels: a steady course of action, the wise use of talent, and governmental reforms. Yuan urged that both those who stir up anti-Manchuism and those officials (such as Tieliang, perhaps?) who harbor "biases about Manchus and Han" should be firmly punished. He also recommended that the various proposals that others had advanced in recent years to eliminate Manchu-Han differences should be screened for presentation to the court for adoption. This was the first occasion on which Yuan, despite the key role he had played in retraining the Metropolitan Banners, discussed Manchu-Han relations.[139]

Duanfang, the one Manchu among the three, had, on his return from the constitutional study tour a year earlier, called on Cixi (with some success) to eliminate ethnic slots and (with no success) to abolish the provincial banner garrisons. His memorial, submitted on 31 July, forwarded a petition from a constituent, the licentiate Li Hongcai from De County, Anhui. Although Duanfang at this time offered no advice of his own, it seems that he fully supported the ideas in Li's petition, which appears among Duanfang's collection of memorials as if it were one of his own. Like Yuan Shikai, Li Hongcai took note of the recent upsurge in activity among the revolutionaries, who were spreading rumors, selling bonds, smuggling arms, allying with bandits, and "even assassinating high officials." He contended that the main reason for such unrest was the "pretext" of Manchu-Han differences and that therefore the only way to restore peace was to eliminate those differences. The court, he said, must clearly state its intention not to exalt Manchus and belittle Han (*zhong-Man qing-Han*) and not to use Manchus to defend against Han (*yi-Man fang-Han*). Duanfang's surrogate concluded by suggesting (as will be discussed below) several specific reforms in Manchu-Han relations.[140]

Zhang Zhidong, of course, had long been an advocate of reducing Manchu-Han differences. His recommendations, which curiously were made indirectly in response to a query from the Ministry of Foreign Affairs rather than directly to the court's edict, were sent on 7 August. The ministry had asked him for his opinion regarding the implications for China's security of a recent agreement between Japan and France. Zhang replied that, apart from diplomatic maneuvers, "if one wishes to strengthen frontier defenses, one must first pacify the domestic turbulence. At present the revolutionary party is active everywhere, and the people's minds are disturbed." The only solution was for the court to issue a proclamation "eradicating the boundaries between Manchus and Han" (*huachu Man-Han zhenyu*) and ordering all governmental agencies to recommend concrete reform proposals for immediate implementation. "Once such an edict is issued," Zhang asserted, "the people's minds will be settled, and the rebel party and wicked people will have no further excuse [for making trouble]."[141] Five days earlier, on 2 August, Zhang Zhidong's trusted subordinate, the Hubei provincial judge Liang Dingfen (1859–1919), had submitted a very similar memorial. Referring approvingly to the court's recent abolition of the Manchus' monopoly of posts in the banner organization, Liang asked the court (in words that were almost identical to those of Zhang Zhidong) to go further and issue a decree "eliminating the boundaries between Manchus and Han" (*huachu Man-Han jiexian*). He noted that this was a matter that "all officials have wanted to speak about, but they have kept silent. If, however, the empress dowager and the emperor were to speak out, then it would be done."[142]

It was Liang Dingfen's memorial that prompted the empress dowager on 10 August to issue a second edict. Unlike the previous decree of a month before, this one focused specifically on Manchu-Han relations. Cixi maintained, yet one more time, that the Qing dynasty throughout its long history had always treated Manchus and Han impartially, both as officials and as subjects. Nor had it, in recent appointments to the banner system, distinguished between Manchus and Han. These were perilous times when everyone should be working together to devise solutions. How could there be any lingering prejudice? Echoing the advice of Zhang Zhidong and Liang Dingfen, she then called on all officials to offer suggestions on "how to totally eradicate the boundaries between Manchus and Han."[143]

Whereas Cixi's first edict had elicited only a trickle of memorials, the second decree produced a torrent. The memorialists included Manchus and Han, high- and low-ranking bureaucrats, administrators and censors, officials and scholar-commoners. Many cited the revolutionaries' propaganda and deeds as the compelling reason for the court to take corrective action. For example, Heilongjiang governor Cheng Dequan, the first Han to be appointed to a banner post, referred to "desperadoes" who, ignoring the fact that for over two hundred years the court had treated the Han (Hanren) no differently than it treated Manchus (Manren), preached anti-Manchuism and revolution. The only way to dissipate such talk was to institute constitutionalism, including the elimination of the distinction between Manchus and Han.[144] Most of the memorialists urged reform, though a few did not. Collectively they touched on every aspect of Manchu-Han relations, save one. Some focused on matters that were primarily of symbolic importance; others, on issues of substance involving the Eight Banner system itself. Some revisited old ideas previously discussed during the Tongzhi Restoration, the Hundred Days, or the early post-Boxer period; others brought up totally new ones.[145]

One old issue of symbolic importance was the distinctive name-giving practice among Manchu men, who generally suppressed their family name in public and used only their given name. The censor Guixiu recommended that all Manchus (Manzhou) adopt the Han style by prefacing their disyllabic personal name with a surname, as many Hanjun already did. (Guixiu, judging from his name, may have been a bannerman; if so, he was not practicing what he preached.) Another largely symbolic issue in Manchu-Han relations raised by the memorialists concerned the different style of address used by Manchu and Han officials when memorializing the throne. Whereas Han officials referred to themselves as "your minister" (*chen*), Manchus called themselves "your slave" (*nucai*). Li Hongcai, speaking perhaps for Duanfang, said that it was demeaning for Manchus (Manren), even if they were imperial princes, to identify themselves as slaves. Zhao Bingjun, the junior vice-president of the Ministry of Civil Affairs, recommended that Manchu officials adopt the Han terminology. Yet another old issue, but one that was of more than symbolic significance, was the continuing rarity of Manchu-Han marriages despite the lifting of the ban in 1902. The Hanlin scholar Zheng Yuan called on the Qing to do more to popularize intermarriage as a means of reducing Manchu-Han differences. Zheng thought that the court should take the lead in actively arranging marriages between the children of top Manchu and Han officials. As the practice spread among the aristocracy, lower officials would begin to follow suit on their own without compulsion.[146]

A more substantive matter concerned racial quotas in the bureaucracy. This was not an entirely new concern, since the court, when it reorganized the central administration the year before, had abolished dyarchy in the core agencies and had promised to make its appointments, at least to the top metropolitan posts, "without distinction between Manchus and Han." Several memorialists urged that ethnic considerations be completely disregarded when making all future appointments. Li Hongcai noted that the 1906 reorganization of the metropolitan bureaucracy had excluded the Grand Council, Grand Secretariat, and Hanlin Academy, where dyarchy still prevailed; he asked that they be put on the same footing as the ministries by eliminating their ethnic slots. Hu Qian, a mid-level functionary at the Ministry of Personnel, added that dyarchy existed at the Censorate as well and also that at all ministries many lower-ranking positions, particularly that of Manchu-language scribe, were still reserved exclusively for Manchus. Such remaining ethnic distinctions should be done away with gradually. One memorialist, a provincial degree holder from Hunan named Li Weiran, ventured to propose not only that the post of Manchu-language scribe be eliminated but that the Manchu language itself be abolished. According to Li,

> The founding emperors of the dynasty were unable to coerce the country's ministers and people to learn the national writing and national speech [*guowen guoyu*]. Today not even those of banner registry [*qiji*] necessarily know them. They long ago became a formality. Regardless of imperial edicts, they have

become in the eyes of the people of the country one more relic of the division between Manchus and Han [*Man-Han fenjie*].[147]

Whereas Li Weiran and many others favored narrowing Manchu-Han differences by having the Manchus become more like the Han (for example, by adopting Han-style surnames or abandoning the Manchu language), a few memorialists proposed the opposite course. Guixiu recommended that Manchu literature (Manwen) be made a compulsory subject in all schools so that everyone in China, Han as well as Manchu, could learn the language and thus "protect the national essence," and he proposed that the Han emulate the Manchus' "everyone-a-soldier" tradition as a way of strengthening China militarily. Li Hongcai similarly urged the court to reissue and enforce its 1902 edict prohibiting footbinding, a common practice among Han women, and thus bring the Han into conformity with the Manchus.[148]

Another issue that the memorialists brought to the attention of the court was the differential treatment of Manchus and Han under Qing law. The official who was most concerned about this was Shen Jiaben (1840–1913), the junior vice-president of the Ministry of Laws and, since 1902, a commissioner for revising and codifying the laws. Shen recommended that the way to pacify popular discontent was to ensure that the laws were uniform. He was referring, of course, to the provisions in the Qing code that permitted banner persons who had been convicted of a crime to have their punishment commuted. Shen was particularly aggrieved that only five months earlier his ministry had upheld the banner population's right of commutation. He urged instead that the banner people be subject to the same law as the civilian population.[149]

As few had dared before, a surprisingly large number of memorialists called for the partial or even total dismantling of the Eight Banner system as the ultimate solution to the problem of Manchu-Han differences. Cheng Dequan, in two separate memorials, proposed four reforms: disbandment of the Metropolitan Banners and all provincial garrisons; subordination of the banner people (*qiren*) to the jurisdiction of local civil officials; abolition of the posts of banner commander, company captain, and garrison general; and elimination of the distinct legal categorization of Manchus and Han and their reclassification alike as "citizens" (*guomin*). Duanfang submitted a long memorial, this time in his own name, with four similar proposals. First, the entire banner population, both in the capital and in the provinces, should be transferred to the jurisdiction of local civil officials. Second, the banner soldiers in the provincial garrisons should be demobilized gradually, with each disbanded soldier given ten years' worth of stipends to help him prepare a new means of livelihood. Third, the Metropolitan Banners should, with official assistance, be resettled in Manchuria (Manzhou), which, because of the earlier ban on Han immigration, was still relatively sparsely populated and had plenty of arable land. Last, all bannermen office-holders should contribute 10 percent of their salary for the next ten years to generate some of the funds needed for the disbandment of the provincial garrisons and the resettlement of the Metropolitan Banners.[150]

Zhao Bingjun asserted that a hereditary military caste such as the banner people was incompatible with the constitutionalist regime China aspired to be. He proposed a three-step process of disbandment. The first step was to conduct a thorough census of the entire banner population to determine who was or was not receiving a stipend. The second was to confer special (nonmonetary) honors upon those banner people whose families had rendered meritorious service to the dynasty in the past. The final step was to enlist all able-bodied adult bannermen as New Army soldiers, policemen, or servants at court. Those stipendiaries who were old and weak would be paid until they died. Those who were young would be sent to a school or workshop to learn how to make a living; after a specified number of years, when they should have acquired a vocational skill, their stipends would cease. As for the unsalaried (or idle) bannermen, they could either make their own way in the world or be sent to the northeast, where, with government assistance, they would cultivate the barren land.[151]

The memorialist who provided the most thoughtful analysis of the economic ramifications of disbanding the Eight Banners was Xiong Xiling (1870–1942), who drew upon Meiji Japan's prior experience with demobilizing the samurai.[152] A metropolitan graduate of 1895, Xiong had been purged in 1898 for participating in the radical reform movement in his native Hunan. Following his political rehabilitation in 1905, he had accompanied Duanfang on his constitutional study tour of Japan and the West. According to Xiong,

> Those who today speak of eliminating Manchu-Han differences [huachu Man-Han] advocate adopting Han-style surnames, intermarrying, and eliminating [ethnic] slots. All these are easy decisions. What is difficult is abolishing the provincial garrisons and reorganizing the Metropolitan Banners. These matters affect the very lives of several hundred thousand Manchu, Mongol, and Hanjun [banner soldiers] and cannot all be resolved in one day.

If, on the other hand, the garrisons were not abolished and the Metropolitan Banners reorganized, then "the Han [Hanren] would distrust the Manchus [Manren] because they have fewer rights and privileges, and the Manchus would resent the Han because they are less well off economically."

Xiong found fault with three existing proposals for financing the disbandment of the banners. One proposal, similar to Duanfang's, was to pension off each banner soldier with ten years' worth of stipends. However, the annual cost of the stipends was about ten million taels, which multiplied ten times would be a hundred million taels. When the samurai were abolished in 1876, the Meiji government had spent two hundred million yen. As there were "several times" more banner soldiers than there had been samurai, the Qing government could not possibly afford this huge sum of money. Such being the case, a second proposal was to pay off the banner soldiers with interest-bearing bonds, as was done in Japan. But given the lack of popular confidence in the government's bonds, this was tantamount to "exchanging a solid stipend for an empty certificate." A third proposal was to resettle the banner population in the barren wastes along China's frontier, giving each male adult several hundred *mu* of land on which they could feed themselves and their families ever after. This had been tried previously and without success. If it were to succeed now, this third option would require a vast infrastructure including transportation, irrigation, markets, and agricultural implements, none of which was presently in place. Furthermore, none of these three proposals addressed the greatest difficulty of all, the habit of dependence that had built up among the banner people over two hundred years. Even if commanded to be economically independent, they simply would not be able to comply.

Xiong Xiling then offered his own three-pronged long-term program for overcoming these various difficulties: establishment of factories and vocational schools throughout the country to teach the young and vigorous banner soldiers the skills they needed to make their own living; investment of half of the banner soldiers' lump-sum severance pay in a bank, for which they would receive interest-bearing bonds and which would also develop among the banner population the habit of saving money (this was modeled after Okuma Shigenobu's plan in Japan to found a national bank so as to provide for the livelihood of the Meiji aristocracy); and investment of another part of their severance pay in the building of railroads in Manchuria and Mongolia, thus facilitating the movement of settlers into those regions. Furthermore, annual dividends from their railroad stock, according to Xiong's wildly optimistic estimate, would equal half of the banner soldiers' former stipends.

To be sure, not every memorialist responding to Cixi's edict of 10 August favored eliminating Manchu-Han differences; there were a few who bucked the trend. Enming's successor as Anhui governor, Feng Xu (1843–1927), himself a Han, attributed accusations that the court favored Manchus at the expense of Han to unspecified "outsiders who make use of such talk to stir up our revolutionaries" and then take advantage of the resultant unrest. In any case, such allegations of differential treatment, Feng said, were baseless. For example, many Manchus (Manren), including members of the imperial clan, were much less well off economically than the Han (Hanren). The court should concern itself only with selecting benevolent officials without regard to whether they were Manchu or Han. If this were done, the Manchu-Han issue would disappear on its own. If, however, the court merely published paper directives removing Manchu-Han differences, the issue would remain for the revolutionary party to exploit. In other words, official misconduct, not Manchu-Han differences, was what needed to be addressed. The censor Jiang Chunlin, most likely a Han, made much the same point. Jiang explicitly dismissed most of the proposed reforms, including the adoption of Han-style surnames and the abolition of the banners, as unnecessary and irrelevant. He insisted that differences and rivalry (between groups such as Manchus and Han) were natural and inevitable, as they were within a family. All that the court had to do, according to Jiang, was to be impartial. While he conceded that there was a preponderance of Manchus in the most "attractive" posts, which needed to be redressed, he did not think it was necessary to do away with the distinction between Manchu and Han (*Man-Han zhi jie*). Indeed, as he concluded somewhat cryptically, if that distinction were abolished, then "those who were distant" (the Han?) might not feel grateful, while "those who were near" (the Manchus?) would have been dispersed.[153]

Finally, despite the volume and range of reform proposals, there was one aspect of Manchu-Han relations that no memorialist in 1907 addressed, not even obliquely: the wearing of the queue. It, along with the dress code, had been modified in the early post-Boxer years for some social groups, but remained a contentious matter. When the army and police were reorganized, it became immediately apparent that the Manchu hairstyle did not fit well with the new Japanese-style uniforms. Soldiers in the New Army therefore obtained imperial permission to shorten, though not remove, the queue. So too did policemen, who were authorized to reduce the length of their braid by two-thirds. In Beijing, where most of the police were bannermen, the order to shorten the queue went out late in 1905 and, according to Edmund Backhouse, "caused great heart-burnings in many cases. At one barracks the men refused to obey until their officers had had their own queues taken off. The children in the streets call out foreign devil at them and it is amusing to see how indignant this makes them." As the army and police adopted the modified queue, students in the new schools, who often wore a Manchu-style jacket and gown topped by a Japanese-type cap, similarly chafed at the odd appearance that the long, trailing braid presented (see plate 7) They began on their own to shorten and even to remove their plaits. In April 1906, when several students at the

Shuntian Middle School in Beijing took advantage of the switch to new-style drill caps to cut off their braids, the school director cautioned them to wait until a clear directive had come from above. Though never sanctioned, the new fashion was sufficiently widespread for foreign minister Lü Haihuan to complain in 1907 that students, especially those who had returned from abroad, were recklessly discarding the queue and changing their costume.[154]

At the same time that students began acting on their own, nonofficial reformist voices were also calling for the abandonment of the queue. In the lead commentary in its September 1907 issue, the Shanghai monthly *Eastern Miscellany* listed "changing the queue" among four specific reforms that would help resolve the "Manchu-Han conflict" (*Man-Han zhi zheng*) and speed the way toward the realization of constitutionalism. (The others were adopting Han-style surnames, reclassifying banner people as civilians, and eliminating ethnic slots.)[155] Adding to the urgency of the queue question at this moment was the widely circulated news from Korea that King Sunjong, newly installed by his Japanese overlords, had on 16 August cut off his topknot and called on all of his subjects to wear their hair short in the Japanese style. The involuntary nature of Sunjong's tonsorial decree was a painful warning to Chinese newspaper readers of the price to be paid for failing to reform in time. As the Manchu daily *Beijing Women's News* commented, "Alas! Only when the nation was entirely lost did they know to reform! It's too late!"[156] Yet, despite these events at home and abroad, not one of the memorialists in the summer of 1907 recommended any change in the Manchu-imposed hairstyle. Such caution on their part could have been due only to a sense that although every other aspect of Manchu-Han relations, including the banner system itself, was open to reform, the queue requirement was not.

Contributing to the debate about constitutionalism and Manchu-Han relations that the edicts of 8 July and 10 August set in motion was a new journal of political opinion, *Great Harmony Journal* (Datongbao), which began publishing in Tokyo on 25 June 1907; by late September it had produced three lengthy issues, each over a hundred pages. (It was to put out four more issues before it ceased publication on 30 May 1908.) *Great Harmony Journal* differed from all of the other Chinese-language periodicals that proliferated in Japan during the post-Boxer decade in that it was published by Manchus and was devoted largely to an examination of what it itself called the "Manchu-Han question" (*Man-Han wenti*). Its entire editorial staff was Manchu; its two most prolific writers were Hengjun of the imperial clan and Wuzesheng of Jilin, both then students at Waseda University in Japan.[157]

Like many Chinese political journals since the mid-1890s, *Great Harmony Journal* protested the widespread apathy of the Chinese people in the face of the imperialist threat. According to Wuzesheng's "Preface to *Great Harmony Journal*" in the inaugural issue, the reason for such apathy was China's two-thousand-year-old "despotic polity," under which the ruler alone possessed absolute power and the people were deprived of a sense of responsibility. There was, however, a means of salvation: constitutionalism. In a constitutional polity, there is no differentiation between ruler and ruled, and both share the responsibility for the conduct of national affairs. If China were a constitutional country, the foreign powers would no longer be able to throw their weight around. Whereas formerly they might have been able to intimidate one or two officials in the government, they could not do the same to one hundred million aroused citizens. Therefore, if China were to avoid being partitioned by the foreign powers, it had to change to a constitutional polity and empower its citizens. What, Wuzesheng asked, differentiates a constitutional from a despotic polity? Not a constitution, but a parliament. Parliament provides a channel for expressing the citizens' opinions and also for cultivating their sense of unity and political consciousness. It allows the people to assume responsibility. Without a parliament there can be no "responsible government." Consequently, the first two of the four stated objectives of *Great Harmony Journal* were "Establish a constitutional monarchy" and "Summon a parliament in order to create a responsible government."[158] In this regard, *Great Harmony Journal* closely paralleled the views of Yang Du (1875–1931), then based also in Tokyo, who was the organizer of the Seminar on Constitutional Government (Xianzheng Jiangxihui) and editor of the monthly *China New Journal* (Zhongguo xinbao). *Great Harmony Journal* not only carried in its inaugural issue a congratulatory message from Yang, in which he stated that its goals were entirely congruent with his, but later also published his lengthy analysis, "Parliament and the Banner People."[159]

The other two objectives of *Great Harmony Journal* were "Establish equality between the Manchu and Han people" (*Man-Han renmin pingdeng*) and "Unify Manchus, Han, Mongol, Muslims, and Tibetans as one citizenry," both of which were intended to answer the self-posed Manchu-Han question.[160] According to Hengjun, in a multipart article titled "China's Future," the Manchu-Han question was of recent origin. It had arisen only after 1895, when concerned citizens petitioned the government for reforms, only to provoke a conservative opposition, which in turn created an anti-Manchu backlash among many Han.[161] Then, as anti-Manchuism intensified after the Boxer troubles, it engendered an anti-Han reaction among some Manchus. Thus, the Manchu-Han question had two components, anti-Manchuism among Han and anti-Hanism among Manchus. According to Wuzesheng, in the fifty-page essay "The Manchu-Han Question," the ultimate aim of the anti-Manchus was republicanism; that of the anti-Han, increased despotism. Neither was so desirable as a constitutional monarchy.[162] Both Hengjun and Wuzesheng acknowledged that differences existed between Manchus and Han, but felt that such differences lay not in immutable racial characteristics but only in "obligations and privileges." For example, as members of the banner system, Manchus were universally obliged to serve as soldiers, in return for which they were paid a stipend by the state. Han, on the other hand, were obliged to pay taxes, but they were free from military duty.[163]

Great Harmony Journal urged that, at the very least, these differences in obligations and privileges be eliminated, so that equality between the two peoples could be established. More importantly, it favored the abolition of the Eight Banner system itself. Wuzesheng, in one short but pregnant sentence near the end of "The Manchu-Han Question," declared that the only way to get rid of all of the differences between Manchus and Han was for the court to "do away with the peculiar institution [tebie zhidu] in order to demonstrate its absolute impartiality."[164] Yang Du, in "Parliament and the Banner People," provided a detailed justification for the abolition of the banners.[165] Finally, at the heart of Great Harmony Journal's analysis of the Manchu-Han question was its definition of China in political rather than ethnic terms. To be sure, it recognized the existence of different "races" (zu) within China, specifically five—Manchus, Han, Mongol, Muslims (Hui), and Tibetans. This may seem to be no more than a restatement of the Qianlong emperor's self-image as the all-encompassing ruler of these same five subject peoples, but it had been modified in one very significant way: these peoples now owed their loyalty not to the Qing empire but to China. Hengjun rejected the concept of the anti-Manchus that "China ought to be based upon the Han people." He also denied the parallel concept, attributable to the anti-Han, that "China belonged not to the Han but to the Manchus." He insisted instead that members of all five races were "Chinese." Whatever their ethnic differences, they were all "citizens" of China.[166]

Whether Great Harmony Journal, as the voice of young reform-minded Manchus, had much influence on the memorialists in the summer of 1907 is unclear, though some of its ideas paralleled those of Xiong Xiling, who likewise called for disbanding the banner system. In any case, Cixi's court referred all of their memorials to the Office of Governmental Affairs for consideration. The office, created in 1901 to oversee every aspect of administrative reform, was then composed of eight regular members: two grand councilors (Yikuang and Lu Chuanlin); one grand secretary (Sun Jia'nai); two ministers (Rongqing, education; and Tieliang, army); and three governors-general (Xu Shichang, Manchuria; Zhang Zhidong, Hu-Guang; and Yuan Shikai, Zhili). They were divided among three Manchus and five Han.[167] In order for them to participate in these important deliberations, two of the three provincial officials, Zhang Zhidong and Yuan Shikai, were transferred to Beijing, where both were named to the Grand Council and given top posts in the metropolitan administration. Zhang became supervisor of the Ministry of Education, and Yuan, president of the Ministry of Foreign Affairs (replacing Lü Haihuan). (These appointments would appear to contravene the 1906 rule that prohibited a ministry head from holding another important office. However, Zhang's post as supervisor may not have qualified technically as a ministry head, though he, like Yikuang at the Ministries of Foreign Affairs and Army, outranked the minister; Yuan's position in the Ministry of Foreign Affairs was the one specific treaty-imposed exception to the rule.)[168] The appointment of Zhang and Yuan to the Grand Council was another facet of the political storm of 1907, as they were replacements for the powerful Qu Hongji, purged in June, and his ally Lin Shaonian, removed two months later. The expanded six-man Grand Council—consisting of Yikuang, Zaifeng, Shixu, Lu Chuanlin, Zhang Zhidong, and Yuan Shikai—was evenly divided between Manchus and Han. Zaifeng had been added to the council as a probationary member in June.[169]

Beginning in late August 1907, around the time that Zhang Zhidong and Yuan Shikai arrived in the capital, members of the Office of Governmental Affairs met frequently to discuss the various proposals for the reform of Manchu-Han relations as well as other suggestions for the realization of constitutional government. At these meetings, according to at least one news report, Army Minister Tieliang vigorously opposed any precipitous action to do away with the banner soldiers' stipends and other privileges of the banner population as contrary to the wishes of the dynastic founders.[170]

A month later the court issued two edicts, ten days apart, that resolved to drastically change, though not abolish, the Eight Banner system. The first edict, handed down on 27 September, ordered, much as Duanfang had suggested, that the provincial garrisons be disbanded over a ten-year period and their inhabitants be prepared to make their own living. It directed the commander of each garrison, together with the appropriate provincial officials, to take a census of the banner soldiers and then to distribute enough farmland (along with tools, etc.) to each of them so that they might provide for themselves and their families. The officials were to start by dividing up the garrison's own horse pastures and farm land. At a garrison without any land of its own or with an insufficient amount, they were to purchase the land (at the market price) from farmers in the vicinity. Each year about 10 percent of the banner soldiers at a garrison were to receive land, which they would hold in perpetuity but without the right to sell or mortgage to others. As they were resettled on their allotted land, they would stop receiving their stipends, and they would pass from the jurisdiction of the banner officials to that of the local civil officials and would thenceforth be subject to the same treatment, including the same land taxes and the same laws, as the civilian population. The funds for demobilizing the provincial garrisons would come from the Ministry of Finance and from the savings from the termination of the stipends. The second edict, issued on 9 October, dealt with the customary and legal differences between Manchus and Han, such as the length of the mourning period and the commutation of punishments. It called on the Ministry of Rites together with the Commissioners for Revising and Codifying the Laws (Xiuding Falü Dachen) to draw up a set of ceremonies and penal codes that would apply uniformly to Manchus and Han, excepting only the imperial lineage.[171]

These two edicts thus accepted many of the proposals advanced by the memorialists after Enming's assassination. On the face of it, they would have greatly changed the banner system and Manchu-Han relations by disbanding the provincial garrisons and by eliminating the social and legal differences separating Manchus and Han. However, by no means did these two edicts embrace all of the proposed reforms. In particular, they did not heed Xiong Xiling's call for the disbandment of the Metropolitan Banners, who accounted for half the total banner population. They did not abolish the many remaining ethnic slots in the metropolitan government. Finally, since no memorialist had called for it, they did not, of course, alter the queue requirement. Indeed, in response to Lü Haihuan's complaint about rampant queue-cutting, the government in the summer of 1907 reiterated its commitment to the requirement. In a joint memorial, the Ministries of Education and the Army, both headed by Manchus (Rongqing and Tieliang), promised to crack down on returned students and soldiers who had removed their queue.[172]

Meanwhile, in response to the growing demands of the constitutionalist reformers (as exemplified, for example, by *Great Harmony Journal*), Cixi, in her own name, issued two other edicts that clarified the vague promise that she had made a year earlier to institute a constitutional regime. On 20 September 1907 she declared that her ultimate intention was to establish "a bicameral deliberative body." As a preparatory step, she ordered the immediate creation of a Consultative Assembly (Zizhengyuan), appointed the fourth-rank prince Pulun (1874–1926) and the elderly grand secretary Sun Jia'nai as its co-presidents, and charged them, together with the Grand Council, to draw up a detailed plan for this new national assembly. A month later, on 19 October, she authorized the formation of provincial deliberative assemblies as well.[173] Afterward, she sent Pulun to Japan to learn more about constitutional government at first hand.[174]

CONCLUSION

The Qing court's New Policies initially emphasized military and educational reform, a carryover from the era of Self-Strengthening. It was only after 1906 that they went beyond such old concerns and ventured into the uncharted territory of political reform. As the military and educational systems changed in the early and middle years of the post-Boxer decade, the Manchus adapted to them no less than did the general population. They formed a new military unit (the Metropolitan Banners Standing Army, which became the First Division of the national New Army) and new police forces (notably Beijing's Inner City police). They founded new schools, both military and civilian, including the Nobles Military School in Beijing and the Huixing Girls School in the Hangzhou garrison, and they sent students to study abroad, principally to Japan. And they founded their own newspapers and journals (*L'Impartial* in Tianjin, *Beijing Women's News* in the capital, and *Great Harmony Journal* in Tokyo) to present their views on current affairs. In short, the Manchus were active participants in the post-Boxer reforms.

Meanwhile, despite the revolutionaries' often valid indictment of the Manchus, the early post-Boxer court was remarkably slow to address what *Great Harmony Journal* itself called the "Manchu-Han question." On the eve of Enming's assassination in July 1907, it had lifted the ban on Manchu-Han intermarriage, but to little effect. It had appointed a few Han officials to posts in the banner system and to the new provincial administration in Manchuria. It had abandoned the mounted archery component of the Manchus' ancestral tradition, but not that of "national speech." And it had abolished the institution of dyarchy and, with it, the practice of assigning officials to posts that were reserved for specific ethnic or status groups, but only among some agencies of the newly reorganized metropolitan government. A survey of the reform proposals offered by the memorialists in the summer of 1907 shows clearly that as late as the penultimate year of Cixi's rule, numerous and substantial differences still divided Manchus and Han.

Indeed, the elimination of ethnic slots, which many reformers recommended as an effective way of reducing Manchu-Han differences, had the opposite effect. It made the imbalance among high officials more, rather than less, favorable to Manchus at the expense of Han. Previously, under the institution of dyarchy, the officials at the top of the metropolitan administration had been evenly split between the two groups. At the end of 1906, however, when the metropolitan administration was restructured and dyarchy curbed, the thirteen ministry heads were divided between eight Manchus and only five Han.

A year later, in late 1907, the Manchu preponderance had become even greater: nine Manchus and four Han. The Manchus were Yikuang and Natong (at Foreign Affairs), Shanqi (Civil Affairs), Zaize (Finance), Puliang (Rites), Rongqing (Education), Tieliang (Army), Puting (Agriculture, Industry, and Commerce), and Shouqi (Colonial Affairs). The four Han were Yuan Shikai (Foreign Affairs), Lu Runxiang (1841–1915; Personnel), Dai Hongci (Laws), and Chen Bi (1852–1928; Posts and Communications).[175] Furthermore, the trend toward greater princely participation in state affairs had become more pronounced. Thus, among the nine Manchus who were ministerial heads in late 1907, three were imperial princes: Yikuang, Shanqi, and Zaize. A year earlier, only two princes—Yikuang and his son Zaizhen—served as ministry heads. (Zaizhen was subsequently removed from the Ministry of Agriculture, Industry, and Commerce for his involvement in a scandal.) The same trend was evident at the Grand Council. In late 1906 only one of the four grand councilors, Yikuang, was an imperial prince; a year later two of the six, Yikuang and Zaifeng, were princes.[176]

The Qing court did finally awaken to the seriousness of the Manchu-Han question after Governor Enming was assassinated in July 1907. It was then and only then that Empress Dowager Cixi issued her two edicts calling for a substantial revision of the banner system, which the Manchu reformer Wuzesheng called the "peculiar institution," and the elimination of social and legal differences between Manchus and Han. These edicts did not order the complete abolition of the Eight Banners or the elimination of all Manchu-Han differences. Nevertheless, limited as these mandated reforms were, they were more far-reaching than any of the reforms previously attempted, including those promulgated during the Hundred Days. In 1898 the Guangxu emperor had merely called for lifting the ban on outside employment by the banner people and exploring the possibility of resettling the banner population. His order had greatly alarmed the banner population and was, in part, responsible for the termination of those reforms and the emperor's removal from power. Now, almost exactly nine years later, the empress dowager had more than come around to his view.

3 / Zaifeng and the "Manchu Ascendency"

A little more than a year after she issued her two edicts in September and October 1907 on the provincial banner garrisons and Manchu-Han relations, the seventy-three-year-old empress dowager died, ending nearly a half century of court domination. In her last year she made some effort to carry out those decrees, but she expired before much had been accomplished. The task of dealing with the Manchu-Han question and other issues passed to the twenty-five-year-old Zaifeng, who became regent for his young son Puyi when the childless Guangxu emperor died the day before Cixi. Zaifeng, the former Prince Chun, began his regency well regarded as a reformer. However, in less than three years he had dissipated whatever initial goodwill he had by his tendency toward vacillation (as epitomized in his handling of Manchu-Han relations), his disinclination to yield to popular pressure in a timely fashion (as in his repeated confrontations with the constitutionalist reformers), and, perhaps most damagingly, his impolitic attempt to amass power not simply in the central government (as Cixi had done) but in the Qing court itself (such as by organizing a new division-strength palace guard that was under his exclusive control). Moreover, it was during Zaifeng's regency that, in continuing disregard of the revolutionaries' anti-Manchu propaganda, the Qing government became more dominated by Manchus than at any other time since at least the mid-eighteenth century.

CIXI'S LAST YEAR

Having ordered the gradual disbandment of the provincial garrisons and the abolition of legal and customary differences between Manchus and Han, Cixi had considerable trouble getting her decrees implemented. She also had problems dealing with the constitutional reformers, who, though gladdened by her recent commitment to a national consultative assembly, now began agitating for the early convening of a fully legislative parliament. Shortly after agreeing to a nine-year timetable for the realization of a constitutional regime, she passed away, one day after the Guangxu emperor, whom she had held captive since

1898. Before she died, Cixi had arranged to designate Puyi as the new emperor, with his father as regent.

Cixi's edict of 27 September 1907 calling for the gradual dismantling of the provincial garrisons caused, not surprisingly, widespread unease among the banner population, not unlike the Guangxu emperor's decree ten years earlier. Li Guojie, the brigade-general of the Hanjun detachment at Guangzhou and one of the first Han appointed to a banner post, immediately warned that the banner soldiers in the provinces would be greatly upset on learning that their stipends were about to be discontinued; he urged the court to proceed with caution. A couple of months later Lieutenant-General Tingjie of Rehe confirmed that his garrison had greeted the decree with much anxiety. On 18 January 1908 at Chengdu, when it was rumored that the court was about to issue another edict that would strip the banner soldiers of their stipends immediately and require them to fend for themselves unassisted, the unrest erupted into a riot. A crowd of several hundred banner personnel, including women, converged angrily on the office of General Chuohabu to demand that the stipends be continued. In their rage, they smashed the side entrance to the main hall and pummeled one of the banner captains. They were not appeased until the Sichuan governor-general, Zhao Erfeng, himself a Hanjun, arrived and convinced them that they had been misinformed.[1] The banner people's anxiety did not, however, deter Cixi from pressing ahead with the proposed reform. Despite Li Guojie's plea from Guangzhou for caution, the court stood by the original decree. On 30 September 1907, it reiterated its plan to allocate farmland to banner soldiers and, as this was done, to phase out the stipends; it called on garrison and provincial officials to put the program into effect earnestly but at the same time to explain its righteous intent to the affected banner people so as to allay their unease. On 16 January 1908 the court brushed aside another memorial, this one from the commander of the Jingzhou garrison, raising doubts about how the disbandment policy would be implemented.[2]

However, the core of the new policy—resettling the banner population on nearby farmland—proved at once to be impractical, especially within China proper. As garrison after garrison reported, little or no banner land was available for resettlement, or, if the land existed, it was usually not suitable for cultivation. The small Kaifeng garrison in Henan said it had absolutely no farm or pasture land of its own; so, too, did the much larger garrison at Guangzhou. In Shandong, both the Qingzhou and Dezhou garrisons had some pasture land, but it was either unsuited for agriculture (as was the case for Qingzhou) or it had been leased to (presumably Han) tenants, whom it would not do to evict because their rents helped to pay for Dezhou's military modernization. In Chengdu, as in Dezhou, the garrison's land, totaling 7,470 *mu* (roughly 1,250 acres), had all been rented out, and it would cost two hundred thousand taels in rental deposits to reclaim it. The only garrisons to report that they had arable land on which to resettle their banner personnel were those in Chahar and Heilongjiang, both beyond the Great Wall. Even some of the garrisons out-side China proper were short on land. The Liangzhou and Zhuanglang gar-risons, in Gansu, owned pastures in Yongchang and Pingfan Counties respectively, but they too were ill-suited for agriculture and settlement.³

Where banner land was not available for resettlement, Cixi's edict had rec-ommended that garrisons purchase land from nearby farmers at the market price, but that expedient proved to be chimerical as well. Officials from such widely scattered garrisons as Chengdu, Qingzhou, and Liangzhou all reported that the land was much more expensive than they could afford. The Chengdu general, for example, estimated that he would need more than twenty thou-sand *mu* (about 3,500 acres) of land to distribute to his personnel and that the price of land in Sichuan was between sixty and seventy taels per *mu*; this worked out to a total of about 1,300,000 taels, which his treasury did not have. The Guangzhou general implied that even if the funds were available, there might not be enough agricultural land close by to accommodate the 33,965 people in his garrison if each individual were to receive ten *mu* (1.7 acres). No such vast quantity of land was for sale in the vicinity. (Actually, the edict had said that land should be given not to all banner people or even all bannermen but only to banner soldiers, of whom there were about five thousand in Guangzhou, and it had not specified the size of the land allotment.) Furthermore, a group of twenty-five leading Manchus in Beijing, headed by the imperial clansman Wenbin, jointly warned that the court's land-repurchasing idea might cause resentment among Han landowners and thus prove counterproductive to the ultimate aim of easing tensions between Manchus and Han.⁴

Yet another alternative was to resettle the population of the provincial gar-risons in the outlying regions of the empire. This had been the proposed solu-tion to the "Eight Banners' livelihood problem" all through the nineteenth century, and it was again advanced by two or three officials. The Zhili provin-cial treasurer, the Mongol bannerman Zengyun (d. 1921), noted that although land was expensive and scarce within China proper, it was quite otherwise along China's frontiers, where the price might be five hundred to a thousand times less. Zhirui (1852–1912), the acting general of the Ningxia garrison, proposed that banner people from garrisons with little or no land be sent to Gansu or along the great northern bend of the Yellow River to help develop those sparsely populated regions.⁵ Long-distance resettlement, however, had been conspic-uously absent from the court's original edict, which had emphasized keeping each garrison's populace close to home. The Office of Governmental Affairs responded to Zengyun's and Zhirui's suggestions without enthusiasm. It declared that because of transportation difficulties, emigration to the northwest was impractical. And while it conceded that one feasible destination, due to newly built railroads, was the northeast—especially Heilongjiang, where, according to Governor-General Xu Shichang, there was a large surplus of undeveloped land—it stressed that if such emigration were to take place, it should be entirely voluntary, not coerced.[6]

Since most garrison officials found the resettlement scheme sanctioned by the September edict unrealistic, they turned to other remedies that might accomplish the same result, which was to make the banner people economically independent and thus facilitate the eventual disbandment of the provincial garrisons. In Suiyuan, General Yigu, in addition to resettling 5,100 bannermen on 120,000 *mu* (20,000 acres) of not very fertile land nearby, initiated three other types of economic development for his garrison. One was vocational training: he founded workshops that taught useful skills to a hundred young bannermen, and factories that made clothing and caps for the army, employing forty orphans and widows. Another was education, both military and civilian: he established eighteen schools, including a military middle school and several regular primary schools, which enrolled eight hundred students. The third was military service: he formed a battalion of 120 soldiers, and he proposed to organize a police force as well. Yigu's efforts were hardly novel; they were no more than a systematization of reforms that various garrisons had tried out in the early post-Boxer years. Nevertheless, the Qing court ordered that Yigu's account of his program be circulated to the other garrisons for their consideration. While the Office of Governmental Affairs continued to regard the "conferring of land and a return to farming" (*shoutian guinong*) as the fundamental solution to the economic problems of the banner people, it admitted that the encouragement of industry and the promotion of education were also important.[7]

Thus, various banner garrisons, following Yigu's model in Suiyuan, actively pursued vocational, educational, and military reforms. In most instances, they simply built upon earlier efforts. The Taiyuan garrison in Shanxi had already organized a standing army detachment and founded a senior primary school; it now planned to start an agricultural and industrial training course (including an experimental farm plot and a workshop) for qualified bannermen, with an attached lecture hall to provide some rudimentary vocational information to less qualified bannermen as well as to orphans, widows, and banner women in general. The Kaifeng garrison in Henan had previously established a crafts office and a sericulture bureau offering vocational training and had retrained about eight hundred banner soldiers; it now proposed to reorganize and expand its school system to include a new middle school. The Rehe garrison, which earlier had reorganized about a thousand of its banner soldiers (or half the garrison) into three battalions of standing army, now planned to transform them into the core of the New Army division that had been assigned to the territory; it was also going to set up a workshop to teach bannermen who were not suited for the army how to weave and dye.[8]

All of these local reform programs were hindered by a shortage of funds. Cixi's original edict had promised that the initial cost of resettling the banner soldiers would be borne by the Ministry of Finance. Perhaps because relocation proved to be impractical, the government subsequently rejected nearly all requests for financial assistance from the center. The court did direct the ministry to allocate two hundred thousand taels to Suiyuan and one hundred thousand to Chahar, but otherwise, as the Office of Governmental Affairs bluntly informed the general at Chengdu, each garrison was responsible for financing its efforts with its own resources.[9] With money in short supply, the reforms, understandably, made slow progress. Indeed, shortly before her death in November 1908, Cixi reportedly expressed her impatience to the Grand Council. It had been over a year since the decree to "confer land and return [the banner people] to farming" had been issued. Why, she asked, had so few garrisons made any headway in its implementation?[10]

Cixi's court had somewhat greater, though still mixed, success at implementing her other edict, which directed the Commissioners for Revising and Codifying the Laws and the Ministry of Rites respectively to abolish various legal and social differences that still separated Manchus and Han. The former responded promptly; the latter did not. The three-person legal commission—consisting of Shen Jiaben (the junior vice-minister of laws), Yu Liansan (a former provincial official who, incidentally, had helped Enming's assassin get his position at the Anhui police academy), and Yingrui (a Manchu bannerman and president of the newly reorganized Supreme Court of Justice [Daliyuan])—made two proposals for legal reform.[11] One followed up on the court's decree of 27 September to subject the provincial garrison personnel, as they were disbanded, to the same treatment as the general population. This was an issue on which Shen Jiaben had recently memorialized. Shen and his fellow commissioners thus recommended that henceforth banner people be dealt with the same as civilians not only in punishments but in all other aspects of the law, and that furthermore *all* banner personnel, not simply the provincial banner people as they were demobilized, should come under the jurisdiction of the new hierarchy of civilian courts that was being set up. The only ones exempted were the imperial lineage, who heretofore had been subject to the Imperial Clan Court, and their exemption was temporary and partial. For the time being, they would be free from the supervision of the lower courts; they would instead be dealt with by the Supreme Court of Justice. The legal commissioners' other proposal, which was supported by the Ministry of Finance as well, urged that the prohibition of transfer of property from banner people to civilians be abolished without equivocation. They noted that because of conflicting rulings in the past by the Boards of Revenue and Punishments, considerable uncertainty existed as to whether the ban was still in effect. In any case, they contended that the prohibition was disadvantageous to the banner population because it restricted their economic opportunities. In January 1908 Cixi's court approved both proposals from the legal commission.[12]

Ostensibly, this meant that the legal differences between Manchus and Han had been eliminated. Indeed, it would appear that as the new three-tier court system was gradually put into place, Manchus increasingly were subject to the same judicial process as Han. Leading the way was Beijing, with the establishment in December 1907 of one Higher Court for the entire metropolitan region and, inter alia, one district and three local courts for the Inner City. The regulations for these courts stated explicitly that they were accessible to everyone, "without distinction between banner people and Han or between officials and subjects" (wulun qi-Han guanmin).[13] Later, when the system had been extended to other locations with banner garrisons, the Ministry of Civil Affairs proposed that the courts in those cities similarly assume jurisdiction over the local banner people.[14]

Unlike the Commissioners for Revising and Codifying the Laws, the Ministry of Rites was unable to agree on any reforms. It had been asked to recommend ways of eliminating such customary differences between Manchus and Han as the length of the mourning period, the use (or non-use) of surnames, the term by which memorialists referred to themselves when addressing the throne, and the style of women's clothing. All of these issues provoked strong, conflicting opinions among the leaders of the ministry. Regarding the mourning period, for example, the minister, the imperial clansman Puliang, reportedly favored universalizing the Manchu practice of mourning for only one hundred days, while the two vice-ministers, both Han, adamantly objected to any departure from the traditional Han mourning period of twenty-seven months.[15] As a result of such disagreements, the ministry made no recommendation at this time.

Cixi also had to contend in her last year with the growing number of political reformers who were impatient with the court's slowness to fulfill its promise of a constitutional regime. In the fall of 1907 she had ordered the creation of a national assembly and authorized the formation of provincial assemblies, but then nothing more happened. Presumably her officials were deliberating among themselves about how best to proceed. While they dallied, the court came under increasing pressure from below, as three groups of activists organized a sophisticated campaign to pick up the pace of reform. One was Yang Du's Seminar on Constitutional Government, which relocated from Tokyo to Hunan and Beijing following Yang's return to China in December 1907 and was renamed the Association for Constitutional Government (Xianzheng Gonghui). Another was the Association for Constitutional Preparations (Yubei Lixian Gonghui), headed by Zhang Jian, Zheng Xiaoxu (1860–1938), and Tang Shouqian (1856–1917) in Shanghai. The third was the Political Information Institute (Zhengwenshe), founded by Liang Qichao in Tokyo, which moved its headquarters to Shanghai in February 1908 (though without Liang, who was still persona non grata with the Qing).[16] Reform-minded Manchus were involved in all three groups. Yang Du's Association for Constitutional Government included the imperial clansman Hengjun, a founding editor of the Tokyo-based *Great Harmony Journal*, which, as noted, had close ties to Yang. Zhang Jian's Association for Constitutional Preparations included Ruicheng (1863–1912), grandson of Qishan (1790?–1854), Lin Zexu's successor as imperial commissioner at Guangzhou during the First Opium War; he was to be the governor-general at Wuchang when the 1911 Revolution broke out. And one member of Liang Qichao's Political Information Institute in Beijing was Changfu, the imperial clansman who had studied police matters in Japan and been active there in the 1903 anti-Russian agitation.[17]

To influence the desultory official deliberations in Beijing, these three groups, first separately and then together, launched a historic lobbying effort. They found justification for their activism in Cixi's edict of 8 July 1907, which, in soliciting suggestions for constitutional reform, had opened up the channel of communications beyond those normally authorized to submit memorials. The campaign began in October with Yang Du's group, then still based in Tokyo, which sent a four-person delegation (including Hengjun) to Beijing with a petition claiming to represent the thousands of Chinese students in Japan. Their petition, addressed to the Censorate, urged the court to respond to China's external dangers and internal unrest by establishing a "popularly elected deliberative assembly" (*minxuan yiyuan*) and to do so within a year or two. Among its several advantages, such an assembly would help to overcome the differences between the banner people and "ordinary people" by equalizing the obligations and privileges of the two populations; it would also help to bring unity to China's five major ethnic groups—Manchus, Han, Mongols, Muslims, and Tibetans. Both ideas, of course, echoed the editorial stance of Hengjun's *Great Harmony Journal*.[18] Following the presentation of the petition, Hengjun, instead of returning to Japan, remained behind in the capital, where early in 1908 he founded a daily newspaper, the *Central Great Harmony Daily* (Zhongyang datong ribao), which, like its Tokyo namesake, favored constitutional-ism and an end to Manchu-Han differences.[19] (The Tokyo journal ceased pub-lication at the end of May.) By then, too, Yang Du had relocated to Beijing, where he and Hengjun established a branch of their Association for Consti-tutional Government.[20]

The Qing court tried to nip this incipient campaign in the bud, but with-out success. In late December 1907 Cixi issued two decrees within a day of each other that restated the traditional prohibition of students' and commoners' meddling in "national and political matters."[21] The edicts did not have the desired effect, as the petition movement gathered strength amidst news reports that high government officials were finally considering constitutionalism seri-ously. In early June 1908 members of the Bureau for the Implementation of Constitutional Government (Xianzheng Bianchaguan), the agency charged with overseeing the transition to the new regime, began meeting almost daily at the Yiheyuan Summer Palace, where Cixi and the Guangxu emperor were then in residence.[22] Moreover, what they were discussing was no longer whether to make the change but when. They were reportedly considering a wide range of dates, from five to twenty years. Pulun and Sun Jia'nai, the co-presidents of the National Assembly, noted, for example, that it had taken Japan nineteen years (1871–90) to convene its parliament.[23] To the constitutional reformers outside the government, nineteen years, or even five, was much too long. Zhang Jian's Association for Constitutional Preparations and Liang Qichao's Political Information Institute separately petitioned the bureau urging that Parliament be summoned no later than within two or three years.[24]

In late July and early August, Zhang Jian's Association for Constitutional Preparations finally took the initiative to coordinate the heretofore disorga-nized petition movement. The result was a series of similarly worded petitions from various provincial groups, who moreover began to converge on Beijing. This effort culminated on 11 August in a joint petition from these provincial delegations asking for an early parliament. Among the petitioners were a num-ber of Manchus. The delegation from the Eight Banners was headed by the imperial clansman Hengjun; the one from Zhili included Wuzesheng, his col-league from *Great Harmony Journal*; and the one from Jilin was headed by Songyu, who earlier had founded the Jilin Local Self-Government Society.[25]

The Qing court reacted to this unprecedented agitation by, on the one hand, cracking down and, on the other, making concessions. A couple of days after the joint petition, it issued a decree proscribing Liang Qichao's Political Information Institute, which it denounced as "claiming to research current affairs while conspiring to foment unrest," and ordering the arrest of its mem-bers. Two months later, on 11 October, it disbanded Songyu's Jilin Local Self-

Government Society because of its involvement in the petition movement.[26] The court did not, however, take action against the other two main organizations in the movement, Zhang Jian's Association for Constitutional Preparations and Yang Du's Association for Constitutional Government. To the contrary, it had by then managed to co-opt Yang into the Qing government. Previously, in April, on the joint recommendation of Grand Councilors Zhang Zhidong and Yuan Shikai, Yang was appointed a mid-level adviser to the Bureau for the Implementation of Constitutional Government. He was to remain a strong supporter of a constitutional monarchy down to the end of the dynasty.[27]

As Yang Du's appointment to a government post had perhaps foreshadowed, the Qing court also responded to the petition movement by yielding to some of its demands. On 27 August, two weeks after the joint petition, Cixi, in her own name, agreed for the first time to set a deadline for the realization of constitutionalism. She also gave her approval to two documents drawn up by the Bureau for the Implementation of Constitutional Government: the Constitutional Outline (Xianfa Dagang) and a nine-year plan for the formation of a "deliberative assembly" (*yiyuan*), in other words, a parliament. The Constitutional Outline included as one of its guiding principles "dissolution of the boundaries between Manchus and Han" (*ronghua Man-Han zhenyu*), and one of the tasks specified for the first year (1908) of the Nine-Year Plan was the creation of the Banner Reorganization Office (Biantong Qizhi Chu), whose dual missions were to arrange for the Eight Banners' livelihood and to eliminate Manchu-Han differences.[28] The nine-year timetable, of course, disappointed many of the petitioners, who had called for summoning Parliament within no more than two or three years, but Yang Du, who personally had pushed for a three-year schedule but who now spoke for the government, pleaded with them to give the court the benefit of the doubt.[29]

Cixi's edict approving the constitutional timetable was one of her last important acts, for she died less than three months later, on 15 November, one day after her nephew, the Guangxu emperor. Their deaths from the beginning spawned widespread suspicions of foul play. On the face of it, the youthful emperor's dying within one day of his aged captor stretches the limits of coincidence and credulity. It often has been suggested that the thirty-seven-year-old emperor was murdered—or, at the very least, his death hastened—so as to prevent him from outliving Cixi, regaining control of the court, and exacting revenge on her many supporters, particularly those (such as Yuan Shikai) who had sided with her against him during the 1898 coup.[30] Given the murderous climate of the Qing court under Cixi, such suspicions can easily be believed. Indeed, two scholars who examined the manuscript notebooks on the emperor's daily activities commented, in an aside, that "the notebooks for

1908 raise a mysterious question about the death of the Kuang-hsü [Guangxu] emperor, for he was reported officially as having been regularly attending Peking opera performances until only a few days before his death—apparently in fair health all along."[31] However, more recently, investigators with access to the emperor's original medical records, including the diagnoses and prescriptions of his various doctors, show rather convincingly that the emperor did die of natural causes and that he died at the time originally reported. He had been in ill health for at least a year and began to deteriorate in the spring of 1908. His doctors were pessimistic about his chances for recovery. From their diagnoses for the five days prior to his demise, there is no sign of any dramatic turn for the worse that might have indicated that he had been poisoned; he went into a coma around midnight on 13 November and died the following evening at his residence in the Forbidden City. The cause of death was progressive failure of heart and lungs.[32] In sum, there is no evidence to substantiate the rumors that the emperor actually died *after* the empress dowager and that he was done away with in order to keep him from regaining control of the court.

As the Guangxu emperor lay dying, Cixi, though in weak health herself, arranged for his succession. Such a last-minute decision was not at all unusual in the Qing dynasty. Since the Kangxi emperor's troubled experience in the early eighteenth century with a designated heir, each Qing ruler had delayed announcing a successor until the ruler was on his own deathbed. Like the Tongzhi emperor before him, the Guangxu emperor was childless. According to dynastic as well as Confucian custom, his successor was supposed to come from the following generation, that is, a member of the imperial clan whose given name began with the character *pu*. Cixi considered at least four candidates: Pulun, Puwei (1880–1937), an unnamed son of Zaizhen, and Puyi. Pulun, the National Assembly's co-president, was the oldest of the four; he had been considered once before, in 1875, as successor to the Tongzhi emperor. Puwei, twenty-eight years old, was Yixin's grandson, who on Yixin's death in 1898 had inherited his title as the second Prince Gong. Zaizhen's unnamed son, perhaps Puzhong (b. 1897), was, of course, a grandson of the influential prince Yikuang, but of the four he was the farthest removed from the deceased emperor. Finally, Puyi was the two-and-a-half-year-old son of Zaifeng.[33] Cixi, after consulting with most of the grand councilors, selected Puyi. According to information given to the British legation by Yuan Shikai, she made her decision on the morning of 13 November, as the emperor's condition worsened. That evening, in an edict issued in her own name, Cixi announced that Puyi would be brought into the palace to be raised and educated; an accompanying edict named his father, Zaifeng, as "prince regent" (*shezhengwang*). When the Guangxu emperor died the following day, Puyi became the eleventh ruler of the Qing dynasty. He was designated to succeed both the Guangxu and Tongzhi emperors.[34]

Cixi's selection of Puyi as emperor and his father as regent seems, in retrospect, to have been preordained. She had been exceptionally close to Puyi's grandfather, Yihuan, who was married to her younger sister and to whom she may have felt a debt of gratitude for having gone along in 1875 with her controversial choice of his son Zaitian as successor to the Tongzhi emperor. The selection of Zaitian had defied dynastic tradition and Confucian norms because he was of the same generation as his predecessor; nevertheless, it had allowed Cixi to renew her de facto regency and prolong her control of the court. Zaifeng himself, Puyi's father, was born in 1883, twelve years after the Guangxu emperor, who was his full brother. When Yihuan died in 1891, Zaifeng inherited his princedom, becoming the second Prince Chun. He first became politically prominent in 1901 when he was sent on the mission of apology to Germany. The following year he was married to Ronglu's daughter, who gave birth to Puyi, her first child, in February 1906. Immediately upon his birth, Puyi seemingly became the top candidate to succeed the Guangxu emperor. Indeed, even before he was born, Edmund Backhouse had prophesied to G. E. Morrison that "should Prince Ch'un unexpectedly have a son, he would be the heir."[35] It was after Puyi's birth that Zaifeng, then twenty-three years old, began his rapid political rise. He received his first substantive assignment six months later when he chaired the committee that reviewed the findings of the constitutional study commissioners. In May 1907 he was appointed, along with Grand Secretary Sun Jia'nai, to investigate the accusations of corruption and abuse of power that had been lodged against Yikuang and his son Zaizhen, as a result of which Zaizhen was dismissed as minister of agriculture, industry, and commerce. (Zaizhen's impeachment may have doomed his unnamed son's chance of being chosen emperor.)[36] A month later, on 19 June 1907, Zaifeng was appointed a probationary member of the Grand Council; he became a full member on 2 February 1908.[37] In other words, Zaifeng's political advancement seemingly foreshadowed the eventual choice of Puyi.

Puyi, in his autobiography, confirms that Cixi chose him primarily because of his father: like Yihuan before him, Zaifeng was expected to be so docile that she could continue "to listen to government from behind the screen." Puyi wrote, "I do not believe that she thought herself fatally ill on the day she proclaimed me successor to the throne." Zaifeng's younger brother, Zaitao (1887–1970), likewise suggests that Zaifeng, who supposedly was already known for his indecisiveness, was selected because as regent he would defer to her and allow her to govern as before.[38] Thus, on 14 November, right after Zaifeng's son was named emperor, Cixi added "administrator of the realm" (*jianguo*) to his day-old title of "prince regent" and empowered him, during his son's minority, to act on "all military and governmental matters." However, he was to do so only under her "instructions."[39] But then Cixi's own health gave out. On 15 November, in the early afternoon, she too died.

VACILLATION AND RETREAT

Zaifeng was regent for all but the last two months of his young son's three-year reign as the Xuantong emperor (see plate 8). It fell to him to try to follow through on the promises that Cixi had made in her last years about constitutional preparations and reform of Manchu-Han relations. During the first two years of the regency, Zaifeng performed reasonably well with regard to constitutional preparation but much less so on the Manchu-Han question.

Cixi's death freed Zaifeng from the constraints that she had imposed on his exercise of power. On 13 December 1908, one month after he took over, he issued a lengthy sixteen-point "protocol" (*lijie*) that spelled out in detail his prerogatives as regent. The second point of the protocol restated his authority, via the issuance of edicts, to decide on all matters of military and governmental affairs, including the appointment and dismissal and the reward and punishment of all officials, while the fifth point asserted his supreme command, as regent for the emperor, over all of the naval and military forces of the country. Nevertheless, extensive as his powers were, Zaifeng was obliged to share some authority at the Qing court with his sister-in-law, the widow of the former emperor, upon whom the epithet Longyu was later bestowed. Unlike Cixi, her aunt, Empress Dowager Longyu (1868–1913) was not allowed to "listen to government from behind the screen." But, according to the sixteen-point protocol, Zaifeng acknowledged that there might be some "weighty and major issues" where it would be incumbent upon him to solicit an edict from her; if so, only he and no one else was authorized to consult with her on such matters. Although Empress Dowager Longyu was to play a critical role during the last stages of the negotiations leading to the Qing abdication in 1912, until then she largely stayed in the background.[40]

The initial public reaction to the designation of Zaifeng as regent was positive among both foreigners and Chinese. According to E. G. Hillier, the Beijing agent of the Hong Kong and Shanghai Banking Corporation, Zaifeng was "a serious-minded young fellow, of clean life and irreproachable integrity, and full of sincere zeal for the good of his country." To Isaac Taylor Headland (1859–1942), an American missionary educator in Beijing, he was "the wisest choice that could be made at the present time." The American minister W. W. Rockhill (1854–1914) was equally impressed. He thought that Zaifeng had conducted his mission of apology to Germany in 1901 "with conspicuous ability and great dignity" and that during his recent, if brief, service on the Grand Council he had "shown sound judgment and been a strong advocate of liberal policies."[41]

Among the constitutionalist reformers, hopes ran high, especially when it seemed that Zaifeng intended (in the parlance of the later Communists) to "reverse verdicts" on the 1898 reforms. One of his first acts as regent was to get rid of Yuan Shikai, whose military support had been crucial to the success of Cixi's coup. Reportedly in fulfillment of his brother's deathbed command, Zaifeng on 2 January 1909 issued an edict abruptly relieving this powerful official of his posts on the Grand Council and at the Ministry of Foreign Affairs on the contrived excuse of a "foot ailment."[42] The dismissal of Yuan was followed by a purge of many of his supporters within the metropolitan and provincial bureaucracies. Xu Shichang, for example, was transferred in February from the important governor-generalship of Manchuria to become the minister of posts and communications; Zhao Bingjun, who had helped to reform the Beijing police, was dismissed in March as junior vice-minister of civil affairs. Yuan's influence over his old Beiyang Army was likewise diminished, as Tieliang's Ministry of the Army removed his protégés from command positions and replaced them with fellow graduates of the Japanese Army Officers School, such as Wu Luzhen (1880–1911), who had no personal allegiance to Yuan.[43] However, attempts to dislodge Yikuang, Yuan's strongest backer at court, from his many powerful positions failed. When Censor Jiang Chunlin in February boldly criticized Yikuang for numerous failings, Zaifeng's court denounced the accusations as baseless and demanded that they be retracted. When the censor refused, he was discharged. Yikuang, whose princedom had been elevated to one in perpetuity at the beginning of the regency, became more entrenched in power than ever before.[44]

The dismissal of Yuan Shikai and his cohorts was paralleled by a movement to rehabilitate politically those victims of the 1898 purge who were still under a cloud. Previously, in June 1904, Cixi had issued an edict pardoning all those involved in the "1898 affair," except Kang Youwei and Liang Qichao (along with Sun Yat-sen). Despite the edict, several officials, including Weng Tonghe (1830–1904; the Guangxu emperor's former tutor) and Chen Baozhen (1831–1900; the governor of Hunan), were not fully exonerated. In response to petitions from their defenders, in July 1909 and January 1910 Zaifeng issued edicts posthumously restoring Weng and Chen to their last official posts.[45] Similar efforts to secure a pardon for the main leaders of the 1898 reforms, Kang and Liang, were, however, unsuccessful. The initial opposition came from Zhang Zhidong, who had been as critical of the reforms as had Yuan Shikai. Zhang was the "certain grand councilor" whom the Manchu-founded anti-Cixi news-paper, *L'Impartial*, denounced in July 1909 for blocking a current move to reha-bilitate Kang and Liang. Even after Zhang died on 6 October and talk of a pardon revived, Zaifeng was unable or unwilling to push for this ultimate reversal of verdict on 1898, and therefore it did not happen. The translator (and by then national assemblyman) Yan Fu (1853–1921), writing to G. E. Morrison a month after the start of the 1911 Revolution, thought that Zaifeng's failure at the begin-ning of his regency to grant amnesty to Kang and Liang and allow them to return to China had been a monumental mistake because it dampened the enthusiasm of the constitutionalist reformers. If he had acted otherwise, Yan wrote, "nothing of the present revolt could happen."[46] Thus, Zaifeng's han-dling of this controversy involving the 1898 reformers was one indication of his indecisiveness, which his brother Zaitao claimed was why Cixi had selected him as regent in the first place and which was to characterize much of the rest of his three-year rule.

If the constitutionalist reformers were discouraged by Zaifeng's irresolu-tion about pardoning Kang and Liang, they were, on the other hand, heart-ened by his adherence to Cixi's Nine-Year Plan for constitutional reform, which he publicly reaffirmed on 3 December 1908, less than three weeks after he took power.[47] In 1909, as required by the plan, he ordered the establishment of the provincial assemblies, which were elected in a two-stage process that summer and which met for the first time in all provinces (except Xinjiang) on 14 October. A year later, on 3 October 1910, as the provincial assemblies began their sec-ond annual session, Zaifeng, again as scheduled, convened the first meeting of the National Assembly.

The provincial assemblies and the National Assembly that were formed in 1909–10 involved the banner people no less than the rest of the population, and, once convened, they provided an additional forum for the discussion of Manchu-Han issues. The assemblies were organized at a time when, as the drafters of the regulations for the provincial assemblies noted, the court had promised "to do away with Manchu-Han differences and to abolish the ban-ner system in the future." Should there be special provisions, then, to ensure that the minority Manchu population would be represented? The drafters decided to treat Manchuria and China proper differently. In the three north-eastern provinces, "the banner people and the Han ought to be dealt with alike"; therefore, no seats were reserved in those assemblies for the numerous Manchus in the region "in order to set an example for the elimination of [Manchu-Han] differences." In those provinces of China proper with banner garrisons, however, additional seats were created for the local banner popu-lace. Thus, the 140–member assembly for Zhili Province was allotted ten extra representatives for the Metropolitan Banners as well as an additional two for Miyun, the largest of the capital region garrisons; assemblies in other provinces were similarly allocated one to three extra seats to be elected from the garrisons. These special seats, according to the regulations, were supposed to be only a "temporary" expedient. Nevertheless, Meng Sen (1868–1938), editor of the Shanghai reformist journal *Eastern Miscellany*, criticized them as harmful to the fostering of "a sense of commonality between banner people and Han" and likely to cast doubt on the court's stated intention of reorganizing the banner system.[48]

Within China proper, the election of the assemblymen from the banner garrisons in 1909 was basically the same as that among the general populace. The educational and financial qualifications for voting and serving were the same for both the banner people and the civilian population; also, the elections at a banner garrison were generally held at the same time as those of the neighboring jurisdiction. There was, however, a tremendous difference between the two in the ratio between the electorate and the elected. In Guangdong Province, for example, the ratio was 1,556 voters to each assemblyman; in the Guangzhou garrison, it was 123 voters.[49] In short, the Manchus were greatly overrepresented within China proper. On the other hand, in Manchuria, where the electoral process did not distinguish between banner and non-banner people, Manchu representation in the assemblies may have been more in line with the relative size of their population. From their Manchu-style names it would appear that perhaps as many as seven of the fifty-three people elected to the Fengtian assembly were bannermen; similarly, six of the thirty representatives in Jilin and five of the thirty in Heilongjiang may also have been Manchus.[50]

Finally, the social background of the Manchu assemblymen was similar to that of their Han colleagues. Many were members of the scholar-official elite. The three bannermen in the Shandong assembly—two from the Qingzhou garrison and one from Dezhou—were all licentiates. Similarly, according to unpublished documents in the archives of the Bureau for the Implementation of Constitutional Government, the one representative elected to the Henan assembly from the Kaifeng garrison was a regular provincial degree holder; both of those elected to the Sichuan assembly from the Chengdu garrison were provincial degree holders, one from the literary examinations and the other from the translation examinations; and the three elected to the Fujian assembly from the Fuzhou garrison included a regular provincial degree holder, a translation provincial degree holder, and a licentiate. The twelve Manchus in the Zhili assembly were composed of one provincial degree holder, six licentiates, one school graduate, and four low-ranking metropolitan officials (three Manchu-language scribes and one ceremonial usher).[51]

When the provincial assemblies convened for their first session in October 1909, some of them took advantage of this new arena for public debate and included on their agenda issues relating to Manchu-Han relations. The Shandong assembly considered a "vocational plan to mitigate Manchu-Han differences and enhance the banner people's livelihood." The Zhejiang assembly debated, and defeated, a proposal to turn wasteland held by the Hangzhou garrison into a marketplace. The Zhili assembly discussed and agreed not to reserve any places on its standing committee, which conducted the assembly's business between annual sessions, for its twelve Manchu members; the stated reason was "to eliminate [Manchu-Han] differences."[52] The most acrimonious Manchu-Han dispute during the first session of the provincial assemblies occurred in Guangdong. The controversy, perhaps similar in content to the one in Zhejiang, centered on the erection by some banner personnel of a market in the drill field in front of the new provincial assembly hall. One of the assembly's three Manchus, the Hanjun Cuizhen, defended the market as a worthwhile effort to promote the banner population's livelihood. Other assemblymen complained that it obstructed access to the assembly hall and demanded its removal. Some also argued that the drill field on which the market was located was public land and ought not to have been used for the sole benefit of the banner people; they contended that such a private venture on public property ran counter to the court's current policy of "eliminating [Manchu-Han] differences" and warned darkly that if the garrison insisted on making a distinction between Manchus and Han, then "the future of China may not be what the banner people wish." In the end, all of the twenty-seven assemblymen present, except Cuizhen, voted against the market. The garrison authorities later agreed to relocate it elsewhere.[53]

Whereas Manchus were only a small (but over-represented) minority among the provincial assemblymen, they made up a much larger proportion (though still a minority) of the National Assembly. According to the regulations, half of the assembly's two hundred members were to be designated by the emperor and half by the provincial assemblies. The imperial appointees, whom Zaifeng named in May 1910, were drawn from seven categories of people and were composed of thirty-eight Manchus, forty-six Han, and fourteen others. The thirty-eight Manchus included fourteen "hereditary princes of the blood" (*zongshi wanggong shijue*; e.g., Yikuang's disgraced son Zaizhen), six other "members of the imperial lineage" (*zongshi jueluo*), seven of the twelve "Manchus and Han holding hereditary titles" (*Man-Han shijue*), and eleven of the thirty-two mid-level metropolitan officials. (One of these officials was the imperial clansman Changfu, a department director at the Ministry of Foreign Affairs; he had studied police matters in Japan in 1901 and had been a member of Liang Qichao's Political Information Institute in 1907–8 before it was banned.) The forty-six Han assemblymen who were imperially appointed included five holders of hereditary titles, twenty-one mid-level metropolitan officials, ten "eminent scholars" (e.g., the jurist Shen Jiaben and the translator Yan Fu), and ten large taxpayers. The fourteen "others" were Mongols, Muslims, and Tibetans who were "hereditary princes of the outer dependencies" (*waifan wanggong shijue*). As for the one hundred national assemblymen who were selected by the provincial assemblies, perhaps only three were, judging from their names, Manchus—one from each of the three northeastern provinces. Together with co-president Pulun, Manchus accounted for forty-two of the two hundred members of the National Assembly. It may be noted, as did Jinliang, the young reform-minded Manchu bannerman from Hangzhou, with a trace of bitterness, that the seven status categories that were allotted seats in the National Assembly as imperial appointees did not include the Eight Banners; thus, the bannermen in the National Assembly, unlike those in the provincial assemblies, were representatives of some other constituency.[54]

If Zaifeng may be credited with adhering to Cixi's timetable for constitutional preparations, he was far less scrupulous about following through on her concomitant pledge to "abolish Manchu-Han differences." Cixi, in the last year or so of her life, had committed the Qing court to four sets of reforms in Manchu-Han relations: it would set up in the first year of the Nine-Year Plan a Banner Reorganization Office; it would phase out the banner soldiers' stipends in the provincial garrisons and resettle the soldiers and their dependents on nearby farmland as a long-term solution to the "Eight Banners' livelihood problem"; it would eventually disband the provincial garrisons and perhaps ultimately dissolve the Eight Banner system altogether; and finally, it would eliminate existing social and legal differences between Manchus and Han.

In dealing with Manchu-Han relations, Zaifeng got off to a quick and seemingly promising start. On 17 December 1908, one month after taking charge, he created the Banner Reorganization Office, thus meeting the deadline for its establishment. The main goals of the office were to "provide for the Eight Banners' livelihood" and to "eliminate Manchu-Han differences" by no later than 1915. To supervise its work in consultation with the Grand Council, he appointed Pulun, Zaize, Natong, and three other leading Manchu officials. He urged them not to tarry.[55] However, the Banner Reorganization Office, once founded, was largely inactive. Soon after it was set up, it rehashed some old ideas for reducing Manchu-Han differences, such as making Manchu men's names more like Han names and encouraging Manchu-Han intermarriage. The office also sent out directives to various banner units requesting an up-to-date census of their personnel and an accounting of their land holdings, both of which would be needed if and when their banner soldiers were resettled. It reportedly urged each garrison to establish its own Banner Affairs Office as well. It did hardly anything more. *Eastern Miscellany*, which closely monitored the course of constitutional reforms, reported month after month little to no progress at the office. On more than one occasion, even the regent was said to have been discouraged at its slow pace of work.[56]

Yet, if anyone was to be blamed for the inactivity of the office, it was Zaifeng himself, because after fulfilling the first of Cixi's four promised reforms in Manchu-Han relations, he proceeded to gut the others and left the agency with nothing to do. His edict of 17 December 1908 creating the Banner Reorganization Office had caused considerable consternation among the banner population, who once again were worried that the banner soldiers' stipends would soon stop. Whereas in late 1907 Cixi, in the face of similar anxiety, had stood firm, Zaifeng hurriedly backed off. Nine days later, on 26 December, he issued another edict stating that his previous decree had not been entirely "clear." He now wished to assure the banner people that distribution of their stipends of money and grain would continue indefinitely. Rather than curbing the stipends, he told them, the Banner Reorganization Office should focus on finding ways of "nurturing" the banner soldiers' "self-strength and self-reliance" (*ziqiang zili*).[57]

Armed with such vague instructions, the Banner Reorganization Office, not surprisingly, provided no leadership in solving the long-standing "Eight Banners' livelihood problem," the second of Cixi's four promised reforms, but instead left the problem in the lap of the local banner authorities. In one instance, General Qingrui of the Nanjing garrison, pressed by a lack of funds in his treasury, seemed to have thought about implementing Cixi's idea on his own. In April 1909 he drafted a set of regulations terminating the disbursement of rations to his banner soldiers and ordering them to set up "agricultural colonies" where they could make their own living. However, when news of these regulations spread to other garrisons, they caused an uproar. The "gentry and students" at the Hangzhou garrison sent a telegram to Qingrui voicing their fear lest by his actions their country's "sublime policy" (of eliminating Manchu-Han differences?) turn into a "tragedy of racial extinction" (*mie zhong zhi canhuo*). Qingrui, in response, reassured his critics that the controversial regulations were only a draft and had not, in fact, been promulgated.[58]

Elsewhere, both in Beijing and in the provincial garrisons, local banner officials as well as private individuals attempted a variety of programs to alleviate the banner population's continuing, indeed worsening, economic hardships. As before, these programs typically involved vocational education, military retraining, and resettlement. In Beijing, for example, Shaoying, the former constitutional study commissioner whose injury from Wu Yue's assassination attempt had kept him from making the tour and who was now the senior vice-minister of finance, solicited funds—including funds from the Ministry of Agriculture, Industry, and Commerce—to establish an industrial workshop for banner women. Located near the southwest corner of the Inner City, the Capital Number One Women's Factory (Shoushan Diyi Nü Gongchang) began operation in January 1909. It offered two tuition-free courses, each enrolling eighty applicants. One was a three-year comprehensive course for twelve- to fifteen-year-old girls; the other, a one-year accelerated course for those who were sixteen to twenty-five. Graduates of both courses could either teach at other vocational schools or stay on at the factory to work.[59]

The most ambitious and systematic local effort at banner reform at this time took place in Fengtian, where Governors-General Xu Shichang and Xiliang had put Jinliang, the Manchu from Hangzhou, in charge of the provincial Banner Affairs Office.[60] Under Jinliang, the office established workshops in different garrison towns throughout Fengtian offering year-long and half-year training courses to the banner population in a variety of useful crafts. The main workshop, set up in early 1909 in Shengjing, enrolled five hundred young male apprentices, while a branch shop in Jinzhou trained another hundred bannermen from the Liaoxi corridor. Two years later it was proposed that two additional workshops be founded in Liaoyang and Niuzhuang for bannermen living in those parts of the province. Meanwhile, in Shengjing, a "training institute for banner women workers" was similarly instructing one hundred women in rug weaving, knitting, sewing, and brocading. The women's institute was such an immediate success that a few months later it was slated to be relocated and expanded.[61] Aside from vocational schools, Jinliang also proposed the establishment in Shengjing of a Manchu- and Mongol-language middle school that, beginning in the spring of 1910, would enroll two hundred students from among the banner population.[62] Although military reform was not part of Jinliang's duties, he nevertheless found an excuse—that the security at the three imperial mausoleums near Shengjing needed to be improved—in order to recruit and train one regiment of banner soldiers. He insisted that, as in the New Army, these recruits be school graduates; he later claimed that they became the best-trained soldiers in Shengjing.[63] The Fengtian Banner Affairs Office under Jinliang also fostered resettlement: as a pilot project, perhaps in 1910, it sent three hundred banner households to the slopes of Changbaishan, in newly organized Antu County, Jilin, and gave each household three "sections" (*jian*) of housing, five hundred *mu* (eighty acres) of land, fodder, and seeds, as well as travel expenses.[64] Finally, Jinliang's office in 1911 attempted to establish in

Shengjing an Eight Banner Industrial Development Bank, but it was not so well capitalized from the sale of banner land as he had hoped.[65]

Zaifeng's edict of "clarification" on 26 December 1908 represented a retreat not only from Cixi's promise to solve the "Eight Banners' livelihood problem" but also from her third promise, to disband the provincial garrisons and perhaps the banner system itself. The retreat worried *Central Great Harmony Daily*, the reformist newspaper in Beijing founded by the same group of Manchus who had published *Great Harmony Journal* in Tokyo. In a commentary addressed to the Banner Reorganization Office, the paper conceded that the continuation of the stipends might have been politically necessary in order to pacify the disgruntled banner population, but it hoped that this action would not delay the abolition of the banner system. Like its Tokyo-based predecessor, *Central Great Harmony Daily* contended that the dismantling of the Eight Banners was a prerequisite for the realization of constitutionalism; if the banner system were not done away with promptly, then Manchu-Han differences would not be eliminated by the end of the Nine-Year Plan, as called for by the plan.[66] Such criticisms had no visible effect on the Banner Reorganization Office.

Finally, with regard to the elimination of Manchu-Han differences (the last of Cixi's four promised reforms), Zaifeng's performance was equally spotty. For example, he continued and extended Cixi's administrative changes in Manchuria by abolishing most of the remaining brigade-general posts. As a result, the banner population in the northeast, who previously had been governed by their own hierarchy of banner officials, now came under the jurisdiction of the new regular civilian administration. As with its three provincial assemblies, where banner people were given no special considerations, Manchuria was supposed to set an example in Manchu-Han relations for the rest of China. In this instance, however, Zaifeng did not go much beyond what Cixi had already done, because the reforms in the northeast were not extended into China proper, where no administrative positions in the provincial garrisons were eliminated.[67]

In another instance, Zaifeng not only did not go beyond Cixi, but he backed off. In January 1908 Cixi had endorsed the recommendation of the Commissioners for Revising and Codifying the Laws to put most banner people under the jurisdiction of the new court system and to subject them to the same legal treatment as the civilian population. Zaifeng went along with this important reform, but then failed to follow through on Cixi's policy with regard to members of the imperial lineage. Taking note of their exalted status, the legal commissioners had proposed—and Cixi had agreed—that as a temporary measure, members of the imperial lineage would be exempt from the jurisdiction of the local-level civilian courts and instead would have their legal cases decided directly by the Supreme Court of Justice. In mid-1910, however, the Imperial Clan Court objected to turning over its control of the imperial lineage to the Supreme Court. Zaifeng caved in to those objections and actually reversed Cixi's decision (as well as a previous decree of his own) sanctioning the legal commissioners' original plan. Consequently, members of the imperial lineage remained under the Imperial Clan Court, where they were, of course, treated differently not only from the Han but from other banner people as well.[68]

Unlike the legal commissioners, who had responded promptly to Cixi's request for proposals to reduce Manchu-Han differences, the Ministry of Rites had dragged its feet because of internal dissension; it was unable to come up with any proposal until 25 March 1909, when it memorialized with regard to the mourning period. Noting that the ban on Manchu-Han intermarriage had been lifted, that ethnic slots had been (partially) abolished, and that the banner system was to be reorganized, the ministry asserted (with dubious accuracy) that the only remaining Manchu-Han difference was the length of the mourning period, which was twenty-seven months for Han officials and one hundred days for Manchus. Previously, the leaders of the ministry had been split on the issue, with the Manchu minister favoring the Manchu custom and his two Han vice-ministers opposed. In the end the two Han officials evidently prevailed, because the ministry's memorial recommended that all officials follow the Han custom and be required to mourn for twenty-seven months. Zaifeng's edict of the same day, approving the ministry's recommendation, ordered that henceforth all officials in mourning, whether Manchus or Han, should resign their posts for the duration of their twenty-seven months' mourning period. At least three Manchu officials promptly quit in order to comply with the new policy.[69]

Once again, however, Zaifeng, having made a decision, began to back off right away. In the very same edict that approved the uniform length of mourning, he introduced a major loophole: he declared that officials in essential posts might request an exemption. Many officials, as a result, petitioned for and were granted permission to remain in office while in mourning. While at least one of them (Wang Shizhen) was a Han, most were Manchus, among whom were Natong (the grand councilor) and Yulang (commandant of the Metropolitan Banners Infantry Division).[70] It thus appears that Zaifeng's decree calling for a uniform mourning period for Manchus and Han had no real effect upon most officials. With some exceptions on both sides, most bannermen, taking advantage of the loophole, were allowed to follow the old Manchu practice of mourning for only one hundred days, while most Han officials, as before, resigned their posts and mourned for twenty-seven months.

Concerning the term of address used by officials to refer to themselves in memorials to the throne, Zaifeng adopted a stance that was similarly inconsistent. On 10 March 1910 he issued an edict that all officials, whether metropolitan or provincial, Manchu or Han, civil or military, should henceforth style themselves in the Han fashion as "your minister." This change, he explained, would "eliminate partiality" at this time of constitutional preparations as well as demonstrate the court's regard for uniformity and universality. As before, Zaifeng vitiated the reform almost at once. On the very next day he issued another, somewhat confusing, edict stating that, in certain situations, "Manchu officials [Manyuan] should still refer to themselves as *aha* ["slave," in Manchu]."[71] Though Manchus thereafter generally referred to themselves as ministers and no longer as slaves, nevertheless the distinction between Manchus and Han with regard to the form of self-address had not been, contrary to Zaifeng's original edict, entirely eliminated.

In sum, in the first two years of his regency Zaifeng repeatedly expressed a willingness to abide by Cixi's general promise, as stated in the Nine-Year Plan, to solve the "Eight Banners' livelihood problem" and to eliminate Manchu-Han differences, and he did in fact carry out the first of her four specific aims (and, along the way, comply with the requirements of the constitutional timetable) by establishing the Banner Reorganization Office in late 1908. As for her other three aims, Zaifeng's accomplishments were extremely limited. He backed off from Cixi's stated intention of phasing out the banner soldiers' stipends. He evinced no interest in disbanding the provincial garrisons, let alone the entire banner system. And he did very little toward eliminating Manchu-Han differences. At best, he continued reforms already begun by Cixi; he introduced few innovations of his own. At worst, he undid some of what Cixi had initiated. With such an unenviable record of inaction, it is hard to disagree with his detractors' opinion that Zaifeng's major problem was his indecisiveness, his capacity to contradict himself with seeming disregard, his tendency to bend with the wind. However, as we shall soon see, the prince regent could be very determined and focused on other issues when he wanted to be.

REIMPERIALIZATION OF MILITARY AND POLITICAL AUTHORITY

One main purpose of Cixi's New Policies, as Enming's assassin Xu Xilin and other critics had pointed out, was to recentralize political and military authority, to reverse the half-century drift of power away from Beijing to the provinces dating from the suppression of the Taiping Rebellion. The high point of Cixi's recentralization effort came in late 1906 when Zhili governor-general Yuan Shikai was forced to turn four of the six Beiyang divisions that he had personally organized and trained over to the Ministry of the Army. However, while this transfer of control clearly enhanced the authority of the central government, it did not necessarily strengthen the imperial court. For its own protection, for instance, the Qing still relied upon an ad hoc palace guard that was drawn from the First Division, which, though predominantly Manchu in personnel, was nevertheless controlled by the Ministry of the Army and not the court. Upon becoming regent, Zaifeng set about not only to recentralize authority but also to "reimperialize" it. Reimperialization, too, had begun under Cixi—who, beginning in the 1860s, had reversed the mid-Qing tradition of princely abstention from state affairs—but it greatly accelerated under Zaifeng. He reorganized the top command of China's armed forces, created a new palace guard, and revitalized the navy, all under his direct control. As he did so, he leaned heavily on a coterie of Manchus, including such imperial kinsmen as his two half-brothers, Zaixun (1885–1949) and Zaitao, who were even younger and less experienced than he. So dependent was he upon these bannermen that contemporary diplomats and journalists as well as later historians speak of a "Manchu ascendency" and a "Manchu cabal." Yet Zaifeng was deterred neither by these criticisms nor by a rash of assassination attempts, including one on himself. His determination to stick to this unpopular course of action stood in sharp contrast to his irresolution in the handling of Manchu-Han issues.

Like Cixi, Zaifeng was intent on recentralizing authority, particularly over the military. Thus, on 26 September 1910, he issued an edict that extended the control of the Ministry of the Army over all six Beiyang divisions. Previously, the ministry, by way of the Metropolitan Training Office headed by Tieliang's Hanjun protégé Fengshan, had controlled only the four divisions (the First and Sixth in Beijing, the Third in Manchuria, and the Fifth in Shandong) that Yuan Shikai had turned over in 1906. The Second and Fourth Divisions, in Zhili, had remained under the jurisdiction of the local governor-general, even after Yuan had been called to Beijing and then subsequently dismissed. Zaifeng's edict of September 1910 put all six divisions under the "direct control" of the Ministry of the Army. The Metropolitan Training Office was abolished, and its head, Fengshan, was sent off to Jingzhou and then to Guangzhou, where he was later killed by revolutionaries.[72]

Zaifeng, however, wanted to reconcentrate authority not simply in the central government but in the court as well. According to the Constitutional Outline promulgated by Cixi, one of the prerogatives of the emperor was to "command the army and navy and to design the military system." The outline further stated that "the emperor possesses total authority to dispatch the military forces of the entire nation and to specify the number of regular soldiers" and that "the [future] parliament absolutely must not interfere in any military matter."[73]

When Zaifeng became regent, he immediately reasserted the emperor's (hence his own) claim to be the supreme military commander. Thus, the sixteen-point protocol issued by the court on 13 December 1908 enumerating the rights and duties of the regent reiterated that

> the emperor possesses the authority to command the naval and military forces of the entire nation. Whatever authority regarding military affairs the Constitutional Outline specified for the emperor is entrusted to the prince regent. The prince regent may control and assign all banner and Green Standard units and all naval and military troops, whether in the capital or in the provinces.[74]

According to the subsequent testimony of both his brother and his son, Zaifeng's interest in and concern with the role of the emperor as supreme commander dated from his 1901 mission of apology to Germany, where he was exposed to the Prussian command structure, in which the military was directly controlled by the emperor. During his three weeks in Germany (which turned out to be his only travel outside China), Zaifeng observed several military reviews, in one of which both Kaiser Wilhelm and Prince Heinrich personally participated. He came away greatly impressed by the notion that the imperial family should play a direct and active part in military matters.[75]

Empowered by Cixi's Constitutional Outline and persuaded by his Prussian mentors, Zaifeng proceeded to assert the court's authority over China's armed forces. On 15 July 1909 he designated himself, during the emperor's minority, as the acting generalissimo (*dayuanshuai*) of the army and navy of the Great Qing Empire (Da-Qing Diguo). This prompted widespread criticisms. Grand Councilor Zhang Zhidong, shortly before his death, reportedly protested that it would concentrate all military power in the regent's hands, while Meng Sen, editor of the *Eastern Miscellany*, commented that the decree was superfluous since the monarch's authority in China was theoretically unlimited anyway. Meng compared Zaifeng unflatteringly to such previous would-be strongmen as Wuzong, an irresponsible, fun-loving ruler of the mid-Ming with an inordinate interest in the military.[76]

On the same date, to assist him in his added responsibility, the regent revamped the military command structure by converting the General Staff Council (Junzichu) from the French to the Prussian model. Previously, the council, founded in November 1906, was subordinate to the Ministry of the Army and headed by two military professionals, Feng Guozhang and Ha Hanzhang. Feng, a former military underling of Yuan Shikai, was then the superintendent of the Nobles Military School, while Ha was a graduate of the Japanese

Army Officers School. When Zaifeng transformed the council to the Prussian model, he brought it under the direct authority of the emperor, making it independent of and superior to the Ministry of the Army, and he superimposed upon the council's existing staff two new "directors" (*guanli dachen*), Yulang and Zaitao, imperial princes with little or no military experience. Yulang, the former head of the Beijing Inner City's police, had risen on the death of his father in 1907 from a ninth-rank noble to a third-rank prince; he was one of those officials granted an exemption from the newly enacted universal mourning period of twenty-seven months. Zaitao, also a third-rank prince, was the regent's half-brother; his only prior military "experience" was the auditing of classes at Feng's Nobles Military School. (To make way for Zaitao to take control of the army, Yikuang resigned as supervisor of the Ministry of the Army.) Feng Guozhang and Ha Hanzhang, the council's incumbent leaders, were retained, but they now answered to the two princes. In thus restructuring the General Staff Council, Zaifeng was guided by not only Hohenzollern Germany but also Meiji Japan, which had made a similar shift from the French to the Prussian military system in the late 1870s.[77]

When he reorganized the General Staff, Zaifeng had already set in motion a related plan to create a new, separate palace guard that would also be under his personal control. Since the collapse of the Metropolitan Banners during the Boxer troubles, the court had first depended for security on the Sixth Division and then on the First, which patrolled the palace precincts on a rotating basis. However, the First Division, though predominantly Manchu, was never intended as a permanent palace guard. As early as December 1905, the Board of War had made it clear that a new palace guard should be created apart from the First Division. During the next three years, there were recurrent press reports that Cixi's court was about to organize such a guard.[78] But nothing happened until Zaifeng became regent, when on 25 December 1908, in one of his very first acts, he ordered the formation of the new Palace Guard (Jinweijun).[79]

Unlike the ad hoc palace guard from the First Division, the new Palace Guard was to be independent of the Ministry of the Army and under the direct command of the regent. A special training commission was set up to oversee its establishment. The original commission was composed of the two imperial princes, Yulang and Zaitao, who six months later were to be named directors of the General Staff Council, along with army minister Tieliang. Yulang's limited and Zaitao's nonexistent military experience have already been noted. Only Tieliang, a Manchu commoner, was truly qualified in military matters. Yet, despite his military background and a proven record of advancing Manchu interests that had earned him the particular enmity of such anti-Manchu revolutionaries as Wu Yue and Xu Xilin, Tieliang's tenure as a Palace Guard training commissioner lasted less than two months. On 19 February 1909, ostensibly so that he could help revitalize the navy, Tieliang was dropped from the commission. Zaifu (1887–1933), a noble of the ninth rank, who was Yikuang's second son, eventually took Tieliang's place, but he was never very active. As a result, the work of overseeing the organization of the new Palace Guard was borne largely by Zaitao and Yulang, especially Zaitao after August 1910, when Yulang, on his appointment to the Grand Council, was removed from the Palace Guard commission (but not the General Staff Council).[80] Subordinate to the commissioners, and to a great extent remedying their lack of expertise, were six staff members. The highest ranking among them was Putong (1871–1952), a ninth-rank noble, a brother of the National Assembly co-president Pulun, who seems to have been no more than a figurehead. He achieved minor (and fleeting) fame when a couple of years later he helped Yan Fu, then of the Ministry of the Navy, compose the new dynastic anthem. Of the other five members of the Palace Guard commission staff, two—Xu Zhishan and Tian Xianzhang—were products of the civil service examination system, and three—Ha Hanzhang, Zhang Yujun, and Wenhua—were graduates of the Japanese Army Officers School. All five had previously served either at the Ministry of the Army or on the old General Staff Council. Thus, unlike the commission itself, the training staff was (except for Putong) composed of experienced military personnel, and only Putong and Wenhua were Manchus.[81]

The Palace Guard commissioners quickly formulated a plan to create a division-strength force modeled on the post-Boxer New Army. They also sketched out a two-year timetable, which was divided into four stages, each lasting half a year and each devoted mainly to organizing one infantry regiment and one cavalry division. The process would begin at once and, if all went well, would be completed by January 1911.[82] The regent's edict had specified that the Palace Guard would be recruited from among the banner soldiers. This prompted criticisms, for example in the *Peking Times* (Shuntian shibao) in January 1909, that an all-banner force would run counter to various recent efforts by the court to eliminate Manchu-Han differences. Ignoring such comments, the commissioners decided that the rank and file would be recruited from the banner divisions and garrisons in the Beijing area, and the noncommissioned officers from the predominantly Manchu First Division. The commanding officers, however, would be selected without ethnic distinction.[83]

The Palace Guard commissioners were able to stick to their plan with regard to the timetable but not, in the end, to the ethnic composition of the force. To form the infantry regiment and cavalry division specified in the first stage of recruitment, they simply went to the First Division and, by prior arrangement with Tieliang and the Ministry of the Army, stripped it of all the soldiers and officers required. (The First Division subsequently replenished its depleted ranks with new banner recruits.)[84] During the second and third stages of recruitment in late 1909 and early 1910, the commissioners recruited among the banner population in the metropolitan area following the same procedure that Yuan Shikai and Tieliang had used in organizing the First Division. They circulated among the banner divisions and garrisons a set of their requirements and solicited lists of qualified candidates. Nominees were supposed to be between seventeen and twenty-five years old, of a minimum height, and of a clean family background, with no addictions, "hidden illnesses," or criminal record.[85] However, because of increasing difficulty in attracting able banner personnel, when the fourth and final stage of recruitment was upon them in the last half of 1910, the commissioners were obliged to depart from their original plan. In the name of "impartiality" (*tongren*), they opened up the ranks of the Palace Guard to non-bannermen. They recruited the fourth infantry regiment from among the Han population of Shuntian, the metropolitan prefecture, and the two nearby provinces of Zhili and Shandong, and a new cavalry division from among the Mongol herders of Inner Mongolia.[86] As a result, the Palace Guard, though still predominantly Manchu in makeup, was no longer the all-banner unit that the regent had originally envisaged.

Officers for the Palace Guard came from several different sources. The six Beiyang divisions were one source. During the first stage of recruitment, the First Division provided the Guard with not only its soldiers but its officers as well. Subsequently, a wider range of units, both banner and non-banner, was canvassed. Even so, most of those who passed the written qualifying examinations evidently came from the six Beiyang units, with a disproportionate number still coming from the First Division. In June 1910, when twenty-two battalion-level officers were chosen by examination, ten were from the First Division; the other twelve were about equally divided among the Second, Fourth, and Fifth Divisions.[87] Returned military students were another source of officers. At the end of 1909 the Palace Guard brigade commander was able to secure the services of eighteen graduates of foreign (probably Japanese) military academies. Similarly, a year later Commissioner Zaitao selected for the Guard twenty out of one hundred returned military students.[88] A third source was China's own Nobles Military School, which graduated its first class in July 1909, just as the new Palace Guard was being formed. Of its ninety-eight graduates, ten were assigned immediately to the Guard.[89] (The following year, the Nobles Military School enrolled a second class, with 240 students in a five-year course. The new superintendent of the school, succeeding Feng Guozhang, was

Grand Councilor Natong's brother, Najin; replacing Yikuang as overseer was another imperial prince, Zairun [1878–1963].)[90]

Palace Guard officers, unlike the soldiers, were supposed to have been chosen without ethnic distinction. In practice, there was, as among the rank and file, a pronounced preference for Manchus. The ten graduates of the Nobles Military School who were assigned to the Guard all had Manchu-style names; so did the ten officers from the First Division who were picked by examination in 1910. Also, the contingent of foreign military graduates who were sent to the Palace Guard at the end of 1909 was headed by Shiming, of the Japanese Army Officers School, who was probably a bannerman; although in the end Shiming himself was excused from reporting for duty, most or all of the eighteen who did show up were quite possibly bannermen as well. According to the recollections of the late-Qing military commander Yun Baohui, a majority of the company and platoon leaders in the Palace Guard were Manchus.[91]

Manchus figured prominently among the Palace Guard's top command as well. Because Prince Regent Zaifeng himself was nominally its supreme leader, the Guard did not have an overall division commander. Its highest ranking officers— Liangbi and Wang Tingzhen, one a Manchu and the other a Han— were the commanders of its two constituent brigades. Liangbi, it may be recalled, was a collateral member of the imperial lineage from the Jingzhou (Hubei) garrison and a graduate of the Japanese Army Officers School. He had become a close associate of Tieliang and indeed was thought by revolutionaries such as Wu Yue to be the mastermind behind the army minister's alleged pro-Manchu, anti-Han policy; by 1907 he was head of the Department of Military Education in the ministry. In 1909 Liangbi was appointed commander of the Palace Guard's First Infantry Regiment and then of the First Brigade, as these units were organized. Wang Tingzhen was likewise a product of the Japanese Army Officers School, a 1902 graduate of the cavalry class; on his return to China, he had become chief of staff of the First Division. In the Palace Guard, he was initially commander of the First Cavalry Division and then, in late 1910, of the newly formed Second Brigade. Of the two, Liangbi was by far the more influential. Not only did he, as commander of the First Brigade, have seniority over Wang Tingzhen, but also, as an imperial kinsman, he worked very closely with the Palace Guard commissioner, Zaitao. He thus accompanied Zaitao during the latter's five-month military tour of Japan, the United States, and Europe in mid-1910. As advisor to the inexperienced Zaitao, he wielded enormous influence over both the Palace Guard and the General Staff Council.[92] Below Liangbi and Wang Tingzhen were the five regimental commanders, three of whom were Manchus. The four infantry regiments were commanded by, respectively, Zhonghe (or Guan Zhonghe), Chongen (or, as he is also identified,

Chonglin), Zhalafen, and Tian Xianzhang. The only non-bannerman among them, Tian Xianzhang, who was formerly with the Palace Guard training staff, led the one infantry regiment that was made up of Han recruits. The commander of the cavalry regiment, following Wang Tingzhen's promotion, was Hua Zhenji, probably another Han.[93]

After two years, the Palace Guard reached full strength in early 1911, only a couple of months behind schedule. On 26 March the entire division, two brigades strong, conducted a full-scale review at its temporary encampment at Nanyuan, the imperial park to the south of the capital. (It was due to move to its permanent quarters at Changchunyuan after the war games in the fall.) According to the American military attaché, the infantry and artillery were fully equipped; the only deficient unit was the cavalry, which "has the complement of men but the third squadron, the Mongol squadron, is not yet mounted." On 16 September, less than one month before the outbreak of the revolution, the Palace Guard was formally commissioned. At a majestic ceremony held at a drill field in the northern suburbs outside Desheng Gate, the regent, in his capacity as the unit's commander, personally inspected the troops. Pleased by what he saw, Zaifeng complimented the two remaining Palace Guard commissioners, Zaitao and Zaifu, for having organized the force so expeditiously. He praised the officers and soldiers for their martial appearance and reminded them of their unique and exalted status. Unlike the New Army, he told them, they had the responsibility of defending not only the country but the throne as well. Indeed, by then the Palace Guard had already taken on the mission for which it was created; it had relieved the First Division of its palace guard duty.[94]

In his alternate capacity as naval commander-in-chief, Zaifeng also attempted to revitalize the navy. With the defeat in the Sino-Japanese War in 1894–95, the core of the navy, Li Hongzhang's fleet, had been destroyed, and the Navy Yamen, which Zaifeng's father had headed, disbanded. For the next decade and a half China, in effect, lacked a navy; it had warships, but no organized naval force. It was not until Zaifeng became regent that plans were developed to revive the navy. On 19 February 1909, responding to a memorial from Shanqi, who was then the minister of civil affairs and who earlier had helped create the Beijing police force, the regent appointed a committee to formulate those plans. The four-person committee consisted of Shanqi, Minister of Finance Zaize, Minister of the Army Tieliang, and the commander of the Guangdong fleet, Sa Zhenbing (1859–1952), with Yikuang in his customary role as overseer. (It was at this point that Tieliang was relieved of his post with the Palace Guard training commission in order that he might concentrate on this new assignment.)[95]

On 15 July, six days after the committee made its report and at the very same time that he both declared himself generalissimo and restructured the General Staff Council, Zaifeng created the Navy Commission (Chouban Haijun Shiwuchu) as a step toward forming a full-fledged Ministry of the Navy. To head the new body, he named the third-rank prince Zaixun and Sa Zhenbing. A graduate of the Fuzhou Naval Shipyard School who afterward studied in Britain, Sa was selected for the commission, as he had been for Shanqi's committee, because of his extensive experience in naval affairs; soon afterward he was promoted from the position of commander of the Guangdong fleet to that of commander-in-chief of the entire naval force (*haijun tidu*) and transferred to Shanghai. On the other hand, Zaixun, who had not served on Shanqi's committee and who heretofore had not been even tangentially involved in naval matters, was designated because he was, like Zaitao, the regent's half-brother.[96] A month later the Navy Commission, together with the Ministry of the Army, presented the court with a seven-year plan for the revitalization of the navy. The two commissioners then set off on the first of several whirlwind inspection tours, which eventually took them to Europe in late 1909 and to the United States and Japan in late 1910. On their return from Japan, Zaixun and Sa Zhenbing recommended that the Navy Commission be converted into a Ministry of the Navy, as a counterpart to the Ministry of the Army. On 4 December 1910 the regent so ordered, and appointed Zaixun as minister.[97]

The major accomplishment of Zaifeng's naval reform was to unify China's separate fleets. Soon after the Navy Commission was set up, it grouped the existing ships into a sea-going and a Yangzi River fleet. Subsequently, in December 1910, when the commission became a ministry, the former commissioner Sa Zhenbing was appointed as overall commander of both fleets, with his headquarters still in Shanghai.[98] The pride of the sea-going fleet was its four cruisers: the 4,300–ton British-built *Haiqi* (with a crew of 439) and the 2,950–ton German-built *Haichou*, *Haishen*, and *Hairong* (each with a crew of 279). All had been ordered in 1896, following the debacle of the Sino-Japanese War, and delivered in 1898–99. (The Chinese had bought a fifth cruiser, the *Haitian*, from the British, but it had sunk in 1907 after running aground in a fog off Shanghai.)[99] While Sa and the two fleet commanders were Han, several Manchus (graduates of the evanescent Kunming Lake Naval School of the Self-Strengthening period) held leading posts aboard these cruisers.[100] Perhaps the most remarkable achievement in Zaifeng's naval modernization program was the historic round-the-world voyage of the *Haiqi* in 1911. After steaming to London for the coronation of King George V, it went on to New York, where the sea-going fleet commander paid a call on President William Howard Taft, and to Havana to "show the flag" to the Chinese community in Cuba.[101]

Zaifeng's heavy reliance upon various imperial princes and other Manchus in these efforts to recentralize and reimperialize military authority gave rise to much talk among contemporary diplomats, officials, and journalists as well as later historians of what British minister John Jordan (1852–1925) called the "Manchu ascendency." In a dispatch of 16 March 1909, Jordan noted that "there has been a marked revival of Manchu ascendency in the councils of the Empire" and that no consideration was now given to a fusion of Manchus and Han and the elimination of the Manchus' privileged position. He worried that Zaifeng was coming under the influence of a "camarilla"—composed of Zaifeng's brothers Zaixun and Zaitao, his "cousin" Zaize (then minister of finance), and his "kinsman" Tieliang (minister of the army)—who Jordan claimed were collectively known as the "Inner Grand Council." The *North-China Herald*, in August 1909, commented in a similar vein on the supremacy of the Manchu party: "In doing away with all distinctions between Manchus and [Han] Chinese, the important posts in the Government have been gradually filled by Manchus." Zhang Zhidong, shortly before his death, reportedly also warned the regent (in Daniel Bays' words) about the "Manchu clique" surrounding him. Historian Jerome Ch'en refers to it as the "Manchu Cabal," which he asserts was formed around 1905 by Tieliang "in an attempt to strengthen Manchu power in both the government and the army."[102]

This "Manchu ascendency" was not, contrary to the thrust of Minister Jordan's remarks, a new departure for Zaifeng but rather a continuation and extension of a trend begun by Cixi after the reorganization of the metropolitan bureaucracy in 1906. Previously, guided by the principle of dyarchy, the number of Manchus and Han among the top metropolitan officials had been more or less equal; by late 1907, however, the Manchus had gained a clear majority of nine to four over the Han among the thirteen ministry heads (including the two supervisors at the Ministry of Foreign Affairs), though they were still evenly matched with the Han on the six-member Grand Council. Zaifeng proceeded to appoint even more Manchus than Cixi had, particularly at the Grand Council, where after a major shakeup in August 1910 they outnumbered the Han three to one. (The three Manchus were Yikuang, Natong, and Yulang; the solitary Han was Xu Shichang, the former governor-general of Manchuria, who had managed to escape from under the still-dark shadow of his former patron, Yuan Shikai.) And among the (by now) fourteen ministry heads, the Manchu majority had increased by one, to become ten to four.[103]

Still, the "Manchu Cabal" was hardly monolithic. Zaifeng, in his official appointments, may have preferred Manchus over Han, but he did not indiscriminately favor all Manchus. In particular, two bannermen officials who had prospered under Cixi—Duanfang and Tieliang—did not fare well, ultimately at least, under Zaifeng. When Duanfang, formerly at Liang-Jiang, was promoted to the position of Zhili governor-general in June 1909, his appointment was cited as one more sign of the Manchu ascendency under Zaifeng. John Jordan noted that until then a Han had occupied the important Zhili post continuously since Zeng Guofan's appointment in 1868. (The British minister was slightly mistaken: two Manchus, Ronglu and Yulu [1844?–1900], had been Zhili governor-general briefly during the 1898–1900 period of reaction.)[104] Less than five months later, however, Duanfang, who seems to have been fascinated with modern gadgets, was denounced by a Han official, Li Guojie, the former brigade-general at Guangzhou, for three major ritual improprieties during the recent funeral for Cixi: he had authorized his subordinates to photograph the funeral procession; he had on one occasion ridden in a sedan chair when other mourners were on foot; and he had strung up telegraph wires within the geomantic (or spirit) screen forming the enclosure around the mausoleum. Duanfang was consequently removed (and replaced by, it might be noted, a Han, Chen Kuilong [1856–1948]).[105] Like Yuan Shikai, Duanfang left office quietly and retired to Beijing to devote his attention to promoting education and collecting ancient art, of which he was said to be a connoisseur. Subsequent efforts to recall him to office foundered, or so it was reported, on the opposition of Empress Dowager Longyu, who allegedly and for unspecified reasons was the one at court who had insisted on his dismissal in the first place. Duanfang's involuntary retirement lasted until May 1911, when he was named director-general of the newly nationalized railroads.[106] This assignment was to cost him his life.

Tieliang, whom Jerome Ch'en credits as the founder and leader of the Manchu Cabal, similarly, though not so suddenly, lost the considerable power that he had amassed during the last years of Cixi. Following Zaifeng's elevation as regent, Tieliang continued as army minister and indeed was given a couple of additional military assignments, first as Palace Guard training commissioner and then as a member of Shanqi's committee to decide on naval reorganization. However, even as Minister Jordan was claiming in March 1909 that he was part of an all-Manchu "Inner Grand Council," Tieliang's control over the military was being curtailed by Yulang and Zaitao, the two imperial princes on the General Staff Council. Finally, in August 1909, claiming illness, Tieliang submitted his resignation as army minister, which was accepted the following March. He was replaced at the ministry by another Manchu, Yinchang, Zaifeng's interpreter during his mission of apology, who had just returned from an extended stint as Chinese minister to Germany. Tieliang was subsequently, in September 1910, sent away from Beijing and given the relatively inconsequential post of general of the Nanjing banner garrison.[107]

Tieliang had been an effective agent of Cixi's policy of recentralization, but he did not have the princely credentials to fit into Zaifeng's effort at reimperialization. He was only an ordinary Manchu bannerman and not, as British Minister Jordan described him, Zaifeng's "kinsman." This may explain why he felt estranged from the regent and his inner circle. For Zaifeng drew his support not so much from Manchus in general as from the imperial clan and, more narrowly, from the princes who were a subset of the clan. This political dependence on imperial princes, again, was not new with Zaifeng. Over the course of Cixi's long rule, dating from the early 1860s, more and more princes had been appointed as grand councilors and ministry heads, in contravention of the mid-Qing tradition of princely nonparticipation in state affairs. Zaifeng simply, and in the end self-destructively, carried this process one step further. Whereas in 1907, under Cixi, three of the thirteen ministry heads were imperial princes, in 1910, under Zaifeng, it was four of fourteen (Yikuang, Shanqi, Zaize, and Zaixun); similarly, at the Grand Council, one-third of the members (two of six) under Cixi were imperial princes, while it was one-half (two of four) under Zaifeng (Yikuang and Yulang). The princes on whom Zaifeng relied most heavily were Yikuang, Shanqi, Zaize, Yulang, and most notably, his two brothers, twenty-four-year-old Zaixun and twenty-year-old Zaitao, whom he had put in charge of the navy and army respectively. (Zaitao, unlike the others, was neither a grand councilor nor a ministry head, but he supervised the General Staff Council and headed the Palace Guard training commission.) In January 1910 the Shanghai reformist daily, the *Eastern Times* (Shibao), reported from the capital that "the power of the imperial relatives has increased enormously. Formerly there were only Prince Qing [Yikuang] and his son; now there are the three third-rank princes: Zaixun, Zaitao, and Yulang." The censor Jiang Chunlin submitted a memorial also cautioning the Prince Regent against relying so heavily upon his brothers.[108]

The princes themselves did not necessarily form a monolithic bloc any more than did the Manchus as a whole. While the divisions within the Qing court are obscure, they did exist. The former split between the "emperor's faction" and the "empress's faction" had not disappeared with the deaths of the Guangxu emperor and Cixi; it persisted into the regency. On one side were Zaifeng, Zaixun, and Zaitao, all brothers of the former emperor. Shanqi, who had opposed Cixi's embrace of the Boxers, may also have been aligned with this faction. On the other side were former supporters of Empress Dowager Cixi, who included the new empress dowager Longyu (Cixi's niece), Zaize (married to Longyu's younger sister), and Yikuang.[109]

One consequence of the notoriety achieved by the imperial princes under Zaifeng was that they became tempting marks for assassins. The first assassination attempt was directed at Zaixun, the naval commissioner, who on his return from his European tour at the beginning of 1910 was targeted once, possibly twice, by the revolutionaries. In late January, shortly after he left Harbin on a train bound for Beijing, the authorities in Manchuria arrested a suspected revolutionary, Xiong Chengji (1887–1910). Xiong confessed to having played a role in the abortive 1908 mutiny in Anqing, Anhui, which he proudly acknowledged was intended as a "political revolution"; he denied, however, that he had left his refuge in Japan in order to kill Zaixun. Despite his claim of innocence with regard to Zaixun, Xiong Chengji was executed a month later. Although he apparently was telling the truth when he said that he had come to Manchuria only to do business with some Russians, his hagiographic biographers insist otherwise. Given his admitted role in the Anqing mutiny, they regard his presence in Harbin just as Zaixun was passing through as no mere coincidence. So too did the contemporary press. *Eastern Miscellany*, for example, included in its account of his arrest and execution the unconfirmed report that he had told an associate in Changchun (who subsequently betrayed him) that he was going to Harbin for the sole purpose of murdering the regent's brother.[110]

Whatever Xiong Chengji's intentions may have been in Harbin, other revolutionaries led by Wang Jingwei were waiting for the unscathed Zaixun in Beijing. Wang, a close ally of Sun Yat-sen, had become discouraged by the failure of the series of Alliance-organized revolts in south China in 1907–8 and, like Wu Yue before him, had turned to assassination. He and several other like-minded revolutionaries in Japan formed an assassination corps to kill high-ranking Manchu officials in Beijing. In the fall of 1909, one member of the group, Huang Fusheng (1883–1948), went ahead and set up a photographic studio in the Outer (or "Chinese") City as a front. Wang and the others followed. With Zaixun about to arrive in Beijing, they decided to try to toss a bomb at him at the railroad station. It was dusk, however, when the prince arrived, and Wang was unable to pick him out from the crowd of high officials. So Zaixun was, perhaps for the second time, spared.[111]

The disappointed assassins, after considering other potential targets, including Yikuang, chose the regent himself as the new victim. Their plot was to attack Zaifeng during his daily trip from his mansion in the northwestern part of the Inner City into the Forbidden City. It so happened that Zaifeng's customary and well-guarded route down the broad avenue past the Drum Tower had been torn up for road repair, and he was obliged to make a detour. The assassins buried a canister of explosives under a small bridge along the detour and planned to detonate it as he passed over. Unfortunately for the revolutionaries, as they were making their final preparations on the night of 2 April, the canister was discovered. The police found out that it was of local manufacture and even-

tually traced the assassins to their photographic studio. The two revolutionaries who had remained in Beijing, Wang Jingwei and Huang Fusheng, were
arrested.[112]

Wang Jingwei readily confessed that he was a former editor of *The People's
Journal* and that he had come to the Chinese capital to do something that would
"startle the world." He displayed no particular animus toward the regent personally nor toward the Manchus in general; unlike Xu Xilin in 1907, he did not
dwell on the state of Manchu-Han relations to any extent. Indeed, the only time
he touched on the Manchu question in his confession was when he offered reas-
surance to the Manchu populace and the Qing emperor about their future in
a republic if they were to give up peacefully. He promised the Manchus
(Manren) that they would be treated as equal citizens, and he warned the
Manchu monarch that it would be far preferable for him to be toppled by the
native Han people than by a foreign power. He contrasted the fate of the imperial rulers of Annam and Korea after their countries had been overrun by foreigners with that of the shogun following the domestic revolution in Japan.
Whereas under the French and the Japanese, the Nguyen and Yi emperors
respectively were regarded as old "worn-out shoes," in Japan the Tokugawa
shogun, after giving up power, had been treated with respect. Instead of
Manchu-Han relations, Wang Jingwei focused on the futility of the constitutionalist cause under the Qing as well as on the continuing threat of partition
by the foreign powers. Citing historical precedents from France, Britain,
Germany, and Japan, he insisted that genuine constitutionalism could come
about only after a revolution. He questioned the naive faith of the constitutionalist reformers in the efficacy of a parliament, for which they were then agitating, as a bulwark against imperial autocracy.[113] Because of the blackout
imposed by the authorities, Wang's confession, unlike Xu Xilin's, did not become
public. Even so, some news of the failed assault did get into the newspapers.[114]

In view of the high status of their intended victim, Wang Jingwei and Huang
Fusheng were treated with extraordinary leniency. They were not executed, as
Xiong Chengji had been less than two months earlier. Instead, on 29 April the
new Supreme Court of Justice sentenced them to life imprisonment.[115] By all
accounts it was Shanqi, the minister of civil affairs, who was responsible for
their relatively light sentences. Shanqi, perhaps to gather intelligence and perhaps also to ingratiate himself with them, had secretly cultivated contacts with
various oppositional groups for several years. He was on good terms with the
exiled monarchists Kang Youwei and Liang Qichao, who in 1907 had sought
his help to counter Yuan Shikai and Yikuang and return the Guangxu emperor
to power. He was in touch with the republicans as well, particularly via a staff
member, Cheng Jiacheng (1872–1914), who as a student in Japan had joined

the Alliance. According to the later accounts of Feng Ziyou and Song Jiaoren, in 1908 or 1909 Shanqi had sent Cheng to Japan to offer the leaders of the Alliance a sizable amount of money to buy them off. For their part, the revolutionaries too, like Kang and Liang, tried to persuade the prince to work for them. In 1909 Zhang Binglin, then head of the organization in Tokyo, appealed to Shanqi's self-image by inviting him to join the Alliance and urging him to emulate Prince Kropotkin of Russia by taking the lead in the coming revolution. Zhang also assured Shanqi that the revolutionaries did not want a racial massacre but only a "return of sovereignty to us [Han]." Zhang stated (as he had once before, in the 1907 *Heaven's Punishment* supplement to *The People's Journal*) that the Manchus would be allowed to "return to the east," to Manchuria, where they could maintain their own separate, racially homogeneous "empire" (*diguo*) adjacent to the Han republic within China proper.[116]

After Wang Jingwei and Huang Fusheng were arrested, Shanqi, whose ministry oversaw the Beijing police, talked with the prisoners at least twice prior to their sentencing. He was particularly impressed by Wang's confession and engaged in an extended political dialogue with him. According to Huang's recollection, the prince said that he had long been an avid reader of *The People's Journal*. He told Wang that its espousal of the Three People's Principles was too narrow; he recommended instead the "great harmony of the five races" (*wuzu datong*), a rival concept that the Manchu publication *Great Harmony Journal* advocated. When Wang replied that he had no wish to repudiate *The People's Journal*'s position, Shanqi commended him for sticking by his principles even as he faced the prospect of execution. Afterward, perhaps mindful of the negative publicity that the vengeful execution of Xu Xilin and Qiu Jin had produced in 1907 and perhaps under the influence of his staff member Cheng Jiacheng, Shanqi convinced Zaifeng that too severe a punishment might be counterproductive; it would stir up the revolutionaries to make new attempts and also needlessly antagonize the constitutionalist reformers. The regent thereupon agreed to the reduced sentence of life imprisonment for Wang and Huang.[117]

Six months later, on 6 October 1910, Zaixun was once more the intended victim of an assassination attempt. It happened in Oakland, California, as he was completing his naval tour of the United States. The would-be assassin was a thirty-one-year-old U.S.-born Chinese American, George Fong (Kuang Zuozhi), who had been stirred to action by the revolutionaries' propaganda on the "racial question" (*zhongzu wenti*). As he explained at his trial, he had wanted to "help China free itself from the clutches of the Manchus" by killing the regent's brother, whose naval purchases abroad were meant not to strengthen China but to suppress the revolutionary party. He and an associate had planned to shoot the navy commissioner at the Oakland docks as he was welcomed by the leaders of the Chinese community. However, the security at the scene was tight, and Fong was spotted by an American detective, who disarmed him before he could draw his pistol. His subsequent trial in an American court was widely publicized in China. His anti-Manchu declarations appeared, for example, in *Eastern Miscellany*, as did his predictions about the imminence and the inevitability of a republican revolution. On 13 January 1911, he was found guilty of assault and sentenced to fourteen years' imprisonment.[118]

Finally, two months after Fong's assault on Zaixun, there was yet another attempted assassination of a Manchu prince. The target this time was Yikuang, whom Wang Jingwei had considered but given up because he was so well protected. On 3 December 1910, as Yikuang was returning from the Forbidden City to his home in the northern part of the Inner City, one or more individuals fired a pistol and tossed a bomb at his horse-drawn carriage. Amidst the confusion caused by terrified horses and bewildered bodyguards, the assassin(s) escaped. Although the attempt failed, it too received wide publicity.[119] No one ever took credit for the attack.

CLASHES WITH THE NATIONAL ASSEMBLY

Zaifeng's efforts to impose his authority over the army and navy and to create a new, imperially controlled palace guard had, by and large, succeeded by late 1910; he had met with some criticisms, particularly from the now relatively unfettered press, but not enough to deter him from his course. Then, on 3 October 1910, the day that the provincial assemblies began their second annual session, the National Assembly convened in Beijing, as Cixi's Nine-Year Plan had specified. Zaifeng himself attended its inaugural meeting. In a departure from custom, the assemblymen did not kneel in his presence but remained standing through his welcoming speech.[120] Thereafter life was never again the same for Zaifeng. The assembly, which opened with the fourth-rank prince Pulun as president and the judicial reformer Shen Jiaben (replacing the deceased grand secretary Sun Jia'nai) as vice-president, was in session for three months, during which time it clashed with the regent over a number of different issues, such as whether to expedite the summoning of a parliament, how to make the Grand Council behave like a "responsible cabinet," whether (once more) to pardon Kang Youwei and Liang Qichao for their role in the 1898 reforms, and how to react to an unprecedented lobbying effort from below to change the queue requirement. In coping with these controversies, Zaifeng took—as he had in reimperializing authority—a determined, even tough, stance. When the assembly finally adjourned in January 1911, the regent got no relief, as his naming of a cabinet in May created the biggest controversy yet. All of these issues raised in late 1910 and early 1911 impinged, some more directly than others, upon the Manchu-Han question.

The first controversy pitting the regent against the National Assembly arose out of the ongoing movement to expedite the summoning of a parliament. The assembly itself was only an advisory body, with no authority to make laws; according to the Nine-Year Plan, it was not until the plan's final year (1916) that a parliament, with legislative powers, would be elected. Ever since the Nine-Year Plan was promulgated in 1907, political reformers had been lobbying the court to shorten the constitutional timetable, just as they had previously pressured it to issue the timetable in the first place. In the year since the provincial assemblies first met in the fall of 1909, the reformers, including organized groups of Manchus, had mounted two new nationwide petition drives, in November 1909 and again in June 1910, pleading with the court to hasten the formation of Parliament. Zaifeng, however, had curtly rebuffed both efforts; on the second occasion, he softened the rejection by reminding the petitioners that the National Assembly was due to open in less than four months.[121]

The assembly's inauguration did not appease the agitators for a constitutional government. Snubbed in June, they came right back in October with a third petition, this time addressed to the assembly itself rather than, as before, to the Censorate. They demanded the summoning of a true parliament by the very next year (1911) and the concurrent formation of a "responsible cabinet." They asserted, as had the Manchu publication *Great Harmony Journal* previously, that "only where there is a responsible cabinet is there a constitutional government . . . and only where there is a parliament is there a responsible cabinet." On 22 October, amidst joyous shouts of "Long live the Parliament! Long live the Great Qing State! Long live the constitutional polity of the Great Qing State!" the assembly gave its unanimous approval to the petition, which was subsequently recast as a memorial and forwarded to the throne.[122]

Meanwhile, a majority of top provincial officials, headed by Governor-General Xiliang of Manchuria, had submitted a joint telegram to the Grand Council in full support of the National Assembly's memorial. Citing the case of the last Ming emperor, whose caution had doomed the dynasty, they warned against needless delay. The telegram was signed by four of the nine governors-general and all but two of the governors, with Manchus ranged on both sides of the issue. Xiliang and Ruicheng (Hu-Guang) were two of the four governors-general who signed, while Changgeng (Shaan-Gan), Zhao Erxun (Sichuan), and Songshou (Min-Zhe) were three of the five who refused. However, the most adamant opponents of Xiliang's telegram were two Han governors-general: Chen Kuilong of Zhili and Zhang Renjun of Liang-Jiang. Unlike Xiliang, who called for the simultaneous creation of a parliament and a cabinet, Chen Kuilong sought to separate the two. He cited the example of Meiji Japan, which did not convene a parliament until after a cabinet had been installed. Chen's recommendation to the throne was to appoint a "responsible cabinet" the next year (1911) but hold off on a parliament until 1913, when the National Assembly's term of office was due to expire. In the meantime, the assembly could, if necessary, perform some of the functions of a parliament.[123]

Zaifeng asked the Office of Governmental Affairs for its advice before making a decision. According to published news reports, the office conceded that the court could no longer adhere to the original Nine-Year Plan; it was inclined toward Chen Kuilong's alternative proposal. Dismayed by such press accounts, the parliamentary petitioners immediately intensified their lobbying for a parliament by no later than 1911. They denied that it was unfeasible to draw up the necessary regulations within a year, and they questioned whether China, in view of its perilous condition abroad and financial needs at home, could afford the three years' delay in opening a parliament. Governor-General Xiliang and other supportive provincial leaders also took issue with the Meiji precedent that Chen Kuilong had cited. According to their reading of recent Japanese history, it was precisely the Sat-Chō oligarchs' naming of a cabinet in 1885 without convening a parliament at the same time that had caused so much unrest (presumably the popular rights movement), which was not dissipated until the Diet opened in 1890.[124] Ignoring these last-minute appeals, Zaifeng accepted the compromise solution recommended by Chen Kuilong and the Office of Governmental Affairs. On 4 November he agreed to advance the summoning of Parliament to 1913 and to name a cabinet some time before then. He insisted that the preparatory work could not be expedited any further. In a separate edict, he told the Ministry of Civil Affairs and the provincial authorities to notify the petitioners of his decision and to order them to disperse. Two days later, he appointed National Assembly president Pulun and Minister of Finance Zaize, both imperial princes, to take charge of drafting a constitution. A month later, he called on the Bureau for the Implementation of Constitutional Government to revise the constitutional timetable.[125]

Zaifeng's concessions did not suffice to placate the parliamentary petitioners. Rather than giving up, as he had demanded, the petitioners reorganized themselves as the Society of Comrades (Tongzhihui), then announced that they would continue to agitate for the speedy convening of a parliament. The National Assembly too was dissatisfied; on 10 November it submitted a memorial questioning the wisdom of quibbling over a couple of years.[126] The delay in summoning Parliament was most intensely felt among the concerned citizens of Fengtian, who three months earlier had seen Japan annex their neighbor, Korea. They claimed that their province could be rescued from the rapacious imperialists only if a parliament were formed immediately. With Governor-General Xiliang's blessings, a delegation of protesters went to Beijing to present their case directly. On 20 December, having arrived in Tianjin, where they were joined by several thousand local supporters, they marched on Chen Kuilong's yamen to demand that he wire the court to convene a parliament the next year. The Zhili governor-general agreed to forward their petition, though, unlike Xiliang, he did not endorse its content. Zaifeng's response was to insist once more that, because of the complex preparations required, Parliament could not be opened any sooner. When publication of this edict failed to keep defiant students from meeting to plan future protests, Governor-General Chen sent soldiers and the police to disperse the gathering. The regent not only approved Chen's resort to force, he directed the Ministry of Civil Affairs and the Infantry Division of the Metropolitan Banners to do likewise, if necessary, to send the Manchurian petitioners back home. He had been patient enough, he said.[127] Only then did the agitation to hasten the summoning of Parliament die down.

Meanwhile, following the initial confrontation in October over when to summon Parliament, Zaifeng clashed again with the National Assembly over the latter's parallel demand that the cabinet that the regent had promised to create be a "responsible" one. When Zaifeng declared on 4 November that he would not open Parliament until 1913, the assembly began aggressively staking out a claim that it itself deserved to be treated not merely as an advisory group but as a fully legislative body to which the four-member Grand Council, as a protocabinet, ought to be responsible. The assembly seized on three provincial disputes that had been appealed to it to make good its claim.

The first dispute originated in Hunan, where Governor Yang Wending had contracted for a public loan without securing the assent of the provincial assembly. The National Assembly, by a three-to-two majority, voted to support the objections of the Hunan Assembly; it asked the court to order the governor to submit the loan agreement to his provincial assembly for its decision. Zaifeng responded on 8 November that Yang's failure to consult his assembly had been an "oversight," but that since the loan had been approved by the Ministry of Finance, it should stand as contracted. Many National Assembly members were incensed that what they considered Yang's "gross abuse of authority" had been minimized as a mere "oversight." They summoned the grand councilors, who had helped draft the regent's response, to come to the assembly to explain their action in person; for reasons of political prudence, they did not attack the regent himself. The councilors—Yikuang, Yulang, Natong, and Xu Shichang—ignored the demand.[128]

Less than two weeks later, the National Assembly clashed again with the

Grand Council on two other provincial issues. One involved Yunnan, where the governor-general had raised the price of salt without the consent of the provincial assembly; the other concerned Guangxi, where the governor had permitted students from other provinces to attend its Higher Police School in disregard of his provincial assembly, which wanted to limit enrollment to natives of the province. On 20 November the National Assembly memorialized on the two matters, where it, as before in the Hunan loan case, supported the provincial assemblies against the provincial governors. Zaifeng's court, rather than immediately accepting the National Assembly's recommendations, issued an edict referring the issues to the Salt Gabelle (Yanzhengchu) and the Ministry of Civil Affairs respectively for their consideration. Once more, the assembly was outraged that its will had been ignored. Members complained that the executive organs of government were trampling on the "independence of the legislative organ." They voted to impeach the entire Grand Council for its role in drafting the edict.[129]

The prospective impeachment of the grand councilors dramatically escalated the conflict between the National Assembly and the regent. Zaifeng tried at once to defuse the situation, but without success. On 25 November, on the advice of the Salt Gabelle and the Ministry of Civil Affairs, he adopted the assembly's original recommendations on both matters.[130] Furthermore, he had the edict rushed over to the assembly, hoping that it would sidetrack the pending effort to draft the articles of impeachment. Indeed, one imperially appointed member (the Mongol bannerman Wenpu, an official at the Foreign Ministry) argued that since in the end the court had done what the assembly wanted, the impeachment was moot; another imperial appointee (Lu Zongyu [1876–1958], an "eminent scholar") questioned whether the two cases were important enough to justify impeachment. A majority, however, pointed out that these were not the only instances in which the Grand Council had ignored the National Assembly. They asserted that the assembly should be vigilant against any and all such displays of "irresponsibility" (*bufu zeren*) so as to set a worthy example for the future parliament. The assembly consequently voted to draw up a revised memorial condemning the Grand Council for its "irresponsibility." The modified memorial, debated and approved two weeks later, did not so much impeach the council as complain about its ill-defined authority. It claimed that while the assembly was faithfully exercising its representative and legislative functions, the Grand Council had been derelict in fulfilling its executive responsibilities. It saw a need for a prime minister both to shield the emperor from criticisms and to unite the government under a single leader. It asked Zaifeng to appoint a cabinet speedily and, until then, to define clearly the Grand Council's duties.[131]

Finally, when the four grand councilors jointly offered to resign, Zaifeng told the National Assembly to mind its own business. Rejecting the resignations, he rebuked the assembly on 18 December for encroaching on the throne's exclusive authority, as set forth in the Constitutional Outline, to create government offices and make official appointments. He asserted that whether the Grand Council was "responsible" and whether to set up a "responsible cabinet" were entirely up to him. The National Assembly could not decide on an appropriate response. At a meeting on 19 December, some assemblymen saw no alternative but to resign in order to defend the honor and integrity of their institution. Others urged making one more effort at impeaching the grand councilors, this time individually rather than as a group, before taking the ultimate step of mass resignation. On a vote, 102 assemblymen favored one last attempt at impeachment. In the following days, however, the assembly seemingly had second thoughts. On 26 December a majority even voted to drop the matter lest it provoke the dissolution of the body. When this failure of nerve was roundly criticized by the press, the assembly changed its mind yet again and on 30 December voted out a memorial of impeachment. Zaifeng now simply ignored their action. Instead of dissolving the assembly, as some of its members had feared, he shelved its memorial, which was never officially published nor acted upon. On this inconclusive note, the controversy petered out, as the assembly's scheduled three-month session came to an end soon afterward.[132]

Amidst the rancorous debates about speeding up the summoning of Parliament and impeaching the Grand Council, the National Assembly also took up the still unresolved issue of pardons for Kang Youwei and Liang Qichao. Previous efforts had succeeded in "reversing verdicts" for almost all of the disgraced reformers of 1898, but not for Kang and Liang or the six officials who had been executed. Leading the new attempt was the Society of Comrades, the former parliamentary petitioners, who appealed to the regent's brother and general staff councilor, Zaitao, who was thought to be sympathetic to the reform cause in general. The society said that with the edict of 4 November advancing the opening of Parliament to 1913, it was essential that political parties be permitted to play an active and open role; they therefore asked that the traditional ban on political organizations be lifted. Furthermore, they urged that those 1898 reformers who were still in exile be summoned home; in an open letter to the general public, they specifically named Kang Youwei and Liang Qichao as deserving of pardons. At the National Assembly an imperially appointed member, Chen Baochen (1848–1935; one of the "eminent scholars"), likewise proposed memorializing the court to pardon the 1898 reformers. Now was the appropriate time, Chen said, because the current agitation for a parliament had its beginnings in the Hundred Days. He also claimed that the

Censorate was in possession of a handwritten edict from the former emperor exonerating the six executed men. As a result, on 3 January 1911 the assembly approved a memorial asking that the six martyrs of 1898, along with other unspecified political offenders, be pardoned. One assemblyman argued that their political rehabilitation would help do away with Manchu-Han differences (*pochu Man-Han zhi jie*) as well as demonstrate the court's magnanimity. It was another of the assembly's memorials that Zaifeng brushed aside.[133]

The last controversy that pitted the regent against the National Assembly—the one that touched most directly upon Manchu-Han relations—concerned the dynasty's hairstyle for its adult male subjects and dress code for its officials. With the turn of the twentieth century, as more and more Chinese went abroad as diplomats, students, and workers and also as China itself began to industrialize, an increasing number of reformers had joined the revolutionaries in opposing the queue and the long-sleeved loose gown. Unlike the revolutionaries, who objected because they were badges of Han servitude to Manchu rule, the reformers complained that the two Manchu impositions were out of step with the Western-influenced mores of the modern world. In partial recognition of the changing times, the post-Boxer court itself had modified the hair requirement for its soldiers and police personnel (but not students), who, as they adopted military-style uniforms and caps, were permitted to shorten (but not remove) their queue. Nevertheless, as of late 1909 very few Chinese, except for the revolutionaries and an occasional press commentator, had dared to advocate getting rid of the braid completely or changing the official costume.

The first high-level officials to discuss openly the queue and costume question and to urge a change were two Han reformers: Wu Tingfang (1842–1922), the Chinese minister to the United States; and Tang Shouqian, the Jiangxi education commissioner, who late in 1909 submitted separate memorials on the subject. Wu Tingfang claimed to be speaking on behalf of the seventy thousand Chinese residents in the United States, who found the queue particularly irksome. It made them look outlandish in the eyes of other Americans, and it endangered their lives if it got caught in a piece of operating machinery. They asked their envoy to petition the Qing court to abolish the queue and also to adopt the Western style of dress. Wu, in his memorial, supported the Chinese in America halfway; he agreed with them about the hairstyle but not clothing. He saw no need to abandon the existing Chinese attire, which was inexpensive and suitable for all seasons; he claimed that the Japanese had retained their native clothing after the Meiji Restoration and had adopted Western attire only for formal functions. The queue, however, was without any redeeming value. Wearing it had no bearing whatsoever on one's loyalty to the emperor or nation. It was only a matter of fashion, and fashions change. Western men at one time had worn braids too, but no longer. As Chinese increasingly emulated the Westerners, the pace of queue-cutting would inevitably accelerate regardless of official policy. It would be better for the court to take the lead. Wu Tingfang thus called for "cutting the hair but not changing the attire" (*jianfa buyifu*).[134] On the other hand, Tang Shouqian, Zhang Jian's colleague at the Association for Constitutional Preparations, advocated, as one of eight reform proposals, not only cutting the hair but changing the attire as well. He claimed that the official robe was just as ridiculous looking in foreign eyes as the braided hair, and the long sleeves of the gown were just as likely to get caught in a piece of moving machinery. He urged the regent to set an example for the scholar-official elite by cutting his queue and wearing Western-style dress. The rest of the population could follow or not as they pleased.[135]

The memorials from Wu Tingfang and Tang Shouqian had a delayed impact. Because the court did not respond to either of them at the time they were submitted, their contents were not known until months later. Their subsequent publication touched off a year-long debate about the hair and dress code of the Qing. In the spring of 1910, when Tang Shouqian's memorial appeared, the Shanghai newspaper *Eastern Times* carried a series of satirical cartoons on the "uses of the queue" (see plates 9 and 10).[136] It was, however, the publication of Wu Tingfang's memorial in August that had the greater effect, largely because it coincided with the return of Zaitao, the regent's reform-minded brother, from his five-month military tour overseas. The prince was widely thought to favor changing the queue requirement.[137] By mid-September, according to the *Eastern Times*, there was so much talk in the capital of changing the hairstyle that it overshadowed all other topics. The paper reported, apparently correctly, that even newly appointed army minister Yinchang had, without adverse consequence, removed his queue. It expressed amazement at the large number of men who now dared to appear in public in short hair. As they had in 1906–7, many students began cutting their hair in anticipation of a change in the requirement. When students at the Hunan Military Primary School in Changsha were reprimanded for being queueless, they cited the example of army minister Yinchang as justification.[138]

The agitation for cutting the hair and altering the dress code did not go unchallenged. Some were opposed because it was contrary to "ancestral customs." Former Grand Councilor Shixu, when told that the abolition of the queue would not necessarily lead to the extinction of the nation, retorted, "Though China might not perish, the Great Qing State would surely be done for."[139] However, the main opponents were not Manchu traditionalists but some Han merchants and manufacturers, who were guided not by politics but by economics and were more concerned about the costume than the hairstyle.

The merchants feared that if the hair requirement were changed, so would the dress code, and as the Western style of dress was adopted, imported wool would replace native silk as a basic clothing material. Pawnshop operators, too, were worried that they might be stuck with a vast stock of traditional-style clothes, shoes, and caps that no one would want to redeem. In Hangzhou the silk, shoe, and hat merchants and the pawnbrokers met on 25 September 1910 to voice their concern over the effect that a change of dress requirements would have on their business. The General Chamber of Commerce in Wuchang expressed similar reservations. These groups' anxieties reached the Qing court in the form of a memorial from the Ministry of Agriculture, Industry, and Commerce that warned that any change in the hairstyle or costume would ripple through the economy with devastating effect.[140]

Although the popular agitation for cutting the queue and changing the dress code had already developed considerable momentum by the time the National Assembly convened in early October, the assembly itself did not take up the matter until well into its three-month session. On 2 December, while debating whether to impeach the Grand Council, it voted to appoint a committee to examine a member's proposal that called for changing the hairstyle and the dress code. The committee, perhaps in deference to the merchants' concerns, decided to delete from the original bill the requirement that the costume be altered. On 15 December, after a lively debate, the assembly passed the amended bill by a vote of 102 to 28. It had three provisions: One made queue-cutting mandatory for officials, soldiers, police, and students, and optional for the rest of the population. Another asked the court to conduct a thorough study of ceremonial costumes at home and abroad, and it stipulated that if the dress code were to be changed in the future, only the official attire and not casual dress would be affected, and the material used in new costumes would be entirely of native origin. The third provision called on the regent and the emperor to take the lead in adopting the customary ways of the foreigners, as had the Meiji emperor of Japan and King Wuling of Zhao during the ancient Warring States era. The proposal, as passed, was sent to another committee to be rewritten as a memorial for presentation to the court.[141]

Before the National Assembly had had a chance to ratify the text of its memorial, however, Zaifeng suddenly injected himself into the debate and, rather than settling it, caused an uproar. Responding to the earlier memorial from the Ministry of Agriculture, Industry, and Commerce, he issued a preemptive edict on 21 December declaring that the Manchu-imposed dress code was of long standing and ought not to be tampered with lightly. He therefore ordered that with the exception of soldiers and the police (whose uniforms had already been altered), everyone (including specifically officials and students) should adhere to the "established system."[142] What was odd about this decree was that it addressed only the issue of costume, which the National Assembly had already decided to leave alone, without making clear whether the hairstyle too was a part of the "established system." Five days later the assembly went ahead and approved its own memorial calling for the abolition of the queue. Zaifeng's reply to the assembly, issued on 30 December, was brief and even more puzzling: "The Ministry of Agriculture, Industry, and Commerce has already memorialized on the subject and elicited a clear decree. Let matters be handled according to the previous edict. There is no need to deliberate on this memorial."[143] The previous edict, of course, had been silent on the queue. According to some news reports, the regent personally favored altering the hairstyle, but he had been dissuaded by finance minister Zaize and others. Yet, as a biting commentary in the *Eastern Times* on 25 January 1911 noted, his evasion on the queue question exposed him to criticism from both sides. Opponents of the plait denounced him for not heeding public opinion; supporters, for not defending the "national essence." There was no clear policy, the newspaper complained. Some people argued that Zaifeng, by his silence, had sanctioned queue-cutting so long as the traditional costume was retained; others contended that without his explicit permission, queue-cutting was still illegal. Each person made his own decision, leading to anarchy. The government spoke daily of centralization of authority, but it did not make use of the authority that it already possessed.[144]

In the absence of a clear and unambiguous directive, the queue-cutting movement continued and intensified. Wu Tingfang, who since his return from the United States had been living in Shanghai, had his own queue cut privately on 14 January 1911. On the following day, he organized a large public ceremony in Shanghai, at which thirty barbers sheared off between three hundred and a thousand braids as a crowd of several thousand watched and cheered. Students in growing numbers joined the movement. In Nanjing, Japanese barbers, who were experienced in cutting short hair, reportedly did a thriving business among students. In Beijing, at the School of Mongolian and Tibetan, the School of Financial Administration, and even the Nobles Military School, most students had cut their braid.[145] This wave of accelerated activity finally led the minister of education, Tang Jingchong, in mid-January to issue an order to all schools throughout the country demanding that queue-cutting stop immediately.[146] It was this decree by the Ministry of Education, rather than the court's edict three weeks earlier, that finally caused the wave of queue-cutting to subside.

As the queue agitation died down in early 1911, public attention turned once again to the issue of a "responsible cabinet." The National Assembly's condemnation of the grand councilors as "irresponsible" had been shelved as the first session of the assembly adjourned on 11 January. Six days later Zaifeng approved a new constitutional timetable that the Bureau for the Implementation of Constitutional Government had, at his request, drawn up. The revised schedule provided for the establishment of a cabinet in 1911, the proclamation of a constitution in 1912, and the convening of a bicameral parliament in 1913. It also called for continuing efforts by the Banner Reorganization Office "to arrange for the Eight Banners' livelihood," but, much to the frustration of the Eight Banners Association for Constitutional Government (Baqi Xianzheng Hui), a new Manchu political group that had recently criticized the office for inactivity, it gave no specifics.[147] On 8 May, in accordance with the new timetable's requirements for 1911, the regent dramatically restructured the metropolitan government along the lines that had been discussed during the previous reorganization effort in the fall of 1906. The Grand Council, the Grand Secretariat, and the Office of Governmental Affairs were all abolished and replaced by a new cabinet, which was to be headed by a prime minister and one or two associate prime ministers and which would be composed of the ten ministry heads. (Two existing ministries, Personnel and Rites, were eliminated.) Reflective of the regent's desire to assert the primacy of imperial control in military matters, the army and navy ministers were to be, as in Meiji Japan, responsible not to the prime minister but to the throne directly.[148]

To the bitter disappointment of the reformers who had hoped that the implementation of constitutionalism would herald the dawn of a new political day, Zaifeng's appointments to the new cabinet were nearly all holdovers from the former regime. Unpopular as they were to the National Assembly, three of the four grand councilors were appointed as cabinet heads. Yikuang was named prime minister, and Natong and Xu Shichang, associate prime ministers. The only grand councilor not named to the new cabinet was Yulang, but he kept his post on the powerful General Staff Council, which became the General Staff Office (Junzifu) with no change in duties. Furthermore, all but one of the ten cabinet ministers were incumbents. (At the Ministry of Foreign Affairs, Liang Dunyan [1872–1924] replaced Zou Jialai [1853–1921].) Yikuang, the prime minister, continued as the supervisor of the Ministry of Foreign Affairs. The Manchu-Han ratio among the top officials of the new government was, consequently, no different from before. The cabinet in the spring of 1911 was composed of nine Manchus and four Han, which was practically identical to the ratio of eleven Manchus to five Han among the grand councilors and ministry heads who held office the previous fall. The one major difference was that the imperial princes were even more numerous than before. Whereas there had been four princes among the top metropolitan officials in the fall of 1910, in the spring of 1911 there were five. They were Yikuang as prime minister, Shanqi at the

Ministry of Civil Affairs, Zaize at Finance, Zaixun at Navy, and Pulun at Agriculture, Industry, and Commerce. (Pulun had been president of the National Assembly, but after its first tumultuous session he had been replaced by Shixu, the conservative former grand councilor, whom the court expected to be less inclined to side with the assembly.)[149]

Zaifeng's appointments were not entirely unexpected; they were much as the *Eastern Times* had predicted six months earlier.[150] Nevertheless, the new cabinet was a blow to the reformers, who objected especially to the preponderance of princes. It came to be called the "imperial kinsmen's cabinet" (*huangzu neige*). By running a full-page display of photographs in its May issue under the heading "imperial relatives in the political world," *Eastern Miscellany* at once drew attention to the prominent role that the princes were playing in Zaifeng's government. The photographs (plate 11) were of Yikuang, Zaixun, Zaitao, Pulun, Yulang, and Puwei (the opium prohibition commissioner). The *Eastern Times* similarly complained that of the cabinet's thirteen members, only four were Han, and that all of the most important posts had been assigned to imperial relatives (*qingui*). In early July it warned that these appointments were playing straight into the hands of the republican revolutionaries: "The revolutionary party constantly preaches anti-Manchuism. If the prime minister is a member of the imperial lineage, then they will use the excuse that the court discriminates in favor of Manchus [Manren] to sow doubt." Zhang Jian, the constitutionalist leader from Shanghai, privately deplored that "the government, as is evident in their control of the navy and army and the top ministerial posts, was entirely in the hands of imperial relatives [*qingui*]. This is contrary to the ancestral tradition."[151]

Most of the criticism, however, focused not so much on the number of Manchus or even princes in the new cabinet as on the appointment of an imperial kinsman, Yikuang, as prime minister. (This was the central point of the *Eastern Times* commentary in July.) Within four days of the naming of the cabinet, members of the Confederation of Provincial Assemblies (Ziyiju Lianhehui) were meeting in Beijing to vent their frustration.[152] In mid-June the confederation submitted via the Censorate a petition contending that the naming of an imperial kinsman as prime minister was incompatible with the basic idea of a constitutional monarchy, which was that the prime minister and the cabinet should insulate the monarch from partisan politics. Otherwise, it could pose an insoluble dilemma. If an imperial kinsman headed the cabinet and then the cabinet were overturned, this action would tarnish the monarch; if, on the other hand, a cabinet could not be overturned because it was headed by an imperial kinsman, this would not be a constitutional system. The confederation also argued that Zaifeng's appointment of Yikuang as prime minister (and indeed of the other princes as ministry heads) contravened the dynasty's own "ancient system," namely, that "imperial princes do not serve on the Grand Council." The complainants did not mention that the court had repeatedly contravened this tradition since Yixin's reappointment to the Grand Council in 1861; they chose, instead, to cite the Jiaqing emperor's edict of 1799 canceling the appointment of his brother Yongxing to the council, and they suggested that this mid-Qing prohibition on princely participation in state affairs was even more appropriate for the new cabinet than for the old Grand Council. Finally, they called for Yikuang to be replaced as prime minister by some other high official "who was outside the ranks of the imperial lineage."[153] Although the confederation did not specify that the new prime minister be a Han, Zhang Jian, Tang Shouqian, and other reformers in Shanghai urged Zaifeng to do as Cixi had done fifty years earlier when confronted by the Taiping Rebellion: appoint an experienced and well-educated high official who was Han. The man they probably had in mind was the disgraced Yuan Shikai, who, unlike Duanfang, still had not been recalled to office.[154]

Zaifeng refused to reconsider. He shelved the petition from the Confederation of Provincial Assemblies, and he rebuked one of his own high officials, Governor Sun Baoqi (1867–1931) of Shandong, who had submitted a similar memorial opposing the "participation of imperial relatives, both direct and collateral, in government." (Sun was an unlikely source for such criticism, as he was related to Yikuang by marriage; his was one of the rare instances of Manchu-Han intermarriage. His memorial stirred press speculation of a Machiavellian plot, engineered perhaps by Yikuang himself to strengthen his political stance. On the other hand, Sun had challenged the regent at least once before; an earlier memorial had discussed the benefits of cutting the queue and altering the dress code.)[155] Undeterred by the regent's nonresponse, the confederation in late June submitted a second petition, which stated that the naming of an imperial kinsman as prime minister had caused ridicule abroad and despair at home; it repeated its previous criticism that the appointment was contrary to the essence of a constitutional monarchy and called again for someone other than an imperial kinsman as prime minister. Shortly afterward the confederation issued a long public statement expressing its distress on six broad public issues, including foreign loans and railroad nationalization; the statement also complained that the court still had not responded to its two petitions regarding the prime ministership. It asserted that the new cabinet was no different from the old Grand Council, which the National Assembly had only recently impeached. "In name, it is a cabinet; but in substance, it is the Grand Council. In name, it is constitutionalism; but in substance, it is autocracy." The confederation called for the naming of a "complete cabinet" (wan-

quan neige), guided by the principle that "in a constitutional monarchy members of the imperial lineage cannot serve on the cabinet [as prime minister]." On 5 July Zaifeng finally responded to the confederation. He gave the group the same answer that he had given to the National Assembly in December, when it tried to impeach the Grand Council. Referring to the Constitutional Outline, the regent insisted, once more and for the last time, that the appointment of officials was the prerogative of the court and could not be infringed upon.[156]

The confederation was not, of course, satisfied with this response, but thereafter complaints about the new cabinet were eclipsed by the uproar that greeted Zaifeng's other two decisions in May, the nationalization of the trunk railroad lines and the agreement for a large foreign loan with which to build those railroads. As is well known, opposition to railroad nationalization and the foreign loan quickly spread throughout the country; by early September it had escalated into a provincewide rebellion in Sichuan. Finally, when New Army troops from Hubei were sent up the Yangzi River to quell the rebellion, it helped trigger the Wuchang Revolt and the onset of the 1911 Revolution.

CONCLUSION

The Qing dynasty began with Dorgon's regency (1643–50), and it was to end with another, Zaifeng's. Zaifeng had come to power because Cixi, thinking that she would outlive the dying Guangxu emperor, wanted another infant emperor with a compliant father as regent who would allow her to continue to "listen to government from behind the screen." Her unexpected death only one day after Puyi's ascension as the Xuantong emperor thrust the young and inexperienced Zaifeng into a complex and rapidly changing political scene that perhaps no one, not even Cixi herself, could have understood and mastered.

In some respects, Zaifeng simply continued and extended policies that Cixi had begun. It was Cixi who first stripped Yuan Shikai of his control over four of his six Beiyang divisions and turned them over to the Ministry of the Army; Zaifeng merely completed the process by imposing the ministry's control over the remaining two divisions. Similarly, it was Cixi who, when she abolished some ethnic slots and promised to make appointments "without distinction between Manchus and Han," began to appoint more, not fewer, Manchus to the top positions of the metropolitan government; Zaifeng, again, did as she had done previously. Thus, the Manchu-dominated cabinet that the regent appointed in May 1911 was not significantly different, except in degree, from the Manchu-dominated government that the empress dowager had named in late 1906 following the reorganization of the metropolitan administration.

In other respects, Zaifeng went beyond Cixi. Cixi's intent, as epitomized by her attempt to undercut Yuan Shikai's military independence, had been to recentralize power, to reassert the authority of the central government over the increasingly autonomous provinces. Zaifeng continued this policy, as seen, for example, in his reorganization of the Chinese navy and in his nationalization of the trunk railroad lines, but he went one step further. He wanted to reassert the authority not just of the central government but of the Qing court; he wanted not only to recentralize authority but to reimperialize it. This was a goal that Cixi shared, as reflected in the long-term trend that she had initiated and fostered of appointing more and more imperial princes to top government positions. Zaifeng perpetuated this trend as well, which culminated in the naming of the "imperial kinsmen's cabinet" in May 1911, but he went much further than Cixi had. Thus, he shifted the General Staff Council that Cixi had created as a subordinate agency of the Ministry of the Army, brought it under the direct control of the court, and made it independent of the central government. Similarly, even though the First Division was predominantly Manchu, he was not satisfied with its serving as an ad hoc palace guard because it was controlled by the Ministry of the Army. He therefore set out to organize another division-strength force that would be under his direct command. The formation of the new Palace Guard was one of the major accomplishments of Zaifeng's regency. In these efforts to reimperialize authority, he was guided by the proven successes of Japan under the Meiji emperor and Germany under the two Wilhelms.

Zaifeng, however, lacked Cixi's steadiness of purpose. On occasion, he was determined and strong-willed, even stubborn. Thus, he dismissed Yuan Shikai, who was then the second most powerful official in the country (after Yikuang). Despite extraordinary lobbying from all sides, he refused to pardon Kang Youwei and Liang Qichao; he refused to abandon the Manchu-imposed official dress code and queue requirement; and he refused to reconsider his appointments to the cabinet. On other occasions, however, the regent vacillated and yielded to pressure easily. Thus, he backtracked from Cixi's edict of late 1907 to disband the provincial banner garrisons, and, by granting exceptions from the mourning requirement to numerous Manchu officials, he made a mockery of his own decree ordering Manchus and Han to observe a uniform period of mourning for their parents.

As a result of such half measures, Zaifeng did little to resolve the Manchu-Han question. His main achievement on this front was to follow through on another of Cixi's decrees and subject the general banner population (though not the imperial lineage) to the same laws as the Han; by so doing, he erased the legal separation of Manchus and Han. Other forms of Manchu-Han differences, however, persisted. As of 1911 the Eight Banner system had not been disbanded or otherwise reconstituted, as under Zaifeng the Banner Reorganization Office was absolutely inert. Manchus were still classified as banner people, with most other Chinese classified as civilians. Except in Manchuria, the banner people were still subject to the jurisdiction of their own banner officials and independent of the regular civilian administration. The banner soldiers among them were still stipendiaries of the Qing state. The banner people still lived apart from Han in their own separate Manchu cities. Though no longer prohibited by imperial decree, they still, by and large, did not intermarry with Han. They still observed different social customs from the Han. Manchu women did not bind their feet; they dressed in "banner gowns" and wore their hair in a "bat-wing shaped" style. Manchu men referred to themselves by their personal name and did not use their family name in public. In sum, nearly all of the differences that had been highlighted during the late-1907 debate on Manchu-Han relations following the assassination of Governor Enming—differences that Cixi seemingly had promised to eliminate—still existed four years later, on the eve of the revolution.

If Manchu-Han differences remained, so too did the bitter enmity that many Han revolutionaries bore toward the Manchus. Wang Jingwei, the would-be assassin of the regent, was atypical in his lack of outrage at the state of Manchu-Han relations. More typical was George Fong, who, like Enming's assassin, Xu Xilin, had been obsessed with what he himself called the "racial question." In his 1910 attempt to kill the regent's brother, Fong had hoped to free China "from the clutches of the Manchus." This continuing, visceral hatred for the Manchus erupted yet once more on 8 April 1911, when the general of the Guangzhou garrison, the Manchu bannerman Fuqi, was shot to death by an overseas Chinese worker from Southeast Asia, Wen Shengcai (1870–1911). Before he was executed a week later, Wen repeatedly stated that he had killed Fuqi solely because he was a banner person and that by so doing, he hoped to gain revenge for his four hundred million (Han) compatriots; he called on others to take up where he had left off.[157] Six months later, Wen Shengcai got his wish, as the revolution for which he, Wu Yue, and Xu Xilin had sacrificed themselves finally began.

4 / The 1911 Revolution

The 1911 Revolution, which brought down the Qing dynasty and ended 268 years of Manchu rule over China, began with the Wuchang Revolt on 10 October 1911 and ended four months later with the abdication of the Xuantong emperor on 12 February 1912. The emperor's father, Prince Regent Zaifeng, making use of the new powers that he had amassed, mounted a reasonably effective military response to the initial uprising, but he fell afoul of the numerous political problems that had been left unresolved from the first session of the National Assembly. Within a month after the outbreak of the revolution, Zaifeng was forced to backtrack from the controversial "imperial kinsmen's cabinet" and yield to demands for the speedy summoning of a parliament. In the meantime, the revolution had spread beyond Hubei, and as it did so it engulfed the various banner communities in other provinces. Given the anti-Manchu rhetoric and deeds of the revolutionaries in the past, the banner garrisons in the affected regions faced the very real prospect of racial annihilation, which each had to deal with on its own. Some garrisons managed to survive the revolution relatively unscathed; others did not. Finally realizing the futility of the struggle, the Qing court entrusted its fortunes to Yuan Shikai, whom it had been forced to recall to office. Yuan, from the north, opened negotiations with the Republicans in the south. These negotiations led eventually, but not without several delays, to the abdication of the Qing.

THE COURT'S MILITARY RESPONSE

The Wuchang Revolt, which began on the night of 10 October, is perhaps the most written-about event in all of Chinese history, but in the voluminous celebratory accounts there is hardly any mention of how the Qing responded militarily to the uprising and the subsequent revolution. In fact, the imperial army and navy, on which Zaifeng and his two brothers had lavished much attention since the beginning of the regency, acquitted themselves quite well during the first three weeks. They launched an effective counteroffensive against the revolutionaries, culminating in the recovery of Hankou from the insurgents on 1 November.

The authorities in Beijing learned of the revolt in Wuchang early the following afternoon, on 11 October; it took them another day to make some sense out of what was happening. Associate Prime Minister Natong was entertaining some foreign diplomats at a hotel on the 11th when the French minister handed him the news. Leaving his guests, Natong hurried to the home of the prime minister, Yikuang, where other cabinet members and high officials had already gathered. There they spent the rest of the day and night, as more bad news poured in.[1] By the morning of the 12th, the entire Wuhan tri-city complex—Wuchang, Hankou, and Hanyang—had fallen into the hands of the revolutionaries. Most of the Hubei New Army had defected, and one of its two commanders, Li Yuanhong (1864–1928) of the Twenty-first Mixed Brigade, had been persuaded to join the mutineers and to head up their new Military Government, which soon also included leading members of the gentry and merchant elite. Only two battalions and Li's counterpart at the Eighth Division, Zhang Biao, had remained loyal to the Qing; they had retreated to the village of Liujiamiao (Liu Family Shrine), six miles north of the terminus of the Beijing-Hankou railroad. Meanwhile, from his refuge aboard a gunboat in the middle of the Yangzi River, Governor-General Ruicheng, the reform-minded Manchu bannerman who previously had been a member of Zhang Jian's constitutionalist group, wired Beijing asking that a "high official" be sent with a large contingent of "crack troops."[2]

The prince regent (and self-proclaimed generalissimo) ordered immediate military and naval reinforcements to Wuchang. His principal advisers were Zaitao and Yulang of the General Staff Office, navy minister Zaixun, and army minister Yinchang. All were Manchus, and all except Yinchang were imperial princes. On their advice, on 12 October Zaifeng put Yinchang in charge of the military operations and authorized him to take two New Army divisions to Hubei. He also directed both components of the reorganized Chinese navy, the sea-going fleet under naval commander-in-chief Sa Zhenbing and the Yangzi River fleet under Cheng Yunhe, to proceed up the Yangzi from Shanghai as quickly as possible.[3] Two days later Zaifeng tried, unsuccessfully, to enlist Yuan Shikai's help as well. After he was forced out in January 1909 on the trumped-up excuse of a foot ailment, the organizer of the Beiyang divisions had been living in comfortable retirement at his country home at Zhangde (now Anyang), in northern Henan. In the past there had been numerous suggestions that he be recalled to office; most recently, during the controversy over the "imperial kinsmen's cabinet," he was the unspoken choice among some critics of the cabinet to replace Yikuang as prime minister. Heretofore the regent had turned a deaf ear to all such proposals. Now he was driven to issue an edict naming Yuan governor-general of Hubei and Hunan (in place of the cashiered Ruicheng) and giving him the right of joint command with army commander Yinchang and naval commander Sa. Claiming that he had not fully recovered from his affliction, Yuan declined the appointment. However, from his personal telegraph office at his country estate, he began to offer suggestions, particularly regarding personnel, which the court eagerly accepted.[4]

Yinchang was a controversial choice to lead the military operations against the revolutionaries in Hubei. He was a Manchu bannerman with a dual career in diplomacy and military affairs. An early product of the Beijing Translators College, he was one of the first Chinese to study abroad (in Germany). In the late 1880s and the 1890s, he headed Li Hongzhang's Tianjin Military Preparatory School. He translated at the negotiations of the Boxer settlement and for Zaifeng during his visit of apology to Germany, and he was twice China's minister to Germany. (He was even married to a German.) He became army minister in 1910, when his predecessor Tieliang, frustrated at being eclipsed by the imperial princes Yulang and Zaitao, resigned. To his critics, Yinchang was more a diplomat than a military professional, as most of his military career, limited as it was, had been spent behind a desk. Liangbi, commander of the First Brigade of the Palace Guard, thought that Yinchang's reputation as a military expert rested upon his foreign studies and was undeserved. Nevertheless, as the incumbent army minister and as a Manchu, he was not an illogical selection as field commander.[5]

On the 14th Zaifeng and his advisers decided which troops to send with Yinchang to Hubei and what use to make of the other forces at their disposal. Due to the recent efforts at recentralizing and reimperializing the military, the Ministry of the Army had direct control over the first six divisions of the New Army (those that formerly constituted Yuan Shikai's Beiyang Army) while the regent himself had control over the new Palace Guard, whose commissioning ceremony he had attended less than a month before. It so happened that at this time five of these seven units, along with a mixed brigade from the Twentieth Division, were gathered together at Luanzhou (now Luanxian), east of Beijing, for the annual war games, which were scheduled to begin on 17 October. Canceling the war games, Zaifeng quickly recombined these units into three corps (*jun*). The First Corps was the force that Yinchang was to take to Hubei and was made up of the Fourth Division and the two mixed brigades from the Second and Sixth Divisions. The two divisions that were predominantly Manchu in personnel, the Palace Guard and the First Division, were designated as the Third Corps and assigned to defend the capital; they were recalled to Beijing and put under the command of Zaitao, the regent's brother, who had overseen the formation of the Guard and was cohead of the General Staff Office. The remaining troops, consisting of the mixed brigade from the Twentieth Division at Luanzhou and two units who were not at Luanzhou—the Fifth Division at Ji'nan, Shandong, and the Third Division at Changchun, Jilin— were grouped together as the Second Corps. Commanded by Feng Guozhang of the General Staff Office, they were to act as a backup to Yinchang's First Corps.[6] Zaifeng's decision to keep the predominantly Manchu Third Corps close to home while sending the First Corps, which was composed of Han soldiers, off to the front clearly smacked of "using Han to fight Han," which the revolutionaries had long accused the Qing court of doing as a matter of policy.

Yinchang was able to get his troops, numbering as many as twenty-five thousand, from the mock war at Luanzhou to the real war at Wuhan with remarkable speed. They went by train via the Beijing-Shenyang line (on which Luanzhou is situated) and then the Beijing-Hankou line, a trip of over six hundred miles that took only about forty hours. The first contingent of soldiers left for the south as early as 13 October; parts of the Twenty-second Infantry Regiment began arriving at the northern outskirts of Hankou two days later.[7] Yinchang himself departed Beijing on the 15th. As he passed through northern Henan, he paused to confer with Yuan Shikai at Zhangde. Yuan, who had turned aside the offer of joint command a day or two before, cautioned the Manchu commander not to take the revolution lightly. Reaching Xinyang in southern Henan on the night of the 17th, Yinchang stopped to await the passage of his main force, the Fourth Division.[8] As he waited, the Qing suffered a minor setback on the 18th, as the revolutionaries launched a surprise attack on Zhang Biao's small detachment of loyalist soldiers at Liujiamiao.[9] Zhang's group, however, retreated only a short distance northward to Shekou, and the Qing military buildup resumed. The Fourth Division, led by brigade commander Wang Yujia, arrived at Shekou on the 21st; two days later, Yinchang moved his command post forward to Xiaogan, only forty-five miles from Hankou. Meanwhile, Sa Zhenbing, coming up the Yangzi from Shanghai, had arrived off Wuhan with the first of his cruisers from the sea-going fleet, the *Haichen* (whose captain, Rongxu, was a Manchu), accompanied by a small flotilla of about ten gunboats and torpedo boats.[10]

By 21 October or soon thereafter, the Qing forces, both military and naval, were thus poised for a counterattack on the revolutionaries in Wuhan; yet the attack itself did not begin until the 27th. The delay proved to be extremely costly, perhaps even fatal, to the dynasty because it was during those six days that the revolution began to spill out of Hubei Province, to Changsha in Hunan and Xi'an in Shaanxi on the 22nd and to Jiujiang in Jiangxi on the 24th. Why the critical delay? Perhaps it was due to Yinchang's excessive caution and his inexperience as a field commander. Perhaps, as is most commonly alleged, it was also due to footdragging among his subordinates, many of them protégés of Yuan Shikai, who awaited their mentor's return from exile.[11] Certainly, as the revolutionaries hung on in Wuhan and as their sympathizers began to rise up in other provinces, the Qing court intensified its efforts to recall Yuan to office. According to a widely repeated (but poorly substantiated) account, after Yuan turned down his appointment as governor-general, Prime Minister Yikuang sent his deputy, Associate Prime Minister Xu Shichang, to confer secretly with his old patron. After visiting Zhangde on the 20th, Xu reported that Yuan insisted that the court commit itself to six reforms before he would agree to return to office, two of which were that he be given supreme, not simply joint, command over all land and naval forces and that he be guaranteed adequate funding. The accuracy of this account is difficult to verify.[12] In any case, Zaifeng soon gave in. On 27 October he issued an edict naming Yuan Shikai "imperial commissioner" with complete authority over all military and naval forces in Hubei. On Yuan's previous recommendation, he recalled Yinchang to the capital, ostensibly so that he could concentrate on his duties as army minister, and replaced him as commander of the First Corps with Feng Guozhang; Zaifeng also named Duan Qirui to succeed Feng at the Second Corps and placed both Feng and Duan under Yuan's supreme command. Feng Guozhang, formerly superintendent of the Nobles Military School, was then chief of the chancery at the General Staff Office; both he and Duan were old associates of Yuan dating back to the mid-1890s. The regent told Yinchang to wait for Yuan before leaving for Beijing.[13]

By no coincidence perhaps, the Qing counterattack on Wuhan began on the very day, 27 October, that Yuan was appointed imperial commissioner, but with Yinchang still in the field as commander. It was, from the Qing perspective, a huge success. On land, Wang Yujia's Fourth Division and Wang Zhanyuan's (1861–1934) mixed brigade from the Second Division, reinforced from the Yangzi River by Sa Zhenbing's fleet of ships, advanced southward from Shekou along either side of the Beijing-Hankou railroad tracks. Despite spirited opposition, the Qing forces pushed the Republicans steadily back to Hankou. By the end of the third day, they had reached the terminus of the railroad, having carefully skirted the foreign concessions lining the Yangzi waterfront. This was the first real battlefield experience for the Beiyang Army, and they had acquitted themselves very well. In Ralph Powell's estimation, "the tactics used were those of the contemporary Occident. Covered by artillery fire and the guns of the imperial squadron [i.e., Sa's navy], the royalists deployed a line of skirmishers followed by troops formed in close-order company fronts. As the skirmishers advanced, making use of cover, they were supported by volley fire from the main line." Only when they had fought their way back to Hankou did Yinchang, on 30 October, turn over command of the First Corps to Feng Guozhang. As he returned to Beijing with the dynasty's much-desired victory, he crossed paths at Xinyang with Yuan Shikai, who had finally accepted his appointment as imperial commissioner and was headed south toward the Hubei front.[14]

When Feng Guozhang took over from Yinchang, one section of Hankou still to be recovered was the Chinese City (Huajie), a walled area along the Han River opposite Hanyang. Some revolutionaries had sought refuge in its crowded quarters, while others continued to put up a stout, if disorganized, resistance. Ignoring Yuan's earlier advice to proceed cautiously, Feng pressed ahead with the attack on the Chinese City. As he did so, the Qing artillery, whether by design or by accident, set off a number of fires, which rapidly turned into a conflagration. According to various descriptions, Hankou's Chinese City became a "raging furnace," an "absolute inferno," and, later, "scorched earth." As two Western doctors from the Red Cross Association reported a couple of weeks later, three-quarters of the city had been leveled, and although relatively few lives had been lost, most of the population had become refugees. Feng Guozhang's perhaps wanton destruction of Hankou provoked a political furor at the newly reconvened National Assembly and served to tarnish the Qing triumph. It did, nevertheless, force the Republican defenders out of the city. On 1 November, as the last revolutionaries retreated to Hanyang, the Qing was once again master of all of Hankou.[15]

Yuan Shikai, however, failed to follow up the Qing victory at Hankou. With the revolutionaries in disarray and on the defensive and with his own troops more numerous and better armed and trained, he could probably have retaken Hanyang and Wuchang rather easily. Naval commander Sa Zhenbing, for one, was convinced that at this point the battle for Wuhan could have been won for the Qing. Yuan, though, claimed that the northern troops were exhausted and needed a rest. Intent on maximizing his own power in his ongoing negotiations with the Qing court, he reined Feng Guozhang in and ordered him to pause.[16]

However, the victory at Hankou, even if it had been followed by success at Hanyang and Wuchang, might have come too late to save the Qing by military means. Between 27 October and 1 November, during which time Hankou was recovered, the overall situation for the dynasty had worsened. The revolution, which had already spread beyond Hubei to Changsha, Xi'an, and Jiujiang, now encompassed three more cities in two new provinces: Taiyuan in Shanxi, Kunming in Yunnan, and Nanchang in Jiangxi (again). The insurrection in Shanxi, on 29 October, was particularly ominous because of Taiyuan's proximity to Beijing. It, moreover, coincided with the Luanzhou "armed remonstrance," in which New Army commanders in Zhili demanded that the Qing make extensive political changes. Thus threatened at close quarters from both the west and the east, Zaifeng's court finally realized the need to deal with the revolutionary outbreak as not only a military but a political problem as well.

THE COURT'S POLITICAL RESPONSE

The Wuchang Revolt on 10 October, coupled with the scheduled reconvening of the National Assembly twelve days later, revived various political controversies that had been quiescent since the previous spring, particularly the agitation against the "imperial kinsmen's cabinet" and for a parliament. As before, the regent was loath to make concessions. Nevertheless, by the end of October, as the overall military situation began to deteriorate, he had no alternative but to give in to long-standing demands for a complete restructuring of the government. Still unresolved, however, were other issues concerning Manchu-Han relations.

Soon after the outbreak at Wuchang, the agitation against Yikuang's cabinet and in favor of a parliament started up again after several months of sullen resignation. On 16 October Governor Cheng Dequan of Jiangsu submitted a memorial, drafted for him at his request by the Shanghai reformer Zhang Jian, calling on the Qing court to make two basic changes to regain the trust of the people and prevent the current "political revolution" from turning into a "racial revolution." One was to dissolve the "imperial kinsmen's cabinet" and appoint a "worthy and competent" person to form a new cabinet with full responsibility to act for the emperor; the other was to hasten the promulgation of the promised constitution, which the regent had already moved forward from 1916 to 1912. Yuan Shikai, from his retirement home at Zhangde, allegedly gave the court similar advice. When Xu Shichang saw him on 20 October, if the report of the visit is correct, Yuan demanded not only that he be given supreme military authority at the Hubei front and be assured of adequate supplies, but also that the court yield on four other issues of a general political nature, namely, that it "summon a parliament [guohui] next year, form a responsible cabinet, be lenient toward the people who have risen up at this time, and lift the ban on political organizations."[17]

When the National Assembly reconvened as scheduled on 22 October, with the Hanjun Li Jiaju (b. 1870) acting as president for the ailing Shixu, it quickly took up these same issues, which had been left unresolved from the first session. On 26 October it submitted a memorial asking that a "completely responsible cabinet" be formed quickly, that the summoning of Parliament be advanced from 1913 to 1912, and that the assembly be permitted to "discuss" (*huiyi*) the text of the constitution that Prince Pulun and others were supposed to be drafting prior to its promulgation by the throne. Three days later, it submitted three more memorials that made significant new demands. The first memorial, calling for a responsible cabinet, now insisted that imperial relatives be prohibited from serving not only as prime minister but also as cabinet ministers. This change, it contended, would accord with the basic principles of monarchical constitutionalism as well as with the dynasty's own "established institutions" (that is, as laid down by the Jiaqing emperor). The second memorial, concerning the drafting of the constitution, demanded that the draft be presented to the assembly to be "ratified" (*xiezan*), not merely "discussed," before it could be promulgated. The result would thus be a compact (*xintiao*) between the monarch and his subjects rather than a decree from above like the constitutions of Meiji Japan and Czarist Russia, which the assembly claimed were universally regarded as deficient. The third memorial, in addition to requesting an end to the ban on political organizations, also asked for a pardon not only for those involved in the current revolt but for all political offenders dating back to the 1898 reforms (such as Kang Youwei and Liang Qichao).[18]

Regent Zaifeng's response until now had been to shelve all such demands for further political reform. He had pigeonholed Cheng Dequan's memorial by "retaining it in the palace" (*liuzhong*). While granting Yuan Shikai's requests for military authority and financial support, he had done nothing about his four proposals for political change. Similarly, he had ignored the National Assembly's recommendations of 26 October. It is doubtful that Zaifeng would have been any more tolerant of its demands on 29 October, except that on that very same day the assembly unexpectedly received a major boost from a nearby source, a threatened mutiny known as the Luanzhou "armed remonstrance" (*bingjian*).

The chief "remonstrator" was Zhang Shaozeng (1879–1928), commander of the Twentieth Division, which had remained at Luanzhou, ninety-five miles east of Beijing, following the cancellation of the war games. Scholars disagree as to why Zhang, a graduate of the Japanese Army Officers School, threatened to mutiny at this time. Some say that he was sympathetic to the revolution and hoped to relieve the military pressure on the beleaguered revolutionaries in Wuhan then under attack by Yinchang; others say that he was at heart a constitutionalist reformer and that he took advantage of the insurrection at Wuchang to pressure the Qing court to reform.[19] Whatever his motivation, Zhang Shaozeng, together with two associates and two subordinates, submitted a joint memorial to the court on 29 October. They noted that in the almost three weeks since the Wuchang uprising, the court had responded to the insurrection only in a military way without any attempt as yet to correct the root causes, which they said were political. Contending that repression would only intensify revolution, they asked instead for reforms in the polity, which they spelled out in a twelve-point "political program." These reforms would help eliminate "racial differences" yet would not harm the "dignity of the emperor's position."[20]

The Luanzhou remonstrators' twelve-point program was similar to the National Assembly's three memorials of the same date, but on some points it was considerably more far-reaching. It called for the naming of a responsible cabinet in which members of the imperial lineage would be barred from being prime minister or cabinet members, the drafting of a constitution that would be subject to "discussion and decision" (*yijue*) by Parliament (not the National Assembly), and the pardoning of political criminals. It also called for the rapid convening of Parliament, not the following year but by the end of "the present year." Where it differed most from the National Assembly's memorials was in its claim for the supremacy of the popularly elected Parliament, which would have the sole authority, inter alia, to amend the constitution and elect the prime minister.[21] To get the attention of the regent and lend weight to his demands, Zhang Shaozeng ignored an order to take his troops from Luanzhou to the south.[22]

The Luanzhou armed remonstrance, occurring east of the capital, coincided with the revolutionary uprising in Taiyuan, to the west, which greatly magnified the military and political pressure on the Qing court. The threat from Taiyuan was particularly acute because of the relative ease with which the rebels could march out of the Taihang Mountains at Niangziguan onto the North China Plain, capture the strategic rail center at Shijiazhuang on the Beijing-Hankou line, and thus threaten not only the imperial forces at Hankou but the imperial court itself in Beijing. To deal with the problems in Shanxi, the regent named Wu Luzhen, commander of the Sixth Division at Baoding, to replace the murdered Shanxi governor and sent him (with troops) to Shijiazhuang to block any rebel attempt to march on Beijing.[23] Wu was to die about a week later under mysterious circumstances.

Thus, despite the victory at Hankou, Zaifeng was obliged by the military threat from Luanzhou and Taiyuan to yield to the steadily growing demands for political reforms. On 30 October, one day after receipt of the National Assembly's three memorials and the remonstrance from Zhang Shaozeng, the Qing court responded with an extraordinary edict issued in the name of the emperor. In it the five-year-old boy was made to take upon himself the blame for the outbreak of the revolution and its rapid spread. Replying to the chorus of criticisms about the cabinet, he acknowledged having exercised poor judgment in official appointments, especially in employing an excessive number of imperial relatives. He promised, "in cooperation with the soldiers and people of my country, to make a new beginning and implement constitutional government." Noting that his predecessor, the Guangxu emperor, had issued several edicts to "eliminate differences between banner people and Han" (*huachu qi-Han*), he vowed to put those edicts into effect.[24]

Aside from having the emperor take the blame for the current troubles and promise a new start, Zaifeng at last acceded to most of the National Assembly's repeated demands, particularly the three that had been singled out in its most recent memorials. First, he directed Pulun, who had been put in charge of drafting the constitution, to do so in accord with the Constitutional Outline and to submit the text of the constitution to the assembly for its careful "examination and discussion" (*shenyi*) prior to its promulgation by the emperor. "Examination and discussion," however, was less than the "ratification" that the assembly had asked for. Second, Zaifeng agreed that it was contrary both to the practices of constitutional states and to the "established institutions of our dynasty" to have "close relatives" (*yiqin*) of the emperor serving as cabinet members. He promised that as soon as the military and political situation had become more settled, the court would designate a worthy person to organize a "complete cabinet" and that thereafter it would not appoint an imperial relative (*qingui*) to the cabinet ever again. Third, the regent agreed to pardon three broad categories of political offenders: those guilty of "political coups" dating from 1898, those forced into exile because of "political revolution," and those who voluntarily repented their waywardness in the current "disturbance." Thus, Kang Youwei and Liang Qichao were finally pardoned. Though the regent did not explicitly revoke the traditional ban on political organizations, he promised to protect all legal activities and to stop making arbitrary arrests.[25] Perhaps because it was not among the assembly's most recent proposals, he said nothing about advancing the date for the summoning of Parliament.

The edicts of 30 October dealt with the stated concerns of the National Assembly but not those of the Luanzhou remonstrators. Indeed, Zaifeng at first tried to brush aside their twelve-point political program; he asserted that he had already incorporated into his earlier decrees those that were acceptable.[26] Zhang Shaozeng was not satisfied; on 1 November he wired the court again with another petition. Regarding the cabinet, he asked that the court not wait until conditions had stabilized before removing its imperial kinsmen members. According to Zhang, so long as the cabinet remained unchanged, the domestic disturbance would not subside. He repeated his previous demand that the prime minister be "popularly selected." With reference to the constitution, he asked that the Constitutional Outline of 1908 be scrapped altogether

1. Ming official in court dress. (From Zhou Xibao, *Zhongguo gudai fushi*, 392)

2. Ming scholar in informal dress. (From Zhou Xibao, *Zhongguo gudai fushi*, 401)

3. Qing official in court dress.
(From Zhou Xibao, *Zhongguo
gudai fushi*, 475)

4. Two Qing scholars in informal
dress. (From Zhou Xibao,
Zhongguo gudai fushi, 475)

5. Manchu woman and two Han women examining a shoe for a bound foot. (From Wu Youru, *Wan-Qing shehui fengsu baitu*, no. 75)

6. Empress Dowager Cixi, attended by court ladies, 1903. The Guangxu emperor's wife, the future Empress Dowager Longyu, is at the right. (From Bland and Backhouse, *China Under the Empress Dowager*, 256)

7. Schoolboy with a queue and military-style cap, wearing a long gown and "horse jacket." (From H. Y. Lowe, *The Adventures of Wu*, 5)

8. Zaifeng (holding Pujie) with Puyi, circa 1908. (From Bland and backhouse, *China Under the Empress Dowager*, 4)

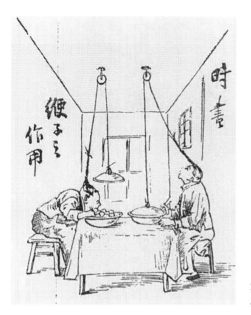

9. "Uses for the queue (1)." (From *Shibao*, XT 2/3/4 [13 April 1910], 2)

10. "Uses for the queue (2)." (From *Shibao*, XT 2/3/6 [15 April 1910], 2)

11. "Imperial relatives in the political world." *From top to bottom, left to right:* Yikuang, Zaitao, Zaixun, Puwei, Yulang, and Pulun. (From *DFZZ* 8, no. 2 [XT 3/2; April 1911]. Courtesy of East Asian Library, Columbia University)

12. "Banner woman altering her dress (1)." (From *Shibao*, XT 3/9/6 [27 Oct. 1911] supplement. Courtesy of Jiao Tong University Library)

13. "Banner woman altering her dress (2)." (From *Shibao*, XT 3/9/6 [27 Oct. 1911] supplement. Courtesy of Jiao Tong University Library)

14. "Banner woman after altering her dress. (From *Shibao*, XT 3/9/7 [28 Oct. 1911] supplement. Courtesy of Jiao Tong University Library)

15. Prominent Manchus with Premier Zhou Enlai, 1961. *First row, from left*: Puyi (second), Lao She (third), Zaitao (fourth), Zhou (sixth), and Pujie (last). (From *China Pictorial*, 1979, no. 8: 39)

rather than serve as the basis for the future constitution, and also that Parliament, not Pulun, be responsible for drawing up the new constitution.[27]

Perhaps as a result of Zhang Shaozeng's second petition but probably mostly because of Yuan Shikai's calculated foot-dragging at the Hubei front, the Qing court did act on the "imperial kinsmen's cabinet" without waiting for conditions to settle down. On 1 November, the day of Zhang's petition, Yikuang's cabinet resigned. Taking note of the emperor's penitential edict, Yikuang and his two associate prime ministers, Natong and Xu Shichang, said that they, rather than the emperor, should be blamed for the worsening crisis. They asked to be relieved of their positions so that a "worthy and capable" person could be appointed quickly to organize a "complete cabinet." In a separate memorial, the four other imperial princes besides Yikuang who were cabinet ministers—Zaize, Zaixun, Pulun, and Shanqi—likewise resigned. Zaifeng promptly accepted their resignations as well as those of the rest of the cabinet. At the same time, he named Yuan Shikai as prime minister and authorized him to organize a "complete cabinet." Yuan, who was to retain his position as commander-in-chief of all military and naval units at the Hubei front, was to come to the capital as soon as he had taken care of the situation at Wuhan. In a show of appropriate modesty, Yuan declined his new appointment several times. Pending his acceptance and arrival, Yikuang's cabinet continued as before. Meanwhile, other princes who were high-ranking metropolitan officials similarly gave up their positions. Thus Zaitao, the regent's brother, resigned on 1 November as one of the two chiefs of the General Staff Office and was replaced by army minister Yinchang, a Manchu bannerman but not of the imperial lineage. Whereas Zaitao seems to have quit of his own volition, it appears that his colleague at the General Staff, Yulang, refused to do the same; he was dismissed ten days later and succeeded by Xu Shichang, the former associate prime minister.[28]

On 2 November, the following day, Zaifeng took up the other main issue in Zhang Shaozeng's second petition, the procedure for writing the constitution. Previously, the regent had entrusted a committee headed by Pulun with the task of drawing up the document, which then was to be "examined and discussed" by the National Assembly; now, in response to Zhang's petition, the regent authorized the assembly itself, rather than Pulun's committee, to "draft" the constitution. In this same edict, Zaifeng praised Zhang Shaozeng and his military associates for the "sincerity of their patriotism." He also pointed out to them that, with the replacement of Yikuang by Yuan Shikai as prime minister, he had met their call for a new cabinet. He clearly hoped that he was done with the Luanzhou armed remonstrance.[29]

Zhang Shaozeng, however, was still not satisfied. On 3 November he submitted a third petition expressing frustration with the court's incomplete response to his original twelve-point political program, especially with regard to the cabinet and the constitution. He noted that although the "imperial kinsmen's cabinet" had resigned, the prime minister was still imperially appointed rather than designated by a popularly elected parliament. He also was displeased with the new arrangement for drawing up the constitution, which should be written by the future parliament and not by the current National Assembly. The assembly was an "organ of the old government, incapable of representing the entire country." Any constitution that it drew up would lack input from the nation's citizens and thus would still be "imperially decreed." Zhang Shaozeng therefore called for the immediate formation of a "provisional government" (by which he seems to have meant a parliament) as well as a military cease-fire. He bluntly stated that "if [the court] cannot summon parliament, if it cannot enact a constitution, if it cannot elect a prime minister, then it cannot solve its basic problem."[30]

In contrast, the National Assembly did not share Zhang Shaozeng's disappointment with Zaifeng's response to the demands for political reforms. On the contrary, its members (at least those ninety or so assemblymen who were still in attendance) were exceedingly pleased with the regent's decision to assign them the task of drafting the new constitution. Meeting on 2 November, they greeted his edict with applause, with some shouting, "Long live the country and the Emperor!" Furthermore, they accomplished their assignment with extraordinary dispatch. Realizing that it would take too long to write a whole new constitution, they opted on 3 November for a stop-gap measure, a Nineteen-Article Compact (Shijiu Xintiao) that would serve as the basis of the constitution that they would enact later. They asked the court to publish the document and to swear adherence to it at the dynasty's Temple of Ancestors (Taimiao). This, the assembly said, would unite the nation and protect the imperial household (huangshi). Zaifeng's court did as the assembly requested. It proclaimed the compact at once, and it promised to pledge allegiance to it at the Temple of Ancestors at a later date, which Zaifeng eventually did on 26 November.[31]

Although Zhang Shaozeng had opposed entrusting the enactment of the constitution to the National Assembly because it was not a popularly elected body, the Nineteen-Article Compact fulfilled nearly all of the stated aims of his armed remonstrance. Many of the compact's nineteen articles were virtually identical in wording to Zhang's twelve-point political program, which may explain how the compact could have been written in only one or two days. The compact recognized the exalted status of the Qing emperor but circumscribed in various ways his authority over the constitution and Parliament. Thus, the emperor would command the army and navy but could not use them in a domestic situation without the prior approval of Parliament. The emperor could not legislate by decree. The National Assembly would "discuss and decide" (*yijue*) the constitution, which subsequently only Parliament could amend. Parliament would approve annual budgets as well as ratify international treaties. Parliament would also elect the prime minister, who in turn would nominate the members of his cabinet. The compact reiterated the court's newly decreed prohibition of imperial kinsmen from serving on the cabinet and barred them from senior provincial posts as well. Pending the election of Parliament, the National Assembly would exercise all of its responsibilities.[32]

Still, the convening of Parliament had not been advanced any closer than 1913. The National Assembly, despite its general satisfaction with the Nineteen-Article Compact, pressed the regent once more for an earlier date. In response, Zaifeng on 5 November authorized the assembly to enact as soon as possible the requisite regulations for the organization of Parliament and the election of its members. He pledged that once those laws were passed and the elections held, he would convene Parliament.[33] Thus, with the regent's embrace of the Nineteen-Article Compact and his promise to convene Parliament speedily, the Luanzhou armed remonstrance came to an end. By then only one of Zhang Shaozeng's original demands—that the constitution be drawn up by a popularly elected parliament rather than by the National Assembly—had not been met. On 5 November Zhang Shaozeng was removed as commander of the Twentieth Division, given an ostensible promotion, and transferred to the Yangzi valley, where it was hoped that he would use his now considerable reputation to soothe the rebels. He left Luanzhou four days later.[34]

Meanwhile, the National Assembly was also demanding that Zaifeng make good on his promise of 30 October to pardon political criminals. At this time, the most prominent political offender under custody was Wang Jingwei, the regent's would-be assassin, who was imprisoned in Beijing. On 2 November and again a couple of days later, members of the assembly asked why Wang had not been released; it claimed that his confession had contained no "wild words" and had expressed only a desire to "stimulate the spirit of constitutionalism." On 6 November Zaifeng ordered Wang's immediate release and directed that he be returned to his native Guangdong.[35] Once freed, Wang Jingwei remained in Beijing, where he was to play a role in the subsequent negotiations between the revolutionaries and the court.

Politically, the first month after the Wuchang Revolt was concerned mostly with the "imperial kinsmen's cabinet," the drafting of a constitution, and the summoning of Parliament. Nevertheless, despite being overshadowed by other issues, questions about Manchu-Han relations continued to be raised at the National Assembly. On 27 October Assemblyman Mou Lin (from Guizhou) repeated the common complaint that the Banner Reorganization Office, in the three years since its establishment, had done nothing toward eliminating Manchu-Han differences, which he claimed had become more numerous than before. Another assemblyman, Wang Jilie, likewise called for the elimination of Manchu-Han differences, notably in name-giving practices. On 2 November, Assemblyman Gao Lingxiao from Sichuan introduced a proposal to "dissolve Manchu-Han differences" (*ronghua Man-Han*) so as to "melt away racial boundaries" (*huachu zhongzu jiexian*). Gao proposed several specific reforms, none of which was new, though none had yet been implemented: banner personnel should add Han-style surnames; Manchu women should adopt the "common" costume of Han women, which would facilitate intermarriage; provincial banner garrisons should be abolished, and Manchu cities opened up for residence to everyone; officers and able-bodied soldiers of the garrisons should be incorporated into regular military units, while the old and weak should be given a one-time grant of grain. When another assemblyman, Li Shangwen of Hunan, suggested adding queue-cutting to the list of proposed reforms, Gao Lingxiao fended off the amendment. A majority of the assembly then voted in favor of Gao's original resolution. It would appear that even at this late date, queue-cutting was regarded as an issue so controversial that it might sidetrack all the other reforms.[36]

In response to such pleas for improving Manchu-Han relations, Zaifeng's court continued to be evasive. On the one hand, the boy emperor, in his penitential edict of 30 October, acknowledged that his predecessor, the Guangxu emperor, had issued several unspecified edicts to "eliminate differences between banner people and Han," which he now promised to put into effect. On the other hand, in another edict that was likewise issued in his name, the emperor on 4 November fell back on traditional generalities about the dynasty's impartiality. He enumerated the various concessions the court had made as China embarked on the difficult transition from despotism to constitutionalism. He insisted that only a minority of the populace were spreading the slander of "racial revolution." Denying that the Qing had ever practiced discrimination, he noted that Shun was a Yi from the east and Yu was a Qiang from the west, but (despite their alien origins) both had become sage rulers of China (Zhong-Xia).[37] In the end, Zaifeng failed to act on any of the specific reform proposals that Assemblyman Gao Lingxiao had advanced; nor, of course, did he on his own revisit the issue of the queue.

In sum, by early November, the Qing court had been induced to make numerous important political concessions. In particular, when it dissolved Yikuang's controversial cabinet and replaced it with one that was free of imperial kinsmen, it had put an end to Zaifeng's three-year effort at reimperializing authority and to Cixi's fifty-year trend toward greater and greater princely involvement in governmental affairs. However, four weeks into the revolution, the Qing court still had not done anything more to reduce, let alone eliminate, the considerable differences that continued to separate Manchus and Han. To the court, "racial revolution" may have been merely slanderous talk; to the banner garrisons in the provinces, it was a threat to their very lives.

ANTI-MANCHU VIOLENCE

Zaifeng's political concessions at the beginning of November may have defused the Luanzhou armed remonstrance, but they did not halt the spread of revolution. Despite the recovery of Hankou from the revolutionaries in Hubei and the dispatch of Wu Luzhen to open up a second front along the Taihang Mountains bordering Shanxi, the Qing steadily lost ground elsewhere, as more and more cities, especially in central and south China, went over to the Republican side. A large number joined the revolution in early November, including Hangzhou (5 November), Zhenjiang (7 November), Fuzhou (8 November), and Guangzhou (9 November). Others followed later: Chengdu (27 November), Nanjing (2 December), Jingzhou (17 December), and Yili (7 January 1912). Along with Xi'an and Taiyuan, which had defected in late October, all of these were banner garrison cities with sizable Manchu populations.

The 1911 Revolution, after a slow start, gathered strength so rapidly that it is easy to overlook the violence it unleashed. Popular as it may have been, it was by no means bloodless. This aspect of the revolution, however, has been minimized in nearly all the retrospective accounts. The revolution's most likely victims were the Manchus in the banner garrison cities. Despite a decade of criticisms from both revolutionaries and constitutionalists and of repeated promises by the court to reform, the gulf between Manchus and Han had not significantly narrowed by the time the revolution broke out. Nor, notwithstanding the mellow note of Wang Jingwei's confession in 1910, had the anti-Manchu rhetoric of the republicans been significantly toned down. The result was a wave of anti-Manchu violence, which began with the outbreak of the revolution in Wuchang and which later engulfed the banner garrisons at Xi'an, Taiyuan, Zhenjiang, Fuzhou, and Nanjing. Furthermore, the Jingzhou garrison was besieged for nearly a month, during which it suffered enormous casualties, though in the end it avoided a massacre. Other garrisons escaped relatively unscathed, though never without first confronting the threat of racial annihilation. Individual Manchus in isolated situations, away from their home garrisons, faced the same threat.

The first outburst of anti-Manchu violence occurred at the very beginning of the revolution. Wuchang was not, of course, a banner garrison city; nevertheless, a large group of Manchus were living in the Hubei capital in 1911 as a result of one of the early post-Boxer reforms. Since 1904 the provincial authorities and the Jingzhou garrison commanders had arranged for a thousand banner soldiers from Jingzhou to train with the New Army in Wuhan, where they constituted about 10 percent of the Hubei New Army. A majority of the banner soldiers seems to have been concentrated in the Thirtieth Infantry Regiment in Zhang Biao's Eighth Division. Two of the four companies in the regiment's First Battalion and one each in the Second and Third Battalions were headed by officers with Manchu-style names. So was one other unit in the division, the Second Battalion of the Thirty-second Regiment. If these five companies, each with about 150 soldiers, were composed entirely of bannermen, they would have accounted for three-fourths of the banner soldiers in Wuhan. The rest were in the military police, which was predominantly Manchu, or scattered among the other units of the Hubei New Army. The Military Middle School, outside Wuchang, also had "several tens" of students from the Jingzhou garrison.[38]

The three companies in the First and Third Battalions of the Thirtieth Regiment and the military police were the ones who bore the initial brunt of the revolutionaries' anti-Manchu fury because their barracks were located inside Wuchang near the armory, which was the rebels' immediate objective on the night of the 10th. (The other two companies led by officers with Manchu-style names were outside Wuchang and in Hankou.)[39] As the revolutionaries headed for the arsenal to arm themselves, one of their rallying cries was "Slay the Manchu officials and the banner people!" (Shalu Manguan qiren). Although the banner soldiers in the Thirtieth Regiment offered little or no resistance, many were killed. The barracks of the predominantly Manchu military police were also overrun and destroyed, and at least ten banner soldiers were beheaded. By the next morning, bodies of dead banner people littered the streets of their neighborhood.[40]

The Hubei Military Government, newly proclaimed on 11 October, seemed intent to avenge the three captured revolutionaries whom Governor-General Ruicheng and his military adviser Tiezhong, both Manchus, had executed the previous morning. Its declared goal was to "elevate the Han and exterminate the Manchus" (xing-Han mie-Man). It consequently wiped out four leading Manchu families (Zha, Bao, Tie, and Bu) in Wuchang and confiscated their property. It tore down the Eight Banners Guildhall (Baqi Huiguan), the meeting place and hostel for banner personnel in the Wuhan area. Finally, on 12 October, after its headquarters at the Provincial Assembly had come under attack from a ragtag group of banner soldiers led by a loyalist Han battalion commander, it initiated a witch hunt for surviving Manchus in Wuchang. Revolutionary soldiers began systematically stopping people on the streets simply because they looked or sounded different and subjecting them to a quick quiz intended to reveal whether they were Manchus. According to Li Lianfang, "Those people whose head was flat in the back were ordered to pronounce the number 666 [*liubailiushiliu*] and if they said *niu* rather than *liu*, they were executed." (The Manchus' flat head was supposedly due to the unusual hanging cradle in which they spent their infancy; their accent bespoke their social segregation from their neighbors.) No one failing the test was spared.

> One banner woman, about to be killed, piteously cried, "We are guiltless; we detest our ancestors for their mistreatment of the Han people." Another old woman pleaded, "What is to be gained by murdering us worthless women and children? Why not release us as a show of your magnanimity?" The soldiers, though moved, dared not reply but killed them anyway.

Xiong Bingkun (1885–1969), a leader of the uprising, confirms that the anti-Manchu violence peaked on 12 October, when many Manchus were seized and killed. The bloodshed that day was so appalling that over a hundred of the city's merchants and gentry members jointly asked the Military Government to prohibit its soldiers from entering private homes in search of Manchus. The government refused at first on grounds of military necessity.[41]

It was only following the intervention of the eleven foreign consuls in Hankou, so it is said, that the Military Government called a halt to this reign of terror. On the 13th, while considering a request from the revolutionaries to remain neutral in the nascent struggle against the Qing, the consuls purportedly asked them to stop the wanton murder of the Manchus. The revolutionaries acquiesced, but with obvious reluctance. As one of their later proclamations explained, "They [the Manchus] have seized our lands and taken away our rights. Now in order to seek our revenge, we rightly ought to exterminate them with all our might and so dissipate the pent-up hatred of our compatriots." Such savagery, however, it went on to say, might make the foreign powers ridicule their cause. Consequently, the Hubei Military Government did as the consuls asked and issued an order prohibiting further vengeance against the "banner people." The decree told the citizenry instead to hand over suspected Manchu spies to the Military Government for trial. Otherwise, as another directive warned, anyone found harboring a Manchu (Manren) would be beheaded.[42]

As a result of the proclamation of 13 October, but also because the revolutionaries had, for the moment at least, consolidated their control over Wuhan, the worst of the violence against the Manchus came to an end. By then hundreds of Manchus had been massacred. One representative of the Military Government toured Wuchang and calculated that no fewer than four hundred to five hundred "banner people" had been killed during the first three days of the revolt. Their bodies were still lying around and threatened to spread disease; they were eventually buried. A correspondent for the Reuters news agency, visiting Wuchang on the 14th, "found corpses of Manchus everywhere" and estimated that eight hundred had been slain. Cao Yabo asserts that altogether four hundred "banner soldiers" were killed during the uprising and another three hundred "persons of banner classification" (*qiji renyuan*) were arrested and detained at the Wuchang prison. About a hundred of these detainees were released in the spring of 1912, after the revolution had succeeded, and safely returned to Jingzhou. They thus avoided the tragic fate of seven captured banner soldiers who were released prematurely and were murdered on their way home. The rest of the Manchus in the Wuhan tri-city complex, particularly those fortunate ones who were not trapped inside Wuchang when the revolution began, fled.[43] Noting that all the high-ranking Manchu officials in Wuchang—including Governor-General Ruicheng, Provincial Treasurer Lianjia, and the military adviser Tiezhong—had likewise escaped, Li Lianfang, despite his own account of the vigilante justice meted out to Manchus, concludes that "the arrests and the killings were not so extreme as described in popular accounts." Joseph Esherick is probably closer to the truth when he says that what happened to the banner people in Wuchang "approached racial slaughter."[44]

The first city with a full-fledged banner garrison to experience large-scale anti-Manchu violence was Xi'an; it was also the scene of the bloodiest encounter between the banner people and the revolutionaries. The population of the garrison in 1911 was probably twenty thousand. They lived, well defended, inside their spacious walled compound in the northeastern sector of Xi'an City.[45] The revolution came to Shaanxi on 22 October, when sympathizers in the New Army, after persuading Chief of Staff Zhang Fenghui (1881–1958) to join their cause, rose up in support. Unlike in Wuchang, where elements of the New Army were stationed inside the city and were thus able to seize it from within, the Shaanxi Mixed Brigade was quartered about a mile outside Xi'an, while the arsenal—which, as at Wuchang, was the revolutionaries' first objective—was located inside Xi'an (but outside the Manchu City). At midday on the 22nd, revolutionary soldiers split up into small groups and made their way into Xi'an City undetected by the banner soldiers guarding the city's west and south gates. They then gathered at the arsenal and easily captured it from its surprised defenders. Fortified by the Mauser and Mannlicher rifles stored at the armory, they quickly overran most of the city. The only part of Xi'an that the revolutionaries did not immediately take was the Manchu City. Its commanding general, Wenrui, ordered all the gates closed and posted soldiers atop the walls.[46]

The following morning, the revolutionaries launched a concerted assault on the Manchu City, with one group, led by the New Army officer Zhang Fenghui, attacking from the south and another group, headed by a leader of the Elder Brothers Society (Gelaohui), Zhang Yunshan (1877–1915), from the west. The banner soldiers were no match for their opponents. About two thousand banner soldiers (one-third of the garrison's statutory strength) had received some modern training as a result of reforms in the 1890s, but they were poorly armed. The three thousand modern rifles that Ronglu had purchased fifteen years earlier had been sold off. Thus, in contrast to the revolutionaries with their modern rifles, the Manchus were using ancient muzzle-loaders and obsolete breech-loading rifles. Yet the banner soldiers resisted fiercely. The fighting lasted all day. Finally, Zhang Fenghui discovered a weak spot along the Manchu City's south wall, while Zhang Yunshan succeeded in capturing one of the two gates along its west wall. By then, though, it was late in the day. To avoid killing their own people in the approaching darkness, the revolutionaries decided to hold off their final assault until morning.[47] Meanwhile, in the name of the Han Restoration Army of Shaanxi and Gansu (Qin-Long Fu-Han Jun), they issued a brief announcement that various provinces had risen up to "expel the Manchus" (*paichu Manren*) and that this was in accord with both heaven's will and popular sentiments. The proclamation vowed to protect the citizenry (*min*), merchants, and foreigners and to regard Han and Muslims as one, but it pointedly did not extend protection to the Manchus. It can thus be seen as sanctioning the bloodbath that ensued.[48]

The next day, the 24th, Xi'an's Manchu City fell. As the revolutionaries poured in from the south and west, they looked upon all its trapped inhabitants as potential enemies and slaughtered them indiscriminately. According to J. C. Keyte, a British missionary who investigated the scene several months later,

Old and young, men and women, little children, were alike butchered. . . . Houses were plundered and then burnt; those who would fain have lain hidden till the storm was past, were forced to come out into the open. The revolutionaries, protected by a parapet of the wall, poured a heavy, unceasing, relentless fire into the doomed Tartar city. Those who tried to escape thence into the Chinese city were cut down as they emerged from the gates.

Two junior officers in the New Army concede, retrospectively, that the Republicans "unnecessarily killed a number of banner soldiers and their dependents."[49]

The slaughter was merciless and thorough. According to Keyte,

> When the Manchus found that further resistance was useless, they in many cases knelt on the ground, laying down their weapons, and begged the soldiers for life. They were shot as they knelt. Sometimes there was a whole line of them. In one doorway a group of between ten and twenty were thus killed in cold blood.

Some of the banner people attempted to flee, but, as in Wuchang, it was difficult for them to escape detection.

> They were known by their clothing, by their cast of countenance, by their speech. Their fondness for reds and yellows, their use of white linings, their high collars and narrow sleeves . . . their belts, their shoes; all gave them away. With the women the unbound feet were the fatal distinction. Their peculiar headdress, their clothing they might change, but there was no disguising their natural-sized feet.

As at Wuchang, suspected Manchus were subject to a pronunciation test, though, as Keyte noted, "this often meant danger for Chinese of other provinces, especially Chihli [Zhili]," because they too spoke standard Chinese with a Beijing accent. Many banner people, seeing that there was no escape, committed suicide. Some set fire to their houses and burned to death; others cut their own throats; yet others threw themselves down deep wells—until the wells were choked with the dead and the dying. Chang'an county magistrate Derui, after killing his wife and children, tried to set himself on fire; when that failed, he grabbed a knife and stabbed himself to death. General Wenrui threw himself down a well and drowned; his principal subordinates, the garrison's two brigade-generals, also committed suicide.[50]

On the 25th, after three days, the revolutionaries decreed an end to the violence.[51] By then, according again to Keyte, the total casualties were "not less than ten thousand who were either killed or took their own lives to escape a worse fate." If the population of the banner garrison was twenty thousand, then half had perished. Furthermore, the Manchu City had been systematically plundered. Those banner personnel who survived the massacre were rounded up. Well-to-do survivors, such as the provincial judge Xitong and the industrial intendant Guangzhao, were held for ransom. Little girls were abducted by the rich as household servants and slaves, while young women were claimed as wives by poor Han soldiers who otherwise could not have afforded to marry. Others were expelled from the city and told to find their own living.[52]

Taiyuan, capital of Shanxi Province, was the second garrison city to feel the wrath of the revolutionaries. One of the smaller garrisons in China proper, it had a statutory strength of only 644 banner soldiers and was headed by Commandant Zengxi. The tiny Manchu City was nestled inside the high city walls at the southwestern corner of Taiyuan City. The revolution came early on the morning of 29 October, one week after Xi'an fell, when units of the provincial New Army defied an order transferring them to the southwest to stop the anticipated spread of the revolution from neighboring Shaanxi. The mutinous troops forced their way into Taiyuan City, killed the governor and the New Army brigade commander (both of them Han), then headed for the Manchu City. They placed guns atop the city walls and began bombarding the still-sleeping banner people below. The Manchus could only offer brief and sporadic resistance; the commandant surrendered. As a result, perhaps no more than twenty or twenty-five of the Manchus were killed. Those who survived, however, either fled or were driven away. The Manchu City was looted and, according to two resident Westerners, "utterly destroyed."[53]

The next Manchu City where many were killed was Zhenjiang, the treaty port in Jiangsu where the Grand Canal crosses the Yangzi. The garrison had a statutory strength of 1,692 soldiers and was commanded by Brigade-General Zaimu, an imperial clansman. Unlike in Wuchang, Xi'an, and Taiyuan, the anti-Manchu violence in Zhenjiang occurred not during but after the city had been "restored" to Han rule on 7 November. Three days earlier, following the fall of Shanghai, the scholars and merchants of Zhenjiang had opened negotiations with the brigade-general in an attempt to forestall the two New Army regiments outside the south gate from rising up and attacking the city in support of the revolution. These negotiations led to a public meeting at the Self-Government Office on 6 November, where Zaimu agreed to surrender the garrison in return for a guarantee of safety for the lives and property of its inhabitants. The banner soldiers afterward turned over their weapons and ammunition to the Self-Government Office. Thus, the garrison had already been disarmed before the New Army mutinied on the 7th and the city joined the revolution. Furthermore, the newly formed Zhenjiang Military Government, on the advice of the local elite, had agreed to give the banner soldiers three months' supply of rations and help them find alternative employment.[54]

Unfortunately, due to a series of misunderstandings, the new regime's policy of tolerance toward the surrendered garrison did not last. On 9 November, when Republican soldiers attacking Nanjing were driven off and fell back to Zhenjiang to regroup, they took out their frustration and rage on the local banner people, unaware that their safety had been guaranteed. By the time the retreating troops were ordered to desist, they had killed twenty to thirty of the Manchus and ransacked their quarters. Feeling betrayed, Brigade-General Zaimu committed suicide, while other banner soldiers attempted, unsuccessfully, to bombard the revolutionaries' headquarters. The Military Government, in turn, revoked its earlier policy of leniency and evicted the rest of the banner people from the Manchu City. Moreover, once they left the relative safety of the Manchu City, the banner people were hunted down by rebel soldiers and by bandits masquerading as soldiers. Finally, at the request of the Self-Government Office, the Military Government issued a new decree asking that the banner people not be harmed. By then, the Manchus had been ousted from Zhenjiang and an untold number killed.[55]

Fuzhou, another garrison city, was restored to Han rule the day after Zhenjiang. Its statutory strength was about 2,200 banner soldiers, nearly all of whom had received some modern training in recent years. The garrison commander was Pushou, but he shared power with another Manchu bannerman, Governor-General Songshou.[56] In the three or four weeks since the uprising at Wuchang, particularly as the revolution began to spread to east China, Songshou and Pushou together had taken several precautionary measures. On the one hand, they tried to disarm the local New Army detachment, the Tenth Division, by removing the ammunition from their encampment outside the city. On the other, they distributed a foreign rifle and three hundred bullets to every bannerman over the age of thirteen and a small sword to every banner woman. These measures spawned alarming rumors about the Manchus' ultimate intentions. It was said that they had organized a "Han-killing gang" composed of five hundred bannermen and led by the regimental colonel, Wenkai, and that they had mounted big guns and buried land mines within the Manchu City and, if attacked, were prepared to take the rest of Fuzhou and its Han residents down to destruction with them.[57]

As tension mounted, the city's elite (as previously in Zhenjiang) attempted a last-minute effort to avert bloodshed. On the afternoon of 7 November, a couple of days after neighboring Zhejiang had peacefully declared for the Republic, the Fujian Provincial Assembly approved a like-minded proposal that the province issue a declaration of "independence and self-protection" and establish a new government. The assembly asked Governor-General Songshou the next day to accede to the new authorities, and it requested General Pushou to order the banner personnel to hand over their arms and ammunition. In return, the assembly promised "henceforth to treat Manchus and Han without distinction" and also "to continue distributing the Manchus' salaries as before." The garrison commander, Pushou, refused to go along with the proposal.[58]

That night, soldiers of the Tenth Division rose up against the Manchus. Despite the officials' precautions, they had managed to acquire weapons and ammunition smuggled out to them from the city. Thus armed, they headed for and, with little difficulty, captured the artillery emplacement on Mount Yu, from which they could bombard the Manchu City below. As at Xi'an, the banner population at Fuzhou did not give up without a fight. Several hundred soldiers, led by Wenkai of the "Han-killing gang," attempted unsuccessfully to recapture the guns on Mount Yu and suffered heavy casualties. Other banner people, in a vengeful mood, hosed down neighboring Han homes with kerosene and set the area ablaze. The fighting between the rebels and the Manchus lasted into the following day. By the afternoon of 9 November, it appeared as if the Manchus had had enough; they sued for peace and agreed to a cease-fire. The cease-fire, however, did not hold, as on the morning of the 10th about one hundred banner soldiers made a final, desperate lunge at the revolutionary line. They were beaten off. The recalcitrant Pushou was found, arrested, and held at Mount Yu, where, according to his nephew, he was killed as he fought his captors and "cursed them as insubordinate bandits." His body was hacked into four pieces and left on the side of the mountain. With Pushou's death, the Manchus' resistance came to an end. Meanwhile, during the three days of fighting, many other banner people had lost their lives. Some were slain as they resisted the revolutionaries or defended the Manchu City. Others killed themselves rather than be captured. Governor-General Songshou committed suicide by swallowing gold; regimental colonel Dingxuan strangled himself; Lang Le'e, an officer in the garrison's semimodernized force, and more than ten members of his family covered themselves with oil-soaked blankets and burned themselves to death; several hundred other banner soldiers and their dependents cast themselves down wells or into the Min River and drowned.[59]

However, when the revolutionaries took over on 11 November, they, unlike those at Xi'an, treated the defeated banner population with remarkable leniency. They gave medical attention to wounded Manchus. They provided appropriate burials to those who had been killed. They even held a memorial service for Governor-General Songshou, and they permitted General Pushou's family to retrieve his broken remains. They allowed many captured garrison officers, including the organizer of the "Han-killing gang," Wenkai, to go free. Finally, although they disregarded the Provincial Assembly's pledge to continue the banner soldiers' stipends indefinitely, an offer that had been rendered moot by the Manchus' resistance, they nevertheless gave each of the several hundred surrendered banner soldiers one silver dollar and a peck of rice before sending him out to make his own way in the world.[60]

The Manchus in Nanjing, when the city fell to the revolutionaries on 2 December, were not nearly so fortunate. The post-Taiping strength of the garrison, located in the southeast corner of the city, was 2,424 soldiers. The garrison commander was Tieliang, the former grand councilor and army minister who had run afoul of the regent's program of reimperializing authority and been sent away from the capital in September 1910. He shared power with two Han officials: the Liang-Jiang governor-general Zhang Renjun and Zhang Xun (1854–1923), the commander of the old-style Yangzi patrol troops.

In the weeks following the outbreak of the revolution at Wuchang, the Nanjing authorities had taken a number of precautions similar to those at Fuzhou. On the one hand, they had strengthened their own defenses by bringing Zhang Xun's ill-trained but loyal troops into the city. On the other, they had disarmed the local New Army unit, the Ninth Division, whose reliability was questionable, and relocated it twenty miles to the south.[61] Nonetheless, the atmosphere in Nanjing became increasingly tense among both Han and Manchus as the revolution spread into Jiangsu Province, particularly after Shanghai fell on 4 November. Greatly contributing to the anxiety of the Han inhabitants was Tieliang's well-known reputation as pro-Manchu and anti-Han. As in Fuzhou, it was rumored that the Manchus had mounted guns on the city walls and mined the approaches to the banner quarters and had vowed to bring down all of Nanjing with them. Although Tieliang issued a public denial, it is doubtful that he was believed. Indeed, these rumors circulated so widely that British diplomats at the time and some historians subsequently have accepted them as true.[62] At the same time, the Manchus in Nanjing, mindful of what the Taipings had done to them sixty years earlier, were no less fearful. According to the recollections of a Han telegraph operator,

> Entire families of Manchus cried bitterly every day. The women were especially frightened, because they did not bind their feet and did not dress the same as the Han. They would go to used-clothing stores to buy Han women's apparel and make themselves up as Han; they would even force girls who were already about ten years old to bind their feet. The men, too, changed their names [probably by adopting surnames] so as to pass for Han.[63]

At this critical juncture, the elite of Nanjing, like those at Zhenjiang and Fuzhou, sought to mediate a peaceful solution, but without success. On 6 November the vice-chair of the Provincial Assembly met with Governor-General Zhang Renjun and urged him to abandon the Qing cause, declare his province independent, and so avoid a military confrontation with the revolutionaries. The governor-general was amenable to this course of action, but he was overruled, not by the Manchu Tieliang, as some sources state, but by the Han commander of the Yangzi patrol forces.[64] Zhang Xun, shunting aside both Zhang Renjun and Tieliang, took control of Nanjing's defenses and immediately initiated a witch hunt against suspected Republicans, which lasted two days. According to Percy Horace Kent,

> The search for revolutionaries resolved itself into a hunt for students and queueless men, and for persons showing signs of the white badge of revolt, or anything that by any stretch of imagination might be so considered. On the night of the 8th alone it was said that four hundred suspects were executed, and their heads hung over the doors of their own homes.[65]

Murderous Zhang Xun held off the revolutionaries for a month. Repulsed on 7 November, the Republicans withdrew downriver to Zhenjiang, where they regrouped and awaited reinforcements. (It was then that they attacked the unfortunate Manchus at that garrison.) With Nanjing increasingly isolated, time was on their side. When they returned two and a half weeks later, they had put together a large army of about thirty thousand soldiers, as opposed to Zhang Xun's force of about twenty thousand (including two thousand banner soldiers). On 24 November the Republicans began a concerted assault on Nanjing along a wide front, aiming initially to capture the artillery batteries atop the several mountains ringing the city. Despite the spirited opposition of Zhang Xun's troops, they took Mount Mufu to the north on the 25th and Purple Mountain to the east on 1 December. Zhang Xun, in the end, sued for peace. On 1 December he made three requests of the revolutionaries: that he be allowed to leave Nanjing with his Yangzi patrol force, that Zhang Renjun and Tieliang be permitted to return north, and that the local banner people be spared. The Republicans were willing to let the governor-general and garrison commander go and to spare the Manchus, but they refused to permit Zhang Xun to depart with his army intact. Yet that very night Zhang Xun and two thousand of his troops were able to sneak out of the city, cross the Yangzi, and retreat northward along the tracks of the Tianjin-Pukou railroad; they wound up at Xuzhou, in northern Jiangsu. Zhang Renjun and Tieliang, too, managed to flee, escaping to Shanghai aboard Japanese gunboats.[66] The revolutionaries took over Nanjing on 2 December.

The subsequent massacre of the Manchus in Nanjing occurred even though, unlike in Xi'an and Fuzhou, they had not been in the forefront of the resistance against the revolutionaries. The principal opposition had come from Zhang

Xun and his army, who were Han. Nevertheless, it was the Manchus, defenseless since the abrupt departure of their leaders, who fell victim to the revolutionaries' pent-up rage. On 3 December elements of the Republican army, particularly those under the command of Su Liangbi, entered the Manchu City and went on a rampage. As a soldier belonging to another unit recalled, Su's army "burned, killed, and plundered" at will. According to Fernand Farjenel, a visiting French scholar, "The revolutionary troops set fire to [the Manchu City] and surrounded the burning buildings, firing on every Tartar who sought to save a few of his belongings. Those who fled empty-handed got away with their lives." Fearing the wrath of the revolutionaries, some banner people killed themselves by bashing their heads into mail boxes and steel poles. Others gathered at the arsenal and set themselves on fire, igniting an explosion that rocked the city and blackened the sky for a day. Order was not restored until later in the day, when the Republican commander-in-chief issued a proclamation promising safety to surrendered banner people. Su Liangbi was arrested and his marauding troops disbanded. By then, however, an "incalculable number" of banner persons had been killed and the Manchu City reduced to "scorched earth." In March 1912 Farjenel found that "of the Tartar quarter not one stone is left standing. We went for a drive among the ruins, and saw nothing but charred and crumbling walls, every house having been systematically burned to the ground." Only two grinning stone lions on pedestals remained outside a former yamen.[67]

The victory at Nanjing is often described as the last important battle of the revolution.[68] It did indeed lead to a general truce between the Republicans and the Qing, which was to be extended repeatedly until the court's abdication the following February. Still, despite the truce, there was one other major military confrontation between the revolutionaries and the Manchus that did not end until two weeks later. This was the month-long battle for Jingzhou, up the Yangzi from Wuchang. Commanded by General Liankui, the garrison in 1911 had a population of twenty-seven thousand. They occupied the entire eastern half of Jingzhou City and accounted for nearly half of the city's total population.[69] Aside from Beijing, no other place in China proper had proportionately as large a Manchu population.

Although the battle for Jingzhou did not begin until 19 November, pressure on the garrison had been building steadily for over a month. On 18 October revolutionaries led by a local New Army officer, Tang Xizhi, had risen up and captured Yichang, from which they gradually extended their influence. By 5 November they had all of Yichang Prefecture under their control, except for Jingzhou and the adjacent treaty port of Shashi.[70] In the meantime, attempts to persuade the garrison to join the revolution had been unsuccessful. The head of the Hubei Military Government, Li Yuanhong, had sent a telegram to Liankui on 26 October promising that if his banner soldiers surrendered their weapons to the approaching Republican troops, they would be well cared for. The Manchus would be treated the same as the Han people and their private property would be protected. Subsequent appeals by the revolutionaries to the Jingzhou garrison explained that though they were "anti-Manchu" (*pai-Man*), they aimed "only to overthrow the government and not to wipe out the banner people." The garrison commanders rejected the Republicans' appeal. Their reply questioned the sincerity of Li's promise and his political motives. While they applauded his intention to "reform the government," they asked why he persisted in rebellion when the Qing court had on 3 November already given its assent to the Nineteen-Article Compact. And they deplored the ferocity of the anti-Manchu massacre at Wuchang, whose victims were from the Jingzhou garrison. Claiming that pregnant women and infants in swaddling clothes had been indiscriminately killed, they asked what murdering these women and children had to do with "reforming the government." At Jingzhou, they claimed, "banner soldiers" and Han people had lived together in peace for more than two hundred years. They got along well with each other and over time had eliminated various (unspecified) racial differences. The revolutionaries should withdraw to Yichang to await the outcome of the revolution.[71]

When Tang Xizhi and the Republicans began attacking Jingzhou on 19 November, the banner forces, which included at least one well-armed regiment of newly trained troops, resisted fiercely. They initially staked out a forward position ten or more miles away from the city, but in a week of fighting, in which they suffered heavy casualties, they were successively driven back toward Jingzhou. By 26 November they were trapped inside the city. On the 27th, as they had done at least twice before, General Liankui and his subordinates sent out a desperate plea to the court for help. Jingzhou, they said, was surrounded. With Wuchang and Yichang in the hands of the revolutionaries, they were cut off from their food supply. Their ammunition was depleted. They asked that the recently victorious Qing troops at Hankou be sent to their rescue. As before, no aid was forthcoming. The garrison authorities began confiscating goods from the city's inhabitants, including wood products to use for fuel.[72]

The Manchus withstood the siege for two weeks. They defended themselves at first by holding the Han residents in the western half of the city hostage. After about ten days the Han, through the mediation of a resident Franciscan priest, Marcel Sterkendries, convinced the officials to allow them to leave, though without their personal belongings. The departure of the Han from Jingzhou, however, left the Republicans free to bombard the Manchus. On 9 December they pounded the city with an artillery shelling that lasted ten hours and caused numerous casualties. The garrison's will to fight began to crumble. The main proponent of resistance had been one of the two brigade-generals, Hengling. As the battered garrison ran out of ammunition, food, and firewood, the survivors went to Hengling and implored him to surrender. Bereft of support, the brigade-general killed himself on 10 December. General Liankui then asked for peace. In the ensuing negotiations, which were mediated by the Franciscan priest as well as by the Japanese consul and the customs commissioner at Shashi, the two sides arrived at a six-point agreement. For their part, the Manchus agreed to give up their arms and ammunition, turn over their public lands and public property, and obey the Hubei Military Government. The revolutionaries, in return, promised to protect the lives and private property of individual banner people, provide "charitable rations" to all impoverished banner people for a period of six months, and allow banner people to attend Republican schools. On the basis of this agreement, Liankui went to the Catholic mission on 13 December to surrender. Four days later, as agreed upon, Tang Xizhi and the revolutionaries entered Jingzhou City without incident. Unlike in Xi'an, Zhenjiang, and Nanjing, they exacted no retribution against the surviving Manchus.[73]

Elsewhere in China, four other banner garrisons—in Hangzhou, Guangzhou, Chengdu, and Yili—experienced the revolution at first hand, but unlike the others they did so relatively peacefully, with little or no bloodshed but scarcely any less anguish. In Hangzhou the vice-chair of the Zhejiang Provincial Assembly and other civic leaders had gone to their governor, the Mongol bannerman Zengyun, on 3 November to urge him to issue a preemptive declaration of independence and also to tear down the internal wall separating the Manchu City from the rest of Hangzhou and reclassify the banner people as Han. When Zengyun refused, the New Army rose up the following night in support of the revolution. Subsequent efforts to persuade the garrison to surrender foundered on the opposition of the regimental colonel, Guilin, the Manchu bannerman who four years earlier had gained national prominence for his vigorous support of women's education and the Huixing Girls School. However, once the Republicans began on the 5th to shell the Manchu City from gun emplacements on Mount Wu, the garrison's acting commander, Deji, gave up, in return for a pledge from the new Military Government to spare the banner populace and to continue, at least for a while, to distribute the customary rations to the banner soldiers. Unreconciled to the settlement, regimental colonel Guilin held back a large quantity of arms and ammunition in hopes of continuing the struggle. When discovered a couple of days later, he was arrested and executed. Zengyun and Deji, on the other hand, were well looked after.[74]

Guangzhou, of course, had been a center of revolutionary activity since Sun Yat-sen led an abortive uprising there in 1895; most recently, in April 1911, it was the scene of General Fuqi's assassination. Fuqi's successor, Fengshan, the Hanjun who in 1907 had been the pawn in the struggle between Tieliang and Yuan Shikai over control of the Beiyang divisions, was himself gunned down on 25 October, as he arrived to take up his new post. The banner populace of Guangzhou had ample reason to fear the revolutionaries, who were beginning to converge on the provincial capital. While some Manchus favored taking up arms to defend themselves and holding the rest of the city hostage, most favored cooperating with the local elite to try to forestall a revolutionary assault with a declaration of provincial autonomy. These talks bore fruit on 9 November, when a mass meeting at the Provincial Assembly proclaimed Guangdong's independence from the Qing empire and its adherence to the new republic. One of the ten resolutions passed by the meeting provided that "all banner people and Manchus [qi-Manren] would be dealt with the same [as the Han]." The revolutionaries took over the city the following day, unopposed and with no further bloodshed.[75]

Chengdu, where the revolution may be said to have begun with the railroad protection protests in the summer, did not declare for the Republic until 27 November. As in Guangzhou and other provincial capitals, this declaration resulted from negotiations between the officials and the local elite. Governor-General Zhao Erfeng, himself a Hanjun, had asked that "there be no animosity toward the Manchus [Manren]" and that "the livelihood of the banner people be provided for." The elite readily promised that the banner soldiers would continue to receive their rations pending future arrangements for their livelihood and that "Manchus, along with Mongols and Muslims, would be treated exactly the same as the Han, without any distinction."[76] Accordingly, Zhao Erfeng on 27 November issued a declaration of provincial autonomy and sanctioned the formation of a new government, jointly headed by the chairman of the Provincial Assembly, Pu Dianjun (1876–1934), and the commander of the New Army's Nineteenth Division, Zhu Qinglan (1874–1941). The former governor-general, despite his immense unpopularity for his harsh treatment of the railroad protesters, was permitted to remain in Chengdu so as to continue to oversee affairs relating to the Tibetan border. The new regime in Chengdu, however, proved incapable of controlling the various revolutionary "people's armies" as they poured into the capital demanding to be paid. On 8 December, with the treasury exhausted, some of the soldiers mutinied and drove Pu Dianjun and Zhu Qinglan out. When order was restored, the superintendent of the Military Primary School, Yin Changheng (1886–1953), had taken over as the new military governor. Two weeks later, on 22 December, Yin accused former governor-general Zhao of plotting a counterrevolution and had him arrested and beheaded, thus "avenging a great hatred among us Sichuanese."[77] Afterward the Chengdu banner garrison, which up to this point had been left undisturbed, was disarmed. Negotiations between Governor Yin and the garrison's commander, Yukun, secured an arrangement by which the Manchus surrendered their weapons in return for a pledge from the new government to help provide for their livelihood.[78]

The last banner garrison to be restored to Han rule before the Qing abdication was Yili, in far-off Xinjiang. The revolution at Yili began, as elsewhere, with a mutiny by local New Army soldiers, which occurred on the night of 7 January 1912. From their encampment outside Huiyuan (now Yining) City, they easily forced their way into and took over the "Old Manchu Camp" in the eastern half of the city, including General Zhirui's yamen. They encountered stiff resistance, however, from the Xibe banner soldiers in the "New Manchu Camp" in the western half of the city. When it became apparent that the New Manchu Camp would not give up easily, the revolutionaries agreed to a mediation effort by the garrison's former commanding general, Guangfu. With the apparent assistance of the local chamber of commerce, Guangfu arranged for the banner soldiers to turn over their weapons and for the revolutionaries to stop fighting. The Republicans, rather remarkably, then selected Guangfu as the first head of the new Yili Military Government. He remained military governor for several months, though it appears that real power was exercised by the revolutionaries and the New Army commanders. Because of the conciliatory outcome of the revolution, only a few Manchus were killed; among these, though, was the reform-minded Zhirui, who was executed.[79]

Manchus in banner garrisons were not the only ones threatened by anti-Manchu violence; so were individual bannermen on official assignment in various localities in central and south China. The highest ranking among such individual victims of the revolution was Duanfang, who had only recently been politically rehabilitated following his dismissal as Zhili governor-general in 1909 because of ritual infractions at Cixi's funeral. Duanfang was en route from Chongqing to Chengdu to take over from Zhao Erfeng as Sichuan governor-general when on 27 November, at Zizhou, the detachment of New Army troops that he had brought with him from Hubei mutinied and placed him under arrest. According to some sources, Duanfang pleaded for his life by claiming, correctly, that though he was a Manchu bannerman, his ancestry was originally Han, and by asking that he be allowed to reclaim his Han status. He also sought clemency on the grounds that he had always been an upright official. As with Governor Enming in 1907, Duanfang's captors acknowledged that he had been a fair-minded official but insisted that their quarrel with him was not a private matter but one of "national revenge." They hacked Duanfang and his brother to death.[80]

Numerous other Manchus serving as provincial and local officials met a similarly violent end. Some were slain while resisting the rebels, as happened to Dehu, prefect of Fengxiang, Shaanxi, and to Rongjun, an expectant magistrate at Tianmen, Hubei. Some were murdered after they joined the revolution. For example, Qilin, prefect of Shunning, Yunnan, complied with the provincial declaration of secession but was nevertheless shot and eviscerated when rebellious bandits took over the town. Yet others committed suicide. These included Guiyin, prefect of Anlu, Hubei; Laixiu, prefect of Tingzhou, Fujian; and Ronglin, a tax collector at Baihe, Shaanxi. Another suicide was the naval officer Jisheng, first mate of the cruiser *Hairong*, after the sea-going fleet had defected to the Republicans at Jiujiang in early November; he killed himself by jumping into the Yangzi. Such anti-Manchu violence extended to the dependents of bannermen officials. When Prefect Dehu was killed, so were his two young sons. Before the Jiahe (Hunan) magistrate Zhonglin committed suicide, he bound his wife to a bed and set it ablaze. At Yichang, Hubei, five Manchu women were executed and their blood smeared on the local yamen doors.[81]

However, not all Manchu officials in rebel territory died or were killed. Many managed to flee before the revolutionaries took over. These included the circuit intendant at Jiujiang, Jiangxi; the prefect of Hengzhou and the county magistrate of Youxian, both in Hunan; and about forty expectant officials living at the Eight Banners Guildhall at Suzhou. Others, though captured by the revolutionaries, were spared and allowed to leave. At Nanchang, Jiangxi, five banner men and women were arrested, turned over to the local military government, and eventually expelled from the province. Similarly, following the defection of the sea-going fleet at Jiujiang, the two Manchu captains of the *Hairong* and *Haichen* (Xichang and Rongxu respectively) were sent off to Shanghai. Like Duanfang, Captain Xichang had pleaded for mercy with a partial denial of his ethnic heritage: "Although I am a Manchu, my ancestors were Han and our original surname was He." Finally, in a few instances, individual Manchus were allowed to remain where they were, as was the case with Chunliang, magistrate of Yongshun County, Hunan, after he was reclassified from bannerman to civilian and had adopted the new Han-style surname of Wu.[82]

In sum, the Manchus responded to the revolution in various ways. Some garrisons mounted a spirited defense. Two garrisons—Ningxia and Suiyuan, both along the northern frontier—actually succeeded in beating off the Republicans.[83] Otherwise, the most effective opposition was at Jingzhou, which held off the Hubei revolutionaries for three and a half weeks. Xi'an, Fuzhou,

Hangzhou, and Yili also fought back. On the other hand, garrisons such as Taiyuan, Zhenjiang, Guangzhou, Nanjing, and Chengdu did not resist. (In the case of Nanjing, where there was resistance, it had come not from the Manchus but rather from the Han soldiers of Zhang Xun.) At some garrison cities the local elite, represented by the provincial assembly and/or the chamber of commerce, sought to mediate between the revolutionaries and the banner populace. Some of these efforts, as in Zhenjiang, Guangzhou, Chengdu, and Yili, succeeded in arranging a peaceful transfer of power. Some, as in Fuzhou, Hangzhou, and Nanjing, failed to prevent the two sides from clashing.

The extent of anti-Manchu violence varied, too, but with no clear correlation with the degree of resistance. The Guangzhou and Chengdu garrisons, neither of which resisted, experienced hardly any violence. In several other garrisons where there was resistance—notably Fuzhou, Hangzhou, Jingzhou, and Yili—once the fighting stopped, so, by and large, did the killing. Though a few leaders were executed—such as Regimental Colonel Guilin at Hangzhou, Governor-General Zhao Erfeng at Chengdu, and General Zhirui at Yili—the banner populace were left alone after they had capitulated to the Republicans. On the other hand, the garrisons at Xi'an, Taiyuan, Zhenjiang, and Nanjing along with the banner detachment at Wuchang suffered horribly from anti-Manchu violence. At Wuchang, Xi'an, and Taiyuan the banner soldiers had resisted, but those at Zhenjiang and Nanjing had not. Whatever the provocation, if any, the Manchus in those five places were slaughtered, driven to commit suicide, or expelled and their residential quarters looted and destroyed. The slaughter was indiscriminate and was directed at not only the soldiers but also their dependents, including women and children. They were essentially victims of genocide. It is thus clear that for many revolutionaries, the anti-Manchu element of their ideology was no mere rhetorical flourish.

The often-futile efforts of the banner people to save themselves by passing for Han also clearly show that at the time of the revolution, there were still some very obvious differences separating Manchus and Han. Manchus were easily identifiable by their place of residence, their speech (not Manchu, but the Beijing dialect of standard Chinese), their naming practice, and, in the case of women, their dress and the size of their feet. As depicted in a series of three cartoons in the *Eastern Times* in late October 1911, the women sought to blend in by replacing their one-piece gown with the two-piece blouse-and-trouser outfit worn by Han women, getting rid of their elaborate wire-framed headdress, cutting their hair short and wearing it in a bun, and, finally, shedding their platform shoes and even trying belatedly to bind their feet (see plates 12, 13, 14).[84] As was evident at Wuchang, Xi'an, and Nanjing, such efforts at concealment were usually ineffectual.

Finally, the anti-Manchu violence was largely confined to the southern, central, and northwestern parts of China proper, where the Republicans were most active. Banner garrisons in north China, Beijing, and Manchuria—where as many as two-thirds of all the banner people lived but where the revolutionaries were relatively weak—were spared almost entirely. Undoubtedly they too would have been exposed to the threat of anti-Manchu violence if the revolution had continued and spread. However, by the time Han rule was restored to Yili in January 1912, the Qing court (with Yuan Shikai now acting on its behalf) was actively engaged in negotiations with the Republicans that soon led to the abdication of the emperor and the end of the revolution.

THE NORTH-SOUTH NEGOTIATIONS

By early November 1911, the confusion of the first three weeks of the revolution had, to a great extent, settled down. It was evident by then that the revolution would not succeed easily, for the Qing court under Zaifeng had made considerable headway in coping with its military and political challenges. Specifically, with Yinchang and then Feng Guozhang in command of the First Corps, it had recaptured Hankou from the Republicans, and by approving the Nineteen-Article Compact, it had agreed to most of the political reforms that the constitutional monarchists had been demanding for years. However, it was also clear that the revolution had substantial support across the country and among a broad spectrum of social groups and would not be easy to defeat, for by then the Republicans and their sympathizers in the New Army and the provincial assemblies had extended their control from Wuchang in Hubei to the capitals of five other provinces. As the Qing and the Republicans headed toward a stalemate, the two sides gingerly entered into negotiations, seeking to break the deadlock. These tentative talks culminated in the convening of a formal parley in Shanghai in mid-December.

In Beijing the months of November and December were dominated by the steady ascendency of Yuan Shikai. When first named on 1 November as prime minister to succeed Yikuang, Yuan, who was then at the war front in Hubei, had declined. In line with the demands of the constitutionalist reformers for a responsible cabinet, he insisted that his appointment come not from the emperor but from Parliament. The ninety-two remaining members of the National Assembly, which under the Nineteen-Article Compact was empowered to act as a provisional parliament, obliged on 8 November by electing Yuan prime minister. The court ratified the assembly's action the following day.[85] Only then did Yuan accept the appointment. Surrounded by two thousand bodyguards, he arrived in Beijing on the afternoon of the 13th. An edict of the same day conferred upon him full military authority around the capital, including "all divisions in the metropolitan region." The one unstated exception was the new division-strength Palace Guard, which remained under the direct control of the court, with Zaifeng still its nominal commander.[86]

Once installed in Beijing, Yuan Shikai further extended his power at the expense of Zaifeng and the Qing court. On 22 November he persuaded the court to grant him the authority to make decisions in most matters (except those involving the imperial household) that previously had been the jealously guarded prerogative of the throne. Specifically, all memorials and petitions would henceforth be addressed to the cabinet and not the emperor. At the same time, Yuan obtained permission to excuse himself and his cabinet from the necessity of daily audiences at court.[87] On 6 December, with the apparent support of Empress Dowager Longyu, widow of the Guangxu emperor, he engineered the resignation of the prince regent, who was blamed for all of the shortcomings of the past three years. Zaifeng reclaimed his former title as Prince Chun, with an annual pension of fifty thousand taels from the imperial household account, but was barred from "any further participation in government." Longyu, emulating Cixi perhaps, took over from Zaifeng the conduct of court affairs, though no new regent was appointed for the child emperor.[88] Finally, Yuan succeeded in stripping the Palace Guard from the control of the court. On 9 December an imperial edict, issued at the request of Yuan's cabinet, removed Zaifeng's brother, Zaitao, from the Guard's training commission, with which he had been associated since its inception, and appointed Feng Guozhang, the First Corps commander and Yuan's former subordinate, as the unit's new commander in place of the former regent. (Succeeding Feng at the Hubei front was another of Yuan's protégés, Duan Qirui.) Another edict dismissed the young, Japanese-trained imperial clansman Liangbi as commander of the Palace Guard's First Brigade and transferred him to a high-sounding position of no real authority at the General Staff Office. Feng Guozhang formally took command of the Palace Guard from Zaitao on 21 December.[89] Not only had Yuan Shikai regained control over his Beiyang divisions, but he had dealt yet another blow to the Qing court's recent efforts to reimperialize military authority.

Meanwhile, Yuan Shikai, acting on behalf of the court, sought out the revolutionaries concerning a military cease-fire and, possibly, a negotiated political settlement. Yuan had failed to follow up on the Qing recovery of Hankou and instead had ordered his troops on 4 November to halt their advance on Hanyang. At the same time, he directed one of his subordinates, Liu Cheng'en (a native of Hubei), to write to Li Yuanhong, head of the Hubei Military Government, urging him to accept a "peaceful resolution" to the crisis and to allow the chastened Qing court an opportunity to reform itself. A week later, when the Republicans had not responded, he sent his private secretary, Cai Tinggan (1861–1935), to go with Liu Cheng'en to Wuchang to meet personally with Li Yuanhong. Feng Guozhang, then still the Qing commander at the Hubei front, disapproved of these initial contacts with the revolutionaries.[90]

Yuan Shikai also enlisted the aid of Wang Jingwei, the revolutionary Alliance leader who had been imprisoned for the attempted assassination of the prince regent in 1910. Released on 6 November, Wang, rather than going south to join his fellow revolutionaries, remained in Beijing and soon linked up with Yang Du, the former advocate of constitutional and banner reform, who had become a trusted member of Yuan's political entourage. Wang had known Yang in Japan several years earlier, when both were students at Hōsei University. Perhaps in line with a strategy of "allying with Yuan to overthrow the Qing," he joined Yang Du on 15 November in publishing a manifesto, issued in the name of the Society for the Joint Resolution of National Problems (Guoshi Gongji Hui), in which Wang claimed to speak for the "democratic constitutionalist party" and Yang, the "monarchical constitutionalist party." Though differing over the form of the polity, Wang and Yang declared that they both were committed to constitutional government and popular rights. Their manifesto called on the Qing and the Republicans to stop fighting, lest the foreign powers step in and partition China, and also to agree to the summoning of a "provisional citizens' assembly" that would choose between the two types of constitutional regime.[91]

The two sides eventually agreed to a cease-fire, but not for another three weeks. The revolutionaries were initially disinterested because, after the setback at Hankou, they had regained their momentum. By late November every province along the Yangzi River and south of it had declared for the revolution, as had Shaanxi and Shanxi in north China. At the end of November, however, they suffered two military setbacks. In Hubei, Li Yuanhong and Huang Xing (1874–1916) were unable to hold onto Hanyang, which Feng Guozhang's First Corps retook on 27 November; in Shanxi, the rebels along the Taihang Mountains buckled under the attack of Cao Kun, whose forces eventually (on 12 December) recaptured the strategic pass at Niangziguan and thus relieved the military pressure on Beijing. These reverses on the Republican side were matched on the imperial side by the fall of Nanjing to the revolutionaries on 2 December. Their offsetting defeats convinced the two sides to stop fighting and start negotiating. On 1 December the revolutionaries at Wuchang had already agreed with Yuan's emissaries to a three-day local cease-fire. On 7 December, one day after Zaifeng's resignation as regent, the court consented to a formal parley with the rebels.[92] Except at Jingzhou and Yili, the military phase of the revolution was, by and large, over.

Even before the formal talks began at Shanghai in mid-December, each side had begun to stake out its negotiating position. As Yang Du and Wang Jingwei had put it, the choice was between monarchical constitutionalism and democratic (or republican) constitutionalism. The Qing court, by November, had gone a long way toward converting itself from an autocratic to a constitutional regime. It had, for example, agreed to a proto-constitution in the form of the Nineteen-Article Compact and to a "responsible cabinet" headed by an elected (rather than appointed) prime minister; it had also empowered the prime minister to deal with nearly all aspects of governmental administration. Yuan's emissaries, in their exploratory talks with Li Yuanhong in early November, contended that by these reforms the aims of the revolution had been mostly met. As Liu Cheng'en told Li, "The court still retains the position of emperor nominally, . . . but all power is in the hands of the Han people."[93]

The Qing sought to bolster its case for monarchical constitutionalism by facing up to the revolutionaries' well-worn accusations of racial discrimination. The court, in two edicts issued in early November, repeated its customary denial that such discrimination existed—insisting that, for example, "Manchus and Han are all children of the court" (*Man Han jie chaoting chizi*)—and it deplored the rebels' attempts to fan the flames of racial hatred. One of the edicts, promulgated on 10 November, seems to have been occasioned by the sensational murder three days earlier of Wu Luzhen, the Sixth Division commander, at Shijiazhuang.[94] Together with the Eleventh Brigade from his own division and the Third Regiment from the predominantly Manchu First Division, Wu Luzhen had been sent to recover Shanxi Province from the revolutionaries and relieve the military threat from the west to Beijing. The politically independent commander quickly earned the enmity of both Yuan Shikai and leading Manchus. On the one hand, Wu publicly criticized Yuan's campaign against the revolutionaries in Hubei (particularly the "inhumane" burning of the Chinese City at Hankou) and threatened to halt the southward-bound supply trains as they passed through Shijiazhuang; on the other, he secretly plotted with Yan Xishan (1883–1960) and the Shanxi revolutionaries against the Manchu court. On 7 November two disgruntled subordinates shot Wu to death at his field office at the Shijiazhuang railroad station. In retrospect, it appears that it was not the Manchus but Yuan Shikai, concerned that Wu might block him from proceeding to Beijing to take up his new post as prime minister, who was behind the murder; the immediate press reports, however, almost unanimously blamed it on Manchu soldiers from the First Division.[95] The 10 November edict, though it did not refer to the circumstances of Wu Luzhen's death, seems to have been intended to allay anxiety among the Han population of possible Manchu intransigence. Wu Luzhen's place at the Shanxi front was taken by Cao Kun, who managed to fend off Yan Xishan and his rebel army a month later.

Yuan Shikai, as prime minister, tried to back up the Qing court's rhetoric of racial impartiality by disposing of two contentious issues in Manchu-Han relations, the "imperial kinsmen's cabinet" and the queue. Though Yikuang and his ministers had tendered their resignation on 1 November, they were not replaced until the 16th by Yuan's cabinet, which was strikingly different in membership from its predecessor. Not only was the new cabinet not headed by an imperial prince, but it contained no imperial kinsman at all. (The appointment of someone other than a prince as head of the Ministry of Foreign Affairs violated the Boxer Protocol, as the diplomatic corps pointed out, but the legations eventually went along with the change.)[96] Also, unlike the two-to-one preponderance of Manchus over Han under Yikuang, Yuan's ten-member cabinet had only one Manchu as minister (Dashou at Colonial Affairs, with jurisdiction over the non-Han peoples of outer China).[97] Furthermore, Yuan's cabinet, unlike Zaifeng's court the year before, responded positively to a new initiative by the National Assembly to amend the dynasty's hairstyle ordinance. In late November the assembly voted once more in favor of a bill that would make queue-cutting mandatory for officials, soldiers, teachers, and students and optional for all others. On 7 December the cabinet, which had now replaced the court as the decision maker on matters of governmental policy, agreed to do away with the queue requirement, but without making its abolition in any way mandatory; instead, it made queue-cutting optional for all by permitting everyone, officials and commoners alike, "freely to cut their hair." Many Qing officials, including reportedly all two hundred top officials at the Ministry of Foreign Affairs, quickly shed their plait, but not everyone did so.[98] Yuan Shikai, for one, kept his until the end of the dynasty.

The revolutionaries, of course, were unimpressed by the dynasty's deathbed conversion to the cause of monarchical constitutionalism. What they wanted was "democratic" constitutionalism, which meant the overthrow of the Qing dynasty, the end of the monarchy, and the establishment of a republic. At his meeting on 11 November with Yuan Shikai's two emissaries, Li Yuanhong of the Hubei Military Government questioned the sincerity of the Manchu rulers and wondered how Yuan, in view of how shabbily he had been treated in 1909, could have any trust in them. He told Liu Cheng'en and Cai Tinggan that "the Manchus [Manren] are bandits, while we are the hosts. We have been robbed by the bandits; our women and children and all our belongings have been taken by the bandits." Li and other revolutionaries insisted that Manchu reformism was insufficient, that the Manchus themselves must go. However, in the interest of bringing the revolution to a quick and successful conclusion, the more moderate elements among the Republicans were willing to make significant concessions to Yuan Shikai, to the Qing imperial house, and to the general Manchu population if they all would agree to the establishment of a republic. As early as 11 November, during his meeting with Liu and Cai, Li Yuanhong stated that if Yuan would defect from the Qing, his government was prepared to recognize him as president of the new republic.[99]

The revolutionaries also promised, though rather vaguely, to reward the Qing court if it would step aside in favor of a republic. Li Yuanhong, at the 11 November meeting, told Yuan's emissaries that the court "would be guaranteed pensions and bodily protection"; he also asked Yuan to forward a letter to then Prince Regent Zaifeng in which he repeated the offer "guaranteeing the Throne, if it would abdicate, a pension and honourable treatment." Li Yuanhong subsequently, on 23 November, pledged publicly "to give favorable treatment to the Qing imperial household" in return for its support for a republican regime.[100] The revolutionaries in Shanghai, who did not always see eye to eye with those in Hubei, likewise promised to treat the court well if it would abdicate. On 11 November, the same day that Li Yuanhong in Wuchang made his offer to Yuan Shikai, four prominent Shanghai leaders—Wu Tingfang, Zhang Jian, Tang Wenzhi (1865–1954), and Wen Zongyao (1876–1946), all recent converts from monarchical to democratic constitutionalism—wired a message to Zaifeng arguing that a constitutional monarchy was no longer tenable in China and calling on him to follow the example of the ancient sage kings, Yao and Shun. If the Qing were to abdicate, they said, "the citizenry of China would assuredly reward the imperial household with safety, riches, honor, and glory."[101]

The revolutionaries expressed a similar willingness to treat the general banner populace favorably. Thus, the four Shanghai leaders offered, as well, to "safeguard the Manchus and banner people" (*anquan Man-qi*). Three days later, responding to expressions of concern from some foreign missionaries (notably Gilbert Reid [1857–1927]) about the continued warfare and the plight of the Manchus, Wu Tingfang and Wen Zongyao jointly published an open letter in English addressed "To Our Foreign Friends," in which they declared anew their "guarantee of full protection for the life and property not only of the Imperial family, but of all Manchus." They promised, in particular, that "the Manchus may remain in full enjoyment of citizenship, will be entitled to the fullest equality and freedom, and are urged to rest in possession of their lands and property for the future good of the state."[102]

These informal and indirect talks in November paved the way for the formal, direct negotiations in Shanghai, which the two sides agreed to in early December. On 7 December the Qing court, now headed by Empress Dowager Longyu, bestowed upon Prime Minister Yuan Shikai "complete authority" and asked him to designate a representative to meet with the southerners to "discuss the general situation." Yuan appointed Tang Shaoyi (1860–1938), a long-time associate and veteran diplomatic negotiator, as his envoy plenipotentiary. Named to accompany Tang were, among others, Yang Du and Wang Jingwei, who a few days earlier had disbanded their Society for the Joint Resolution of National Problems, when it had become apparent that neither side was then willing to let a citizens' assembly decide the issue. The revolutionaries, meeting at Wuchang, named Wu Tingfang as their negotiator, with Wen Zongyao as one of his advisors.[103]

The Qing court's agreement on 7 December to negotiate with the southerners, coupled with the forced resignation of Zaifeng as regent the day before, unsettled a number of imperial kinsmen. They were particularly troubled by the appointment of Tang Shaoyi as the negotiator for their side. In the two months since the outbreak of the revolution, he had shown an alarming lack of commitment to the dynasty. According to the British minister John Jordan, Tang in mid-November had spent "several hours with Prince Ch'ing [Qing] endeavouring to convince him that the Court ought to make a graceful exit and facilitate a settlement." Then in early December, taking advantage of the cabinet's recent decision, he had cut off his braid. Pulun, the fourth-rank prince who had been minister of agriculture, industry, and commerce in Yikuang's cabinet, told the visiting American financier Willard Straight that "Yuan's choice of T'ang to represent the government at the Shanghai conference was most unfortunate and has given rise to much suspicion regarding Yuan himself." Indicative of their concern, these leading Manchus insisted that Tang's delegation, which included someone from each province, be enlarged to include a representative of the banner people as well. Zhang Furong, a Hanjun from the Hangzhou garrison, was so designated.[104]

After stopping in Wuchang to meet with Li Yuanhong, Tang Shaoyi and his entourage arrived in Shanghai on 17 December, where he began immediately to confer with the revolutionaries. He met publicly with Wu Tingfang at a series of open sessions held at the Town Hall of the International Settlement's Municipal Council. However, through the mediation of Wang Jingwei, who on his arrival in Shanghai was appointed an adviser to the southern side as well, Tang also conferred privately with Wu and a wide range of other Republicans at the home of a mutual acquaintance. It was at these nightly meetings that the real negotiations took place. The Town Hall sessions during the day were a mere formality; they repeated in public what the two envoys had already agreed to in private.[105]

By the time the formal parley began on the afternoon of 18 December, the negotiating stance of the two sides had been staked out. The irreducible demand of the revolutionaries was the establishment of a republic, which necessarily included the termination of the Qing dynasty and the monarchy. However, as various Republican groups had made clear for over a month, if Yuan Shikai were able to arrange for the Qing court to abdicate, they would make him president of the new republic. Furthermore, if the emperor were to step aside voluntarily, the revolutionaries would reward the court as well as the general Manchu populace with favorable treatment. On the other side, what the Qing dynasty (though not necessarily Yuan himself) wanted was the maintenance of the dynasty and the monarchy, even if much of its power were circumscribed within a constitutional framework. Thus, at issue at the Shanghai conference were one main and two subsidiary questions. The main question was whether to keep the current constitutional monarchy or adopt a republican polity. If a republic was agreed upon, the subsidiary questions were how to bring about the abdication of the Qing and what sort of favorable treatment to accord the Qing court and the banner populace.

The main issue, that of choosing between the monarchy and a republic, came up early in the talks and was decided with surprising alacrity. At their second public session, held on 20 December, the Republican negotiator Wu Tingfang asserted that the Qing dynasty had lost all credibility because of its repeated governmental failures and that China was now ready for "republican constitutionalism." He promised that if the Qing were to abdicate, both the imperial household and the banner soldiers would be provided for. He sought to allay the Manchus' anxiety, as conveyed by Tang Shaoyi, that the revolutionaries intended to "drive out the Manchus" (*jinzhu Manren*) from the eighteen provinces of China proper. "We do not hate Manchus," Wu Tingfang said reassuringly; indeed, "after the changeover, there will be no discrimination whatsoever between Manchus and Han." Tang Shaoyi, to the dismay but perhaps not surprise of many members of the Qing delegation (including the bannerman Zhang Furong), made no effort at all to argue the case for continuing the monarchy. Instead, he told Wu that he personally agreed that a republic was the only peaceful outcome to the revolutionary crisis. Tang proposed, however, that the decision as to whether China should adopt monarchical rule or "democratic" rule be made by a "national convention," thus reviving the discarded proposal of Yang Du and Wang Jingwei. While such a meeting would unquestionably decide in favor of democratic rule, it would make the change of regime easier for the Qing to stomach. Tang asked for a week's recess in the talks, during which he would attempt to persuade Yuan Shikai and the court.[106]

The Qing court was understandably upset at the conciliatory stance taken by its negotiator at Shanghai. In desperation, it asked Yuan Shikai, who professed to be still committed to a "limited monarchy," to sound out the British and Japanese ministers to see if their home governments, both constitutional monarchies, would intervene on its behalf in opposition to the Republican cause in China. Though the Japanese were interested, the British were not. John Jordan, instead, threw his diplomatic weight behind Tang Shaoyi's idea of leaving the choice to a national convention.[107] Meanwhile, the week's recess in the talks was up. On 27 December Tang wired Yuan Shikai urgently requesting a decision. Sun Yat-sen's return from his years of exile and his arrival in Shanghai two days earlier had introduced a new, possibly complicating element into the negotiations. Furthermore, the military cease-fire to which Tang and Wu had agreed was due to run out on the 31st; Tang doubted that the Republicans would accept an extension in the absence of a decision. If the negotiations were to fail and fighting resumed, "no one can foretell," he warned, "whether the ancestral cults [zongshe] will survive or perish." He urged the prime minister to obtain an imperial edict summoning what he now called a "provisional parliament" to decide between monarchical and democratic rule.[108]

On 28 December Yuan Shikai and his cabinet submitted a memorial communicating the substance of Tang Shaoyi's telegram and requesting a meeting with the court. They reiterated Tang's argument that even if the proposed parliament decided in favor of a republic, it would, in gratitude, treat the imperial household generously. On the other hand, if the negotiations ended and fighting broke out again, there was no guarantee that the throne and the aristocracy could be protected. This was not an issue that the cabinet could decide on its own; it required the attention of the court. Empress Dowager Longyu immediately convened a formal court conference, which was attended by at least eight imperial princes (Zaifeng, Yikuang, Shanqi, Zaixun, Zaitao, Pulun, Zaize, and Yulang) as well as by Yuan and his cabinet. The cabinet, as in its memorial, once again asked the court to go along with Tang Shaoyi's proposal. Otherwise, the court would have to make substantial contributions from its private funds to help with the military expenses, once the fighting resumed. If the court did neither, the cabinet could not continue to function. Faced with such bleak alternatives, most of the princes said nothing. Only Yikuang, with a long history of cooperation with Yuan, spoke in favor of the cabinet's plan, while two princes—the former grand councilor Yulang and the former finance minister Zaize—were opposed. After five hours of inconclusive debate, Longyu herself made the decision to do as Tang Shaoyi had proposed. She issued an edict in her own name expressing disappointment that the Nineteen-Article Compact had failed to still the political agitation. She authorized the cabinet to summon a provisional parliament that would decide between monarchical and republican constitutionalism.[109] Since fourteen provinces were now in the hands of the revolutionaries, how Parliament would decide was never in doubt.

With the court having thus capitulated to Tang Shaoyi's face-saving mechanism for effecting the Qing dynasty's abdication, the formal negotiations at Shanghai, suspended since the 20th, resumed on 29 December. At this session and additional meetings the following two days, Tang Shaoyi and Wu Tingfang agreed to an extension of the cease-fire beyond the end of the month. They also agreed on the makeup of the "national convention" (not "provisional parliament") that would decide China's future polity, and they discussed, but without initial agreement, the site and date of the convention. Wu wanted to hold it in Shanghai as soon as 8 January; Tang said he would confer with Yuan Shikai, who wanted it held in Beijing but doubted that it could meet quite so soon.[110] Finally, Wu Tingfang, with scarcely any public comment from Tang, produced two sets of terms, each with five clauses, concerning the future disposition of the Qing emperor and of the Manchus and other non-Han peoples. The emperor would be accorded the same treatment as that given to the monarch of a foreign country; would retire to the Yiheyuan Summer Palace; would be given an annual subsidy, the size of which would be decided by the future parliament; could continue to perform sacrifices at his ancestral tombs and shrines; and could retain his private wealth. With regard to the "Manchus, Mongols, Muslims, and Tibetans" (Man-Meng-Hui-Zang), they would be treated on a basis of equality with the Han; they could retain their private wealth; the Eight Banner soldiers would continue to receive their grain stipends until a way was found to ensure their livelihood; all previous occupational and residential restrictions on the banner populace would be eliminated; and all ranks and titles of nobility would continue as before.[111]

Thus, by the last day of December 1911, the Qing court had all but agreed to abdicate; in return, the revolutionaries had clarified their previously vague promises of favorable treatment for the emperor and the banner populace. Only one procedural step remained: the holding of a convention that would formalize the passing of the mandate from the monarchy to a republic. It was generally assumed that this was only a few days off.

ABDICATION AND ITS TERMS

Abdication, however, did not occur for another six weeks. It was delayed because of a couple of unexpected hurdles, the first erected by Yuan Shikai and the second by diehard Manchu royalists. Additional negotiations were required, focusing on the terms of the abdication agreement. As a result of these talks, the final settlement was even more favorable toward the Qing and the Manchus than what Tang Shaoyi and Wu Tingfang had agreed to originally.

The Tang-Wu agreement to which the Qing court had reluctantly given its assent aroused considerable opposition from both ends of the political spectrum. At one end, the more radical elements among the Republicans, including Sun Yat-sen, were outraged that Wu Tingfang had yielded too much to the Qing. They were particularly incensed that he had gone along with Tang's proposal to wait for a national convention to decide China's future polity. They refused to wait. On 29 December, four days after Sun's arrival at Shanghai, representatives from the pro-Republican provinces elected him provisional president; on 1 January 1912, with the adoption of the solar calendar symbolizing the beginning of a new era, they formally proclaimed the establishment of the Republic of China (Zhonghua Minguo), with its capital at Nanjing.[112] At the other end, supporters of the Qing, many of them Manchus, were no less upset that Tang Shaoyi, whose loyalty had long been in doubt, had not stood firm for the cause of the monarchy. In late December a group in Beijing founded the Society for Monarchical Constitutionalism (Junzhu Lixian Zancheng Hui). The society was headquartered at a shrine for the Eight Banners (Baqi xianxian ci), and most of its members were banner people. It later came to be known as the Royalist Party (Zongshedang), dedicated to the preservation of the dynasty's "ancestral temples and cults of the earth" (zongmiao sheji).[113]

Seemingly in sympathy with the Qing loyalists, Prime Minister Yuan Shikai on 2 January abruptly dismissed Tang Shaoyi as his negotiator, charging that he had exceeded his authority, and repudiated the Tang-Wu agreement. Applauding the move were fifteen northern generals, among them Feng Guozhang, the newly installed commander of the Palace Guard, who jointly wired Yuan's cabinet voicing their steadfast backing for a constitutional monarchy. They swore that they were willing to fight to the death, and they called on the court nobles and high officials to do their part as well, by paying the costs of continued resistance from their private wealth, including the thirty to forty million taels reportedly on deposit at various foreign banks in Beijing.[114]

However, Yuan, unlike the Manchu loyalists, was less concerned about the fate of the monarchy than about his own future. His anger was directed not at the Tang-Wu agreement itself but at what he saw as the perfidy of the radical Republicans. He asserted, with some justification, that their formation of the Republic of China violated the provision in the Tang-Wu agreement that China's future polity would be settled by the yet-to-be-held national convention. He probably wondered if Sun's election had negated the revolutionaries' oft-stated promise to make him president if he were to secure the Qing abdication. He was later reassured by Sun Yat-sen himself that Sun would step aside for him if and when he brought an end to the Qing.[115]

With his future status clarified, Yuan Shikai changed course again. He resumed talking with the Republicans while trying, once more, to persuade the Qing to abdicate. Because the formal face-to-face parley at Shanghai had ended with Tang's dismissal, the subsequent negotiations were conducted by telegraph between Yuan himself and Wu Tingfang, who despite his differences with Sun's Republican government remained as its chief negotiator. Tang Shaoyi, too, though disavowed, continued to serve as Yuan's now unofficial representative in Shanghai.[116] The Tang-Wu agreement formed the basis for the new round of talks. The Republicans made it clear that they were still prepared to treat the Qing court and the Manchus generously if the emperor were to abdicate. On 10 January, according to news reports, they wired Beijing the text of a settlement agreement that was virtually identical to what Wu Tingfang had previously presented to Tang Shaoyi. The new proposal differed from the old in only one respect: it called for the emperor, following the abdication, to move to his summer retreat at Rehe, outside the Great Wall, rather than to the Yiheyuan Summer Palace.[117]

For his part, Yuan Shikai had come around to the view of the radical Republicans that a convention to decide between the monarchy and the Republic was an unnecessary delay. He now pressed the Qing court to accept the revolutionaries' offer and abdicate at once. By mid-January Yuan seemingly had convinced the court to do as he recommended. On the 14th one of his secretaries (probably Cai Tinggan) informed British minister John Jordan that Empress Dowager Longyu would issue an edict in a few days announcing the emperor's abdication and putting Yuan in temporary charge of the government. On the morning of the 16th, Yuan personally delivered to Longyu a secret memorial asserting that popular opinion had turned irretrievably away from the Qing. He warned against continued resistance, to avoid the fate of Louis XVI in the French Revolution.[118] By coincidence, as if to underline the immediacy of the revolutionary threat, Yuan himself, as he left the Forbidden City to return to his office, was nearly killed in an unsuccessful assassination attempt. Three local members of the revolutionary Alliance were seized and executed by strangulation.[119]

With Empress Dowager Longyu in charge, the Qing court met the following day, 17 January, to discuss Yuan's alarming memorial. Both Yikuang and Pulun spoke in favor of the prime minister's implicit recommendation, which was to abdicate without waiting for a national convention. Yikuang, Yuan's ally among the princes, reviewed the terms of the Republicans' offer, while Pulun, notwithstanding his own earlier doubts about Tang Shaoyi's defeatist attitude, supported Yuan's assessment that the Qing cause had become militarily and politically hopeless. Even if a convention were held, it would decide against the Qing; it was prudent, therefore, to accept the Republicans' promise of generous treatment in return for abdication. The other princes at the conference said nothing. Only Nayantu (b. 1873), the Khalka Mongol prince, spoke in favor of continued resistance. Nayantu's objections seem to have stemmed from worries that Russia would (as it, in fact, later did) take advantage of the Qing abdication to incite the Mongols to become independent of China. Because of Nayantu's concerns, the conference failed to act on Yuan's memorial; it adjourned for two days.[120]

As the court deliberated, Yuan Shikai and the Republicans worked on finalizing the terms of the abdication settlement. On 18 January Wu Tingfang presented a revised draft of the settlement, which was very similar to the two previous versions of 30 December and 10 January. The major changes were four additions to the section about the emperor. One provided that he would be styled as the "abdicated emperor" (*rang huangdi*) and that his title would be inheritable. Another permitted him to reside "temporarily" in the Forbidden City before moving to the Yiheyuan Summer Palace, thus dropping for good the idea of his retiring to the distant retreat at Rehe. The third specified that his annual stipend, to be set by Parliament, would not be less than three million taels. The fourth was a new clause that the Republic would pay for completing the Guangxu emperor's tomb, then under construction, as well as for his interment.[121]

Neither side was entirely happy with Wu Tingfang's draft. Some radical Republicans were again upset at Wu's concessions to the Qing. Both Sun Yat-sen and Huang Xing complained about the continued use of the title "emperor" and the inheritability of the title, the emperor's residence (if only temporary) in the Forbidden City, and the Republic's responsibility for burying the former emperor. Wu Tingfang replied that Sun himself had earlier consented to the use of the term "abdicated emperor" (*rang di*) or "Qing emperor" (*Qing di*) as the future title for the emperor and that, in any case, the title was a mere formality, devoid of significance. Wu also explained that the emperor would delay his move from the Forbidden City to the Yiheyuan only until the end of winter. As for the entombment of the Guangxu emperor, on previous occasions of dynastic change, the victors had always paid for the burial of the vanquished; the Republic should do no less. Tang Shaoyi, representing the Qing side, likewise objected to the term "abdicated emperor" as the future designation of the emperor, presumably because it was insufficiently august.[122]

In hopes of expediting a decision, Wu Tingfang then made a couple of last-minute alterations to the settlement offer. To meet the objections of Tang Shaoyi, he changed the title of the monarch after abdication to "Qing emperor." And to meet those of the radical Republicans, he changed, with Tang's approval, the future status of the emperor's title: it was no longer "inheritable through the generations without being abolished" (*xiangchuan bufei*); instead it would be only "retained without being abolished" (*rengcun bufei*), that is, it could not be passed to the next generation. These changes were incorporated into the set of agreements that Wu Tingfang, with Sun Yat-sen's blessings, sent to Yuan Shikai on 20 January.[123]

However, by the time Wu's new settlement offer was ready for presentation, the attitude of the Qing court had hardened dramatically, thus creating the second of the two hurdles on the road to abdication. The apparent inclination of the court to step down without any resistance, not even requiring a vote by a national convention, had stirred some imperial princes and their outside supporters to belated action. They directed their anger at Yikuang, who at the court conference on 17 January had spoken approvingly of the Republicans' offer. On the evening of the 18th, representatives of the Society for Monarchical Constitutionalism went to Yikuang's mansion and loudly denounced him for supporting republicanism; the next day the society issued a fiery proclamation accusing the aged prince of having been bought off by "traitors." The intimidation had its desired effect. At the next court conference, on the 19th, Yikuang disavowed his former support for abdication. Afterward both he and Pulun, who previously had also favored abdication, asked for and were given several days' leave.[124]

The main obstacles to an early abdication were the two predominantly Manchu military units in Beijing, the First Division and especially the Palace Guard, many of whose soldiers were members of the Society for Monarchical Constitutionalism. In mid-January soldiers of the Palace Guard's First Brigade put out a statement criticizing the revolutionaries for disregarding the court's political concessions and declaring their continued adherence to a constitutional monarchy, for which they said they were prepared to die; they even asked to be transferred to the Hubei front to help "eradicate the wild bandits." At this time, soldiers of the Palace Guard were meeting almost daily to vent their anger and frustration. Fanning the soldiers' discontent from behind the scenes were the two Japanese-trained Manchu loyalists who had been most responsible for organizing and training these two units—Liangbi (former commander of the Palace Guard's First Brigade) and Yuan Shikai's old nemesis, Tieliang (former commander of the Nanjing banner garrison, who had just returned to the capital). Both of them were, according to G. E. Morrison, "in close intercourse with the Japanese," who were known to be cool to republicanism, and both were actively "inspiring in the Manchus distrust of Yuan Shih-kai."[125]

Feng Guozhang, Yuan's appointee as commander of the Palace Guard, insisted on being kept informed but otherwise did little to curb the loyalist activities of his troops.[126] Indeed, he himself may have shared their monarchist leanings. Although Feng had begun his military career in Yuan's service, he had more recently been superintendent of the Nobles Military School and had served on the General Staff Council under the imperial princes Yulang and Zaitao. He had led the First Corps to its two victories on the Hubei front—the recapture of Hankou and then of Hanyang—and he had disapproved of Yuan's peace overtures to the Hubei revolutionaries. The court, in an unusual show of gratitude, had bestowed upon him the rank of baron, for which he must have been appreciative. Unlike Tang Shaoyi, he had not removed his queue. Finally, Feng Guozhang was one of the fifteen northern generals who on 2 January had proclaimed their support for the Qing, and he was a founder of a group in Beijing called the Alliance of Comrades (Tongzhi Lianhehui), whose purpose was to promote monarchical constitutionalism.[127]

At court, the most outspoken opponent of abdication was Puwei, Yixin's grandson and his successor as Prince Gong. In a public letter addressed to the Society for Monarchical Constitutionalism, Puwei explained that he had been on leave at the time of the first court conference on the 17th but that he had become enraged by newspaper accounts that some of the princes in attendance had been recommending republicanism. He vowed to make his case at the next conference. He performed as promised. On the 19th Puwei got into an angry argument with three members of Yuan Shikai's cabinet. (Yuan himself was absent; though unhurt, he was supposedly recovering from the attempted assassination.) The cabinet members had come with a strange new proposal from Yuan, which called for forming a provisional government in nearby Tianjin. Puwei argued instead for unrelenting military resistance. The Taiping and Nian rebels, he said, had posed a more serious threat, yet the Qing had fought them for almost twenty years; there had been no thought then of negotiating with the rebels or establishing a new government. Why bother to recall Yuan Shikai to office, he asked, if all he did was sue for peace at the first sign of trouble? When Yuan's foreign minister, Hu Weide (1869–1933), objected that the foreign powers were opposed to a resumption of fighting, Puwei brushed the objection aside by insisting that this was China's internal matter and doubting that the powers would interfere. Several other princes, including Yulang, Zaize, and Zaitao as well as the Mongol prince Nayantu, joined Puwei in opposing an abject capitulation. However, perhaps because of qualms on the part of Empress Dowager Longyu, the conference again adjourned without a decision.[128]

At the next court conference, held on the morning of 22 January, Puwei once more urged a policy of armed resistance. He claimed, allegedly on the authority of Feng Guozhang, that troops (presumably the Palace Guard and the First Division), if adequately funded, were available to defend the dynasty. When the empress dowager expressed her worry that if the Qing fought and lost, the Republicans' offer of favorable treatment would no longer be on the table, Puwei questioned whether the Republicans could be trusted to fulfill the terms of any agreement; in any case, it was ignoble to accept such an offer from the enemy. It would be better to die than abdicate. His views were supported again by Zaize and Nayantu and now by Shanqi as well. Once more, however, there was no decision.[129]

Puwei and other intransigents evidently believed that if the Qing court resisted and failed, it could still flee Beijing and seek refuge elsewhere, as it had twice done in recent decades. Xi'an, to which the court had fled in 1900 during the Boxer troubles, was out of the question this time because it had been in Republican hands since late October. Nevertheless, there were several possible sanctuaries. One was Gansu, where Governor-General Changgeng was rallying loyalist forces. Another was Rehe, the Qing summer retreat beyond the Great Wall, where the Xianfeng emperor had found refuge in 1860 during the Second Opium War. For about a month the new Rehe lieutenant governor, Xiliang, had been preparing for the arrival of the court. A third possible refuge for the court was Manchuria, the ancestral home of the Manchus, whose governor-general was the Hanjun Zhao Erxun, brother of the murdered Zhao Erfeng. Banner officers in Fengtian reportedly had the approval of Governor-General Zhao to finance and train enough soldiers to form a twenty-battalion army to "rescue the emperor." A leading proponent of loyalism and resistance in Fengtian was the Manchu reformer Jinliang, whom the *Eastern Times* called a "second Liangbi."[130]

However, to organize a military resistance or prepare a place of refuge would take time. This may explain the conciliatory tone that Puwei, the outspoken champion of armed resistance, adopted in an interview with Gilbert Reid on 22 January, the day of his verbal outburst at court. Puwei suggested that he was opposed not so much to the abdication itself as to the abject means by which it would be accomplished if his opponents had their way. He told the American missionary that he wanted to adhere to the formula originally devised by Tang Shaoyi and Wu Tingfang of leaving the decision to a national convention. According to Reid, Puwei thought that

> the dynasty had already yielded too much to the revolutionists. If more was yielded, it should not be under pressure, but in accordance with the distinct wish of the people. . . . There ought to be a representative assembly to express the people's will. Abdication would be reasonable if the assembly so decided.[131]

To convene a large representative assembly would, of course, buy the Qing court some valuable time.

The intransigents, in the end, successfully sidetracked the abdication that had seemed all but certain in mid-January. On 24 January Empress Dowager Longyu, despite her personal misgivings, issued an edict that essentially embraced Puwei's views as expressed in his interview with Reid. Contrary to what the British legation had been told earlier to expect, she did not accede to Yuan Shikai's recommendation to abdicate without delay. Nor did she take up the abdication agreement that Wu Tingfang had presented on the 20th. Instead, she retreated to her decision of late December to have the question of China's polity be decided by a national convention, and she called on Yuan Shikai to negotiate with the Republicans about a date and a site, which had been left in abeyance when the Tang-Wu talks were halted.[132]

The last-minute refusal of the Qing to heed his advice stunned Yuan Shikai, who promptly orchestrated a campaign to pressure the court to reverse its decision. He himself, on 25 January, responded to Longyu's edict by warning her of its likely consequences. If a national convention were held, it would most certainly insist on ratifying the terms of any abdication agreement that he and the Republicans had negotiated. If this were to happen, he "dared not predict" whether that convention would be so generous to the court as the Republicans had been thus far. In short, as others had already pointed out, it would be far wiser for the court to accept the Republicans' current settlement offer by abdicating at once than to leave the decision to the caprices of a popular assembly.[133]

Yuan's military and civilian supporters likewise castigated the court for its intransigence. On 26 January more than forty Qing generals and military officers joined the new First Corps commander, Duan Qirui, in sending a telegram to Yuan's cabinet as well as to various imperial princes expressing their displeasure at the court's delay in abdicating, which they blamed on the mischievous machinations of the princes Zaize and Puwei. It would take months, they said, to convene a national assembly, during which time military defections, popular uprisings, banditry, and even intervention and partition by the foreign powers could occur. If fighting broke out and the Qing forces were defeated, it would then be difficult to provide for "the honor of the imperial household and the livelihood of the imperial clan and the colonial peoples" (*huangshi zunrong zongfan shengji*). If an assembly were convened, it would in all likelihood opt for a republican polity. Why not, therefore, spare the country several months of turmoil? Why not anticipate the assembly's decision and establish a republic now? Of the fifteen northern generals who two and a half weeks earlier had pledged to fight to the death for a constitutional monarchy, only two had not changed their tune. One was the Palace Guard commander, Feng Guozhang, and the other was Zhang Zuolin (1875–1928) in Manchuria.[134]

Yuan's civilian supporters also began to abandon the Qing. Yang Du, who in late November had been the self-appointed monarchist in the Society for the Joint Resolution of National Problems, on 26 January organized in Beijing the Society for the Advancement of Republicanism (Gonghe Cujin Hui). Yang's new group, which included among its leading members Wuzesheng, the former editor of the Manchu reformist publication *Great Harmony Journal*, castigated the imperial princes for having dragged their feet all along. When the people wanted monarchical constitutionalism, the princes had clung to monarchical autocracy; now, when the people demanded democratic republicanism, the princes belatedly embraced monarchical constitutionalism. Yang's group warned that if the emperor did not abdicate, the revolutionaries might repudiate their settlement offer.[135] Indeed, the Republicans were, at this time, making precisely such a threat. On 27 January Wu Tingfang notified Yuan Shikai that the settlement agreement presented on the 20th would be withdrawn if the Qing had not announced its abdication by the time the current cease-fire expired on the morning of the 29th.[136]

Despite the warnings of Yuan Shikai and his supporters and the threat of the Republicans, the opponents of an immediate abdication held firm for another two or three days. They were undoubtedly emboldened by the apparent loyalty of Feng Guozhang and the Palace Guard to the Qing cause. Feng had conspicuously failed to join Duan Qirui in voicing support for republicanism, while soldiers of the Palace Guard in late January publicly reiterated their commitment to a "monarchical constitutionalist polity."[137] What finally took the wind out of the Manchu resistance and cleared the way for the abdication was the assassination of Liangbi. Liangbi, who together with Tieliang had been most responsible for stirring up the Palace Guard, was assaulted by a revolutionary on the night of 26 January, as he was returning home from a visit to Shanqi, another Manchu loyalist. (It is possible that Yuan Shikai connived in the attack.) He died of his wounds several days later. Liangbi's murder, coupled with the threatening telegram from Duan Qirui, finally convinced the intransigents, including those in the Palace Guard, that their cause was lost. Tieliang fled Beijing.[138]

There ensued another series of court conferences, this time to discuss how to respond to Duan Qirui. The previously announced plan to let a convention decide China's polity was abandoned for good; so was the idea of armed resistance. However, the princes still could not agree on what to do instead. Empress Dowager Longyu was left to make the decision. On the advice of Zaifeng and Yikuang, who were in frequent touch with Yuan Shikai, she gave "full authority" to the prime minister to make whatever deal he could with the Republicans. She announced her decision at a court conference on 2 February and formalized it in an edict the next day. (Puwei and Zaize, the two princes who had led the resistance, were noticeably absent from the conference, while for Yuan it was his first trip back to the Forbidden City since the attempt on his life two weeks earlier.) In her edict to Yuan, the empress dowager said that the court could not bear to bring misery to the multitude just for the sake of the "glory and honor of a single lineage." She asked him to arrange in advance the terms for the future treatment of the imperial household, the imperial lineage, the Eight Banners, and the Mongols, Muslims, and Tibetans.[139]

Having finally secured full power from the court, Yuan Shikai proceeded, as directed, to reopen negotiations with the Republicans on the terms of the abdication. The court was dissatisfied with the agreement that Wu Tingfang had presented on 20 January; for example, it objected to the use of the term "abdication" (*tuiwei*) in the document.[140] Consequently, Yuan, working closely with the empress dowager, drew up his own version of an abdication agreement, which he forwarded to the Republicans on 3 February.[141] Yuan's counterproposal was quite different from Wu's last offer. Overall, it consisted of three sections rather than Wu's two. As in Wu's version, the first section pertained to the emperor. Reflecting the sensitivity of the court, Yuan's proposal omitted all mention of "abdication." It referred to the emperor as "emperor of the Great Qing" (*Da-Qing huangdi*) rather than simply as "Qing emperor." The emperor's title would be inheritable through the generations, rather than retained only for the duration of the present reign. His annual subsidy would be at least four (not three) million taels, with extra appropriations as needed for special ceremonies. The emperor might choose to reside at the Forbidden City or the Yiheyuan Summer Palace rather than be required to move to the Yiheyuan. Finally, in new provisions not found in Wu's version, the emperor might retain the use of various officials, servants, and guards, including specifically the Palace Guard, who in a separate clause were assured that their size and pay would be unchanged. (This clause was clearly added to reduce the intransigence of the Palace Guard soldiers by allaying anxiety about their future.)

The second section in Yuan's counterproposal dealt separately with the imperial lineage, a group not covered in Wu's version except broadly among the non-Han nobility. Their titles would continue and be inheritable, and their "public rights" would be the same as other citizens, except that they would be exempt from military duty. Finally, the third section—dealing with the Manchus, Mongols, Muslims, and Tibetans—was largely the same as Wu's, except for the addition of two clauses. One provided for the economic well-being of the nobility separately from the Eight Banners, whose stipends, in both versions, would continue pending the resolution of their livelihood problem; if the nobles were to fall into economic difficulty, they would be given grants of official property that would be inheritable. The other additional clause specified that the non-Han peoples would enjoy religious freedom.

Because of the substantial differences between what Yuan now proposed and what the Republicans had offered two weeks earlier, Wu Tingfang took Yuan's draft to Nanjing to show to Sun Yat-sen and his Republican government. On 5 February the Republican Senate agreed to substitute Yuan's version for Wu's as the basis for the next round of negotiations, but then demanded a number of revisions, some of which were new additions and others were restorations from Wu's discarded version.[142] Most of the changes were made in the section dealing with the emperor, some of them substantive and others semantic. Of the substantive changes, the Republicans added a prefatory clause to Yuan's text declaring that "the Qing emperor recognizes the Republican polity," and they specified that the emperor's "preferential treatment" was conferred on him by the Republic of China, an entity that Yuan had not recognized. They rejected the provision in the Beijing text that the emperor's title was inheritable; they insisted, as Wu had, that only the present emperor might retain the title after his abdication. They agreed nominally with Yuan to increase the emperor's subsidy from three to four million but effectively kept it at about the same amount by changing the monetary unit from taels to dollars; they refused to assume the extra costs of special ceremonies.

The Republican Senate refused also to allow the emperor to choose his residence; they insisted, as Wu had, that he retire to the Yiheyuan, though he could stay in the Forbidden City "temporarily." They agreed with Yuan's additional provisions about the emperor's servants and guards but insisted that no more eunuchs be brought into the palace; and while they consented to the continued existence of the Palace Guard, they demanded that the unit, which had been under the separate control of the court, be brought under the authority of the Ministry of the Army. Among the semantic changes, one was to insist that the monarch be styled simply "Qing emperor," as Wu had wanted, and not the more august "emperor of the Great Qing." Another was to reinsert into the document references to the Qing's "abdication," though Wu's term *tuiwei* was replaced with the comparable *sunwei*. In the rest of the document, the Nanjing Senate accepted the addition of a separate section for the imperial lineage, but was willing to assume only a vague obligation to provide for the welfare of the non-Han nobility. It rejected outright the inheritability of the titles and ranks belonging to the imperial lineage and the non-Han nobility. It did, however, agree to continue to distribute the banner soldiers' stipends pending a solution to the long-standing Eight Banners' livelihood problem.

A day later Wu Tingfang wired the amended text of the abdication agreement back to Yuan Shikai, who in turn presented it to Longyu and the Qing court. The court found most of Nanjing's revisions tolerable, but objected to the apparent reduction in the size of the emperor's subsidy as well as a few other changes, including some of the changes in phrasing. Yuan asked Wu to make several modifications in the Nanjing draft. He suggested that the emperor's subsidy of four million be paid first in taels, at least until the new dollar currency had been put into effect. He continued to insist that the emperor be addressed as "emperor of the Great Qing," not simply as "Qing emperor," and that the title be inheritable. He asked that the repugnant term "abdication" (*sunwei*) be deleted or at least replaced by "resignation" (*zhizheng*). He also opposed transferring control of the Palace Guard from the court to the Ministry of the Army. At Yuan's instigation, the northern generals, with Feng Guozhang and Duan Qirui now in agreement, wired Wu Tingfang with their objections as well; they too protested against the noninheritability of the emperor's title and the inclusion of the objectionable term for "abdication."[143]

On 9 February Wu Tingfang, acting on the limited authority given to him by the Republican Senate, replied that he was willing to make some, but not all, of the changes that Yuan asked for. On the one hand, he bowed to Yuan's insistence that the emperor be given the title "emperor of the Great Qing," and he accepted Yuan's suggestion that the emperor's stipend be paid initially in taels and only afterwards in dollars. On the other hand, he was unwilling to delete the term "abdication" or replace it with "resignation," though he proposed substituting *ciwei* (with its connotation of a voluntary stepping down) for *sunwei* (which, like *tuiwei*, implies a degree of coercion). He did not budge from the Republicans' insistence that the emperor's title be noninheritable and that he be required to move to the Yiheyuan. Nor did he compromise on the demand that the Palace Guard be transferred to the authority of the Ministry of the Army.[144]

Wu Tingfang reminded Yuan and the court that there were limits to the concessions the Republicans could make and that the more radical elements among the Republicans thought that those limits had already been exceeded. In Guangdong both the military governor and the Provincial Assembly were outraged. Governor Chen Jiongming (1878–1933) on 8 February sent a public telegram protesting the emperor's retention of his title and continued residence in Beijing; the assembly objected to the continuance of the Palace Guard and called for the resumption of military action against the Qing if the terms were not changed. The veteran revolutionary Tan Renfeng (1860–1920) similarly complained that the preferential treatment promised the emperor was unnecessary and unwise. In Shanghai the newly founded Socialist Party (Shehuidang) on 10 February hosted a public meeting to denounce Wu Tingfang and the Republican Senate for their spineless behavior.[145] Wu conceded that the terms were extraordinarily generous, but so long as they did not conflict with the principle of republicanism, he told Li Yuanhong, he was willing to offer them in the interest of securing an early abdication. His colleague in the negotiations, Wang Jingwei, replied in a similar vein to Governor Chen Jiongming, the Guangdong assembly, and other critics within the revolutionary Alliance.[146]

As the Qing abdication became likely, Yuan Shikai took precautions against unrest in Beijing among those who might still be opposed. He transferred certain units of the Palace Guard and the First Division out of the capital and replaced them with Han units from the Third and Twentieth Divisions and from Jiang Guiti's troops. He also directed Feng Guozhang, who had come to accept the inevitability of republicanism, to pacify the Palace Guard. Feng went to their new barracks at Changchunyuan, assembled all the officers and soldiers, and patiently explained to them the terms of the proposed abdication agreement, including the clause promising their unit's continued existence. He told them that nothing more could be done to protect the imperial household.[147] As a result, soldiers of the Palace Guard in early February announced that they no longer were opposed to the court's abdication. At about the same time, the Society for Monarchical Constitutionalism conceded that the trend toward republicanism was inexorable and promised that it would disband once the court had acted.[148]

Bowing to the inevitable, the Qing dynasty abdicated on 12 February 1912, five days shy of the lunar new year, as Empress Dowager Longyu issued three edicts. One was the abdication edict itself, which was drafted by Zhang Jian for the Republicans and revised by Yuan Shikai. In it the empress dowager admitted that the Qing had lost the Mandate of Heaven; she therefore transferred the emperor's sovereignty to the "entire nation" and established a "constitutional republican polity." In a proviso inserted by Yuan without the prior consent of the revolutionaries, she conferred "full authority" upon Yuan Shikai to organize a provisional republican government and instructed him to negotiate with the "people's army" so as to bring about the reunification of north and south. She ended with the hope that the "territories of the five ethnic groups [wuzu]—Manchu, Mongol, Han, Muslim, and Tibetan—would unite to form one great Republic of China." Longyu's second edict called on all officials, in Beijing and in the provinces, to maintain peace and order during the critical transitional period. The third edict sanctioned the terms of the abdication agreement on which Wu Tingfang and Yuan Shikai had labored for more than five weeks.[149]

The abdication agreement in its final form consisted of three sections. The first section, known as the Articles of Favorable Treatment (Youdai Tiaojian), concerned the "emperor of the Great Qing." It provided that following his "stepping down" (*ciwei*) he would retain his imperial title throughout his life and the Republic of China would treat him with the same degree of ceremony shown monarchs of foreign countries, that the Republic of China would bestow upon him an annual subsidy of four million taels (to be changed to dollars when a new currency system had been adopted), that he could reside "temporarily" in the Forbidden City but "at a later date" would move to the Yiheyuan Summer Palace, and that the Republic of China would offer special protection to all of his private property. It also provided that the emperor would "retain and use as customary" his attendants and bodyguards as well as all other categories of service personnel, except that no more eunuchs could be recruited. It promised that the Republic of China would provide military protection for the perpetual observances at the imperial temples and tombs and would pay for the completion of the Guangxu emperor's tomb and for his funeral. Finally, it stated that the Palace Guard would be placed under the jurisdiction of the Ministry of the Army of the Republic of China but that their statutory strength and stipends would remain as before.

The other two sections of the abdication agreement covered the Qing imperial lineage (*Qing huangzu*) on the one hand, and the Manchu, Mongol, Muslim, and Tibetan ethnic groups (*minzu*) on the other. The section on the imperial lineage specified that the princes and hereditary nobles would continue as before, that the imperial lineage would possess the same public and private rights under the Republic of China as would all other citizens, that all their private possessions would be protected, and that they were exempt from the obligation of military service. The section on the Manchus, Mongols, Muslims, and Tibetans provided that the Republic of China would treat them on an equal basis with the Han, protect their private property, permit the princes and hereditary nobles to continue as before, and allow them freely to practice their native religions. It also promised to devise methods of livelihood for princes experiencing economic difficulty as well as for members of the Eight Banner system and, furthermore, until solutions to the economic problems of the Eight Banners were found, to distribute the rations to the Eight Banner soldiers as of old. Finally, it abolished all of the former restrictions on the banner people's occupation and residence and allowed them to be registered with their local administrative unit.

By these edicts, China passed from a monarchy to a republic. The Republicans were, of course, incensed by Yuan Shikai's last-minute move, in which he received his authority to form a new government from the Qing. All along they had said that they would accept Yuan as president but that he must derive his authority from them and not from the Qing. Nevertheless, despite their misgivings about his intentions, they followed through on their own promises. On 13 February, the day after the Qing abdication, Sun Yat-sen resigned his post, and on the 15th, the Republican Senate unanimously elected Yuan as the new provisional president of the Republic of China. Also on that day, Sun Yat-sen and a large entourage traveled to the tomb of the Hongwu emperor near Nanjing and solemnly announced to the spirit of the founder of the Ming dynasty that the Qing conquest of Ming China had been avenged and that finally, after 268 years, the shameful occupation of China by the "Eastern Barbarians" (Donghu) had come to an end.[150]

CONCLUSION

The Qing abdicated four months and two days after the Wuchang Revolt. The rapidity of its collapse did not mean that the Qing had failed to mount a credible military and political response to the revolution. To the contrary, the court succeeded within days of the outbreak of the revolution in sending a large force to Hubei and by the end of November had recaptured two of the three Wuhan cities; it had also opened up a second front against the revolutionaries in Shanxi and managed eventually to drive them out of the capital city of Taiyuan. Politically, by the terms of the Nineteen-Article Compact, the Qing had transformed itself from an autocratic to a constitutional monarchy. Yuan Shikai, elected prime minister by the National Assembly, headed a "responsible cabinet" that performed nearly all of the executive and administrative functions formerly monopolized by the throne. The Qing also finally did away with the controversial queue requirement. If these concessions had been made months and years earlier, they might well have taken the wind out of the revolutionary sail. However, by the time they were made in November and December 1911, they were much too late. In one provincial capital after another, the civil and military elite, as represented by the chairman of the Provincial Assembly and the commander of the local New Army respectively, scarcely hesitated before throwing in their lot with the revolutionaries. It was their defection, born of repeated disappointments with the Qing, that doomed the dynasty and brought about its speedy demise.

Brief as it was, the revolution was hardly bloodless; it was far from a "very minor affair" in which (according to a recent study) "no more than 1,000 to 2,000 died."[151] The casualties among the banner people at Xi'an alone were several times that. A disproportionate number of the people killed and wounded during the revolution were Manchus, victims of the virulent racist rhetoric that had been a staple of the revolutionaries' ideology for over a decade. As the Republicans neared success, some of them, as had Wang Jingwei in 1910, toned down the racial element of their message. Thus, to a group of Manchu students stranded in Japan by the outbreak of the revolution, the veteran firebrand Zhang Binglin offered reassurances that the revolutionaries had no intention of massacring them to pay back their ancestors' atrocities against the people of Yangzhou.[152] On the other hand, the blood-curdling rhetoric and the racist talk had by no means disappeared. For example, in early November 1911 the Shanghai Military Government announced that "in carrying out its heavy responsibility of restoration [*guangfu*], it could avenge the bitter hatred of the Han race [Hanzu] only by wiping out [*shajin*]" the Manchus. As late as the day before the Qing abdication, Sun Yat-sen was still referring to the Manchus by the derogatory term "caitiff" (*lu*), as when he renamed the Republicans' northern expeditionary troops the "army to quell the caitiffs" (*taolujun*).[153] Indeed, several days later at Hongwu's tomb, he again denigrated them as the "Eastern Barbarians." Stirred by such inflammatory messages, some of the revolutionaries, not surprisingly, sought to carry out genocide. At the same time, many banner people, fearing that the Republicans were as anti-Manchu as they professed, were driven to suicide lest they fall into the hands of their bloodthirsty enemy. It is also clear from the numerous instances of hapless Manchus who tried to pass themselves off as Han that despite extensive and long-term acculturation, there remained certain identifying signs—such as residence, speech, dress, and the size and shape of women's feet—that until 1911 continued to separate Manchus from Han. It was not until the abdication agreement itself that the residential and occupational restrictions on the banner people were, at long last, removed.

Finally, as some radical Republicans complained, the abdication agreement that capped the success of the revolution was extraordinarily favorable to the Manchus. Unable to capture or depose the Xuantong emperor (who had just turned six when he abdicated), the revolutionaries allowed him to keep a semblance of his former title and to continue to live at one of his palace complexes, and they even granted him and his household an enormous annual pension. When the journalist G. E. Morrison first learned that the Qing wanted a subsidy of four million taels, which by one estimate was equivalent to more than 1 percent of China's national revenue, he dismissed it as a "quite preposterous amount"; hardly a Republican sympathizer, he thought that one million was more than ample, especially since the Qing itself had pensioned off the former prince regent with fifty thousand taels.[154] The Republicans, however, consented to the larger sum. They also promised to keep up, at least for a while, the monthly payments to the Eight Banner soldiers. These terms in the abdication agreement were the product of genuine give-and-take between the Republicans and the Qing that lasted over three months; they were not imposed by the victorious revolutionaries upon a vanquished foe. While the public talks at Shanghai in December between Tang Shaoyi and Wu Tingfang may indeed have been no more than a public-relations ploy and a facade, the subsequent long-distance negotiations between Yuan Shikai and Wu Tingfang were real enough. The Republicans' eventual generosity, seemingly at odds with their long-standing diatribes against the "Tartar caitiffs," was surely motivated by the desire to avoid a prolonged military struggle and with it the possibility of foreign intervention. From their perspective, it was a small price to pay to persuade the Qing dynasty to give up and accept the inevitable sooner rather than later.

5 / Court and Manchus after 1911

The new Republican regime, which its supporters had fervently hoped would usher in an age of democratic constitutionalism and national independence, quickly turned out to be a bitter disappointment. Under Yuan Shikai the "liberal republic," as Ernest Young characterizes it, soon led to another autocracy and even to two attempts at reviving the monarchy.[1] The first, in 1915–16, sought to make Yuan the new emperor; the second, in 1917, after Yuan's death, aimed to restore the Qing. Neither succeeded, and the facade of the Republic was preserved. By then, though, China was plunged into the decade of political and military disorder known as warlordism, which did not end until the Nationalist Party (Guomindang; Kuomintang) came to power in 1927–28.

If the political aspirations of the revolution had come up short, what of its anti-Manchu aims? The revolutionaries had previously accused the Manchus of seven sets of misdeeds, which they were now in a position to correct or undo. However, in their desire to bring the revolution to a speedy and successful conclusion, they had also promised the banner people as well as the Qing court that both would be safeguarded and provided for indefinitely. Given such seeming contradictions and in view of the political turmoil of the times, to what extent was the new regime able, on the one hand, to cleanse the crimes of the Manchus and, on the other, to fulfill the pledges of favorable treatment in the abdication agreements? How, in other words, did the Qing court and the banner people fare in the new era, both during the early Republic (1912–28) and under subsequent regimes? How, too, did the concept of the Manchus change over time?

THE QING COURT AND THE EARLY REPUBLIC

With the seven-count indictment as their justification, the republican revolutionaries had called for the overthrow of the Manchu rulers, but in order to avoid a prolonged conflict, they had settled for a negotiated arrangement. In return for the dynasty's transferring its authority to the Republic, they promised, in the Articles of Favorable Treatment, to deal generously with the abdicated emperor. Though the settlement had troubled some Republicans as far too generous, it was to remain in effect by and large until, and even after, Puyi's expulsion from the palace in 1924.

During the first two years of the Republic, when President Yuan Shikai operated within the "liberal" political framework that the former revolutionaries and constitutional reformers had erected (including a provisional constitution and an elected bicameral parliament, which replaced the revolutionaries' ad hoc senate), the new regime made a conscientious effort to fulfill its obligations under the abdication agreement. Indeed, in one respect it treated the Qing court more favorably than promised, by not requiring the emperor to leave the Forbidden City. Originally his stay there was supposed to be only temporary. At an unspecified "later date," which Wu Tingfang publicly stated would be no later than the end of winter, he would transfer to the Yiheyuan Summer Palace in the northwestern suburbs. As spring approached, however, Yuan, citing the turmoil in Beijing caused by the mutiny of Cao Kun's Third Division on 29 February 1912, consented to a postponement. (He used the same excuse to rebuff the Republican Senate's command that he relocate his government to Nanjing.) In the following months, though the newspapers repeatedly reported that the emperor was about to move to the Yiheyuan, he never did. Perhaps Yuan found it easier to keep the court under his watchful eyes when it was nearby rather than out in the suburbs.[2]

The Qing court after its abdication occupied only a small portion of its former holdings in Beijing. Previously, the palace complex comprised not only the Forbidden City but the encompassing Imperial City as well, including such facilities as Prospect Hill (Jingshan, also known as Coal Hill) to the north, the Three Seas (Sanhai) to the west, and the Altar of Harvests and Temple of Ancestors to the south. The abdication agreement permitted the court to remain only within the Forbidden City; the rest of the complex would be conveyed to the Republic. Accordingly, on New Year's Day 1913 the court threw open to the public the long, stone-paved Imperial Way, south of Tiananmen (the Gate of Heavenly Peace), which previously had been sealed off from the outside world. Two months later it turned over the Three Seas, including Yingtai Palace in the South Sea (Nanhai), which in April became the new presidential headquarters and remained so until 1925. Also in 1913 the Republican government converted a section of the Altar of Harvests into Central Park (Zhongyang Gongyuan), a public facility with paid admission. (It was renamed Zhongshan Park, in honor of Sun Yat-sen [Sun Zhongshan], after the triumph of the Nationalists.) However, the adjacent Temple of Ancestors, because of its intimate ties to the dynasty, stayed under the control of the court, as did Prospect Hill, though it was open to the public on a restricted basis.[3]

Within the Forbidden City itself, the Qing gave up most of its southern half, known as the "outer court." Thus, Yuan Shikai's inauguration as president on 10 October 1913, following his perfunctory election by the new parliament, took place within the Hall of Supreme Harmony (Taihedian), where Qing emperors had been enthroned. Other buildings in the outer court that were ceded to the Republic included the Wenhua and Wuying Palaces, near Meridian Gate (Wumen), where civil and military officials used to await audiences with the emperor. Soon afterward, in 1914, these two "waiting palaces"—together with the nearby Taihe, Zhonghe, and Baohe throne halls—became a public museum, the Exhibition Hall of Antiquities (Guwu Chenliesuo), displaying treasures from the palaces at Shenyang (formerly Shengjing) and Rehe. The Qing was left with only the "inner court," north of the Qianqing Gate, and portions of the outer court on either side of the three main throne halls. The Gate of Spiritual Valor (Shenwumen) along the north wall of the Forbidden City replaced Meridian Gate on the south as the formal entrance into the diminished Qing court. In addition to these reduced holdings in Beijing City, the Qing also controlled the Yiheyuan Summer Palace, to which it might still be expected to move one day.[4]

The Republic, as agreed upon, treated the former Qing household with the same degree of ceremony and formality as would have been shown to a foreign monarch. It addressed Puyi as "Emperor of the Great Qing," and it dealt the same way with Longyu, who since the resignation of Zaifeng as regent had dominated court affairs. Thus, on 15 February 1913, on the occasion of the ailing empress dowager's forty-fifth birthday, Yuan Shikai sent his chief secretary, Liang Shiyi (1869–1933), to the palace to offer his congratulations. While Longyu sat on the throne, Liang bowed three times and presented an official message to "Empress Dowager Longyu of the Great Qing." When she died a week later, Yuan's cabinet ordered all government offices throughout the country to fly their flags at half staff and all civil and military officials to wear mourning for twenty-seven days. With Longyu's demise, formal leadership of the court during Puyi's minority passed to the four dowager consorts—the three concubines of Tongzhi and one of Guangxu.[5]

The court's principal intermediaries with the new regime were former grand councilor Shixu, who was then the chief minister of the Imperial Household Department, and Prince Pulun. Thus, Shixu represented the Qing at Yuan's inauguration as provisional president on 10 March 1912. When Sun Yat-sen and Huang Xing visited Beijing six months later, both Shixu and Pulun were dispatched to welcome them on behalf of the court. Pulun hosted a large party for the two leaders of the revolution, while Shixu escorted them on a tour of the Forbidden City and the Yiheyuan. At Yuan's installation as president a year later at the Taihe throne hall, it was Pulun's turn to represent the court. In the receiving line he was placed right after the diplomatic corps, as if the Qing were of nearly equal standing with a foreign country.[6]

The new regime also attempted to fulfill its financial promises to the Qing court. The chief obligation was the annual stipend of four million taels (later on, dollars). It was Shixu's responsibility, as the lead minister of the imperial household, to dun President Yuan for the money.[7] Though financially strapped, the Republic did pay much, though not all, of the obligated sums. In April 1912, for example, the Ministry of Finance turned over 150,000 taels; in October, 600,000 taels; and in December, $200,000. As the North-China Herald commented in early 1913, "There is nothing to show that Republican promises have been broken with regard to allowance and dignities." When Yuan contracted the controversial Reorganization Loan in April 1913, one of its purposes was to pay the expenses of the imperial household, which for the six months from April to September were estimated at $2,777,777.[8] Another obligation to the Qing was the completion of the Guangxu emperor's tomb. This was an even larger (though one-time) expenditure for which the Reorganization Loan was earmarked: $4,611,537. Construction of the tomb, interrupted by the revolution, resumed in the spring of 1913. Despite complaints of cost overruns, the mausoleum was completed, and the Guangxu emperor was formally interred on 13 December 1913.[9]

Finally, Yuan Shikai's government took the Palace Guard away from the Qing court and placed it under the Ministry of the Army, but, as promised, preserved its organizational integrity. Over the objections of some Republican critics, the unit was not disbanded; thus, another intended use of the Reorganization Loan was to advance $1,243,196 to the Ministry of the Army to pay for the Palace Guard. It was one of the largest military units in the capital. When President Yuan reviewed the troops on the first anniversary of the revolution, the Guard's contingent of three thousand soldiers in the parade was second in size only to his own six-thousand-person force, the Gongweijun. Except for the Fourth Infantry Regiment, which from its inception was mostly Han, the Palace Guard also remained a Manchu army. Initially, at least, when new soldiers were recruited, they were drawn, as before, from the ranks of the Metropolitan Banners. As the Beijing correspondent for the North-China Herald noted in October 1912, "The organization and composition of [the Palace Guard] remains practically unchanged, except that many of the principal Manchu officers have been replaced by [Han] Chinese. Nevertheless, the division is still mainly Manchu." Actually, even among the officers, the Manchu presence continued to be strong. In 1913 the commander of the First Brigade was Guan Zhonghe, who previously had led the First Regiment, and the commander of the Second Regiment was, as before, Chonglin (or Chongen). Thus, at least two of the top eight or ten leaders of the Palace Guard were Manchus.[10]

The Palace Guard in the early years of the Republic continued to function as the emperor's bodyguard and kept its distinctive imperial name. In 1913 the predominantly Han Fourth Regiment was sent off to Zhangjiakou to combat Mongol bandits, but most of the rest of the division remained at their new Changchunyuan barracks in the northwestern suburbs. It was the particular responsibility of Chonglin's Second Regiment to stand guard at the main gates leading to the Imperial and the Forbidden Cities, including those gates that had been opened to the public.[11] However, the Palace Guard, in addition to continuing its ties to the Qing court, also became increasingly identified as Feng Guozhang's army and was the foundation on which Feng's growing political power rested. He had been its commander since the resignation of Zaifeng as regent in December 1911. Even when he was appointed military governor of Zhili Province in September 1912 and was replaced as leader of the Palace Guard by Wang Tingzhen, Guan Zhonghe's predecessor at the First Brigade, Feng Guozhang remained as the unit's supreme commander. Although he took only one hundred of its soldiers with him to Tianjin, he retained ultimate authority over the entire Palace Guard. On at least a couple occasions in 1913, he returned to Beijing to take care of Palace Guard matters.[12] Because Feng Guozhang had for several years been closely associated with the Qing court and, as most recently demonstrated during the abdication crisis, was extremely solicitous of its welfare, the Palace Guard's dual ties to the court and to Feng Guozhang were not necessarily in conflict.

The Qing court, for its part, tried to stay in the good graces of the new republic by assiduously keeping its distance from the restorationist activities of some of its adherents. During the first few months after the abdication, the newspapers were full of stories of counterrevolutionary intrigues, many of them attributed to the Royalist Party. Its leading members were said to include those Manchus who had been most opposed to the court's capitulation to the Republicans. When the dynasty abdicated, most of them had fled Beijing and found refuge in various foreign-controlled areas of China. Shanqi went to Lüshun (Port Arthur) in the Japanese leased territory of Guandong in Fengtian; Puwei, to the German leasehold of Qingdao in Shandong; and Tieliang, to the Japanese concession in Tianjin. From their foreign sanctuaries, they tried to rally support to renew the struggle against the Republic and restore the Qing dynasty. The royalists were particularly active in Manchuria and Beijing, both with large Manchu populations who might be inclined to support their aims.

The most ambitious of these early restorationist plots was that of Shanqi (Prince Su), working in conjunction with the Japanese adventurer Kawashima Naniwa, with whom he had collaborated ten years earlier in organizing the Beijing police. In 1912 Shanqi and Kawashima sought to set up a Japanese protectorate in that part of Inner Mongolia bordering on Manchuria where Puyi could be returned to power. However, this effort to create what Marius Jansen calls the "first Manchukuo" collapsed when the Japanese government withdrew its support in favor of working with Yuan Shikai. Shanqi retired to Lüshun, where he died in 1922; he never reconciled with the Republic.[13]

In Beijing the Palace Guard, which had opposed the Qing abdication until almost the very end, was widely suspected of harboring restorationist sentiments. In April 1912 a group of forty or more soldiers from Chonglin's Second Regiment marched on the office of the staunchly pro-Republican *China Daily* (Zhonghua ribao) and dragged its editor off to their headquarters because the newspaper had refused to retract some hostile comments about the banner people. The incident immediately gave rise to a rumor that the Palace Guard was plotting an armed uprising with the royalists. This in turn obliged the Palace Guard soldiers to issue a statement denying the rumor and vowing support for the Republic. There is, indeed, no evidence that the royalists were ever deeply involved with the Guard.[14]

Nevertheless, Yuan's government warned the Qing court to rein in its adherents. Around the end of March 1912, Empress Dowager Longyu accordingly ordered the Royalist Party to disband. She worried that its activities could lead to the revocation of the Articles of Favorable Treatment as well as to foreign intervention. She instructed the imperial princes to leave their foreign sanctuaries and return to Beijing.[15] Although Longyu's decree did not stop the restorationists, she had at least indicated to the Republic that they were acting independently of the court.

The liberal republic soon gave way to a dictatorship. During the first year and a half of his presidency, Yuan Shikai had ruled with the grudging support of the former republican revolutionaries, who, however, grew increasingly suspicious of his autocratic ambitions. In the summer of 1913, following his complicity in the assassination of Song Jiaoren (1882–1913) in March and his attempt a month later to conclude the Reorganization Loan without consulting Parliament, they finally rose up against the president in the so-called Second Revolution. Yuan, however, was able to crush his opponents and force Sun Yat-sen and others to flee China once more. From then on Yuan steadily extended his despotism. In November 1913 he banned the Nationalist Party; in January 1914 he dissolved Parliament; in May he replaced the provisional constitution of 1912 with a "compact" (*yuefa*) that gave him almost unlimited power.

During the period of Yuan Shikai's dictatorship in 1914–15, the Articles of Favorable Treatment for the Qing emperor remained in full force. Indeed, Yuan earned the gratitude of the Qing court when he instructed the committee drafting the new compact to insert an explicit stipulation (Article 65) that the articles and the two other abdication agreements "would be effective forever without change."[16] On 26 December 1914, however, Yuan himself initiated a major modification of the articles by imposing upon the Qing a supplemental agreement known as the Reconstruction Plan (Shanhou Banfa).[17] It is not entirely clear why he took this action at this time. The court's possible involvement in a much-publicized plot by Song Yuren (1857–1931) to restore the Qing may have been the immediate cause. The first article of the Reconstruction Plan pointedly reminded the court of its place within the Republican polity: "The Qing imperial household should respect the sovereignty of the Republic of China, and, except for what is specified in the Articles of Favorable Treatment, it must curtail all activities that contravene present laws."

To judge from the rest of the plan, a more general cause may have been the accumulation of minor misdeeds that the court, willfully or otherwise, had committed over the previous three years. Thus, Article 2 required that the court, in its communications with the government and in other public documents, stop using the lunar calendar and the old system of dating by dynastic reign (i.e., Xuantong) and instead adopt the solar calendar and date by the year of the Republic. Article 3 prohibited the court from conferring posthumous titles and other intangible honors (e.g., permission to ride a horse in the Forbidden City) upon officials and citizens of the Republic, though material rewards were allowed. Article 4 designated the Ministry of Internal Affairs as the Republican unit responsible for protecting the imperial temples and tombs and the court's private property, while Article 5 confirmed the Imperial Household Department as the agency to oversee affairs of the court. Article 6 entrusted the policing of the inner court to a new palace guard. Article 7 reiterated that all court personnel were concurrently citizens of the Republic; therefore, except for such occasions as court ceremonies, they should abide by the dress code of the Republic. In sum, the Reconstruction Plan served primarily to define more precisely than before the limits of the court's authority vis-à-vis the Republic.

Otherwise, Yuan Shikai as dictator treated the Qing court much as he had during the liberal republic. While he himself resided in the Yingtai Palace in the Imperial City, he allowed the emperor to remain in the inner court of the Forbidden City and made no effort to shift him to the Yiheyuan. The court's main representatives in its dealings with Yuan's government at this time continued to be Pulun and Shixu. It was they, along with Zaifeng (Prince Chun) and Shaoying, who hosted a banquet in April 1914 to thank the committee that drew up the constitutional compact for binding the Republic to the Articles of Favorable Treatment in perpetuity. Yuan later added Pulun to his interim legislature, the Council of State (Canzhengyuan). Most important, Yuan continued to pay the Qing court at least some of the annual subsidy due to it. For example, in November 1915, his Ministry of Finance distributed to the imperial household $700,000, almost one-fifth of that year's allocation.[18]

Aside from the Reconstruction Plan, one other change affecting the Qing court during Yuan's dictatorship was the transfer of the bulk of the Palace Guard away from Beijing, a move that emphasized its transformation from the emperor's bodyguard to Feng Guozhang's personal army. In July 1913 Feng was sent from Tianjin to the lower Yangzi valley to help put down the Second Revolution, after which he was appointed military governor of Jiangsu. In January 1914 a mixed brigade of the Palace Guard, led by the divisional commander Wang Tingzhen, joined him in Nanjing. Subsequently, another detachment of the Guard, the Fourth Infantry Regiment, was also posted to Jiangsu and was stationed in Suzhou. Except for the Fourth Regiment at Suzhou, which had always been Han, the Palace Guard soldiers in Jiangsu were, as before, predominantly Manchu, and the commander of the First Brigade was still Guan Zhonghe. The only Palace Guard unit left in the capital was the Second Regiment, which despite its distance from him remained under the overall command of Feng Guozhang. Its mission was unchanged: to stand guard at the palace gates.[19]

The Yuan Shikai presidency evolved in 1915–16 into the Yuan Shikai monarchy. This was a restoration of the monarchy rather than of the Qing dynasty. Nevertheless, the imperial household and other Manchus were expected to play their assigned roles. Early champions of the movement at the local level included Wuzesheng and Hengjun, the two chief editors of the late-Qing Manchu reformist publication *Great Harmony Journal*, the former as a representative from Jilin and the latter from "Manchuria" (Manzhou). Another was Guan Zhonghe of the First Brigade, along with a host of other (non-Manchu) Palace Guard commanders in Nanjing. When Yuan's operatives had produced a show of popular support, the Qing court joined in as well. On 12 December 1915 Pulun, too, urged the president to heed the will of the people and become emperor. Yuan, with appropriate modesty, finally consented. He announced that with the new year, the Republic of China would be reconstituted as the Empire of China (Zhonghua Diguo). The Qing court on 16 December gave Yuan its blessings. Pulun, however, may have overstepped the authority bestowed upon him by the court when he ceremoniously performed the kowtow to Yuan.[20]

The Qing's primary concern during the monarchical restoration, about which Shixu inquired, was the future status of the Articles of Favorable Treatment. Would they be voided by the restoration? Yuan's government replied that though the polity might change, the articles would not. On 16 December, in return for the court's support, Yuan declared that the new constitution that he planned to have drawn up would incorporate Article 65 of the constitutional compact; that is, the abdication agreements were permanent and immutable.[21] Yet, the Qing court realized that with the imminent reestablishment of the monarchy it did need to make at least one change. As it would have been inappropriate for Yuan as emperor to live anywhere else, it was finally time for the Qing to leave the Forbidden City. The court could, as originally intended, relocate to the Yiheyuan or, perhaps, switch residences with Yuan by moving to the South Sea.[22] However, before either the new constitution had been drafted or the court had left the Forbidden City, Yuan's monarchical scheme crashed amidst an unexpected groundswell of opposition from both military and civilian leaders throughout China, many of them his former supporters. One of Yuan's key opponents was Feng Guozhang in Nanjing, even though most of Feng's subordinates in the Palace Guard earlier had signed a petition favoring the monarchical restoration.[23] On 22 March 1916 Yuan Shikai hastily decreed a return to the Republic; less than three months later, he died.

In the immediate aftermath of Yuan's failed effort to revive the monarchy and then of Yuan's death, political power at the national level was divided among Li Yuanhong (Yuan's successor as president), Duan Qirui (the prime minister and concurrently minister of the army), and Feng Guozhang (the Palace Guard commander in Nanjing, whom the reconvened Parliament elected to replace Li Yuanhong). As the new vice-president, Feng Guozhang should have gone to Beijing, but, in recognition of his independent power base, he was given special dispensation to stay in Jiangsu, where he also kept his position as provincial military governor.[24] Relations among the three leaders, all militarists, were tense. Li Yuanhong and Duan Qirui in Beijing feuded over the relative power of the president and the prime minister, while the rivalry between Duan and Feng Guozhang, already in evidence during the abdication crisis in 1911–12, was beginning to split Yuan's Beiyang Army into the competing Anhui (or Anfu) and Zhili cliques respectively.

With Yuan Shikai gone, the Qing court lost its most influential patron, but his immediate successors were not inclined to disturb the status quo. One change during Li Yuanhong's presidency that impinged upon the court was the decision of the newly recalled Parliament (elected in 1912–13 but dissolved by Yuan) to write a new constitution. Unveiled in September 1916, the draft of the constitution said nothing about the abdication agreements; Article 65 of Yuan's compact promising that the agreements were forever immutable had been deleted. The Qing court and its outside supporters, including Vice-President Feng Guozhang and former grand councilor Xu Shichang, busily lobbied Parliament to reinsert the pledge into the final version of the document. Xu contended that to fail to do so would create unsettling doubts that the Articles of Favorable Treatment had been scrapped. Despite their efforts, the new constitution as proclaimed in May 1917 did not reaffirm the articles.[25]

Although the failure of this lobbying campaign suggests a decline in top-level support for the Qing court, it did not mean, as Xu Shichang had feared, that the immediate post-Yuan leaders denied the continuing validity of the abdication agreements. To the contrary, Li Yuanhong's government seems to have observed the Articles of Favorable Treatment more or less faithfully. It did not force the Qing to follow through on its recent offer to Yuan Shikai to vacate the Forbidden City. It also continued to treat the court with respect and dignity. Thus, on 10 October 1916, the first anniversary of the Republican revolution since Yuan's fall, the president included Shixu and Prince Zaitao among those on whom he bestowed special honors. Pulun, who might otherwise have been honored alongside Shixu, had fallen out of favor with the Qing court because of his close, even sycophantic, relationship with the former president; he died in Beijing in 1926.[26]

Li Yuanhong's presidency ended after only one year, when Zhang Xun abruptly restored the Qing. The defender of Nanjing during the revolution had never reconciled himself to the Republic; his army, which had withdrawn to Xuzhou in northern Jiangsu, was known as the "pigtailed army" because his soldiers were not allowed to cut their queue. In June 1917 Zhang was summoned to Beijing to mediate in the worsening dispute between the president and Duan Qirui, whom Li Yuanhong had just dismissed as prime minister. On 16 June Zhang, in Qing court attire, paid a ceremonial visit to the eleven-year-old Puyi at the Mind Nurturing Hall (Yangxindian) in the inner court. Two weeks later, now joined by his troops from Xuzhou and with several Qing loyalists (all of them, like Kang Youwei, Han) in tow, he proclaimed the resurrection of the Great Qing Empire and coerced Republican president Li to turn his authority over to the restored Xuantong emperor. Zhang named himself an adviser. As he explained to a reporter, the republican form of government had not suited China; only a restoration of the emperor could save the country from its many perils.[27]

On the same day and at Zhang's urging, the boy emperor issued a nine-point public proclamation that spelled out the guidelines of the new regime. It would be a "constitutional monarchy" and would embrace those reforms of the late Qing that had curbed the "Manchu ascendency" and reduced Manchu-Han differences. Thus, "in accordance with the ancestral traditions of the dynasty, imperial relatives must not interfere in governmental affairs." Also, "all Manchu-Mongol governmental positions [i.e., ethnic slots] that had previously been abolished would not be revived." Though the proclamation said nothing explicit about the Articles of Favorable Treatment and the associated Reconstruction Plan, the emperor's restoration logically meant that both had been canceled. Puyi was no longer confined to the inner precincts of the Forbidden City; for example, his second audience with Zhang Xun, on 1 July, was held in the outer court, in the Hall of Central Harmony (Zhonghedian). His proclamation was dated according to his reign era (the ninth year of Xuantong), and it used the lunar rather than the solar calendar. His decree did, however, allude to one provision of the Articles of Favorable Treatment. It specified that the allocation to the imperial household should be the "previously agreed figure of $4 million a year."[28]

Zhang Xun's attempt to restore the Qing was no more successful than Yuan Shikai's to revive the monarchy a year and a half earlier. Zhang, too, lacked the support of other military leaders. Feng Guozhang in Nanjing was again in the opposition, even though a majority of the soldiers in his Palace Guard were Manchus and, as such, were widely suspected of favoring the Qing restoration. The First Brigade commander, Guan Zhonghe, himself a bannerman, acknowledged that the very name of his unit would lead naturally to such an idea. To calm popular anxiety in Nanjing, Feng Guozhang and the divisional commander Wang Tingzhen temporarily disarmed the Palace Guard soldiers and transferred them out of the city to Pukou on the other side of the Yangzi River. They also distributed a joint statement by Wang and Guan reassuring the public that the Palace Guard was against the restoration and had communicated its opposition to Zaifeng at court. However, it was not Feng Guozhang in distant Nanjing but Duan Qirui in nearby Tianjin who undid the work of Zhang Xun. Putting together an "army to suppress the traitor," Duan handily defeated Zhang, who on 12 July fled for safety to the Dutch legation. The Qing restoration had lasted twelve days.[29]

Zhang Xun's crushing defeat left the political scene more confused than ever, with two regimes now claiming to represent China. In the north, a succession of militarists from competing factions were dominant. Vice-President Feng Guozhang (of the Zhili clique) initially came to Beijing to serve as acting president in place of Li Yuanhong, whom Zhang Xun had compelled to resign, but, as Feng soon discovered, it was Duan Qirui (of the Anhui clique), triumphant over Zhang, who held real power. In October 1918 Duan forced Feng to retire at the end of his abbreviated term and replaced him as president with Xu Shichang, the former Qing grand councilor. Duan's control of the Beijing government, however, lasted only until July 1920, when the Zhili clique, now led by Cao Kun after Feng Guozhang's death in 1919, got its revenge; in the so-called Zhili-Anhui War, Cao, supported by Zhang Zuolin of the Fengtian clique, vanquished Duan and ended the hegemony of the Anhui clique. However, the two victors over Duan soon began a power struggle of their own that occupied the next couple of years. At last, in April 1922, during the first of two Zhili-Fengtian wars, Cao Kun, together with his increasingly powerful subordinate Wu Peifu (1874–1939), defeated their former ally Zhang Zuolin and sent him back to southern Manchuria. Cao and Wu proceeded to rule over Beijing jointly until 1924. Meanwhile, in south China, other warlords, initially opposed to Duan Qirui in 1917, had set up a rival government in Guangzhou, whose nominal head, off and on, was Sun Yat-sen. Sun was finally able in March 1923 to entrench himself in Guangzhou, where with Soviet help he reorganized his Nationalist Party and created an independent revolutionary regime with its own army.

The emperor's involvement in Zhang Xun's failed effort led many people, for the first time since 1912, to demand that the Articles of Favorable Treatment be abrogated in order to punish the court. They contended that Zhang could not have gotten as far as he had without the active cooperation of the Qing, which therefore was no less culpable than the general. On 7 July, during the restoration, a group of sixty parliamentarians exiled in Tianjin, most of them fervent republicans, proposed a set of nine reforms for the post-Zhang era, one of which was that the abdication agreement be set aside:

> The Articles of Favorable Treatment were a gesture of extraordinary generosity on the part of the Republic. As no other ruler of a defunct country in history ever enjoyed such treatment, there was never any justification for them from the very beginning. Now that the court has rebelled against the state, they should of course be canceled; if they were to be retained, it would be the same as rewarding rebels. The baleful consequences hardly bear thinking about.

The four people who were most deeply involved in negotiating the agreement—not only for the Republic (Wu Tingfang, Wen Zongyao, and Wang Jingwei) but also for the Qing (Tang Shaoyi)—wholeheartedly agreed. In a telegram sent after the restoration had been crushed, they declared that "since the Qing emperor has usurped power, the Articles of Favorable Treatment are obviously invalid." Even a group of northern generals, reportedly on the initiative of Feng Yuxiang (1882–1948), circulated a telegram making similar demands: the articles should be abrogated and the annual allocation of $4 million cease. Puyi should be stripped of his title as the Xuantong emperor and never again be allowed to address the Manchu and Mongol peoples as emperor; his status should be reduced to that of an ordinary citizen. Furthermore, all the palaces, public lands, and gardens belonging to the Qing household in and beyond the capital should be turned over to the nation for the use of the people as a whole. Feng Yuxiang and his fellow generals asserted that if the Qing court were not abolished, it would continue to serve as a rallying point for dissidents: "We fear that while one Zhang Xun has been eliminated, countless other Zhang Xuns will arise in the future."[30]

The Qing court itself expected that it would have to pay a heavy price for its foolhardy collaboration with Zhang Xun. It even drafted an edict in which Puyi would announce his abdication. Fortunately for the court, Duan Qirui's government chose to depict the emperor as a passive, hence largely blameless, victim of Zhang's machinations. It was indeed true that Zhang Xun's effort had been more an expression of Qing loyalism than of Manchu restorationism. It had thus been notably lacking in Manchu participation. No more than five or six of the numerous appointees to the restored imperial government, among them former army minister Tieliang, were Manchus; all the others were Han. Hardly anyone closely identified with the old Royalist Party, such as Puwei, took part in the restoration. Realizing its quixotic nature, Shixu, head of the Imperial Household Department, had been opposed from the beginning; he repeatedly refused to heed Puyi's summons to court. In view of such circumstances, Duan Qirui treated the Qing leniently. He took the abdication edict that the Qing court had prepared for Puyi and "revised" it substantially. The edict, as issued on 17 July, put the blame entirely on Zhang Xun and portrayed the young emperor as utterly naive and helpless. Noting that in the six previous years the Qing court had been extremely well cared for under the Articles of Favorable Treatment, the decree implicitly hoped that such treatment would continue.[31]

The Articles of Favorable Treatment did remain in effect during the rule of Feng Guozhang, Duan Qirui, and Cao Kun from 1917 to 1924. These northern warlords allowed Puyi, after his bold venture into the outer portion of the Forbidden City, to return to his accustomed, if confined, quarters in the inner court; they did not press him to move to the Yiheyuan. They recognized his status and title as emperor of the Qing. They invited imperial representatives to Republican functions such as Xu Shichang's presidential inauguration in October 1918. Similarly, they dispatched Republican representatives to court ceremonies; for example, they sent Yinchang, the former army minister who, though a Manchu, had become a high-ranking military adviser to President Yuan Shikai and his successors, to attend Puyi's wedding in 1922. As Puyi recalls in his autobiography, Yinchang first "congratulated me formally as he would have done a foreign sovereign. When he had finished bowing to me he announced, 'That was on behalf of the Republic. Your slave will now greet Your

Majesty in his private capacity.' With this he knelt on the floor and kotowed to me." When the court stepped out of line, however, the warlords did not hesitate to rein it back in. Thus, in October 1921 Cao Kun reminded the Imperial Household Department that according to the Reconstruction Plan of 1914, its personnel, when communicating with Republican officials, were supposed to date their documents by the solar calendar.[32]

The northern warlords also kept up the payments to the Qing court, though not the full amount of $4 million a year, and never without (in Reginald Johnston's words) "groveling appeals to the republican government." When Puyi married in 1922, Cao Kun's officials apologized that

> as they were having difficulties at the moment in meeting their expenditure they were unable to pay in full the annual subsidies stipulated in the Articles of Favourable Treatment; they would, however, make a special payment from tax revenue of 100,000 dollars to help with the Grand Nuptials, of which 20,000 dollars was to be regarded as a present from the Republic.

In other words, the other $80,000 would be counted against the court's subsidy. Furthermore, Johnston alleges, the Republicans reneged on an agreement regarding the more than seventy thousand imperial items that had been transferred in 1914 from the Shenyang and Rehe palaces and put on display in the Exhibition Hall of Antiquities in the outer court of the Forbidden City. The contract, signed in 1916, stipulated that these treasures were the private property of the Qing imperial household; that they were to be purchased by the Republic, whenever its finances permitted, at a price to be determined by independent experts; and that meanwhile they were considered to be on loan to the Republic from the Qing. The value of these treasures was later set at $3.5 million. According to Johnston, not one dollar of this amount was ever paid.[33] Due to high court expenditures and reduced incomes, the Qing Imperial Household Department was increasingly driven to selling and pawning other portions of its vast art collection.[34]

Finally, the northern warlords continued into the early 1920s to maintain the Palace Guard as a separate military unit, as promised in the Articles of Favorable Treatment. Its personnel were still predominantly Manchu; in mid-1917 Feng Guozhang, its supreme commander, stated that "half were of banner registry [qiji]." The unit, however, suffered from the vicissitudes of warlord politics. Stationed in Nanjing at the time of Zhang Xun's restoration attempt, the Palace Guard returned to Beijing when Feng became acting president after Zhang's defeat in mid-1917. It was the core of Feng Guozhang's military power and it became, along with the Fifteenth Division, a part of his presidential guard. Only then, in a transparent effort to rid itself of the imperial stigma that had bedeviled it during both of the recent restoration attempts, was the Palace Guard renamed the Sixteenth Division, which brought its nomenclature into conformity with the rest of China's national army. (Informally, however, the division was still known as the Palace Guard.) Wang Tingzhen continued as the division commander, and Guan Zhonghe as the commander of the First Brigade, now redesignated the Thirty-first Brigade. Even after Feng Guozhang had been forced to retire as president a year later, the division stayed in close touch with him. Following Feng's death in December 1919, the Sixteenth Division was transferred to Chahar and its commander Wang Tingzhen appointed Chahar lieutenant-general. Wang himself, though, fell from power the next summer during the Zhili-Anhui War, in which the coalition of Zhili and Fengtian forces led by Cao Kun and Zhang Zuolin defeated the Anhui clique of Duan Qirui. As a former subordinate of Feng Guozhang, Wang Tingzhen should have been a part of the winning Zhili faction, but, in a gross miscalculation, he had switched sides. As a result, he lost his command of the division, which passed into the control of a Fengtian-clique general, Zou Fen. Two years later, during the First Zhili-Fengtian War, Zou Fen made a timely defection to the Zhili side, helping to cause Fengtian to lose. Though it was once again part of the dominant Zhili faction, the division was nevertheless "reorganized" out of existence and its predominantly Manchu soldiers "scattered." The disbanding of the bulk of the old Palace Guard in Chahar in 1922 did not, however, affect its Second Regiment in Beijing, which in 1924 was still protecting the palace gates.[35]

The northern warlords' indulgence toward the Qing court did not lack critics, particularly after August 1922, following Cao Kun's victory over Zhang Zuolin, when the old Parliament, dissolved in 1917, was once again reconstituted in Beijing. On at least two occasions, a radical minority in the Parliament urged that the Articles of Favorable Treatment be abrogated. Parliamentarian Deng Yuanpeng was bothered by the pomp and ceremony of Puyi's wedding in December 1922, when yellow dragon flags and other imperial symbols were displayed throughout the capital; he likened the situation to Zhang Xun's restoration and called it tantamount to rebellion. In early 1924 another parliamentarian, Li Xieyang, likewise suggested that the abdication agreement be set aside. According to such critics, the emperor's own recent behavior amply justified canceling the arrangement. Not only had Puyi violated the original 1912 articles by colluding with Zhang Xun to overturn the Republic in 1917, but he had also contravened Article 3 of the 1914 Reconstruction Plan by granting Zhang, on his death in September 1923, a posthumous title. Another cause for public outrage in the early 1920s was the selling and pawning of the palace treasures by the imperial household to cover its expenses. The Archeological Society of Beijing University published a manifesto attacking Zaixun, the former navy minister and Puyi's uncle, for destroying state property. The court insisted that these treasures were part of what the Articles of Favorable Treatment recognized as the imperial household's private property and therefore it could dispose of them as it wished. The critics, on the other hand, contended that they belonged to the Chinese people. Meanwhile, in Guangzhou, the position of the southern regime, unlike that of its conservative rival in the north, was that the court's complicity in Zhang Xun's restoration had rendered the abdication agreements null and void. Sun Yat-sen's government thus called for an end to the Articles of Favorable Treatment and the reduction of Puyi's status to that of an ordinary citizen.[36]

At the same time, significant changes were occurring within the Qing court, where Puyi was fast growing up. In November 1918, when Puyi was twelve years old, Duan Qirui's government arranged for Reginald F. Johnston, a British diplomat, to be his English tutor. Johnston eventually came to exercise considerable influence over the emperor; in about 1921, for example, he persuaded Puyi to cut off his queue, which led nearly everyone else at court to follow suit. In December 1922, when Puyi was almost seventeen, he married, taking two Manchu banner women, Wanrong (1906–46) and Wenxiu (1909–53), as his wife and concubine respectively. Soon afterward, encouraged by Johnston, he began to assert personal control over the management of the Qing court. In July 1923, suspicious that they were enriching themselves at his expense by stealing and selling court treasures, Puyi expelled nearly all of the thousand and more eunuchs from the palace; he kept only about a hundred to look after the dowager consorts.[37]

The following year Puyi attempted to reorganize the Imperial Household Department, which since the death of Shixu in January 1922 had been led by Shaoying. In the spring of 1924 he replaced Shaoying with Zheng Xiaoxu, Zhang Jian's constitutionalist colleague, who became the first Han in the history of the dynasty to head the agency. Zheng, like Johnston, favored extensive changes at court. Both recommended that Puyi relocate to the Yiheyuan Summer Palace, in part because such a move might undercut the growing popular opposition to the Articles of Favorable Treatment. If the court would finally fulfill its promise in the Articles to leave the Forbidden City, then perhaps the Republic would be more inclined to honor the rest of the agreement. Zheng Xiaoxu put Johnston in charge of making the Yiheyuan ready for its new occupants, and he arranged for Puyi to tour the summer palace. However, the prospect of the court's departure from the Forbidden City greatly alarmed the entrenched interests of the Imperial Household Department, who in the end prevailed. After only three months, Zheng Xiaoxu was forced to resign as head of the department, and Shaoying was returned to the post. The plan for the court to move to the Yiheyuan was abandoned.[38]

The court soon paid for its intransigence. In late 1924, during the Second Zhili-Fengtian War, Cao Kun and Wu Peifu of the ruling Zhili clique were defeated when Wu's leading subordinate, Feng Yuxiang, went over to the side of Zhang Zuolin and the Fengtian clique. Feng's army drove Wu's out of Beijing, forced Cao to resign as president, and replaced him with a "caretaker cabinet" headed by Huang Fu (1880–1936). Feng Yuxiang and Zhang Zuolin were to rule Beijing jointly for the next year. Feng, though a northern warlord, had long chafed at the continued presence of the Qing court at the heart of the capital. Seven years earlier, following Zhang Xun's attempted restoration, he had led a group of other northern generals in calling for the revocation of the Articles of Favorable Treatment and the reduction of Puyi's status to that of an ordinary citizen. His caretaker cabinet noted that the court had had ample time (thirteen years) to make good on its original promise to leave the Forbidden City. Feng Yuxiang promptly and unilaterally changed the terms of the Qing court's relationship with the Republic. On 5 November, two weeks after his entry into Beijing, one of his subordinates and twenty soldiers forced their way into the inner court of the Forbidden City and delivered an ultimatum from Feng addressed to "Mr. Puyi" (Puyi Xiansheng) demanding that he leave the premises within three hours. Feng also imposed upon Puyi a "revised" set of Articles of Favorable Treatment. The revised articles required that the "Xuantong emperor" forever give up his imperial title and instead enjoy the same legal status as any other citizen of the Republic of China; the Republic reduce the annual subsidy to the Qing imperial household from four million to half a million dollars (which would be in addition to a special, one-time allocation of $2 million to operate workshops for the poor people of Beijing, with priority given to the banner people); the Qing imperial household leave the Forbidden City and resettle wherever they wish, with the Republic still responsible for their personal safety; the Republic continue to provide military protection for the perpetual sacrifices at the imperial temples and tombs; and the Republic offer special protection for the imperial household's private property but take possession of all of their public property.[39]

Puyi had no choice but to leave the Forbidden City, followed soon after by his two young wives and the two surviving dowager consorts. He first went to his father Zaifeng's house, north of the Forbidden City, then to the Japanese legation in the diplomatic quarters of Beijing, and eventually, in February 1925, to the Japanese concession in Tianjin.[40] Other members of the Qing imperial clan likewise departed the capital. Zaifeng went to live in Tianjin too, as did

Zaizhen, Yikuang's eldest son and his successor (since 1918) as Prince Qing.[41] Johnston returned to the British foreign service. Meanwhile, with Puyi's expulsion from the Forbidden City, the mission of the Palace Guard's Second Regiment as the imperial bodyguard finally came to an end. They were demobilized and dispersed, as the rest of the division had been two years earlier.[42]

The eviction of Puyi and the Qing court was generally well received, especially among the old-time revolutionaries and radical republicans in the south, some of whom had objected to the abdication agreement from the first. Asked for his opinion by Shaoying and other members of the Imperial Household Department, the ailing Sun Yat-sen, on his final visit to Beijing two months before his death in March 1925, observed that the Qing itself had failed to live up to the terms of the original Articles of Favorable Treatment and the supplementary Reconstruction Plan. The Qing court had remained in the Forbidden City; it had not stopped dating documents by the imperial calendar; it had not curtailed conferring posthumous titles and other honors (upon non-Manchus such as Zhang Xun); and it had gone along with Zhang Xun's attempt to alter the national polity. Sun concluded that the Qing had no moral or legal grounds for complaint. The veteran anti-Manchu revolutionary Zhang Binglin, using racialist terms from fifteen or twenty years before, congratulated Feng Yuxiang for his long-overdue ejection of the "Qing chieftain" (*Qing qiu*) and the reduction of the "barbarian [*yi*] to a commoner." Indeed, Zhang was of the opinion that Feng's revised articles were still too generous to the Qing, particularly in promising to protect Puyi's considerable private wealth. A group who likewise thought that Feng Yuxiang had not gone far enough was the Grand Alliance to Oppose the Favorable Treatment of the Qing Household (Fandui Qingshi Youdai Datongmeng) in Beijing; according to Johnston, it pressed for the "total abolition of the last vestiges of 'favourable treatment,' including the arbitrarily-imposed 'agreement' of November, 1924, and the drastic punishment and even the execution of all 'monarchists' including the emperor himself."[43]

A minority, however, criticized Feng Yuxiang for having gone too far. Some complained about the way Puyi's expulsion had been carried out. One such critic was, surprisingly, Tang Shaoyi, who in 1917 had joined Wu Tingfang and other negotiators of the original Articles of Favorable Treatment in declaring that by colluding with Zhang Xun, the Qing court had itself nullified the articles. Tang Shaoyi now denounced Feng's action as coercive as well as "inopportune, unequal, and unethical" because he had used military force against a young and defenseless Puyi. If the abdication agreement were to have been changed, Tang contended, it should have been done through negotiation. Hu Shi (1891–1962), the prominent intellectual of the May Fourth New Culture movement, was similarly disturbed that the revision of the articles had been accomplished by "military intimidation"; he called it "the most unsavoury act of the Chinese republic."[44]

Some protested the eviction itself. Apart from Qing loyalists and ex-officials, they included such powerful figures as Duan Qirui and Zhang Zuolin. Duan had been living in retirement in Tianjin since his defeat in the Zhili-Anhui War four years earlier, but with the toppling of the Zhili faction in 1924, he had been brought back as the nominal head of state. Duan, who in 1917 had treated the Qing court's dalliance with Zhang Xun with unusual indulgence, sent Feng Yuxiang a telegram criticizing the expulsion. He viewed the Articles of Favorable Treatment as having the force of a formal treaty between the Republic and the monarchy. In his eyes, not only did Puyi's ouster violate a binding commitment that the Republic had made to the court, but it might also undermine the credibility of the Republic in future diplomatic negotiations with foreign countries. Duan sent word to Puyi personally of his willingness to support the imperial house "with all my strength." Zhang Zuolin, Feng Yuxiang's ally of the moment, reportedly shared many of Duan's misgivings. Those opposed to the expulsion demanded a return to the status quo ante. On 8 November a group of Qing officials, headed by former Zhili governor-general Chen Kuilong, wired Duan and Zhang calling for the immediate restoration of the original Articles of Favorable Treatment. This would have included the return of Puyi to the Forbidden City (or, at least, the Yiheyuan), recognition of his imperial title, and payment of his full annual subsidy of $4 million. In February 1925, at the so-called "aftermath conference" convened by Duan Qirui to set future government policy, numerous Qing loyalist and Manchu groups joined to petition the Republic to "protect Puyi." However, with Feng Yuxiang still in control of Beijing, the campaign went nowhere. Whatever their personal feelings on the matter, Zhang Zuolin and Duan Qirui were unwilling or unable to go against Feng at this time.[45]

Though Puyi had been ejected from the palace, Feng Yuxiang, as Zhang Binglin had complained, had not completely revoked the Articles of Favorable Treatment; he had only "revised" them. According to the new agreement, the Republic promised to give the Qing an annual subsidy of half a million dollars, to differentiate between the imperial household's private property (which would be protected) and its public property (which would be confiscated), and to safeguard the imperial temples and tombs. To what extent did Feng's government fulfill these scaled-back promises? It apparently never paid Puyi any of his reduced subsidy, presumably because the ex-emperor had given up his claim to it by seeking political asylum among the Japanese. Feng's government did, however, make an effort to sort out the complex property holdings of the Qing court so as to determine what was private and what was public. Soon after

Puyi was forced out, the Committee for the Readjustment of the Qing Household (Qingshi Shanhou Weiyuanhui), jointly composed of Republican and Qing appointees, was created to make a complete survey of the court's holdings. The committee sealed up the palaces in the inner court of the Forbidden City on 9 November and began taking inventory; nine months later it had completed its task. Having thus distinguished between the court's public and private property, the government then seized, without compensation, the public holdings, which included all of the palaces of the inner court as well as much of their art treasures. These became the Palace Museum (Gugong Bowuyuan), which opened in October 1925. (The museum subsequently, after the Sino-Japanese War [1937–45], absorbed the Exhibition Hall of Antiquities, which had been set up earlier in the outer court.)[46] The Republic took over the Yiheyuan Summer Palace at this time too. Finally, Feng's government did apparently maintain security at the Qing imperial tombs.

Feng Yuxiang's rule over Beijing lasted only one year, after which his uneasy alliance with Zhang Zuolin fell apart. At the end of 1925 Zhang, joined by Wu Peifu (who was out to avenge his betrayal by Feng the year before), turned against his erstwhile ally and defeated him. As Feng Yuxiang went into temporary exile in the Soviet Union and Duan Qirui was eased out of his posts, Zhang Zuolin took over the northern government and controlled it for the next three years. Supporters of the Qing cause were jubilant, for Zhang, who reportedly had disapproved of Puyi's expulsion, was now in a position to undo what Feng had done. Thus, in July 1926 various Qing loyalists, including Kang Youwei in Shanghai, petitioned Zhang's ally, Wu Peifu, to restore the Articles of Favorable Treatment. However, much to their and Puyi's chagrin, Zhang Zuolin made no effort to comply. In response to the July 1926 petition, his Ministry of Internal Affairs decided that Puyi had forever forfeited his title as emperor as well as nearly all of the property that the Republic had designated as public, and that neither should be returned to him.[47]

Not only did Zhang Zuolin fail to reinstate the original Articles of Favorable Treatment, he even flouted the one still pertinent provision of Feng Yuxiang's "revised" articles, which was to safeguard the Qing tombs. Security at the mausoleums, particularly the Eastern Tombs in Zunhua, eighty miles northeast of Beijing, fell apart after Zhang came to power. In the autumn of 1926, soldiers from his Fengtian clique began cutting down trees at the Eastern Tombs and selling them off as lumber. In the winter of 1926–27, a Fengtian general in pursuit of a local bandit quartered his troops for a while in the outlying buildings of the Eastern Tombs and trashed them. The following spring, thieves broke into the tomb of the Tongzhi emperor's consort, dragged her coffin out, stole the precious burial goods, and abandoned her body. Several perpetrators were captured and turned over to the authorities of Zunhua County, but they went unpunished.[48]

Zhang Zuolin was finally ousted from Beijing and the warlord era ended in mid-1928, as Chiang Kai-shek (1887–1975), successor to Sun Yat-sen and commander of the National Revolutionary Army, completed the Northern Expedition. The Nationalists, who had long called for the revocation of the original Articles of Favorable Treatment, made no effort at all to honor Feng Yuxiang's "revised" articles. They paid Puyi, living in the Japanese concession in Tianjin, no subsidy, and they took no care to protect the Qing tombs. Indeed, their violation of the imperial mausoleums went far beyond what Zhang Zuolin's soldiers had done. In July 1928, as the National Revolutionary Army neared Beijing, units belonging to Sun Dianying's (1889–1947) Twelfth Army, which was operating in Zunhua, particularly Tan Wenjiang's Fifth Division, used cannons and dynamite to break into and plunder the mausoleums of the Qianlong emperor and Empress Dowager Cixi, whose bodily remains were desecrated. Twelve other tombs in the necropolis, though not robbed, were, to varying degrees, damaged. Qianlong's and Cixi's had been targeted probably because their occupants were known for their love of luxury and their burial goods were the most numerous and expensive. One estimate of the value of the plundered goods, hauled off in more than twenty trucks, was in excess of $100 million. They were quickly sold off in the art markets of Beijing.[49]

Puyi and his supporters were outraged at the Nationalists not only for their soldiers' initial acts of sacrilege but also for their government's subsequent lackadaisical handling of the incident. The Qing imperial household sent a delegation, headed by former finance minister Zaize, to the scene to survey the extent of the damage and initiate repairs, and they demanded that the Nationalist government send troops to protect the tombs and to capture and punish the culprits. In response, the Nationalists dispatched investigators to the Eastern Tombs at Zunhua and guards to the Western Tombs in Yi County; they also promised to convene a court-martial to try the case, with division commander Tan Wenjiang as the principal suspect. Thereafter, nothing more happened. The court-martial dragged on and on and never did reach a decision.[50]

The plundering of the Eastern Tombs in 1928, preceded by the expulsion of Puyi from the Forbidden City four years earlier, marked the end of the "favorable treatment" of the Qing emperor that the abdication settlement of 1912 had promised. It is truly remarkable how favorable the treatment had been and how long it had lasted. The abdication settlement, however, included another set of promises concerning the Manchu populace. Was the early Republic equally scrupulous about fulfilling this other pledge?

THE MANCHUS IN THE EARLY REPUBLIC

The success of the revolution in and of itself had rendered moot two of the seven counts in the revolutionaries' indictment against the Manchus. The atrocities that their ancestors had committed against the Chinese during the Qing conquest (count 2) had been more than offset (or "avenged") by those against the banner people during the revolution, and a dethroned Qing was no longer in a position to pursue its former policy of anti-Hanism (count 7). It remained for the early Republic to act on the five other charges.

Count 3 in the indictment accused the Manchus of having barbarized China by imposing their customs—among them the queue, the Manchu language, and the official dress—upon the Han. The new regime lost no time in reversing these instances of Manchufication. The men's hairstyle, which the Qing originally required as a badge of subservience to Manchu rule, was, not surprisingly, the revolutionaries' first target.[51] Despite several years of open agitation by political and social reformers for its removal, the queue requirement had remained in effect until two months into the revolution. Even then the Qing had only permitted, but did not compel, its male subjects to cut their queue and wear their hair short in the Western (and Japanese) style of the day. The Republicans were not satisfied with this eleventh-hour, half-hearted measure; they insisted on universal, mandatory queue-cutting. Thus, in the four months between the Wuchang uprising and the Qing abdication, wherever the revolutionaries took power, one of the first decrees they issued was for the removal of the queue as a sign of loyalty to their regime. In Jiangxi, for example, the new government in mid-December 1911 demanded that its own officials as well as all adult males in the province cut off their braid within five days after receipt of the directive.[52]

To the Republicans' distress, their policy of universal mandatory queue-cutting did not always meet with general approval, not necessarily because the people were opposed to the revolution but because after more than two centuries, they regarded the Manchufied hairstyle as an integral part of their cultural tradition. As a result, the queue-cutting orders were often ignored; their unrealistically short deadlines, unmet. When the directives for voluntary compliance failed of their purpose, the revolutionary governments generally resorted to coercion. In Zhejiang, local officials in Jiaxing and Hangzhou sent out soldiers armed with large shears to cut any remaining braids on sight; they posted such "queue-cutting brigades" at the city gates to catch unwary villagers entering from the countryside.[53] These coercive measures only added to the policy's unpopularity. Merchants closed their shops in protest, farmers withheld their produce from the city, and men hid themselves from scissors-wielding soldiers.[54]

Nevertheless, the revolutionaries refused to back away from the new, short hairstyle. On 5 March 1912, five days before he was formally succeeded by Yuan Shikai as provisional president, Sun Yat-sen issued a decree that made queue-cutting obligatory throughout China. Now that Manchu rule had ended, he explained, it was time to "cleanse the ancient stain and become a citizen of the new nation" by discarding the Manchu-imposed hairstyle. While most people in the large cities had already done so, he conceded that in out-of-the way places "not a few" still had not. Sun therefore directed the provincial military governors to issue proclamations that all adult males within their jurisdiction cut off their plait within twenty days.[55]

Though Yuan Shikai never countermanded Sun's order, he himself seemingly reverted to the permissive policy that he had earlier convinced the Qing court to adopt. While he quietly removed his own queue on 16 February, four days after the Qing abdication, he did not demand that others follow his lead. The commander of the Palace Guard, Feng Guozhang, for example, did not cut his until six months later. Teachers and students, however, were an exception; according to the *Eastern Times*, in May 1912 Minister of Education Cai Yuanpei (1868–1940) ordered them to cut their hair or face expulsion. Otherwise, queue-cutting, after an initial mandatory phase during the revolution, became, in practice, a voluntary program. In late October 1912 the Republican Senate debated, and in the end rejected, a proposal to make cropped hair a prerequisite for the exercise of "public rights," including the right to vote in the upcoming parliamentary elections. President Yuan instead turned the matter over to the provincial authorities and told them to deal with it not by coercion but by persuasion. Yet in June 1914, after the demise of the liberal republic, Yuan's own government evidently embarked on a campaign of mandatory, universal queue-cutting in Beijing. This step may have marked the end of the queue as an officially sanctioned hairstyle.[56]

Even then, the Manchu hairstyle did not disappear entirely from the Chinese scene. Political and social conservatives continued to stick by it. A few members of the political elite—not only Manchus but Han as well—resisted altering their hairstyle, in order to show their undying loyalty to the fallen Qing dynasty. Thus Zhang Xun, leader of the 1917 attempt at a Qing restoration, retained his braid, and he required the soldiers in his army to keep theirs as well. Another well-known Qing loyalist, Wang Guowei (1877–1927), still wore his hair in the Manchu style at the time of his death by suicide in June 1927. By then the Qing emperor himself had cut his hair short. After that there was no longer any compelling reason for political conservatives to adhere to the old style.[57] On the other hand, social conservatives kept their queue because they saw it as part of inherited tradition. They were generally to be found in the interior provinces of China proper and particularly among rural villagers. In Henan, for example, the plait was still so commonly worn in 1922, when Feng Yuxiang became military governor, that he included its elimination (along with that of footbinding among women) in a ten-point reform program. In Sichuan at about the same time, the military rehabilitation commissioner Yang Sen (1884–1977) too called for doing away with the queue, which was "worn by not a few in the rural sections of western China." By the late 1930s, however, though it could be glimpsed occasionally in such remote places as a market town in Anhui, it had become a noteworthy rarity.[58] Otherwise, the hairstyle of Chinese men had been completely "de-Manchufied."

Another change that came with the overthrow of the Qing was the dethroning of Manchu as an official language of the country alongside Chinese. It was no longer required that government documents be rendered in Manchu as well as Chinese. Manchu inscriptions disappeared from the coins issued by the new regime. The teaching of Manchu in Republican schools, as in Aihun, Heilongjiang, was proscribed.[59] The term "national speech" (*guoyu*), which in Qing times referred to Manchu, now came to designate the standard dialect of Chinese. This did not mean, however, that the two-hundred-year dominance of the Manchu language had left no imprint on the language of Republican China. Though relatively few Manchu loan-words made their way into the permanent lexicon of Chinese, a number of linguists suggest that, due to a process called "language shift," the grammatical structure of northern standard Chinese—the model spoken language for the rest of China—had in some important (and generally unacknowledged) ways been fundamentally transformed by the Manchu language.[60]

Finally, in addition to abolishing the queue and removing Manchu as an official language, the new Republic also rid itself of the old equestrian-style dress of the Manchu court and, as some earlier proponents of queue-cutting had advocated, adopted a new official uniform. Out went the full-length robe, close-fitting at the top and loosely flowing below the waist, worn under a half-length "horse jacket"; out, too, went the knobbed hat and long necklace. In came costumes borrowed from the West or from Western-influenced Japan. As is amply documented in contemporary photographs, Sun Yat-sen (e.g., at his inauguration as provisional president in January 1912) and other civilian leaders favored suits and ties and overcoats, while Yuan Shikai and subsequent warlords preferred military uniforms. Sun eventually came up with an amalgam of the two styles that came to be called the "Sun Yat-sen suit" (*Zhongshan zhuang*), which yet later was so closely identified with Communist Party cadres that it is known, in the West, as the "Mao suit."[61]

Unlike queue-cutting, which was mandatory for all males, sartorial de-Manchufication was restricted to men of the official class. Male commoners were not required to abandon the Manchu-style costume that many of them had voluntarily adopted in the course of the two and a half centuries of Qing rule. Thus, during the first two or three decades of the Republic, Chinese men, old and young alike, continued to wear a modified version of the Manchus' full-length gown with long sleeves, with or without the waist-length horse jacket. Known as the *changpao* (long gown), it persisted in the urban areas into the Nationalist era, when it was replaced by Western style trousers and shirts; in rural areas, it lasted even longer. De-Manchufication of the official dress also did not prevent Chinese women, who hitherto had not succumbed to the Manchu attire, from belatedly taking to the *qipao* (banner gown), which, as its name indicates, was of Manchu origin. Even at the end of the Qing dynasty, most Han women were still wearing the Ming-style outfit, consisting of a loose three-quarter-length jacket worn over trousers. Paradoxically, however, within a decade after the revolution, urban middle-class Han women began to reject the old two-piece jacket-and-trousers outfit in favor of the vanquished Manchus' one-piece full-length gown. (They did not adopt the elaborate head-dress and platform shoes that were also distinctive features of Manchu dress.) By the 1930s the *qipao*, notwithstanding its Manchu origins, had become the official women's dress of the Nationalist regime and was widely regarded as the "national" costume of Chinese women. It was only in the 1950s, after the Communist takeover of China, that the *qipao*, along with the similarly Manchu-derived *changpao* of the men, was supplanted by the unisex Sun Yat-sen (or Mao) suit and its variants.[62]

In sum, with regard to count 3 in the revolutionaries' indictment of the Manchus, the principal Manchu impositions upon the Chinese—the queue, the Manchu language, and the official dress—were all revoked at the beginning of the Republic. However, most evidently in the case of the dress of ordinary Chinese men and women and less so in the case of the Chinese language, they did not disappear without leaving a significant trace behind them.

In the four charges of the indictment still to be addressed, the revolutionaries had accused the Manchus of being an alien, barbarian people who did not belong in China (count 1), constituting a privileged minority separate from and superior to the Han Chinese (count 4), functioning as a force of military occupation oppressing the Han (count 5), and benefiting from political discrimination at the expense of the Han (count 6). However, in the "Article of Treatment regarding the Manchus, Mongols, Muslims, and Tibetans," the last of the three abdication agreements, the Republicans also made three promises to the Manchus: to treat them on an equal basis with the Han, to continue to distribute the banner soldiers' stipends pending a resolution of their economic problems, and to abolish the former restrictions on the banner people's occupation and residence. President Yuan Shikai, in Article 65 of his constitutional compact of May 1914, vowed that this agreement, like the rest of the abdication settlement, would be "effective forever without change," and he reiterated the pledge in December 1915 on the eve of his monarchical restoration.[63] Although Yuan's warlord successors through the 1920s never repeated the promise, neither did they repudiate it. As the Republican rulers attempted to avenge or correct the four sets of Manchu misdeeds while grappling to fulfill the three promises of generous treatment for the Manchus, the banner people's relationship to the new state necessarily changed, as did their status and identity in Chinese society.

According to count 4 in the revolutionaries' indictment, the Manchus had been a privileged minority superior to and separate from the Han. As evidence, the indictment cited the stipends that banner soldiers received from the Qing state, the restrictions on bannermen's occupations, the residential segregation of banner and non-banner people, and the ban on Manchu-Han intermarriage. Pursuant to the terms of the abdication agreement, the Republican authorities immediately lifted the former restrictions on the banner people's occupations and residence but continued, until the early 1920s in some areas, to disburse the banner soldiers' stipends.

So long as those stipends were distributed, the Eight Banner system continued to exist and function. President Yuan Shikai more than once pondered what to do with the centuries-old system. In October 1912 his cabinet discussed reorganizing the system; two years later, his government reportedly decided to abolish the twenty-four lieutenants-general—each of whom headed one Manchu, Mongol, or Hanjun banner—and replace them with a special office to oversee banner affairs.[64] No change, though, resulted from these deliberations. Thus, despite the overthrow of the Qing, Yuan and his warlord successors continued to make appointments to the top posts in the twenty-four banners as well as to the Banner Duty Office, the coordinating body for the entire system. For example, on 22 December 1912 President Yuan appointed Pulun lieutenant-general of the Manchu Bordered Red Banner; two weeks later he named Pulun and seven others to the Banner Duty Office. Very often, as in these two instances, the appointees to the banner system were themselves bannermen, including imperial princes such as Pulun. However, in line with one of the post-Boxer reforms, not all banner officials in the early Republic were Manchus; thus, Pulun's predecessor at the Manchu Bordered Red Banner was

Duan Zhigui (1869–1925), a Han. Some appointments to such national banner posts were made as late as the first half of 1924, while some to local posts (e.g., military commandant of the Liaoyang garrison in Fengtian) were made until at least 1919.[65]

The Eight Banner system continued, as before, to serve as the administrative agency that oversaw the affairs of its members. In May 1914, for example, a certain Zhonglu, whose accusations of corruption had led to the dismissal of the head of the Manchu Bordered Blue Banner, was himself judged to be guilty of some infraction and was remanded to his banner with orders to be "kept under strict surveillance."[66] The system was also the institutional device by which backers of Yuan Shikai in late 1915 solicited support among the Manchus for resurrecting the monarchy, as the twenty-four banners were each required to send one delegate to the national convention that elected him emperor.[67] However, the major function of the Republican Eight Banner system, and the main reason why the system survived the revolution, was the role it played in the distribution of the welfare benefits promised to the Manchus by the abdication agreement.[68]

Because the new regime kept its capital in Beijing, it could not easily overlook the Manchus, who were 20 to 25 percent of the city's population in the early 1920s.[69] Consequently, the early Republican governments did make an earnest effort in Beijing to abide by the abdication agreement and continue the distribution of the banner soldiers' stipends of grain and money via the Eight Banner system. According to the recollections of some Manchu old-timers in the 1950s, the banner soldiers at first received both customary types of payments, with the amounts unchanged from the late Qing, but by the end of the liberal phase of Yuan Shikai's presidency around 1913–14, the grain allocation had been stopped. Thereafter they received only the money stipend, paid in silver dollars and then increasingly in copper coins rather than, as previously, in bulk silver. Moreover, after Yuan's death in 1916, the stipends were further reduced in size. Yet, as late as July 1918, when Feng Guozhang was president, tens of thousands of banner people in Beijing were still being paid by the government, as revealed by the account book of the Manchu Plain Red Banner for the month. That banner alone had more than 8,400 people on the payroll. The stipends themselves, specified in taels but paid in dollars at a discount, ranged from a maximum of 3.8 taels monthly for the 420 corporals down to 0.5 taels for a couple of recent widows. The 1,534 privates, who were the common soldiers of the system, received 2.1 taels each. Soon afterward, however, the payment of the stipends became much more erratic and occurred only after repeated requests by the lieutenants-general of the twenty-four banners. Eventually, in the early 1920s, the stipends were restricted to the three great festivals of the lunar year—in the first, fifth, and eighth months—and they amounted to scarcely more than ten debased copper dollars each time.[70]

In the provincial garrisons of China proper, the early Republic was considerably less successful in fulfilling its promise to continue distributing the banner soldiers' stipends. The experiences of the garrisons varied, depending in part on how each had responded to the revolution, but in no case did the stipends continue for long. In those cities where the banner people resisted the revolution to the bitter end—notably Xi'an, Taiyuan, Fuzhou, Zhenjiang, and Nanjing—the stipends stopped immediately and the surviving banner people were left to take care of themselves. In those cities where negotiations led to a peaceful transfer of power, the banner soldiers usually received some form of official assistance, often as part of the negotiated settlement, but never for more than a few months. Thus in Chengdu the Republicans continued to disburse the banner soldiers' stipends for at most one year.[71] In Jingzhou they had promised to provide "charitable rations" to impoverished banner people for six months, but actually distributed only three months' worth. When that proved insufficient, they allocated another $20,000 in relief funds.[72] In Hangzhou, after disbursing the provisions for two months as originally promised, they consented to a three-month extension worth $90,000.[73] And in Guangzhou, they initially agreed to allocate $73,000 a month and to keep intact the garrison's detachment of modern-trained banner troops. But the detachment was disbanded after only three months, with each soldier in the unit who turned in a weapon given $10 in severance pay. Beginning in April 1912 the banner people were each allotted only eighty cents a month for living expenses. Even this paltry payment stopped in the summer of 1913, following the failure of the Second Revolution and the arrival of the warlord Long Jiguang (1867–1925).[74] Finally, in those garrison cities that did not experience the revolution at first hand, some of the new rulers continued to distribute the banner stipends, at least initially; others did not. According to Brigade-General Chuohatai in November 1912, the garrisons at Miyun, Chahar, Rehe, and Suiyuan were still receiving their stipends, but his own garrison at Ningxia no longer did. In the Liangzhou and Zhuanglang garrisons in Gansu, the stipends may have continued until 1914.[75]

Once the banner soldiers' stipends ended, so too did the rationale for the continuance of the banner system. Thus, at most locations, the system collapsed within months after the revolution. By December 1913, as Minister of the Army Duan Qirui informed President Yuan, most banner units in the provinces had disintegrated; only in the capital as well as a few outposts such as Qingzhou, Taiyuan, Ningxia, Liangzhou, and Yili did the Eight Banners remain more or less intact.[76] In Beijing, too, the stipends eventually stopped, though not until late 1924, coincident with Feng Yuxiang's expulsion of Puyi from the Forbidden City and his termination of the Republican subsidy to the Qing court. It was then and only then that the Eight Banner system finally came to an end, and no further appointments to banner posts were made. The Infantry Division of the Metropolitan Banners, for example, was disbanded on 5 October 1924.[77]

The continued disbursement of the banner soldiers' stipends had never been intended as a permanent measure; it was supposed to last only until the new regime had come up with a solution to the long-standing "Eight Banners' livelihood problem." The early Republic made a stab at solving this problem, but it was no more successful than its imperial predecessor had been. Soon after he became provisional president, Yuan Shikai established, within the Ministry of Internal Affairs, the Office to Manage the Eight Banners' Livelihood (Chouban Baqi Shengji Chu), which took over from the Banner Reorganization Office of the late Qing. It may have been at the instigation of this office that Yuan's cabinet in January 1914 proposed to the Political Council (Zhengzhi Huiyi), the quasi-legislative body that briefly succeeded the dissolved Parliament, that China conclude a multiyear loan of £5 million from an international banking consortium in order to finance a massive resettlement scheme. The proposal called for relocating eight hundred thousand people from the Metropolitan Banners in Beijing onto wasteland in Manchuria, Chahar, Suiyuan, and Xinjiang, with the $9 million spent annually on banner stipends serving as the collateral for the loan. Resettlement was hardly a new idea, nor was its outcome any different from before. The Political Council, worried about adding to China's mounting indebtedness, decided that, in the absence of reliable statistics, the project was premature; it called for a census of the banner population in and about Beijing together with an inventory of land available for resettlement along the northern border. Nothing more was heard from the Office to Manage the Eight Banners' Livelihood. As a Manchu complained in late 1914, the office had been in existence for three years and had produced no result worth mentioning.[78]

As before, there were also other, largely unofficial, efforts in the early Republic to solve the banner people's livelihood problem by offering them vocational training. In Beijing the Capital Women's Factory, founded in 1909 by Manchu and Han officials, continued to teach banner women such skills as weaving, sewing, and brocading. Its history, however, reflected the Republic's declining interest in and concern for the Manchus. In 1912 the factory operated six sections, employed more than three hundred women, and maintained a primary school for girls. President Yuan gave it his personal support and authorized a contribution from the government. Throughout the 1910s successive Republican governments supported the factory with an annual contribution of twenty thousand taels, but those contributions ceased after 1923. When Feng Yuxiang evicted Puyi from the Forbidden City a year later, he offered, in the "revised" Articles of Favorable Treatment, to make a one-time allocation of $2 million to open and operate workshops for the poor people of Beijing, with priority given to "those of banner registry" (*qiji*). It does not appear that this public money was ever spent. The Capital Women's Factory managed to survive (to 1929 at least) only as a private philanthropy.[79]

In some provincial garrison cities, there were similar Republican efforts to help the Manchus become self-sufficient. The most ambitious program was at Jingzhou, where the Hubei Military Government under Li Yuanhong in the spring of 1912 appointed Hu Egong (1884–1951), a Japanese-educated Han native of Jingzhou, as his special envoy to arrange for the livelihood of the city's twenty thousand banner people. Hu's plan, which was to be financed partly by public funds and partly by forced contributions from wealthy local Manchus, called for sending the most impoverished of the Manchus off to other parts of the province. They would each be given $30 for start-up expenses, after which they were expected to provide for themselves and never to return. The program began in October 1912, when 1,500 banner persons were dispatched by boat downriver to the tri-city complex of Wuhan, with six hundred to be settled in Wuchang, five hundred in Hankou, and four hundred in Hanyang. By the end of the year, as many as half of the city's Manchus had been sent away. Unfortunately, they had gone off without first acquiring a vocational skill and were therefore unable to earn a living at their new locations. Soon most of the banner people were making their separate ways back to Jingzhou, where they were no better off than before.[80] Some other garrison cities, such as Chengdu, set up offices like the one in Jingzhou to try to help the Manchus adjust to their new situation.[81] As in Beijing and Jingzhou, they were generally ineffective. Yet other cities, such as Guangzhou, made no effort at all.

With the banner soldiers' stipends reduced or eliminated and with the early Republican government unable to devise a long-term solution, the Manchus had no alternative but to make their own way in the world. The abdication agreement had finally lifted the former restrictions on their choice of occupation. As a group, however, they were ill prepared to cope with their newly bestowed freedom. Those in Manchuria may have been the most fortunate and subject to the fewest disruptions. In the past, they had generally lived some distance from the garrison city to which they were attached, and, residing in the countryside, they had been able to supplement their income by farming, hunting, and fishing. They had never been so dependent on the banner soldiers' stipends, nor so indolent, as the banner people in Beijing and the provincial garrisons of China proper.[82]

In Beijing, even during the 1910s when the banner soldiers' stipends were still being distributed, the Manchus had a difficult time adjusting to the unprecedented laissez-faire conditions. Those who had been enrolled in the new military formations of the late Qing were generally able to keep their posts. Until its dispersal in 1922, three of the four infantry brigades of the Palace Guard remained, as previously noted, predominantly Manchu in composition. So, too, was the First Division, for a while at least. Under the command of He Zonglian, it (or a large part of it) was transferred during the revolution from Beijing to Chahar and Zhangjiakou. When it mutinied in June 1914, the division was still made up mostly of banner soldiers. Soon after the mutiny, He Zonglian was replaced as commander by Cai Chengxun (1871–1946), who in 1922 was sent with his troops to Jiangxi. Four years later, while in Jiangxi, the division, now a part of warlord Sun Chuanfang's (1885–1935) forces, was defeated and scattered by Chiang Kai-shek's National Revolutionary Army.[83] Aside from the military, many Manchus in Beijing continued to serve in the metropolitan police. Of the ten thousand policemen in Beijing in the 1920s, "upwards of three-quarters," according to David Strand, "had banner status."[84] For literate bannermen, including the many Manchu-language scribes who had been laid off by the disestablishment of Manchu as an official language, employment as "Chinese secretaries" at the various foreign legations was a possibility. At the British Legation, for example, every post in the Chinese Secretary's Office into the 1930s was filled by a Manchu.[85]

Most of the banner people in Beijing, however, lacked not only the skills but also the motivation to work. Unlike their counterparts in Manchuria, they were unable to overcome the habits of dependency that the Qing ban on alternative occupations had long instilled. Sidney Gamble's social survey of Beijing in the late 1910s confirmed Lao She's portrait of his refined but indolent relatives. According to Gamble,

> Long years of living on government bounty have unfitted most of the Manchus for earning a living, and now many of them would rather starve than go to work. Cases are known where they have been willing to sell even the bricks from their floors before they would do anything to earn money.

Gamble also substantiated the Manchus' reputed fondness for living well. By examining household budgets, he found that they spent a larger portion of their income on luxuries than did Han households and that they were more likely than Han to live beyond their means. Unfortunately, "Manchus willing to work can find employment only in the unskilled lines and that means competition, low wages, a lower standard of living and destitution for those who have known comfort in the past." And, indeed, "a large proportion of the Manchus are destitute."[86]

The Manchus in the former garrison cities of China proper were no better off than those in the capital. They too were generally driven by economic necessity and the lack of vocational skills to compete for low-skilled, labor-intensive jobs with poor pay. The fortunate ones were those who were literate and lived in treaty ports such as Guangzhou and Fuzhou and could work for the foreign consulates and the foreign-run maritime customs and post office. Most, however, lived from hand to mouth. In Guangzhou, according to one rough estimate, 20 percent of the Manchus lived comfortably; 60 percent scraped by as peddlers and laborers; and 20 percent barely survived on odd jobs or by begging.[87] Not everyone survived. The first winter after the revolution was particularly hard for the Manchus in the provinces. Despite efforts by local authorities and elite to distribute rice gruel and padded jackets, many homeless banner people starved or froze to death.[88]

Meanwhile, the system of de jure segregation, by which Manchus were kept separate from Han, had come to an end with the Republic. On 13 April 1912 President Yuan Shikai, noting that Cixi's edict of 1902 had failed to change social behavior, issued a reminder that Manchu-Han marriage was no longer prohibited.[89] Manchu cities, formerly the residential preserves of the banner people, were also abolished. The abdication agreement had lifted the restrictions on the banner people's place of residence, and though promising to protect their private property, it implied that their public property was subject to confiscation. As a result, in those cities with a banner garrison, the Republican authorities quickly extended their control over the Manchu quarters, which were often vast and sparsely populated, and expropriated all the land and buildings that were not privately owned. In Beijing, as noted, they took over most of the Forbidden City, leaving (until 1924) only the portion at the rear of the Qing court; they took over the entire Inner City as well, including (within it) the Imperial City. In Fuzhou the governor in 1912 repudiated land contracts that the banner people had signed and ordered new ones drawn up because the Manchu City was now the property of the new regime.[90] In Hangzhou, the government auctioned off the land in the Manchu quarters and began converting it into the bustling commercial center that it is today. As early as 1913, according to a Western correspondent,

> the plan of the old Manchu city has been published, and . . . building lots are for sale. . . . The Chamber of Commerce has bought most of the lots facing the lake. The few remaining houses belonging to the Tartars are rapidly disappearing, and signs of the making of roads are to be seen.[91]

The walls that formerly separated a Manchu settlement from its host city were, in most instances, removed. In Xi'an the south wall of the Manchu City was torn down in 1912 and replaced by a broad roadway lined on both sides with foreign-style shops. In Jingzhou, Hangzhou, and Chengdu the internal city walls were demolished in either 1912 or 1913. Beijing was an exception; the wall separating the Inner and Outer Cities remained largely intact down to the Communists' Great Leap Forward in the late 1950s.[92]

However, although the de jure segregation of Manchus and Han ended with the revolution, de facto segregation continued. Yuan Shikai's 1912 decree supporting intermarriage was apparently no more effective than Cixi's had been ten years earlier. At Aihun, Heilongjiang, in the early 1920s, Manchus generally married other Manchus (including Hanjun) and only rarely married Han.[93] Furthermore, the banner people still tended to live among themselves on the site of their old Manchu City, even though they no longer were rigidly separated from the Han people. In Beijing in the late 1910s, according to Sidney Gamble's survey, the Manchus were concentrated in five of the ten police districts into which the Inner City was divided. In particular, they were a majority of the population in the two districts that together comprised the Imperial City and they were "a large proportion of the population" in the three northern and northwestern districts of the Inner City. In other words, non-Manchus, who were no longer excluded, had moved in large numbers into the five eastern and southern districts. In Guangzhou, too, the vast majority of the Manchus continued well into the Republic to live where they had previously been confined, in the western half of the Old City.[94]

In sum, with regard to count 4 in the revolutionaries' indictment, the Manchus after the revolution were still, to some degree, segregated from the Han, but they clearly were no longer the privileged elite that they had been under the Qing. Although they had begun to experience economic difficulties long before the revolution, their plight worsened considerably when the new regime eliminated the banner soldiers' stipends altogether, as it did eventually in Beijing and almost immediately everywhere else. The Manchus quickly fell to the lowest stratum of Chinese society. They came to be identified in the public consciousness with poverty and unskilled labor, much as, say, the natives of northern Jiangsu were in Shanghai. Like the Subei people in Shanghai, the Manchus dominated the rickshaw-pulling business in Beijing. In both instances this line of work, viewed as nearly subhuman, epitomized their low status.[95]

Just as the revolutionaries dislodged the banner people from their perch as a privileged minority, so too did they succeed in uprooting them as a military occupation force oppressing the Han—count 5 in their indictment of the Manchus. From the beginning, the Eight Banners had been a military as well as an administrative organization. After the revolution, although the banner system was preserved (in Beijing at least) in order to handle the administrative chores of allocating the soldiers' stipends, the Republican authorities quickly stripped it of its military responsibility. In May 1912 President Yuan's army minister, Duan Qirui, told the Eight Banners that they should discontinue their rifle practices, because under the Republic all military personnel must come from the army, and he ordered the lieutenants-general of the twenty-four banners to return the ten thousand or more rifles that the ministry had given them in the late Qing, when the court had replaced archery with rifle practice.[96] As a result, the Eight Banners in the early Republic ceased to serve, as they nominally still did in the late Qing, any military purpose.

The revolutionaries also ended the preferential treatment that the Manchus had previously enjoyed in the political realm at the expense of the Han (count 6). Throughout the Qing period, bannermen had been disproportionately represented in the central government because of the related institutions of dyarchy and ethnic slots. Though the court in the post-Boxer era had made some progress toward the newly stated goal of appointing officials "without distinction between Manchus and Han," it remained for its Republican successor to do away with dyarchy entirely and abolish most ethnic slots. The Manchu presence in government plummeted as a result, though it did not disappear altogether. When Yuan Shikai became president, he reportedly wanted at least one bannerman in his Republican cabinet. (The cabinet that he, as Qing prime minister, had named also included one Manchu.) His token Manchu was Rongxun, who previously had worked with Beijing's Inner City police; he was, until his death in June 1916, vice-minister of internal affairs. In the decade after Rongxun, at least one other bannerman served in the cabinet of the northern government: Enhua, a Japanese-educated Mongol bannerman from the Zhenjiang garrison, who was vice-minister of laws in 1924.[97]

Below the level of the cabinet, however, several agencies of the government continued to reserve some slots for Manchus. Many of the leading posts in the Eight Banner system, until its complete disbandment in 1924, were held by bannermen. Similarly, the vice-director of the Office for Mongolian and Tibetan Affairs (Meng-Zang Shiwu Yuan), successor to the Qing's Ministry of Colonial Affairs, was almost always a bannerman.[98] And the office for the compilation of *The Draft History of the Qing*, established in Beijing in 1914, was headed by the Hanjun Zhao Erxun, formerly governor-general of Manchuria, and it employed, among others, the Manchu bannerman Jinliang. When Zhao died in 1927, it fell to Jinliang to hasten the completion of the history before Chiang Kai-shek's National Revolutionary Army could reach Beijing and put a stop to their effort.[99]

Surprisingly, the one Manchu official who proved most adept at making the transition from monarchy to republic was Yinchang, the German-educated former minister of the army who commanded the initial military operations against the revolution. When Yuan Shikai appointed Yinchang in September 1912 to succeed Feng Guozhang as head of the military affairs section in the office of the president, many members of the Nationalist Party were predictably upset. Nevertheless, Huang Xing, the party's leading military figure, came to Yinchang's defense and supported his selection. Although at the time of the revolution the Qing loyalist Liangbi had questioned Yinchang's qualifications, Huang lauded him for "his superior knowledge of military affairs, which was internationally recognized," and for "his cosmopolitan point of view." When Yinchang led the Qing troops against the revolutionaries, he was, Huang said, only doing his duty; in any case, it was not he but Feng Guozhang who had been responsible for the bloody assault on Hankou and the destruction of its Chinese City. Yinchang's career as a Republican official continued even after his patron Yuan's downfall, as he held a number of high-ranking advisory military posts until his death in 1928. He often represented the Republic in its formal dealings with the Qing court, such as when he attended Puyi's wedding in 1922.[100]

Finally, though count 1 of the revolutionaries' indictment had charged that the Manchus were an alien, barbarian people who had no place in China, the new regime did not, in fact, expel them. While there were many instances during the revolution when local groups of banner people were driven from their homes, the Republic accepted the presence of the Manchus within China and even promised, in the abdication agreement, that they should be treated on an equal basis with the Han. The agreement officially recognized them as one of the five major ethnic groups (*minzu*) that together made up the new Republic of China. This concept of China as composed of five ethnic groups, which Empress Dowager Longyu also lauded in her valedictory edict, was not new. The "unity of Manchus, Han, Mongol, Muslims, and Tibetans as one citizenry" had been an editorial objective of the Manchu reformist publication *Great Harmony Journal* in 1907. Indeed, the "five-in-one" idea can be traced back to the Qianlong emperor's self-image as the unifier and ruler of a multiethnic empire. However, under the Republic the Manchus were no longer the superior people that they had been during the Qing. Their status had been reduced to, at least, that of equality with the Han and other major ethnic groups. As Article 5 of the Provisional Constitution of March 1912 stated, "Citizens of the Republic of China are in all respects equal, with no distinctions of race [*zhongzu*], class, or religion."[101]

The vision of Republican China as a multiethnic country in which all five major ethnic groups were equal was symbolized by the "five-color flag" that was adopted by President Yuan in June 1912 on the recommendation of the Senate and that remained the emblem of the state until replaced by the Nationalists. The flag consisted of five horizontal stripes of equal width, each of a different color (red, yellow, blue, white, and black) representative of the Han, Manchus, Mongols, Muslims, and Tibetans respectively.[102] The same ideal of ethnic equality was conveyed in the phrase "The five ethnic groups are as one family" (*Wuzu yijia*), which was a constant refrain in the first years of the Republic. A significant extension of the old idea of "Manchus and Han as one family" (*Man-Han yijia*), it was espoused in 1912 by such diverse figures as Longyu, Yuan Shikai, and Sun Yat-sen. When, for example, the empress dowager was urged by leading Manchus at court to protest Yuan's changing the name of the Great Qing Gate (Da-Qing Men) to China Gate (Zhonghua Men) as an unwarranted Republican encroachment upon the imperial precincts, she replied, "The five ethnic groups are as one family. Why distinguish between yours and mine?"[103]

Making good on its professed commitment to ethnic equality and impartiality, the new regime called for an end to the kinds of anti-Manchu writings and activities that had been commonplace recently. The revolution, for example, had unleashed an outpouring of anti-Manchu literature. It included old writings that during the Qing had been proscribed, such as Wang Xiuchu's graphic account of the ten days' massacre at Yangzhou, as well as new writings, such as *A Short History of Slaves* (Nucai xiaoshi), consisting of twenty biographical sketches of incompetent bannermen and corrupt eunuchs, and *Biographies of Avaricious Officials and Corrupt Personnel* (Tanguan wuli zhuan), both compiled by a certain "Lao Li" (Old Servitor) and published in May 1912. In that same month Yuan Shikai issued a presidential decree banning all such anti-Manchu literature as "contrary to the principles of the Republic" and harmful to the "unity of feelings between Han and Manchus." The prohibition broadly targeted books that were "hostile toward the Manchus or slandered the former Qing." Yuan's government also repeatedly warned both individuals and local communities against the illegal confiscation of the banner people's private property and, where this had already occurred, ordered them to return such property to their former owners. The Hubei authorities in 1912 issued a similar proclamation of their own calling on their citizens not to discriminate against Manchu and Mongol "banner people" (*qimin*).[104] Indeed, Manchus were not prohibited from taking the postimperial examinations to select county magistrates. At the third such examination, administered in August 1914, for example, twelve of the 830 (1.4 percent) who passed were "people of banner registry" (*qijiren*) or, in one instance, a Metropolitan Bannerman.[105]

However, although the early Republic seemed to be committed to the goal of impartiality, the Manchus often found it difficult to overcome the stigma left by the revolutionaries' earlier accusation that they were a foreign group who did not belong in China. They claimed, for example, that they alone, among China's five major ethnic groups, were denied adequate representation in the first Republican parliament. In 1912, when the Senate drew up the electoral laws for the legislature to be elected later that year, it allotted a certain number of seats to each province as well as to Mongolia, Tibet, and Qinghai. The Manchus, led by the Association for the Common Advancement of the Manchus (Manzu Tongjin Hui), charged that under this territorial system it was almost impossible for any of them to be elected because in no province were they numerically dominant (as, say, the Mongols were in Mongolia). They asked that the "banner people" (qiren) be given a special, nonterritorial electoral quota, similar to those set aside for educators and overseas Chinese. The Senate, citing Article 5 of the Provisional Constitution with its stipulation that all citizens were equal without racial distinction, rejected the Manchus' plea for special treatment. It asserted that in certain locations, notably Beijing and Manchuria, banner people were sufficiently numerous to be electable under the territorial system. As a matter of fact, the elected bicameral parliament did include among its 862 members at least three with Manchu-sounding names—two senators from Fengtian (Yanrong and Fuyuan) and one representative from Zhili (the imperial clansman and former publisher of *Great Harmony Journal*, Hengjun). Even so, this was far from the fifty-four seats allotted to Mongolia or the twenty to Tibet (not all of which were necessarily held by Mongols or Tibetans). The issue of representation by the banner people came up again in 1914, when a new legislature was to replace the parliament that Yuan Shikai had disbanded. Though that body never left the drawing board, the Manchus were upset once more that the plans under discussion did not include any special quota for them. As a certain Ziwei complained in the new Manchu political journal, *The Banners* (Qizu yuebao), while China's four other major ethnic groups would all be able to express and act on their political views, only the "banner ethnic group" (qizu) was doomed to silence and passivity.[106]

Though the Manchus failed to gain special representation in Parliament, it was clearly not due to a lack of effort. The Association for the Common Advancement of the Manchus, which spearheaded the campaign, was founded in the spring of 1912 specifically to speak for the Manchus (Manzu) in the new explicitly multiethnic environment of the early Republic. In a statement addressed to the "elders and juniors of the Eight Banners," the association dismissed the fear expressed by some that its formation would only stir up the anti-Manchu elements. It asserted that each of the other four major ethnic groups had established its own representative organization and that only the Manchus had abstained from such political activism. If the Manchus wished to save themselves from destruction, they too must unite. The group, whose founding president, Xiyan, had been a metropolitan official in the late Qing, listed four tasks for itself: revive the Manchus' withered spirit; struggle for their legitimate rights; seek a basic level of knowledge; and plan for their future livelihood. It remained the leading representative organization of the Manchus in Beijing until at least 1929. It had, at one time, a branch office in Fengtian as well.[107] Another voice of the Manchus was the above-mentioned *The Banners*, a monthly journal published in Beijing in 1914 and edited by Luo Wanzhang. It was devoted to the affairs of what it itself called the "banner ethnic group"; its sixth issue, dated 5 November 1914, was devoted to an examination of the perennial Eight Banners' livelihood problem.

Not only collectively but also individually, the Manchus suffered much from discrimination and prejudice during the early Republic. The promises in the abdication agreement and the repeated injunctions of the Republican government notwithstanding, most Manchus were powerless to resist when and where local authorities illegally seized their private holdings. Only someone such as Zhisen, a former provincial treasurer with ties to Yikuang, had the political and financial resources to catch the attention of President Yuan and his cabinet and to persist for almost three years in an effort, which in the end was only partially successful, to recover a drugstore that the Zhejiang government in 1912 had expropriated and auctioned off.[108] Furthermore, Manchus desperate for work found that Han employers often refused to hire people whom they knew or suspected to be Manchu—such as someone with an unusual disyllabic name, for many Manchus continued after the revolution to follow the old custom of suppressing their family name and going only by their personal name. Nine of the twelve bannermen who passed the qualifying examination for county magistrates in 1914 had such Manchu-style names.[109]

In an attempt to evade such discrimination, many (though, clearly, not all) Manchus sought to eliminate the obvious indicators of their non-Han origins. Principally, they took advantage of the provision in the abdication agreement allowing them freely to "register with the departments and counties" (i.e., the local civil authorities) so as to change their classification and alter their names. In Beijing, where the Eight Banner system functioned until the mid-1920s, the applicant would petition the Ministry of Internal Affairs, which, if it approved the request, would notify the applicant's original banner as well as the county to which his family registration would be transferred. On 2 March 1913 alone, the *Government Gazette* (Zhengfu gongbao) recorded six directives from the ministry acting on requests from banner people to make changes in their classification and name. In one representative case, Lingshou, a policeman from the Infantry Division, petitioned to switch his registration from "banner person" (*qi*) in Dachonga's company in the Manchu Bordered Blue Banner to "civilian" (*min*) in Wanping County, Zhili; in the same petition, he also asked to adopt Guan as his surname and to change his personal name to Deshou. The ministry approved the request and asked that both the Manchu Bordered Blue Banner and Wanping County be so notified. The name change usually consisted of adding a Han-style surname (such as Guan) to one's given name, but sometimes, as with Lingshou, it involved taking a new personal name as well.[110]

It is noteworthy that the change of registration was from "bannerman" to "civilian" rather than from "Manchu" to "Han." The concept of the Manchus as an ethnic group certainly existed at this time; the third abdication agreement had identified them specifically as one of China's four major non-Han peoples. And as is evident in the name of the Association for the Common Advancement of the Manchus, the term "Manzu" (Manchu ethnic group) was around as well. Nevertheless, the Manchus, by and large, still identified themselves, and were identified by others, not so much as an ethnic group but as members of the Eight Banner system. Thus, in the early Republic, the most common term for the Manchus was not Manzu—or even Manren, which for some reason seems not to have been used so often as before the revolution—but *qiren* (banner people) or one of its variants, including the newly coined *qijiren* (people of banner registry) and *qizu* (banner ethnic group). Owen Lattimore, traveling through Manchuria in 1929–30, found that

> the word "Manchu" was and is almost never used in conversation and comparatively rarely in writing. . . . The term in commonest use was *Ch'i-jen* [*qiren*], "Bannermen," which included both Chinese and Manchu Bannermen. The corresponding term for non-Banner Chinese was *min*, "a commoner," "a civilian."[111]

Of course, as long as the Eight Banner system continued to exist, as it did until 1924, it is understandable that the Manchus would be equated with its membership.

Aside from altering their classification and adopting Han-style surnames, Manchus attempted to hide their origins and pass for Han in yet other ways. Some abandoned their hereditary settlements, including the Manchu cities, to live and try to find work among the Han. At an encampment of the Scouts, one of the three outer divisions of the Metropolitan Banners, for example, of the more than one hundred households who lived there at the end of the Qing, only about twenty were left in the late 1940s; the rest had gone away. Manchus also stopped observing Manchu customs and wearing Manchu dress; they hid their family genealogies; in places where their spoken Chinese set them apart from the local population, they modified their speech (e.g., from standard Chinese to the local dialect); and they even intermarried, usually with Manchu women marrying Han men, because Manchu men often were too poor to attract marriageable partners. In general, they refused to acknowledge, at least to outsiders, that they were Manchus. When Yenching University sociologists in 1928 surveyed a nearby village that belonged to one of the outer divisions of the Metropolitan Banners, they found that less than 3 percent of its 2,437 inhabitants admitted to being Manchu. "We suspect that some of the Manchus have possibly concealed their origin from the investigators as the Manchus usually do not like people to know that they are Manchus." Only by turning their back on their heritage, so a number of Manchus thought, could they make their way in early Republican China. When a Beijing doctor, a member of the Suwan Gūwalgiya lineage, was denied a medical license for no apparent reason other than that he was Manchu, he petitioned the Ministry of Internal Affairs to change his classification from banner person to civilian and to adopt a Han-style three-syllable name (Li Chengyin) for himself. Once the change was confirmed in 1916, he obtained his license.[112]

In sum, the new Republic's treatment of the Manchu people was inconsistent. On the one hand, it made what must be judged a reasonably good-faith effort to continue to distribute, as specified in the abdication agreement, the banner soldiers' stipends, at least in Beijing, where nearly half of the banner people lived; it did not stop the stipends altogether until Feng Yuxiang came to power in 1924. It, admittedly, did not devise a solution to the Eight Banners' livelihood problem, but neither had the Qing. On the other hand, the new regime, in the course of disposing of the revolutionaries' seven-count indictment against them, did not treat the Manchus with the impartiality and equality that the abdication agreement had also promised, or so the Manchus themselves thought. The new government did away with the Manchu impositions upon the Han; it disbanded the Eight Banner system and the banner garrisons; it ended the segregation of Manchus from Han; and it toppled the Manchus from their privileged position in Chinese society. The cost to the Manchus, however, was widespread discrimination, the erosion of their own sense of self, and their seemingly imminent assimilation by the majority Han population.

THE QING COURT AND THE MANCHUS AFTER 1928

Puyi's expulsion from the Forbidden City in 1924 and the desecration of the Qing Eastern Tombs in 1928 coincided with the final distribution of the banner soldiers' stipends in Beijing. Thereafter, both the former imperial household and the general Manchu populace were left entirely on their own. What happened to each of them under the three very different regimes that succeeded the early Republic: the Nationalists, the Japanese puppet state of Manchukuo, and the Communists?

By and large, Chiang Kai-shek and the Nationalists ignored Puyi, who had been living since 1925 in the Japanese concession in Tianjin. It was only when the Japanese had overrun China's northeastern provinces in late 1931 and had approached Puyi to head the puppet state that they were planning that the Nationalists took an interest in him. In an effort to dissuade him from cooperating with the Japanese, Chiang Kai-shek sent an emissary, Gao Youtang, an ex-Qing official who was then a member of the Nationalists' Control Yuan, to Puyi with a startling proposition. According to Gao's published account, which Puyi's autobiography corroborates, Chiang promised to arrange and pay for Puyi to relocate to Beijing or Shanghai, resurrect the Articles of Favorable Treatment if Puyi sincerely supported the Republic, resume payment of an annual subsidy to the Qing court, appoint representatives of the Manchu ethnic group (Manzu) to the highest organs of government, and ensure that the Manchus would be represented in all future political bodies on the same basis as the Mongols and Tibetans. Although Chiang's offer included the restoration of the Articles of Favorable Treatment, it would have been only a partial restoration, as it did not provide for Puyi's return to either the Forbidden City or the Yiheyuan or for the resumption of his imperial title. Puyi, however, doubted whether Chiang would honor his promises. He noted that, notwithstanding the findings of the court-martial, the Nationalists still had not punished the soldiers guilty of looting the Qing tombs.[113] When Puyi decided to go with the Japanese after all, the Nationalists had no further dealings with him.

The Japanese had wanted a member of the Qing imperial clan to head their puppet state in Manchuria, but Puyi was not the only candidate. Shanqi, with whom they had collaborated earlier, would have been a logical choice, but he had died in 1922. Another, self-promoted, candidate was Puwei, who, like Shanqi, had vigorously opposed the Qing abdication and afterward had been closely identified with the antirepublican Royalist Party. Puwei had initially found refuge in the German (later Japanese) leasehold of Qingdao; after Qingdao's return to Chinese control in 1922, he had moved to Dalian in the Japanese leased territory of Guandong in southern Manchuria. When the expansionist-minded Kantō Army captured Shenyang in September 1931, Puwei applauded and eagerly put himself forward to lead a Manchurian independence movement. In October he went to Shenyang, where he convened a large meeting of the city's citizens, took charge of a pro-Japanese support group, and issued a call for cooperation with Japan and for "Manchus to govern Manchuria" (*Manren zhi Man*). He also paid a visit to the nearby tombs of Nurhaci and Hong Taiji, the founders of the Manchu people, to offer sacrifices. The Japanese, however, soon told Puwei they had other plans and speedily sent him back to Dalian. As in 1908, when both had been under consideration to succeed the Guangxu emperor, he had been passed over for Puyi. He died six years later.[114]

Spurning Chiang Kai-shek's appeal, Puyi in mid-November 1931 secretly left Tianjin for Lüshun to negotiate the terms of his collaboration with the Kantō Army. What Puyi and his supporters wanted was a restoration of both the monarchy and the Qing dynasty. The Japanese agreed only to revive the monarchy and, even then, to do so only on a delayed basis. Thus, the new state of Manchukuo, when it was inaugurated on 1 March 1932, started out as a republic, with Puyi as its "chief executive." Only on its second anniversary was it transformed into the "Manchu empire" (*Manzhou diguo*) and Puyi elevated to the position of emperor.[115] In their choice of the name for the new polity and the date of its establishment, the Japanese made deliberate use of the region's historical ties to the Manchus and the Qing heritage. Specifically, "Manzhouguo" (the Manchu state) was the name that Hong Taiji had used for his regime before he adopted the dynastic name "Qing," and the first of March was supposedly an auspicious date for the Qing.[116]

The Japanese, however, drew the line well short of restoring the Qing dynasty. They located the capital of Manchukuo not at Shenyang, the site of Nurhaci's and Hong Taiji's government, but rather at Changchun (renamed Xinjing, "New Capital") in Jilin. They adopted as the emblem of the new state not the dragon flag of the late Qing but a five-color flag that harked back to that of the early Republic. They did not permit Puyi, as he went to take up his new post in 1932, to worship at the Qing tombs outside Shenyang, as his kinsman Puwei had done a few months earlier; all they did was stop the train briefly as he passed the tombs so that he could "do obeisance to the spirits of his forefathers" without getting off. Most tellingly, when Puyi was enthroned in 1934, the Japanese made him emperor not of the Qing but of the "Manchu empire," and they gave him a new reign title, Kangde, in place of his original title, Xuantong. Furthermore, they made him wear a military uniform at the public enthronement ceremony; he was allowed to wear the Qing imperial dragon robe only at an earlier ritual at a makeshift Altar of Heaven, where he announced his accession to heaven.

Finally, when the Japanese in 1937 occupied Beijing, they did not return Puyi to the Forbidden City or extend his imperial authority beyond Manchuria back into China proper.[117]

Although the dynasty was not resurrected, Manchukuo nevertheless attracted the services of several other members of the Qing imperial lineage. Most notable was Puyi's younger brother, Pujie, whom the Japanese married in 1937 to a cousin of Emperor Hirohito and whom they then designated as heir apparent if Puyi were to die without issue. Another imperial kinsman who joined Manchukuo was Xianjun, the twelfth son of the fervently anti-Republican Shanqi, who headed a military hospital. Others of the Aisin Gioro family, however, did not collaborate with the Japanese in Manchuria. Among them were Puyi's own father, Zaifeng, and his uncle, Zaitao. Although they visited him in Manchukuo, they did not stay.[118]

Puyi's reign as the Kangde emperor of Manchukuo ended in 1945, eleven years after it started, with the defeat of his patron state. When he learned that Hirohito had surrendered, he hurriedly issued his second edict of abdication and prepared to flee to Tokyo. He was, instead, captured by advancing Soviet troops and flown to the Soviet Union, where he was detained for five years, mostly at Khabarovsk. In August 1946, while a Soviet detainee, he testified for eight days at the Tokyo War Crimes Trial as a prosecution witness against the Japanese. In July 1950 the Soviets returned Puyi to China and its new Communist masters, who kept him in prison for another nine years. Detained with him at Fushun, Liaoning, were several other members of the Qing imperial family who had collaborated with the Japanese, including his brother Pujie, Shanqi's son Xianjun, and a son of Puwei known as Little Gu. They were all subject to intense ideological remolding.[119]

On 4 December 1959 Puyi was freed as part of the special pardon proclaimed on the tenth anniversary of the founding of the People's Republic. Afterward, for the first time since his expulsion from the Forbidden City thirty-five years earlier, he returned to Beijing, where he was initially assigned to the Beijing Botanical Gardens as a gardener. In 1961 he was transferred to the Historical Materials Commission (Wenshi Ziliao Yanjiu Weiyuanhui) of the National Committee of the Chinese People's Political Consultative Conference as a "literary and historical worker." One of his duties was to organize historical documents from the late Qing and early Republic; another was to revise and expand the confessions that he had written in prison into his autobiography, which was published in March 1964 as *The First Half of My Life* (Wo de qian ban-sheng), or, as it is known in English, *From Emperor to Citizen*. Puyi died on 17 October 1967, at the outset of the Cultural Revolution; he was 61 years old and childless.[120]

The Communists did not, of course, recognize the validity of the 1912 Articles of Favorable Treatment; nevertheless, they treated some surviving members of the Qing imperial household with surprising respect, particularly those who, unlike Puyi, had kept their distance from Manchukuo. Such leniency toward the former dynasty may have been one aspect of the Communists' "united front" policy, by which they sought to distinguish themselves from their predecessors, the Nationalists, who had been uncompromising in their hatred of the Qing. Thus, in the early years of the People's Republic, the Communists gave a prominent, if nominal, political role to Puyi's uncle, Zaitao, who together with Zaixun had dominated the late Qing court during their brother Zaifeng's regency. (Zaixun had died in 1949; Zaifeng, in 1952.) During the regency Zaitao had been considered more open-minded than his brothers; during the Republic, he had not participated in any restorationist plot or in Manchukuo. As a result, he was in relatively good standing with the Communists. Perhaps on account of his youthful involvement with military affairs during Zaifeng's regency, he was assigned to an advisory position in the People's Liberation Army in charge of horses, and he spent some time in the steppes of the northwest. Having attended the second session of the first Chinese People's Political Consultative Conference in June 1950, Zaitao was elected in 1954 to the First National People's Congress from Beijing Municipality as a representative of the Manchus. Thereafter he seems to have traveled around the country as an ambassador of the congress to various Manchu groups; for example, he visited the small Manchu community in Guangzhou in May 1956. He was reelected to the Second and Third National People's Congresses in 1959 and 1964 respectively. He died in September 1970.[121] Zaitao's status as the officially recognized intermediary between the state and the Manchus was not unlike that of Pulun's during Yuan Shikai's presidency.

After the Cultural Revolution Zaitao's nephew Pujie, his past record as a war criminal notwithstanding, emerged to play a very similar role. Released from Fushun prison in 1960, a year after his brother Puyi, Pujie too had been assigned to the Historical Materials Commission; the following year, he and his Japanese wife and mother-in-law, together with Zaitao and Puyi and the Manchu novelist Lao She, all had their photograph taken with Prime Minister Zhou Enlai (plate 15). In 1978 Pujie was elected to the Fifth National People's Congress; he was elevated to the Standing Committee of the next three congresses elected in 1983, 1988, and 1993. With Pujie's death in early 1994 at age 87, the long and often strained relationship between the Qing court and its successor regimes finally came to an end.[122]

Meanwhile, how had the broad masses of Manchus been getting along under these same three post-1928 governments? In general, each regime dealt with the Manchus in accordance with its overall policy on ethnic groups. The Nationalists rejected the ethnic pluralism of the early Republic in favor of assimilationism. The early Republic had recognized the existence within China of five major ethnic groups, of whom the Manchus were one, and it had professed that all were equal; the Nationalists, on the other hand, asserted that China was ethnically homogeneous and denied that the Manchus constituted a separate ethnic group. Their assimilationist policy can be traced back to Sun Yat-sen, though Sun himself had characteristically been on both sides of the issue. Thus, in late 1912, when he met with the Manchus in Beijing, he indicated to them that he too subscribed to the then prevalent concept of "five ethnic groups as one family." Twelve years later, when he was allied with the Communists, he and the reorganized Nationalist Party again acknowledged the existence of various ethnic groups within China and promised, as had the early Republic, to treat them all as equals. In between, however, in June 1921 he asserted that, among his Three People's Principles, that of Nationalism had been no more than partially realized with the overthrow of the "Manchu Qing" (Man-Qing) and that it would be fully achieved only with the creation of a new "Chinese ethnic group" (*Zhonghua minzu*). Modeled on the idea of American ethnicity, this Chinese ethnicity "would take the Han people (Hanzu) as the core and have the other four peoples—Manchus, Mongols, Muslims, and Tibetans—all assimilate to us." Chinese ethnicity was therefore basically synonymous with "we Han people" (*women Hanzu*).[123]

Chiang Kai-shek's policy on ethnic groups was unwaveringly assimilationist. In *China's Destiny* (Zhongguo zhi mingyun), first published in 1943, he insisted that the people of China consisted of a single group, which he too called the "Chinese ethnic group" and which was the product of a long historical evolution during which "various racial stocks [*zongzu*] blended into the Chinese ethnic group." Furthermore, following Sun, Chiang equated this Chinese ethnic group with the Han. When explaining the disappearance of the Xiongnu and other ethnic groups of ancient China, he described their blending into the Chinese ethnic group as identical to their "Hanification" (Hanhua). Like the Xiongnu, the Manchus had been "assimilated into the Chinese ethnic group": "Since the 1911 Revolution, Manchus [Manzu] and Han [Hanzu] have so fused into one entity that there is no trace of distinctiveness." In short, according to Chiang Kai-shek, the Manchus had been so completely assimilated that they no longer existed as a separate entity. They had become an undifferentiated part of the single, all-encompassing Chinese ethnicity that was essentially identical to the Han.[124]

Since they were not recognized as a distinct group, it is hardly surprising that the Manchus received no special consideration from the Nationalists. As with Puyi, the only time that the Nationalists paid them any attention was in late 1931. As part of his appeal to Puyi not to collaborate with the Japanese, Chiang offered to recognize and give the Manchus special representation in various executive and deliberative bodies of the Nationalist regime on the same basis (and for the same kinds of geopolitical reasons) as the Mongols and Tibetans. However, the offer was withdrawn when it failed to deter Puyi from going to Manchuria. Nor did the Nationalists concern themselves with the Manchus' economic plight. They had located their capital in Nanjing; consequently, unlike their predecessors, they did not have to confront on a daily basis the masses of impoverished Manchus still living in the former capital. Although Nanjing too had been a garrison city, its relatively small population of banner people had been all but wiped out during the revolution. Thus, the attitude of the Nanjing government toward the Manchus was one of "out of sight, out of mind."

Due to the Nationalists' assimilationist policy, it became even more urgent than under the early Republic for individual Manchus to hide their ethnic origins and blend into the Han majority, as the regime claimed had already occurred. This was probably why Lao She, one of greatest and most prolific writers of the Nationalist era, did not then acknowledge his Manchu ancestry or include any recognizably Manchu character in the fiction he wrote at that time.[125] This too was probably why in the census of 1953, taken soon after the collapse of Nationalist rule, less than 2.5 million (half the estimated number of banner people in the late Qing) identified themselves as Manchus. How else to explain such an enormous population loss in such a short span of time? Though many Manchus had been killed during the Republican revolution and many more had died of starvation in the following decades, the others had disappeared by passing themselves off as Han.

Much to the annoyance of the Nationalists, who in 1938 angrily accused them of using "self-determination" as a device to divide and conquer China, the Japanese in Manchuria professed the alternate ethnic policy of pluralism. Manchukuo thus assiduously courted the various ethnic groups within its borders, assuring them a happy era of racial equality and harmony. To this end it adopted as its national emblem a five-color flag that, as in the early Republic, symbolized the union of five major ethnic groups. The five constituent groups of Manchukuo, however, differed slightly from those of the early Republic—they were Manchu, Han, Mongol, Japanese, and Korean, with the Japanese and their Korean subjects replacing the Muslims and Tibetans. Unlike Chiang Kai-shek, the Japanese not only reaffirmed the Manchus' status as one of the five major ethnic groups but accorded them the pride of place in the new "Manchu state." The Manchukuo flag, for example, was three-quarters yellow, symbolic of the Manchus, while the remaining quarter, in the upper corner next to the staff, was divided into four horizontal stripes representing the other four groups. Furthermore, according to F. C. Jones, the Japanese "endeavoured ... to stimulate Manchu racial consciousness by the revival of the Manchu spoken language and the Manchu script." They even tried to appeal to the Manchu-speaking Xibe people in far-off Xinjiang, whom one Manchukuo publication in 1939 called "the forgotten Manchus," who allegedly were "gazing in the direction of Manchuria with an intense morbid [sic] longing for their own fatherland." However, the Manchus in Manchukuo were relatively few in number, no more than 3 percent of the population, which was partly because many Han had migrated to the region in recent decades and partly because many Manchus had become largely assimilated to the Han way of life. The Manchukuo journal *Contemporary Manchuria* admitted that only those Manchus in the north still retained "their racial characteristics in the building of homes, clothing, and hair-dressing."[126]

According to Jones, the Japanese, echoing Puwei's espousal of "Manchus governing Manchuria," also "endeavoured to recruit Manchus for the administration of 'Manchukuo.'" Yet, among the initial high-level appointees to the government, only two had Manchu-sounding names. One was the Manchu bannerman Xiqia (1884–1952), a 1911 graduate of the Japanese Military Officers School, who in the twenty years since his return to China had been active in military affairs in the northeast; he was minister of finance in the Manchukuo government and concurrently governor of Jilin, the metropolitan province. The other was Guifu, a privy councilor. It may be symptomatic of Manchukuo's overall failure to attract Manchu commoners to its cause that the Qing loyalist Jinliang, who had been working in Shenyang since 1926 as curator of the Qing archives and an editor of *The Draft History of the Qing*, fled the region in 1931 and retired, penniless, to Beijing, where he lived on proceeds from his calligraphy. He died in 1962.[127]

The Communists, upon coming to power in 1949, likewise pursued a pluralist ethnicity policy. Proclaiming that theirs was a "united, multiethnic state," in December 1952 they formally recognized the Manchus (Manzu) as one of what came to be more than fifty minority ethnic groups in the People's Republic, who together make up about 7 percent of the country's current population. However, because the Manchus had become so assimilated to Han culture, their classification as a distinct group required a rather loose interpretation of the accepted Stalinist definition of a "nationality," or ethnic group. According to Stalin, a "nationality" was supposed to share in common four objective characteristics: language, territory, economic life, and mindset or culture. As field investigators in the mid-1950s found almost everywhere they looked, hardly any Manchus, except for the Xibe in Xinjiang and a few elderly residents along the upper reaches of the Amur River, could still speak or read the Manchu language. Nor were the Manchus concentrated in any one geographical location. Then, too, they lacked a common economic life. And their mindset was scarcely any different from that of the Han. Nevertheless, the Communists found in the Eight Banner system of the Qing the key element that both set the Manchus apart from the Han and most other ethnic groups and unified them into one distinct group. As the authors of the field survey of the Manchus in Beijing in the 1950s explained,

> To be sure, the "Eight Banners" and the "Manchus" are two different concepts, but from the standpoint of the formation of the Manchu ethnic group, the two are inseparable. The Mongols, Han, and other ethnic groups who joined the Eight Banners all experienced the same constraints of the banner system together with its political status and economic benefits; they were basically identical to the Eight Banner Manchus. Over a long period of waging war and earning a livelihood, their living customs, their use of language, and even their mindset became largely the same as those of the Eight Banner Manchus.[128]

In other words, the Qing policy of "Manchufying" the entire membership of the Eight Banner system had imposed upon all of its members a common livelihood, a common language, and a common mindset, thus fulfilling three of the four Stalinist criteria of a "nationality." Only a common territory was lacking.

The late Qing and early Republican concept of the Manchus as banner people thus formed the basis of the Communist definition, but the terminology had changed. The old term "banner people" was set aside, though it did not disappear altogether, particularly in informal speech. According to Yunxiang Yan, who conducted field research in a banner settlement in Shuangcheng County, Heilongjiang, in 1991, Manchus and Han still referred to each other respectively as "banner people" (qiren) and "civilians" (minren).[129] The new term, which was first used in the late Qing and had gained currency during the Nationalist era, was "Manchu ethnic group" (Manzu), and its use was all but compulsory in formal publications. Its correlative, the counterpart to "civilians," was "Han ethnic group" (Hanzu).

There were, however, two exceptions to the Communists' general equation of the Manchu ethnic group with the descendants of the banner people of the Qing. First, descendants of the Mongol banners and the Hanjun could, if they wished, revert to their ancestors' original ethnic affiliation. Thus, in Guangzhou, most descendants of the Hanjun asked to be classified as Han, while in Chengdu, Liu Xianzhi, a former member of the Mongol Bordered White Banner, identified himself as a Mongol. Many others whose ancestors had belonged to the

Mongol banners and the Hanjun chose to be registered as Manchu. For example, according to another field survey of the mid-1950s, of the 226,338 "Manchus" in the Jinzhou region, on the coastal corridor between Liaoning and Hebei, only 10 percent traced their ancestry to the Manchu Eight Banners; all of the rest were descended from the Hanjun.[130]

Second, descendants of five New Manchu groups within the Qing banner system were officially recognized as members of independent ethnic groups that were separate and distinct from the main Manchu group. The anthropologist Fei Xiaotong has described how this decision was reached with regard to the Daur, who live along the Nen River and its tributaries. Because they lived adjacent to Tungusic peoples to their east in Heilongjiang and because in the early Qing they had been incorporated into the Eight Banners, the Daur, based on the general equation of the Manchus and banner people, could justifiably have been classified as Manchu. Or because they lived adjacent to Mongols to their west in Inner Mongolia and because they spoke a language that was a variant of Mongolian, they could just as legitimately have been considered Mongol. Or, finally, they could have been thought of as an independent group that was neither Mongol nor Manchu because, on the one hand, the Mongolian language they spoke differed greatly from current Mongolian speech and, on the other, they had "resisted assimilation by the Tungus-Manchu-speaking peoples in spite of [their] proximity" and in spite of their membership in the banner system. In the end, it was decided that the Daur were sufficiently different from both Manchus and Mongols to constitute a separate group.[131] In addition to the Daur, the Communists also recognized as distinct groups the Xibe in Liaoning and Xinjiang; the Evenki (Ewenke, formerly known as Solun) and the Oroqen, both in northeastern Inner Mongolia; and the Hezhe (or Gold) in northern Heilongjiang.

According to the 1953 census, Manchus totaled 2,418,931, ranking seventh in population among China's ethnic minorities, behind the Zhuang, Uygur, Hui, Yi, Tibetans, and Miao but ahead of the Mongols. The other five groups that had been part of the Qing Eight Banners were minuscule in size. The Daur numbered 44,100; the Xibe, 19,000; the Evenki, 6,200; the Oroqen, 2,200; and the Hezhe, China's smallest minority, 450. Altogether, the six Manchu-related groups totaled 2,490,881, only about half the population of the banner people in the late Qing.[132]

Apart from acknowledging them officially, the Communists gave the Manchus other kinds of recognition and support that had been denied not only under the Nationalists but during the early Republic as well. In particular, they provided for Manchu representation in the country's governmental bodies. For example, eighteen Manchus (including Zaitao) were among the more than 1,200 delegates who attended the First National People's Congress when it met in 1954.[133] The Communists, in a show of turning their back on the anti-Manchu prejudice of the recent past, also attempted to censor certain words that Manchus found offensive. Thus, the State Council in February 1956 ordered book and newspaper publishers to not refer to the Manchus as "Man-Qing." Originally employed by Republican revolutionaries as well as later Nationalists (including Sun Yat-sen) to label the old Manchu regime, the term was later applied to the Manchu people as a whole. Many Manchus objected to the association of the broad masses of Manchu people with the discredited rulers of the Qing dynasty.[134]

In general, the Manchus had reason to be pleased with how the new regime down to the early 1980s treated them. Lao She, for one, no longer hid his ancestry as a Manchu bannerman, as he had under the Nationalists. From 1954 to 1964, under his real name, Shu Sheyu, rather than his pen name, he represented the Manchus as a delegate from Beijing to the first three National People's Congresses. (His Han-style surname, Shu, was derived from the first syllable of his original Manchu surname, Sumuru.) As captured in the 1961 photograph with Prime Minister Zhou Enlai, Lao She—as much as Zaitao, Puyi, and Pujie of the Qing imperial house—came to personify the Manchu people. Also, in contrast to his earlier reticence, he began to write explicitly about his fellow Manchus. His play *Teahouse*, composed in 1957, has as its main characters two bannermen in Beijing, while his novel *Beneath the Red Banner*, written in the early 1960s but not published until long after his death in 1966, is an autobiographical account of his family and relatives among the Manchus of Beijing around the time of his birth in 1899.[135] As other banner people and their descendants likewise stopped concealing their ethnic identity, the precipitous drop in the Manchu population that had occurred during the previous several decades came to a halt and was reversed. By 1982, according to the census, the Manchu population had risen to 4,299,159, almost twice that of 1953. At that time, the Manchus had surpassed the Tibetans but were still outnumbered by the Zhuang, Hui, Uygur, Yi, and Miao. The other five ethnic minorities previously affiliated with the Qing banner system had increased even more, from 71,950 to 202,594. Nevertheless, the total population of Manchus, Daur, Xibe, Evenki, Oroqen, and Hezhe in 1982 was still slightly less than the estimated five million banner people in the late Qing.[136]

In one respect, however, until the 1980s the Communists treated the Manchus significantly worse than they treated other ethnic minorities. The Manchus were unique among the eleven largest minorities in not being permitted to establish any large-scale "autonomous" territory, where they would be ostensibly free to practice and preserve their own lifestyle. They were authorized in 1956 and 1957 to set up only a handful of "ethnic townships" (*minzu xiang*) in Heilongjiang and Hebei, and most of these were dissolved in 1958 and transformed into people's communes. The most obvious reason was that, unlike the other principal minorities, the Manchus were not geographically concentrated. According to the 1982 census, most were located in the three northeastern provinces of Liaoning, Jilin, and Heilongjiang and in Hebei Province and Beijing Municipality. Specifically, 46 percent of all Manchus were in Liaoning, 12 percent in Jilin, and 21 percent in Heilongjiang; in other words, 79 percent were in "Manchuria." Another 9 percent were in Hebei and 3 percent in Beijing. The remaining 9 percent were scattered among the other provinces, especially those where banner garrisons had been situated during the Qing. However, in no province were the Manchus more than a tiny fraction of the total population. Even in Liaoning, where they were most numerous, they constituted only 5.6 percent of the total population of the province. There may have been other reasons as well. According to He Puying, writing in 1987, the question of granting Manchus a higher degree of autonomy was one that "greatly concerned" the Communist leadership during the 1950s, but for "various historical reasons" that the author fails to divulge, it was not resolved at the time.[137]

It was not until the mid-1980s, after Cultural Revolution, that the "historical" obstacles, whatever they may have been, were overcome and Manchus were finally granted autonomy at an administrative level higher than that of a township. Thus, in 1985 and 1986 five Manchu autonomous counties (*Manzu zizhi xian*) were designated, of which three were in eastern Liaoning: Xinbin (where the Manchus were 52.8 percent of the population), Xiuyan (71.7 percent), and Fengcheng (54.5 percent); the other two were in northern Hebei: Qinglong (51.6 percent) and Fengning (48.6 percent). By 1994 eight additional counties had been so designated—five in Liaoning and two in Hebei (one of which, Weichang, was a joint Manchu-Mongol county). Meanwhile, 340 Manchu ethnic townships had also been created. One of these townships, for example, was Dongling, in Zunhua County, northeastern Hebei, where 41.3 percent of the population were Manchus, descendants of the banner garrison guarding the Qing's Eastern Tombs, which the Nationalist troops had desecrated in 1928. In such places, the most evident expression of their putative autonomy was that the signs on public buildings were written in Manchu alongside Chinese.[138]

The 1980s also witnessed an unprecedented explosion of interest among the Manchus in their own history and culture. Publications about the Manchus, often written by Manchus, proliferated. Foremost among them was the quarterly journal *Manchu Studies* (Manzu yanjiu), founded in 1985. Other pioneering publications of the time included anthropological descriptions of individual

Manchu communities, such as *The History and Livelihood of the Manchus* (Manzu de lishi yu shenghuo), about Sanjiazitun, a village in Fuyu County, Heilongjiang, and *The Manchus at Xiuyan* (Manzu zai Xiuyan), on one of the Manchu autonomous counties in Liaoning; these two accounts were published in 1981 and 1984 respectively. Another anthropological study, appearing in 1985, was *Investigations into the Society and History of the Manchus* (Manzu shehui lishi diaocha), a compilation of excerpts from the field surveys done in various Manchu communities in the late 1950s. Less scientifically detached and more personal were the two series of articles by Jin Qicong on the Manchus in and about Beijing that ran in *Manchu Studies* from 1985 to 1989; both focused on the early Republican period and drew upon Jin's own experiences as a Metropolitan Bannerman. A similar account from another part of the country was *A Short History of the Manchus in Guangzhou* (Guangzhou Manzu jianshi), written by Wang Zongyou, a Manchu Bordered Red Bannerman from the local garrison, and published in 1990.

Another manifestation of the growing interest in Manchu culture was the attempt to preserve and perhaps even revive their ancestral language. The Manchus as a group had long since ceased to speak and write Manchu. In the 1980s the only large group of people who still used the Manchu language were the Xibe in the Yili valley of western Xinjiang, who despite their ancestral membership in the Qing banner system had been recognized as an ethnic group separate from the Manchus. Organized into Qapqal (Chabuchaer) Xibe Autonomous County, they even published a newspaper in the Xibe variant of the Manchu language.[139] To remedy this deficiency, nine Manchus and one Mongol in 1985 founded the Beijing Manchu Language School (Beijing Manwen Xueyuan) as a "spare-time school" (which students attend when not at work) with an enrollment of about 150; over half of the students were Manchus, mostly in their twenties and early thirties. The school's first class, a two-year course, graduated in 1987.[140] However, perhaps because Manchu is not widely spoken, it does not appear on banknotes along with Mongol, Tibetan, Uygur, and Zhuang minority scripts.

The most dramatic indicator of the Manchus' flourishing state in the 1980s was the tremendous increase in their population, which rose from 4,299,159 in 1982 to 9,821,180 in 1990. In the thirty years prior to 1982, their population had risen 78 percent; in the following eight years, it rose by 128 percent! Whereas their annual growth rate between 1952 and 1982 had been 2 percent, it was 10.9 percent between 1982 and 1990. Among all fifty-six of the officially recognized ethnic groups in China, Manchus were the fourth fastest-growing during that period. As a result, they became the second-largest minority in China, having outstripped the Yi, the Uygur, the Miao, and even the Hui. Only the Zhuang, in Guangxi, were still more numerous. The five ethnic groups who in the past had been affiliated with the Manchus in the banner system—the Xibe, Daur, Evenki, Oroqen, and Hezhe—also registered above-average gains; together, in 1990 they numbered 331,729. They and the Manchus collectively totaled more than 10 million, or roughly 1 percent of China's population.[141] Because the Manchus, unlike most other ethnic minorities, were not exempt from the regime's rigorous family planning policies, this extraordinary growth could not have been due to increased fertility. (The annual growth rate for the Han, for example, was only 1.3 percent.) It occurred primarily because of the increased willingness of individual Manchus, who, like Lao She earlier, had formerly passed for Han but who now wanted to acknowledge their ancestry. Just as the 50 percent drop in the Manchu population after the Qing can be attributed to the pattern of anti-Manchu discrimination during the early Republic and the assimilationist policy of the Nationalist government, the 128 percent increase of the 1980s may be explained by the policy of ethnic pluralism and cultural autonomy of the post-Mao era. For example, the daughter of Li Chengyin, the Beijing medical doctor who in 1916 had petitioned to change his classification from bannerman to civilian, took advantage of the relaxed atmosphere in the 1980s to formally reclaim her status as a Manchu (though not her original Manchu surname).[142] As a cumulative result of such individual actions, the Manchus in the 1980s finally recovered all the people they had lost during and after 1911. For the first time since the Republican revolution, there were more Manchus than there had been banner people at the end of the Qing.

CONCLUSION

The history of the Qing court and the Eight Banners thus did not end with the Republican revolution. Both the court and the banner system survived, though in attenuated forms, for more than another decade, as the successive governments of the early Republic made a serious, though diminishing, effort to honor and implement the abdication agreements that had led to the relatively easy success of the revolution. Despite their own financial straits, each continued, as promised, to subsidize both the court and the banner people. For its part, the Qing court, except for its quixotic collaboration with Zhang Xun in 1917, also made a conscientious effort to abide by those agreements. Although the court's continued residence at the rear of the Forbidden City was a clear violation of the agreement, it could not have occurred without the willing consent of the Republican authorities. This modus vivendi between the Republic on the one hand and the Qing court and the banner people on the other finally ended in the mid- and late 1920s, as first Feng Yuxiang evicted Puyi from the

Forbidden City and stripped him of his imperial title and then Nationalist troops desecrated the Qing imperial tombs. At that time appointments to posts in the Eight Banner system ceased, as did distribution of the banner soldiers' stipends as well as the court's subsidy. The personnel of the Qing court, but not the Qing dynasty itself, got a new lease on life, if only for a few years, when the Japanese created Manchukuo. There was, however, no second chance for the banner people, who had to struggle to survive on their own, not only economically but also psychologically. As they did so, they were transformed after 1949 from the hereditary military caste they had been under the Qing into an ethnic group. The "banner people" had evolved into the "Manchus."

Conclusion

China's Republican revolution was a classic example of a revolution of rising expectations. The Qing dynasty was overthrown in 1911–12 not because it was resistant to reform, as it had been in 1898, but because it was not reforming fast enough. In its last decade, following the foreign intervention to suppress the Boxer Rebellion, the incumbent regime under the leadership of the chastened empress dowager Cixi finally recognized the need for change. Known as the New Policies (Xinzheng), the reforms she initiated were so radical and far-reaching that they have been described as revolutionary in and of themselves. Thus, Douglas Reynolds speaks of a "Xinzheng Revolution" that preceded the Xinhai (1911) Revolution in time and perhaps exceeded it in results.[1] As he and others have described them, the New Policies comprised educational reforms and study abroad; reorganization of the army, navy, and police; and administrative and political changes, including plans to transform the millennia-old autocracy into a constitutional monarchy. While they were nationwide in scope, the overall reforms had the greatest impact among China's urban minority. The five million or so Manchus, as a predominantly urban population, were one of the groups most affected by the New Policies. Thus, new schools were founded among the banner people in Beijing and in the provincial garrisons. Manchus were among the first Chinese to go abroad to study in Japan. Parts of the Metropolitan Banners were reorganized into the First Division of the new national army and into the new Beijing police. Manchus were also elected to the provincial assemblies and selected for the National Assembly.

One principal consequence of the post-Boxer reforms, unanticipated and unwelcome by the Qing court, was the politicization of China's urban elite, who ever more boldly demanded a greater role for themselves in their government, whether in the form of a constitutional monarchy or a republic. While few, if any, Manchus were adherents of republicanism, they were not lacking among the reformist critics of the regime. Some took part in the first large-scale popular demonstration of Chinese nationalism, the anti-Russian agitation of 1903; some published periodicals, such as *Beijing Women's News* and *Great*

Harmony Journal, that supported various reformist causes; and some joined protopolitical parties, such as Liang Qichao's Political Information Institute, and participated in the lobbying campaign of 1909–10 for the immediate summoning of a parliament. Thus, the post-Boxer reform movement, unlike the revolutionary movement, was never exclusively Han or inherently anti-Manchu.

It was the inability of the late Qing court to meet the rising expectations that its own reforms had created that estranged the elite from the incumbent regime and allowed the revolution to succeed. The court's shortcomings in this regard were numerous. The most egregious was its steadfast opposition to the growing chorus of demands for a "responsible cabinet" and an elected legislature. It finally did accede to those demands, by proclaiming the Nineteen-Article Compact, but not until three weeks after the revolution had broken out and only after some of its own generals at nearby Luanzhou had threatened to march on the capital; by then it was clearly too little, too late. No less critical to the alienation of the reformers from the court were the attempt by the Qing court to reimperialize authority and its failure to eliminate Manchu-Han differences.

Reimperialization was related to but distinct from the court's concurrent effort in the late Qing to recentralize, to reverse the process of political decentralization that had greatly accelerated in the mid-nineteenth century, when the court had had to rely upon such provincial officials as Zeng Guofan and Li Hongzhang and their armies to suppress the Taiping and other rebellions. During the post-Boxer decade, the Qing, with some success, reclaimed some of the political and military authority that it had previously given up. Most notably, it managed, first, to strip Li's successor, Yuan Shikai, of his command over four of the six New Army divisions that he had personally organized and to turn them over to the Ministry of the Army under Tieliang; then, to remove Yuan and his equally powerful colleague, Zhang Zhidong, from their provincial bases in Tianjin and Wuchang by transferring them both to the capital; and finally, after Cixi's death, to dismiss Yuan from all his posts. Each of these steps served to strengthen the central government at the expense of the provincial authorities and other local interests. The nationalization of the trunk railroad lines in May 1911 had the same centralizing effect, and, as is well known, it provoked such strong opposition among the merchant and gentry elite in the provinces, especially Sichuan, that it led indirectly to the outbreak of the revolution downriver at Wuchang five months later.

Reimperialization, which was no less controversial, aimed to regain power not for the central government but for the Qing court itself. It seems to have been the main policy objective of Prince Regent Zaifeng, who evidently modeled himself after Kaiser Wilhelm of Germany. During the three years that he was in charge, Zaifeng ordered and oversaw the formation of an additional New Army division, the Palace Guard, which was under the direct command of the court rather than under the Ministry of the Army; he appointed his two brothers, Zaitao and Zaixun, to leading posts in the army and navy; he gave himself the title of generalissimo and took over as commander-in-chief of all the armed forces; he transferred control of the army's general staff from the Ministry of the Army to the court; and when responding to the demands of the constitutionalists, he named a cabinet that was headed by Yikuang and included four other imperial princes as ministers. The political ascendency of these princes during Zaifeng's regency was extremely unpopular, as the contemporary press and the debates at the newly convened National Assembly made amply clear.

While Zaifeng carried it to extreme lengths, the attempt to reimperialize authority did not begin with him; it had started half a century earlier, in 1861, when Yixin was named to the Grand Council. Yixin's appointment is usually lauded as critical to the success of the Tongzhi Restoration, but at the same time it was a portentous departure from a dynastic tradition of more than a century's standing—dating from the creation of the Grand Council in the 1720s and 1730s—that no imperial prince should be a council member or, by extension, a ministry head. It marked a return to the practices of the first century of the dynasty, when, under very different circumstances, imperial princes routinely participated in decision-making. Thus, beginning with Yixin in 1861 (aside from one brief break during 1901–3), one prince or another was to serve continuously as grand councilor until 1911. Furthermore, starting with the appointment of Yikuang as supervisor of the Ministry of Foreign Affairs in 1901 and that of his son, Zaizhen, as minister of commerce two years later, the mid-Qing ban on princes as ministry heads was also breached. These were the precedents, both of them set under Cixi, that paved the way for Zaifeng's formation of the "imperial kinsmen's cabinet," with Yikuang as prime minister.

The outcome of the court's efforts at recentralization and reimperialization was mixed. Reimperialization succeeded only in the short run and did not survive the revolution. Soon after the Wuchang uprising, the court was forced to beat a steady retreat. It removed Zaitao and Zaixun from their military and naval positions; it rescinded the appointment of Yikuang and the other princes as cabinet ministers, and, following a vote by the National Assembly, it named Yuan Shikai, recently recalled to office, to head up the new cabinet; it removed Zaifeng as regent; it conferred almost total decision-making authority upon Yuan and his cabinet; and last, at the time of the abdication, it transferred control of the Palace Guard from the court to the Ministry of the Army. On the other hand, though reimperialization obviously had failed, the cumulative effect of the parallel efforts at recentralization continued into the first few years of the new republic. They formed the institutional basis of Yuan Shikai's presidency as a strong, central ruler. Only after Yuan died in 1916 did decentralization regain the upper hand.

Another shortcoming of the late-Qing court that contributed to the alienation of the elite and the success of the revolution was its failure to deliver on its oft-stated promise to "eliminate differences between Manchus and Han." Such differences accounted for a substantial part of the republican revolutionaries' indictment against the dynasty, but they figured in the reformers' critique as well, such as Liang Qichao's essay of 1898 in *The China Discussion* and the Manchus' commentaries in *Great Harmony Journal*. They contradict the widespread belief, embraced by such disparate authorities as Mary Wright and Chiang Kai-shek, that the Manchus had become so assimilated to Han culture that by the late Qing they were no longer identifiably distinct from the Han; they also contradict the corollary of that belief, that the ethnic (or Manchu) issue was irrelevant to the 1911 Revolution. During the 268 years of Qing rule over China proper, the Manchus undeniably absorbed much of Han culture (even as they, to a lesser extent, had an indelible effect upon Han culture as well). After such a long period of sedentary idleness among the seductive pleasures of urban living surrounded by the multitude of Han Chinese, nearly all Manchus eventually turned their backs on the two core elements of the old Manchu way of life, Manchu speech and mounted archery. Yet the Manchus never entirely lost their identity as a separate people either in their own eyes or in the eyes of the Han. The institution of the Eight Banners remained intact down to the end of the dynasty and so did certain cultural markers, such as men's names and women's dress and natural feet, all of which continued to set Manchus apart from Han. It was upon the reality of these few but persistent differences that the revolutionaries based their propagandistic (and sometimes physical) assaults against the Manchus *qua* Manchus.

The late Qing court itself acknowledged the reality of Manchu-Han differences and tried repeatedly to do something about them. On three widely separate occasions—in 1865, 1898, and 1907—it issued decrees that either abolished the occupational and residential restrictions on the banner people or called for the disbandment of at least the provincial banner garrisons. However, none of these three edicts (nor that of 1902 lifting the ban on Manchu-Han marriage) was ever implemented. The banner people, for example, did not gain their freedom to choose where to live and what to do for a living until after the Qing abdication. Here, too, the court's failure was not the fault of Zaifeng alone; Cixi shared in the blame as well.

Yet, when the revolution finally occurred, the Qing court, notwithstanding its unpopularity, fared surprisingly well. Though its overthrow was never in doubt, the terms of its surrender were by no means unconditional or abject. The abdication agreement was a product of genuine negotiations between the court and the Republicans, with Yuan Shikai as intermediary. Consequently, Puyi's postrevolutionary fate contrasts dramatically with that of other deposed monarchs and autocrats of his historical era. He was not imprisoned and executed, as were King Louis XVI of France a century before and Czar Nicholas of Russia a few years later. He was not forever banished from his home country, as was Sultan Mehmed VI of the Ottoman dynasty following the Turkish revolution of 1922–24. Nor was he even obliged to give up his palace and take up residence elsewhere, as happened to the last Tokugawa shogun, Yoshinobu, whose castle in Edo (Tokyo) was turned over to the Meiji emperor while he himself retired to Shizuoka.[2] The Articles of Favorable Treatment for Puyi and his court, which was signed in 1912, remained more or less in effect for over a decade afterward, despite the vicissitudes of warlord politics in Beijing. He was not expelled from the Forbidden City until 1924. Even then, the rest of the tattered agreement was not abrogated until 1928, when the Nationalists' desecration of the Qing Eastern Tombs went unpunished.

It was also not until the mid-1920s that the Eight Banner system of the Qing was totally dismantled, thus hastening the completion of the process by which the Manchus evolved from an occupational caste into an ethnic group. As is evident throughout this study, the question of who the Manchus were is greatly complicated by the fact that the single English term "Manchu" embraces a number of different Chinese terms, ranging from Manzhou, Manzhouren, Manren, and Manzu to *qiren*, *qijiren*, and *qizu*. Although these words all refer to the Manchu people, their meaning could and did vary—sometimes slightly, sometimes greatly—depending on the social or historical context. As the concept of the Manchus changed over time, it helped to define who the Han were as well.

During the Qing, the question of Manchu identity was inextricably interwoven into the history and structure of the banner system, resulting initially in three concentric circles of meaning. First, in the narrowest as well as the earliest sense, the Manchus were the Manzhou, descendants of the Jurchen, whose scattered tribes in what was later called Manchuria (also Manzhou in Chinese) were unified by Nurhaci beginning in the 1590s and organized by him in 1615 into the Eight Banners. In 1635 Hong Taiji bestowed upon them the name Manju, from which is derived the Chinese transliteration Manzhou. To distinguish them from later additions to the Manchu banners, they were also known as the Old Manchus (Fo Manzhou, in Chinese). They and their descendants were the core element of the banner system. Throughout the Qing period, in the eyes of successive emperors they were the most highly esteemed, most trusted contingent of the system. The emperor himself was always one of them. It was their ancestral language and their equestrian lifestyle that constituted the essence of the "Manchu way." Second, in a broader (and slightly later) sense, the Manchus were the Eight Banner Manchus (Baqi Manzhou). These included not only the Old Manchus but also the New Manchus (Yiche Manzhou), the nearby Tungusic and Tungusized Mongol peoples who were added to the Manchu banners after the Qing invasion of China proper in 1644.

Finally, in the broadest sense, the Manchus were the banner people (*qiren*), particularly when they were being contrasted to the Han. It is clear from the pronouncements of the Qing rulers themselves that when referring to Man-Han, they usually meant by "Man" not only the Old Manchus nor even the Eight Banner Manchus but the membership of the entire Eight Banner system, which Hong Taiji had enlarged by creating two new contingents in 1635 and 1642 respectively, the former made up of Mongols and the latter of captured or surrendered Han Chinese. Thus, in this sense, the Manchus embraced all three ethnic components of the banner system—the Manchu banners, the Mongol banners, and the Hanjun—as well as the bondservants. By this formulation, the Manchus were identical to the people who hereditarily belonged to one or another of the twenty-four banners and as such were officially classified as banner people, while the non-banner people, the vast majority of whom were Han, were generally classified as civilians (*min*). Since the Qing emperors and their officials used these two sets of terms—Man-Han and *qi-min*—more or less interchangeably, therefore just as the banner people corresponded to the Manchus, so the civilian population were, practically speaking, synonymous with the Han.

If, as this study contends, the Manchus are best viewed as equivalent to the banner people, then they were, during most of the Qing period, not so much an ethnic group as an occupational caste. In origin, the banner people were a multiethnic group. Not only were they divided among the three ethnic divisions, but the Eight Banner Manchus were divided between the Old and the New Manchus, and the New Manchus were divided among different groups themselves. As a whole, the banner people lacked the racial, linguistic, and cultural homogeneity of the original Old Manchus. While subsequent Qing rulers made an effort to Manchufy the entire banner population by requiring them all to learn and absorb the "national speech and mounted archery" tradition of the Old Manchus, in the end what differentiated the Manchus as banner people from the Han as civilians was not ethnicity or (as some have stated) political status, but occupation.[3] From the very beginning, the primary function of the Eight Banner system was military. The core members of the system were the banner soldiers, who provided the main fighting force for the Qing conquest of China and who thereafter were required to protect and maintain the Qing dynasty from their more than ninety garrisons in Beijing, in their northeastern homeland, and in various strategic centers within China proper and across China's northern frontier. Except for office-holding (which was rare) and in some cases farming, bannermen were prohibited from other employment, so as to better hold themselves in military preparedness. In return, the banner soldiers received a stipend of money and grain from the Qing state. The banner system, however, included not only the banner soldiers but also their families as well as numerous other relatives and dependents. By the end of the dynasty, when the banner population totaled five or six million, the ratio of banner soldier to banner people was roughly one to twenty. Every banner person (whether soldier or dependent) belonged to a banner company and was subject to the jurisdiction of his or her company captain and the banner's lieutenant-general. Finally, membership in the banner system was hereditary and had been closed off to outsiders soon after the invasion of China proper. Intermarriage with non-banner people was prohibited and seldom occurred. In short, the Manchus as banner people can be characterized occupationally as a hereditary military caste, similar to the samurai of Tokugawa Japan.

The transformation of the Manchus from an occupational caste to an ethnic group began during the watershed decade of the late 1890s and early 1900s, when a growing number of Chinese scholars and officials were compelled by the threat of foreign imperialism to begin to think of their country no longer as a cultural sphere but rather in political and territorial terms as a nation-state. Heretofore, Chinese thinkers had viewed both themselves and others largely in cultural terms. They themselves were the "inner, civilized" people originating from the Central Plain of north China who called themselves Hua and/or Xia; the others were various "outer, barbarian" peoples, such as the Yi to the east and the Di to the north. It was, as is well known, Liang Qichao who was most responsible for redefining the notion of China from a civilization (indeed, the one and only civilization) to a territorial state (one among many). As part of that redefinition, Liang also reconceptualized the Manchus as a racial group. According to his late 1898 essay on Manchu-Han relations, just as the yellow race and the white race were locked in a life-or-death "racial conflict," so too were the Manchus and Han, two subgroups of the yellow race within China. When referring to the Manchus and Han, Liang pointedly eschewed the traditional cultural terms (such as Yi-Di and Huaren) in favor of two essentially new terms, Manren and Hanren. (Though obviously derived from the established combination Man-Han, their usage as separate words had been infrequent in the past.) Liang, furthermore, equated the Manren with the banner people, the "five million people" who for two centuries had "eaten without farming and been clothed without weaving."

Liang Qichao's social Darwinist redefinition of Manchus and Han carried the day. In the late Qing and early Republic, Manchus and Han were increasingly differentiated from each other along racial rather than—as in the past— either occupational or cultural lines, though the old concepts and the associated terminology lingered on. Thus, Wu Yue, the assassin of 1905, and *Great Harmony Journal*, the Manchu reformist publication of 1907, as well as the abdication agreement of 1912 all called the Manchus an ethnic group (*zu* or *minzu*). Yet the combined term "Manzu" (Manchu ethnic group), which clearly existed at the time, was rarely used as a reference for the Manchus. (It figured most prominently in the name of the Manchus' main lobbying organization in the 1910s and 1920s, the Association for the Common Advancement of the Manchus.)[4] Instead, the two most commonly used terms by which to refer to the Manchus in the late Qing and early Republic were "Manren" and *qiren*. The former, popularized by Liang Qichao, was favored by revolutionaries such as Zou Rong; the latter, by Qing administrators. Also, "Manren" seems to have been more popular before the revolution; *qiren*, or its variant *qijiren* (people of banner registry), more popular afterward. In addition to these terms, there were yet others in common use, particularly among the republican revolutionaries of the post-Boxer era. Chen Tianhua, for one, almost always used "Manzhouren," which can be translated either as "Manchu people" (with "Manzhou" referring to the Eight Banner Manchus) or "people of Manchuria" (with "Manzhou" referring to China's northeastern territory). Others drew upon China's rich and ancient store of culturalist epithets. Thus, Zhang Binglin loved to vilify the Manchus as Donghu (Eastern Barbarians) and as *lu* (caitiffs), while others denigrated them as Dada (Tartars) and Dalu (Tartar caitiffs). In short, even as a consensus was emerging that the Manchus should be considered an ethnic group, there was as yet no agreement on what to call them.

As to who the Manchus were, the general view in the late Qing and early Republic was, following Liang Qichao, that they were synonymous with the total membership of the Eight Banners—in other words, the banner people. Thus, the revolutionaries' seven-point indictment of the "Manchus" in the post-Boxer decade was, at heart, a condemnation of them as members of the banner system. This equation of the Manchus with the banner people lasted well into the early Republic, as did, of course, much of the banner system itself. Thus the Republican government, despite its recognition of the Manchus as an ethnic group, continued the Qing practice of classifying them as "banner people," except in those cases where individual Manchus formally petitioned to have their status changed. (The change, though, was not from "Manchu" to "Han," but from "banner person" to "civilian.") This was why Manchus were so commonly referred to then as "people of banner registry." Indeed, a group of politically active Manchus in 1914 even proposed *qizu* (banner ethnic group or "nationality") as yet another name for themselves. Though it combined the old (Manchus as the banner people) and the new (Manchus as an ethnic group), the term did not catch on.

If there was no agreement about what to call the Manchus, there was no such problem with regard to the Han, who, following Liang Qichao, were almost universally known in the late Qing and early Republic as Hanren. For example, in contrast to their proclivity for labeling the Manchus as barbarians, the revolutionaries hardly ever utilized the correlatives Hua and/or Xia to refer to themselves; instead, they nearly always called themselves Hanren. (It is thus all the more surprising that when the Republic was established, they chose to use the traditional-sounding "Zhonghua" in its name.) As to who was meant by "Hanren," here, too, Liang Qichao's lead was followed. In his account of the racial competition within China, he focused on only two contestants—the Manchus and the Han. Since the Manchus were equated with the five million banner people, the Han were, by implication, the rest of China's vast population, the four hundred million non-banner "civilians" of the *qi-min* dichotomy.

Finally, what was the proper place for the Manchus? Where in late Qing and early Republican China did they fit in? The concept of China among the republican revolutionaries in the post-Boxer decade was that of a unitary nation-state. Geographically, it encompassed China proper, where nearly all the residents were Han and where the Han should rule. As Chen Tianhua asserted, "China belongs to the Han people." In a China so defined, the Manchus, simply because they were non-Han, had no rightful place; they should be, according to the manifesto of the revolutionary Alliance, "expelled." As Zhang Binglin more than once intimated, the appropriate refuge for the Manchus was Manchuria, their ancestral homeland, where they could create a nation-state of their own, as the Japanese later on tried to do in their name. The Qing, on the other hand, regarded China as a multiethnic empire, of which Han-populated China proper was but one region. The Qing empire, in this view, also included Manchuria, Mongolia, Turkestan, and Tibet, all of which, along with China proper, owed equal but separate obeisance to the emperor. The peoples of these different regions were administered separately. Whereas the Han were governed by the regular civil bureaucracy and the Manchus by the Eight Banners, the Mongols, Muslims, and Tibetans were subject to the Court of Colonial Affairs. The Qianlong emperor, who was instrumental in subjugating Turkestan and bringing it firmly within the Qing empire, took particular delight in his self-image as ruler and unifier of the five peoples. During the post-Boxer decade, the Manchu reformers associated with *Great Harmony Journal* reiterated the Qianlong ideal when they sought to "unify the Manchus, Han, Mongols, Muslims, and Tibetans as one citizenry."

By the time Qing rule was overthrown in 1912, however, the republicans had abandoned their earlier, narrowly defined view of "China proper for the Han Chinese." They did not, for example, drive the Manchus back to Manchuria but generally allowed them to remain where they were. Instead, they came around to a modified version of the Qing's expansive concept of China as a multiethnic state. Sanctioned by Empress Dowager Longyu's abdication decree, the new regime claimed to be the legitimate successor to the Qing and hence to all of its far-flung territories and variegated populations. (Not everyone heeded its claim, as the Mongols in Outer Mongolia refused to transfer their allegiance from the Qing empire to the Republic.) The revolutionaries' previous view of China as caught in a struggle between two groups, Han and Manchus, was replaced by the concept of the Republic of China (no longer the Qing empire) as composed of five peoples. This idea, recycled from the Qing, was symbolized by the five-bar flag of the early Republic. Moreover, it was explicitly spelled out in the abdication agreements, which referred to the four major non-Han peoples—Manchus, Mongols, Muslims, and Tibetans—as ethnic groups and promised that they would be treated on an equal basis with the Han people (Hanren). Such, at least, was the stated aim of the early Republic, even if the reality for the Manchus was quite otherwise.

Temporarily rejected by Chiang Kai-shek and the Nationalists, the early Republic's ideal of China as a multiethnic state was resurrected by the Communists. Chiang and the Nationalists, successors to the republican revolutionaries, insisted that China was a unitary nation-state, populated by one undifferentiated "Chinese ethnic group" (*Zhonghua minzu*) that was essentially synonymous with the Han. Though they referred to the Manchus as Manzu, as if they were a separate entity, they viewed them as having been completely assimilated with "us Han." The People's Republic, on the other hand, proclaimed itself a multiethnic state, and the number of officially recognized ethnic groups ballooned from five to fifty-six as ethnographers differentiated the Chinese population more carefully, more precisely than before. For example, during the early Republic the sizable Muslim population, most of whom are concentrated in the northwest, were considered one ethnic group, the Hui. Under the Communists, they were divided on the basis of linguistic and cultural differences into ten separate groups, and the term "Hui" came to be reserved for the Chinese-speaking Muslims, who were now called "Huizu." The

Han, however, did not undergo a similar subdivision, as the regime refrained from recognizing as official ethnic groups such distinct groups as the Hakka and the Subei people. Instead, much like Liang Qichao, the Communists consider the Han, with 93 percent of China's total population, one huge, undifferentiated mass of people.[5]

Like the Hui and unlike the Han, the Manchus too multiplied amoebalike under the Communists. What in the early Republic had been one people, based on common membership in the Eight Banner system, became six: the Xibe, Daur, Evenki, Oroqen, Hezhe, and, of course, the Manchus. As in the late Qing, ancestral membership in the Eight Banners is again the defining characteristic of the Manchu ethnic group, but it is now shared with five other groups. Though *qiren* is still used informally in some localities to refer to the Manchus, it has by and large been supplanted by the single term "Manzu," thus ending the terminological confusion of the late Qing and early Republic. In short, the banner people (*qiren*) have completed their transformation from the hereditary military caste that they were during the Qing, to the broad but vaguely construed ethnic group whom the republican revolutionaries and others in the late Qing and early Republic called "Manren," and finally to the narrowly defined, officially recognized Manchu ethnic group (Manzu) that they are under the Communists.

Notes

INTRODUCTION

1. Liang Qichao, *Yinbingshi wenji*, part 1, 77–83. See also Pusey, *China and Charles Darwin*, 181–84.

2. Hsieh, *Chinese Historiography*; Xiao Yishan, *Qingdai tongshi*.

3. Esherick, *Reform and Revolution*; Hou Yijie, *Ershi shiji chu*.

4. Wright, *Last Stand*; Kwong, *Mosaic of the Hundred Days*.

5. Bland and Backhouse, *China under the Empress Dowager*; for an all-too-brief scholarly look at Cixi, see Chung, "Much Maligned Empress Dowager."

6. Bays, *China Enters*; Powell, *Rise of Chinese Military Power*; J. Ch'en, *Yuan Shih-k'ai*; MacKinnon, *Power and Politics*.

7. Mark Elliott, in almost identical terms, likewise speaks of the apparent disappearance of the Manchus by the end of the dynasty. See his "Resident Aliens," xi.

8. R. Lee, *Manchurian Frontier*; Des Forges, *Hsi-liang*; Crossley, *Orphan Warriors*.

9. Zheng Tianting, *Tanweiji*, 176; Ch'en Chieh-hsien, "Decline of the Manchu Language," 144; Wright, *Last Stand*, 53.

10. Zou Rong, *Gemingjun*, 1 (based on Lust's translation, 58).

11. Wright, "Introduction," 21–23.

1 / SEPARATE AND UNEQUAL

1. This definition of anti-Manchuism is much narrower and more specific than that offered by Kauko Laitinen, who defines it simply as "advocation (propaganda) by the Chinese in favour of overthrowing the Manchus" (*Chinese Nationalism*, 2).

2. Zou Rong, *Gemingjun*, 5 (based on Lust's translation, 65).

3. Zhang Nan and Wang Renzhi, *Xinhai Geming qianshinianjian*, 1: 60.

4. Luo Baoshan, "Guanyu Zhang Binglin," 56–62; Zhang Nan and Wang Renzhi, *Xinhai Geming qianshinianjian*, 1: 94–99, 752–64. On Zhang Binglin's anti-Manchuism, see Wong, *Search for Modern Nationalism*, esp. 61–64; and Laitinen, *Chinese Nationalism*.

5. On Zou Rong, see Lust's introduction to Tsou, *The Revolutionary Army*.

6. See Young, "Problems of a Late Ch'ing Revolutionary."

7. For a somewhat different analysis of the revolutionaries' anti-Manchuism, based on articles in *The People's Journal* after 1905, see Gasster, *Chinese Intellectuals*, chap. 3.

8. Zhang Nan and Wang Renzhi, *Xinhai Geming qianshinianjian*, 1: 686.

9. Zou Rong, *Gemingjun*, 22 (based on Lust's translation, 80).

10. See Tao Jing-shen, "Barbarians or Northerners," 84 n. 43.

11. Laitinen, *Chinese Nationalism*, 66, 83; on the term "Shina," see Fogel, "Sino-Japanese Controversy."

12. Chen Tianhua, *Chen Tianhua ji*, 107–8; Zou Rong, *Gemingjun*, 29–32.

13. Chen Tianhua, *Chen Tianhua ji*, 153.

14. Zou Rong, *Gemingjun*, 17 (based on Lust's translation, 76); Zhang Nan and Wang Renzhi, *Xinhai Geming qianshinianjian*, 1: 754.

15. Zou Rong, *Gemingjun*, 20–21 (based on Lust's translation, 79).

16. Zou Rong, *Gemingjun*, 9 (based on Lust's translation, 68); Chen Tianhua, *Chen Tianhua ji*, 57, 117, 118.

17. Chen Tianhua, *Chen Tianhua ji*, 117; Zou Rong, *Gemingjun*, 8–9 (based on Lust's translation, 68); Zhang Nan and Wang Renzhi, *Xinhai Geming qianshinianjian*, 1: 684.

18. Zou Rong, *Gemingjun*, 6–8 (based on Lust's translation, 66–68); Chen Tianhua, *Chen Tianhua ji*, 118.

19. Liang Qichao, *Yinbingshi wenji*, part 5: 35.

20. Zou Rong, *Gemingjun*, 22 (based on Lust's translation, 80).

21. The reputed source of the quote, leaving aside the issue of its authenticity, is in dispute. Liang Qichao, in *Wuxu zhengbian ji* (An account of the 1898 coup) as reprinted and abridged in *Wuxu bianfa*, 1: 290, attributes the quote to Gangyi; Zou Rong, *Gemingjun*, 19, to Cixi's confidant Ronglu; and S. L. Tikhvinsky, according to Lust's introduction to his translation of Tsou, *The Revolutionary Army*, 95 n. 121, to Yihuan (Prince Chun). See also Min Tu-ki, "Wuxu bianfa shiqi," 383–84, who goes along with Liang.

22. Chen Tianhua, *Chen Tianhua ji*, 36; Zou Rong, *Gemingjun*, 5. My thanks to Weikun Cheng for his help in locating the Zou Rong citation.

23. Aixin Jueluo Zongkui, "Manzu jiusu," 264; J. Lee and R. Eng, "Population and Family History," 8. See also Elliott, "Resident Aliens," 499–501. I am grateful to Robert Eng for making his copy of Zongkui's article available to me.

24. *Da-Qing huidian*, 84: 1a; R. Lee, *Manchurian Frontier*, 24–25; Spence, *Ts'ao Yin*, 2–9; Chen Jiahua, "Baqi zhidu," part 1.

25. Brunnert and Hagelstrom, *Present Day Political Organization*, no. 97; *Lishi dang'an*, 1989, no. 2: 51, 106.

26. *Qingshigao*, 130: 3880–89. See also *Da-Qing huidian*, 84: 3a-4b; 86: 17b.

27. Chen Jiahua, "Baqi zhidu," part 1: 114.

28. *Da-Qing huidian*, 84: 3a-3b; Wang Zhonghan, "Qingdai Baqi," part 1: 37–42; W. Wu, "Development and Decline," 22 n. 68.

29. R. Lee, *Manchurian Frontier*, 14–16, 33–34; Wang Zhonghan, "Guanyu Manzu," 8–10; Chen Jiahua, "Baqi zhidu," part 2: 118–19; Wu Zhichao, "Lüelun 'Xin Manzhou.'"

30. Zhang Deze, *Qingdai guojia jiguan*, 169; Brunnert and Hagelstrom, *Present Day Political Organization*, nos. 39–40; Naquin and Rawski, *Chinese Society*, 116; J. Lee et al., "Last Emperors," 363 n. 13; Telford and Finegan, "Qing Archival Materials," 94–95.

31. Brunnert and Hagelstrom, *Present Day Political Organization*, nos. 16–27, 41.

32. Hummel, *Eminent Chinese*, 964–65; Wei Xiumei, *Qingji zhiguan biao*, "Renwulu," 224; Shen Yunlong, "Zhangwo wan-Qing zhengbing," 70; *Qingdai renwu zhuan'gao*, 9: 149–56.

33. *Qingshigao*, 470: 12,799; Hummel, *Eminent Chinese*, 387, 598.

34. R. Lee, *Manchurian Frontier*, 16, 34–35; Chen Jiahua, "Baqi zhidu," part 1: 114–15. On Xiliang, see Des Forges, *Hsi-liang*.

35. Pamela Crossley and Mark Elliott render Hanjun as "Chinese-martial" and "Han-martial" respectively. Both terms strike me as awkward sounding and hardly more meaningful than the original Chinese.

36. R. Lee, *Manchurian Frontier*, 35; Wang Zhonghan, "Qingdai Baqi," part 2: 62–66; Chen Jiahua and Fu Kedong, "Baqi Hanjun"; Crossley, *Manchus*, 7.

37. *Qingdai renwu zhuan'gao*, 5: 98.

38. R. Lee, *Manchurian Frontier*, 26; Wang Zhonghan, "Guanyu Manzu," 14–16; Spence, *Ts'ao Yin*, 6–18; *Manzu shehui lishi*, 226.

39. Crossley, *Manchus*, 7.

40. *Da-Qing huidian*, 84: 1a; *Manzu shehui lishi*, 85; Brunnert and Hagelstrom, *Present Day Political Organization*, nos. 719, 720.

41. *Da-Qing huidian*, 86: 20b-21a; Zhang Deze, *Qingdai guojia jiguan*, 92; Brunnert and Hagelstrom, *Present Day Political Organization*, no. 718.

42. Zheng Tianting, *Tanweiji*, 172; Hummel, *Eminent Chinese*, 600; *Manzu shehui lishi*, 84. The Chinese system, as seen for example at the Altar of Harvests (Shejitan) in Beijing, associated red with south, blue or blue-green with east, white with west, black with north, and yellow with the center. See Smith, *China's Cultural Heritage*, 102; *Beijing mingsheng*, 152. The Mongol system, on the other hand, associated red with south, white with east, black with west, yellow with north, and blue with the center (Atwood, "National Questions," 44).

43. Hu Jieqing and Shu Yi, "Ji Lao She."

44. Zheng Tianting, *Tanweiji*, 172–73; Ma Xiedi, "Qianlun Qingdai zhufang," 194.

45. Jin Qicong, "Jingqi de Manzu," 1988, no. 3: 65; Rozman, *Urban Networks*, 292.

46. *Da-Qing huidian*, 84: 3a-4b; *Manzu shehui lishi*, 85; Brunnert and Hagelstrom, *Present Day Political Organization*, no. 722.

47. Rozman, *Urban Networks*, 292.

48. Zhang Deze, *Qingdai guojia jiguan*, 90; Brunnert and Hagelstrom, *Present Day Political Organization*, nos. 726–27; Fu Kedong and Chen Jiahua, "Qingdai qianqi de zuoling," 168.

49. Zhang Deze, *Qingdai guojia jiguan*, 90; Qin Guojing, "Qingdai de Baqi," 15.

50. *Da-Qing huidian*, 84: 8b-9a; J. Lee and R. Eng, "Population and Family History," 9–10; Telford and Finegan, "Qing Archival Materials," 87–90; *Manzu shehui lishi*, 85.

51. *Da-Qing huidian*, 84: 12a-13a. See also Torbert, *Ch'ing Imperial Household Department*, 72–77.

52. *Qingshigao*, 130: 3887–89. Actually, when the bondservant companies, which are broken down by banners in *The Draft History of the Qing*, are added up, the total is 105. However, in this listing the Plain Blue Banner is credited with only six companies, even though it reportedly had 2,704 soldiers, for an average of 451 soldiers per company. By contrast, each of the other seven banners had between eleven and twenty-one companies, averaging 167 soldiers per company. Perhaps the Plain Blue Banner should have been credited instead with sixteen (not six) companies, which would bring its soldier-to-company ratio down to 169, which is comparable to that of the other banners. The adjusted total of bondservant companies would then be 115.

53. Wade, "Army of the Chinese Empire," 254; Wang Zhonghan, "'Guoyu qishe,'" 205; Yang Du, *Yang Du ji*, 425; *Qingshigao*, 130: 3889. *The Draft History of the Qing* arrived at its total by adding up the strength of all the specialized units except the Escorts, Infantry, and Light Cavalry (36,118), the bondservant companies (20,413), and the twenty-four banners (70,272), along with a detachment of forty-eight soldiers and three officers guarding the tomb of Yihuan. (These figures actually add up to 126,854, a discrepancy of 135.) It should be noted that the *Draft History* total includes the more than 20,000 members of the bondservant companies, which are not normally considered a part of the regular banners; if the bondservant companies are not counted, then the *Draft History* total for the Metropolitan Banners would be about 106,500. Its exclusion of the Light Cavalry and the Infantry, the two largest service branches, seems to be based on the premise that they overlap with the twenty-four banners.

54. *Da-Qing huidian*, 84: 4b.

55. Brunnert and Hagelstrom, *Present Day Political Organization*, nos. 744–46.

56. Ma Xiedi, "Zhufang Baqi," 19–21.

57. *Da-Qing huidian*, 84: 5b; 86: 7a; *Hubei tongzhi*, 64: 1a-2a. See also Pan Honggang, "Xinhai Geming," 21. *The Collected Statutes* errs in crediting the Jingzhou garrison with only one brigade-general. Also *The Collected Statutes*, though reissued in 1899, does not (unlike the Hubei gazetteer) include the 1,560 soldiers who were added to the garrison in 1815, 1833, and 1861. According to the gazetteer, the garrison numbered 7,228 soldiers.

58. On Tieliang, see Zha Shijie, "Qingmo de Zongshedang," 132; *Qingdai renwu zhuan'gao*, 8: 117–19.

59. Elliott, "Resident Aliens," 178–90, 204–9.

60. Zhang Yutian, "Wan-Qing qiying," 56–60; *Hangzhoufu zhi*, 41: 12b-13a; *Jiangningfu zhi*, 3: 2a-3b.

61. On the establishment of the provincial garrisons and their distribution in China proper, see Elliott, "Resident Aliens," chap. 2. See also Ding Yizhuang, *Qingdai Baqi zhufang*, 215–17. My thanks to Ding Yizhuang for sending me a copy of her book.

62. *Da-Qing huidian*, 84: 2a, 2b, 4b, 8a; 86: 4b-5a, 8a-8b; Ma Xiedi, "Zhufang Baqi," 20; Wade, "Army of the Chinese Empire," 314–18; Brunnert and Hagelstrom, *Present Day Political Organization*, nos. 569, 748, 893, 897, 898.

63. *Da-Qing huidian*, 84: 2a-3a, 4b-7a; 86: 5a-6a, 7b-8b; Ma Xiedi, "Zhufang Baqi," 19–20; Fu Kedong, "Baqi shuishi," 19–20; Wade, "Army of the Chinese Empire," 323–29; Zhang Deze, *Qingdai guojia jiguan*, 237–42. The total of 125 companies in Fengtian was arrived at by adding up the number of companies assigned to each garrison as listed in *The Collected Statutes of the Great Qing*. This, however, may be an undercount, as at least five garrisons—Tieling, Xingjing, Fushun, Niuzhuang, and Gaizhou, which together had 1,583 soldiers—were not credited with any company at all. Furthermore, the Xiongyue garrison, with 954 soldiers, was credited with only one company.

64. *Da-Qing huidian*, 84: 2a-3a, 5b-6a; 86: 7a-7b; Ma Xiedi, "Zhufang Baqi," 20; Wade, "Army of the Chinese Empire," 321–23.

65. *Da-Qing huidian*, 84: 2a-2b, 5b-6a; 86: 6a-7b; Ma Xiedi, "Zhufang Baqi," 20; Wade, "Army of the Chinese Empire," 318–21.

66. Wang Zhonghan, "'Guoyu qishe,'" 205; Zheng Tianting, *Tanweiji*, 173–74; R. Lee, *Manchurian Frontier*, 32; Ma Xiedi, "Zhufang Baqi," 19; Ding Yizhuang, *Qingdai Baqi zhufang*, 2; Liu Fenghan, "Qingji Ziqiang Yundong," 346; Elliott, "Bannerman and Townsman," 40 n. 8.

67. Aixin Jueluo Zongkui, "Manzu jiusu," 264; *Da-Qing huidian*, 84: 9a; Brunnert and Hagelstrom, *Present Day Political Organization*, no. 732a; R. Lee, *Manchurian Frontier*, 28.

68. China, Baqi Dutong Yamen Archives, *juan* 8, "Qiwu"; Fu Kedong and Chen Jiahua, "Qingdai qianqi de zuoling," 168.

69. *Manzu jianshi*, 100; Wang Zonghan, "'Guoyu qishe,'" 205.

70. *Manzu shehui lishi*, 35; Zhang Qizhuo, *Manzu zai Xiuyan*, 13–14; J. Lee and R. Eng, "Population and Family History," 12.

71. Zheng Chuanshui, "Qingmo Manzu shehui," 61. The authors of the 1959 field survey of the Manchus in Beijing greatly understate the numerical gap between banner soldiers and banner people in the late Qing when they assert that each soldier had only five dependents (*Manzu shehui lishi*, 85). Liu Fenghan is much closer to the mark. He estimates that by the mid-nineteenth century each banner soldier was responsible for the livelihood of "more than ten or even several tens of family members" ("Qingji Ziqiang Yundong," 352).

72. *SL/TZ*, 144: 2b-3b; Wright, *Last Stand*, 53–54.

73. Evelyn Rawski, too, describes the status of what she calls "the conquest elite" as "separate and unequal" ("Reenvisioning the Qing," 832).

74. Hua Li, "Cong qiren biancha baojia"; Zhang Qizhuo, *Manzu zai Xiuyan*, 6–7.

75. W. Wu, "Development and Decline," 103–4; Wakeman, *Great Enterprise*, 468.

76. Ma Xiedi, "Baqi zhidu," 32–33; R. Lee, *Manchurian Frontier*, 31; Jin Qicong, *Manzu de lishi*, 23–24; China, Baqi Dutong Yamen Archives, no. 4, "Qiwu," Shandong governor Zhang to the lieutenant-general of the Hanjun Bordered Red Banner, communication, GX 14/3/15.

77. Ding Yizhuang, *Qingdai Baqi zhufang*, 162–68; S. Chang, "Morphology of Walled Capitals," 92. For a slightly different typology of Manchu cities, see Elliott, "Resident Aliens," 132–42.

78. Jin Qicong, "Jingqi de Manzu," 1988, no. 3: 63–65; Wakeman, *Great Enterprise*, 477–79.

79. Ma Xiedi, "Qianlun Qingdai zhufang," 194. On Suiyuan and Urumqi, see Gaubatz, *Beyond the Great Wall*, 66–68, 71–74. On Qingzhou, see S. Chang, "Morphology of Walled Capitals," 92; Williamson, *Journeys in North China*, 1: 104. On Ningxia, see Huang Guangyun and Chen Jinming, "Ningxia minjun," 500.

80. On Kaifeng, see map in *Henan tongzhi*, 2: 2b-3a. On Zhenjiang, see Elliott, "Bannerman and Townsman," 37.

81. Elliott, "Resident Aliens," 133–39. On Jingzhou, see map at front of *Jingzhoufu zhi*. On Xi'an, see map in *Shina shōbetsu zenshi*, 7: 26. On Guangzhou, see Rhoads, "Merchant Associations," 98. On Nanjing, see *Jiangningfu zhi*, 3: 1b-2b; Spence, *God's Chinese Son*, 187. On Taiyuan, see *Yangquxian zhi*, 3: 2b-3a.

82. Wakeman, *Great Enterprise*, 477–79; Elliott, "Bannerman and Townsman," 43; idem, "Resident Aliens," 138–39.

83. Wakeman, *Great Enterprise*, 478 n. 158; Dai Xueji, *Huhehaote jianshi*, 59; Elliott, "Bannerman and Townsman," 43.

84. Jin Qicong, "Jingqi de Manzu," 1988, no. 3: 65; *Beijing mingsheng*, 154.

85. Ma Xiedi, "Qianlun Qingdai zhufang," 196; Wakeman, *Great Enterprise*, 478 n. 158; Rozman, *Urban Networks*, 291–92. See also Williamson, *Journeys in North China*, 2: 322.

86. Wang Jun, "1908-nian Beijing," 103; *Neige guanbao*, XT 3/7/25 and 7/26, 539–41.

87. Rozman, *Urban Networks*, 292–93; Wang Jun, "1908-nian Beijing," 103.

88. On Guangzhou, see Rhoads, "Merchant Associations," 97. On Xi'an, see Keyte, *Passing of the Dragon*, 113. On Chengdu, see Kendall, *Wayfarer in China*, 174.

89. Li Jieren, *Sishui weilan*, 211–12, as translated (with slight modifications) by Hu Zhihui in *Chinese Literature*, Dec. 1981, 29; for a map of the Manchu City, see Chen Yishi and Wang Duanyu, "Qingdai Chengdu," 78.

90. Chen Yishi and Wang Duanyu, "Qingdai Chengdu," 72, 75.

91. Wakeman, *Great Enterprise*, 469–71; Ma Feng-ch'en, "Manchu-Chinese Social and Economic Conflicts," 335–40.

92. Malone, *History of the Peking Summer Palaces*, 55–56; "Beijingshi Haidianqu Huoqiying," 89; *Manzu shehui lishi*, 226, 232; J. Lee and R. Eng, "Population and Family History," 8.

93. R. Lee, *Manchurian Frontier*, 78–79, 183. See also Edmonds, *Northern Frontiers*, 56–70.

94. Hosie, *Manchuria*, 211; R. Lee, *Manchurian Frontier*, 102; Edmonds, *Northern Frontiers*, 78–81; Zhao Zhongfu, "Qingdai Dongsansheng," 299.

95. Fletcher, "Sino-Russian Relations," 332–33.

96. R. Lee, *Manchurian Frontier*, 103, 119.

97. Zhang Qizhuo, *Manzu zai Xiuyan*, 83–85; Ding Yizhuang, *Qingdai Baqi zhufang*, 215–17. See also Zheng Tianting, *Tanweiji*, 59–61; Wang Zhonghan, "Qingdai Baqi," part 1: 42–45; Y. Yan, *Flow of Gifts*, 39.

98. Pan Honggang, "Xinhai Geming," 27; *Manzu shehui lishi*, 199–200; Franck, *Wandering in Northern China*, 374. See also Wang Zongyou, *Guangzhou Manzu*, 80–81. My thanks to Harry Lamley for drawing my attention to Wang's book and for making his copy of it available to me.

99. *Manzu shehui lishi*, 87; Zhang Qizhuo, *Manzu zai Xiuyan*, 7.

100. Chen Yishi and Wang Duanyu, "Qingdai Chengdu," 74; Bodde and Morris, *Law in Imperial China*, 96, 97, 351–52.

101. Wang Dezhao, *Qingdai keju zhidu*, 33, 39, 51–52; Shang Yanliu, *Qingdai keju kaoshi*, 54, 105; Huang Guangliang, *Qingdai keju zhidu*, 150–52. On Duanfang and Natong, see Wei Xiumei, *Qingji zhiguan biao*, "Renwulu," 39, 52.

102. Shang Yanliu, *Qingdai keju kaoshi*, 202–10; R. Chu and Saywell, *Career Patterns*, 49. See also Crossley, "Manchu Education," 351–52. On Fengshan, see Wei Xiumei, *Qingji zhiguan biao*, "Renwulu," 32.

103. Li Hong, "Qingdai bitieshi," 91; Chen Wenshi, "Qingdai de bitieshi," 69–72. On Fuqi, see Wei Xiumei, *Qingji zhiguan biao*, "Renwulu," 23. On Songshou, see Shang Binghe, *Xinren chunqiu*, 44: 1a.

104. On Ronglu, see Hummel, *Eminent Chinese*, 405; Liu Fenghan, *Wuweijun*, 23–31. On Zhao Erfeng, see *Qingdai renwu zhuan'gao*, 5: 98. On *yinsheng*, see Brunnert and Hagelstrom, *Present Day Political Organization*, no. 958.

105. MacKinnon, *Power and Politics*, 14–15; Hummel, *Eminent Chinese*, 950; Brunnert and Hagelstrom, *Present Day Political Organization*, no. 137A.

106. R. Chu and Saywell, *Career Patterns*, 49–50, 68.

107. Chen Wenshi, "Qingdai Manren," 551–53.

108. Fairbank, "Manchu-Chinese Dyarchy," 270; Zhang Deze, *Qingdai guojia jiguan*, 115–16.

109. Kessler, "Ethnic Composition," 493. See also Elliott, "Resident Aliens," 369.

110. Bartlett, *Monarchs and Ministers*, 35–41, 242, 374 n. 42. See also Sun, "Board of Revenue," 177–79.

111. Zhang Deze, *Qingdai guojia jiguan*, 6, 43; Brunnert and Hagelstrom, *Present Day Political Organization*, nos. 131–35, 288, 290–92; Chen Wenshi, "Qingdai Manren," 568, 570.

112. Li Hong, "Qingdai bitieshi"; Chen Wenshi, "Qingdai de bitieshi"; R. Chu and Saywell, *Career Patterns*, 52; Zhang Deze, *Qingdai guojia jiguan*, 43.

113. Chen Wenshi, "Qingdai Manren," 556–57; Zhang Deze, *Qingdai guojia jiguan*, 145–46. See also Ning, "Li-fan Yuan," 32–33.

114. Chen Wenshi, "Qingdai Manren," 572–75.

115. Ibid., 552; Zhang Qizhuo, *Manzu zai Xiuyan*, 7–8; R. Lee, *Manchurian Frontier*, 128–29.

116. Wei Xiumei, "Cong liang de . . . jiangjun dutong," 194; idem, "Cong liang de . . . fudutong," 396.

117. Kessler, "Ethnic Composition," 509; Li Guoqi and Zhou Tiansheng, "Qingdai jiceng difangguan," 302, 305. See also R. Chu and Saywell, *Career Patterns*, 38–39, 66.

118. Kessler, "Ethnic Composition," 509; Li Guoqi and Zhou Tiansheng, "Qingdai jiceng difangguan," 319.

119. *Manzu shehui lishi*, 87; Brunnert and Hagelstrom, *Present Day Political Organization*, no. 979; Elliott, "Bannerman and Townsman," 61–62 n. 120; Lui, *Hanlin Academy*, 109–10; Wei Xiumei, "Cong liang de . . . jiangjun dutong," 224; idem, "Cong liang de . . . fudutong," 427.

120. Kessler, "Ethnic Composition," 502; Zhang Deze, *Qingdai guojia jiguan*, 269.

121. Rhoads, "Self-Strengthening"; Wang Jiajian, *Zhongguo jindai haijun*, 216–21; Qian Shifu, *Qingji xinshe zhiguan*, 61.

122. Zheng Chuanshui, "Lun Qingchao de qixiang," 77–78; Luo Bingmian, "Zongli Yamen," 177; Guo Taifeng, "Baqi Lüying fengxiang," 107.

123. Yi Baozhong, "Shilun Qingdai Manzu," 29; Wang Zhonghan, "Qingdai qidi," 133; *Manzu shehui lishi*, 206.

124. Zheng Chuanshui, "Xinhai Geming," 34; R. Lee, *Manchurian Frontier*, 37; Zhao Zhongfu, "Qingdai Dongsansheng," 298–300.

125. Yang Shusen, *Qingdai liutiaobian*, 99; R. Lee, *Manchurian Frontier*, 79; *Manzu jianshi*, 150; Yi Baozhong, "Shilun Qingdai Manzu," 28; Li Guilian, *Shen Jiaben*, 111–12; Y. Yan, *Flow of Gifts*, 26. See also Zhao Zhongfu, "Qingdai Dongsansheng," 293–94.

126. Ma Xiedi, "Baqi zhidu," 32; Wang Zongyou, "Erbainianlai Guangzhou Manzu," 250; China, Huiyi Zhengwuchu Archives, *juan* 137, Beishou, memorial, GX 34/8/9.

127. W. Wu, "Development and Decline," chap. 6.

128. Ibid., chaps. 7–8; Zheng Chuanshui, "Lun Qingchao de qixiang," 78–80. On the eventual outcome of one resettlement program, see Y. Yan, *Flow of Gifts*, 24.

129. Wang Zongyou, "Erbainianlai Guangzhou Manzu," 252; Zheng Chuanshui, "Lun Qingchao de qixiang," 79. See also *Manzu shehui lishi*, 89.

130. Lao She, *Beneath the Red Banner*, 13, 31–32, 38, 39, 89.

131. Wu Wo-yao, "Bannerman at the Teahouse." See also Crossley, *Orphan Warriors*, 176–77.

132. Hosie, *Three Years in Western China*, 86–87; Kendall, *Wayfarer in China*, 174–75; Henry, *Ling-nam*, 46.

133. Muramatsu, "Banner Estates," 12–13; Jin Qicong, *Manzu de lishi*, 23–25; J. Lee and R. Eng, "Population and Family History," 12; *Manzu shehui lishi*, 92. For a conflicting view of the economic situation among the "frontier Manchus," see Rigger, "Voices of Manchu Identity," 199–201.

134. As translated by Oxnam, *Ruling from Horseback*, 36, but slightly modified.

135. For a fuller, and slightly different, discussion of the "Manchu Way," see Elliott, "Resident Aliens," 403–47.

136. Zhang Jie, "Qingdai dongbei Manzu," 31–32; Elliott, "Resident Aliens," 428–30; Zhang Guochang, "Manzu jiaoyu," 57–58; Lei Fangsheng, "Jingzhou qixue," 57.

137. Ch'en Chieh-hsien, "Decline of the Manchu Language," 139–40; *DFZZ* 4, no. 5: "Junshi," 33–34 (GX 33/5); Wang Zhonghan, "'Guoyu qishe,'" 197.

138. Wu Yuanfeng and Zhao Zhiqiang, "Xibozu you Keerqin Mengguqi," 66.

139. Ch'en Chieh-hsien, "Decline of the Manchu Language," 139–41; Hao and Liu, "Importance of the Archival Palace Memorials," 82; *Manzu jianshi*, 184–85; Li Lin, "Cong jiapu," 64; Lao She, *Beneath the Red Banner*, 50.

140. Williamson, *Journeys in North China*, 2: 39; Hosie, *Manchuria*, 26; Ch'en Chieh-hsien, "Decline of the Manchu Language," 143; Su Jing, *Qingji Tongwenguan*, 14, 125; *Yangwu yundong*, 3: 510. On the earlier history of Manchu as a "security language in military affairs," see Crossley and Rawski, "Profile of the Manchu Language," 70–71.

141. Aixin Jueluo Yingsheng, "Tantan Manzuren de xingming," 56–58. On the Suwan branch of the Gūwalgiya lineage, see Crossley, *Orphan Warriors*, 39–46.

142. Aixin Jueluo Yingsheng, "Tantan Manzuren de xingming," 56–59; Liu Qinghua, "Manzu xingshi," 69–70; Wang Huo, "Qingdai Baqi zhong Gaoliren," 47–49. On Duanfang's family name, see Hummel, *Eminent Chinese*, 780.

143. Spence, *Ts'ao Yin*, 18–27; Fang Zhaoying, *Qingmo Minchu yangxue*, 22–23, 69–72; Su Jing, *Qingji Tongwenguan*, 174–78.

144. Zhang Qizhuo, *Manzu zai Xiuyan*, 142.

145. Ch'en Chieh-hsien, "Sinification of Manchu Names," 5–12; Aixin Jueluo Yingsheng, "Tantan Manzuren de xingming," 59.

146. Zhang Qizhuo, *Manzu zai Xiuyan*, 142; Li Lin, "Cong jiapu," 67. See also He Puying, "Manzu Tatalashi jiapu," 49–50.

147. Zhang Qizhuo, *Manzu zai Xiuyan*, 142; Hummel, *Eminent Chinese*, 248.

148. Wang Zhonghan, "Qingdai Baqi," part 2: 60; Liu Qinghua, "Manzu xingshi,"

69; Ch'en Chieh-hsien, "Sinification of Manchu Names," 12–13. On the Niohuru clan and the transformation of their surname into Lang, see Hummel, *Eminent Chinese*, 221; Jin Qicong, "Jingqi de Manzu," 1989, no. 2: 68, 70.

149. Luo Bingmian, "Zongli Yamen," 167; Rong Tiegeng, "Qingdai Beijing," 36; Lei Fangsheng, "Jingzhou qixue," 59; Zhang Jing'ai, "Manzu de qishe," 72–73; Wang Dezhao, *Qingdai keju zhidu*, 52; Pan Honggang, "Xinhai Geming," 23.

150. Elliott, "Resident Aliens," 311–25; *Da-Qing huidian*, 87: 1a-1b; Zhang Jing'ai, "Manzu de qishe," 72; *Manzu shehui lishi*, 34, 213; Jin Qicong, *Manzu de lishi*, 25; R. Lee, *Manchurian Frontier*, 68.

151. Wang Zhonghan, "'Guoyu qishe,'" 198, 201–2; Cheng Changfu et al., "Mulan weichang," 27, 28; R. Lee, *Manchurian Frontier*, 68. See also Menzies, *Forest and Land Management*, chap. 3.

152. Lao She, *Beneath the Red Banner*, 24.

153. Fay, *Opium War*, 342–44, 352–53; Zhang Yutian, "Wan-Qing qiying," 56–58; *Manzu shehui lishi*, 192; Zou Shencheng, "Zhapu zhanyi"; Elliott, "Bannerman and Townsman," 46–63; Waley, *Opium War*, 197–221; Jin Qicong, *Manzu de lishi*, 26.

154. Jen, *Taiping Revolutionary Movement*, 118, 371–72, 436, 442; Crossley, *Orphan Warriors*, 128–38; Zhang Yutian, "Wan-Qing qiying," 59–60.

155. Zhang Yutian, "Wan Qing qiying," 60–61; R. Lee, *Manchurian Frontier*, 116–17; Ma Xiedi, "Zhufang Baqi," 23; *Qingmo choubei lixian*, 937.

156. Kuwabara, "Zhongguo bianfa shi"; Wakeman, *Great Enterprise*, 648–50; Struve, *Southern Ming*, 60–63; Ye Hao, "Cong 'changmao,'" 50; Hummel, *Eminent Chinese*, 95; Kuhn, "Political Crime," 88 n. 28; Naquin and Rawski, *Chinese Society*, 82. On the Turks, see Millward, "Beyond the Pass," 271–75. My thanks to Don Sutton for the information about the Miao and to Robert Entenmann for making available to me two of his unpublished papers on the history of the queue. For a recent study of the queue, see Godley, "The End of the Queue."

157. See, for example, the preface to Hu Yunyu, "Fa shi," 449–50.

158. Zheng Tianting, *Tanweiji*, 83; Struve, *Southern Ming*, 63; Zhou Xibao, *Zhongguo gudai fushi*, 378–413; Garrett, *Chinese Clothing*, 11–14.

159. Zheng Tianting, *Tanweiji*, 83; Zhou Xibao, *Zhongguo gudai fushi*, 449–84; Garrett, *Chinese Clothing*, 31–32, 42–45, 65–74; Scott, *Chinese Costume*, 5.

160. Zheng Tianting, *Tanweiji*, 84–87; Huang Zhangjian, *Wuxu bianfa shi*, 365. My thanks to Huang Zhangjian for locating the Liu Zhenyu reference.

161. Vollmer, *Decoding Dragons*, 15–16; Garrett, *Chinese Clothing*, 76–79; Wang Yunying, "Shilun Qing ruguan qian," 74.

162. Fairbank and Teng, "On the Types and Uses," 45–54; Ch'en Chieh-hsien, "Decline of the Manchu Language," 137, 141. See also Crossley and Rawski, "Profile of the Manchu Language," 65–80, 91.

163. Lui, *Hanlin Academy*, 66–67; Crossley and Rawski, "Profile of the Manchu Language," 84–85; Waley, *Opium War*, 12.

164. Aixin Jueluo Yingsheng, "Manyu he Hanyu"; Guan Jixin and Meng Xianren, "Manzu yu Shenyangyu, Beijingyu"; Wadley, "Altaic Influences."

165. Scott, *Chinese Costume*, 29–33; Zhou Xibao, *Zhongguo gudai fushi*, 484–504; Garrett, *Mandarin Squares*, 30; and idem, *Chinese Clothing*, 56–61, 84–93.

166. *Qingmo choubei lixian*, 952; *SL/XT*, 30: 25b-26a.

167. Jin Qicong, *Manzu de lishi*, 35.

168. *Qingmo choubei lixian*, 952; Crossley, *Manchus*, 145; Cao Xueqin, *Story of the Stone*, 186, 203.

169. *SL/GX*, 412: 14a-15b. See also Pomerantz-Zhang, *Wu Tingfang*, 104.

170. *Wuxu bianfa*, 3: 181–83; Tang Zhijun, *Wuxu bianfa renwu*, 347–48. See also Pusey, *China and Charles Darwin*, 116–17.

171. *Wuxu bianfa*, 3: 181–83; Tang Zhijun, *Wuxu bianfa renwu*, 347–49, 688. See also Pusey, *China and Charles Darwin*, 116–17; Crossley, *Orphan Warriors*, 166–67.

172. *Wuxu bianfa*, 3: 200–201; Wang Ermin, "Duanfa yifu gaiyuan," 60–62.

173. Huang Zhangjian's comments on the paper by Wang Ermin, in *Zhongguo jindai de weixin yundong*, 88; Kwong, *Mosaic of the Hundred Days*, 192–94.

174. *Wuxu bianfa*, 2: 227–30, 237–40, 263–65.

175. *Wuxu bianfa dang'an*, 44–45. On Zhang Yuanji, see Tang Zhijun, *Wuxu bianfa renwu*, 245–51; Wu Fang, *Renzhi de shanshui*.

176. *SL/GX*, 425: 22a-22b. On Yuan Chang, see Hummel, *Eminent Chinese*, 945–48.

177. Lao She, *Beneath the Red Banner*, 58 (with slight modification); idem, *Teahouse*, 18.

178. See also Crossley, *Manchus*, 7–8.

179. Powell, *Rise of Chinese Military Power*, 56.

2 / CIXI AND THE "PECULIAR INSTITUTION"

1. *SL/GX*, 427: 12a; 428: 6b, 7a; Tang Zhijun, *Wuxu bianfa renwu*, 248; Hummel, *Eminent Chinese*, 947.

2. *SL/GX*, 430: 20b-21a.

3. Ibid., 432: 11b-12b; 444: 1a-1b; Powell, *Rise of Chinese Military Power*, 102–3; Liu Fenghan, *Wuweijun*, 67, 86–88, 335–45; idem, *Yuan Shikai*, 108.

4. Hummel, *Eminent Chinese*, 393–94; Bays, *China Enters*, 64–65. See also Chung, "Much Maligned Empress Dowager," 190–96.

5. Headland, *Court Life*, 161–63.

6. Crossley, *Orphan Warriors*, 174–75; Malone, *History of the Peking Summer Palaces*, 208; Duiker, *Cultures in Collision*, 103, 116.

7. *SSJY*, 1900–1901: 272; Liu Fenghan, *Wuweijun*, 752–54.

8. Gan Haifeng, *Lao She nianpu*, 1–2; Tang Zhijun, *Wuxu bianfa renwu*, 349.

9. Tan, *Boxer Catastrophe*, 159–61; *SSJY*, 1900–1901: 237–38, 354, 363, 369; Shiro-kogoroff, *Social Organization*, 4.

10. *SL/GX*, 468: 3a-3b; *SSJY*, 1900–1901: 357, 395, 467. On Yinchang, see Su Jing, *Qingji Tongwenguan*, 171–72.

11. *SL/GX*, 470: 1b-2a; 477: 9b-11a; 488: 11b-12b; Tan, *Boxer Catastrophe*, 216–22.

12. Dai Xueji, *Huhehaote jianshi*, 75–79.

13. *SL/GX*, 477: 11a-11b.

14. Zaifeng, "Chun qinwang"; Hummel, *Eminent Chinese*, 385.

15. Tan, *Boxer Catastrophe*, 236.

16. *SL/GX*, 476: 8a-10b.

17. *SL/GX*, 481: 4b-5a; Zhang Deze, *Qingji guojia jiguan*, 282.

18. *SL/GX*, 476: 8b-9a; 530: 4b; Wu Fang, *Renzhi de shanshui*, 82.

19. Morrison, *Correspondence*, 155–56; Bays, *China Enters*, 103.

20. Zhang Zhidong, *Zhang Wenxiang gong*, 53: 22a-24a; Bays, *China Enters*, 108.

21. Zhang Bingduo, *Zhang Zhidong*, 273.

22. Zhou Fu, *Zhou Queshen gong*, "Zougao," 2: 41a.

23. Zhang Bingduo, *Zhang Zhidong*, 273.

24. *SL/GX*, 492: 9b.

25. *Beijing nübao*, GX 33/3/15, 2; *NCH*, 12 July 1907, 79–80; 30 May 1908, 545; *DFZZ* 2, no. 1: "Shiping," 6 (GX 31/1). On Li Guojie, see Wei Xiumei, *Qingji zhiguan biao*, "Renwulu," 60.

26. R. Lee, *Manchurian Frontier*, 140–41; Wei Xiumei, *Qingji zhiguan biao*, 960, 1057; idem, "Cong liang de . . . fudutong," 427.

27. *SL/GX*, 553: 3b; 564: 18a-18b; Gongsun Hong, *Feng Guozhang nianpu*, 7; *Manzu shehui lishi*, 85.

28. *Manzu jianshi*, 150; Yi Baozhong, "Shilun Qingdai Manzu," 28.

29. *Manzu shehui lishi*, 209; *Manzu jianshi*, 150–51.

30. R. Lee, *Manchurian Frontier*, 152–55; *Beijing nübao*, GX 33/3/23, 3.

31. Zhang Deze, *Qingdai guojia jiguan*, 282–84, 287–88; Brunnert and Hagelstrom, *Present Day Political Organization*, no. 305.

32. *Guangxu zhengyao*, 31: 67a-69a.

33. Wei Xiumei, *Qingji zhiguan biao*, 487–97.

34. *Qingmo choubei lixian*, 597; Fu Zongmao, *Qingdai junjichu*, 184; Bartlett, *Monarchs and Ministers*, 144–48, 238, 373 n. 28.

35. Zhang Deze, *Qingdai guojia jiguan*, 22; Hummel, *Eminent Chinese*, 380; China, Junjichu Lufu Zouzhe, "Nongmin yundong lei," *juan* 1696, no. 10, Liu Tingchen, memorial, XT 3/9/8; Qian Shifu, *Qingji zhongyao zhiguan*, 54–72. Rawski, *The Last Emperors*, takes no notice of this mid-Qing tradition.

36. Qian Shifu, *Qingji zhongyao zhiguan*, 47–50. On Shiduo, see Hummel, *Eminent Chinese*, 80; and "Qingmo bufen Baqi dutong," 37.

37. Qian Shifu, *Qingji zhongyao zhiguan*, 72–98; idem, *Qingji xinshe zhiguan*, 1–13, 61.

38. Qian Shifu, *Qingji zhongyao zhiguan*, 50; Hummel, *Eminent Chinese*, 385.

39. Zhang Deze, *Qingdai guojia jiguan*, 283; Qian Shifu, *Qingji zhongyao zhiguan*, 99–104; idem, *Qingji xinshe zhiguan*, 30–32. On Zaizhen, see *Qingdai renwu zhuan'gao*, 9: 157–61. Contrary to Qian Shifu, Yulang (the senior vice-minister of police in 1905) was not then an imperial prince. The son of a second-rank prince, Yulang did not inherit his father's princedom, on a descending scale, as a prince of the third rank, until the latter's death in 1907; meanwhile, he was only a noble of the ninth rank. On Yulang, see Hummel, *Eminent Chinese*, 729; Tahara, *Shinmatsu Minsho*, 653.

40. *SL/GX*, 532: 15a; *DFZZ* 2, no. 4: "Neiwu," 62–63 (GX 31/4); *Donghualu*, 5684–85; 5699.

41. Crossley, *Orphan Warriors*, 175; *Beijing nübao*, GX 33/7/16; *Manzu shehui lishi*, 93.

42. *DFZZ* 1, no. 2: "Shiye," 18 (GX 30/2); 1, no. 6: "Shiye," 95 (GX 30/6); 2, no. 12: "Junshi," 384 (GX 31/12); Zhou Fu, *Zhou Queshen gong*, "Zougao," 2: 40b.

43. Duanfang, *Duan Zhongmin gong*, 4: 44a; 8: 55b; 11: 25a; *DFZZ* 2, no. 12: "Junshi," 385 (GX 31/12); 4, no. 9: "Zazu," 21 (GX 33/9); *NCH*, 20 Sept. 1907, 676; 18 Oct., 152; 1 Nov., 276.

44. *DFZZ* 1, no. 9: "Shiye," 160 (GX 30/9); 3, no. 8: "Shiye," 169 (GX 32/7); Duanfang, *Duan Zhongmin gong*, 7: 12a–12b; Zheng Chuanshui, "Lun Qingchao de qixiang," 80.

45. Liu Fenghan, *Wuweijun*, 461–62; MacKinnon, *Power and Politics*, 129; Yuan Shikai, *Yuan Shikai zouzhe*, 319–20; *DFZZ* 2, no. 4: "Junshi," 146–48 (GX 31/4); Wu Zhaoqing, "Yuan Shikai," 105–6.

46. *SL/GX*, 507: 6b–7a; Powell, *Rise of Chinese Military Power*, 140–43.

47. Yuan Shikai, *Yangshouyuan zouyi*, 21: 4b–5a.

48. *Zhongguo jindaishi cidian*, 582; Tahara, *Shinmatsu Minsho*, 793; Zha Shijie, "Qingmo de Zongshedang," 132; MacKinnon, *Power and Politics*, 78; Fang Zhaoying, *Qingmo Minchu yangxue*, 48; *Saishin Shina*, 392.

49. *SL/GX*, 515: 5a; Zhang Deze, *Qingdai guojia jiguan*, 289; Powell, *Rise of Chinese Military Power*, 166–67; Fung, *Military Dimension*, 36–38.

50. Tahara, *Shinmatsu Minsho*, 793; Guo Tingyi, *Jindai Zhongguo shishi*, 1188; Gongsun Hong, *Feng Guozhang nianpu*, 6.

51. Yuan Shikai, *Yangshouyuan zouyi*, 21: 4b–5a; Fung, *Military Dimension*, 21–22; MacKinnon, *Power and Politics*, 100; Morrison, *Correspondence*, 202; *DFZZ* 1, no. 1: "Zazu," 1 (GX 30/1).

52. *SL/GX*, 525: 8b; 532: 13b–14a; Powell, *Rise of Chinese Military Power*, 204–9; *DFZZ* 2, no. 8: "Zazu," 59 (GX 31/8); 2, no. 12: "Junshi," 386–87 (GX 31/12); Wen Gongzhi, *Zuijin sanshinian*, "Junshi," 3–4; *Guangxu zhengyao*, 31: 69a–72b.

53. Fung, *Military Dimension*, 33; USDS, Numerical File, 2106/2–5, undated report, "The Chinese Army," 170–73; Yuan, *Yangshouyuan zouyi*, 41: 2a-8a.

54. Fung, *Military Dimension*, 26; *DFZZ* 1, no. 12: "Junshi," 452 (GX 30/12).

55. Zhang Bofeng and Li Zongyi, *Beiyang junfa*, 1: 91; USDS, Numerical File, 1518/38–29, Rockhill to State, 7 Feb. 1907; Fung, *Military Dimension*, 33. On Cao Kun, see *Minguo renwu zhuan*, 1: 172. On Wang Tingzhen and He Zonglian, see Tahara, *Shinmatsu Minsho*, 35–36, 196. On all three, see Zhang Bofeng and Li Zongyi, *Beiyang junfa*, 5: 370–71, 442, 518–19.

56. *Donghualu*, 5429–32; Zhang Bofeng and Li Zongyi, *Beiyang junfa*, 1: 91–92.

57. *DFZZ* 1, no. 1: "Zazu," 1 (GX 30/1); China, Baqi Dutong Yamen Archives, "Jiaoyu," file no. 698, communications from the Banner Duty Office to the Hanjun Bordered Red Banner, GX 29/7/— and from Tieliang to the lieutenant-general of the Hanjun Bordered Red Banner, GX 29/7/4.

58. Fung, *Military Dimension*, 63–66; *DFZZ* 1, no. 12: "Jiaoyu," 274–79 (GX 30/12); 2, no. 6: "Jiaoyu," 109–23 (GX 31/6); Guo Fengming, *Qingmo Minchu lujun*, 78–86.

59. *SL/GX*, 540: 8a; *Donghualu*, 5300–5301.

60. China, Baqi Dutong Yamen Archives, "Jiaoyu," file no. 698, memorial from Office of Military Training and Board of War, GX 32/+4/1, enclosed in communication from Banner Duty Office to the Manchu Bordered Yellow Banner, GX 32/+4/—; *DFZZ* 2, no. 12: "Jiaoyu," 321–32 (GX 31/12); 3, no. 6: "Zazu," 32 (GX 32/5); *SL/GX*, 549: 13a-13b; 553: 3b; *SL/XT*, 28: 2a-2b; Brunnert and Hagelstrom, *Present Day Political Organization*, no. 713a. On Feng's background, see "Feng Guozhang zaoqi lüli."

61. Fung, *Military Dimension*, 69–70; *DFZZ* 2, no. 12: "Jiaoyu," 321–32 (GX 31/12); *ZZGB*, XT 1/9/4, 5–7.

62. *DFZZ* 1, no. 4: "Jiaoyu," 97–101 (GX 30/4); Shu Xincheng, *Jindai Zhongguo liuxue*, 56–64; Fung, *Military Dimension*, 71–72.

63. Shu Xincheng, *Jindai Zhongguo liuxue*, 63–64; Guo Fengming, *Qingmo Minchu lujun*, 72–73; *DFZZ* 2, no. 12: "Jiaoyu," 348 (GX 31/12).

64. *SL/GX*, 483: 8a; 494: 13a-13b; 498: 8a; Han Yanlong and Su Yigong, *Zhongguo jindai jingcha*, 80–101; Hunt, "Forgotten Occupation," 513–14; Morrison, *Correspondence*, 614.

65. Strand, *Rickshaw Beijing*, 69–70; *DFZZ* 1, no. 10: "Neiwu," 135–36 (GX 30/10); 3, no. 8: "Junshi," 134–35 (GX 32/7).

66. *SL/GX*, 498: 8a, 9a; Bai Jie, "Qingmo zhengtan," 36–37. On Shanqi, see *Aixin Jueluo jiazu*, 3: 213–14; on his ancestry, see Hummel, *Eminent Chinese*, 280–81.

67. *SL/GX*, 524: 2a; 525: 8b; Shen Yunlong, *Xu Shichang*, 24. On Natong, see "Qing Waiwubu," 42. On Yulang, see "Xunjingbu zhuyao guanyuan," 63, 79.

68. Strand, *Rickshaw Beijing*, 67; Shen Yunlong, *Xu Shichang*, 24; *Zhongyang jingguan xuexiao*, 11, 17–20; Jansen, *Japanese and Sun Yat-sen*, 138; Han Yanlong and Su Yigong, *Zhongguo jindai jingcha*, 233–38; Wang Jiajian, *Qingmo Minchu woguo jingcha*, 28, 46, 242; "Youguan Chuandao Langsu."

69. Jansen, *Japanese and Sun Yat-sen*, 138; Bai Jie, "Qingmo zhengtan," 37; Shen Yunlong, *Xu Shichang*, 24; "Youguan Chuandao Langsu," 67–68. See photograph in Reynolds, *China, 1898–1912*, 166, where Shanqi is misidentified as Yikuang.

70. Wang Jiajian, *Qingmo Minchu woguo jingcha*, 29, 242–43; Fang Zhaoying, *Qingmo Minchu yangxue*, 22–24; *Subao*, 12 June 1903, 1–2. On the Kōbun Institute, see Harrell, *Sowing the Seeds*, 34; Huang Fu-ch'ing, *Chinese Students*, 103–5.

71. Sang Bing, "Guimao yuanri," 75–76; Yang Tianshi and Wang Xuezhuang, *Ju-E yundong*, 127–28; Chen Tianhua, *Chen Tianhua ji*, 157. See also Rankin, "Manchurian Crisis."

72. Sang Bing, "Guimao yuanri," 76; Zhang Pengyuan, *Lixianpai*, 320; Shen Yunlong, *Xu Shichang*, 24.

73. "Youguan Chuandao Langsu," 69–70; Wang Jiajian, *Qingmo Minchu woguo jingcha*, 46; *Zhongyang jingguan xuexiao*, 20–23.

74. Han Yanlong and Su Yigong, *Zhongguo jindai jingcha*, 110–19.

75. Fung, *Military Dimension*, 34.

76. *DFZZ* 1, no. 4: "Junshi," 183 (GX 30/4); *Guangxu Zhengyao*, 31: 10b-11a; Fung, *Military Dimension*, 115. See also Su Yunfeng, "Hubei xinjun," 373; Su, however, estimates that the garrison provided only 4 percent of the Hubei Standing Army in 1905.

77. *DFZZ* 1, no. 12: "Jiaoyu," 275–76 (GX 30/12); 2, no. 6: "Jiaoyu," 109–11 (GX 31/6); 4, no. 9: "Jiaoyu," 204–7 (GX 33/9). On the Jingzhou school, see also Lei Fangsheng, "Jingzhou qixue," 58–59; and Zhou Wuyi, "Lujun disan zhongxue," 11.

78. *DFZZ* 1, no. 7: "Jiaoyu," 159 (GX 30/7); *Saishin Shina*, 392–93; Fang Zhaoying, *Qingmo Minchu yangxue*, 8–9, 48–49.

79. *DFZZ* 1, no. 4: "Jiaoyu," 98 (GX 30/4); 2, no. 12: "Jiaoyu," 348 (GX 31/12).

80. *DFZZ* 2, no. 1: "Zazu," 10 (GX 31/1); 2, no. 10: "Neiwu," 201 (GX 31/10); 3, no. 4: "Neiwu," 105 (GX 32/4); Fang Zhaoying, *Qingmo Minchu yangxue*, 24.

81. *SL/GX*, 546: 11a-11b; *Donghualu*, 5431.

82. *DFZZ* 4, no. 5: "Junshi," 28–30 (GX 33/5); 4, no. 7: "Junshi," 63–65 (GX 33/7); *Beijing nübao*, GX 34/2/21, 2; 3/1, 4.

83. Morrison, *Correspondence*, 345.

84. *SL/GX*, 493: 9b; Zhuang Jifa, *Jingshi Daxuetang*, 138; Brunnert and Hagelstrom, *Present Day Political Organization*, no. 717a; *DFZZ* 1, no. 10: "Jiaoyu," 235 (GX 30/10); *Beijing nübao*, GX 31/10/25, 3.

85. *DFZZ* 2, no. 6: "Jiaoyu," 157 (GX 31/6); 3, no. 12: "Jiaoyu," 369 (GX 32/11).

86. *SL/GX*, 493: 9b-10a.

87. Duanfang, *Duan Zhongmin gong*, 3: 27a-29a, 60a-61b; *DFZZ* 1, no. 7: "Jiaoyu," 157–59 (GX 30/7); Lei Fangsheng, "Jingzhou qixue," 58.

88. *DFZZ* 3, no. 3: "Jiaoyu," 55 (GX 32/3).

89. Biggerstaff, *Earliest Modern Government Schools*, 136–39; Zhuang Jifa, *Jingshi*

Daxuetang, 28–29, 81–82, 138, 167–95; Fang Zhaoying, *Qingmo Minchu yangxue*, 69–139, 145–53.

90. Fang Zhaoying, *Qingmo Minchu yangxue*, 26, 136–39; *DFZZ* 2, no. 6: "Jiaoyu," 101–3 (GX 31/6); Chou, "Frontier Studies," 298.

91. *Beijing nübao*, GX 34/1/21, 1–2; 1/22, 2; 1/26, 2–3; 11/1, 1–2.

92. Duanfang, *Duan Zhongmin gong*, 7: 21b.

93. *DFZZ* 3, no. 5: "Jiaoyu," 103–4 (GX 32/+4); *Beijing nübao*, GX 32/3/22, 3; Crossley, *Orphan Warriors*, 195; Zheng Yunshan et al., *Hangzhou yu Xihu*, 93–94.

94. Jinliang, *Guang-Xuan xiaoji*, 100; *Beijing nübao*, GX 33/3/24, 4; 3/29, 1–2; *Shibao*, 10 Nov. 1915, 2; Zheng Yunshan et al., *Hangzhou yu Xihu*, 94.

95. Beahan, "Feminism and Nationalism," 408–10.

96. *Beijing nübao*, GX 31/10/18.

97. Ibid., GX 34/5/15, 1–2; 5/16, 1–2.

98. Beahan, "Feminism and Nationalism," 408–9; *Beijing nübao*, GX 34/10/27, 1.

99. Ding Shouhe, *Xinhai Geming shiqi*, 5: 1–32; Boorman and Howard, *Biographical Dictionary*, 4: 56–58; Britton, *Chinese Periodical Press*, 117; Zhao Shu, "Xinhai Geming qianhou," 16.

100. China, Baqi Dutong Yamen Archives, "Jiaoyu," file no. 698, Banner Duty Office to the Manchu Bordered Red Banner, GX 34/5/—; *Beijing nübao*, GX 33/6/18, 3; *DFZZ* 4, no. 11: "Jiaoyu," 256–57 (GX 33/11).

101. Lei Fangsheng, "Jingzhou qixue," 58.

102. *DFZZ* 4, no. 9: "Jiaoyu," 202–3 (GX 33/9); 4, no. 11: "Jiaoyu," 256–57 (GX 33/11); Wang Di, "Qingmo xinzheng," 258.

103. *DFZZ* 4, no. 5: "Junshi," 33–34 (GX 33/5).

104. Bays, *China Enters*, 127–28. As Bays points out, the text of this memorial has not been located.

105. Zhang Jian, "Seweng ziding nianpu," 58; Zhang Yufa, *Qingji de lixian tuanti*, 311–12. On contacts between Zhang Jian and Tieliang, see S. Chu, *Reformer in Modern China*, 61, 65.

106. *SL/GX* 546: 8a, 15a. On Shaoying, see Wei Xiumei, *Qingji zhiguan biao*, "Renwulu," 188. On Zaize, see *Qingdai renwu zhuan'gao*, 9: 192–97.

107. *XHGM*, 2: 382–85, 432; *Minguo renwu zhuan*, 2: 46–49; Feng Ziyou, *Geming yishi*, 3: 197–204.

108. *DFZZ* 2, no. 12: "Zazu," 77 (GX 31/12).

109. Wang Jiajian, *Qingmo Minchu woguo jingcha*, 35–38; *Minguo renwu zhuan*, 2: 182; Brunnert and Hagelstrom, *Present Day Political Organization*, nos. 339, 501.

110. *SL/GX*, 550: 16b–17b.

111. Hou Yijie, *Ershi shiji chu*, 59–60; Sun, "Chinese Constitutional Missions," 253–57; Pan Chongxiong, "Duanfang yu yubei lixian," 433–36.

112. Sun, "Chinese Constitutional Missions," 260–62.

113. *DFZZ*, special issue, "Zouyi," 4–7 (GX 32/12). (In the bound reprint edition, this issue is misplaced at the end of vol. 5, after the GX 34/12 issue.)

114. *XHGM*, 4: 39–47; Guo Tingyi, *Jindai Zhongguo shishi*, 1258. This important memorial, curiously, does not appear in the volume of Duanfang's collected memorials.

115. *SL/GX*, 562: 4b, 8a-9b; Guo Tingyi, *Jindai Zhongguo shishi*, 1248, 1257; Sun, "Chinese Constitutional Missions," 266.

116. *SL/GX*, 562: 9b-10a.

117. Li Jiannong, *Zuijin sanshinian*, 121; Zhang Yufa, *Qingji de lixian tuanti*, 313. See also Pan Chongxiong, "Duanfang yu yubei lixian," 438–39.

118. *Donghualu*, 5559–61.

119. *SL/GX*, 564: 11b-14a.

120. *SL/GX*, 564: 14b-15a. On Shixu, see *Qingdai renwu zhuan'gao*, 9: 198–201.

121. Zhang Deze, *Qingdai guojia jiguan*, 291–95.

122. *SL/GX*, 564: 15b-16a; Qian Shifu, *Qingji zhongyao zhiguan*, 105. At least one source, Lao Li, *Nucai xiaoshi*, 14b, claims that Lu Chuanlin (at Personnel) was a Hanjun. This may explain why a number of accounts (e.g., Hummel, *Eminent Chinese*, 299) assert that nine, not eight, of the thirteen ministry heads were bannermen. However, other, more authoritative sources, including *Qingshigao*, 438: 12387, state that Lu Chuanlin was a native of Zhili and say nothing about his being a Hanjun.

123. *Minbao*, no. 10 (20 Dec. 1906): 57–65.

124. MacKinnon, *Power and Politics*, 81–82, 114; Li Zongyi, *Yuan Shikai zhuan*, 152.

125. Powell, *Rise of Chinese Military Power*, 216; MacKinnon, *Power and Politics*, 82, 114–15.

126. *ZZGB*, XT 2/8/25, 8–9; *DFZZ* 4, no. 1: "Zazu," 1 (GX 33/1).

127. Zhang Bofeng and Li Zongyi, *Beiyang junfa*, 1: 92.

128. MacKinnon, *Power and Politics*, 82–89.

129. *SL/GX*, 571: 13a; China, Junjichu Xianzheng Zhuanti, no. 144, Yuan Shikai, memorandum enclosed in memorial, GX 33/6/19; Hou Yijie, *Yuan Shikai*, 93–94; Powell, *Rise of Chinese Military Power*, 218, 251–52; *DFZZ* 4, no. 11: "Zazu," 27 (GX 33/11).

130. Hou Yijie, *Yuan Shikai*, 94; *DFZZ* 4, no. 11: "Zazu," 28 (GX 33/11); *SL/GX*, 575: 18a; 581: 15b-16a; Zhang Bofeng and Li Zongyi, *Beiyang junfa*, 1: 92–93; Powell, *Rise of Chinese Military Power*, 250; *NCH*, 8 Nov. 1907, 353; MacKinnon, *Power and Politics*, 116.

131. *Minguo renwu zhuan*, 1: 58–61; Rankin, *Early Chinese Revolutionaries*, 147–48, 164–71, 178–85; Wang Daorui, "Xinfaxian."

132. Ding Shouhe, *Xinhai Geming shiqi*, 5: 8.

133. *Qingshigao*, 469: 12783–84.

134. Feng Ziyou, *Geming yishi*, 5: 85–87.

135. *Beijing nübao*, GX 33/6/13, 3.

136. FO 405/175, no. 80, Jordan to Grey, 20 Aug. 1907; no. 85, Jordan to Grey, 21 Aug.;

USDS, Numerical File, 215/66–67, Rockhill to State, 9 Aug. 1907. On the lingering effect on Duanfang's nerves of Wu Yue's bombing, see Morrison, *Correspondence*, 624, 721; and *Beijing nübao*, GX 33/7/4, 5.

137. *Beijing nübao*, GX 33/7/10, 3; *NCH*, 23 Aug. 1907, 431.

138. *SL/GX*, 574: 8a-8b.

139. China, Junjichu Xianzheng Zhuanti, no. 144, Yuan Shikai, memorandum enclosed in memorial, GX 33/6/19; *SL/GX*, 575: 16a-17a. This long and important memorial does not appear in Yuan's collected memorials (*Yangshouyuan zouyi*) or in the documentary collection *Qingmo choubei lixian*.

140. *Qingmo choubei lixian*, 915–18; Duanfang, *Duan Zhongmin gong*, 8: 37b-41a.

141. Zhang Zhidong, *Zhang Wenxiang gong*, 85: 35b-36b; Hu Jun, *Zhang Wenxiang gong nianpu*, 6: 5b-6a.

142. *SL/GX*, 575: 19a; Wu Tianren, *Liang Jiean*, 223–25.

143. *SL/GX*, 576: 1a-1b.

144. *Qingmo choubei lixian*, 257.

145. For a slightly more detailed analysis of the various reform proposals, see Rhoads, "Assassination of Governor Enming," 10–19 .

146. *Qingmo choubei lixian*, 916, 919–21, 938.

147. Ibid., 916, 952, 954.

148. Ibid., 917, 921–22.

149. Ibid., 940–42.

150. Ibid., 257, 926–31, 948–49.

151. Ibid., 937–38.

152. Ibid., 943–44. On Xiong Xiling, see Boorman and Howard, *Biographical Dictionary*, 2: 108–10.

153. *Qingmo choubei lixian*, 939–40, 946–48.

154. *DFZZ* 2, no. 1: "Zazu," 7 (GX 31/1); 3, no. 2: "Neiwu," 79 (GX 32/2); 4, no. 7: "Neiwu," 347–48 (GX 33/7); Morrison, *Correspondence*, 354; *Beijing nübao*, GX 32/3/29.

155. *DFZZ* 4, no. 7: "Sheshuo," 117–19 (GX 33/7).

156. *Beijing nübao*, GX 33/7/14, 2.

157. Ding Shouhe, *Xinhai Geming shiqi*, 2: 518–33; *Datongbao*, 1: 19 (GX 33/5/15); Yang Du, *Yang Du ji*, 411; Tahara, *Shinmatsu Minsho*, 304, 382.

158. *Datongbao*, 1: 13–21 (GX 33/5/15).

159. Yang Du, *Yang Du ji*, 411–12; Ding Shouhe, *Xinhai Geming shiqi*, 2: 518–19; Zhang Yufa, *Qingji de lixian tuanti*, 370–73.

160. *Datongbao*, 1: 20 (GX 33/5/15).

161. Ibid., 5: 4–5 (GX 33/11/28).

162. Ibid., 1: 76, 90 (GX 33/5/15).

163. Ibid., 1: 19, 97–99 (GX 33/5/15); 5: 7–9 (GX 33/11/28).

164. Ibid., 1: 100 (GX 33/5/15).

165. Yang Du, *Yang Du ji*, 435–59.

166. *Datongbao*, 1: 55 (GX 33/5/15); 5: 1–3 (GX 33/11/28). On Qianlong's self-image as ruler of a multiethnic empire, see Millward, "Beyond the Pass," 268–71; Zhang Yuxin, "Qingdai qianqi ge minzu," 35–37. My thanks to Evelyn Rawski for drawing my attention to Millward's study.

167. Qian Shifu, *Qingji xinshe zhiguan*, 54.

168. Guo Tingyi, *Jindai Zhongguo shishi*, 1282, 1284, 1286, 1288. See also Bays, *China Enters*, 190–92.

169. Wei Xiumei, *Qingji zhiguan biao*, 60.

170. *NCH*, 30 Aug. 1907, 520.

171. *SL/GX*, 578: 4b-5b; 579: 2a.

172. *DFZZ* 4, no. 7: "Neiwu," 347–52 (GX 33/7).

173. *SL/GX*, 577: 11b; 579: 14b-15a.

174. *NCH*, 18 Oct. 1907, 153; 22 Nov., 445; 20 Dec., 720.

175. Qian Shifu, *Qingji zhongyao zhiguan*, 106.

176. Ibid., 51.

3 / ZAIFENG AND THE "MANCHU ASCENDENCY"

1. *SL/GX*, 578: 7b; *ZZGB*, GX 33/10/28, 9–10; 34/6/29, 11–13; FO 405/182, no. 166, Jordan to Grey, 4 June 1908, summary of events for May 1908.

2. *SL/GX*, 578: 7b-8a; 581: 10b-11a; *ZZGB*, GX 33/12/18, 6–7.

3. *ZZGB*, GX 33/11/30, 10–11; 34/2/21, 12–14; 3/26, 6–8; 4/30, 12–13; 8/6, 5–6; 8/22, 5–8; China, Huiyi Zhengwuchu Archives, *juan* 149, no. 1059, General Chuohabu, memorial, GX 34/2/21.

4. China, Huiyi Zhengwuchu Archives, *juan* 149, no. 1059, General Chuohabu, memorial, GX 34/2/21; *ZZGB*, GX 33/10/12, 10–12; 34/8/22, 5–8.

5. *ZZGB*, GX 33/10/10, 5–9; 12/22, 14–15.

6. Ibid., GX 33/12/19, 8–10; 12/22, 14–15.

7. Ibid., GX 33/11/1, 7–12; 34/4/24, 5–6; *SL/GX*, 581: 16b.

8. *ZZGB*, GX 33/10/28, 9–11; 11/26, 11–13; 12/26, 14–15; 34/4/30, 12–13.

9. Ibid., GX 33/11/1, 7–12; 34/3/6, 5–7; 4/24, 5–6.

10. *DFZZ* 5, no. 10: "Jizai," 115 (GX 34/10).

11. On the Commissioners for Revising and Codifying the Laws, see Brunnert and Hagelstrom, *Present Day Political Organization*, no. 174; Qian Shifu, *Qingji xinshe zhiguan*, 57.

12. *Donghualu*, 5794–95, 5813–14; Shen Jiaben, *Shen Jiyi*, "Wencun," 1: 11a-14b; Li Guilian, *Shen Jiaben*, 110–13.

13. *DFZZ* 5, no. 2: "Neiwu," 101–8, 135 (GX 34/2); *Donghualu*, 5769–70; *ZZGB*, GX 33/11/7, 19 (p. 579 in the bound reprint edition); Hou Yijie, "Yubei lixian," 110. On the

new court system, see Brunnert and Hagelstrom, *Present Day Political Organization*, nos. 758–61.

14. *Shibao*, XT 2/8/2, 2.

15. Hu Jun, *Zhang Wenxiang gong nianpu*, 6: 8a-8b.

16. Zhang Yufa, *Qingji de lixian tuanti*, 348–56, 365–73.

17. Ibid., 350–52, 367; Zhang Kaiyuan, *Xinhai Geming*, 323. On Ruicheng (often mis-transliterated as "Ruizheng"), see Wei Xiumei, *Qingji zhiguan biao*, "Renwulu," 193; Hummel, *Eminent Chinese*, 128.

18. *Qingmo choubei lixian*, 609–17; Hou Yijie, "Qingmo yubei lixian," 103.

19. *DFZZ* 5, no. 1: "Jiaoyu," 42–43 (GX 34/1); *Datongbao*, 7: 69–94 (GX 34/5/1). On *Central Great Harmony Daily*, see also Fang Hanqi, *Zhongguo jindai baokan*, 588.

20. *Beijing nübao*, GX 34/6/6, 3; 6/12, 2–3; Hou Yijie, "Qingmo yubei lixian," 104.

21. *SL/GX*, 583: 5b-7b.

22. Yang Du, *Yang Du ji*, 811–12. On the bureau, see Zhang Deze, *Qingdai guojia jiguan*, 285–86.

23. *NCH*, 4 July 1908, 26; *ZZGB*, GX 34/6/15, 4–5.

24. *DFZZ* 5, no. 7: "Jizai," 10–11 (GX 34/7); Li Shoukong, "Zhengwenshe," 631.

25. Zhang Yufa, *Qingji de lixian tuanti*, 384–85; *DFZZ* 5, no. 7: "Jizai," 2 (GX 34/7); 5, no. 8: "Jizai," 35–38, 61–62 (GX 34/8). On Songyu, see *DFZZ* 5, no. 2: "Neiwu," 141 (GX 34/2).

26. *SL/GX*, 594: 12b-13a; Li Shoukong, "Zhengwenshe," 632; *DFZZ* 5, no. 10: "Jizai," 95–96 (GX 34/10).

27. Yang Du, *Yang Du ji*, 811; Hou Yijie, "Yang Du er ti," 237–44. For a biographical sketch of Yang Du, see Boorman and Howard, *Biographical Dictionary*, 4: 13–16.

28. *SL/GX*, 595: 1a-3a; *ZZGB*, GX 34/8/2, 5–18.

29. Hou Yijie, "Qingmo yubei lixian," 106–7.

30. See, e.g., Hummel, *Eminent Chinese*, 733.

31. Hao and Liu, "Importance of the Archival Palace Memorials," 88–89.

32. Zhu Jinfu and Zhou Wenquan, "Cong Qinggong yian."

33. *NCH*, 19 Dec. 1908, 697. On Pulun and Puwei, see Hummel, *Eminent Chinese*, 378, 383. On Puzhong, see Li Zhiting, *Aixin Jueluo jiazu*, 2: 357.

34. Xiao Yishan, *Qingdai tongshi*, 2488–93; FO 405/183, no. 127, Jordon to Grey, 14 Nov. 1908; *SL/GX*, 597: 9a, 10a.

35. Morrison, *Correspondence*, 308–9.

36. Guo Tingyi, *Jindai Zhongguo shishi*, 1274; Tianjia, *Man-Qing waishi*, 70–71.

37. *SL/GX*, 573: 10b; 586: 1b.

38. Aisin-Gioro, *From Emperor to Citizen*, 18; Zaitao, "Zaifeng yu Yuan Shikai," 79.

39. *SL/GX*, 597: 10a-10b.

40. *SL/XT*, 3: 5b-11b; 25: 7a. See also Zairun, "Longyu yu Zaifeng," 76–77.

41. FO 405/190, no. 58, Hillier to Addis, 5 Jan. 1909; Headland, *Court Life*, 171; USDS, Numerical File, 14911/40–52, Rockhill to State Department, 17 Nov. 1908.

42. *SL/XT*, 4: 24b; Zaitao, "Zaifeng yu Yuan Shikai," 80–81. For more on Yuan's dismissal, see Hou Yijie, *Yuan Shikai*, 101–3.

43. Li Zongyi, *Yuan Shikai zhuan*, 158.

44. Shen Yunlong, "Zhangwo wan-Qing zhengbing," 74–76; *SSJY*, 1910: 36–37, 42–43; *SL/XT*, 3: 33a.

45. On Weng Tonghe, see *SL/XT*, 14: 8a; *DFZZ* 6, no. 7: "Jizai 1," 331 (XT 1/6); Hummel, *Eminent Chinese*, 861. On Chen Baozhen, see *Guofengbao* 1, no. 3: 127–29 (XT 2/2/1).

46. Ding Shouhe, *Xinhai Geming shiqi*, 5: 8; Bays, *China Enters*, 59–61, 211–12; *NCH*, 16 Oct. 1909, 134; Li Jiannong, *Zuijin sanshinian*, 150–51; Morrison, *Correspondence*, 653–54.

47. *SL/XT*, 2: 16b-17b.

48. *ZZGB*, GX 34/6/26, 7; *DFZZ* 6, no. 6: "Jizai 1," 298 (XT 1/5).

49. *DFZZ* 6, no. 7: "Jizai 1," 351 (XT 1/6). On the electoral process in Guangdong, see Rhoads, *China's Republican Revolution*, 155–58.

50. Zhang Pengyuan, *Lixianpai*, 248–52.

51. *DFZZ* 6, no. 7: "Jizai 1," 351 (XT 1/6); China, Xianzheng Bianchaguan Archives, "Kaocha choubei xianzheng," file 19.

52. *DFZZ* 6, no. 13: "Jizai 1," 480, 482 (XT 1/12); FO 405/199, no. 26, annex 1, "Matters discussed in the Chekiang Provincial Assembly."

53. *Shibao*, XT 1/11/1, 5; China, Xianzheng Bianchaguan Archives, "Kaocha choubei xianzheng," file 28, undated memorial from Governor-General Yuan Shuxun and General Zengqi, enclosed in a communication from Governor-General Yuan, XT 1/12/3.

54. *ZZGB*, XT 1/7/11, 6; Brunnert and Hagelstrom, *Present Day Political Organization*, no. 167; *SL/XT*, 34: 1a-3a; 35: 3b-4a; China, Junjichu Xianzheng Zhuanti, no. 448, Jinliang, petition, XT 3/4/3; Zhang Pengyuan, *Lixianpai*, 313–20.

55. *SL/XT*, 3: 17b-18b; *ZZGB*, GX 34/8/2, 13, 17.

56. *Zhongyang datong ribao*, GX 34/12/2, 3; 12/4, 3; 12/15, 3; 12/20, 3; *STSB*, XT 1/3/22, 4; 4/12, 4; 8/5, 7.

57. *SL/XT*, 4: 7a-7b.

58. *DFZZ* 6, no. 5: "Jizai 1," 227–28 (XT 1/4); *STSB*, XT 1/3/3, 7.

59. *Beijing nübao*, GX 34/12/11, 1, 2; Zhao Shu, "Xinhai Geming qianhou," 15.

60. Jinliang, *Guang-Xuan xiaoji*, 121–22; Crossley, *Orphan Warriors*, 193.

61. *ZZGB*, XT 1/3/9, 5–7; 12/13, 9; 2/4/5, 16; 12/29, 14–15; Jiang Xiangshun, "Jindai Shenyang Manzu," 34.

62. *ZZGB*, XT 1/12/13, 8.

63. Jinliang, *Guang-Xuan xiaoji*, 143.

64. Ibid., 139–40; *STSB*, XT 2/5/25, 7.

65. *ZZGB*, XT 2/12/29, 15; 3/+6/13, 13; *Shibao*, XT 3/6/17, 2.

66. *Zhongyang datong ribao*, GX 34/12/9, 2.

67. Zhang Bofeng, *Qingdai gedi*, 59–61, 105–6, 151–52; *ZZGB*, XT 2/3/26, 12–13.

68. *STSB*, XT 2/4/3, 7; 6/17, 7; *SL/XT*, 36: 37a-38a; 37: 10a.

69. *ZZGB*, XT 1/+2/5, 6–10; *SL/XT*, 9: 6a-6b; *DFZZ* 6, no. 4: "Jizai 1," 163 (XT 1/3).

70. *SL/XT*, 9: 6a-6b; *DFZZ* 6, no. 4: "Jizai 1," 163 (XT 1/3).

71. *SL/XT*, 30: 25b-26a; 31: 1a. On *aha* as "slave," see Norman, *Concise Manchu-English Lexicon*, 7.

72. *SL/XT*, 41: 17b-18a; *ZZGB*, XT 2/8/25, 8–9.

73. *ZZGB*, GX 34/8/2, 9.

74. *SL/XT*, 3: 7a-7b.

75. Zaitao, "Jinweijun zhi jianli," 237; Aisin-Gioro, *From Emperor to Citizen*, 21; Zhang Guogan, "Qingmo Jinweijun," 23. According to Zaitao, his brother's interest in the emperor's military role was intensified when Prince Heinrich paid a return visit to China in April 1905. However, the German prince who visited China then was not Heinrich but Friedrich Leopold. See *NCH*, 14 April 1905, 61.

76. *SL/XT*, 14: 20b-21b; Bays, *China Enters*, 213; *DFZZ* 6, no. 7: "Jizai 1," 332–33 (XT 1/6). On Wuzong, see Goodrich and Fang, *Dictionary of Ming Biography*, 311–12; R. Huang, *1587*, 96–99.

77. *SL/XT*, 14: 21a, 25b; 15: 7b; Brunnert and Hagelstrom, *Present Day Political Organization*, no. 184a; *ZZGB*, XT 1/8/23, 4–8; Qian Shifu, *Qingji xinshe zhiguan*, 60; Powell, *Rise of Chinese Military Power*, 264–65; Zheng Huaiyi and Zhang Jianshe, *Modai huangshu*, 33–35; *Beijing nübao*, GX 34/12/18, 4. On the Japanese precedent, see Hackett, *Yamagata Aritomo*, 82–83; Presseisen, *Before Aggression*, 59–67.

78. *NCH*, 26 July 1907, 228; *Beijing nübao*, GX 34/5/16, 3; 5/26, 3.

79. *SL/XT*, 4: 3a.

80. Ibid., 4: 3a; 7: 34b-35a; 14: 21b; 38: 36b; Zhang Guogan, "Qingmo Jinweijun," 23; Qian Shifu, *Qingji xinshe zhiguan*, 60.

81. *STSB*, XT 1/+2/2, 7; China, Jinweijun Xunlianchu Archives, *juan* 1, memorial, n.d.; Zhang Guogan, "Qingmo Jinweijun," 23; Tahara, *Shinmatsu Minsho*, 74, 315; *Saishin Shina*, 392–93. On Putong, see Morrison, *Correspondence*, 768–69; *STSB*, XT 3/8/17, 7; Xin Ping et al., *Minguo shehui daguan*, 35.

82. China, Jinweijun Xunlianchu Archives, *juan* 1, memorial and memorandum responding to an edict of GX 34/12/3; Wu Zhaoqing, "Qingmo Jinweijun," 13–14, 20; Powell, *Rise of Chinese Military Power*, 294; Fung, *Military Dimension*, 21–22.

83. *SL/XT*, 4: 3a; *STSB*, GX 34/12/12, 2; China, Jinweijun Xunlianchu Archives, *juan* 1, memorial responding to an edict of GX 34/12/3; Wu Zhaoqing, "Qingmo Jinweijun," 19.

84. China, Jinweijun Xunlianchu Archives, *juan* 1, memorial responding to an edict of GX 34/12/3; *juan* 3, "Ribaobiao" for XT 1/4; *SL/XT*, 16: 20a; Wu Zhaoqing, "Qingmo Jinweijun," 19; *STSB*, XT 1/5/3, 7; 8/4, 7; 8/13, 7.

85. Wu Zhaoqing, "Qingmo Jinweijun," 19.

86. *ZZGB*, XT 2/9/30, 4–5; *SL/XT*, 41: 18b.

87. China, Jinweijun Xunlianchu Archives, *juan* 3, "Ribaobiao" for XT 1/7 and 1/8; *Shibao*, XT 2/5/13, 2.

88. China, Jinweijun Xunlianchu Archives, *juan* 3, "Ribaobiao," XT 1/10/16, 10/25; United States, War College Division of the General Staff, 6283/4, monthly report of military events, 30 Nov. 1910.

89. *SL/XT*, 21: 21a; *ZZGB*, XT 1/9/4, 5–7.

90. *SL/XT*, 17: 29b-30a; 28: 2a-2b; *Shibao*, XT 2/1/29, 2; 2/8, 3; *Neige guanbao*, XT 3/7/29, 375–76. On Zairun, see Li Zhiting, *Aixin Jueluo jiazu*, 3: 171–72.

91. *SL/XT*, 21: 21a; *Shibao*, XT 2/5/13, 2; China, Jinweijun Xunlianchu Archives, *juan* 3, "Ribaobiao," XT 1/10/16, 10/25; *Saishin Shina*, 397; Yun Baohui, "Xinhai Feng Guozhang," 119.

92. *SL/XT*, 21: 34a; Wu Zhaoqing, "Qingmo Jinweijun," 20; Liang Xuyi, "Liangbi zhuan," 28–30; Tahara, *Shinmatsu Minsho*, 35–36. On Zaitao's military tour, see *Guofengbao* 1, no. 6: 67 (XT 2/3/1).

93. Zaitao, "Jinweijun zhi jianli," 239; Zhang Guogan, "Qingmo Jinweijun," 23; Yun Baohui, "Xinhai Feng Guozhang," 119; Wu Zhaoqing, "Qingmo Jinweijun," 20, 22.

94. United States, War College Division of the General Staff, 6283/8, "Monthly Report of Military Events," 20 April 1911; *SL/XT*, 59: 19a-19b; *DFZZ* 8, no. 8: "Zhongguo dashiji," 13 (XT 3/8); *STSB*, XT 3/6/18, 7; 6/21, 7; 7/25, 7; Wu Zhaoqing, "Qingmo Jinweijun," 20–23.

95. *SL/XT*, 7: 34b-35a; Bai Jie, "Qingmo zhengtan," 38.

96. *SL/XT*, 14: 9a-12a, 21b-22a; 16: 29a. On Sa Zhenbing, see Tahara, *Shinmatsu Minsho*, 766; *Zhongguo jindaishi cidian*, 615–16.

97. *DFZZ* 6, no. 9: "Jishi," 253–54 (XT 1/8); Lin Xianxin, "Zaixun Sa Zhenbing," 846–49; *SL/XT*, 44: 3b-4b, 9a.

98. Lin Xianxin, "Zaixun Sa Zhenbing," 846; *SL/XT*, 44: 9b-10a.

99. Zhang Xia et al., *Qingmo haijun*, 171–72, 850–52, 893, 898.

100. Yan Shouhua, "Hairong deng jian," 706; Zhang Xia et al., *Qingmo haijun*, 444, 591–92, 597.

101. Lin Xianxin, "Zaixun Sa Zhenbing," 849.

102. FO 405/190, no. 150, Jordan to Grey, 16 Mar. 1909; *NCH*, 21 Aug. 1909, 413–14; 28 Aug., 477–78; Bays, *China Enters*, 214; J. Ch'en, *Yuan Shih-k'ai*, 60.

103. Qian Shifu, *Qingji zhongyao zhiguan*, 51, 109. I have included the Ministry of the Navy in this analysis, even though it was not created until a few months later.

104. FO 405/191, no. 33, Jordan to Grey, 15 July 1909; Qian Shifu, *Qingji zhongyao zhiguan*, 138–60.

105. *DFZZ* 6, no. 12: "Jizai 1," 437 (XT 1/11); *ZZGB*, XT 1/10/14, 9–10.

106. FO 405/191, no. 153, Jordan to Grey, 26 Nov. 1909; *STSB*, XT 2/7/23, 7; *Shibao*, XT 2/1/8, 2; *SL/XT*, 53: 4b.

107. *NCH*, 7 Aug. 1909, 328; *SL*/XT, 31: 11b; 40: 7a; *Qingdai renwu zhuan'gao*, 8: 110.

108. *Shibao*, XT 1/11/28, 2; *DFZZ* 7, no. 4: "Wenjian 1," 49–50 (XT 2/4).

109. Zhang Kaiyuan, *Xinhai Geming*, 332, 337; Bai Jie, "Qingmo zhengtan," 38.

110. Zhu Lanting and Xu Fengchen, "Xiong Chengji"; Lü Jian, "Guanyu Xiong Chengji"; Feng Ziyou, *Geming yishi*, 5: 187–94; *DFZZ*, 7, no. 2: "Jizai 3," 45–46 (XT 2/2). Feng's account errs in identifying Xiong's intended victim as Zaitao.

111. *SSJY*, 1910: 87–88; Feng Ziyou, *Zhonghua minguo*, 2: 230–35.

112. Feng Ziyou, *Zhonghua minguo*, 2: 235–38; *SSJY*, 1910: 88–89, 104–6; *DFZZ* 7, no. 3: "Jizai 1," 47–48 (XT 2/3); Jin Xiangrui, "Wo shi zenma."

113. Feng Ziyou, *Zhonghua minguo*, 2: 238–45. See also "Qingmo Wang Zhaoming."

114. *DFZZ* 7, no. 3: "Jizai 1," 47–48 (XT 2/3).

115. "Qingmo Wang Zhaoming," 21; *Shibao*, XT 2/3/16, 2; *NCH*, 13 May 1910, 374.

116. Zhang Kaiyuan, *Xinhai Geming*, 317–40; Feng Ziyou, *Geming yishi*, 5: 251–54; 6: 50–51; Bai Jie, "Qingmo zhengtan," 38. See also *XHGM*, 2: 290.

117. Feng Ziyou, *Zhonghua minguo*, 2: 246, 251–54; *SSJY*, 1910: 108–9.

118. *DFZZ* 7, no. 11: "Jizai 3," 359–61 (XT 2/11); Feng Ziyou, *Geming yishi*, 2: 287–89; *New York Times*, 7 Oct. 1910, 1.

119. *DFZZ* 7, no. 12: "Jizai 1," 169 (XT 2/12).

120. Farjenel, *Through the Chinese Revolution*, 21.

121. Li Shoukong, "Gesheng ziyiju lianhehui," 321–38; Zhang Yufa, *Qingji de lixian tuanti*, 393–405; *Shibao*, XT 1/12/14, 2; *DFZZ* 7, no. 1: "Wenjian 1," 17–20 (XT 2/1); *STSB*, XT 2/6/8, 4; 6/9, 4; *SL*/XT, 36: 28a-30a.

122. *DFZZ* 7, no. 11: "Jizai 1," 143–51 (XT 2/11); *Shibao*, XT 2/9/25, 2.

123. *DFZZ* 7, no. 11: "Jizai 1," 151–57 (XT 2/11); Des Forges, *Hsi-liang*, 171–72.

124. *DFZZ* 7, no. 11: "Jizai 1," 154–56 (XT 2/11).

125. *SL*/XT, 43: 2b-5b, 6b; 44: 9a-9b.

126. *DFZZ* 7, no. 11: "Jizai 1," 158–59 (XT 2/11); Li Shoukong, "Gesheng ziyiju lianhehui," 346.

127. *DFZZ* 7, no. 12: "Jizai" 1, 178–80 (XT 2/12); *SL*/XT, 45: 11a-11b, 14b-16a; *Guofengbao* 1, no. 32: 109–10 (XT 2/11/21).

128. *DFZZ* 7, no. 11: "Zhongguo dashiji buyi," 85 (XT 2/11); 7, no. 12: "Zhongguo dashiji buyi," 104–6 (XT 2/12); *SL*/XT, 43: 15b-16a.

129. *DFZZ* 7, no. 11: "Zhongguo dashiji buyi," 85–86 (XT 2/11); *SL*/XT, 43: 30b-31a.

130. *SL*/XT, 43: 34a; *DFZZ* 7, no. 11: "Zhongguo dashiji buyi," 86 (XT 2/11).

131. *Guofengbao* 1, no. 30: 89–90 (XT 2/11/1); *DFZZ* 7, no. 12: "Jizai 1," 170–74 (XT 2/12); *NCH*, 16 Dec. 1910, 660.

132. *SL*/XT, 45: 1a-2a; *DFZZ* 7, no. 12: "Jizai 1," 174–77 (XT 2/12); FO 405/204, no. 89, Jordan to Grey, 31 Jan. 1911.

133. *DFZZ* 7, no. 11: "Jizai 3," 326–27 (XT 2/11); *Guofengbao* 1, no. 32: 92–93 (XT 2/11/21); *STSB*, XT 2/12/4, 7.

134. *DFZZ* 7, no. 8: "Wenjian 1," 98–100 (XT 2/8); *NCH*, 5 Aug. 1910, 309–10; Pomerantz-Zhang, *Wu Tingfang*, 186–88.

135. *DFZZ* 7, no. 3: "Wenjian 1," 40–41 (XT 2/3); *NCH*, 18 Dec. 1909, 660.

136. *Shibao*, XT 2/3/4, 2; et seq.

137. *NCH*, 13 Nov. 1909, 364; FO 405/199, no. 162*, "Summary of the Peking press" for April 1910; *Shibao*, XT 2/3/17, 2; 7/3, 2.

138. *Shibao*, XT 2/8/9, 2; 9/7, 3.

139. Ibid., XT 2/7/27, 2.

140. Ibid., XT 2/8/21, 2; 8/24, 3; 9/2, 3; *DFZZ* 7, no. 9: "Jizai 3," 261 (XT 2/9); *ZZGB*, XT 2/11/23, 7–8.

141. *Shibao*, XT 2/11/3, 2; 11/7, 2; 11/9, 1; 11/22, 1; 11/24, 5.

142. *SL/XT*, 45: 10b-11a.

143. *Shibao*, XT 2/11/26, 2; *SL/XT*, 45: 20a.

144. *Shibao*, XT 2/12/3, 2; 12/9, 2; 12/25, 1.

145. *NCH*, 20 Jan. 1911, 148–49, 158–59; *Shibao*, XT 2/12/6, 3; 12/12, 2.

146. *Shibao*, XT 2/12/17, 2; *STSB*, XT 2/12/25, 4.

147. *DFZZ* 8, no. 1: "Zhongguo dashiji," 4 (XT 3/2). On the Eight Banners Association for Constitutional Government, see *Guofengbao* 1, no. 29: 81 (XT 2/10/21), and *Shibao*, XT 2/10/29, 1.

148. *DFZZ* 8, no. 4: "Zhongguo dashiji," 2–3 (XT 3/5); *NCH*, 13 May 1911, 391, 436.

149. Qian Shifu, *Qingji zhongyao zhiguan*, 110–11.

150. *Shibao*, XT 2/10/5, 2.

151. *DFZZ* 8, no. 1 (XT 3/2) (p. 19,069 in the Taiwan reprint edition); *Shibao*, XT 3/4/12, 1; 4/14, 1; Li Shoukong, "Gesheng ziyiju lianhehui," 358; Zhang Jian, *Seweng ziding nianpu*, 66.

152. *SSJY*, 1911: 246–47.

153. *DFZZ* 8, no. 5: "Zhongguo dashiji," 7–9 (XT 3/6).

154. Zhang Jian, *Seweng ziding nianpu*, 66.

155. *SL/XT*, 54: 23a-23b; *NCH*, 24 June 1911, 833; *Shibao*, XT 2/12/9, 2.

156. *Qingmo choubei lixian*, 577–79; *Guofengbao* 2, no. 14: 70–73 (XT 3/5/21); *SL/XT*, 55: 11b-12a.

157. Lingnan Banweng, "Wen Shengcai," 699–703.

4 / THE 1911 REVOLUTION

1. Shang Binghe, *Xinren chunqiu*, 3: 4a; *DFZZ* 8, no. 9: "Geming zhanshi ji," 20 (XT 3/9).

2. Dutt, "First Week of Revolution," 395–413; Esherick, *Reform and Revolution*, 178–92; *SL/XT*, 61: 24b-25a.

3. *STSB*, XT 3/8/22, 7; 8/23, 7; *SL/XT*, 61: 25a-25b.

4. *SL/XT*, 61: 34a–34b, 73b–75a; 62: 3a–4a, 8b–9b; Kent, *Passing of the Manchus*, 101–2; Hou Yijie, *Yuan Shikai*, 117–20.

5. Zhang Bofeng and Li Zongyi, *Beiyang junfa*, 6: 543; Jinliang, *Guang-Xuan xiaoji*, 153.

6. *SL/XT*, 51: 10b–11a; 53: 4b–5a; 57: 20a; 61: 28b–29a, 34b–35a; *STSB*, XT 3/6/9, 7; Ding Shiyuan, "Meileng zhangjing," 256–57; Luo Zhengwei, "Luanzhou geming," 335–39; United States, War College Division of the General Staff, 6780–42, "Notes on the Chinese Revolution of 1911–12."

7. *NCH*, 21 Oct. 1911, 141; *SL/XT*, 61: 28b, 70a; *DFZZ* 8, no. 9: "Geming zhanshi ji," 21 (XT 3/9).

8. *STSB*, XT 3/8/26, 7; *NCH*, 21 Oct. 1911, 146, 152; *SL/XT*, 61: 69b–70b; Kent, *Passing of the Manchus*, 134; Ding Shiyuan, "Meileng zhangjing," 258–59. Ding (1879–1945) was a high-ranking staff officer at the Ministry of the Army and traveled south with Yinchang; his first-hand account is quite informative and detailed, but strangely is often inaccurate as to dates. For example, he says Yinchang left Beijing on the 13th and arrived at Xinyang on the 15th.

9. Li Lianfang, *Xinhai Wuchang*, 140b–144a.

10. Shang Binghe, *Xinren chunqiu*, 3: 6a; *NCH*, 28 Oct. 1911, 217; *DFZZ* 8, no. 9: "Geming zhanshi ji," 21 (XT 3/9); Chen Chunsheng, "Xinhai Geming haijun," 697; Zhang Yibo, "Xinhai haijun," 471–72.

11. See, e.g., Li Jiannong, *Zuijin sanshinian*, 191; Xiao Yishan, *Qingdai tongshi*, 2648; Tao Juyin, *Beiyang junfa*, 1: 77.

12. Hou Yijie, *Yuan Shikai*, 120–21. Although numerous other authors discuss this critical episode—Xu's visit to Yuan and Yuan's six demands—in almost identical terms, the credibility of this standard account is open to question for at least three reasons. First, most authors, including Hou Yijie, cite no source. Second, when authors do cite a source, the citation does not support the claim. For example, J. Ch'en (*Yuan Shih-k'ai*, 86) refers to Tao Juyin (*Beiyang junfa*, 1: 76), but Tao's own account is unsubstantiated; Ch'en also cites Zhang Guogan (*Xinhai Geming*, 106–10), but Zhang makes no reference to either Xu's visit or Yuan's demands. Other accounts (e.g., Wang Shounan, "Xinhai Wuchang," 86) cite Li Lianfang (*Xinhai Wuchang*, 145b); Li does indeed quote Yuan's six demands, but he neither dates them nor links them to any visit by Xu Shichang. Third, Zaitao ("Zaifeng yu Yuan Shikai," 82) expresses doubts about "stories of Xu Shichang's secretly going to Zhangde to negotiate terms [with Yuan Shikai]"; he categorically states that "at the time, I never heard of Xu's going to Zhangde." On the other hand, the contemporary press, not always a reliable source, does offer some independent confirmation for Xu's visit and Yuan's demands. *Shibao* (XT 3/8/27 [18 Oct. 1911], 2) reported that Xu, accompanied by an unidentified fourth-rank prince, visited Yuan at Zhangde to urge him not to turn down his appointment as governor-general; and *STSB* (XT 3/8/30 [21 Oct.], 7) carried an item saying that Yuan

had submitted a secret eight-point memorial in which he, inter alia, asked for full power for himself.

13. *SL/XT*, 62: 14a-14b, 28a-28b, 38a-38b.

14. Li Lianfang, *Xinhai Wuchang*, 153b-158a; Wang Shu'nan, "Wuhan zhanji," 231–32; Kent, *Passing of the Manchus*, 139–45; Powell, *Rise of Chinese Military Power*, 323; *SL/XT*, 62: 55b-56b; Ding Shiyuan, "Meileng zhangjing," 267.

15. Shang Binghe, *Xinren chunqiu*, 3: 6b; Hou Yijie, *Yuan Shikai*, 122; Shen Yunlong, "Beiyang zhi 'gou,'" 49; *NCH*, 4 Nov. 1911, 294; 11 Nov., 355, 357, 358; 25 Nov., 508, 511; *DFZZ* 8, no. 9: "Geming zhanshi ji," 23–24 (XT 3/9); Kent, *Passing of the Manchus*, 148–56.

16. Shang Binghe, *Xinren chunqiu*, 24: 3b; *SL/XT*, 63: 6b, 17a.

17. Zhang Guogan, *Xinhai Geming*, 271–73; Zhang Jian, *Seweng ziding nianpu*, 70; Li Lianfang, *Xinhai Wuchang*, 145b; Hou Yijie, *Yuan Shikai*, 120–21.

18. *SSJY*, 1911: 735–36, 754–58; *STSB*, XT 3/9/7, 7; 9/8, 7.

19. For conflicting views of Zhang Shaozeng's motivations, see Dong Fangkui, "Lun 'Luanzhou bingjian'"; and Du Chunhe, "Zhang Shaozeng."

20. *SSJY*, 1911: 753–54, 803–5. The text of Zhang's memorial here is strangely dated XT 3/9/13 (3 Nov.); an abbreviated version of the memorial, correctly dated, appears in Zhang Guogan, *Xinhai Geming*, 197–98.

21. Zhang Guogan, *Xinhai Geming*, 198–99, trans. in Fung, *Military Dimension*, 218–19.

22. Du Chunhe, "Zhang Shaozeng," 259. See also *NCH*, 4 Nov. 1911, 285.

23. Zhang Guogan, *Xinhai Geming*, 202–3.

24. *SL/XT*, 62: 49a-50b, trans. in Kent, *Passing of the Manchus*, 160–61.

25. *SL/XT*, 62: 50b-53b, trans. in Kent, *Passing of the Manchus*, 162–64.

26. *SL/XT*, 62: 55a.

27. *SSJY*, 1911: 779.

28. *Qingmo choubei lixian*, 598–600; *SL/XT*, 63: 1a-2a, 5a; 64: 2b.

29. *SL/XT*, 63: 5b-6a.

30. *SSJY*, 1911: 807–8.

31. *NCH*, 4 Nov. 1911, 296; *SSJY*, 1911: 805–6; *SL/XT*, 63: 10b.

32. *DFZZ* 8, no. 9: "Zhongguo dashi ji," 8–9 (XT 3/9), trans. in Kent, *Passing of the Manchus*, 169–70.

33. *NCH*, 11 Nov. 1911, 358; *SL/XT*, 63: 23a.

34. *SSJY*, 1911: 830–31; Du Chunhe, "Zhang Shaozeng," 275.

35. *STSB*, XT 3/9/13, 7; 9/15, 7; 9/25, 5; *SL/XT*, 63: 27a; "Qingmo Wang Zhaoming," 21–22.

36. *STSB*, XT 3/9/7, 7; 9/13, 7; 9/20, 2.

37. *SL/XT*, 63: 16a-18a, trans. in Kent, *Passing of the Manchus*, 171–73.

38. Li Lianfang, *Xinhai Wuchang*, 77a-80a; Fung, *Military Dimension*, 205–6; He Juefei and Feng Tianyu, *Xinhai Wuchang*, 191; Wang Zuancheng, "Xinhai shouyi," 29; Zhou Wuyi, "Lujun Disan Zhongxue," 14.

39. See maps in Fung, *Military Dimension*, 228–29; and He Juefei and Feng Tianyu, *Xinhai Wuchang*, 201.

40. [Li] Jiannong, "Wuhan geming," 171; Esherick, *Reform and Revolution*, 181–82; Dutt, "First Week of Revolution," 399–400; Zhang Guogan, *Xinhai Geming*, 73, 75; Zhou Wuyi, "Lujun Disan Zhongxue," 15.

41. *Shibao*, XT 3/8/28, 3; 9/8, 3; Li Lianfang, *Xinhai Wuchang*, 109b–110a; He Juefei and Feng Tianyu, *Xinhai Wuchang*, 212; Zhang Guogan, *Xinhai Geming*, 85; Kent, *Passing of the Manchus*, 92; Xiong Bingkun, "Wuchang qiyi," 94; [Li] Jiannong, "Wuhan geming," 174. On the Manchus' flat heads, see Crossley, *Manchus*, 20.

42. Yang Tingyuan, "Ji E Junzhengfu," 47; *STSB*, XT 3/9/8, 4; Li Lianfang, *Xinhai Wuchang*, 110a; He Juefei and Feng Tianyu, *Xinhai Wuchang*, 226–27; Cao Yabo, *Wuchang geming*, "Zhengbian," 100–101. I have been unable to locate in American and British diplomatic sources confirmation of consular intervention on behalf of the Manchus.

43. Yang Tingyuan, "Ji E Junzhengfu," 47–48; *NCH*, 21 Oct. 1911, 143; Cao Yabo, *Wuchang geming*, "Zhengbian," 33; *STSB*, 9 April 1912, 4; Wang Zuancheng, "Xinhai shouyi," 29; Li Lianfang, *Xinhai Wuchang*, 113a–113b.

44. Li Lianfang, *Xinhai Wuchang*, 110a; Esherick, *Reform and Revolution*, 182.

45. *Neige guanbao*, XT 3/7/25, 539–40; FO 405/208, no. 65, Jordan to Grey, 29 Dec. 1911.

46. Zhu Xuwu and Dang Zixin, "Shaanxi Xinhai Geming," 4–8; Keyte, *Passing of the Dragon*, chaps. 1–5; Shang Binghe, *Xinren chunqiu*, 43: 5a.

47. Zhu Xuwu and Dang Zixin, "Shaanxi Xinhai Geming," 8–10; Shang Binghe, *Xinren chunqiu*, 4: 1a; 43: 5a; Keyte, *Passing of the Dragon*, 9; *Shaanxi tongzhi gao*, 44: 43b–44a.

48. Guo Xiaocheng, "Shaanxi guangfu," 46; Guo Xiaoren, "Congrong jilüe," 65.

49. Keyte, *Passing of the Dragon*, 42; Zhu Xuwu and Dang Zixin, "Shaanxi Xinhai Geming," 10.

50. Keyte, *Passing of the Dragon*, 43–45; Shang Binghe, *Xinren chunqiu*, 4: 2b, 3b.

51. Guo Xiaocheng, "Shaanxi guangfu," 41–42; Keyte, *Passing of the Dragon*, 48; Guo Xiaoren, "Congrong jilüe," 69.

52. Keyte, *Passing of the Dragon*, 32–33, 44, 48, 53–55; FO 405/208, no. 149, enclosure 2, A. G. Shorrock to Jordan, 1 Dec. 1911; Shang Binghe, *Xinren chunqiu*, 43: 5b; *NCH*, 23 March 1912, 772; Zhu Xuwu and Dang Zixin, "Shaanxi Xinhai Geming," 10, 12.

53. Shang Binghe, *Xinren chunqiu*, 6: 1a–2b; Xue Dubi, "Taiyuan he Hedong," 169–71; Yao Yijie, "Xinhai Taiyuan," 266–68; *NCH*, 25 Nov. 1911, 518–20; Keyte, *Passing of the Dragon*, 174–75, 179.

54. Zhang Liying, "Zhenjiang guangfu," 76–77; Wu Cifan, "Zhenjiang guangfu," 263–67; Xu Chonghao, "Zhenjiang xinjun," 247–50; Guo Xiaocheng, "Jiangsu guangfu," 20; *Shibao*, XT 3/9/18, 3; 9/20, 4.

55. Zhang Liying, "Zhenjiang guangfu," 78; Wu Cifan, "Zhenjiang guangfu," 267–68; Lin Shuqing, "Zhenjun yuan-Ning," 42, 44; *Shibao*, XT 3/9/26, 3; 10/5, 4.

56. Liu Tong, "Xinhai Fujian," 460; Shang Binghe, *Xinren chunqiu*, 44: 1a-3a; Wei Xiumei, *Qingji zhiguan biao*, "Renwulu," 15, 204.

57. *Shibao*, XT 3/10/1, 3; Guo Xiaocheng, "Fujian guangfu," 280; Shang Binghe, *Xinren chunqiu*, 15: 1a; Liu Tong, "Xinhai Fujian," 460.

58. *Shibao*, XT 3/10/6, 3; Guo Xiaocheng, "Fujian guangfu," 280–81; Shang Binghe, *Xinren chunqiu*, 15: 1a-1b; *DFZZ* 8, no. 9: "Geming zhanshi ji," 18–19 (XT 3/9).

59. *Shibao*, XT 3/10/1, 3; 10/6, 3; Guo Xiaocheng, "Fujian guangfu," 281; Liu Tong, "Xinhai Fujian," 461–63; Shang Binghe, *Xinren chunqiu*, 15: 1b-2b; Zheng Quan, "Fujian guangfu," 318–19; China, Junjichu Lufu Zouzhe, "Nongmin yundong lei," *juan* 1736, no. 2, Jingxu, memorial, XT 3/12/12; *STSB*, XT 3/12/19, 7; Gao Shiliang, "Fujiansheng geming," 363, 365.

60. *Shibao*, XT 3/10/1, 3; *STSB*, 3/10/23, 4; 12/19, 7; Gao Shiliang, "Fujiansheng geming," 365 n. 2; Liu Tong, "Xinhai Fujian," 463; Guo Xiaocheng, "Fujian guangfu," 281; Shang Binghe, *Xinren chunqiu*, 15: 2a-2b; Zheng Quan, "Fujian guangfu," 319.

61. Cai Hongyuan and Liu Xiaoning, "Xinhai Nanjing guangfu," 165–66; Kent, *Passing of the Manchus*, 241.

62. Shang Binghe, *Xinren chunqiu*, 13: 3b-4a; FO 405/205, no. 494, Jordan to Grey, 23 Nov. 1911; Fung, *Military Dimension*, 222.

63. Ma Yamin, "Nanjing guangfu," 258.

64. Shang Binghe, *Xinren chunqiu*, 13: 4a; Kent, *Passing of the Manchus*, 241–42; Fung, *Military Dimension*, 222.

65. Kent, *Passing of the Manchus*, 245; Shang Binghe, *Xinren chunqiu*, 13: 5a.

66. Cai Hongyuan and Liu Xiaoning, "Xinhai Nanjing guangfu," 167–72; Kent, *Passing of the Manchus*, 247–52; Zhang Guogan, *Xinhai Geming*, 234–35; Shang Binghe, *Xinren chunqiu*, 13: 6a-6b; Guo Xiaocheng, "Jiangsu guangfu," 17.

67. Xu Chonghao, "Xinhai Zhenjun," 40; Farjenel, *Through the Chinese Revolution*, 106; Zhang Guogan, *Xinhai Geming*, 237; Shang Binghe, *Xinren chunqiu*, 13: 6b; 45: 11b-12a; *STSB*, XT 3/10/16, 7; 11/4, 4; *Shibao*, XT 3/10/18, 4.

68. See, e.g., Fung, *Military Dimension*, 223.

69. China, Maritime Customs, *Returns of Trade, 1911*, part 2: 270.

70. Esherick, *Reform and Revolution*, 195–96; Li Yi, "Jing-Yi-Shi-He," 253; Pan Honggang, "Xinhai Geming," 23–24.

71. Bohai Shouchen, *Xinhai Geming*, 344; Li Yi, "Jing-Yi-Shi-He," 262–67; *STSB*, XT 3/10/16, 2; 10/17, 2.

72. Li Yi, "Jing-Yi-Shi-He," 254–57; China, Junjichu Lufu Zouzhe, "Nongmin yundong lei," *juan* 1718, nos. 8–10, Liankui et al., memorials, XT 3/9/6, 9/28, and 10/7.

73. Li Yi, "Jing-Yi-Shi-He," 257–59; China, Maritime Customs, *Returns of Trade, 1911*, part 2: 270; Shang Binghe, *Xinren chunqiu*, 3: 13b; 42: 7b-9a; Bohai Shouchen, *Xinhai Geming*, 681–82.

74. *DFZZ* 8, no. 9: "Geming zhanshi ji," 17–18 (XT 3/9); Guo Xiaocheng, "Zhejiang

guangfu," 135–36; Shang Binghe, *Xinren chunqiu*, 14: 1a-2b; 44: 4a-5a; Zhang Guogan, *Xinhai Geming*, 238–39; Xu Bingkun, "Hangzhou guangfu," 165–66.

75. Lin Jiayou, "Xinhai Geming qianhou," 210–17; Shu Zhongji, "Xinhai Geming shi"; Wang Zongyou, *Guangzhou Manzu*, 47–54; Da-Han Rexin Ren, "Guangdong duli," 437, 438, 441, 442, 450.

76. *SSJY*, 1911: 1003–4. There exists a curious and suspect document dated 21 Nov., in which the Hanjun of the garrison plead with the Republicans that they be treated more leniently than the Manchus (Manren), that they be allowed to surrender even if other banner personnel do not. They claim that their ancestors had joined the Eight Banners unwillingly and that they now wish to reclaim their original Han status. See *Shibao*, 7 Jan. 1912, 4. The document, however, is probably spurious, because the Chengdu garrison was composed only of Manchu and Mongol banner members; it had no Hanjun.

77. Wei Yingtao, *Sichuan baolu*, 341–53; Qiu Yuanying, "Zhao Erfeng," 127–33; *SSJY*, 1911: 1120–21.

78. Shang Binghe, *Xinren chunqiu*, 2: 17a; Ma Xiedi, "Liu Xianzhi," 46; Qian Anjing and Zhou Xiyin, "Xinhai Geming shiqi," 118; Xiong Kewu et al., "Shu dang," 179; Wang Youyu, "Da-Han Sichuan junzhengfu," 73; *Shibao*, 29 Jan. 1912, 3.

79. Guanglu, *Guanglu huiyilu*, 2–9; Yang Fengchun, "Yili Xinhai Geming," 510–17; Lin Jing, "Yili geming," 429–31; Zhou Xuan, "Zhirui chulun," 54; *Shibao*, 9 March 1912, 3.

80. China, Junjichu Lufu Zouzhe, "Nongmin yundong lei," *juan* 1711, no. 3, Jixian et al., petition, XT 3/11/19; Bohai Shouchen, *Xinhai Geming*, 696–98; Hummel, *Eminent Chinese*, 780–81.

81. Shang Binghe, *Xinren chunqiu*, 24: 3a; 42: 4b-5b, 6b-7a; 43: 6a, 9a; 44: 3a-3b; 44: 16b; 45: 4b, 8a; Bohai Shouchen, *Xinhai Geming*, 692–93; Yang Qingzhen, "Hairong, Haichou, Haichen," 102; *NCH*, 11 Nov. 1911, 360; Esherick, *Reform and Revolution*, 195.

82. *NCH*, 4 Nov. 1911, 283; *Shibao*, XT 3/9/21, 4; 10/8, 3; 21 Jan. 1912, 4; Bohai Shouchen, *Xinhai Geming*, 303, 334; Yan Shouhua et al., "Changjiang jiandui," 58.

83. Huang Guangyun and Chen Jinming, "Ningxia minjun," 500–503; Rong Xiang, "Lüetan Xinhai Geming," 237–42.

84. *Shibao*, XT 3/9/6 and 9/7, supplement.

85. *SSJY*, 1911: 907; *NCH*, 11 Nov. 1911, 366; *SL/XT*, 63: 38a.

86. *SSJY*, 1911: 936; *NCH*, 18 Nov. 1911, 437; *SL/XT*, 64: 6a.

87. *Neige guanbao*, XT 3/10/3, 95–96.

88. *SL/XT*, 66: 1a-2b; FO 405/208, no. 40, Jordan to Grey, 20 Dec. 1911.

89. *SL/XT*, 66: 8a-8b; Liang Xuyi, "Liangbi zhuan," 31–32; *STSB*, XT 3/11/3, 7.

90. Zhang Guogan, *Xinhai Geming*, 278–79; Guo Xiaocheng, "Yihe shimo," 65–67; *SSJY*, 1911: 984.

91. Huang Zhongxing, *Yang Du*, 91–93; Yang Du, *Yang Du ji*, 538–42.

92. *SSJY*, 1911: 1028–29; *SL*/XT, 66: 5b.

93. Guo Xiaocheng, "Yihe shimo," 65–66.

94. *SL*/XT, 63: 16a-18a, 41a-41b.

95. Li Huimin, "Wu Luzhen xunnan"; Zhang Guogan, *Xinhai Geming*, 202–8; *SSJY*, 1911: 781–83, 851–66; *XHGM*, 6: 375; *Shibao*, XT 3/9/21, 2; *NCH*, 11 Nov. 1911, 361, 363, 366; *DFZZ* 8, no. 10: "Zhongguo dashi ji," 1 (April 1912); for conflicting interpretations of Wu Luzhen's political stance, see Dong Fangkui, "Lun 'Luanzhou bingjian,'" and Wu Zhongya, "Wu Luzhen."

96. FO 405/208, no. 123, Jordan to Grey, 13 Jan. 1912.

97. *SL*/XT, 64: 12b-13b; Qian Shifu, *Qingji zhongyao zhiguan*, 112. These figures are somewhat misleading. Because five of his appointees (e.g., Sa Zhenbing and Zhang Jian) were not in Beijing at the time, Yuan designated additional "acting" ministers. Three of the five acting ministers were Manchus: Shaoying, Shouxun, and Xiyan. Thus, in actuality, four (rather than one) of the ten ministers in Yuan's original cabinet were Manchus.

98. *NCH*, 25 Nov. 1911, 509, 512; Williams, *China Yesterday and To-day*, 478–79; *SL*/XT, 65: 2b; 66: 5a; *STSB*, XT 3/11/1, 7.

99. Guo Xiaocheng, "Yihe shimo," 66–67; Zhang Guogan, *Xinhai Geming*, 279–80; *NCH*, 25 Nov. 1911, 511–15.

100. Morrison, *Correspondence*, 661–66; *NCH*, 25 Nov. 1911, 505; *SSJY*, 1911: 986.

101. Wu Tingfang, *Wu xiansheng gongdu*, 1: 1a; Zhang Cunwu, "Wu Tingfang," 102, 110–11; Pomerantz-Zhang, *Wu Tingfang*, 205–6.

102. Wu Tingfang, *Wu xiansheng gongdu*, 1: 1a; *NCH*, 18 Nov. 1911, 445; Zhang Cunwu, "Wu Tingfang," 102–4; Pomerantz-Zhang, *Wu Tingfang*, 203.

103. *SL*/XT, 66: 5b; Zhu Ying, "Tang Shaoyi," 73–74; Yang Du, *Yang Du ji*, 542–43; *SSJY*, 1911: 1052, 1059–60. My thanks to Zhu Ying for making the Tang Shaoyi article available to me.

104. Liu Housheng, *Zhang Jian zhuanji*, 192; Sigel, "Revolution by Diplomacy," 119, 120, 133; Zhang Yuesheng, "Zhuiji Baqi daibiao," 427; *SSJY*, 1911: 1086.

105. Liu Housheng, *Zhang Jian zhuanji*, 182, 192–95; Zhang Guogan, *Xinhai Geming*, 292; Sigel, "Revolution by Diplomacy," 131–32; Pomerantz-Zhang, *Wu Tingfang*, 211.

106. Wu Tingfang, *Gonghe guanjian lu*, 1: 9–16.

107. FO 405/205, no. 575, Jordan to Grey, 22 Dec. 1911; no. 588, Jordan to Grey, 24 Dec.; no. 590, memorandum communicated by Chargé Yamaza, London, 26 Dec.; no. 595, Jordan to Grey, 26 Dec.; no. 597, Grey to Jordan, 26 Dec.; no. 613, Jordan to Grey, 28 Dec.

108. Zhang Guogan, *Xinhai Geming*, 293.

109. *Zhonghua Minguo shi*, 2: 51–52; *STSB*, XT 3/11/10, 7; 11/11, 7; Zhang Guogan, *Xinhai Geming*, 294; *NCH*, 30 Dec. 1911, 870; 6 Jan. 1912, 25; *SL*/XT, 67: 11b-12a.

110. Wu Tingfang, *Gonghe guanjian lu*, 1: 16–30; Zhang Guogan, *Xinhai Geming*, 294–95.

111. Wu Tingfang, *Gonghe guanjian lu*, 1: 18, 21.

112. Pomerantz-Zhang, *Wu Tingfang*, 215–16; *SSJY*, 1912A: 18. On Sun's election and inauguration, see Esherick, "Founding a Republic."

113. *STSB*, XT 3/11/13, 7; 11/18, 2; 11/19, 2; *Qingdai renwu zhuan'gao*, 8: 123; Zha Shijie, "Qingmo de Zongshedang," 126–30; Bai Jie, "Qingmo zhengtan," 39.

114. Zhang Guogan, *Xinhai Geming*, 296–97; Zhu Ying, "Tang Shaoyi," 78–79; *SSJY*, 1912A: 20–21.

115. *STSB*, XT 3/11/18, 7; J. Ch'en, *Yuan Shih-k'ai*, 96; FO 405/208, no. 177, Jordan to Grey, 22 Jan. 1912.

116. Pomerantz-Zhang, *Wu Tingfang*, 219–20.

117. *NCH*, 13 Jan. 1912, 101; *Shibao*, 16 Jan. 1912, 2. This proposal does not appear in Wu Tingfang, *Gonghe guanjian lu*.

118. Zhang Guogan, *Xinhai Geming*, 297–300; FO 405/208, no. 67, Jordan to Grey, 14 Jan. 1912; Morrison, *Correspondence*, 700; Shang Binghe, *Xinren chunqiu*, 26: 16a-18b.

119. *SSJY*, 1912A: 91–97.

120. *STSB*, XT 3/12/1, 7; 12/5, 7; Shang Binghe, *Xinren chunqiu*, 26: 18b-19a; Morrison, *Correspondence*, 703.

121. Wu Tingfang, *Gonghe guanjian lu*, 1: 72–74.

122. Ibid., 1: 72–80, 83–84.

123. Ibid., 1: 81–82.

124. *STSB*, 3/12/2, 7; 12/5, 7; Liang Xuyi, "Liangbi zhuan," 32; Morrison, *Correspondence*, 703; *NCH*, 27 Jan. 1912, 231, 233.

125. *STSB*, XT 3/11/22, 2; 12/5, 7; *Shibao*, 25 Jan. 1912, 3; Liao Yuchun, "Xin Zhongguo," 455; Morrison, *Correspondence*, 706–7.

126. *STSB*, XT 3/12/5, 7.

127. Yun Baohui, "Xinhai Feng Guozhang," 119–20; Zhang Yilin, "Gu daili dazongtong," 17a-17b; Shen Yunlong, "Beiyang zhi 'gou,'" 49; Liao Yuchun, "Xin Zhongguo," 450, 455, 457, 461; Jinliang, *Guang-Xuan xiaoji*, 153–54; *Shibao*, 25 Jan. 1912, 3.

128. *STSB*, 3/12/6, 7; Shang Binghe, *Xinren chunqiu*, 26: 19a-19b; Puwei, "Rangguo yuqian huiyi," 111–12; Xiao Yishan, *Qingdai tongshi*, 2717–18; *NCH*, 27 Jan. 1912, 231–32. Puwei and Xiao Yishan both misdate this meeting; Puwei says it took place on the 17th; Xiao says the 20th.

129. Shang Binghe, *Xinren chunqiu*, 26: 19b; Puwei, "Rangguo yuqian huiyi," 112–14; *STSB*, 3/12/5, 7; 12/6, 7. Puwei again errs in his dating of this meeting.

130. Wan Xiangchun and Deng Xianglin, "Xin-Yi geming"; Liang Xuyi, "Liangbi zhuan," 32; Des Forges, *Hsi-liang*, 183–84; *SL/XT*, 69: 9a-9b; *STSB*, XT 3/12/20, 4; *Shibao*, 21 Feb. 1912, 5.

131. *NCH*, 3 Feb. 1912, 301.

132. *SL/XT*, 69: 13b-14a.

133. *SL/XT*, 69: 14b.

134. Zhang Guogan, *Xinhai Geming*, 304–6; Li Shoukong, "Duan Qirui."

135. *STSB*, XT 3/12/9, 7; Yang Du, *Yang Du ji*, 543–44.

136. Wu Tingfang, *Gonghe guanjian lu*, 1: 87.

137. *STSB*, XT 3/12/10, 7; *Shibao*, 10 Feb. 1912, 2.

138. Liang Xuyi, "Liangbi zhuan," 32; Chang Shun, "Maichen beizha"; *SSJY*, 1912A: 131–38; *STSB*, XT 3/12/20, 7; Morrison, *Correspondence*, 716.

139. Zhang Guogan, *Xinhai Geming*, 309, 311; *STSB*, XT 3/12/12, 7; 12/14, 7; 12/16, 7; 12/17, 7; 12/19, 7.

140. Wu Tingfang, *Gonghe guanjian lu*, 1: 87–88.

141. Ibid., 1: 94–96; Zhang Guogan, *Xinhai Geming*, 311–13.

142. *SSJY*, 1912A: 188–90; Wu Tingfang, *Gonghe guanjian lu*, 1: 96–98; Zhang Guogan, *Xinhai Geming*, 313–14. On the tael-dollar exchange rate (80 taels = 100 yuan), see Yang Xuechen and Zhou Yuanlian, *Qingdai Baqi wanggong guizu*, 367.

143. Wu Tingfang, *Gonghe guanjian lu*, 1: 107–12; *STSB*, XT 3/12/20, 7; 12/23, 7.

144. Wu Tingfang, *Gonghe guanjian lu*, 1: 113–14.

145. Ibid., 1: 117–18, 127–28; *SSJY*, 1912A: 214; *Shibao*, 11 Feb. 1912, 5.

146. Wu Tingfang, *Gonghe guanjian lu*, 1: 127; *Shibao*, 13 Feb. 1912, 1–2.

147. *STSB*, XT 3/12/13, 7; 12/14, 7; 12/15, 7; 12/16, 7; Yun Baohui, "Xinhai Feng Guozhang," 119–20; Zhang Yilin, "Gu daili dazongtong," 17b; Liao Yuchun, "Xin Zhongguo," 462.

148. *Shibao*, 5 Feb. 1912, 2; *STSB*, XT 3/12/20, 7; 12/21, 7; 12/24, 7; 12/27, 5.

149. *SL/XT*, 70: 13b–19a.

150. J. Ch'en, *Yuan Shih-k'ai*, 105; *SSJY*, 1912A: 241–42.

151. Rummel, *China's Bloody Century*, 41.

152. Feng Ziyou, *Geming yishi*, 5: 254–55.

153. *STSB*, XT 3/9/21, 4; *NCH*, 28 Oct. 1911, 227; *SSJY*, 1912A: 224. Due to Qing censorship, the reference to the Manchus in the *STSB* report was deleted.

154. Morrison, *Correspondence*, 770. On the estimated size of the national revenue, see Robert Bredon in *NCH*, 2 March 1912, 554.

5 / COURT AND MANCHUS AFTER 1911

1. On the "liberal republic," see Young, *Presidency of Yuan Shih-k'ai*, chap. 4.

2. J. Ch'en, *Yuan Shih-k'ai*, 106–7; *NCH*, 16 March 1912, 729; 25 Jan. 1913, 262; 22 Feb., 563; 1 March, 645; *STSB*, 7 April 1912, 7; 30 April, 7; 31 Aug., 5; 16 Oct., 7; 21 Dec., 7; *Shibao*, 25 April 1913, 4; Hu Pingsheng, *Minguo chuqi de fubipai*, 389.

3. *STSB*, 24 Dec. 1912, 5; *Shibao*, 7 Jan. 1913, 3; 22 Feb., 3; 7 April, 2; 9 April, 2; Bredon, *Peking*, 84, 119, 134; Gamble, *Peking*, 61, 236–37; Johnston, *Twilight in the Forbidden City*, 178, 305. See also Shi, "From Imperial Gardens."

4. Wu Tingfang, *Gonghe guanjian lu*, 1: 72; *Shibao*, 11 Oct. 1913, 2–3; 24 Oct. 1915, 3; Xin Ping et al., *Minguo shehui daguan*, 952; Bredon, *Peking*, 89; Bonner, *Wang Kuo-wei*, 276 n. 33; Johnston, *Twilight in the Forbidden City*, 169–72, 175, 300–302, 357.

5. *SSJY*, 1913A: 143, 174; Aisin-Gioro, *From Emperor to Citizen*, 80; Yang Xuechen and Zhou Yuanlian, *Qingdai Baqi wanggong guizu*, 376–77; *Shibao*, 10 March 1913, 2; 11 March, 2; Pujie, "Qinggong huiqin jianwen."

6. *Shibao*, 11 March 1912, 2; 15 Sept., 2; 11 Oct. 1913, 2–3; *SSJY*, 1912B: 243–44; *STSB*, 13 Sept. 1912, 2, 7; *NCH*, 18 Oct. 1913, 184–85.

7. See, e.g., *Shibao*, 24 March 1912, 2; 26 May, 2; 14 Aug., 2; 24 Nov., 2; *STSB*, 13 June 1912, 7; 29 Sept., 5; 3 Dec., 5; 21 Dec., 5.

8. *STSB*, 9 April 1912, 7; 13 June, 7; 23 June, 7; 26 Oct., 7; 3 Dec., 5; *Shibao*, 20 April 1912, 2; *NCH*, 1 March 1913, 609; *SSJY*, 1913A: 500.

9. *SSJY*, 1913A: 501; 1913B: 637–38; 1915: 716; Hu Pingsheng, *Minguo chuqi de fubipai*, 57; *Shibao*, 28 Jan. 1913, 2; 14 Nov., 2; 16 Dec., 2.

10. *SSJY*, 1913A: 500; *Shibao*, 17 Oct. 1912, 3; 9 Jan. 1913, 3; 11 Oct., 4; *STSB*, 3 April 1912, 7; 5 May, 2; *NCH*, 19 Oct. 1912, 178; Wu Zhaoqing, "Qingmo Jinweijun," 22.

11. United States, War College Division of the General Staff, 6283–11, "Casual Military Notes," 4 May 1912, enclosure no. 2; *Shibao*, 23 Feb. 1912, 2; 7 Jan. 1913, 3; 9 Jan., 3; 20 Oct., 2; *STSB*, 11 Sept. 1912, 5; 20 Oct., 5; Wu Zhaoqing, "Qingmo Jinweijun," 22; Zaitao, "Jinweijun zhi jianli," 241.

12. *SSJY*, 1912B: 239; *STSB*, 28 Sept. 1912, 7; 24 Nov., 7; *Shibao*, 27 June 1913, 2.

13. Hu Pingsheng, *Minguo chuqi de fubipai*, 33–40; Jansen, *Japanese and Sun Yat-sen*, 137–40; Zha Shijie, "Qingmo de Zongshedang," 132–39; Xianjun, "Su qinwang Shanqi."

14. *STSB*, 18 April 1912, 2; 19 April, 2; 25 May, 5; 26 May, 5; 28 May, 5; *Shibao*, 20 April 1912, 3; Hu Pingsheng, *Minguo chuqi de fubipai*, 3–8.

15. *STSB*, 4 April 1912, 7; 6 April, 7; 7 April, 7; 26 May, 7; *Shibao*, 7 April 1912, 2; *DFZZ* 8, no. 11: "Zhongguo dashiji," 7 (May 1912).

16. *SSJY*, 1914A: 554–56, 588–89, 606, 704–10; Hu Pingsheng, *Minguo chuqi de fubipai*, 383–84; *Shibao*, 28 April 1914, 2; 1 May, 4.

17. Hu Pingsheng, *Minguo chuqi de fubipai*, 63–64, 384; Johnston, *Twilight in the Forbidden City*, 98–100.

18. *Shibao*, 28 April 1914, 2; 1 May, 4; 15 Nov. 1915, 1; *SSJY*, 1914B: 719.

19. *Shibao*, 8 Feb. 1914, 2; 23 Feb., 5; 30 Nov., 4; 19 Feb. 1915, 2; 24 June, 5; 30 Aug., 6; 8 Sept., 4; 25 Dec., 5; Zaitao, "Jinweijun zhi jianli," 240; Zhang Bofeng and Li Zongyi, *Beiyang junfa*, 6: 370; Wu Zhaoqing, "Qingmo Jinweijun," 22.

20. *Shibao*, 27 Aug. 1915, 2; 5 Sept., 2; 8 Sept., 4; 15 Sept., 4; 22 Sept., 3; 18 Dec., 2; 27 Dec., 2; J. Ch'en, *Yuan Shih-k'ai*, 174; Young, *Presidency of Yuan Shih-k'ai*, 215, 222; *SSJY*, 1915: 927; Johnston, *Twilight in the Forbidden City*, 120–21.

21. *Shibao*, 13 Oct. 1915, 2–3; 21 Oct., 2; Hu Pingsheng, *Minguo chuqi de fubipai*, 385.

22. *Shibao*, 26 Sept. 1915, 2; 29 Sept., 3; 15 Dec., 2; *Qingdai renwu zhuan'gao*, 9: 199; Hu Pingsheng, *Minguo chuqi de fubipai*, 389.

23. Boorman and Howard, *Biographical Dictionary*, 2: 16–17.

24. *SSJY*, 1916: 636, 664.

25. *SSJY*, 1916: 513–21, 725; 1917: 40, 320; Hu Pingsheng, *Minguo chuqi de fubipai*, 385–87; Johnston, *Twilight in the Forbidden City*, 105.

26. *SSJY*, 1916: 597; Zhang Bofeng and Li Zongyi, *Beiyang junfa*, 6: 543.

27. Hu Pingsheng, *Minguo chuqi de fubipai*, 212, 223–25.

28. *SSJY*, 1917: 490–91; Hu Pingsheng, *Minguo chuqi de fubipai*, 223–25.

29. *SSJY*, 1917: 555–56; Hu Pingsheng, *Minguo chuqi de fubipai*, 246, 262, 267–68, 339–43.

30. Hu Pingsheng, *Minguo chuqi de fubipai*, 327, 329; *SSJY*, 1917: 581–82; Sheridan, *Chinese Warlord*, 66 note; Feng Yuxiang, *Wo de shenghuo*, 510.

31. Aisin-Gioro, *From Emperor to Citizen*, 94–96; Hu Pingsheng, *Minguo chuqi de fubipai*, 227, 320, 326–30; *Qingdai renwu zhuan'gao*, 9: 200; Xin Ping et al., *Minguo she-hui daguan*, 701–2.

32. Johnston, *Twilight in the Forbidden City*, 142; *SSJY*, 1918B: 373; 1921B: 627–28; Aisin-Gioro, *From Emperor to Citizen*, 120.

33. Aisin-Gioro, *From Emperor to Citizen*, 114, 119; Johnston, *Twilight in the Forbidden City*, 224–25, 300–302; Bonner, *Wang Kuo-wei*, 276 n. 33. Johnston, p. 300, reproduces the document in Chinese; there is, however, no reference to the agreement in Hu Pingsheng, *Minguo chuqi de fubipai*.

34. Aisin-Gioro, *From Emperor to Citizen*, 114.

35. *SSJY*, 1917: 555, 733, 903; 1919A: 75; Hu Pingsheng, *Minguo chuqi de fubipai*, 268; Zaitao, "Jinweijun zhi jianli," 240–41; Zhang Bofeng and Li Zongyi, *Beiyang junfa*, 1: 12, 104; 6: 370–71.

36. Hu Pingsheng, *Minguo chuqi de fubipai*, 387–88; Aisin-Gioro, *From Emperor to Citizen*, 123, 141–42; Boorman and Howard, *Biographical Dictionary*, 1: 72; 3: 81; *SSJY*, 1922B: 161; 1924A: 839–40; Bonner, *Wang Kuo-wei*, 201–4; Johnston, *Twilight in the Forbidden City*, 142–43.

37. Johnston, *Twilight in the Forbidden City*, 163–67, 231–32, 273–74, 337–40; Aisin-Gioro, *From Emperor to Citizen*, 113–21, 132–36, 141; *SSJY*, 1923B: 77.

38. Hu Pingsheng, *Minguo chuqi de fubipai*, 390, 395–97; Aisin-Gioro, *From Emperor to Citizen*, 139–42; Johnston, *Twilight in the Forbidden City*, 354–61, 366–67.

39. Hu Pingsheng, *Minguo chuqi de fubipai*, 407–12; Feng Yuxiang, *Wo de shenghuo*, 509–10; Aisin-Gioro, *From Emperor to Citizen*, 144–49; Johnston, *Twilight in the Forbidden City*, 389–91.

40. Aisin-Gioro, *From Emperor to Citizen*, 148–69; Hu Pingsheng, *Minguo chuqi de fubipai*, 410–11, 416–25.

41. Yang Xuechen and Zhou Yuanlian, *Qingdai Baqi wanggong guizu*, 405, 412.

42. Zaitao, "Jinweijun zhi jianli," 241; *SSJY*, 1924B: 759.

43. Wu Xiangxiang, "Qingdi tuiwei," 118–19; Hu Pingsheng, *Minguo chuqi de fubipai*, 413, 462; Johnston, *Twilight in the Forbidden City*, 439–42.

44. Hu Pingsheng, *Minguo chuqi de fubipai*, 414–15; Johnston, *Twilight in the Forbidden City*, 405–6; Aisin-Gioro, *From Emperor to Citizen*, 157. For a recent study that is likewise critical of Puyi's expulsion, see Yu Dahua, "'Qingshi youdai tiaojian' xinlun," 172–76.

45. Hu Pingsheng, *Minguo chuqi de fubipai*, 414–16, 420; Aisin-Gioro, *From Emperor to Citizen*, 153; Johnston, *Twilight in the Forbidden City*, 410–11; Feng Yuxiang, *Wo de shenghuo*, 510–11. On the "aftermath conference," see Boorman and Howard, *Biographical Dictionary*, 3: 334–35.

46. Hu Pingsheng, *Minguo chuqi de fubipai*, 425–27; Xin Ping et al., *Minguo shehui daguan*, 952; Shi, "From Imperial Gardens," 238–39.

47. Hu Pingsheng, *Minguo chuqi de fubipai*, 463–67, 546; Lo, *K'ang Yu-wei*, 248–49.

48. Hu Pingsheng, *Minguo chuqi de fubipai*, 442–43.

49. Ibid., 443–49, 453–54; Crossley, *Orphan Warriors*, 210.

50. Hu Pingsheng, *Minguo chuqi de fubipai*, 449–57; Aisin-Gioro, *From Emperor to Citizen*, 194–96.

51. For an overview, see Cheng Weikun, "Minchu 'jianbianre.'"

52. *Shibao*, XT 3/9/8, 3; 10/26, 4.

53. *NCH*, 16 Dec. 1911, 738; 23 Dec., 806; *STSB*, XT 3/12/3, 4.

54. *Shibao*, 1 Jan. 1912, 3; 2 Jan., 3; *STSB*, 17 July 1912, 7; 19 July, 7.

55. *SSJY*, 1912A: 312.

56. Morrison, *Correspondence*, 742; Yun Baohui, "Xinhai Feng Guozhang," 119–20; *Shibao*, 6 May 1912, 2; *STSB*, 31 Oct. 1912, 5; *SSJY*, 1912B: 443–44; Young, *Presidency of Yuan Shih-k'ai*, 204–5.

57. Bonner, *Wang Kuo-wei*, 208, 214.

58. Sheridan, *Chinese Warlord*, 113, 116; Franck, *Roving through Southern China*, 551; Cochran and Hsieh, *One Day in China*, 173.

59. Shirokogoroff, *Social Organization*, 4, 148.

60. Wadley, "Altaic Influences."

61. Esherick, "Founding a Republic," 148; Finnane, "What Should Women Wear?" 101, 107; Fitzgerald, *Awakening China*, 23–25.

62. Finnane, "What Should Women Wear?"; Xin Ping et al., *Minguo shehui daguan*, 585–88; Garrett, *Traditional Chinese Clothing*, 15–20. On the persistence and evolution of the *changpao* and *qipao* in the Republican era, see Zhou Xibao, *Zhongguo gudai fushi*, 537, 539–40.

63. *SSJY*, 1915: 942–43.

64. *STSB*, 10 Oct. 1912, 7; *Shibao*, 13 Nov. 1914, 2.

65. Tong Jiajiang, "Qingdai Baqi zhidu," 101–5; *SSJY*, 1912B: 70, 751; 1924A: 77.

66. Tong Jiajiang, "Qingdai Baqi zhidu," 107; *SSJY*, 1914A: 793–94.

67. *SSJY*, 1915: 775, 903–7.

68. Tong Jiajiang, "Qingdai Baqi zhidu," 107.

69. Gamble, *Peking*, 99.

70. *Manzu shehui lishi*, 89, 124–29.

71. *STSB*, 16 Nov. 1912, 4. See also *Manzu jianshi*, 179.

72. *Shibao*, 9 April 1912, 3; 9 May, 3.

73. *STSB*, 14 July 1912, 5.

74. Wang Zongyou, *Guangzhou Manzu*, 64–65; Shu Zhongji, "Xinhai Geming shi," 223.

75. *STSB*, 12 July 1912, 5; 23 Nov., 3; *Shibao*, 15 Nov. 1912, 2; *Manzu jianshi*, 179.

76. Tong Jiajiang, "Qingdai Baqi zhidu," 104–6, 108; *Shibao*, 20 Dec. 1913, 2.

77. *Manzu shehui lishi*, 89; Tong Jiajiang, "Qingdai Baqi zhidu," 104; *SSJY*, 1924B: 789; Han Yanlong and Su Yigong, *Zhongguo jindai jingcha*, 352.

78. *STSB*, 18 April 1912, 2; 18 Aug., 7; *SSJY*, 1914A: 648; 1914B: 530, 971; *Shibao*, 3 Feb. 1914, 4–5; 25 Feb., 3–4; *Qizu yuebao*, no. 6: "Shiping," 1–3 (Nov. 1914).

79. *STSB*, 21 April 1912, 2; 7 Aug., 5; *Yishibao* (Beiping), 18 Feb. 1929, 7; Hu Pingsheng, *Minguo chuqi de fubipai*, 407; Zhou Qiuguang, "Modern Chinese Educational Philanthropy," 61. I am grateful to David Strand for sharing the *Yishibao* reference with me.

80. *Shibao*, 9 May 1912, 3; 25 Dec., 3; 2 Oct. 1915, 5; *STSB*, 9 June 1912, 7; 10 Nov., 4; *Guomin xinbao* (Hankou), 20 May 1918. My thanks to Edward McCord for making the citation from *Guomin xinbao* available to me.

81. *Manzu jianshi*, 179.

82. Ibid.

83. *Shibao*, 1 July 1914, 5–6; Zhang Bofeng and Li Zongyi, *Beiyang junfa*, 1: 92.

84. Strand, *Rickshaw Beijing*, 72–73. See also "Beijingshi Haidianqu Huoqiying," 89.

85. Coates, "Documents in Chinese," 243–44.

86. Gamble, *Peking*, 273–74.

87. Wang Zongyou, *Guangzhou Manzu*, 65–68; *Manzu shehui lishi*, 194.

88. *Shibao*, 31 Dec. 1912, 2, 4.

89. *SSJY*, 1912A: 441.

90. USDS, Decimal File, 893.52/8–10, Consul John Fowler, Fuzhou, 12 Sept., 24 Sept., and 2 Oct. 1912.

91. *NCH*, 8 Nov. 1913, 450; *Shibao*, 16 Sept. 1913, 5; Zheng Yunshan et al., *Hangzhou yu Xihu*, 94.

92. Zhu Xuwu and Dang Zixin, "Shaanxi Xinhai Geming," 9; *NCH*, 10 Aug. 1912, 416; *STSB*, 2 Aug. 1912, 4; *Chengdu chengfang guji*, 100; Cao Zixi and Yu Guangdu, *Beijing tongshi*, 10: 190–91; Yang Dongping, *Chengshi jifeng*, 194–99. My thanks to Mingzheng Shi for the two Beijing references.

93. Shirokogoroff, *Social Organization*, 71.

94. Gamble, *Peking*, 272–73; *Manzu shehui lishi*, 191.

95. Strand, *Rickshaw Beijing*, 30–31; Honig, "Politics of Prejudice," 245–46; Pan Honggang, "Xinhai Geming," 24–25.

96. *STSB*, 25 May 1912, 2.

97. *Shibao*, 17 April 1912, 2; *SSJY*, 1912B: 783–88; 1916: 409; Zhang Bofeng and Li Zongyi, *Beiyang junfa*, 6: 493–94, 507.

98. *SSJY*, 1912B: 784; 1914A: 1021–22; 1914B: 983; 1917: 478, 1119; 1920: 486.

99. Boorman and Howard, *Biographical Dictionary*, 1: 141–42; Crossley, *Orphan Warriors*, 208–9.

100. *STSB*, 29 Sept. 1912, 7; Zhang Bofeng and Li Zongyi, *Beiyang junfa*, 6: 543.

101. *SSJY*, 1912A: 327.

102. Xin Ping et al., *Minguo shehui daguan*, 32–35; *SSJY*, 1912A: 500, 517, 552–53.

103. *SSJY*, 1912B: 325. See also 1912A: 441; and Zhao Shu, "Xinhai Geming qian-hou," 16.

104. *SSJY*, 1912A: 534–35; *STSB*, 4 June 1912, 2; *Shibao*, 2 Sept. 1912, 3; 24 March 1914, 5.

105. *SSJY*, 1914B: 306–25.

106. *STSB*, 16 April 1912, 7; 7 May, 7; 29 June, 5; 25 Sept., 7; *SSJY*, 1912B: 484–85; Zhang Yufa, *Minguo chunian*, 531–66; *Qizu yuebao*, no. 6: "Lunshuo 2," 1–4 (Nov. 1914). On Fuyuan, see Tahara, *Shinmatsu Minsho*, 567.

107. *STSB*, 30 April 1912, 5; 22 May, 2, 4; *Yishibao*, 18 Feb. 1929, 7.

108. *Shibao*, 17 July 1912, 3–4; 27 March 1914, 5; 3 April, 5; 15 Jan. 1915, 3–4; 16 Jan., 4; 17 Jan., 4.

109. Zhao Shu, "Cong yizhang"; *SSJY*, 1914B: 306–25.

110. *SSJY*, 1913A: 200–201.

111. Lattimore, *Manchuria*, 62 n. 2; on *qizu* as a label for the Manchus, see Teng Shaozhen, "Manzhou Manzu" (part 2), 51–52

112. Rong Tiegeng, "Qingdai Beijing," 36; Wang Zongyou, *Guangzhou Manzu*, 70, 77–82; Hsu, *Study of a Typical Chinese Town*, 4; Zhao Shu, "Cong yizhang."

113. Hu Pingsheng, *Minguo chuqi de fubipai*, 485–86; Aisin-Gioro, *From Emperor to Citizen*, 228.

114. Xianjun, "Su qinwang Shanqi," 311, 314; Aisin-Gioro, *From Emperor to Citizen*, 176; USDS, Decimal File, 893.44, Kung Prince/—, Consul J. W. Ballantine, Dalian, 8 Dec. 1922; Hu Pingsheng, *Minguo chuqi de fubipai*, 476–77, 553; Scotland, *Empty Throne*, 68.

115. Hu Pingsheng, *Minguo chuqi de fubipai*, 487–93; Aisin-Gioro, *From Emperor to Citizen*, 239–47, 273–76; Jones, *Manchuria Since 1931*, 40–42.

116. On the historical roots of the Manzhouguo name, see Johnston, *Twilight in the Forbidden City*, 450–51; and Wakeman, *Great Enterprise*, 176. On the symbolism of 1

March, see Hu Pingsheng, *Minguo chuqi de fubipai*, 490; and Jones, *Manchuria Since 1931*, 40. According to Jones, the date was the anniversary of the establishment of the Qing in Beijing in 1644, but none of the key dates in early Qing history—including Nurhaci's proclamation of the Jin in 1616; Hong Taiji's proclamation of the Qing in 1636; and Shunzhi's accession as emperor, entry into Beijing, and enthronement as emperor of China in 1643–44—corresponds to the first day of the third month in either the lunar or the solar calendar.

117. Hu Pingsheng, *Minguo chuqi de fubipai*, 482; Johnston, *Twilight in the Forbidden City*, 450; Jones, *Manchuria Since 1931*, 41–42; Aisin-Gioro, *From Emperor to Citizen*, 273–76.

118. Aisin-Gioro, *From Emperor to Citizen*, 276–77, 289–90, 372; Xianjun, "Su qin-wang Shanqi," 315; Jin Qicong, "Jingqi de Manzu," 1990, no. 4: 36; *Qingdai renwu zhuan'-gao*, 9: 206; Zheng Huaiyi and Zhang Jianshe, *Modai huangshu*, 92–94, 150.

119. Aisin-Gioro, *From Emperor to Citizen*, 319–30, 340, 361, 372.

120. Ibid., 466–67, 472, 478–80; Wang Qingxiang, *Mao Zedong Zhou Enlai*, 337–47.

121. Zheng Huaiyi and Zhang Jianshe, *Modai huangshu*, 105–94; Wang Zongyou, *Guangzhou Manzu*, 180; *Zhonghua renmin gongheguo*, 1: 408; 2: 348, 355.

122. Aixin-Jiaoluo, "My Family and Myself"; Yang Xuechen and Zhou Yuanlian, *Qingdai Baqi wanggong guizu*, 440–41; *Zhonghua renmin gongheguo*, 4: 901–5; *New York Times*, 2 March 1994, B9. For a light-hearted account of a search for Puyi's heir, see Scotland, *Empty Throne*.

123. Li Jiannong, *Zuijin sanshinian*, 560–62; Deal, "'Question of Nationalities,'" 25; *Sanmin Zhuyi cidian*, 64, 436–37. On how Sun's government in Guangzhou dealt with the local Manchus in 1925, see Fitzgerald, *Awakening China*, 183–84.

124. Benson, *Ili Rebellion*, 12–15; Deal, "'Question of Nationalities,'" 25–28; Jiang Jieshi, *Zhongguo zhi mingyun*, 119–20; Chiang, *China's Destiny*, 3–13; *Sanmin Zhuyi cidian*, 64.

125. Shu Yi, "Zaitan Lao She," 62; Vohra, *Lao She*, 162.

126. Deal, "'Question of Nationalities,'" 26; Jones, *Manchuria Since 1931*, 5, 55, 59; "Tungus Race in Manchoukuo," 65–72.

127. Jones, *Manchuria Since 1931*, 59; Hu Pingsheng, *Minguo chuqi de fubipai*, 490; Aisin-Gioro, *From Emperor to Citizen*, 256; Crossley, *Orphan Warriors*, 208–13. On Xiqia, see Zhang Bofeng and Li Zongyi, *Beiyang junfa*, 6: 547–48; Li Zhiting, *Aixin Jueluo jiazu*, 3: 217–18.

128. Zhao Shu, "Jianguo qianhou," 35; Moseley, *Party and the National Question*, 29; Heberer, *China and Its National Minorities*, 30; *Manzu shehui lishi*, 81.

129. Zhao Shu, "Beijing chengqu Manzu," 207; Y. Yan, *Flow of Gifts*, 26, 32–33.

130. Ma Xiedi, "Qingdai Guangzhou Manzu," 65; idem, "Liu Xianzhi," 43; *Manzu shehui lishi*, 204–5.

131. Fei, "Ethnic Identification," 69–71.

132. Banister, *China's Changing Population*, 322–23.

133. Yang Xuechen and Zhou Yuanlian, *Qingdai Baqi wanggong guizu*, 425; *Zhonghua renmin gongheguo*, 1: 407–11.

134. Wang Zongyou, *Guangzhou Manzu*, 74–75; He Puying, "Xin Zhongguo chengli," 90.

135. Vohra, *Lao She*, 162–63; *Zhonghua renmin gongheguo*, 1: 408; 2: 348, 355.

136. Banister, *China's Changing Population*, 322–23.

137. Moseley, *Party and the National Question*, 161–62; Wulaxichun, "Manzu de yuyan," 52; Zhao Shu, "'Wenge' xianhou," 52; *Zhongguo 1982-nian renkou*, table 27; He Puying, "Xin Zhongguo chengli," 91.

138. He Puying, "Xin Zhongguo chengli," 91; Zhao Huansen and Tang Xuekai, "Pengbo fazhan," 42; Zhang Jiasheng, "Wo du 'Dandong Manzu,'" 40; Stary et al., *On the Tracks of Manchu Culture*, 71; "Hebeisheng Zunhuaxian Dongling."

139. Tongjia and Qingfu, "Xinjiang Xibozu"; Yan Xiangdong, "Xinjiang Xiboyu."

140. *Renmin ribao*, 12 May 1986; *China Daily*, 16 July 1987, 5.

141. Zhang Tianlu, *Zhongguo shaoshu minzu*, appendix 2.

142. Zhao Shu, "Cong yizhang," 32.

CONCLUSION

1. Reynolds, *China, 1898–1912*.

2. On the fate of the Ottoman dynasty, see Lord Kinross, *Ataturk*, chaps. 42, 45, 46. On that of the Tokugawa shogunate, see *Kodansha Encyclopedia*, 4: 171; 8: 57.

3. For the dissenting view that Manchus and/or banner people were defined politically, see Rawski, "Ch'ing Imperial Marriage," 180; and Rigger, "Voices of Manchu Identity," 191.

4. On the emergence of the term "Manzu" in the late Qing and early Republic, see Teng Shaozhen, "Manzhou Manzu," part 2: 50–53.

5. See Gladney, *Muslim Chinese*; Constable, *Guest People*; Honig, *Creating Chinese Ethnicity*.

Glossary

Aixin Jueluo (Aisin Gioro) 愛新覺羅

anquan Man-qi 安全滿旗

Baerhu 巴爾虎
baoyi (booi) 包衣
Baqi 八旗
Baqi Huiguan 八旗會館
Baqi Manzhou 八旗滿洲
Baqi shengji wenti 八旗生計問題
Baqi xianxian ci 八旗先賢祠
Baqi Xianzheng Hui 八旗憲政會
Beijing Manwen Xueyuan 北京滿文學院
Beijing nübao 北京女報
beile 貝勒
beizi (beise) 貝子
bianmen 邊門
Biantong Qizhi Chu 變通旗制處
bingjian 兵諫
bitieshi (bithesi) 筆帖式
bufen Man-Han 不分滿漢
bufu zeren 不負責任
Bujunying 步軍營

Cai Chengxun 蔡成勛
Cai Tinggan 蔡廷幹

Cai Yuanpei 蔡元培
canling 參領
Canzhengyuan 參政院
Cao Kun 曹錕
Cao Xueqin 曹雪芹
Cao Yabo 曹亞伯
Chaguan 茶館
Chahaer 察哈爾
changbeijun 常備軍
Changfu 長福
Changgeng 長庚
changpao 長袍
Chaoxian 朝鮮
chen 臣
Chen Baochen 陳寶琛
Chen Baozhen 陳寶箴
Chen Bi 陳璧
Chen Jiongming 陳炯明
Chen Kuilong 陳夔龍
Chen Mingxia 陳名夏
Chen Tianhua 陳天華
Cheng Dequan 程德全
Cheng Jiacheng 程家檉
Cheng Yunhe 程允和
chengshouwei 城守尉
Chongen (or Chonglin) 崇恩（崇林）
Chongshi Xuetang 崇實學堂

Chouban Baqi Shengji Chu 籌辦
八旗生計處
Chouban Haijun Shiwuchu 籌辦
海軍事務處
Chunliang 春梁
Chuohabu 綽哈布
Chuohatai 綽哈泰
ciwei 爵位
Cixi 慈禧
Cuizhen 崔鎮

Dachonga 達崇阿
Dada 韃靼
Dagongbao 大公報
Dai Hongci 戴鴻慈
Daliyuan 大理院
Dalu 韃虜
Daoguang 道光
daqian 打千
Da-Qing Diguo 大清帝國
Da-Qing huangdi 大清皇帝
Da-Qing huidian 大清會典
Dashou 達壽
Datongbao 大同報
Dawoer 達斡爾
dayuanshuai 大元帥
Dehu 德祜
Deng Yuanpeng 鄧元彭
Derui 德銳
diguo 帝國
Dingxuan 定烜
Dongfang zazhi 東方雜誌
Donghu 東胡
Duan Qirui 段棋瑞
Duan Zhigui 段芝貴
Duanfang 端方
dutong 都統

Elunchun 鄂倫春
Eluosi 俄羅斯
Elute 鄂魯特
Enhua 恩華
Enming 恩銘
Ewenke 鄂溫克

Fandui Qingshi Youdai Datong-
meng 反對清室優待大同盟
fangshouwei 防守尉
fangyu 防禦
fanyi 繙譯
fanzi 番子
feiding 廢丁
Feng Guozhang 馮國璋
Feng Xu 馮煦
Feng Yuxiang 馮玉祥
Fengshan 鳳山
Fo Manzhou (fe Manju) 佛滿洲
Foying 佛英
fudutong 副都統
fuguo jiangjun 輔國將軍
Fujun 富俊
Fuqi 孚琦
Fuwen Shuyuan 輔文書院
Fuyuan 富元

Gangyi 剛毅
Gao Lingxiao 高凌霄
Gao Youtang 高友唐
Gelaohui 哥老會
geming pai-Man 革命排滿
Gemingjun 革命軍
Gonghe Cujin Hui 共和促進會
Gongweijun 拱衛軍
Gongxunju 工巡局
Guan Deshou 關德壽

Guan Zhonghe 關忠和
Guangfu 廣福
guangfu 光復
Guangfuhui 光復會
Guangxu 光緒
Guangzhao 光照
guanli dachen 管理大臣
Gugong Bowuyuan 故宮博物院
Guifu 貴福
Guilin 貴林
Guixiu 貴秀
Guiyin 桂蔭
guohui 國會
guomin 國民
Guominbao 國民報
Guoshi Gongji Hui 國事共濟會
guowen guoyu 國文國語
guoyu Manwen 國語滿文
guoyu qishe 國語騎射
Guwu Chenliesuo 古物陳列所

Ha Hanzhang 哈漢章
haijun tidu 海軍提督
Hanhua 漢化
Hanjun 漢軍
Hannü 漢女
Hanren 漢人
Hanren nüzi 漢人女子
Hanzu 漢族
He Zonglian 何宗蓮
Hengjun 恆鈞
Hengling 恆齡
Hezhe 赫哲
Hu Egong 胡鄂公
Hu Qian 胡潛
Hu Shi 胡適
Hu Weide 胡惟德

Hu Yufen 胡燏棻
Hua 華
Hua Zhenji 華振基
huachu Man-Han 化除滿漢
huachu Man-Han jiexian 化除滿漢界限
huachu Man-Han zhenyu 化除滿漢畛域
huachu qi-Han 化除旗漢
huachu zhongzu jiexian 化除種族界限
Huajie 華界
Huang Fu 黃郛
Huang Fusheng 黃復生
Huang Xing 黃興
huangshi 皇室
huangshi zunrong zongfan shengji 皇室尊榮宗藩生計
huangzu 皇族
huangzu neige 皇族內閣
huaqu Man-Han zhenyu 化去滿漢畛域
Huaren 華人
Hui 回
Huixing 惠興
huiyi 會議
Huizu 回族
Hujunying 護軍營
Huoqiying 火器營
Hushenying 虎神營

jia (giya) 佳
jiala (jalan) 甲喇
jianfa buyifu 剪髮不易服
Jiang Chunlin 江春霖
Jiang Guiti 姜桂題
Jiang Shuzi 姜叔子

339

jiangjun 將軍
jianguo 監國
Jianruiying 健銳營
Jianzhou 建州
Jiaqing 嘉慶
Jiaxian Xuetang 嘉憲學堂
jifu 畿輔
Jin Qicong 金啓孮
Jingqi 京旗
Jingqi Changbeijun 京旗常備軍
Jingqi Lianbingchu 京旗練兵處
Jingshi Daxuetang 京師大學堂
Jingshi Gaodeng Xunjing Xuetang
  京師高等巡警學堂
Jingshi zhong 警世鐘
Jingwu Xuetang 警務學堂
Jinji Dulian Gongsuo 近畿督練公
  所
Jinliang 金梁
Jinweijun 禁衛軍
jinzhu Manren 儘逐滿人
Jisheng 吉陞
Jitai 濟泰
Jueluo (Gioro) 覺羅
Junguomin Jiaoyuhui 軍國民教
  育會
Juntong 俊桐
junwang 郡王
Junzhu Lixian Zancheng Hui 君主
  立憲贊戌會
Junzichu 軍諮處
Junzifu 軍諮府

Kaizhilu 開智錄
Kang Youwei 康有為
Kangde 康德
Kangxi 康熙

Kawashima Naniwa 川島浪速
Keerqin 科爾沁
Kuang Zuozhi 鄺佐治
Kungang 崑岡
Kunminghu Shuishi Xuetang 昆明
  湖水師學堂
Kuyala 庫雅喇

Laixiu 來秀
Lang Le'e 郎樂額
Lao Li 老吏
Lao She (Shu Sheyu) 老舍
  (舒舍予)
Li Chengyin 李承蔭
Li Guojie 李國杰
Li Hongcai 李鴻才
Li Hongzhang 李鴻章
Li Jiaju 李家駒
Li Jieren 李劼人
Li Kuiyuan 李奎元
Li Lianfang 李廉方
Li Shangwen 黎尚雯
Li Shengduo 李盛鐸
Li Weiran 李蔚然
Li Xieyang 李爕陽
Li Yuanhong 黎元洪
Lianbingchu 練兵處
Lianfang 聯芳
Liang Dingfen 梁鼎芬
Liang Dunyan 梁敦彥
Liang Qichao 梁啓超
Liang Shiyi 梁士詒
liangbatou 兩把頭
Liangbi 良弼
Lianjia 連甲
Liankui 連魁
Lifanyuan 理藩院

lijie 禮節

Lin Shaonian 林紹年

Lin Zexu 林則徐

lingcui 領催

Lingshou 凌壽

Liu Cheng'en 劉承恩

Liu Kunyi 劉坤一

Liu Xianzhi 劉顯之

Liu Zhenyu 劉震宇

Liutiaobian 柳條邊

liuzhong 留中

Long Jiguang 龍濟光

Longyu 隆裕

lu 虜

Lu Chuanlin 鹿傳霖

Lu Runxiang 陸潤庠

Lu Zongyu 陸宗輿

Lü Haihuan 呂海寰

Lujun Guizhou Xuetang 陸軍貴
州學堂

Luo Wanzhang 羅萬章

Lüying 綠營

magua 馬掛

majia 馬甲

Mancheng 滿城

Man-Han bixu ronghua ye 滿漢
必須融化也

Man-Han fenjie 滿漢分界

Man-Han jie chaoting chizi 滿漢
皆朝廷赤子

Man-Han renmin pingdeng 滿漢
人民平等

Man-Han shijue 滿漢世爵

Man-Han wenti 滿漢問題

Man-Han yijia 滿漢一家

Man-Han zhi jie 滿漢之界

Man-Han zhi zheng 滿漢之爭

Man-Meng-Hui-Zang 滿蒙回藏

Man-Mengwen Gaodeng Xuetang
滿蒙文高等學堂

Man-Qing 滿清

Manren 滿人

Manren zhi Man 滿人治滿

Manwen 滿文

Manyuan 滿員

Manzhou 滿洲

Manzhou diguo 滿洲帝國

Manzhou jiemei 滿洲姊妹

Manzhou nüzi 滿洲女子

Manzhou zhi waizhong 滿洲
之外種

Manzhou zhong 滿州種

Manzhouguo 滿洲國

Manzhouren 滿洲人

Manzu 滿族

Manzu Tongjin Hui 滿族同
進會

Manzu zizhi xian 滿族自治縣

Meiqing Shuyuan 梅青書院

Meng huitou 猛回頭

Meng Sen 孟森

Meng-Zang Shiwu Yuan 蒙藏事物
院

Mianti 緜愭

mie zhong zhi canhuo 滅種之
慘禍

min 民

Minbao 民報

minren 民人

minxuan yiyuan 民選議院

minzu 民族

minzu xiang 民族鄉

Mou Lin 牟琳

Najin 那晉

Natong 那桐

Nayantu 那彥圖

nei zuoling 內佐領

nei-Man wai-Han 內滿外漢

Neiwufu 內務府

niulu (niru) 牛彔

nucai 奴才

Nucai xiaoshi 奴才小史

paichu Manren 排除滿人

pai-Man 排滿

ping Man-Han zhi jie 平滿漢
之界

pochu Man-Han zhi jie 破除滿
漢之界

Pu Dianjun 蒲殿俊

Pujie 溥傑

Pujun 溥儁

Puliang 溥良

Pulun 溥倫

Pushou 樸壽

Puting 溥頲

Putong 溥侗

Puwei 溥偉

Puyi 溥儀

Puzhong 溥忠

qi 旗

Qianfengying 前鋒營

qiang-Man pai-Han 強滿排漢

Qiangxuehui 強學會

Qianlong 乾隆

qibing 旗兵

qi-Han 旗漢

qiji (or qijiren) 旗籍（旗籍人）

Qilin 琦璘

qi-Manren 旗滿人

qimin 旗民

qi-min bujiao chan 旗民不交產

qi-min fenzhi 旗民分治

Qing di 清帝

Qing huangzu 清皇族

Qing qiu 清酋

Qingrui 清銳

Qingshi Shanhou Weiyuanhui 清室
善後委員會

Qingshigao 清史稿

qingui 親貴

Qingwen 清文

Qingyibao 清議報

Qingyu 清語

Qingzi Qingyu 清字清語

Qinjunying 親軍營

Qin-Long Fu-Han Jun 秦隴復
漢軍

qinwang 親王

qipao 旗袍

qiren 旗人

Qishan 琦善

Qiu Jin 秋瑾

Qiwuchu 旗務處

qixia de nüzi 旗下的女子

qizu 旗族

Qizu yuebao 旗族月報

Qu Hongji 瞿鴻禨

quanzhan 圈占

quzhu Dalu 驅逐韃虜

rang di 讓帝

rang huangdi 讓皇帝

rengcun bufei 仍存不廢

renzhong 人種

Riben bianzheng kao 日本變政考

rong Man-Han zhi jian 融滿漢之見

ronghua Man-Han 融化滿漢

ronghua Man-Han zhenyu 融化滿漢畛域

Rongjun 榮濬

Ronglin 榮麟

Ronglu 榮祿

Rongqing 榮慶

Rongxu 榮續

Rongxun 榮勳

Ruicheng 瑞澂

Sa Zhenbing 薩鎮冰

shajin 殺盡

Shalu Manguan qiren 殺戮滿官旗人

Shang Qiheng 尚其亨

Shanhou banfa 善後辦法

Shanqi (Prince Su) 肅親王善耆

Shaoying 紹英

Shehuidang 社會党

Shen Guifen 沈桂芬

Shen Jiaben 沈家本

Shenjiying 神機營

shenyi 審議

shezhengwang 攝政王

Shibao 時報

Shiduo (Prince Li) 禮親王世鐸

Shijiu Xintiao 十九信條

Shiming 世銘

Shitouji 石頭記

Shiwubao 時務報

Shixu 世續

Shizi hou 獅子吼

Shoufu 壽富

Shouqi 壽耆

Shoushan Diyi Nü Gongchang 首善第一女工廠

shoutian guinong 授田歸農

Shouxun 壽勳

shuishiying 水師營

Shuntian shibao 順天時報

Shunzhi 順治

Shushen Nü Xuetang 淑慎女學堂

Sishui weilan 死水微瀾

Song Jiaoren 宋教仁

Song Yuren 宋育仁

Songhua 松華

Songshou 松壽

Songyu 松毓

Songyun 松筠

Su Liangbi 蘇良弼

Subao 蘇報

suiquedi 隨缺地

sula 蘇拉

Sun Baoqi 孫寶琦

Sun Chuanfang 孫傳芳

Sun Dianying 孫殿英

Sun Jia'nai 孫家鼐

Sun Zhongshan 孫中山

sunwei 遜位

Suolun 索倫

Suweiying 宿衛營

Tan Renfeng 譚人鳳

Tan Wenjiang 譚溫江

Tang Jingchong 唐景崈

Tang Shaoyi 唐紹儀

Tang Shouqian 湯壽潛

Tang Wenzhi 唐文治

Tang Xizhi 唐犧支

Tanguan wuli zhuan 貪官污吏傳

taolujun 討虜軍

tebie zhidu 特別制度

Tian Xianzhang 田獻章

Tiantao 天討

Tieliang 鐵良

tiemaozi wang 鐵帽子王

Tiezhong 鐵忠

Tingjie 廷杰

Tingqi 廷啓

Tonggusizu 通古斯族

Tongmenghui 同盟會

tongpan 通判

tongren 同仁

Tongwenguan 同文館

Tongyi Xuetang 通藝學堂

Tongzhi 同治

Tongzhi Lianhehui 同志聯合會

Tongzhihui 同志會

tuiding 退丁

tuiwei 退位

wai zuoling 外佐領

waifan wanggong shijue 外藩王公世爵

Wang Guowei 王國維

Wang Jilie 王季烈

Wang Jingwei 汪精衛

Wang Shizhen 王士珍

Wang Tingzhen 王廷楨

Wang Wenshao 王文韶

Wang Xiuchu 王修楚

Wang Yujia 王遇甲

Wang Zhanyuan 王占元

Wang Zongyou 汪宗猷

Wanguo gongbao 萬國公報

wanquan neige 完全內閣

Wanrong 婉容

Wen Shengcai 溫生才

Wen Zongyao 溫宗堯

Wenbin 文斌

Weng Tonghe 翁同龢

Wenhua 文華

Wenkai 文楷

Wenpu 文溥

Wenrui 文瑞

Wenshi Ziliao Yanjiu Weiyuanhui 文史資料研究委員會

Wenxiu 文秀

Wo de qian bansheng 我的前半生

wo Manzhou genben 我滿洲根本

women Hanzu 我們漢族

Wu Luzhen 吳祿貞

Wu Peifu 吳佩孚

Wu Tingfang 伍廷芳

Wu Yue 吳樾

wulun qi-Han guanmin 無論旗漢官民

wutiandi 伍田地

Wuwei Zhongjun 武衛中軍

Wuzesheng 烏澤聲

wuzu 五族

wuzu datong 五族大同

wuzu yijia 五族一家

Xia 夏

Xianfa Dagang 憲法大綱

Xianfeng 咸豐

xiangchuan bufei 相傳不廢

Xianjun 憲均

xiansan 閑散

Xianzheng Bianchaguan 憲政編查館

Xianzheng Gonghui 憲政公會

Xianzheng Jiangxihui 憲政講習會

xiaoqixiao 驍騎校

Xiaoqiying 驍騎營

Xibo 錫伯

Xichang 喜昌

xieling 協領

xiezan 協贊

Xiliang 錫良

xing-Han mie-Man 興漢滅滿

Xing-Zhong Hui 興中會

Xinjun 新軍

xintiao 信條

Xinzheng 新政

Xiong Bingkun 熊秉坤

Xiong Chengji 熊成基

Xiong Xiling 熊希齡

Xiqia 熙洽

Xitong 錫桐

Xiuding Falü Dachen 修定法律大臣

Xiyan 熙彥

Xu Shichang 徐世昌

Xu Shoupeng 徐壽朋

Xu Xilin 徐錫麟

Xu Zhishan 徐致善

Xuantong 宣統

Yan Fu 嚴復

Yan Xishan 閻錫山

Yang Du 楊度

Yang Sen 楊森

Yang Shixiang 楊士驤

Yang Wending 楊文鼎

yangqiangdui 洋槍隊

yangyubing 養育兵

Yangzheng Xuetang 養正學堂

Yanhong 延鴻

Yanrong 延榮

Yanzhengchu 鹽政處

yi 翼

Yiche Manzhou (ice Manju) 伊澈滿洲

Yi-Di 夷狄

Yigu 貽穀

Yihuan (Prince Chun) 醇親王奕譞

yijue 議決

Yikuang (Prince Qing) 慶親王奕劻

Yilibu 伊里布

yi-Man fang-Han 以滿防漢

yin 廕

Yin Changheng 尹昌衡

Yinchang 廕昌

Ying Lianzhi 英斂之

Yingrui 英瑞

yinsheng 廕生

yiqin 懿親

Yixin (Prince Gong) 恭親王奕訢

yiyuan 議院

Yizhen 宜珍

Yonglin 永璘

Yongxing (Prince Cheng) 成親王永瑆

Youdai Tiaojian 優待條件

youding 幼丁

Yu Liansan 俞廉三

Yuan Chang 袁昶

Yuan Shikai 袁世凱

Yubei Lixian Gonghui 預備立憲公會

yuefa 約法

Yukun 玉崑

Yulang 毓朗

Yulu 裕祿

Yun Baohui 惲寶惠

Zaifeng 載灃

Zaifu 載塨

Zaimu 載穆

Zairun 載潤

Zaitao 載濤

Zaitian 載湉

Zaixun 載洵

Zaiyi (Prince Duan) 端郡王載漪

Zaize 載澤

Zaizhen 載振

Zeng Guofan 曾國藩

Zengxi 增禧

Zengyun 增韞

zeren neige 責任內閣

Zhalafen 扎拉芬

Zhang Biao 張彪

Zhang Binglin 章炳麟

Zhang Deyi (Deming) 張德彝 (德明)

Zhang Fenghui 張鳳翽

Zhang Furong 章福榮

Zhang Ji 張繼

Zhang Jian 張謇

Zhang Renjun 張人駿

Zhang Shaozeng 張紹曾

Zhang Xun 張勛

Zhang Yuanji 張元濟

Zhang Yujun 章通駿

Zhang Yunshan 張雲山

Zhang Zhanyun 張展云

Zhang Zhidong 張之洞

Zhang Zuolin 張作霖

zhangjing (janggin) 章京

Zhao Bingjun 趙秉鈞

Zhao Erfeng 趙爾豐

Zhao Erxun 趙爾巽

Zheng Xiaoxu 鄭孝胥

Zheng Yuan 鄭沅

Zhengfu gongbao 政府公報

Zhenghongqi xia 正紅旗下

zhenguo gong 鎮國公

zhenguo jiangjun 鎮國將軍

Zhengwenshe 政聞社

Zhengwuchu 政務處

Zhengzhi guanbao 政治官報

Zhengzhi Huiyi 政治會議

Zhenwei Xinjun 振威新軍

Zhenwen Nüxue 貞文女學

Zhenyi Nü Xuetang 箴宜女學堂

Zhichi Xuehui 知恥學會

Zhina 支那

Zhinaren 支那人

Zhinianqi 值年旗

Zhirui 志銳

Zhisen 志森

zhizheng 致政

Zhongguo 中國

Zhongguo ribao 中國日報

Zhongguo xinbao 中國新報

Zhongguoren 中國人

Zhonghe (Guan Zhonghe) 忠和 (關忠和)

Zhonghua Diguo 中華帝國

Zhonghua Minguo 中華民國

Zhonghua minzu 中華民族

Zhonghua ribao 中華日報

Zhonglin 鍾麟

Zhonglu 鍾祿

zhong-Man qing-Han 重滿輕漢

Zhongshan zhuang 中山裝

Zhong-Xia 中夏

Zhongyang datong ribao 中央大同日報

zhongzu 種族

zhongzu wenti 種族問題

Zhou Fu 周馥

Zhu Panzao 朱泮藻

Zhu Qinglan 朱慶瀾

zhuangding 壯丁

zhufang 駐防

zhufang zuoling 駐防佐領

Ziwei 子偉

Ziyiju Lianhehui 諮議局聯合會

Zizhengyuan 資政院

zongli 總理

zongli dachen 總理大臣

Zongli Yamen 總理衙門

zongmiao sheji 宗廟社稷

Zongrenfu 宗人府

zongshe 宗社

Zongshedang 宗社党

zongshi 宗室

zongshi jueluo 宗室覺羅

zongshi wanggong shijue 宗室王公世爵

zongzu 宗族

Zou Fen 鄒芬

Zou Jialai 鄒嘉來

Zou Rong 鄒容

zu 族

zuoling 佐領

Bibliography

ABBREVIATIONS

DFZZ   *Dongfang zazhi* (Eastern miscellany), Shanghai. Reprint, Taipei: Taiwan
            Shangwu Yinshuguan, 1971.

FO 405   Great Britain, Foreign Office, Confidential Print, China, FO 405.

GX   Guangxu reign (1875–1908)

KGWX   *Zhonghua minguo kaiguo wushinian wenxian* (Documents commem-
            orating the fiftieth anniversary of the founding of the Republic of
            China). Taipei, 1962–65.

NCH   *North-China Herald and Supreme Court & Consular Gazette: Weekly
            Edition of the North-China Daily News*, Shanghai.

SL   *Da-Qing huangdi shilu* (Veritable records of the Qing emperors).
            Reprint, Taipei: Huawen Shuju, 1964.

SSJY   *Zhonghua minguo shishi jiyao (chugao)* (A chronological history of the
            Republic of China [first draft]). Taipei: Zhonghua Minguo Shiliao
            Yanjiu Zhongxin, 1971–83.

STSB   *Shuntian shibao* ("Peking Times"), Beijing.

TZ   Tongzhi reign (1861–75)

USDS   United States, Department of State. Numerical File, 1906–10; Decimal
            File, 1910–29. National Archives, Record Group 59.

XGHYL   *Xinhai Geming huiyilu* (Memoirs of the 1911 Revolution). Beijing:
            Zhonghua Shuju, 1961–63 (vols. 1–5); and Wenshi Ziliao Chubanshe,
            1981–82 (vols. 6–8).

XHGM   *Xinhai Geming* (The 1911 Revolution). Comp. Zhongguo Shixue Hui.
            Shanghai: Shanghai Renmin Chubanshe, 1957.

XT   Xuantong reign (1908–12)

ZZGB   *Zhengzhi guanbao* (Political gazette), Beijing. Reprint, Taipei: Wenhai
            Chubanshe, 1965.

Aisin-Gioro Pu Yi. *From Emperor to Citizen: The Autobiography of Aisin-Gioro Pu Yi*. Trans. W. J. F. Jenner. Beijing: Foreign Languages Press, 1964–65.

Aixin Jueluo Yingsheng. "Manyu he Hanyu de huxiang yingxiang" (The mutual influence of Manchu and Han speech). *Manzu yanjiu*, 1987, no. 1: 67–72.

———. "Tantan Manzuren de xingming" (A discussion about Manchu people's names). *Manzu yanjiu*, 1985, no. 2: 55–60.

Aixin Jueluo Zongkui. "Manzu jiusu yishu" (Recollections of the Manchus' old customs). *Guangdong wenshi ziliao*, no. 35 (1982): 263–74.

Aixin-Jiaoluo Pu Jie. "My Family and Myself." *China Pictorial*, 1979, no. 8: 38–41.

Atwood, Christopher. "National Questions and National Answers in the Chinese Revolution; Or, How Do You Say *Minzu* in Mongolian?" *Indiana East Asian Working Paper Series on Language and Politics in Modern China* 5 (1994): 35–73.

Bai Jie. "Qingmo zhengtan zhong de Su qinwang Shanqi" (Prince Su, Shanqi, in the late Qing political world). *Manzu yanjiu*, 1993, no. 2: 36–39.

Banister, Judith. *China's Changing Population*. Stanford: Stanford University Press, 1987.

Bartlett, Beatrice S. *Monarchs and Ministers: The Grand Council in Mid-Ch'ing China, 1723–1820*. Berkeley: University of California Press, 1991.

Bays, Daniel H. *China Enters the Twentieth Century: Chang Chih-tung and the Issues of a New Age, 1895–1909*. Ann Arbor: University of Michigan Press, 1978.

Beahan, Charlotte L. "Feminism and Nationalism in the Chinese Women's Press, 1902–11." *Modern China* 1 (1975): 379–416.

Beijing mingsheng guji cidian (A dictionary of famous sites and ancient relics in Beijing). Beijing: Yanshan Chubanshe, 1989.

Beijing nübao (Beijing women's news), Beijing, 1905–9. Available at University of Chicago Library and Beijing University Library.

"Beijingshi Haidianqu Huoqiying Manzu shehui diaocha baogao" (A report of a social survey among the Manchus of the Firearms Division in Beijing's Haidian district). *Manzu yanjiu*, 1988, no. 1: 89–93, 83.

Benson, Linda. *The Ili Rebellion: The Moslem Challenge to Chinese Authority in Xinjiang, 1944–1949*. Armonk, N.Y., and London: M. E. Sharpe, Inc., 1990.

Biggerstaff, Knight. *The Earliest Modern Government Schools in China*. Ithaca: Cornell University Press, 1961.

Bland, J. O. P., and Edmund Backhouse. *China under the Empress Dowager*. London: William Heinemann, 1911.

Bodde, Derk, and Clarence Morris. *Law in Imperial China, Exemplified by 190 Ch'ing Dynasty Cases*. Reprint, Philadelphia: University of Pennsylvania Press, 1973.

Bohai Shouchen (pseud.), comp. *Xinhai Geming shimo ji* (A full account of the 1911 Revolution). Reprint, Taipei: Wenhai Chubanshe, 1969.

Bonner, Joey. *Wang Kuo-wei: An Intellectual Biography*. Cambridge: Harvard University Press, 1986.

Boorman, Howard L., and Richard C. Howard, eds. *Biographical Dictionary of Republican China*. New York: Columbia University Press, 1967–71.

Bredon, Juliet. *Peking*. Reprint, Hong Kong: Oxford University Press, 1982.

Britton, Roswell S. *The Chinese Periodical Press, 1800–1912*. Reprint, Taipei: Ch'eng-wen Publishing Company, 1966.

Brunnert, H. S., and V. V. Hagelstrom. *Present Day Political Organization of China*. Revised by N. Th. Kolessoff; trans. A. Beltchenko and E. E. Moran. Reprint, Taipei: Xinyue Tushu Gongsi, 1964.

Cai Hongyuan and Liu Xiaoning. "Xinhai Nanjing guangfu—Sun Zhongshan jiuren Zhonghua Minguo linshi dazongtong" (The restoration of Nanjing in 1911: Sun Yat-sen's inauguration as provisional president of the Republic of China." In *Xinhai Geming zai gedi* (The 1911 Revolution at various localities), 161–74. Beijing: Zhongguo Wenshi Chubanshe, 1991.

Cao Xueqin. *The Story of the Stone*. Trans. David Hawkes. Vol. 1. Baltimore: Penquin Books, 1973.

Cao Yabo. *Wuchang geming zhenshi* (The true story of the Wuchang revolution). Reprint, Shanghai: Shanghai Shudian, 1982.

Cao Zixi and Yu Guangdu. *Beijing tongshi* (A comprehensive history of Beijing). Beijing: Zhongguo Shudian, 1994.

Chang, Sen-dou. "The Morphology of Walled Capitals." In G. William Skinner, ed., *The City in Late Imperial China*, 75–100. Stanford: Stanford University Press, 1977.

Chang Shun. "Maichen beizha zhuiji" (A posthumous account of the assassination of Liangbi). In *XGHYL*, 6: 389–91.

Chen Chunsheng. "Xinhai Geming haijun fanzheng jishi" (An account of the navy's defection during the 1911 Revolution). In Zhang Xia et al., comps., *Qingmo haijun shiliao* (Historical materials on the late Qing navy), 696–704. Beijing: Haiyang Chubanshe, 1982.

Chen Jiahua. "Baqi zhidu yanjiu shulüe" (A survey of research on the Eight Banner system). *Shehui kexue jikan*, 1984, no. 5: 109–16; and no. 6: 113–20.

———— and Fu Kedong. "Baqi Hanjun kaolüe" (A brief study of the Eight Banner Hanjun). In Wang Zhonghan, ed., *Manzu shi yanjiu ji* (Collected studies on the history of the Manchus), 281–306. Beijing: Zhongguo Shehui Kexue Chubanshe, 1988.

Chen Tianhua. *Chen Tianhua ji* (The collected works of Chen Tianhua). Ed. Liu Qingbo and Peng Guoxing. Changsha: Hunan Renmin Chubanshe, 1982.

Chen Wenshi. "Qingdai de bitieshi" (Manchu-language scribes in the Qing period). *Shihuo yuekan* 4 (1974): 65–76.

————. "Qingdai Manren zhengzhi canyu" (Political participation by Manchus during the Qing period). *Zhongyang Yanjiuyuan Lishi Yuyan Yanjiusuo jikan* 48 (1977): 529–94.

Chen Yishi and Wang Duanyu. "Qingdai Chengdu de 'Mancheng' yu qi-Han fen-

zhi" (The Manchu City in Qing Chengdu and the separate governance of banner people and Han). *Sichuan Daxue xuebao*, 1981, no. 3: 71–78.

Ch'en, Chieh-hsien. "The Decline of the Manchu Language in China during the
Ch'ing Period (1644–1911)." In Walther Heissig, ed., *Altaica Collecta*, 137–54.
Wiesbaden: Otto Harrassowitz, 1976.

———. "The Sinification of Manchu Names: A Study of Personal Names in the
Ch'ing Imperial House and Upper-Class Manchu Society of the Ch'ing Period."
Zhongguo Lishi Xuehui shixue jikan 1 (1969): 1–20.

Ch'en, Jerome. *Yuan Shih-k'ai.* 2nd ed. Stanford: Stanford University Press, 1972.

Cheng Changfu, Bunialin, and Yuan Liping. "Mulan weichang" (The Mulan hunting grounds). *Gugong Bowuyuan yuankan*, 1986, no. 2: 27–32.

Cheng Weikun. "Minchu 'jianbianre' shulun" (An account of the "queue-cutting
rage" in the early Republic). *Shehui kexue yanjiu*, 1987, no. 3: 71–77.

Chengdu changfang guji kao (Investigations into the city walls and ancient relics of
Chengdu). Comp. Sichuansheng Wenshiguan. Chengdu: Sichuan Renmin
Chubanshe, 1987.

Chiang Kai-shek. *China's Destiny.* Trans. Wang Chung-hui. Reprint, New York: Da
Capo Press, 1976. (See also Jiang Jieshi, *Zhongguo zhi mingyun*)

China, The Maritime Customs. *Returns of Trade and Trade Reports, 1911.* Shanghai,
1912.

China, No. 1 Historical Archives. Baqi Dutong Yamen (Office of the Eight Banner
Lieutenants-General) Archives.

———. Huiyi Zhengwuchu (Office of Governmental Affairs) Archives.

———. Jinweijun Xunlianchu (Palace Guard Training Commission) Archives.

———. Junjichu Lufu Zouzhe (Reference Copies of Memorials at the Grand
Council).

———. Junjichu Xianzheng Zhuanti (Grand Council, Special Topic on Constitutional Government).

———. Xianzheng Bianchaguan (Bureau for the Implementation of Constitutional
Government) Archives.

Chou, Nailene Josephine. "Frontier Studies and Changing Frontier Administration
in Late Ch'ing China: The Case of Sinkiang, 1759–1911." Ph.D. diss., University
of Washington, 1976.

Chu, Raymond W., and William G. Saywell. *Career Patterns in the Ch'ing Dynasty:
The Office of Governor-General.* Ann Arbor: Center for Chinese Studies, University
of Michigan, 1984.

Chu, Samuel C. *Reformer in Modern China: Chang Chien, 1853–1926.* New York and
London: Columbia University Press, 1965.

Chung, Sue Fawn. "The Much Maligned Empress Dowager: A Revisionist Study of
the Empress Dowager Tz'u-hsi (1835–1908)." *Modern Asian Studies* 13 (1979): 177–96.

Coates, P. D. "Documents in Chinese from the Chinese Secretary's Office, British Legation, Peking, 1861–1939." *Modern Asian Studies* 17 (1983): 239–55.

Cochran, Sherman, and Andrew C. K. Hsieh, with Janis Cochran, trans. and eds. *One Day in China: May 21, 1936.* New Haven and London: Yale University Press, 1983.

Constable, Nicole, ed. *Guest People: Hakka Identity in China and Abroad.* Seattle: University of Washington Press, 1996.

Crossley, Pamela Kyle. "Manchu Education." In Benjamin A. Elman and Alexander Woodside, eds., *Education and Society in Late Imperial China, 1600–1900,* 340–78. Berkeley: University of California Press, 1994.

————. *The Manchus.* Cambridge, Mass., and Oxford: Blackwell Publishers, 1997.

————. *Orphan Warriors: Three Manchu Generations and the End of the Qing World.* Princeton: Princeton University Press, 1990.

————, and Evelyn S. Rawski. "A Profile of the Manchu Language in Ch'ing History." *Harvard Journal of Asiatic Studies* 53, no. 1 (1993): 63–102.

Da-Han Rexin Ren (pseud.), comp. "Guangdong duli ji" (An account of Guangdong's declaration of independence). *Jindaishi ziliao,* 1961, no. 1: 435–71.

Da-Qing huangdi shilu (Veritable records of the Qing emperors). Reprint, Taipei: Huawen Shuju, 1964.

Da-Qing huidian (Collected statutes of the Great Qing), 1899 ed. Reprint, Taipei: Zhongwen Shuju, 1963.

Dai Xueji. *Huhehaote jianshi* (A short history of Hohhot). Beijing: Zhonghua Shuju, 1981.

Datongbao (Great harmony journal), Tokyo, 1907–8. Available at Beijing University Library and on microfilm at Columbia University's East Asian Library.

Deal, David M. "'The Question of Nationalities' in Twentieth-Century China." *Journal of Ethnic Studies* 12, no. 3 (1984): 23–53.

Des Forges, Roger V. *Hsi-liang and the Chinese National Revolution.* New Haven and London: Yale University Press, 1973.

Ding Shiyuan. "Meileng Zhangjing biji" (Notes of Secretary Meileng). In Wu Xiangxiang, ed., *Zhongguo xiandaishi congkan* (Essays on China's recent history), 5: 235–85. Taipei: Wenxing Shudian, 1964.

Ding Shouhe, comp. *Xinhai Geming shiqi qikan jieshao* (An introduction to the periodicals in the era of the 1911 Revolution). Beijing: Renmin Chubanshe, 1982–87.

Ding Yizhuang. *Qingdai Baqi zhufang zhidu yanjiu* (A study of the institution of the banner garrisons during the Qing period). Tianjin: Guji Chubanshe, 1992.

Dong Fangkui. "Lun 'Luanzhou bingjian' he 'Shiguan sanjie'" (On the "Luanzhou armed remonstrance" and the "three heroes of the Japanese Army Officers School"). *Lishi yanjiu,* 1981, no. 1: 57–72.

Dongfang zazhi (Eastern miscellany), Shanghai, 1904–12. Reprint, Taipei: Taiwan Shangwu Yinshuguan, 1971.

Donghualu Guangxuchao (Donghua records for the Guangxu reign). Reprint, Tainan: Dadong Shuju, 1968.

Du Chunhe. "Zhang Shaozeng yu 'Luanzhou bingjian'" (Zhang Shaozeng and the "Luanzhou armed remonstrance"). *Jindaishi yanjiu*, 1985, no. 3: 259–79.

Duanfang. *Duan Zhongmin gong zougao* (Draft memorials of Duanfang). Reprint, Taipei: Wenhai Chubanshe, n.d.

Duiker, William J. *Cultures in Collision: The Boxer Rebellion*. San Rafael, Calif.: Presidio Press, 1978.

Dutt, Vidya Prakash. "The First Week of Revolution: The Wuchang Uprising." In Mary Clabaugh Wright, ed., *China in Revolution: The First Phase, 1900–1913*, 383–416. New Haven and London: Yale University Press, 1968.

Edmonds, Richard Louis. *Northern Frontiers of Qing China and Tokugawa Japan: A Comparative Study of Frontier Policy*. Chicago: University of Chicago, Department of Geography, 1985.

Elliott, Mark. "Bannerman and Townsman: Ethnic Tension in Nineteenth-Century Jiangnan." *Late Imperial China* 11, no. 1 (1990): 36–74.

———. "Resident Aliens: The Manchu Experience in China, 1644–1760." Ph.D. diss., University of California at Berkeley, 1993.

Esherick, Joseph W. "Founding a Republic, Electing a President: How Sun Yat-sen Became Guofu." In Etō Shinkichi and Harold Z. Schiffrin, eds., *China's Republican Revolution*, 129–52. Tokyo: University of Tokyo Press, 1994.

———. *Reform and Revolution in China: The 1911 Revolution in Hunan and Hubei*. Berkeley: University of California Press, 1976.

Fairbank, John K. "The Manchu-Chinese Dyarchy in the 1840's and '50's." *Far Eastern Quarterly* 12 (1953): 265–78.

———, and S. Y. Teng. "On the Types and Uses of Ch'ing Documents." In idem, *Ch'ing Administration: Three Studies*, 36–106. Cambridge: Harvard University Press, 1960.

Fang Hanqi. *Zhongguo jindai baokan shi* (A history of the press in modern China). Taiyuan: Shanxi Renmin Chubanshe, 1981.

Fang Zhaoying, comp. *Qingmo Minchu yangxue xuesheng timinglu chuji* (A first compilation of directories of students studying abroad in the late Qing and early Republic). Taipei: Zhongyang Yanjiuyuan Jindaishi Yanjiusuo, 1962.

Farjenel, Fernand. *Through the Chinese Revolution*. Trans. Margaret Vivian. New York: Frederick A. Stokes Company, 1916.

Fay, Peter Ward. *The Opium War, 1840–1842*. New York: W. W. Norton & Company, 1976.

Fei Hsiao Tung. "Ethnic Identification in China." In idem, *Toward a People's Anthropology*, 60–77. Beijing: New World Press, 1981.

"Feng Guozhang zaoqi lüli" (An early curriculum vitae of Feng Guozhang). *Lishi dang'an*, 1995, no. 1: 59.

Feng Yuxiang. *Wo de shenghuo—Feng Yuxiang Jiangjun zizhuan* (My life: The auto-biography of General Feng Yuxiang). Reprint, Hong Kong: Bowen Chubanshe, [1974].

Feng Ziyou. *Geming yishi* (An anecdotal history of the revolution). Taipei: Taiwan Shangwu Yinshuguan, 1953, 1965 (vols. 1–5); Beijing: Zhonghua Shuju, 1981 (vol. 6).

———. *Zhonghua Minguo kaiguo qian geming shi* (A history of the revolution before the founding of the Republic of China). Taipei: Shijie Shuju, 1954.

Finnane, Antonia. "What Should Women Wear? A National Problem." *Modern China* 22 (1966): 99–131.

Fitzgerald, John. *Awakening China: Politics, Culture, and Class in the Nationalist Revolution*. Stanford: Stanford University Press, 1996.

Fletcher, Joseph. "Sino-Russian Relations, 1800–62." In John K. Fairbank, ed., *The Cambridge History of China*, vol. 10, *Late Ch'ing, 1800–1911*, part 1, 318–50. Cambridge: Cambridge University Press, 1978.

Fogel, Joshua A. "The Sino-Japanese Controversy over Shina as a Toponym for China." In idem, *Cultural Dimensions of Sino-Japanese Relations: Essays on the Nineteenth and Twentieth Centuries*, 66–76. Armonk, N.Y., and London: M. E. Sharpe, 1995.

Franck, Harry A. *Roving through Southern China*. New York and London: The Century Co., 1925.

———. *Wandering in Northern China*. New York and London: The Century Co., 1923.

Fu Kedong. "Baqi shuishi shilüe" (The Eight Banner water forces). *Manzu yanjiu*, 1986, no. 1: 19–25.

——— and Chen Jiahua. "Qingdai qianqi de zuoling" (The banner company in the early Qing). *Shehui kexue zhanxian*, 1982, no. 1: 164–73.

Fu Zongmao. *Qingdai Junjichu zuzhi ji zhizhang zhi yanjiu* (A study of the organi-zation and functions of the Grand Council in the Qing period). Taipei: Jiaxin Shuini Gongsi Wenhua Jijinhui, 1967.

Fung, Edmund S. K. *The Military Dimension of the Chinese Revolution: The New Army and Its Role in the Revolution of 1911*. Canberra: Australian National University Press, 1980.

Gamble, Sidney D. *Peking: A Social Survey*. New York: George H. Doran Company, 1921.

Gan Haifeng. *Lao She nianpu* (A chronological biography of Lao She). Beijing: Shumu Wenxian Chubanshe, 1989.

Gao Shiliang. "Fujiansheng geming shihua" (Historical anecdotes about the revo-lution in Fujian). In *KGWX*, 2, part 4: 357–65.

Garrett, Valery M. *Chinese Clothing: An Illustrated Guide.* Hong Kong: Oxford University Press, 1994.

———. *Mandarin Squares: Mandarins and Their Insignia.* Hong Kong: Oxford University Press, 1990.

———. *Traditional Chinese Clothing in Hong Kong and South China, 1840–1980.* Hong Kong: Oxford University Press, 1987.

Gasster, Michael. *Chinese Intellectuals and the Revolution of 1911: The Birth of Modern Chinese Radicalism.* Seattle and London: University of Washington Press, 1969.

Gaubatz, Piper Rae. *Beyond the Great Wall: Urban Form and Transformation on the Chinese Frontiers.* Stanford: Stanford University Press, 1996.

Gladney, Dru C. *Muslim Chinese: Ethnic Nationalism in the People's Republic.* Cambridge: Council on East Asian Studies, Harvard University, 1991.

Godley, Michael R. "The End of the Queue: Hair as Symbol in Chinese History." *East Asian History* 8 (1994): 53–72.

Gongsun Hong. *Feng Guozhang nianpu* (A chronological biography of Feng Guozhang). Shijiazhuang: Hebei Renmin Chubanshe, 1989.

Goodrich, L. Carrington, and Chaoying Fang, eds. *Dictionary of Ming Biography, 1368–1644.* New York and London: Columbia University Press, 1976.

Great Britain. Foreign Office, Confidential Print, China, FO 405. Microfilmed ed.

Guan Jixin and Meng Xianren. "Manzu yu Shenyangyu Beijingyu" (The Manchus and Shenyang and Beijing speech). *Manzu yanjiu,* 1987, no. 1: 73–81.

Guanglu. *Guanglu huiyilu* (Memoirs of Guanglu). Taipei: Zhuanji Wenxue Chubanshe, 1970.

Guangxu zhengyao (Essential political documents of the Guangxu reign). Comp. Shen Tongsheng. Reprint, Taipei: Wenhai Chubanshe, 1969.

Guo Fengming. *Qingmo Minchu lujun xuexiao jiaoyu* (Military education in the late Qing and early Republic). Taipei: Jiaxin Shuini Gongsi Wenhua Jijinhui, 1978.

Guo Taifeng. "Baqi Lüying fengxiang zhidu chutan" (A preliminary investigation into the stipend system of the Eight Banners and the Army of the Green Standard). *Fudan xuebao,* 1982, no. 4: 103–7, 33.

Guo Tingyi, comp. *Jindai Zhongguo shishi rizhi (Qingji)* (A chronology of modern Chinese history, the Qing period). Taipei: Zhengzhong Shuju, 1963.

Guo Xiaocheng. "Fujian guangfu ji" (An account of the restoration in Fujian). In *XHGM,* 7: 280–83.

———. "Jiangsu guangfu jishi" (An account of the restoration in Jiangsu). In *XHGM,* 7: 1–33.

———. "Shaanxi guangfu ji" (An account of the restoration in Shaanxi). In *XHGM,* 6: 38–50.

———. "Yihe shimo" (A complete account of the peace talks). In *XHGM,* 8: 65–68.

———. "Zhejiang guangfu ji" (An account of the restoration in Zhejiang). In *XHGM*, 7: 135–49.

Guo Xiaoren. "Congrong jilüe" (A chronicle of taking up arms). In *XHGM*, 6: 60–103.

Guofengbao (Sentiment of the nation), Shanghai, 1910–11. Reprint, Taipei: Hansheng Chubanshe, 1975.

Hackett, Roger F. *Yamagata Aritomo in the Rise of Modern Japan, 1838–1922*. Cambridge: Harvard University Press, 1971.

Han Yanlong and Su Yigong, comps. *Zhongguo jindai jingcha zhidu* (China's modern police system). Beijing: Zhongguo Renmin Gongan Daxue Chubanshe, 1993.

Hangzhoufu zhi (Gazetteer of Hangzhou Prefecture). 1898 ed.

Hao, Yen-p'ing, and Kwang-Ching Liu. "The Importance of the Archival Palace Memorials of the Ch'ing Dynasty: *The Secret Palace Memorials of the Kuang-hsü Period, 1875–1908*." *Ch'ing-shih wen-t'i* 3, no. 1 (1974): 71–94.

Harrell, Paula. *Sowing the Seeds of Change: Chinese Students, Japanese Teachers, 1895–1905*. Stanford: Stanford University Press, 1992.

He Juefei and Feng Tianyu. *Xinhai Wuchang shouyi shi* (A history of the Wuchang uprising in 1911). [Wuhan?]: Hubei Renmin Chubanshe, 1985.

He Puying. "Manzu Tatalashi jiapu zhong de Han wenhua yinsu" (Han cultural elements in the genealogy of the Manchu Tatala lineage). *Manzu yanjiu*, 1993, no. 1: 46–51.

———. "Xin Zhongguo chengli hou Manzu de fazhan" (The development of the Manchus after the establishment of New China). *Manzu yanjiu*, 1987, no. 4: 90–96.

Headland, Isaac Taylor. *Court Life in China: The Capital, Its Officials and People*. New York: Fleming H. Revell Company, 1909.

"Hebeisheng Zunhuaxian Dongling Manzu Xiang" (Dongling Manchu Township, Zunhua County, Hebei). *Manzu yanjiu*, 1989, no. 1: 76.

Heberer, Thomas. *China and Its National Minorities: Autonomy or Assimilation?* Armonk, N.Y., and London: M. E. Sharpe, Inc., 1989.

Henan tongzhi (Gazetteer of Henan Province). 1914 ed.

Henry, B. C. *Ling-nam, or Interior Views of Southern China*. London: S. W. Partridge and Co., 1886.

Honig, Emily. *Creating Chinese Ethnicity: Subei People in Shanghai, 1850–1980*. New Haven: Yale University Press, 1992.

———. "The Politics of Prejudice: Subei People in Republican-Era Shanghai." *Modern China* 15 (1989): 243–75.

Hosie, Alexander. *Manchuria: Its People, Resources and Recent History*. Boston and Tokyo: J. B. Millet Company, 1910.

———. *Three Years in Western China: A Narrative of Three Journeys in Ssu-ch'uan, Kuei-chow, and Yün-nan*. 2nd ed. London: George Philip & Son, 1897.

Hou Yijie. *Ershi shiji chu Zhongguo zhengzhi gaige fengchao: Qingmo lixian yundong shi* (The controversy over political reform in early twentieth-century China: A history of the constitutionalist movement at the end of the Qing). Beijing: Renmin Chubanshe, 1993.

———. "Qingmo yubei lixian shiqi de Yang Du" (Yang Du during the late Qing preparations for constitutionalism). *Jindaishi yanjiu*, 1988, no. 1: 88–114.

———. "Yang Du er ti" (Two questions about Yang Du). *Jindaishi yanjiu*, 1986, no. 6: 236–44.

———. *Yuan Shikai yisheng* (The life of Yuan Shikai). [Zhengzhou?]: Henan Renmin Chubanshe, 1982.

———. "Yubei lixian shi Zhongguo zhengzhi zhidu jindaihua de kaiduan" (Constitutional preparation was the beginning of the modernization of China's political system). *Lishi dang'an*, 1991, no. 4: 104–11, 127.

Hsieh, Winston. *Chinese Historiography on the Revolution of 1911: A Critical Survey and a Selected Bibliography*. Stanford: Hoover Institution Press, Stanford University, 1975.

Hsu, Leonard S. *Study of a Typical Chinese Town: What Survey Revealed in Ching Ho, North China, Which Was Taken as Example*. Peiping: The Leader Press, 1929.

Hu Jieqing and Shu Yi. "Ji Lao She dansheng di" (A note on Lao She's birthplace). In Lao She, *Zhenghongqi xia* (Beneath the Plain Red Banner), 134–42. Beijing: Renmin Chubanshe, 1981.

Hu Jun. *Zhang Wenxiang gong nianpu* (A chronological biography of Zhang Zhidong). Reprint, Taipei: Wenhai Chubanshe, 1967.

Hu Pingsheng. *Minguo chuqi de fubipai* (The restorationist clique in the early Republic). Taipei: Taiwan Xuesheng Shuju, 1985.

Hu Yunyu. "Fa shi" (A history of hair). In *Man-Qing yeshi* (Unofficial histories of the Manchu Qing dynasty), 1: 449–70. Reprint, Taipei: Wenqiao Shuju, 1972.

Hua Li. "Cong qiren biancha baojia kan Qing wangchao 'qi-min fenzhi' zhengce de bianhua" (Changes in the Qing imperial policy of "separate governance of banner people and civilians" as seen from the incorporation of banner people into the *baojia* system). *Minzu yanjiu*, 1988, no. 5: 97–106.

Huang Fu-ch'ing. *Chinese Students in Japan in the Late Ch'ing Period*. Trans. Katherine P. K. Whitaker. Tokyo: Centre for East Asian Cultural Studies, 1982.

Huang Guangliang. *Qingdai keju zhidu zhi yanjiu* (A study of the examination system in the Qing period). Taipei: Jiaxin Shuini Gongsi Wenhua Jijinhui, 1976.

Huang Guangyun and Chen Jinming. "Ningxia minjun qiyi" (The uprising of the people's army in Ningxia). In *XGHYL*, 5: 497–503.

Huang, Ray. *1587, A Year of No Significance: The Ming Dynasty in Decline*. New Haven and London: Yale University Press, 1981.

Huang Zhangjian. *Wuxu bianfa shi yanjiu* (Studies on the history of the 1898 reforms). Taipei: Zhongyang Yanjiuyuan Lishi Yuyan Yanjiusuo, 1970.

Huang Zhongxing. *Yang Du yu Minchu zhengzhi (1911–1916)* (Yang Du and the politics of the early Republic, 1911–16). Taipei: Guoli Taiwan Shifan Daxue Lishi Yanjiusuo, 1986.

Hubei tongzhi (Gazetteer of Hubei Province). 1921 ed.

Hummel, Arthur W., ed. *Eminent Chinese of the Ch'ing Period (1644–1912)*. Washington, D.C.: United States Government Printing Office, 1943–44.

Hunt, Michael H. "The Forgotten Occupation: Peking, 1900–1901." *Pacific Historical Review* 48 (1979): 501–29.

Jansen, Marius B. *The Japanese and Sun Yat-sen*. Reprint, Stanford: Stanford University Press, 1970.

Jen Yu-wen. *The Taiping Revolutionary Movement*. New Haven: Yale University Press, 1973.

Jiang Jieshi. *Zhongguo zhi mingyun* (China's destiny). In *Jiang Xongtong ji* (The collected works of President Jiang), comp. Zhang Qijun, 118–70. Taipei: Guofang Yanjiuyuan and Zhonghua Dadian Bianyinhui, 1960. (See also Chiang, *China's Destiny*)

Jiang Xiangshun. "Jindai Shenyang Manzu de jingji shenghuo he minzu ziben de fazhan" (Economic life and the development of national capitalism among the Manchus of modern Shenyang). *Manzu yanjiu*, 1987, no. 3: 33–37.

Jiangningfu zhi (Gazetteer of Jiangning Prefecture). 1880 ed.

Jin Qicong. "Jingqi de Manzu" (Manchus of the Metropolitan Banners). *Manzu yanjiu*, 1988, no. 3 through 1991, no. 1.

———. *Manzu de lishi yu shenghuo—Sanjiazitun diaocha baogao* (The history and livelihood of the Manchus: A report of a survey at Sanjiazitun). Harbin: Heilongjiang Renmin Chubanshe, 1981.

Jin Xiangrui. "Wo shi zenma zhenpo mouzha shezhengwang yian de" (How I exposed the plot to assassinate the prince regent). In *XGHYL*, 8: 469–74.

Jingzhoufu zhi (Gazetteer of Jingzhou Prefecture). 1880 ed.

Jinliang. *Guang-Xuan xiaoji* (Anecdotes about the Guangxu and Xuantong eras). Reprint, Taipei: Xuesheng Shuju, 1973.

Johnston, Reginald F. *Twilight in the Forbidden City*. London: Victor Gollancz, 1934.

Jones, F. C. *Manchuria Since 1931*. New York: Oxford University Press, 1949.

Kendall, Elizabeth. *A Wayfarer in China: Impressions of a Trip Across West China and Mongolia*. Boston and New York: Houghton Mifflin Company, 1913.

Kent, Percy Horace. *The Passing of the Manchus*. Reprint, Washington, D.C.: University Publications of America, 1977.

Kessler, Lawrence D. "Ethnic Composition of Provincial Leadership during the Ch'ing Dynasty." *Journal of Asian Studies* 28 (1969): 489–511.

Keyte, J. C. *The Passing of the Dragon: The Story of the Shensi Revolution and Relief Expedition*. London: Hodder and Stoughton, 1913.

Kinross, Lord. *Ataturk: A Biography of Mustafa Kemal, Father of Modern Turkey*. New York: William Morrow and Company, 1965.

Kodansha Encyclopedia of Japan. Tokyo and New York: Kodansha, 1983.

Kuhn, Philip A. "Political Crime and Bureaucratic Monarchy: A Chinese Case of 1768." *Late Imperial China* 8, no. 1 (1987): 80–104.

Kuwabara Jitsuzō. "Zhongguo bianfa shi" (A history of the Chinese queue). Trans. Su Qianying. *DFZZ* 31, no. 3 (1934), "Funü yu jiating lan": 15–21.

Kwong, Luke S. K. *A Mosaic of the Hundred Days: Personalities, Politics, and Ideas of 1898*. Cambridge: Council on East Asian Studies, Harvard University, 1984.

Laitinen, Kauko. *Chinese Nationalism in the Late Qing Dynasty: Zhang Binglin as an Anti-Manchu Propagandist*. London: Curzon Press, 1990.

Lao Li (pseud.). *Nucai xiaoshi* (Biographical sketches of slaves). In *Man-Qing bishi* (Unofficial histories of the Manchu Qing dynasty), comp. Lu Baoxuan. Reprint, Taipei: Wenhai Chubanshe, 1970.

Lao She. *Beneath the Red Banner*. Trans. Don J. Cohn. Beijing: Panda Books, 1982.

———. *Teahouse*. Trans. John Howard-Gibbon. Beijing: Foreign Languages Press, 1980.

Lattimore, Owen. *Manchuria: Cradle of Conflict*. New York: Macmillan Company, 1932.

Lee, James, Cameron Campbell, and Wang Feng. "The Last Emperors: An Introduction to the Demography of the Qing (1644–1911) Imperial Lineage." In David S. Reher and Roger Schofield, eds., *Old and New Methods in Historical Demography*, 361–82. Oxford: Clarendon Press, 1993.

Lee, James, and Robert Y. Eng. "Population and Family History in Eighteenth Century Manchuria: Preliminary Results from Daoyi, 1774–1798." *Ch'ing-shih wen-t'i* 5, no. 1 (1984): 1–55.

Lee, Robert H. G. *The Manchurian Frontier in Ch'ing History*. Cambridge: Harvard University Press, 1970.

Lei Fangsheng. "Jingzhou qixue de shimo ji qi tedian" (The history and special character of the banner schools of Jingzhou). *Minzu yanjiu*, 1984, no. 3: 57–59.

Li Guilian. *Shen Jiaben yu Zhongguo falü xiandaihua* (Shen Jiaben and the modernization of China's laws). Beijing: Guangming Ribao Chubanshe, 1989.

Li Guoqi and Zhou Tiansheng. "Qingdai jiceng difangguan renshi shandi xianxiang zhi lianghua fenxi" (A quantitative analysis of the careers of basic-level local officials during the Qing). *Taiwan Shifan Daxue lishi xuebao* 2 (1974): 301–83.

Li Hong. "Qingdai bitieshi" (Manchu-language scribes in the Qing period). *Lishi dang'an*, 1994, no. 2: 89–92.

Li Huimin. "Wu Luzhen xunnan xintan" (A new look at the death of Wu Luzhen). *Zhongguo jindaishi*, 1989, no. 1: 130–36.

[Li] Jiannong. "Wuhan geming shimo ji" (A complete account of the Wuhan revolution). In *XHGM*, 5: 169–84.

————. *Zuijin sanshinian Zhongguo zhengzhishi* (China's political history in the last thirty years). Reprint, Taipei: Taiwan Xuesheng Shuju, 1974.

Li Jieren. "Ripples Across Stagnant Water." Trans. Hu Zhihui. *Chinese Literature*, Nov. 1981: 3–76; Dec. 1981: 3–71.

————. *Sishui weilan* (Ripples across stagnant water). Hong Kong: Xinwenxue Yanjiushe, 1975.

Li Lianfang. *Xinhai Wuchang shouyi ji* (An account of the Wuchang uprising of 1911). Reprint, Taipei: Zhongguo Guomindang Zhongyang Weiyuanhui Dangshi Shiliao Biancuan Weiyuanhui, 1961.

Li Lin. "Cong jiapu zhong tantao Manzu wenhua fazhan" (The evolution of Manchu culture as seen in family genealogies). *Manzu yanjiu*, 1987, no. 4: 64–70.

Li Shoukong. "Duan Qirui yu Xinhai Geming" (Duan Qirui and the 1911 Revolution). *Zhongguo Lishi Xuehui shixue jikan* 6 (1974): 277–97.

————. "Gesheng Ziyiju Lianhehui yu Xinhai Geming" (The Confederation of Provincial Assemblies and the 1911 Revolution). In Wu Xiangxiang, ed., *Zhongguo xiandaishi congkan* (Collected papers on recent Chinese history), 3: 321–73. Taipei: Zhengzhong Shuju, 1961.

————. "Zhengwenshe zhi chengli yu tingbi" (The founding and cessation of the Political Information Institute). In *SSJY*, 1907: 626–33.

Li Yi. "Jing-Yi-Shi-He guangfu ji" (An account of the restoration in Jingzhou, Yichang, Shinan and Hefeng Prefectures). In *XHGM*, 5: 245–85.

Li Zhiting, comp. *Aixin Jueluo jiazu quanshu* (The complete book on the Aisin Gioro family genealogy). Changchun: Jilin Renmin Chubanshe, 1997.

Li Zongyi. *Yuan Shikai zhuan* (A biography of Yuan Shikai). Beijing: Zhonghua Shuju, 1980.

Liang Qichao. *Yinbingshi wenji* (Collected writings from the Ice-Drinker's Studio). Comp. Lin Zhijun. Taipei: Taiwan Zhonghua Shuju, 1970.

Liang Xuyi. "Liangbi zhuan" (A biography of Liangbi). *Shoudu Bowuguan congkan*, 1982, no. 1: 28–32.

Liao Yuchun. "Xin Zhongguo wuzhuang jiejue heping ji" (A chronicle of how New China achieved peace by military means). In *KGWX*, 2, part 2: 419–77.

Lin Jiayou. "Xinhai Geming qianhou Guangzhou Man-Han minzu guanxi shiliao" (Materials on Manchu-Han ethnic relations in Guangzhou before and after the 1911 Revolution). In *Jinian Xinhai Geming qishi zhounian shiliao zhuanji* (A special compilation of historical materials commemorating the seventieth anniversary of the 1911 Revolution), 2: 204–18. Guangzhou: Guangdong Renmin Chubanshe, 1981.

Lin Jing. "Yili geming shimo ji" (A complete account of the revolution at Yili). In *KGWX*, 2, part 5: 428–35.

Lin Shuqing. "Zhenjun yuan-Ning ji" (An account of the Zhenjiang army's assistance at Nanjing). In *KGWX*, 2, part 4: 41–81.

Lin Xianxin. "Zaixun Sa Zhenbing chuguo kaocha haijun" (Zaixun and Sa Zhenbing go abroad to investigate navies). In Zhang Xia et al., comps., *Qingmo haijun shiliao* (Historical materials on the late Qing navy), 846–50. Beijing: Haiyang Chubanshe, 1982.

Lingnan Banweng (pseud.). "Wen Shengcai cisha Guangzhou dutong jian shu jiangjun Fuqi" (Wen Shengcai assassinates Fuqi, the Guangzhou brigade-general and acting general). In *KGWX*, 1, part 13: 697–704.

Lishi dang'an (Historical archives), Beijing.

Liu Fenghan. "Qingji Ziqiang Yundong yu junshi chuqi gaige (1861–1895)" (The Qing's Self-Strengthening Movement and the first period of military reform, 1861–1895). In *Qingji Ziqiang Yundong yanjiu taolunhui wenji* (Essays from the conference on the Qing's Self-Strengthening Movement), 343–93. Taipei: Zhongyang Yanjiuyuan Jindaishi Yanjiusuo, 1988.

———. *Wuweijun* (The Guards Army). Taipei: Zhongyang Yanjiuyuan Jindaishi Yanjiusuo, 1978.

———. *Yuan Shikai yu wuxu zhengbian* (Yuan Shikai and the 1898 coup). Taipei: Zhuanji Wenxue Chubanshe, 1969.

Liu Housheng. *Zhang Jian zhuanji* (A biography of Zhang Jian). Reprint, Shanghai: Shanghai Shudian, 1985.

Liu Qinghua. "Manzu xingshi shulüe" (A brief account of Manchu surnames). *Minzu yanjiu*, 1983, no. 1: 64–71.

Liu Tong. "Xinhai Fujian guangfu huiyi" (Recollections of the restoration in Fujian in 1911). In *XGHYL*, 4: 453–68.

Lo, Jung-pang. *K'ang Yu-wei: A Biography and a Symposium*. Tucson: University of Arizona Press, 1967.

Lowe, H. Y. *The Adventures of Wu: The Life Cycle of a Peking Man*. Reprint, Princeton: Princeton University Press, 1983.

Lü Jian. "Guanyu Xiong Chengji lieshi de xin shiliao" (New historical materials on the martyr Xiong Chengji). *Lishi dang'an*, 1982, no. 3: 120–23.

Lui, Adam Yuen-chung. *The Hanlin Academy: Training Ground for the Ambitious, 1644–1850*. Hamden, Conn.: Archon Books, 1981.

Luo Baoshan. "Guanyu Zhang Binglin zhengzhi lichang zhuanbian de jipian yiwen" (Several unpublished articles concerning the change in Zhang Binglin's political stance). *Lishi yanjiu*, 1982, no. 5: 56–62.

Luo Bingmian. "Zongli Yamen yu Manzu benwei zhengce" (The Zongli Yamen and the policy of Manchu primacy). In *Qingji Ziqiang Yundong yantaohui lunwen ji* (Essays from the conference on the Qing's Self-Strengthening Movement), 161–83. Taipei: Zhongyang Yanjiuyuan Jindaishi Yanjiusuo, 1988.

Luo Zhengwei. "Luanzhou geming jishi chugao (jielu)" (A draft history of the revolution at Luanzhou [extracts]). In *XHGM*, 6: 333–60.

Ma Feng-ch'en. "Manchu-Chinese Social and Economic Conflicts in Early Ch'ing."
In E-tu Zen Sun and John De Francis, eds., *Chinese Social History: Translations
of Selected Studies*, 333–51. Washington, D.C.: American Council of Learned
Societies, 1956.

Ma Xiedi. "Baqi zhidu xia de Manzu" (The Manchus under the Eight Banner system). *Manzu yanjiu*, 1987, no. 2: 28–34.

———. "Liu Xianzhi xiansheng yu 'Chengdu Man-Mengzu shilüe'" (Liu Xianzhi
and his "Short History of the Manchus and Mongols in Chengdu"). *Manzu yanjiu*, 1989, no. 1: 43–47.

———. "Qianlun Qingdai zhufang Baqi" (A brief discussion of the provincial Eight
Banner garrisons during the Qing period). *Shehui kexue zhanxian*, 1986, no. 3:
192–96.

———. "Qingdai Guangzhou Manzu shulüe" (A brief account of the Manchus in
Guangzhou during the Qing period). *Manzu yanjiu*, 1988, no. 1: 61–65.

———. "Zhufang Baqi qiantan" (A brief look at the provincial garrisons of the Eight
Banners). *Manzu yanjiu*, 1985, no. 2: 18–24.

Ma Yamin. "Nanjing guangfu jianwen suoyi" (Trifling memories of the restoration
at Nanjing). In *XGHYL*, 4: 256–62.

MacKinnon, Stephen R. *Power and Politics in Late Imperial China: Yuan Shi-kai in
Beijing and Tianjin, 1901–1908*. Berkeley: University of California Press, 1980.

Malone, Carroll Brown. *History of the Peking Summer Palaces under the Ch'ing
Dynasty*. Urbana: University of Illinois, 1934.

Manzu jianshi (A short history of the Manchus). Beijing: Zhonghua Shuju, 1979.

Manzu shehui lishi diaocha (Investigations into the society and history of the
Manchus). Shenyang: Liaoning Renmin Chubanshe, 1985.

Menzies, Nicholas K. *Forest and Land Management in Imperial China*. New York: St.
Martin's Press, 1994.

Millward, James A. "Beyond the Pass: Commerce, Ethnicity and the Qing Empire
in Xinjiang, 1759–1864." Ph.D. diss., Stanford University, 1993.

Min, Tu-ki. "Wuxu bianfa shiqi de Man-Han guanxi—Yige xiuzheng de kanfa"
(Manchu-Han relations at the time of the 1898 reforms: A revisionist view). In
Zhonghua Minguo jianguo shi taolunji (Conference papers on the history of the
founding of the Republic of China), 1: 380–88. Taipei: Zhonghua Minguo Jianguo
Shi Taolunji Bianji Weiyuanhui, 1981.

Minbao (The people's journal), Tokyo. 1905–07, 1910. Reprint, Beijing: Kexue Chubanshe, 1957.

Minguo renwu zhuan (Biographies of Republican personages). Beijing: Zhonghua
Shuju, 1978–96.

Morrison, G. E. *The Correspondence of G. E. Morrison, 1895–1912*. Ed. Lo Hui-min.
Cambridge: Cambridge University Press, 1976.

Moseley, George. *The Party and the National Question in China*. Cambridge and London: M.I.T. Press, 1966.

Muramatsu, Yuji. "Banner Estates and Banner Lands in 18th Century China—Evidence from Two New Sources." *Hitotsubashi Journal of Economics* 12, no. 2 (1972): 1–13.

Naquin, Susan, and Evelyn S. Rawski. *Chinese Society in the Eighteenth Century*. New Haven: Yale University Press, 1987.

Neige guanbao (Cabinet gazette), Beijing. 1911–12. Reprint, Taipei: Wenhai Chubanshe, 1965.

Ning Chia. "The Li-fan Yuan in the Early Ch'ing Dynasty." Ph.D. diss., Johns Hopkins University, 1991.

Norman, Jerry. *A Concise Manchu-English Lexicon*. Seattle: University of Washington Press, 1978.

North-China Herald and Supreme Court & Consular Gazette: Weekly Edition of the North-China Daily News, Shanghai. 1907–13.

Oxnam, Robert B. *Ruling from Horseback: Manchu Politics in the Oboi Regency, 1661–1669*. Chicago: University of Chicago Press, 1974.

Pan Chongxiong. "Duanfang yu yubei lixian" (Duanfang and the preparations for constitutionalism). *Si yu yan* 22, no. 5 (1985): 425–44.

Pan Honggang. "Xinhai Geming yu Jingzhou zhufang Baqi" (The 1911 Revolution and the Eight Banners' garrison at Jingzhou). *Manzu yanjiu*, 1992, no. 2: 21–28.

Pomerantz-Zhang, Linda. *Wu Tingfang (1842–1922): Reform and Modernization in Modern Chinese History*. Hong Kong: Hong Kong University Press, 1992.

Powell, Ralph L. *The Rise of Chinese Military Power, 1895–1912*. Princeton: Princeton University Press, 1955.

Presseisen, Ernst L. *Before Aggression: Europeans Prepare the Japanese Army*. Tucson: University of Arizona Press, 1965.

Pujie. "Qinggong huiqin jianwen" (Observations from my visits to relatives at the Qing court). In *Wan-Qing gongting shenghuo jianwen* (Eyewitness accounts of court life in the late Qing), 36–47. Beijing: Wenshi Ziliao Chubanshe, 1982.

Pusey, James Reeve. *China and Charles Darwin*. Cambridge: Council on East Asian Studies, Harvard University, 1983.

Puwei. "Rangguo yuqian huiyi riji" (A daily record of the court conferences concerning abdication). In *XHGM*, 8: 110–15.

Qian Anjing and Zhou Xiyin. "Xinhai Geming shiqi Sichuan shaoshu minzu fandi, fanfengjian, fannulizhi de yingxiong douzheng" (The heroic anti-imperialist, antifeudal, antislavery struggles of the minority ethnic groups in Sichuan at the time of the 1911 Revolution). In *Sichuan baolu fengyun lu* (A record of the railroad protection agitation in Sichuan), 108–21. Chengdu: Sichuan Renmin Chubanshe, 1981.

Qian Shifu, comp. *Qingji xinshe zhiguan nianbiao* (Annual personnel tables for the newly created offices in the Qing period). Beijing: Zhonghua Shuju, 1961.

———. *Qingji zhongyao zhiguan nianbiao* (Annual personnel tables for the important offices during the Qing period). In Yang Jialuo, ed., *Xinxiu Qingjishi sajiu biao* (A new compilation of thirty-nine tables on Qing history). Taipei: Dingwen Shuju, 1973.

Qin Guojing. "Qingdai de Baqi zhidu" (The Eight Banner system of the Qing period). *Lishi jiaoxue*, 1981, no. 4: 13–17.

"Qing Waiwubu bufen zhuyao guanyuan lüli" (Curricula vitae of some important officials at the Qing Ministry of Foreign Affairs). *Lishi dang'an*, 1986, no. 4: 40–43, 79.

Qingdai renwu zhuan'gao (Draft biographies of Qing personages). Series B. Shenyang: Liaoning Renmin Chubanshe, 1989–93.

"Qingmo bufen Baqi dutong lüli" (Curricula vitae of some Eight Banner lieutenants-general at the end of the Qing). *Lishi dang'an*, 1989, no. 4: 36–45.

Qingmo choubei lixian dang'an shiliao (Archival materials on constitutional preparations at the end of the Qing). Comp. Gugong Bowuyuan Ming-Qing Dang'anbu. Beijing: Zhonghua Shuju, 1979.

"Qingmo Wang Zhaoming beibu hou de gongdan ji youguan shiliao" (Wang Jingwei's confession after his arrest at the end of the Qing and other related documents). *Lishi dang'an*, 1983, no. 2: 21–24, 20.

Qingshigao (A draft history of the Qing). Comp. Zhao Erxun et al. Beijing: Zhonghua Shuju, 1976.

Qiu Yuanying. "Zhao Erfeng fadong 'Chengdu bingbian' shuo zhiyi" (Doubts about Zhao Erfeng's fomenting the Chengdu mutiny). *Huazhong shiyuan xuebao*, 1982, no. 5: 127–33.

Qizu yuebao ("The Banners"), Beijing. 1914. Available at Beijing Library.

Rankin, Mary Backus. *Early Chinese Revolutionaries: Radical Intellectuals in Shanghai and Zhejiang, 1902–1911*. Cambridge: Harvard University Press, 1971.

———. "The Manchurian Crisis and Radical Student Nationalism, 1903." *Ch'ing-shih wen-t'i*, 2, no. 1 (1969): 87–106.

Rawski, Evelyn S. "Ch'ing Imperial Marriage and Problems of Rulership." In Rubie S. Watson and Patricia Buckley Ebrey, eds., *Marriage and Inequality in Chinese Society*, 170–203. Berkeley: University of California Press, 1991.

———. *The Last Emperors: A Social History of Qing Imperial Institutions*. Berkeley, Los Angeles, and London: University of California Press, 1998.

———. "Reenvisioning the Qing: The Significance of the Qing Period in Chinese History." *Journal of Asian Studies* 55 (1996): 829–50.

Reynolds, Douglas R. *China, 1898–1912: The Xinzheng Revolution and Japan*. Cambridge: Council on East Asian Studies, Harvard University, 1993.

Rhoads, Edward J. M. "The Assassination of Governor Enming and Its Effect on Manchu-Han Relations in Late Qing China." In Etō Shinkichi and Harold Z.

Schiffrin, eds., *China's Republican Revolution*, 3–24. Tokyo: University of Tokyo Press, 1994.

———. *China's Republican Revolution: The Case of Kwangtung, 1895–1913.* Cambridge: Harvard University Press, 1975.

———. "Merchant Associations in Canton, 1895–1911." In Mark Elvin and G. William Skinner, eds., *The Chinese City Between Two Worlds*, 97–117. Stanford: Stanford University Press, 1974.

———. "Self-Strengthening and Manchu-Han Relations." In Hao Yanping (Yen-p'ing Hao) and Wei Xiumei, eds., *Jinshi Zhongguo zhi chuantong yu tuibian* (Tradition and transformation in modern China), 1007–38. Taipei: Zhongyang Yanjiuyuan Jindaishi Yanjiusuo, 1998.

Rigger, Shelley. "Voices of Manchu Identity, 1635–1935." In Stevan Harrell, ed., *Cultural Encounters on China's Ethnic Frontiers*, 186–214. Seattle and London: University of Washington Press, 1995.

Rong Tiegeng. "Qingdai Beijing de Jianruiying" (The Scouts Division of Beijing during the Qing). *Manzu yanjiu*, 1987, no. 2: 35–36.

Rong Xiang. "Lüetan Xinhai Geming qianhou de jiaxiang jiushi" (Tales of home before and after the 1911 Revolution). In *XGHYL*, 5: 231–50.

Rozman, Gilbert. *Urban Networks in Ch'ing China and Tokugawa Japan.* Princeton: Princeton University Press, 1973.

Rummel, R. J. *China's Bloody Century: Genocide and Mass Murder Since 1900.* New Brunswick and London: Transaction Publishers, 1991.

Saishin Shina kanshin roku (The latest directory of Chinese officials and notables). Comp. Pekin Shina Kenkyukai. Tokyo, 1918.

Sang Bing. "Guimao yuanri liu-Ri xuesheng pai-Man yanshuo shishi kaobian" (An examination of the anti-Manchu speeches by students in Japan at the lunar new year of 1903). *Xueshu yanjiu*, 1984, no. 3: 73–77.

Sanmin Zhuyi cidian (A dictionary of the Three People's Principles). Taipei: Zhonghua Congshu Weiyuanhui, 1956.

Scotland, Tony. *The Empty Throne: The Quest for an Imperial Heir in the People's Republic of China.* London: Viking, 1993.

Scott, A. C. *Chinese Costume in Transition.* New York: Theatre Arts Books, 1960.

Shaanxi tongzhi gao (Draft gazetteer of Shaanxi Province). 1934 ed.

Shang Binghe. *Xinren chunqiu* (Annals of 1911–12). Reprint, Hong Kong: Wenyi Shuwu, 1970.

Shang Yanliu. *Qingdai keju kaoshi shulu* (An account of the civil service examinations in the Qing period). Beijing: Sanlian Shudian, 1958.

Shen Jiaben. *Shen Jiyi xiansheng yishu (jiabian)* (Posthumous writings of Shen Jiaben [First collection]). Reprint, Taipei: Wenhai Chubanshe, 1964.

Shen Yunlong. "Beiyang zhi 'gou'—Feng Guozhang" (Feng Guozhang: The Beiyang "dog"). *Zhuanji wenxue* 28, no. 5 (1976): 47–54.

———. *Xu Shichang pingzhuan* (A critical biography of Xu Shichang). Taipei: Zhuanji Wenxue Chubanshe, 1979.

———. "Zhangwo wan-Qing zhengbing zhi Yikuang" (Yikuang, wielder of political power in the late Qing). In idem, *Jindai zhengzhi renwu luncong* (Essays on modern political figures), 1: 70–80. Taipei: Ziyou Taipingyang Wenhua Shiye Gongsi, 1965.

Sheridan, James E. *Chinese Warlord: The Career of Feng Yü-hsiang*. Stanford: Stanford University Press, 1966.

Shi, Mingzheng. "From Imperial Gardens to Public Parks: The Transformation of Urban Space in Early Twentieth-Century Beijing." *Modern China* 24 (1998): 219–54.

Shibao ("The Eastern Times"), Shanghai. 1909–15. Microfilmed ed., Tokyo: Yushodo Film Publications Ltd., 1967.

Shina shōbetsu zenshi (Complete provincial gazetteers of China). Tokyo: Tōa Dobunkai, 1917–20.

Shirokogoroff, S. M. *Social Organization of the Manchus: A Study of the Manchu Clan Organization*. Shanghai: Royal Asiatic Society, North China Branch, 1924.

Shu Xincheng. *Jindai Zhongguo liuxue shi* (A history of study abroad in modern China). Reprint, Taipei: Zhongguo Chubanshe, 1973.

Shu Yi. "Zaitan Lao She xiansheng he Manzu wenxue" (More on Lao She and Manchu literature). *Manzu yanjiu*, 1985, no. 1: 62–67.

Shu Zhongji. "Xinhai Geming shi Guangzhou Baqijun toucheng jingguo" (The surrender of the Eight Banner army in Guangzhou at the time of the 1911 Revolution). In *Jinian Xinhai Geming qishi zhounian shiliao zhuanji* (A special compilation of historical materials commemorating the seventieth anniversary of the 1911 Revolution), 2: 219–23. Guangzhou: Guangdong Renmin Chubanshe, 1981.

Shuntian shibao ("Peking Times"), Beijing. 1908–12. 1908–9 issues available at Beijing Library; 1910–12 issues on microfilm (Washington, D.C.: Center for Chinese Research Materials, Association of Research Libraries).

Sigel, Louis. "Revolution by Diplomacy: A Re-examination of the Shanghai Peace Conference of 1911." *Papers on Far Eastern History* 19 (1979): 111–43.

Smith, Richard J. *China's Cultural Heritage: The Ch'ing Dynasty, 1644–1912*. Boulder, Colo.: Westview Press, 1983.

Spence, Jonathan D. *God's Chinese Son: The Taiping Heavenly Kingdom of Hong Xiuquan*. New York and London: W. W. Norton & Company, 1996.

———. *Ts'ao Yin and the K'ang-hsi Emperor: Bondservant and Master*. New Haven and London: Yale University Press, 1966.

Stary, Giovanni, Nicola Di Cosmo, Tatiana A. Pang, and Alessandra Pozzi. *On the

Tracks of Manchu Culture, 1664–1994: 350 Years after the Conquest of Peking. Wiesbaden: Harrassowitz Verlag, 1995.

Strand, David. *Rickshaw Beijing: City People and Politics in the 1920s.* Berkeley: University of California Press, 1989.

Struve, Lynn A. *The Southern Ming, 1644–1662.* New Haven and London: Yale University Press, 1984.

Su Jing. *Qingji Tongwenguan ji qi shisheng* (The Translators College of the Qing period and its faculty and students). Taipei: Su Jing, 1985.

Su Yunfeng. "Hubei Xinjun (1896–1912)" (The Hubei New Army, 1896–1912). *Lishi xuebao* 4 (1976): 345–80.

Subao (Jiangsu journal), Shanghai. 1903. Reprint, Taipei: Zhongguo Guomindang Zhongyang Weiyuanhui Dangshi Shiliao Biancuan Weiyuanhui, 1968.

Sun, E-tu Zen. "The Board of Revenue in Nineteenth-Century China." *Harvard Journal of Asiatic Studies* 24 (1962–63): 175–228.

———. "The Chinese Constitutional Missions of 1905–1906." *Journal of Modern History* 24 (1952): 251–68.

Tahara Tennan. *Shinmatsu Minsho Chūgoku kanshin jinmeiroku* (A biographical directory of Chinese officials and notables in the late Qing and early Republic). Reprint, Taipei: Wenhai Chubanshe, 1973.

Tan, Chester C. *The Boxer Catastrophe.* New York: W. W. Norton & Company, 1971.

Tang Zhijun. *Wuxu bianfa renwu zhuan'gao* (Draft biographies of the 1898 reformers). Enlarged ed., Beijing: Zhonghua Shuju, 1982.

Tao Jing-shen. "Barbarians or Northerners: Northern Sung Images of the Khitans." In Morris Rossabi, ed., *China Among Equals: The Middle Kingdom and Its Neighbors, 10th-14th Centuries,* 66–86. Berkeley: University of California Press, 1983.

Tao Juyin. *Beiyang junfa tongzhi shiqi shihua* (Tales of the Beiyang warlord era). N.p.: Sanlian Shudian, 1957–59.

Telford, Ted A., and Michael H. Finegan. "Qing Archival Materials from the Number One Historical Archives on Microfilm at the Genealogical Society of Utah." *Late Imperial China* 9, no. 2 (1988): 86–114.

Teng Shaozhen. "Manzhou Manzu mingcheng bianxi" (On the differentiation between the terms Manzhou and Manzu). *Manzu yanjiu*, 1995, no. 3: 45–53; no. 4: 47–54.

Tianjia. *Man-Qing waishi* (An unofficial history of the Manchu Qing dynasty). Taipei: Guangwen Shuju, 1971.

Tong Jiajiang. "Qingdai Baqi zhidu xiaowang shijian xinyi" (A reconsideration of when the Eight Banner system of the Qing withered away). *Minzu yanjiu*, 1994, no. 5: 101–8.

Tongjia and Qingfu. "Xinjiang Xibozu de yuyan yu wenzi" (The speech and script of the Xibe of Xinjiang). *Manzu yanjiu*, 1991, no. 3: 87–96.

Torbert, Preston M. *The Ch'ing Imperial Household Department: A Study of Its Organization and Principal Functions, 1662–1796*. Cambridge: Council on East Asian Studies, Harvard University, 1977.

Tsou Jung. *The Revolutionary Army, A Chinese Nationalist Tract of 1903*. Trans. John Lust. The Hague and Paris: Mouton & Co., 1968.

"The Tungus Race in Manchoukuo." *Contemporary Manchuria*, 3, no. 2 (1939): 47–72.

United States. Department of State, Decimal File, 1910–29. National Archives, Record Group 59. Microfilmed.

———. Department of State, Numerical File, 1906–10. National Archives, Record Group 59.

———. War College Division of the General Staff. National Archives, Record Group 165.

Vohra, Ranbir. *Lao She and the Chinese Revolution*. Cambridge: East Asian Research Center, Harvard University, 1974.

Vollmer, John E. *Decoding Dragons: Status Garments in Ch'ing Dynasty China*. Eugene: Museum of Art, University of Oregon, 1983.

Wade, T. F. "The Army of the Chinese Empire: Its Two Great Divisions, the Bannermen or National Guard, and the Green Standard or Provincial Troops . . ." *Chinese Repository* 20 (1851): 250–80, 300–340, 363–422. Reprint, Tokyo: Maruzen Co., Ltd., and Vaduz: Kraus Reprint Ltd., n.d.

Wadley, Stephen A. "Altaic Influences on Beijing Dialect: The Manchu Case." *Journal of the American Oriental Society* 16 (1996): 99–104.

Wakeman, Frederic, Jr. *The Great Enterprise: The Manchu Reconstruction of Imperial Order in Seventeenth-Century China*. Berkeley: University of California Press, 1985.

Waley, Arthur. *The Opium War Through Chinese Eyes*. New York: MacMillan Company, 1958.

Wan Xiangchun and Deng Xianglin. "Xin-Yi geming shilüe" (A sketch history of the revolution in Xinjiang and Yili). In *KGWX*, 2, part 5: 421–23.

Wang Daorui. "Xinfaxian de Xu Xilin cisha Enming shiliao qianxi" (A brief analysis of a newly discovered document about Xu Xilin's assassination of Enming). *Lishi yanjiu*, 1991, no. 4: 100–103.

Wang Dezhao. *Qingdai keju zhidu yanjiu* (A study of the examination system in the Qing period). Hong Kong: Zhongwen Daxue Chubanshe, 1982.

Wang Di. "Qingmo xinzheng yu jindai xuetang de xingqi" (The New Policies of the late Qing and the rise of modern schools). *Jindaishi yanjiu*, 1987, no. 3: 245–70.

Wang Ermin. "Duanfa yifu gaiyuan—Bianfalun zhi xiangzheng zhiqu" (Queue-cutting, costume change, and calendar reform: Symbolic indicators of reform). In *Zhongguo jindai de weixin yundong—Bianfa yu lixian yantaohui* (The reform movement in modern China: A conference on reform and constitutionalism), 59–73. Taipei: Zhongyang Yanjiuyuan Jindaishi Yanjiusuo, 1982.

Wang Huo. "Qingdai Baqi zhong Gaoliren mingzi de yuyan he minsu tezheng" (Linguistic and folk cultural traits in the names of Koreans in the Eight Banner system of the Qing). *Manzu yanjiu*, 1995, no. 2: 43–49.

Wang Jiajian. *Qingmo Minchu woguo jingcha zhidu xiandaihua de licheng (1901–1928)* (The modernization of our nation's police system in the late Qing and early Republic, 1901–1928). Taipei: Taiwan Shangwu Yinshuguan, 1984.

———. *Zhongguo jindai haijun shi lunwen ji* (Essays on the history of China's modern navy). Taipei: Wenshizhe Chubanshe, 1984.

Wang Jun. "1908-nian Beijing Neiwaicheng de renkou yu tongji" (Population statistics for Beijing's Inner and Outer Cities in 1908). *Lishi dang'an*, 1997, no. 3: 103–8.

Wang Qingxiang. *Mao Zedong Zhou Enlai yu Puyi* (Mao Zedong, Zhou Enlai, and Puyi). Beijing: Renmin Chubanshe, 1993.

Wang Shounan. "Xinhai Wuchang qiyi hou Qingting zhi kunjing yu Qingdi tuiwei" (The Qing court's predicament following the Wuchang uprising in 1911 and the Qing emperor's abdication). *Guoli Zhengzhi Daxue lishi xuebao* 4 (1986): 73–108.

Wang Shu'nan. "Wuhan zhanji" (An account of the battle for Wuhan). In *XHGM*, 5: 229–41.

Wang Youyu. "Da-Han Sichuan Junzhengfu chengli qianhou jianwen" (Observations before and after the establishment of the Great Han Sichuan Military Government). In *XGHYL*, 3: 68–73.

Wang Yunying. "Shilun Qing ruguan qian de yiguan zhi" (On the clothing style of the preconquest Qing). *Liaoning Daxue xuebao*, 1981, no. 5: 71–74.

Wang Zhonghan. "Guanyu Manzu xingcheng zhong de jige wenti" (Several questions concerning the formation of the Manchus). In idem, ed., *Manzu shi yanjiu ji* (Collected studies on the history of the Manchus), 1–16. Beijing: Zhongguo Shehui Kexue Chubanshe, 1988.

———. "'Guoyu qishe' yu Manzu de fazhan" ("National speech and mounted archery" and the development of the Manchus). In idem, ed., *Manzu shi yanjiu ji* (Collected studies on the history of the Manchus), 195–208. Beijing: Zhongguo Shehui Kexue Chubanshe, 1988.

———. "Qingdai Baqi zhong de Man-Han minzu chengfen wenti" (The question of Manchu and Han ethnic elements in the Eight Banners of the Qing period). *Minzu yanjiu*, 1990, no. 3: 36–46, 65; no. 4: 57–66.

———. "Qingdai qidi xingzhe chutan" (An initial investigation into the character of banner lands during the Qing period). *Wenshi* 6 (1979): 127–37.

Wang Zongyou. "Erbainianlai Guangzhou Manzu jingji shenghuo de bianqian" (Changes in the economic life of the Manchus in Guangzhou in the last two hundred years). *Guangdong wenshi ziliao* 35 (1982): 249–62.

———. *Guangzhou Manzu jianshi* (A short history of the Manchus in Guangzhou). [Guangzhou?]: Guangdong Renmin Chubanshe, 1990.

Wang Zuancheng. "Xinhai shouyi Yang-Xia guangfu jishi" (An account of the initial uprising [at Wuchang] and the restoration at Hanyang and Hankou in 1911). In *XGHYL*, 2: 17–46.

Wei Xiumei. "Cong liang de guancha tantao Qingji zhufang fudutong zhi renshi shandi" (A quantitative analysis of the careers of brigade-generals in provincial garrisons during the Qing). *Zhongyang Yanjiuyuan Jindaishi Yanjiusuo jikan*, 13 (1984): 387–428.

———. "Cong liang de guancha tantao Qingji zhufang jiangjun dutong zhi renshi shandi" (A quantitative analysis of the careers of banner garrison generals and lieutenants-general during the Qing). *Zhongyang Yanjiuyuan Jindaishi Yanjiusuo jikan*, 10 (1981): 187–225.

———, comp. *Qingji zhiguan biao* (Tables of Qing officials). Taipei: Zhongyang Yanjiuyuan Jindaishi Yanjiusuo, 1977.

Wei Yingtao. *Sichuan baolu yundong shi* (A history of the railroad protection movement in Sichuan). Chengdu: Sichuan Renmin Chubanshe, 1981.

Wen Gongzhi. *Zuijin sanshinian Zhongguo junshi shi* (A history of military affairs in China during the last thirty years). Reprint, Taipei: Wenhai Chubanshe, 1971.

Williams, Edward Thomas. *China Yesterday and To-day*. London: George G. Harrop & Co., Ltd., [1923?].

Williamson, Alexander. *Journeys in North China, Manchuria, and Eastern Mongolia*. London: Smith, Elder & Co., 1870.

Wong, Young-tsu. *Search for Modern Nationalism: Zhang Binglin and Revolutionary China, 1869–1936*. Hong Kong: Oxford University Press, 1989.

Wright, Mary Clabaugh. "Introduction: The Rising Tide of Change." In idem, ed., *China in Revolution: The First Phase, 1900–1913*, 1–63. New Haven and London: Yale University Press, 1968.

———. *The Last Stand of Chinese Conservatism: The T'ung-chih Restoration, 1862–1874*. 2nd printing, with additional notes. Stanford: Stanford University Press, 1962.

Wu Cifan. "Zhenjiang guangfu huiyi" (Recollections of the restoration at Zhenjiang). In *XGHYL*, 4: 263–68.

Wu Fang. *Renzhi de shanshui: Zhang Yuanji zhuan* (The virtuous delight in mountains, the wise in water: A biography of Zhang Yuanji). Shanghai: Shanghai Wenyi Chubanshe, 1994.

Wu Tianren. *Liang Jiean xiansheng nianpu* (A chronological biography of Liang Dingfen). Taipei: Yiwen Yinshuguan, 1979.

Wu Tingfang. *Wu xiansheng gongdu* (The public papers of Wu Tingfang). Reprint, Taipei: Wenhai Chubanshe, 1971.

————— (Guan Dulu, pseud.). *Gonghe guanjian lu* (A key record of republicanism). Reprint: Taipei: Wenhai Chubanshe, 1981.

Wu, Wei-ping. "The Development and Decline of the Eight Banners." Ph.D. diss., University of Pennsylvania, 1969.

Wu Wo-yao. "A Bannerman at the Teahouse." Trans. Gloria Bien. *Renditions: A Chinese-English Translation Magazine* 4 (1975): 148–50.

Wu Xiangxiang. "Qingdi tuiwei yu chugong jingguo" (The abdication of the Qing emperor and his expulsion from the palace). In idem, *Wan-Qing gongting yu renwu* (The late Qing court and its personnel), 111–19. Taipei: Wenxing Shudian, 1965.

Wu Youru. *Wan-Qing shehui fengsu baitu* (One hundred views of late Qing social customs). [Shanghai?]: Xuelin Chubanshe, 1996.

Wu Yuanfeng and Zhao Zhiqiang. "Xibozu you Keerqin Mengguqi bianru Manzhou Baqi shimo" (A complete account of how the Xibe were detached from the Khorchin Mongol banners and incorporated into the Manchu Eight Banners). *Minzu yanjiu*, 1984, no. 5: 60–66.

Wu Zhaoqing. "Qingmo Jinweijun" (The Palace Guard at the end of the Qing). *Gugong Bowuyuan yuankan*, 1985, no. 2: 12–23.

—————. "Yuan Shikai lian Xinjun gai junzhi ji qi lishi diwei" (Yuan Shikai's training of the New Army and reform of the military system and their place in history). *Lishi dang'an*, 1987, no. 1: 105–11.

Wu Zhichao. "Lüelun 'Xin Manzhou'" (On the "New Manchus"). *Manzu yanjiu*, 1987, no. 1: 92–95, 72.

Wu Zhongya. "Wu Luzhen shi 'lixianpai' ma?" (Was Wu Luzhen a constitutionalist?). *Lishi yanjiu*, 1982, no. 3: 66–82.

Wulaxichun. "Manzu de yuyan he wenhua" (The language and culture of the Manchus). *Manzu yanjiu*, 1992, no. 2: 52–58.

Wuxu bianfa (The 1898 reforms). Shanghai: Shanghai Renmin Chubanshe, 1957.

Wuxu bianfa dang'an shiliao (Archival materials on the 1898 reforms). Comp. Guojia Dang'anju Ming-Qing Dang'anguan. Reprint, Taipei: Dingwen Shuju, 1973.

Xianjun. "Su Qinwang Shanqi de fubi huodong" (Restorationist activities of Prince Su, Shanqi). In *Wan-Qing gongting shenghuo jianwen* (Eyewitness accounts of court life in the late Qing), 308–15. Beijing: Wenshi Ziliao Chubanshe, 1982.

Xiao Yishan. *Qingdai tongshi* (A comprehensive history of the Qing period). Taipei: Taiwan Shangwu Yinshuguan, 1962–63.

Xin Ping, Hu Zhenghao, and Li Xuechang, comps. *Minguo shehui daguan* (An overview of Republican society). Fuzhou: Fujian Renmin Chubanshe, 1991.

Xinhai Geming (The 1911 Revolution). Comp. Zhongguo Shixue Hui. Shanghai: Shanghai Renmin Chubanshe, 1957.

Xinhai Geming huiyilu (Memoirs of the 1911 Revolution). Beijing: Zhonghua Shuju, 1961–63 (vols. 1–5); Wenshi Ziliao Chubanshe, 1981–82 (vols. 6–8).

Xiong Bingkun. "Wuchang qiyi tan" (On the Wuchang uprising). In *XHGM*, 5: 85–98.

Xiong Kewu et al., comps. "Shu dang shigao" (A draft history of the [Nationalist] Party in Sichuan). In *Xinhai Geming shi congkan* 2 (1980): 167–82.

Xu Bingkun. "Hangzhou guangfu zhi ye de yice guanshen jinji huiyi" (An emergency meeting of officials and gentry on the night of Hangzhou's restoration). In *XGHYL*, 4: 165–66.

Xu Chonghao. "Xinhai Zhenjun qiyi kefu Nanjing jingguo ji" (An account of the Zhenjiang army's revolt and its role in the taking of Nanjing in 1911). In *KGWX*, 2, part 4: 36–41.

———. "Zhenjiang Xinjun qiyi he Zhenjun huigong Nanjing jishi" (A record of the mutiny of the Zhenjiang New Army and the Zhenjiang army's assault on Nanjing). In *XGHYL*, 4: 247–55.

Xue Dubi. "Taiyuan he Hedong guangfu de pianduan" (A fragmentary account of the restoration in Taiyuan and the Hedong region). In *XGHYL*, 5: 169–78.

"Xunjingbu zhuyao guanyuan lüli" (Curricula vitae of the important officials at the Ministry of the Police). *Lishi dang'an*, 1994, no. 2: 63, 79.

Yan Shouhua. "Hairong deng jian zai Xinhai Geming zhong jingli" (Activities of the *Hairong* and other ships during the 1911 Revolution). In Zhang Xia et al., comps., *Qingmo haijun shiliao* (Historical materials on the late Qing navy), 704–11. Beijing: Haiyang Chubanshe, 1982.

———, Yang Tinggang, and Lin Shunfan. "Changjiang jiandui xiangying Xinhai Geming de huiyi" (Recollections of the Yangzi River fleet's response to the 1911 Revolution). In *XGHYL*, 7: 56–66.

Yan Xiangdong. "Xinjiang Xiboyu baocun zhi yuanyin" (Reasons for the preservation of the Xibe language in Xinjiang). *Manzu yanjiu*, 1990, no. 2: 67–72.

Yan, Yunxiang. *The Flow of Gifts: Reciprocity and Social Networks in a Chinese Village.* Stanford: Stanford University Press, 1996.

Yang Dongping. *Chengshi jifeng: Beijing yu Shanghai de wenhua jingshen* (Urban monsoons: The cultural ethos of Beijing and Shanghai). Beijing: Dongfang Chubanshe, 1995.

Yang Du. *Yang Du ji* (The collected works of Yang Du). Comp. Liu Qingbo. Changsha: Hunan Renmin Chubanshe, 1986.

Yang Fengchun. "Yili Xinhai Geming gaishu" (An overview of the 1911 Revolution in Yili). In *XGHYL*, 5: 510–22.

Yang Qingzhen. "Hairong, Haichou, Haichen sanjian canyu guangfu jingguo" (The three cruisers *Hairong*, *Haichou*, and *Haichen* join the restoration). In *XGHYL*, 6: 99–103.

Yang Shusen, ed. *Qingdai Liutiaobian* (The Willow Palisade of the Qing period). Shenyang: Liaoning Renmin Chubanshe, 1978.

Yang Tianshi and Wang Xuezhuang, comps. *Ju-E yundong, 1901–1905* (The movement to repel Russia, 1901–1905). Beijing: Zhongguo Shehui Kexue Chubanshe, 1979.

Yang Tingyuan. "Ji E Junzhengfu de chuqi waijiao huodong" (An account of the diplomatic activities of the Hubei Military Government in the early period). In *XGHYL*, 7: 42–55.

Yang Xuechen and Zhou Yuanlian. *Qingdai Baqi wanggong guizu xingshuai shi* (A history of the rise and fall of the Eight Banner princes and nobles during the Qing period). Shenyang: Liaoning Renmin Chubanshe, 1986.

Yangquxian zhi (Gazetteer of Yangqu County). 1843 ed.

Yangwu yundong (The foreign affairs movement). Shanghai: Shanghai Renmin Chubanshe, 1961.

Yao Yijie. "Xinhai Taiyuan gemingjun jilu" (A record of the Taiyuan revolutionary army in 1911). In *KGWX*, 2, part 3: 266–68.

Ye Hao. "Cong 'changmao' tan Taiping Tianguo de fazhi" ("Longhairs": On the hair-style of the Taiping Heavenly Kingdom). *Nanjing shizhi*, 1987, no. 6: 50–51.

Yi Baozhong. "Shilun Qingdai Manzu shibing tudi suoyouzhi de yanbian" (On the evolution of the Manchu soldiers' land system during the Qing). *Manzu yanjiu*, 1987, no. 4: 26–29.

"Youguan Chuandao Langsu de jijian shiliao" (Several documents relating to Kawashima Naniwa). *Lishi dang'an*, 1993, no. 4: 67–71, 66.

Young, Ernest P. *The Presidency of Yuan Shih-k'ai: Liberalism and Dictatorship in Early Republican China.* Ann Arbor: University of Michigan Press, 1977.

———. "Problems of a Late Ch'ing Revolutionary: Ch'en T'ien-hua." In Chün-tu Hsüeh, ed., *Revolutionary Leaders of Modern China*, 210–47. New York: Oxford University Press, 1971.

Yu Dahua. "'Qingshi Youdai Tiaojian' xinlun; jian tan Puyi qianwang dongbei de yige yuanyin" (A new look at the Articles of Favorable Treatment for the Qing imperial household; and an exploration of one reason for Puyi's flight to the northeast). *Jindaishi yanjiu*, 1994, no. 1: 161–77.

Yuan Shikai. *Yangshouyuan zouyi jiyao* (A compilation of Yuan Shikai's important memorials). Comp. Shen Zuxian. Reprint, Taipei: Wenhai Chubanshe, 1966.

———. *Yuan Shikai zouzhe zhuanji* (A special compilation of Yuan Shikai's memorials). Ed. Guoli Gugong Bowuyuan. Taipei: Guangwen Shuju, 1970.

Yun Baohui. "Xinhai Feng Guozhang jietong Jinweijun hou de huodong" (Feng Guozhang's activities after becoming Palace Guard commander in 1911). *Wenshi ziliao xuanji* 9 (1960): 119–20.

Zaifeng. "Chun Qinwang shi-De riji" (Prince Chun's diary of his mission to Germany). *Jindaishi ziliao* 73 (1989): 138–68 (1989).

Zairun. "Longyu yu Zaifeng zhi maodun" (Contradictions between Longyu and

Zaifeng). In *Wan-Qing gongting shenghuo jianwen* (Eyewitness accounts of court life in the late Qing), 76–78. Beijing: Wenshi Ziliao Chubanshe, 1982.

Zaitao. "Jinweijun zhi jianli yu gaibian" (The creation and transformation of the Palace Guard). In Zheng Huaiyi and Zhang Jianshe, *Modai huangshu Zaitao chenfu lu* (The vicissitudes of Zaitao, the last emperor's uncle), 237–42. Beijing: Qunzhong Chubanshe, 1989.

———. "Zaifeng yu Yuan Shikai de maodun" (Contradictions between Zaifeng and Yuan Shikai). In *Wan-Qing gongting shenghuo jianwen* (Eyewitness accounts of court life in the late Qing), 79–83. Beijing: Wenshi Ziliao Chubanshe, 1982.

Zha Shijie. "Qingmo de Zongshedang" (The Royalist Party at the end of the Qing). *Guoli Taiwan Daxue Lishi Xuexi xuebao* 5 (1978): 125–39.

Zhang Bingduo. *Zhang Zhidong pingzhuan* (A critical biography of Zhang Zhidong). Taipei: Taiwan Zhonghua Shuju, 1972.

Zhang Bofeng, comp. *Qingdai gedi jiangjun dutong dachendeng nianbiao* (Annual personnel tables of garrison generals, lieutenants-general, and other regional officials during the Qing period). In Yang Jialuo, ed., *Xinxiu Qingji sajiu biao* (A new compilation of thirty-nine tables on the Qing dynasty). Taipei: Dingwen Shuju, 1973.

——— and Li Zongyi, comps. *Beiyang junfa (1912–1928)* (Beiyang warlords, 1912–1928). Wuhan: Wuhan Chubanshe, 1990.

Zhang Cunwu. "Wu Tingfang yu Xinhai Geming" (Wu Tingfang and the 1911 Revolution). *Zhongguo xiandaishi zhuanti yanjiu baogao* (Research reports on topics in China's modern history) 6: 94–122. Taipei: Zhonghua Minguo Shiliao Yanjiu Zhongxin, 1976.

Zhang Deze. *Qingdai guojia jiguan kaolüe* (A brief study of the governmental institutions in the Qing period). Beijing: Zhongguo Renmin Daxue Chubanshe, 1981.

Zhang Guochang. "Manzu jiaoyu zai Qingdai" (Manchu education in the Qing period). *Manzu yanjiu*, 1986, no. 3: 56–63.

Zhang Guogan. "Qingmo Jinweijun" (The Palace Guard at the end of the Qing). In Zhang Bofeng and Li Zongyi, comps., *Beiyang junfa, 1912–1928* (Beiyang warlords, 1912–1928), 1: 22–24. Wuhan: Wuhan Chubanshe, 1990.

———, comp. *Xinhai Geming shiliao* (Historical materials on the 1911 Revolution). Shanghai: Longmen Lianhe Shuju, 1958.

Zhang Jian. *Seweng ziding nianpu* (Zhang Jian's self-compiled chronological biography). In Zhang Xiaoruo, *Nantong Zhang Jizhi xiansheng zhuanji* (A biography of Zhang Jian of Nantong). Reprint, Taipei: Taiwan Xuesheng Shuju, 1974.

Zhang Jiasheng. "Wo du 'Dandong Manzu'" (My reading of "The Manchus of Dandong"). *Manzu yanjiu*, 1994, no. 4: 40–41.

Zhang Jie. "Qingdai dongbei Manzu wenhua jiaoyu jianlun" (A brief discussion of Manchu culture and education in the northeast during the Qing period). *Manzu yanjiu*, 1995, no. 2: 30–32.

Zhang Jing'ai. "Manzu de qishe" (The Manchus' horsemanship and archery). *Manzu yanjiu*, 1987, no. 4: 71–73.

Zhang Kaiyuan. *Xinhai Geming yu jindai shehui* (The 1911 Revolution and modern society). Tianjin: Tianjin Renmin Chubanshe, 1985.

Zhang Liying. "Zhenjiang guangfu shiliao" (Historical materials on the restoration at Zhenjiang). *Jindaishi ziliao*, 1957, no. 6: 75–80.

Zhang Nan and Wang Renzhi, comps. *Xinhai Geming qianshinianjian shilun xuanji* (Selected political commentaries from the decade before the 1911 Revolution). Hong Kong: Sanlian Shudian, 1962.

Zhang Pengyuan. *Lixianpai yu Xinhai Geming* (The constitutionalists and the 1911 Revolution). Taipei: Zhongguo Xueshu Zhuzuo Jiangzhu Weiyuanhui, 1969.

Zhang Qizhuo. *Manzu zai Xiuyan* (The Manchus at Xiuyan). Shenyang: Liaoning Renmin Chubanshe, 1984.

Zhang Tianlu, comp. *Zhongguo shaoshu minzu shequ renkou yanjiu* (Studies on the population of China's ethnic minority communities). Beijing: Zhongguo Renkou Chubanshe, 1993.

Zhang Xia et al., comps. *Qingmo haijun shiliao* (Historical materials on the late Qing navy). Beijing: Haiyang Chubanshe, 1982.

Zhang Yibo. "Xinhai haijun juyi ji" (An account of the navy's uprising in 1911). In *XHGM*, 7: 471–77.

Zhang Yilin. "Gu daili dazongtong Fenggong shizhuang" (An account of the late Acting President Feng Guozhang). In idem, *Xintaipingshi ji* (Collected works of Zhang Yilin), 4: 14a–20b. Reprint, Taipei: Wenhai Chubanshe, 1966.

Zhang Yuesheng. "Zhuiji Baqi daibiao Zhang Furong suotan Nanbei yihe de yilin banzhao" (A note on the comments of Zhang Furong, representative of the Eight Banners, regarding the North-South peace talks). In *XGHYL*, 6: 427–28.

Zhang Yufa. *Minguo chunian de zhengdang* (Political parties in the early years of the Republic). Taipei: Zhongyang Yanjiuyuan Jindaishi Yanjiusuo, 1985.

———. *Qingji de lixian tuanti* (Constitutionalist groups of the Qing period). Taipei: Zhongyang Yanjiuyuan Jindaishi Yanjiusuo, 1971.

Zhang Yutian. "Wan-Qing qiying de bianqian he moluo shulüe" (A brief account of the reform and decline of the banner forces in the late Qing). In *Manzu luncong* (Essays on the Manchus), 55–76. Shenyang: Liaoning Daxue Chubanshe, 1986.

Zhang Yuxin. "Qingdai qianqi ge minzu tongyi guannian de lishi tezheng" (Historical features of the idea of unity among the various ethnic groups in the early Qing). *Qingshi yanjiu*, 1996, no. 2: 30–38.

Zhang Zhidong. *Zhang Wenxiang gong quanji* (The complete works of Zhang Zhidong). Reprint, Taipei: Wenhai Chubanshe, 1963.

Zhao Huansen and Tang Xuekai. "Pengbo fazhan de Kuancheng Manzu zizhixian"

(The flourishing Manchu autonomous county of Kuancheng). *Manzu yanjiu*, 1994, no. 4: 42–43.

Zhao Shu. "Beijing chengqu Manzu shenghuo suoji" (Notes on the livelihood of the Manchus in Beijing). *Beijing wenshi ziliao* 55 (1997): 202–39.

———. "Cong yizhang Hongxian yuannian pishi kan dangshi Beijing Manzu zhuangkuang" (The Manchus' condition in Beijing as seen in a directive of 1916). *Manzu yanjiu*, 1986, no. 3: 32.

———. "Jianguo qianhou de Beijing Manzuren" (Beijing's Manchus before and after the founding of the state). *Manzu yanjiu*, 1992, no. 2: 32–37.

———. "'Wenge' xianhou de Beijing Manzuren" (Beijing's Manchus before and after the Cultural Revolution). *Manzu yanjiu*, 1993, no. 1: 52–56.

———. "Xinhai Geming qianhou de Beijing Manzuren" (Beijing's Manchus before and after the 1911 Revolution). *Manzu yanjiu*, 1989, no. 3: 15–19.

Zhao Zhongfu. "Qingdai Dongsansheng de diquan guanxi yu fengjin zhengce" (Land tenure in the three northeastern provinces during the Qing and the policy of immigration prohibition). *Zhongyang Yanjiuyuan Jindaishi Yanjiusuo jikan* 10 (1981): 283–302.

Zheng Chuanshui. "Lun Qingchao de qixiang zhengce ji qi yingxiang" (On the Qing dynasty's program of banner stipends and its consequences). *Liaoning Daxue xuebao*, 1985, no. 2: 76–80.

———. "Qingmo Manzu shehui tedian chutan" (A preliminary investigation into the social peculiarities of the Manchus at the end of the Qing). *Xueshu yuekan*, 1982, no. 2: 60–66.

———. "Xinhai Geming yu Baqi zhidu de bengkui—Lüelun Xinhai Geming dui Manzu de yingxiang" (The 1911 Revolution and the collapse of the Eight Banner system: On the effect of the 1911 Revolution upon the Manchus). *Liaoning Daxue xuebao*, 1982, no. 1: 30–35.

Zheng Huaiyi and Zhang Jianshe. *Modai huangshu Zaitao chenfu lu* (The vicissitudes of Zaitao, the last emperor's uncle). Beijing: Qunzhong Chubanshe, 1989.

Zheng Quan. "Fujian guangfu shilüe" (A brief account of the restoration in Fujian). In *KGWX*, 2, part 4: 314–21.

Zheng Tianting. *Tanweiji* (Explorations in minutiae). Beijing: Zhonghua Shuju, 1980.

Zheng Yunshan, Gong Yanming, and Lin Zhengchiu. *Hangzhou yu Xihu shihua* (Historical anecdotes about Hangzhou and West Lake). Shanghai: Shanghai Renmin Chubanshe, 1980.

Zhengzhi guanbao (Political gazette), Beijing. 1907–11. Reprint, Taipei: Wenhai Chubanshe, 1965.

Zhongguo 1982-nian renkou pucha ziliao (Dianzi jisuanji huizong) (1982 population census of China [Results of computer tabulation]). Ed. Guowuyuan Renkou Pucha

Bangongshi and Guojia Tongjiju Renkou Tongjisi. Beijing: Zhongguo Tongji Chubanshe, 1985.

Zhongguo jindai de weixin yundong—Bianfa yu lixian yantaohui (The reform movement in modern China: A conference on reform and constitutionalism). Taipei: Zhongyang Yanjiuyuan Jindaishi Yanjiusuo, 1982.

Zhongguo jindaishi cidian (A dictionary of China's modern history). Shanghai: Shanghai Cishu Chubanshe, 1982.

Zhonghua Minguo kaiguo wushinian wenxian (Documents commemorating the fiftieth anniversary of the founding of the Republic of China). Taipei, 1962–65.

Zhonghua Minguo shi dang'an ziliao huibian (A compilation of archival materials on the history of the Republic of China). N.p.: Jiangsu Renmin Chubanshe, 1979, 1981.

Zhonghua Minguo shishi jiyao (chugao) (A chronological history of the Republic of China [first draft]), from 1894–97 to 1928. Taipei: Zhonghua Minguo Shiliao Yanjiu Zhongxin, 1971–83.

Zhonghua Renmin Gongheguo lishi changbian (A comprehensive history of the People's Republic of China). Nanning: Guangxi Renmin Chubanshe, 1994.

Zhongyang datong ribao (Central great harmony daily), Beijing. 1908–9. Available at Beijing University Library.

Zhongyang Jingguan Xuexiao xiaoshi (A history of the Central Police Academy). Taipei: Mei Kewang, 1967.

Zhou Fu. *Zhou Queshen gong quanji* (The complete works of Zhou Fu). Reprint, Taipei: Wenhai Chubanshe, 1966.

Zhou Qiuguang. "Modern Chinese Educational Philanthropy: Xiong Xiling and the Xiangshan Children's Home." Trans. Edward A. McCord. *Republican China* 19, no. 1 (1993): 51–83.

Zhou Wuyi. "Lujun Disan Zhongxue canjia Wuchang qiyi jingguo" (The Third Military Middle School's participation in the Wuchang uprising). In *XGHYL*, 7: 10–18.

Zhou Xibao. *Zhongguo gudai fushi shi* (A history of ancient Chinese costumes). Beijing: Zhongguo Xiju Chubanshe, 1984.

Zhou Xuan. "Zhirui chulun" (An initial discussion of Zhirui). *Manzu yanjiu*, 1988, no. 4: 49–54.

Zhu Jinfu and Zhou Wenquan. "Cong Qinggong yian lun Guangxudi Zaitian zhi si" (The death of the Guangxu emperor, Zaitian, as seen from the medical records of the Qing court). *Gugong Bowuyuan yuankan*, 1982, no. 3: 3–13.

Zhu Lanting and Xu Fengchen. "Xiong Chengji mouci Zaixun bianxi" (A critical review of Xiong Chengji's plot to assassinate Zaixun). *Jindaishi yanjiu*, 1988, no. 6: 56–60.

Zhu Xuwu and Dang Zixin. "Shaanxi Xinhai Geming huiyi" (Recollections of the 1911 Revolution in Shaanxi). In *XGHYL*, 5: 1–49.

Zhu Ying. "Tang Shaoyi yu Xinhai Nanbei yihe" (Tang Shaoyi and the 1911 North-South peace talks). *Guangdong shehui kexue*, 1989, no. 2: 73–81.

Zhuang Jifa. *Jingshi Daxuetang* (The Metropolitan University). Taipei: Guoli Taiwan Daxue Wenxueyuan, 1970.

Zou Rong. *Gemingjun* (The Revolutionary Army). In Tsou Jung, *The Revolutionary Army: A Chinese Nationalist Tract of 1903*. Trans. John Lust. The Hague and Paris: Mouton & Co., 1968.

Zou Shencheng. "Zhapu zhanyi shishi buyi" (An addendum to the historical record of the battle of Zhapu). *Lishi jiaoxue*, 1980, no. 8: 39–40.

Index